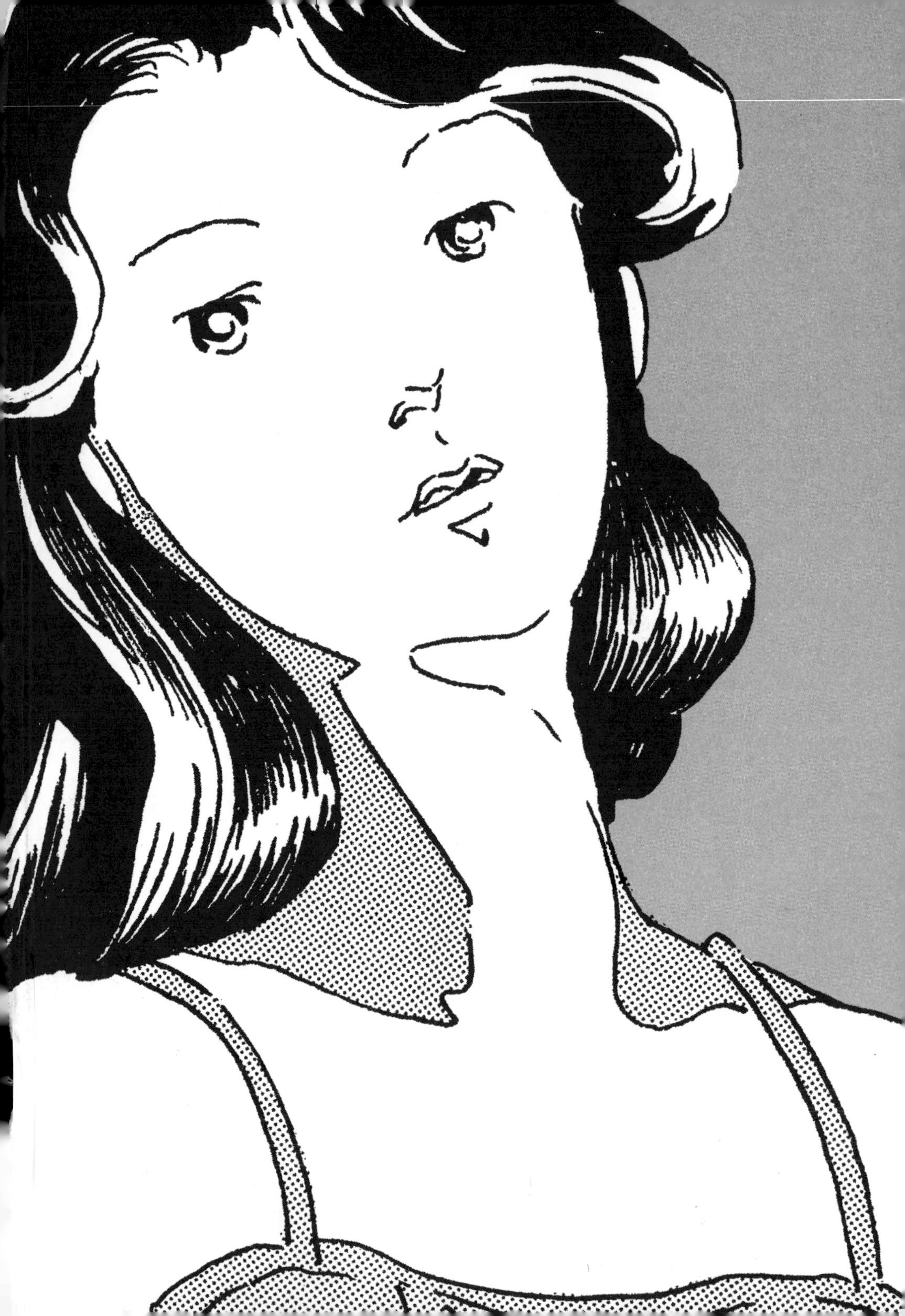

YAMADA MURASAKI

Talk To My Back

Translated by Ryan Holmberg

Drawn & Quarterly

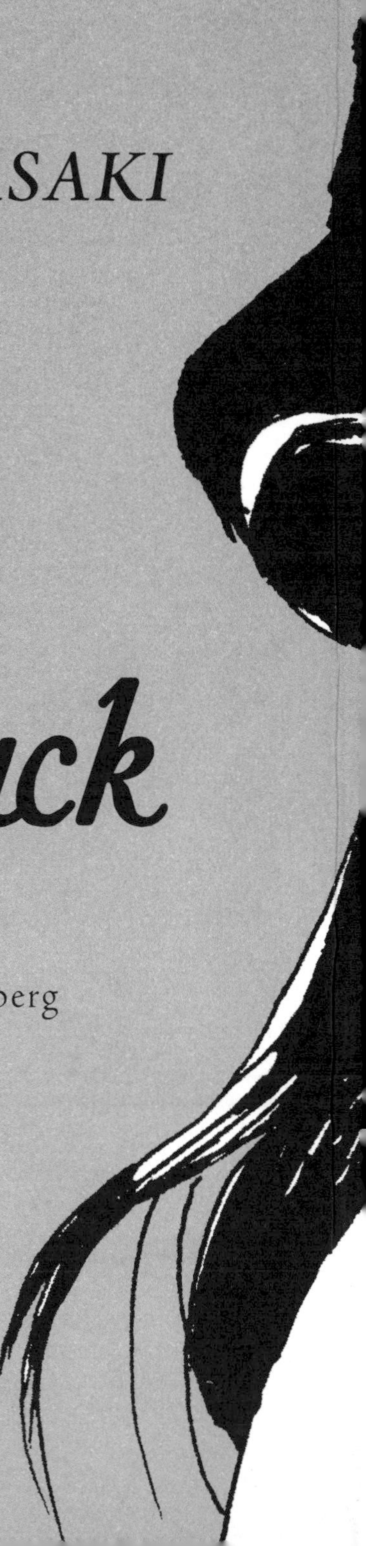

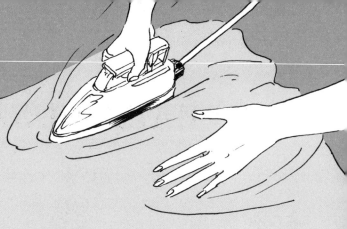

Contents

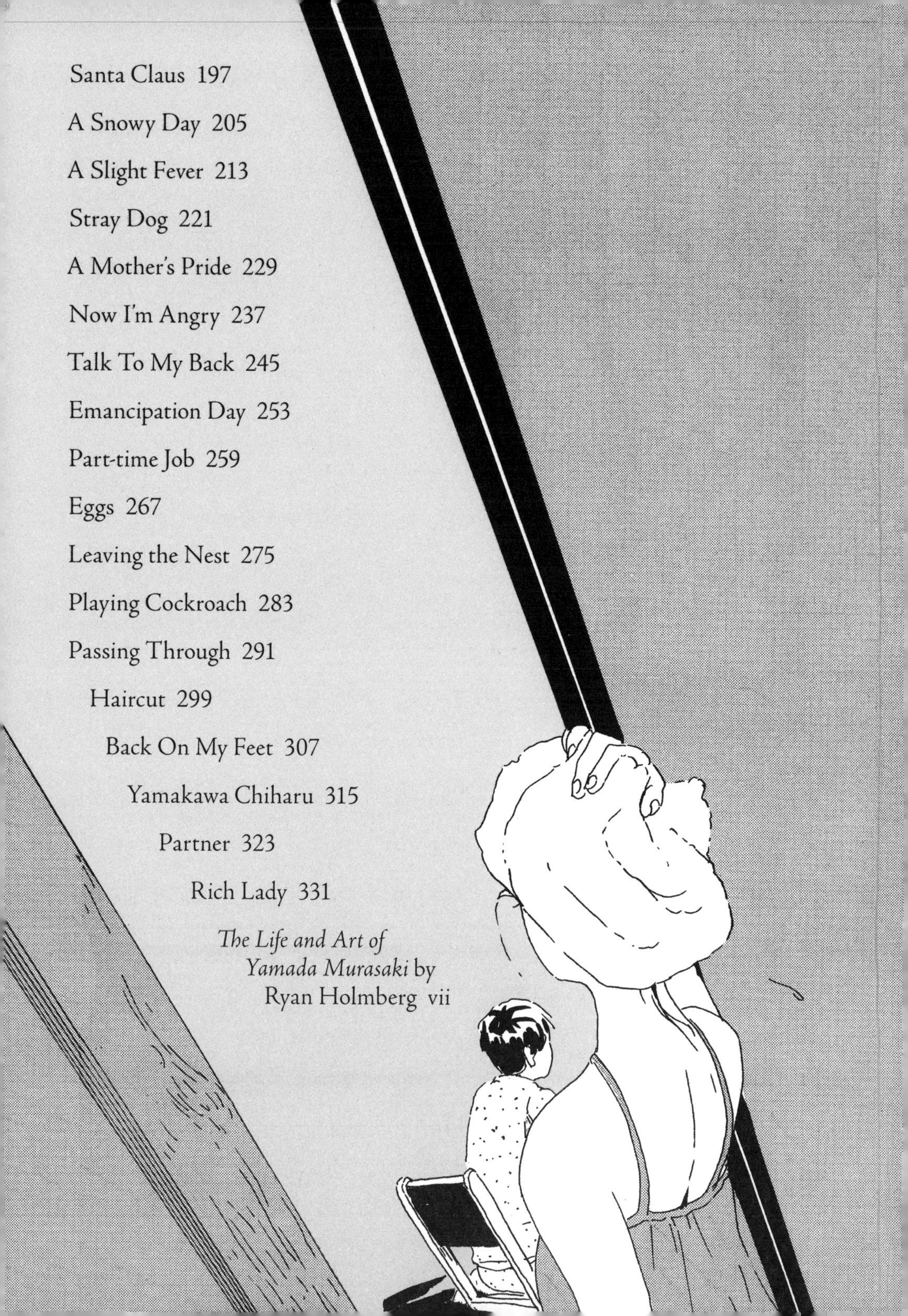

Nanohana

Entranced in a trance, enveloped in mustard flower blossoms
Might a little devil appear?

That mustard blossom, swaying, hides the little devil
Enraptured in a field of mustard flowers

The little devil catches a glint of pale blue through the mustard flower
Off a human's ear

Twilight expands outward from a field of milkvetch, but the mustard field
With the little devil is slower to darken

The little devil is alone, covered to its neck by the mustard blossoms
Alone, crouching, waiting among the mustard

The little devil, as devils will, is alone, waiting there alone and quiet
In a field of mustard flowers, among blossoms of mustard

It shoots a sparrow dead with a grass-arrow, and doesn't the mustard field
Absorb a real drop of blood?

Might be the kind of little devil that wants to pluck and squeeze the juice out of
Dozens of patches of flowers

Pushing its way through the weight and darkness of the mustard blossoms
With a dejected breast, the little devil is soaked in dew

by Kawano Yūko, translated by Steve Ridgely

Lonely Cinderella

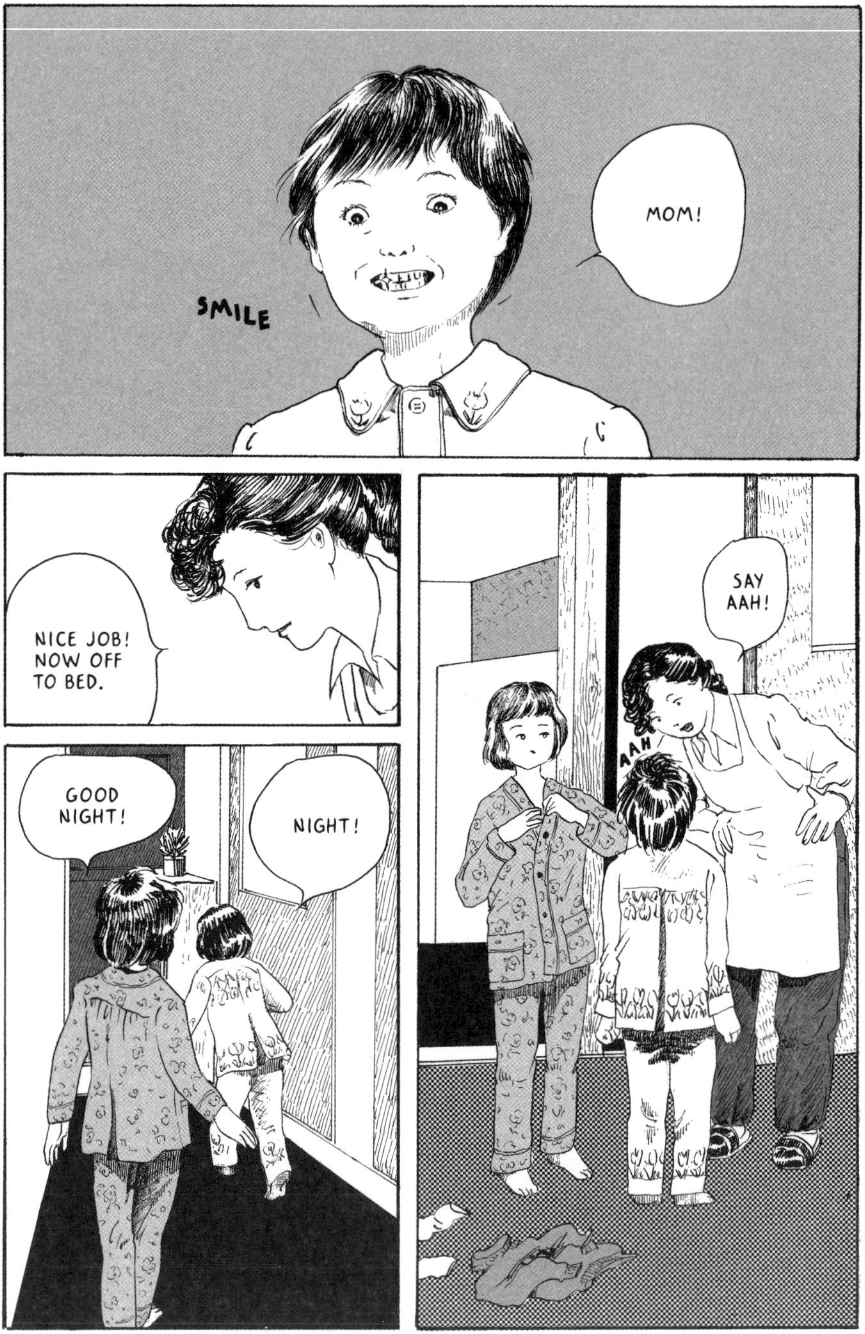
MOM!
SMILE
SAY AAH!
AAH
NICE JOB! NOW OFF TO BED.
NIGHT!
GOOD NIGHT!

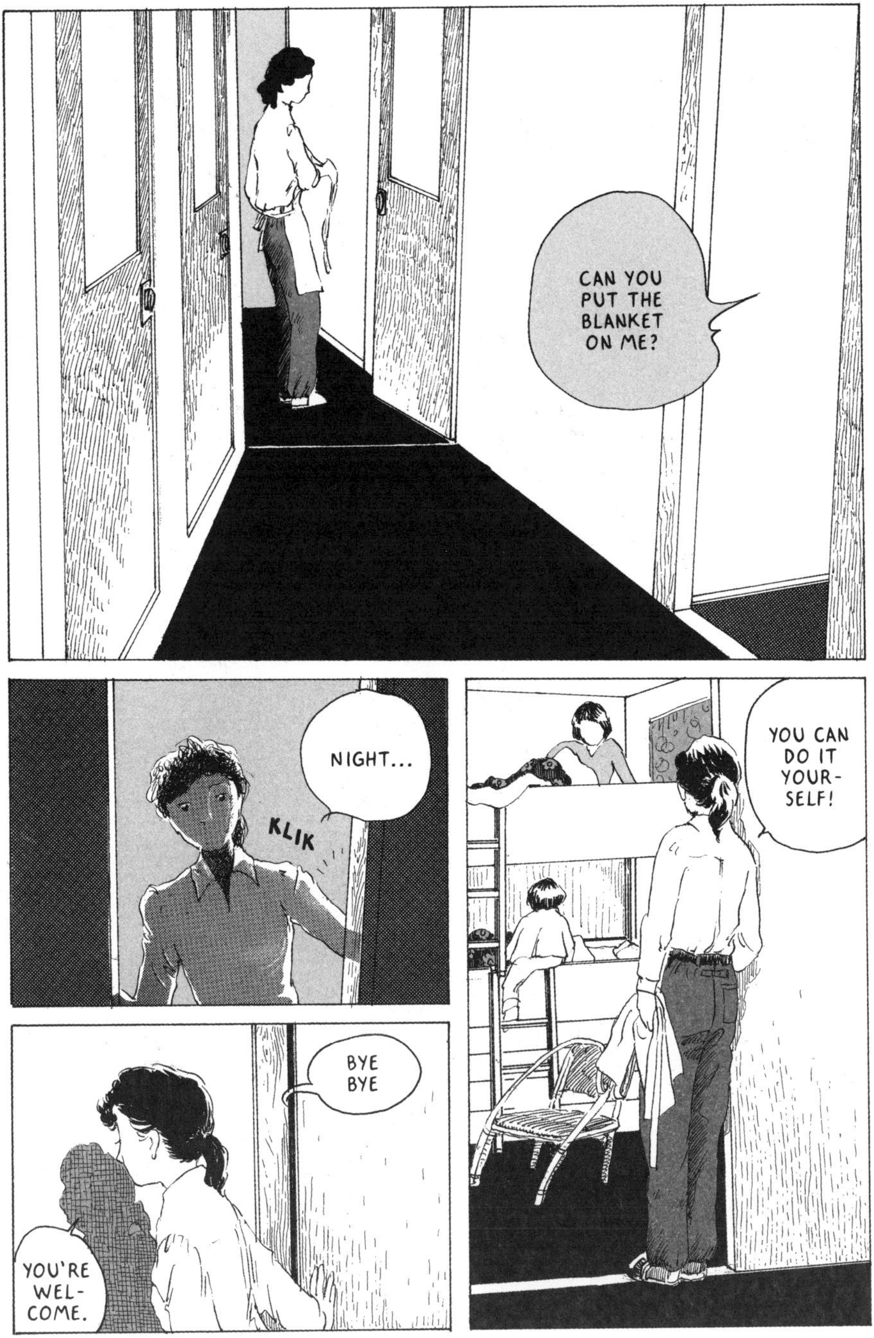
CAN YOU PUT THE BLANKET ON ME?
YOU CAN DO IT YOURSELF!
NIGHT...
KLIK
BYE BYE
YOU'RE WELCOME.

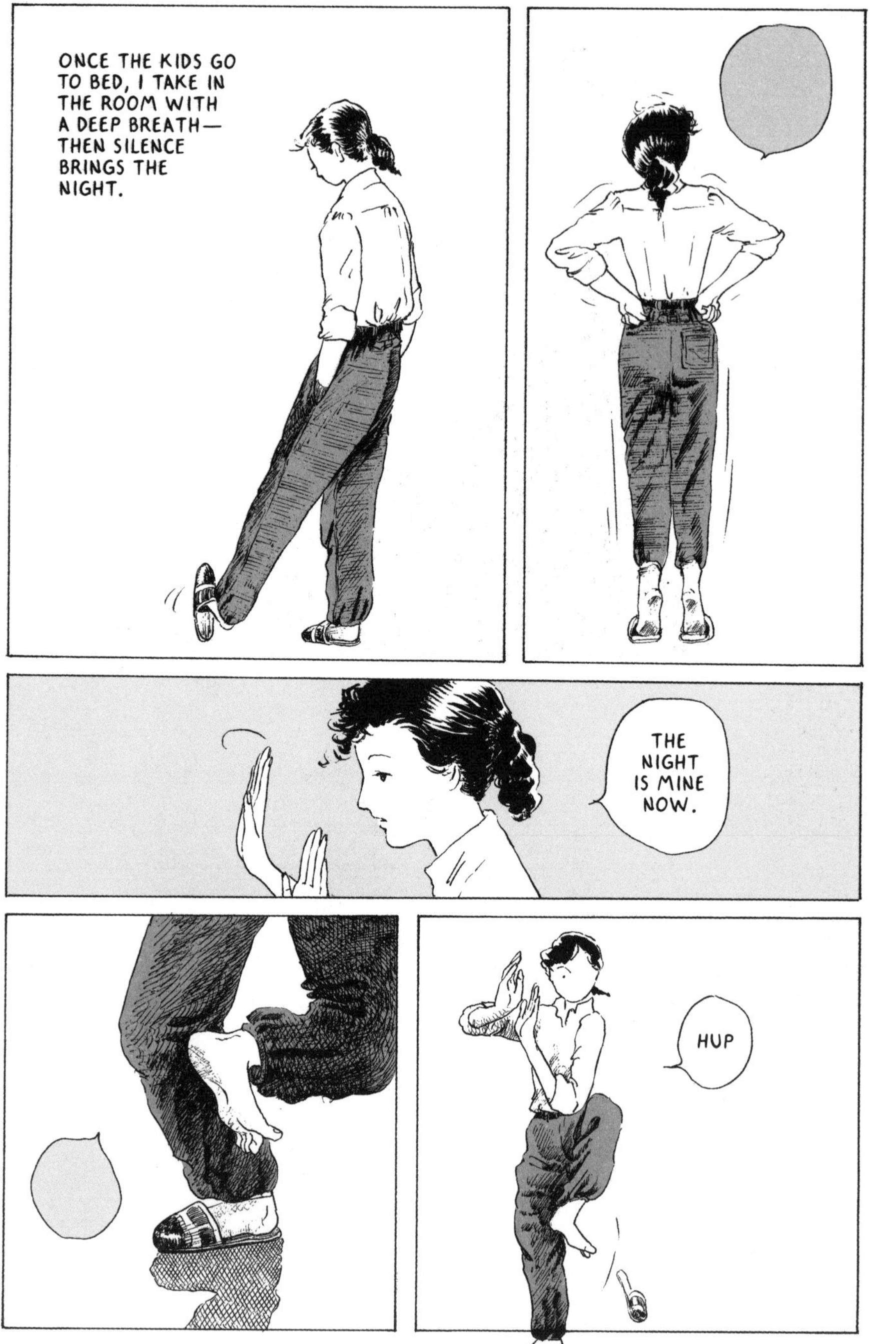
ONCE THE KIDS GO TO BED, I TAKE IN THE ROOM WITH A DEEP BREATH— THEN SILENCE BRINGS THE NIGHT.
THE NIGHT IS MINE NOW.
HUP

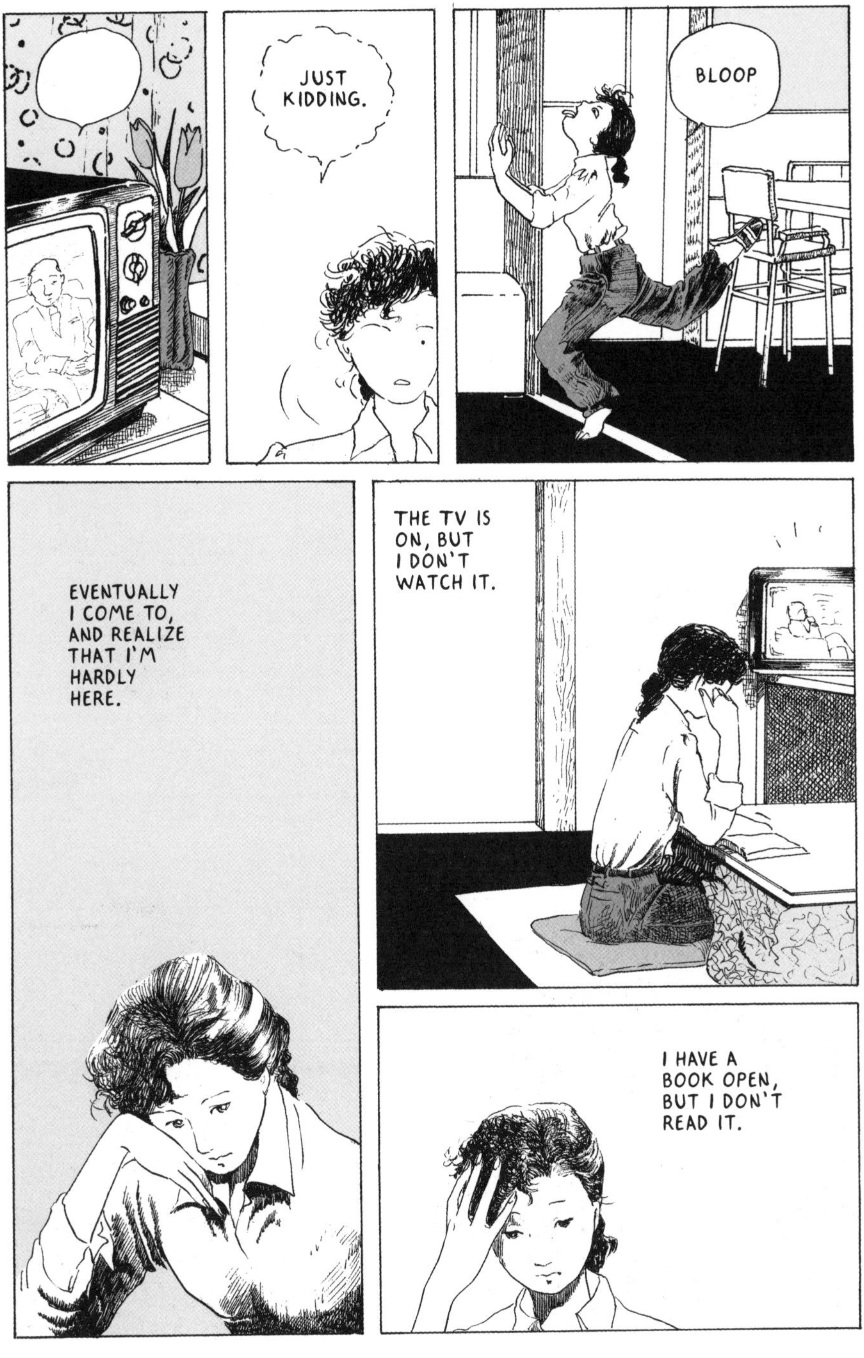
BLOOP
JUST KIDDING.
THE TV IS ON, BUT I DON'T WATCH IT.
I HAVE A BOOK OPEN, BUT I DON'T READ IT.
EVENTUALLY I COME TO, AND REALIZE THAT I'M HARDLY HERE.

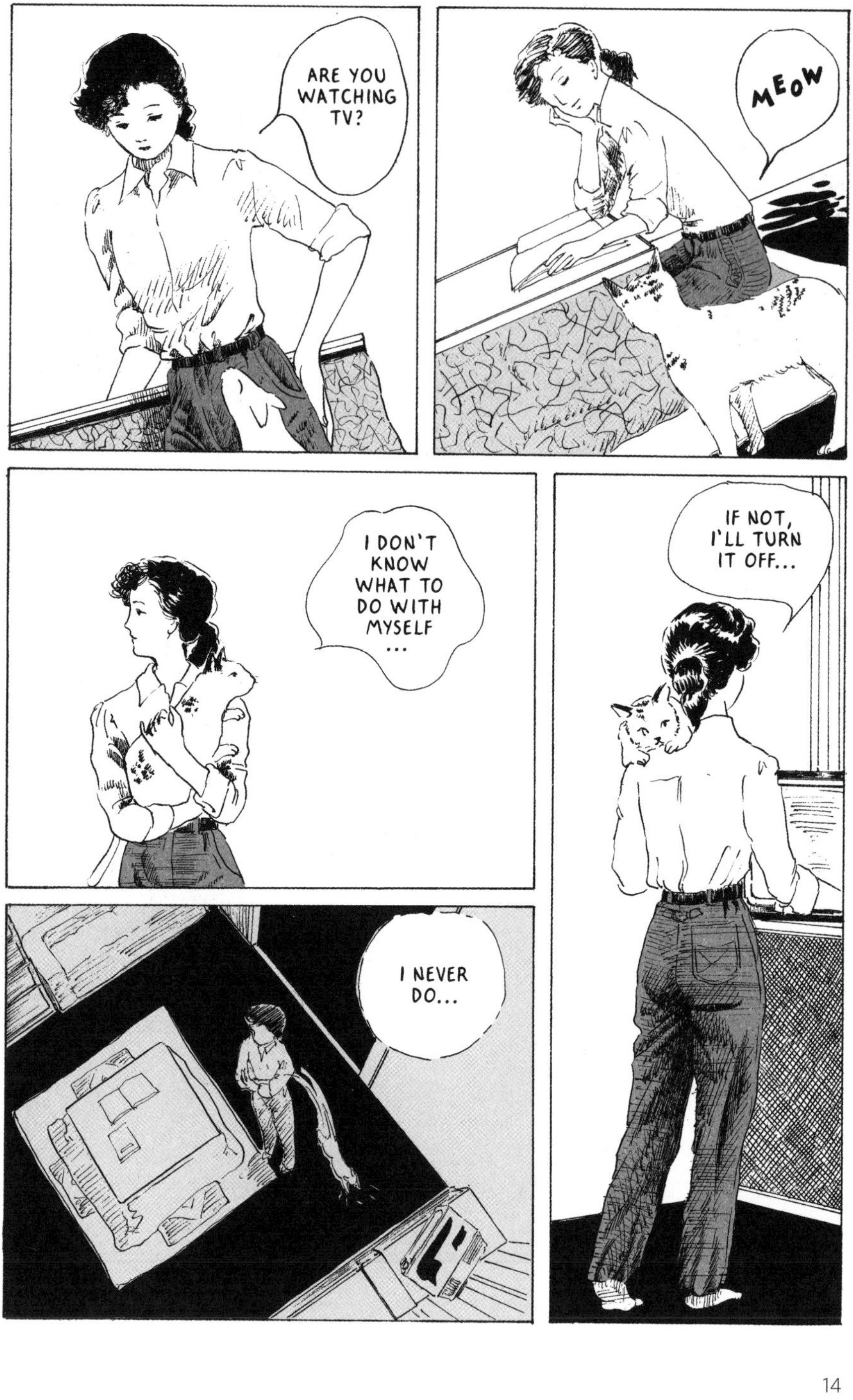
MEOW
ARE YOU WATCHING TV?
IF NOT, I'LL TURN IT OFF...
I DON'T KNOW WHAT TO DO WITH MYSELF ...
I NEVER DO...

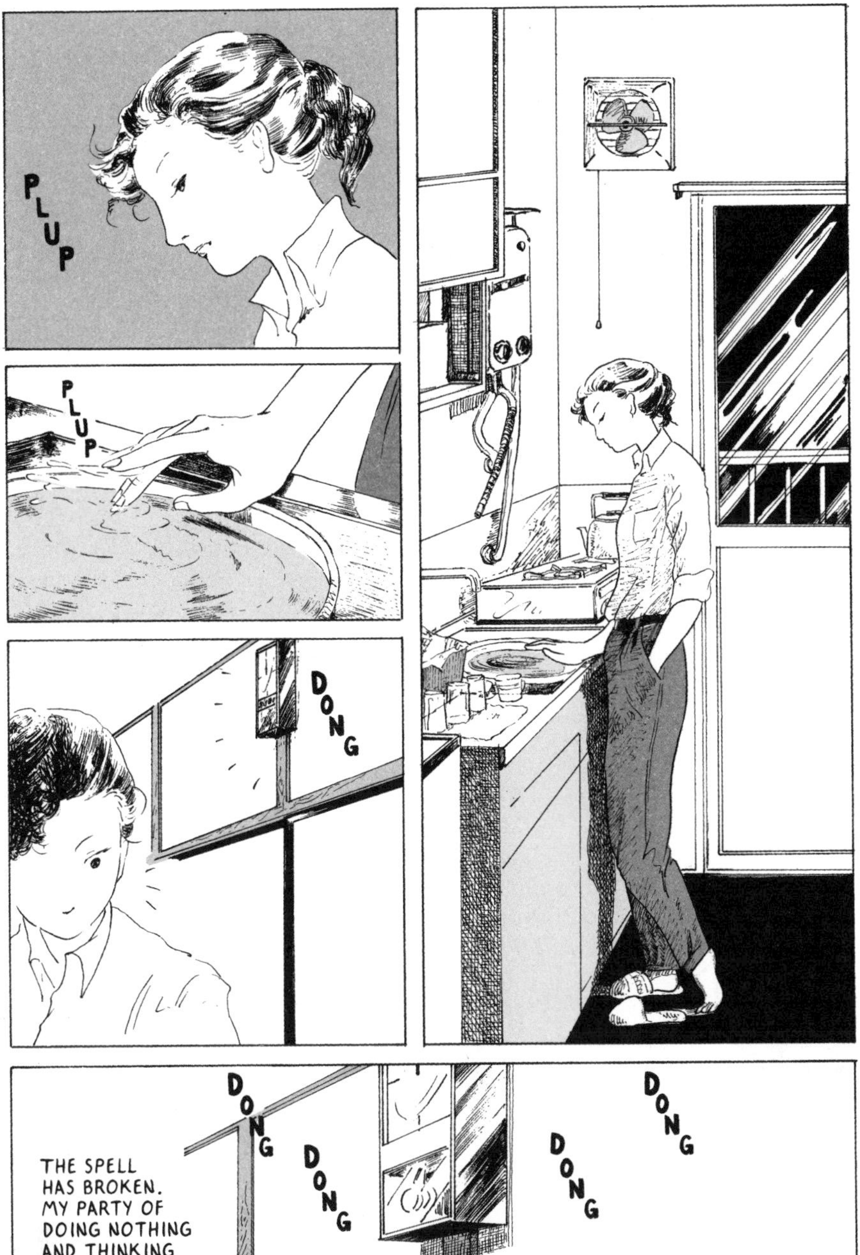
PLUP
PLUP
DONG
DONG
DONG
DONG
DONG
THE SPELL HAS BROKEN. MY PARTY OF DOING NOTHING AND THINKING ABOUT NOTHING IS OVER.

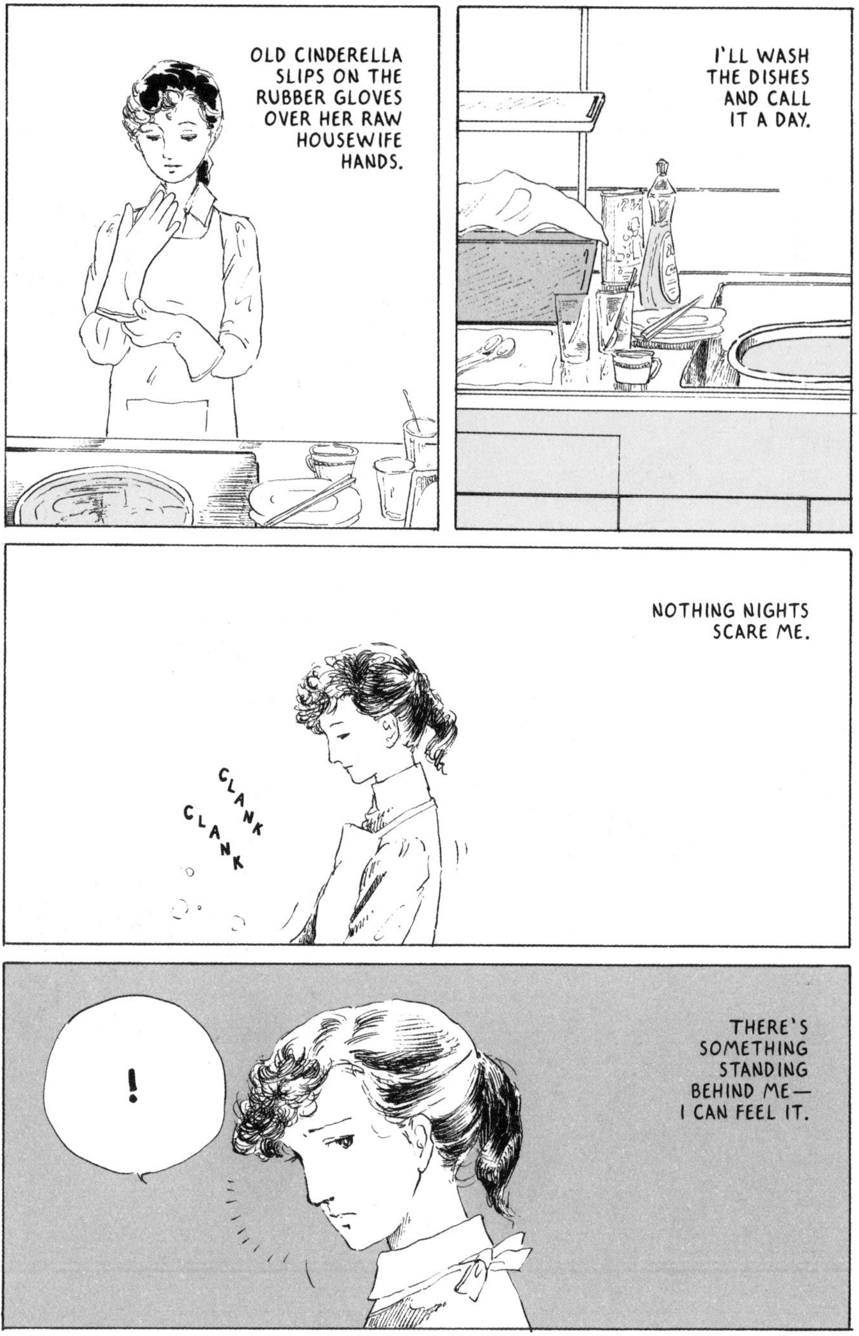
I'LL WASH THE DISHES AND CALL IT A DAY.
OLD CINDERELLA SLIPS ON THE RUBBER GLOVES OVER HER RAW HOUSEWIFE HANDS.
NOTHING NIGHTS SCARE ME.
CLANK
CLANK
THERE'S SOMETHING STANDING BEHIND ME— I CAN FEEL IT.
!

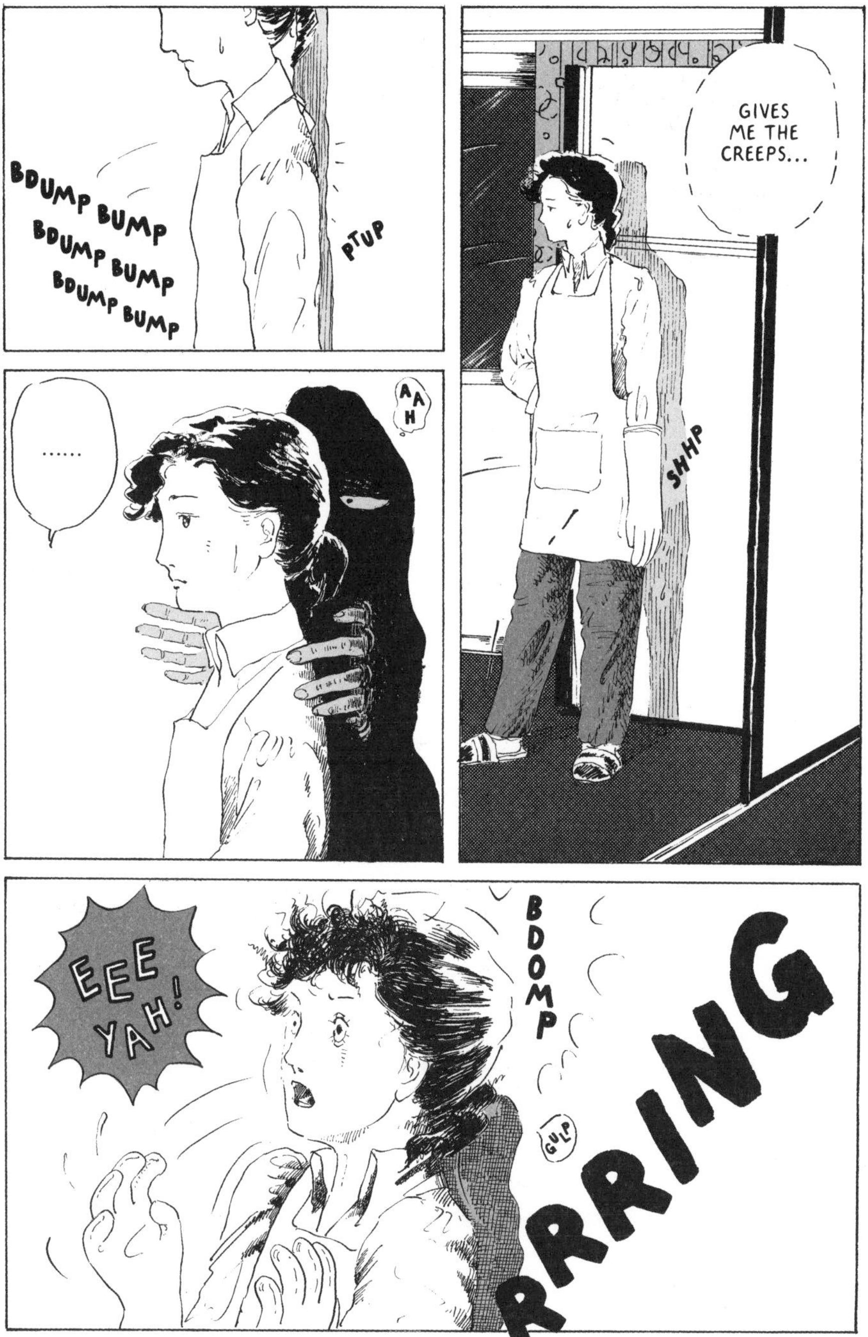
GIVES ME THE CREEPS...
SHHP
PTUP
BDUMP BUMP
BDUMP BUMP
BDUMP BUMP
AAH
......
RRRING
BDOMP
GULP
EEE YAH!

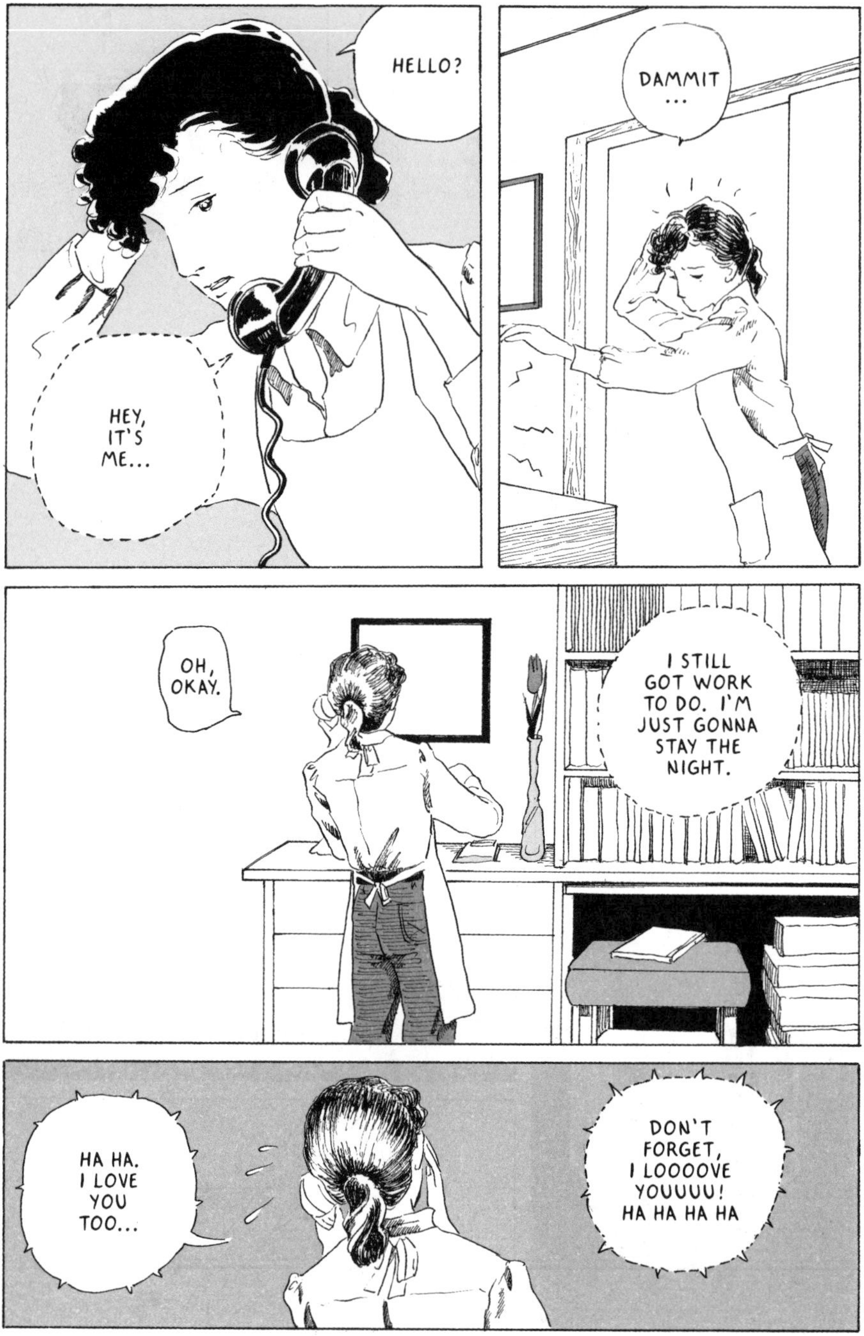
DAMMIT ...
HELLO?
HEY, IT'S ME...
I STILL GOT WORK TO DO. I'M JUST GONNA STAY THE NIGHT.
OH, OKAY.
DON'T FORGET, I LOOOOVE YOUUUU! HA HA HA HA
HA HA. I LOVE YOU TOO...

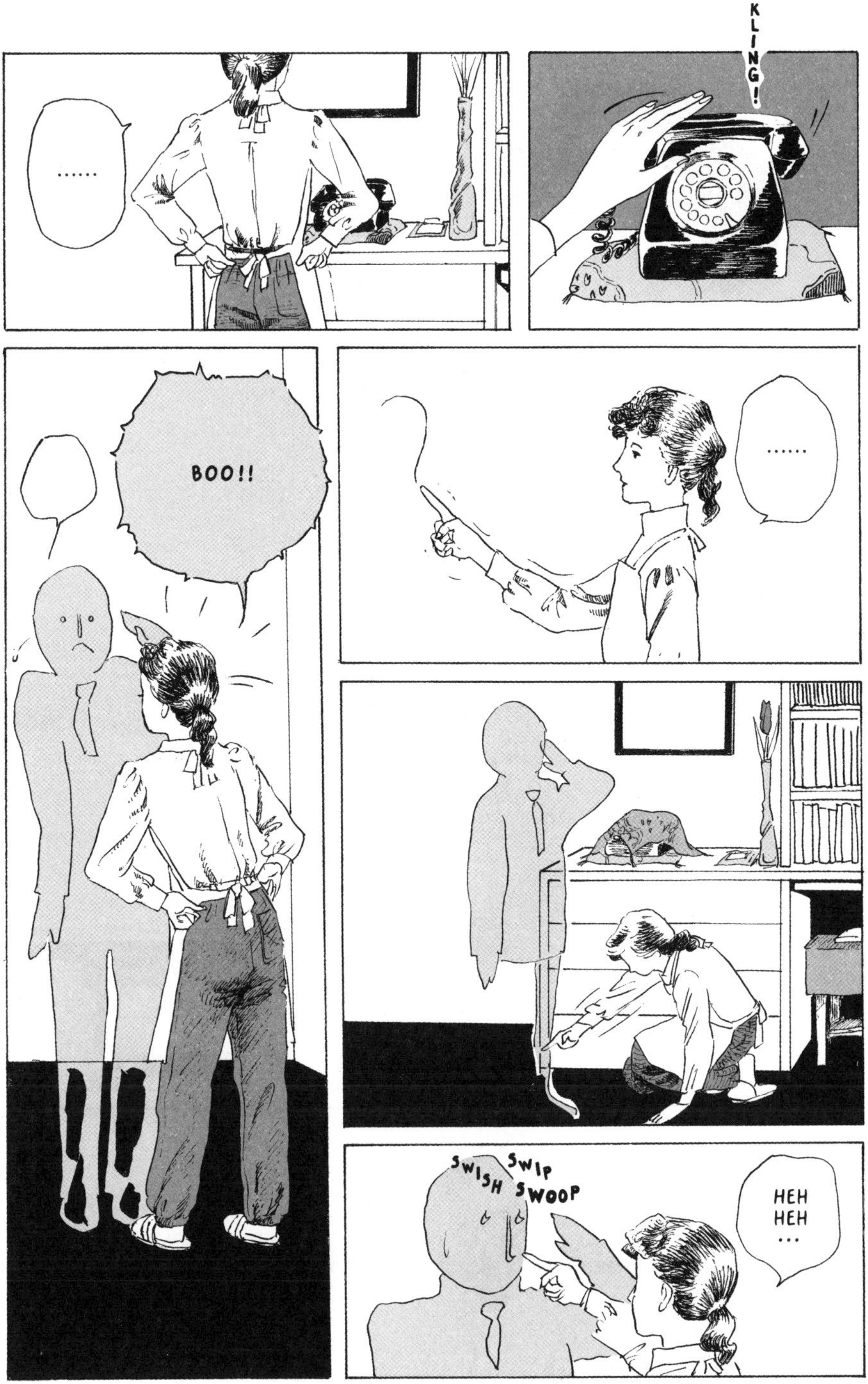
KLING!
......
......
HEH HEH ...
SWIP SWOOP
SWISH
BOO!!

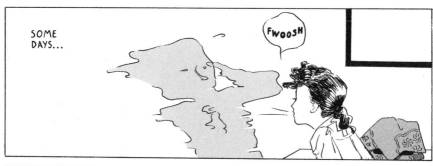

SOME DAYS...

FWOOSH

......

INTOLERABLY...

ARE JUST SO...

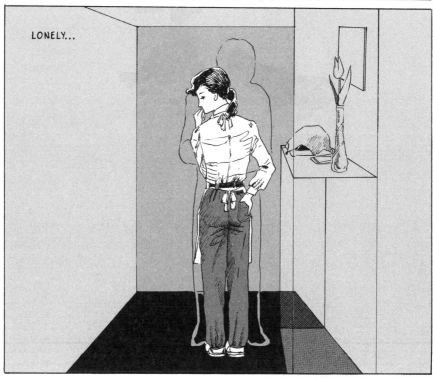

LONELY...

Walking Alone

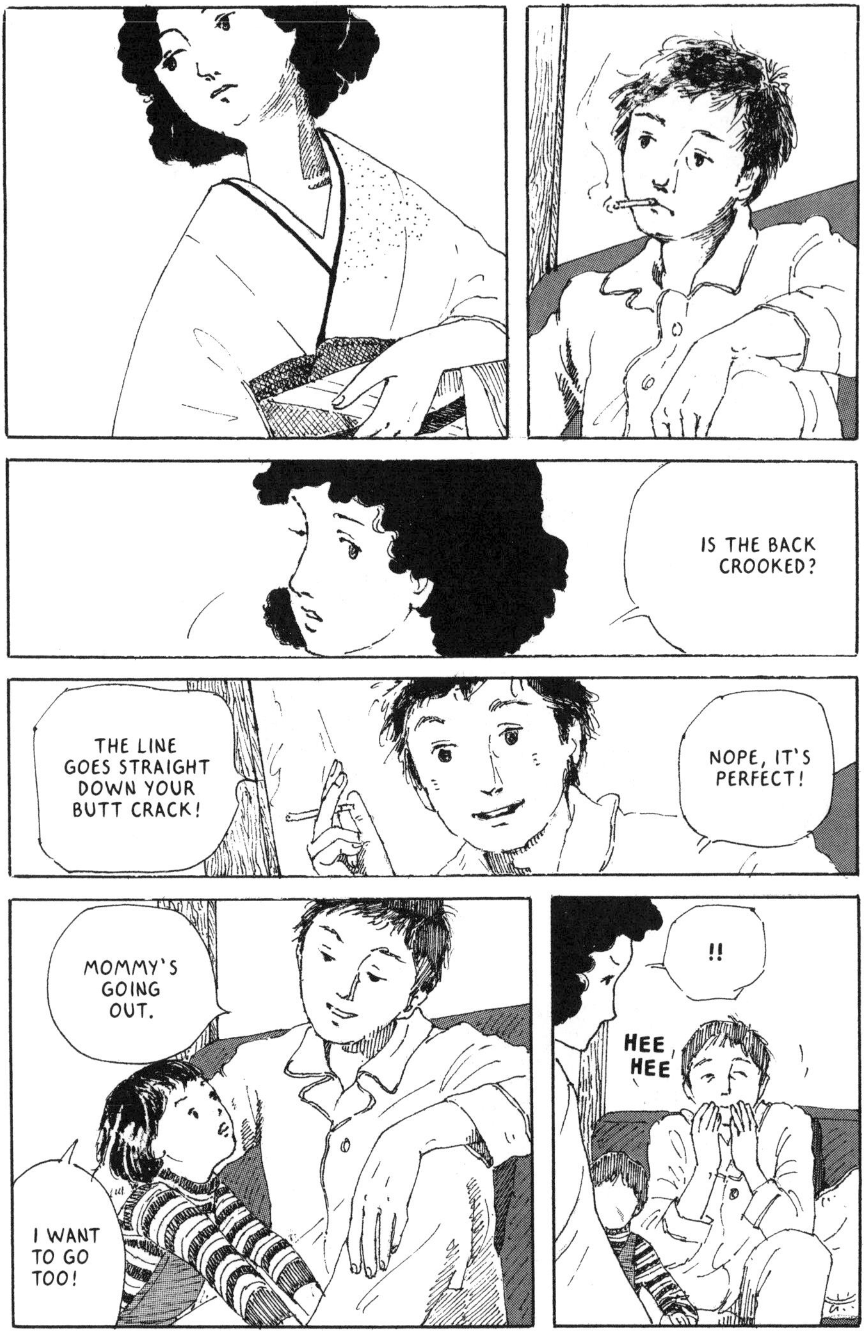
IS THE BACK CROOKED?
NOPE, IT'S PERFECT!
THE LINE GOES STRAIGHT DOWN YOUR BUTT CRACK!
!!
HEE HEE
MOMMY'S GOING OUT.
I WANT TO GO TOO!

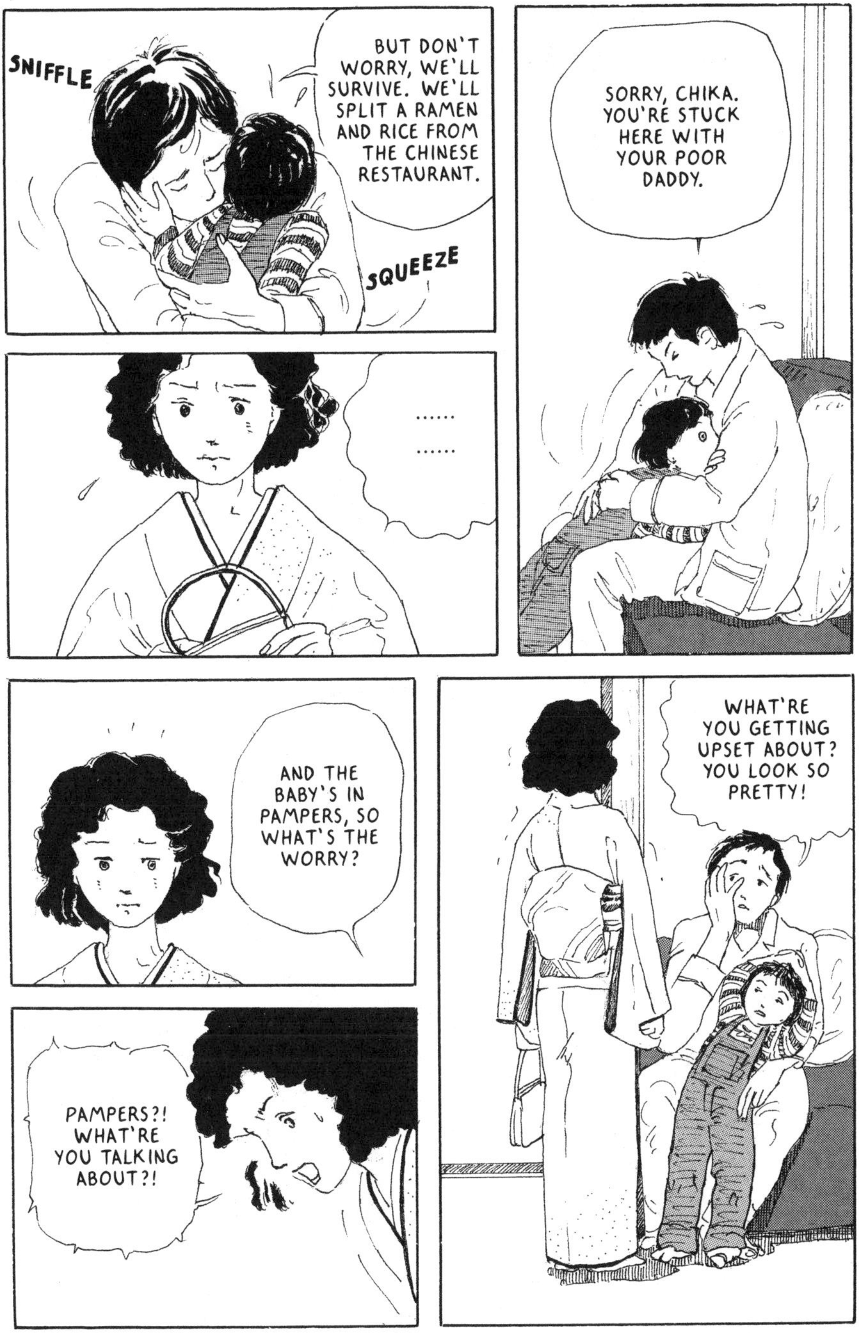
SORRY, CHIKA. YOU'RE STUCK HERE WITH YOUR POOR DADDY.
SNIFFLE
BUT DON'T WORRY, WE'LL SURVIVE. WE'LL SPLIT A RAMEN AND RICE FROM THE CHINESE RESTAURANT.
SQUEEZE
......
......
WHAT'RE YOU GETTING UPSET ABOUT? YOU LOOK SO PRETTY!
AND THE BABY'S IN PAMPERS, SO WHAT'S THE WORRY?
PAMPERS?! WHAT'RE YOU TALKING ABOUT?!

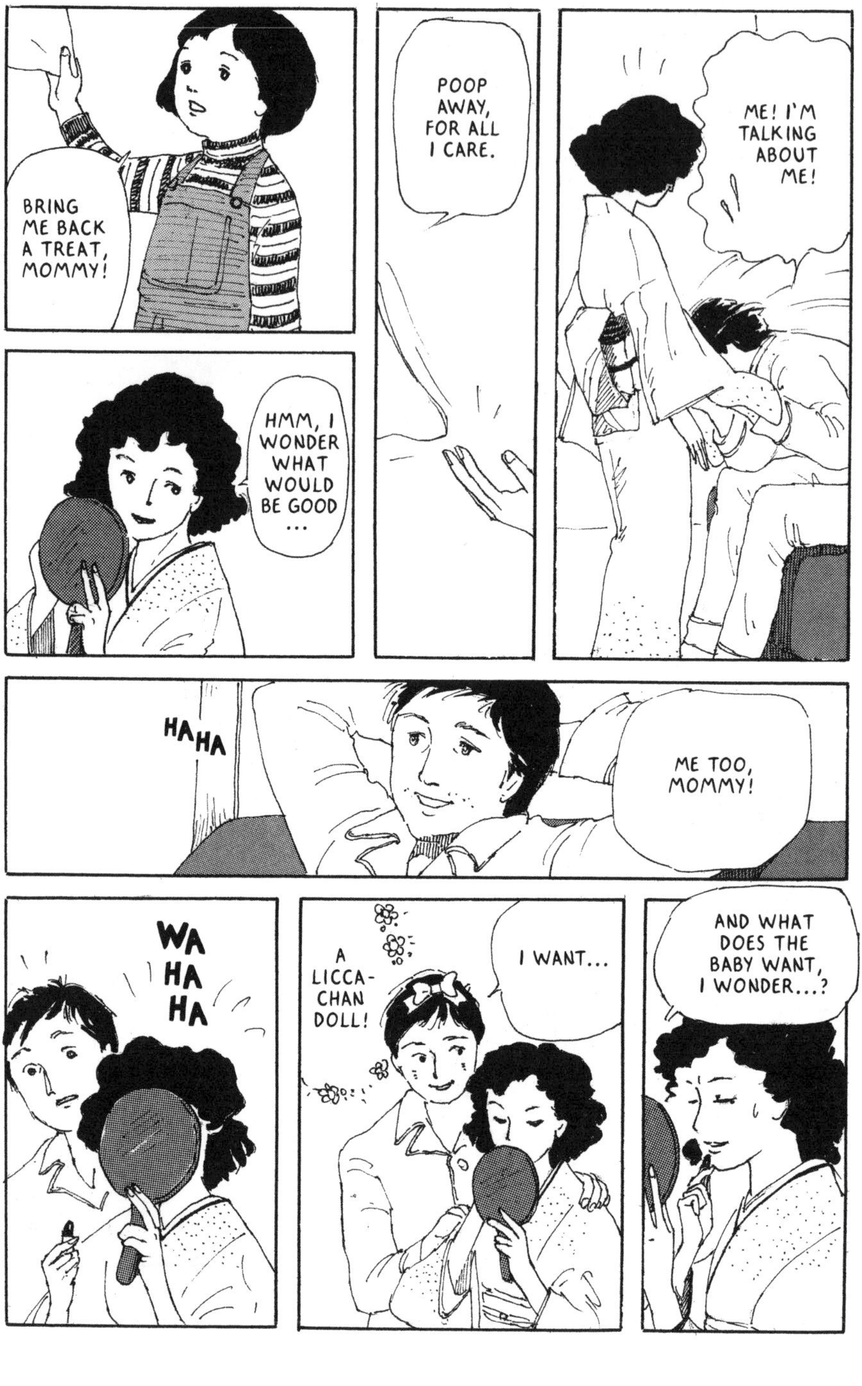
ME! I'M TALKING ABOUT ME!
POOP AWAY, FOR ALL I CARE.
BRING ME BACK A TREAT, MOMMY!
HMM, I WONDER WHAT WOULD BE GOOD...
ME TOO, MOMMY!
HAHA
AND WHAT DOES THE BABY WANT, I WONDER...?
I WANT...
A LICCA-CHAN DOLL!
WA HA HA

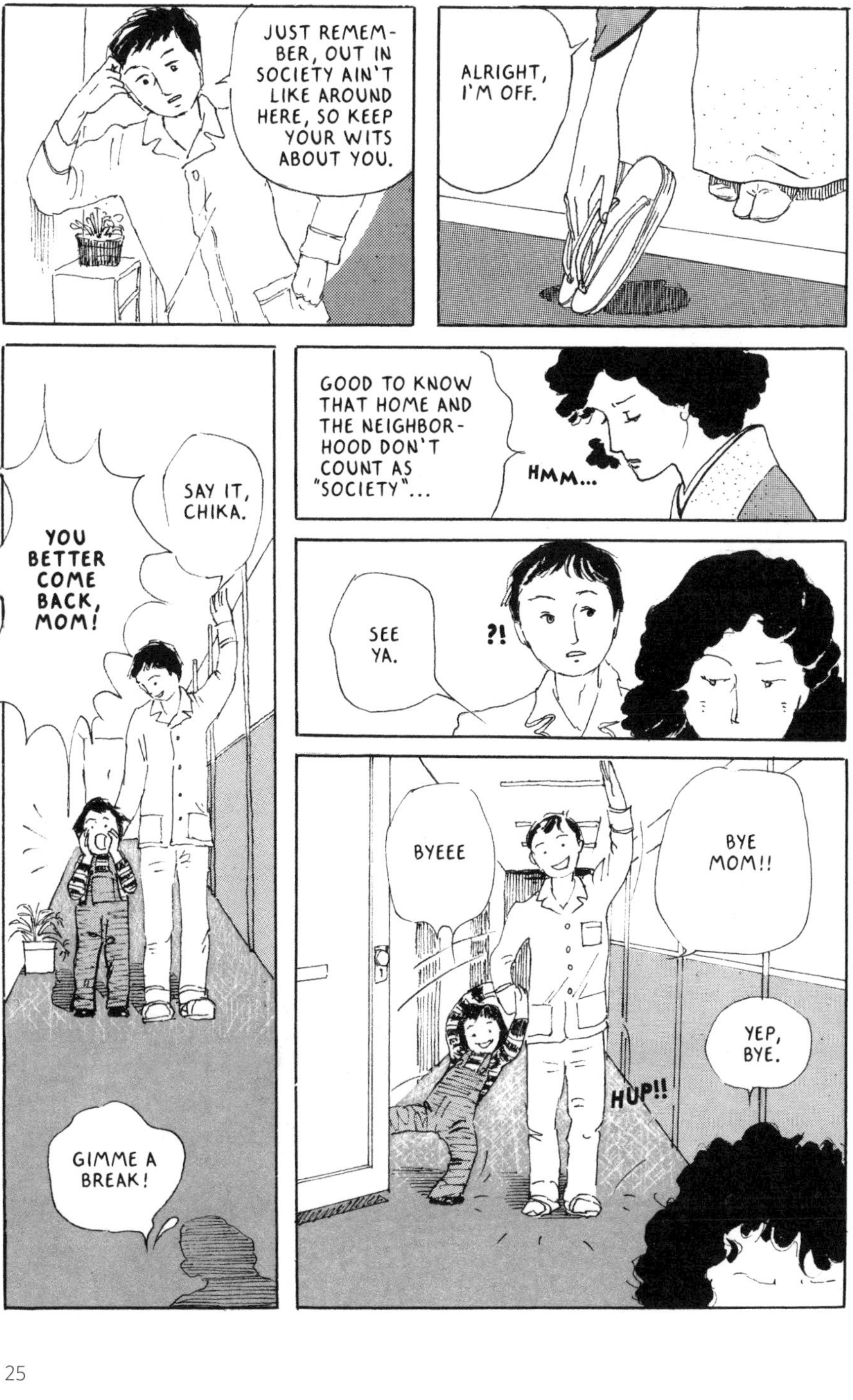
ALRIGHT, I'M OFF.
JUST REMEMBER, OUT IN SOCIETY AIN'T LIKE AROUND HERE, SO KEEP YOUR WITS ABOUT YOU.
GOOD TO KNOW THAT HOME AND THE NEIGHBORHOOD DON'T COUNT AS "SOCIETY"...
HMM...
?!
SEE YA.
BYE MOM!!
BYEEE
YEP, BYE.
HUP!!
SAY IT, CHIKA.
YOU BETTER COME BACK, MOM!
GIMME A BREAK!

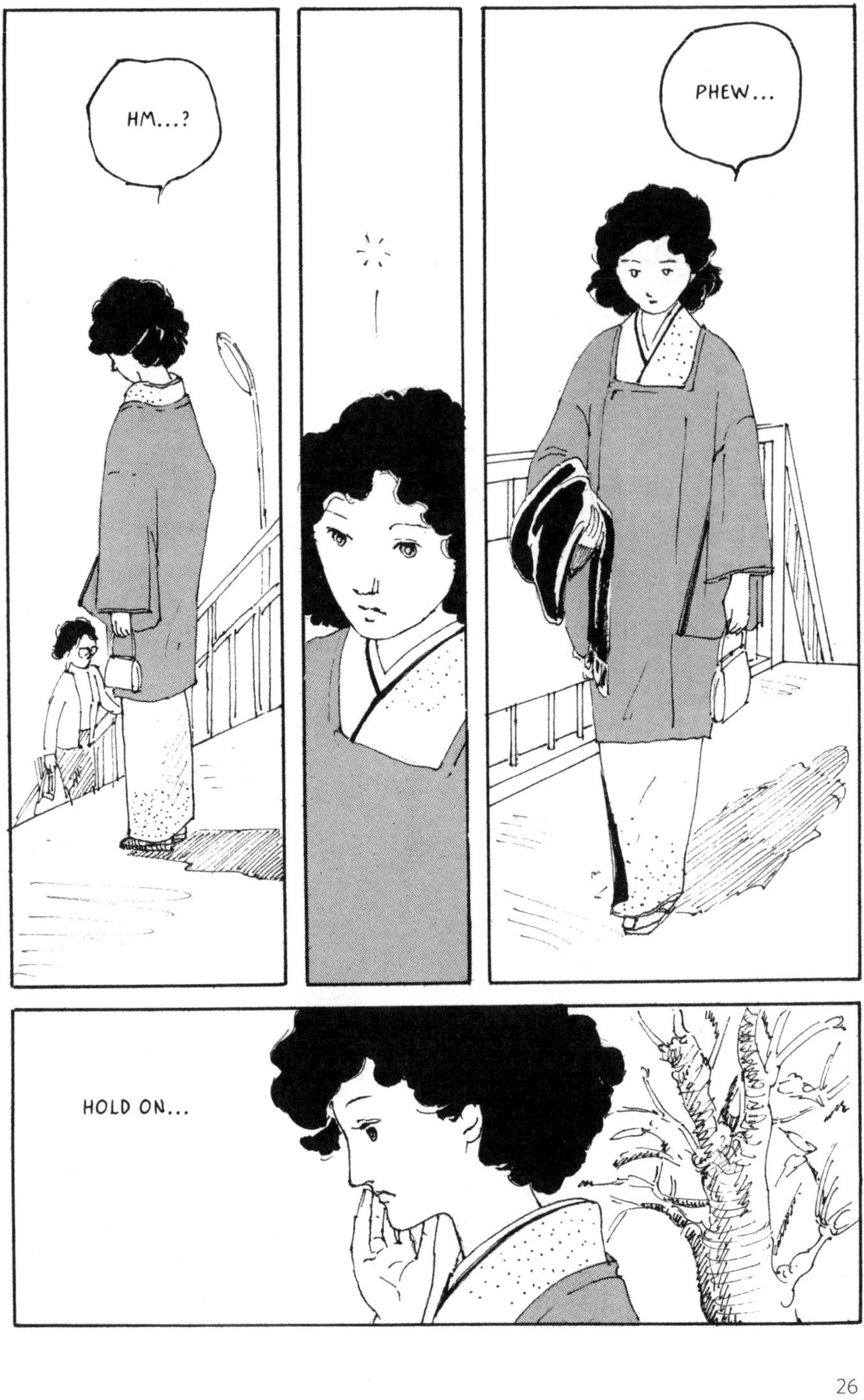
PHEW...
HM...?
HOLD ON...

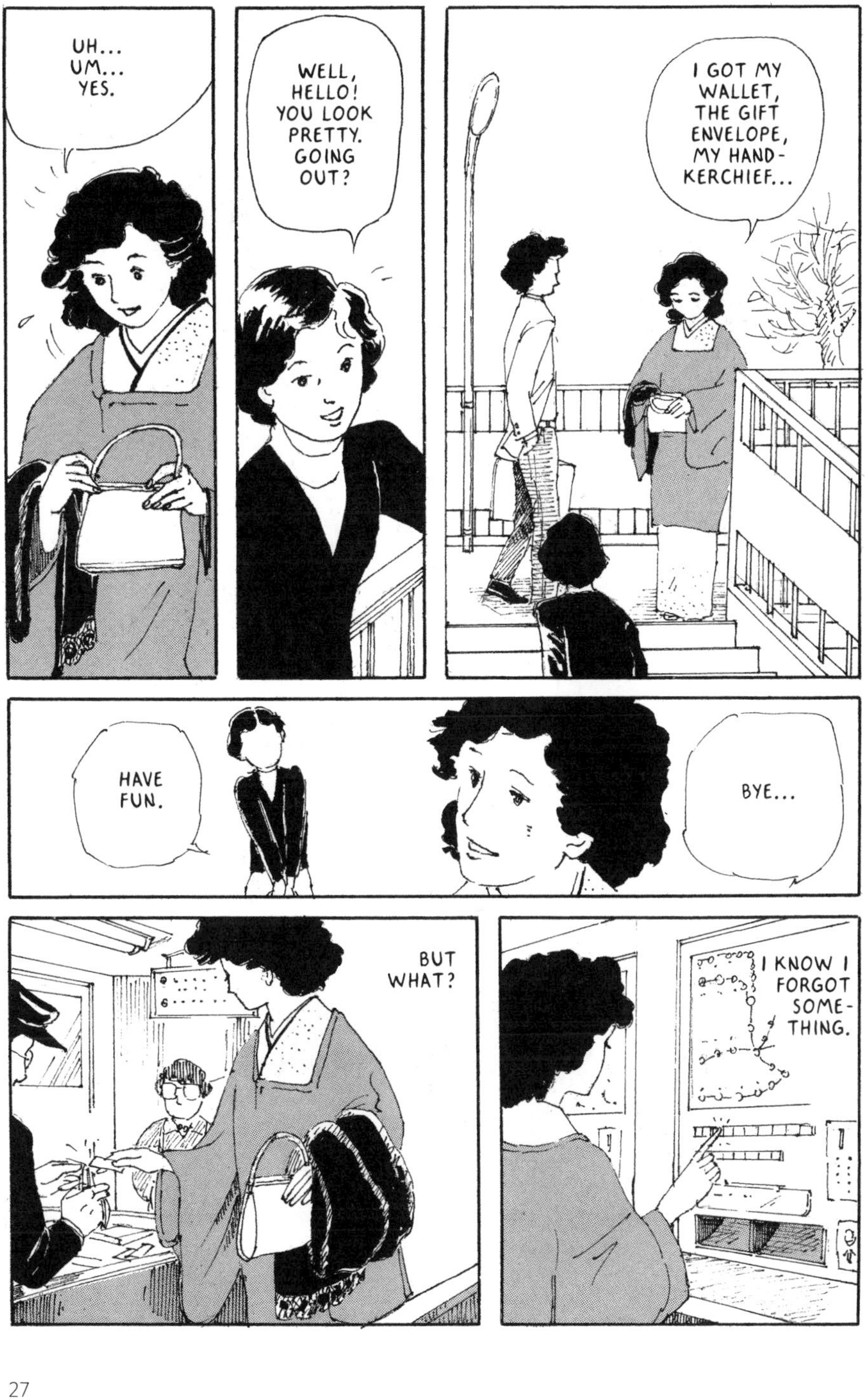
I GOT MY WALLET, THE GIFT ENVELOPE, MY HAND-KERCHIEF...
WELL, HELLO! YOU LOOK PRETTY. GOING OUT?
UH... UM... YES.
BYE...
HAVE FUN.
I KNOW I FORGOT SOMETHING.
BUT WHAT?

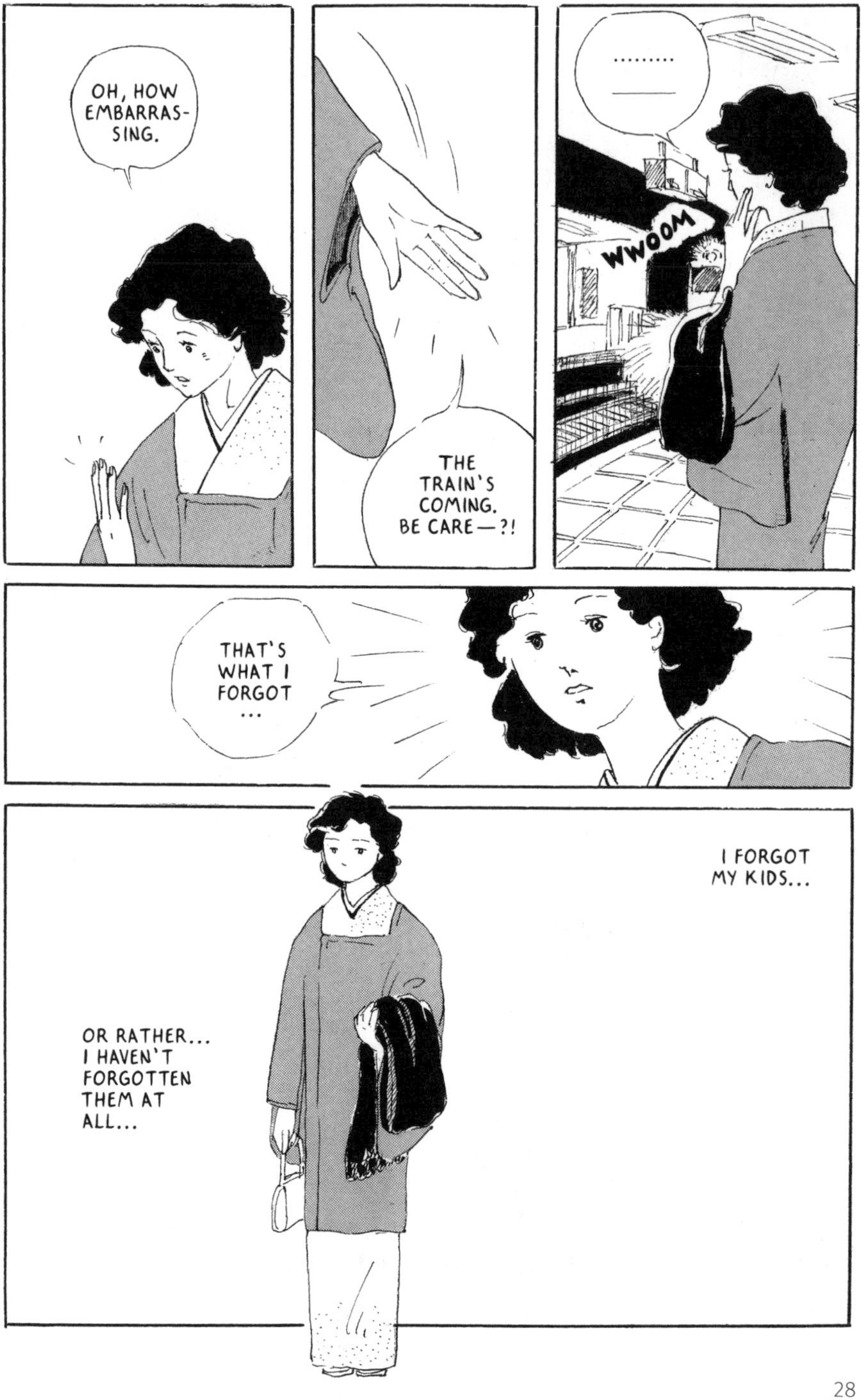
....
———
WWOOM
THE TRAIN'S COMING. BE CARE—?!
OH, HOW EMBARRAS-SING.
THAT'S WHAT I FORGOT ...
I FORGOT MY KIDS...
OR RATHER... I HAVEN'T FORGOTTEN THEM AT ALL...

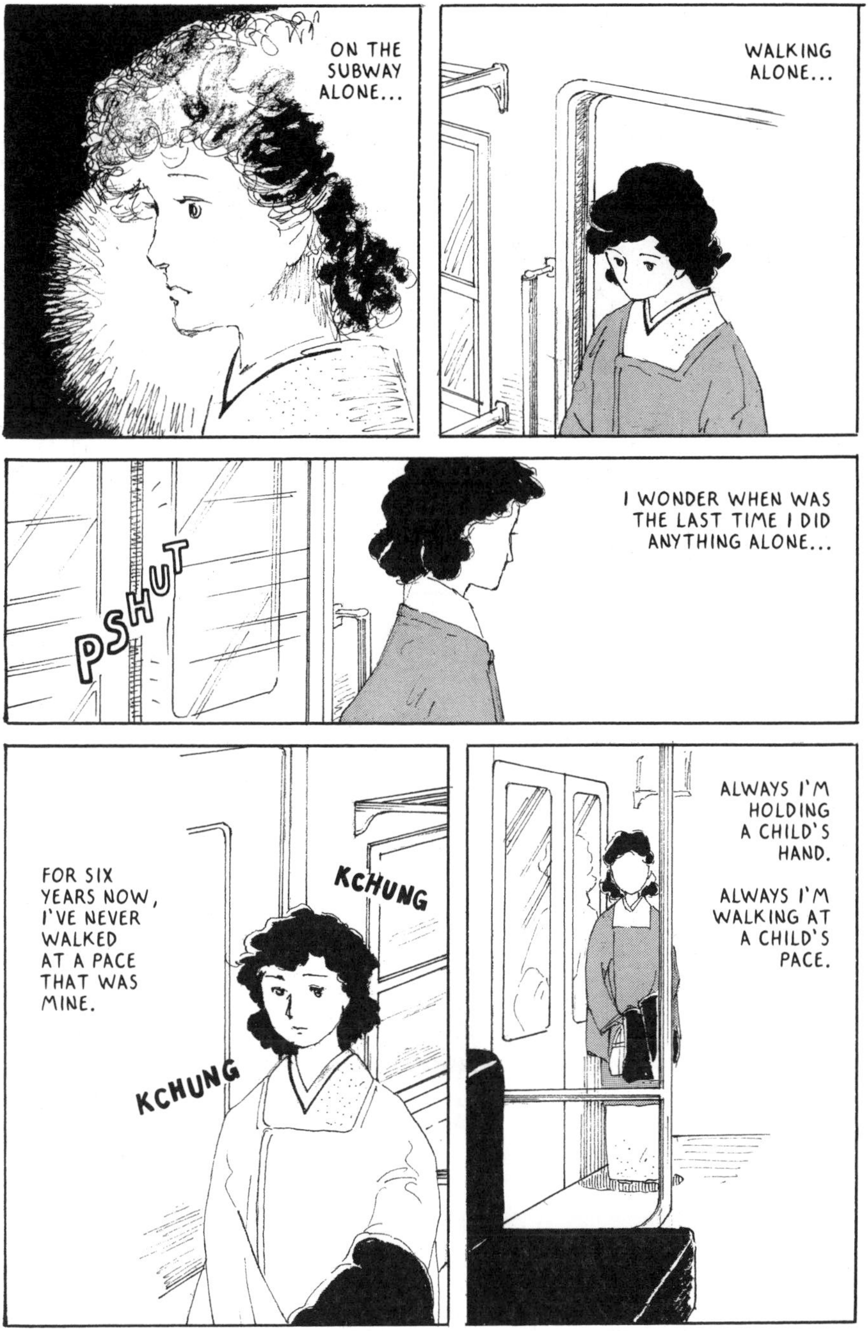
WALKING ALONE...
ON THE SUBWAY ALONE...
I WONDER WHEN WAS THE LAST TIME I DID ANYTHING ALONE...
PSHUT
ALWAYS I'M HOLDING A CHILD'S HAND.
ALWAYS I'M WALKING AT A CHILD'S PACE.
KCHUNG
FOR SIX YEARS NOW, I'VE NEVER WALKED AT A PACE THAT WAS MINE.
KCHUNG

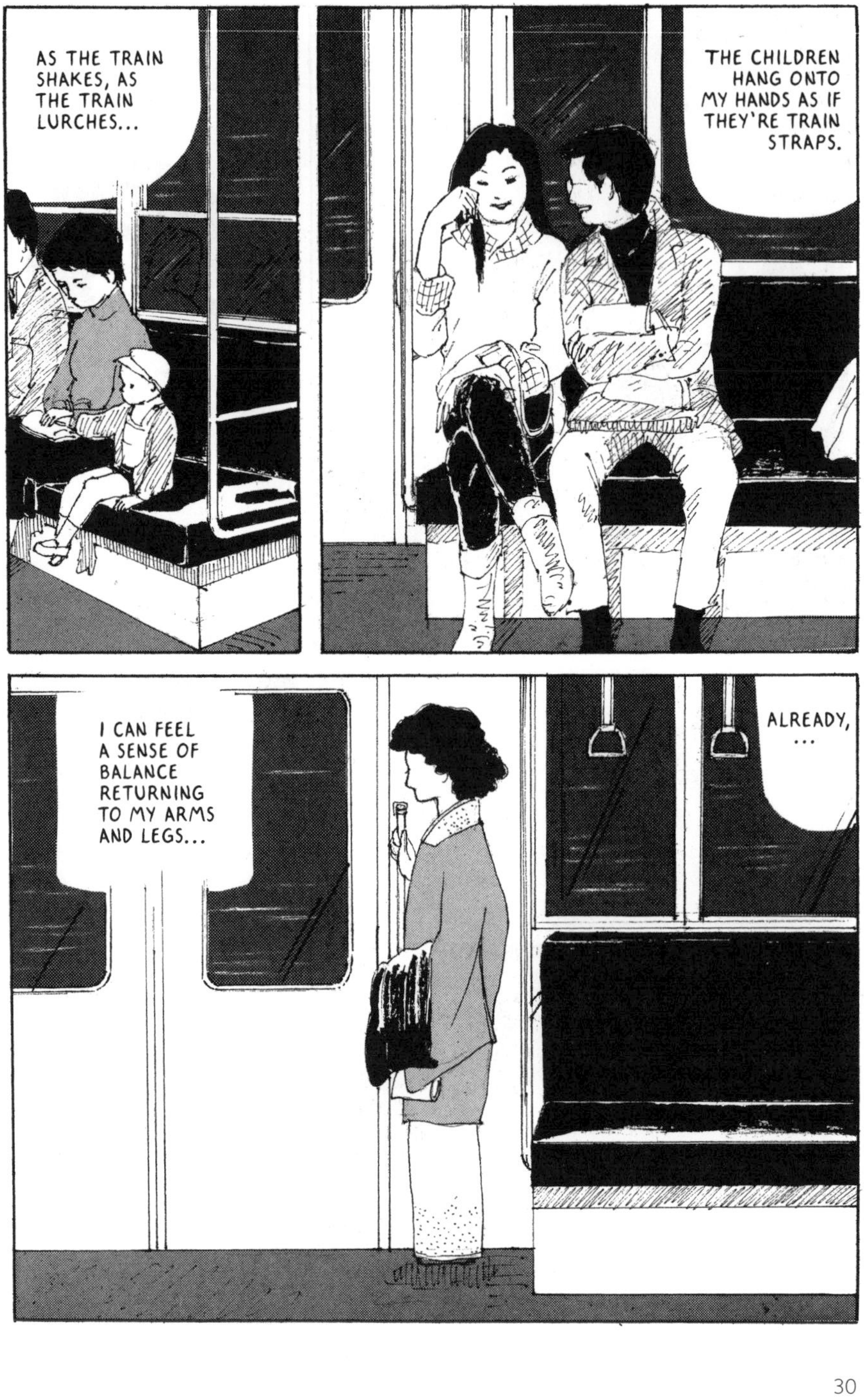
THE CHILDREN HANG ONTO MY HANDS AS IF THEY'RE TRAIN STRAPS.
AS THE TRAIN SHAKES, AS THE TRAIN LURCHES...
ALREADY, ...
I CAN FEEL A SENSE OF BALANCE RETURNING TO MY ARMS AND LEGS...

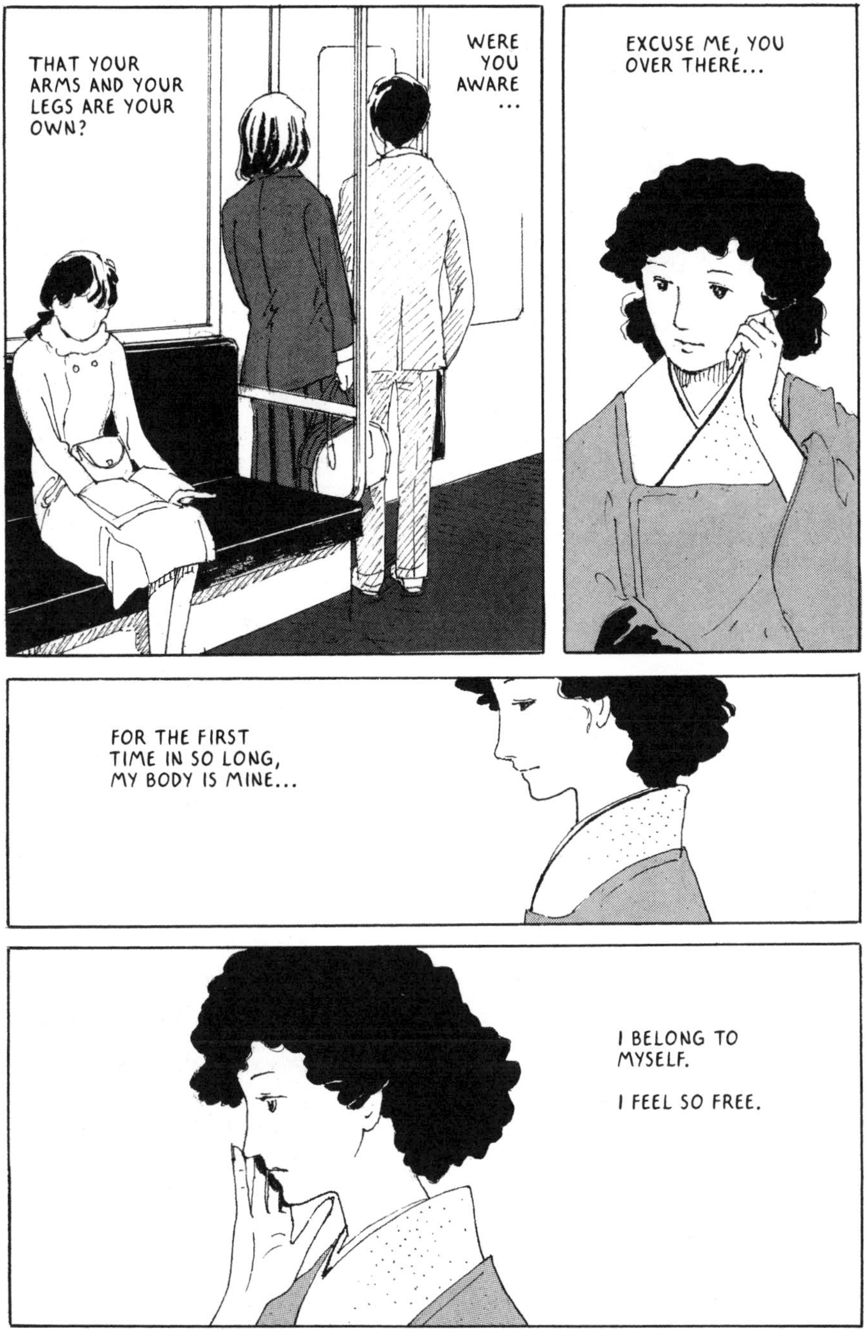
EXCUSE ME, YOU OVER THERE...
WERE YOU AWARE ...
THAT YOUR ARMS AND YOUR LEGS ARE YOUR OWN?
FOR THE FIRST TIME IN SO LONG, MY BODY IS MINE...
I BELONG TO MYSELF.
I FEEL SO FREE.

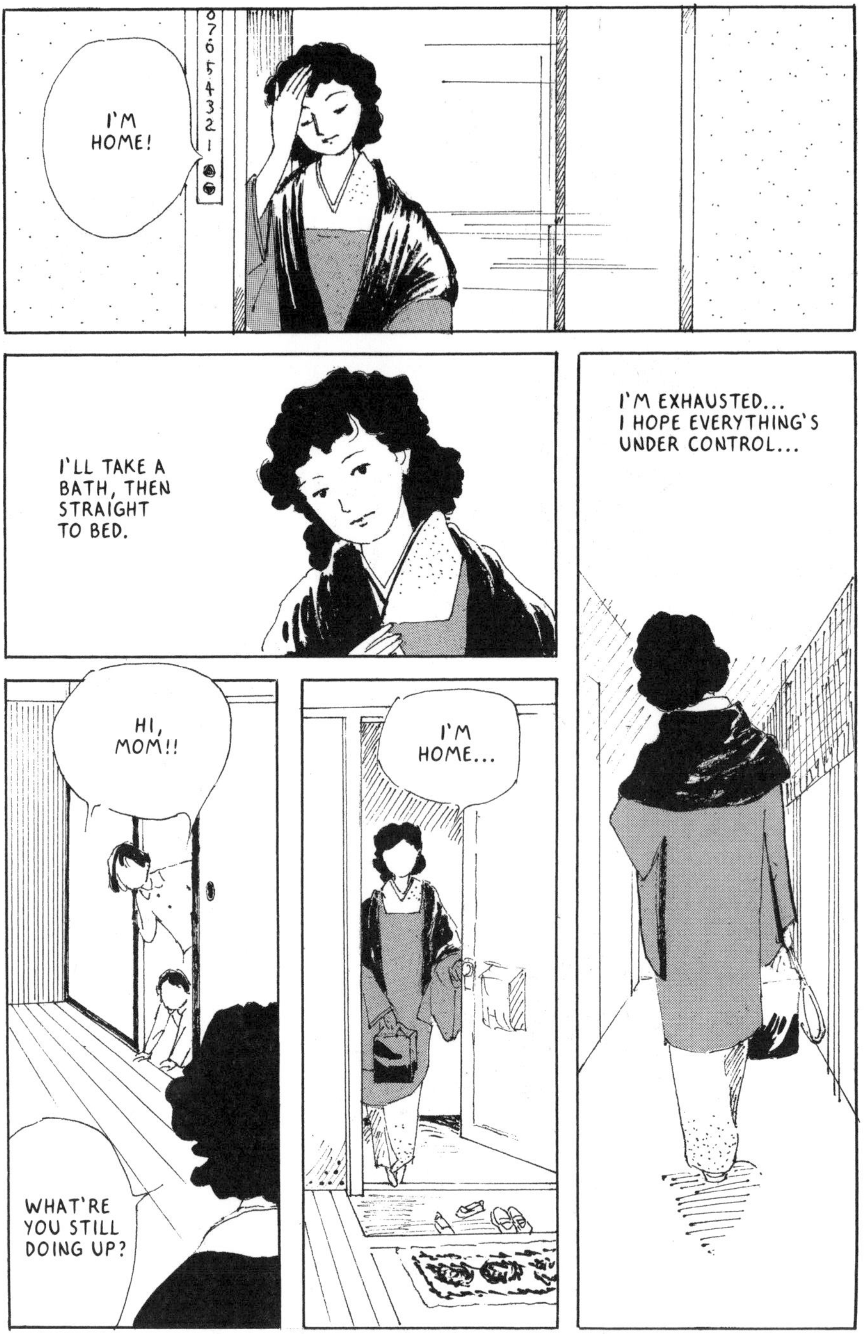
I'M HOME!
I'M EXHAUSTED... I HOPE EVERYTHING'S UNDER CONTROL...
I'LL TAKE A BATH, THEN STRAIGHT TO BED.
I'M HOME...
HI, MOM!!
WHAT'RE YOU STILL DOING UP?

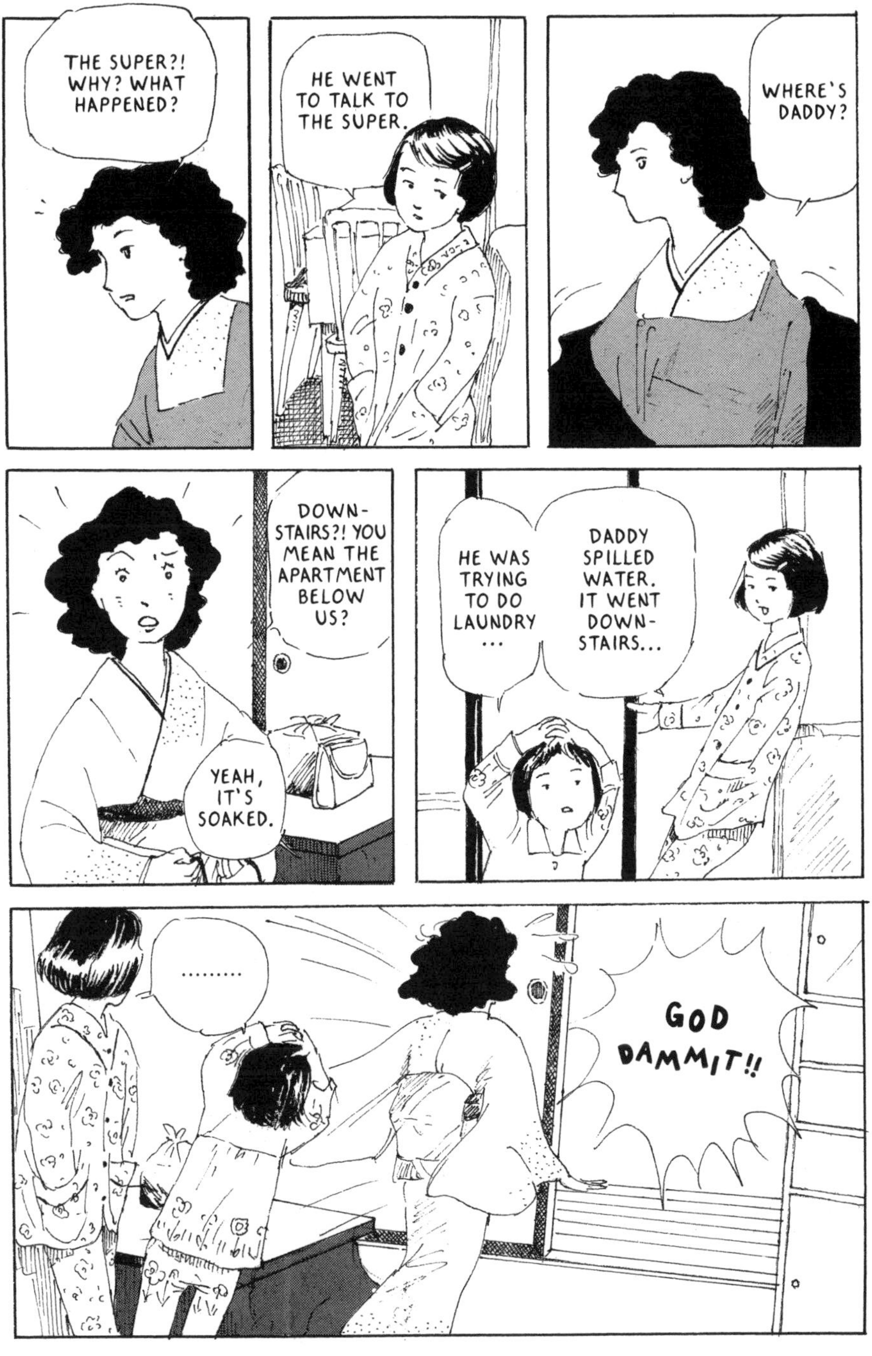
WHERE'S DADDY?
HE WENT TO TALK TO THE SUPER.
THE SUPER?! WHY? WHAT HAPPENED?
DADDY SPILLED WATER. IT WENT DOWN-STAIRS...
HE WAS TRYING TO DO LAUNDRY ...
DOWN-STAIRS?! YOU MEAN THE APARTMENT BELOW US?
YEAH, IT'S SOAKED.
GOD DAMMIT!!
....

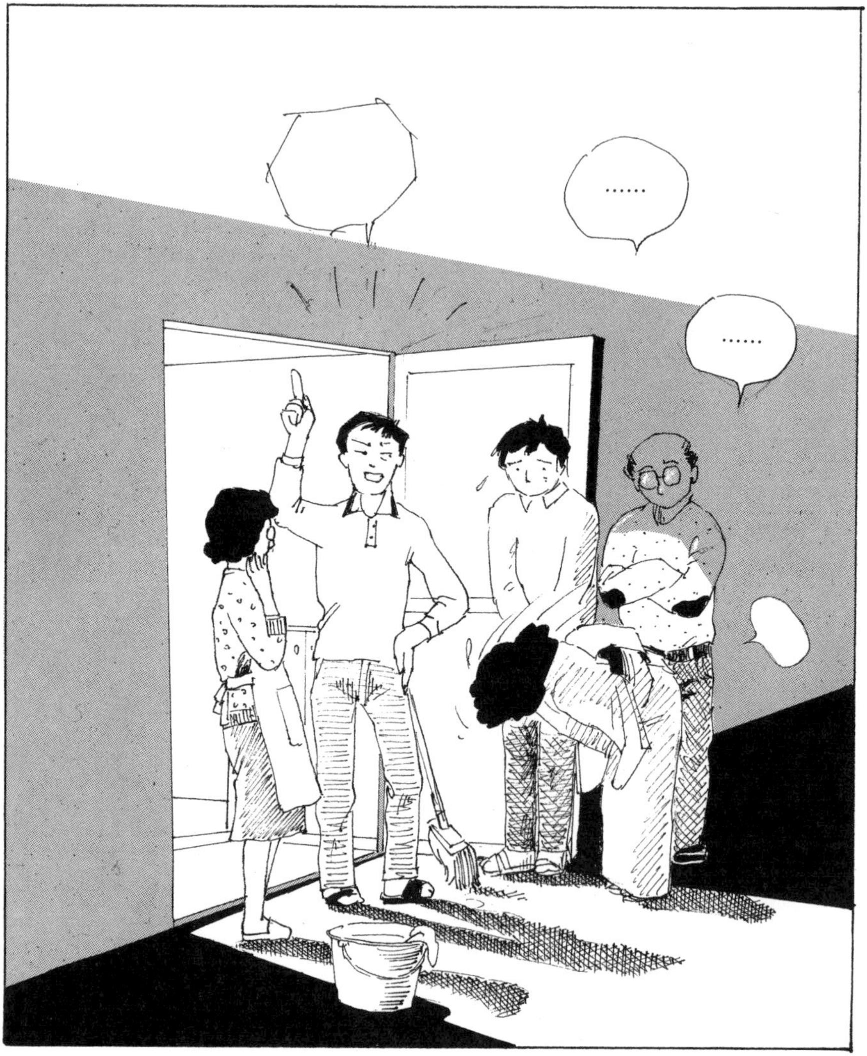
......
......

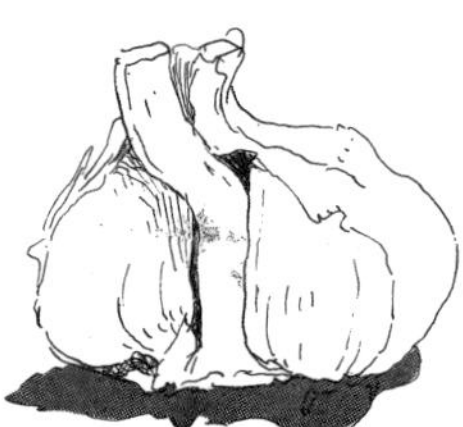

Hold Me Tight

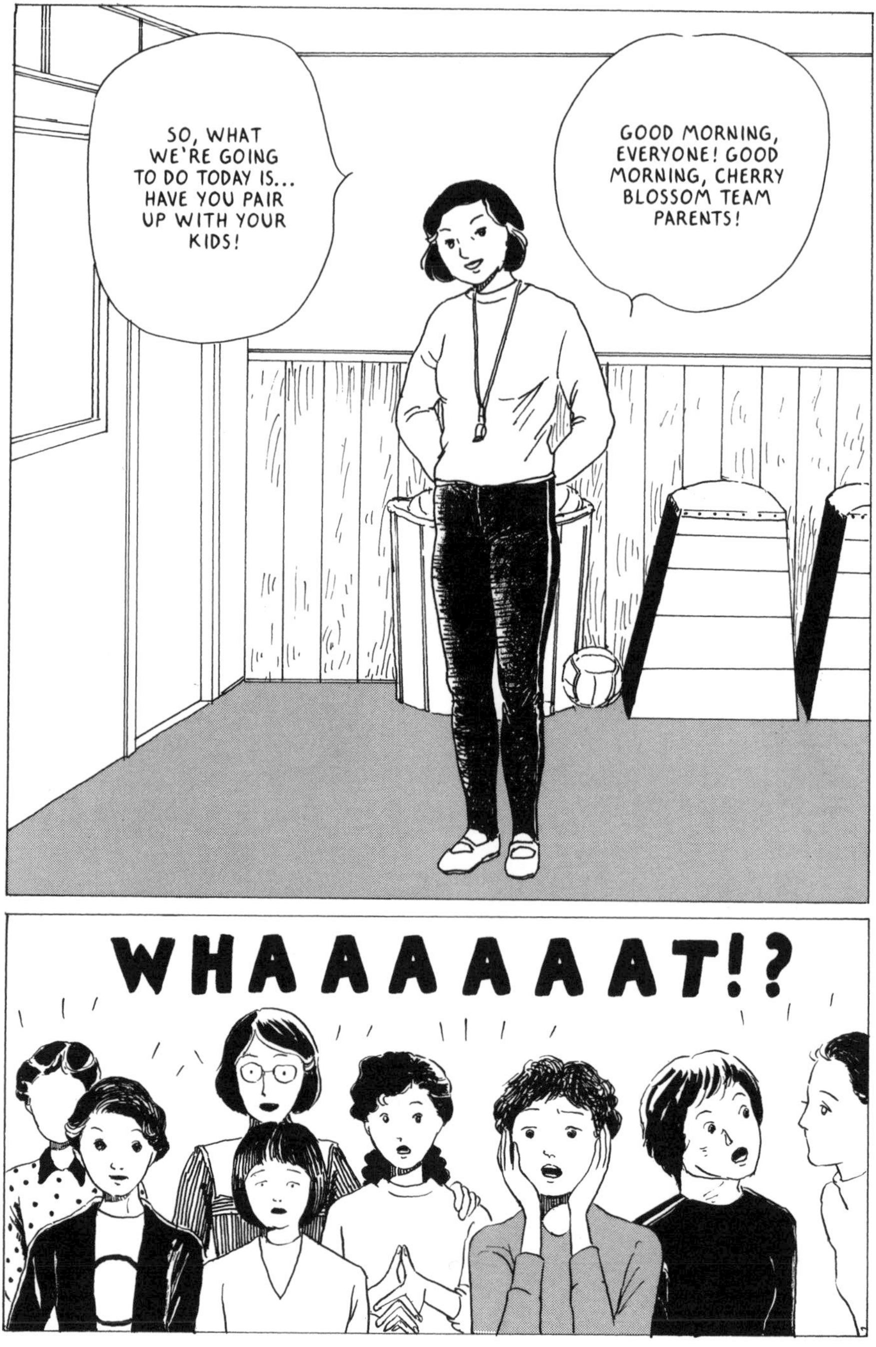
GOOD MORNING, EVERYONE! GOOD MORNING, CHERRY BLOSSOM TEAM PARENTS!
SO, WHAT WE'RE GOING TO DO TODAY IS... HAVE YOU PAIR UP WITH YOUR KIDS!
WHAAAAAAT!?

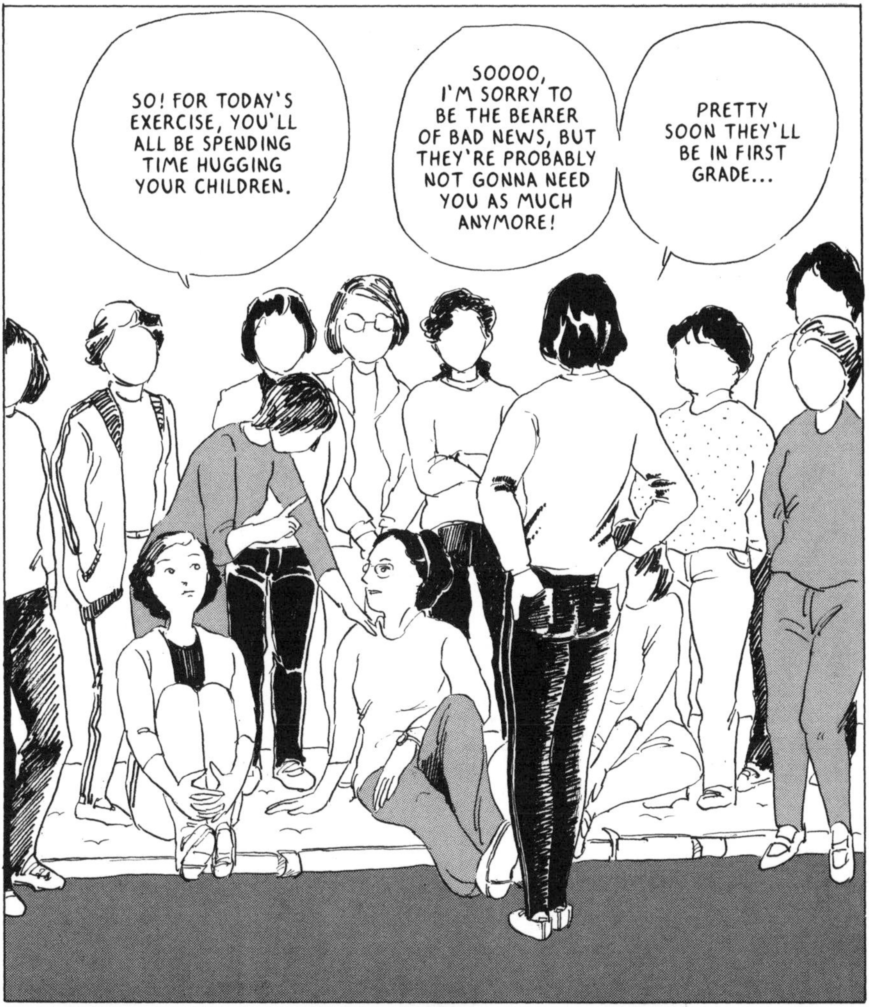
PRETTY SOON THEY'LL BE IN FIRST GRADE...
SOOOO, I'M SORRY TO BE THE BEARER OF BAD NEWS, BUT THEY'RE PROBABLY NOT GONNA NEED YOU AS MUCH ANYMORE!
SO! FOR TODAY'S EXERCISE, YOU'LL ALL BE SPENDING TIME HUGGING YOUR CHILDREN.

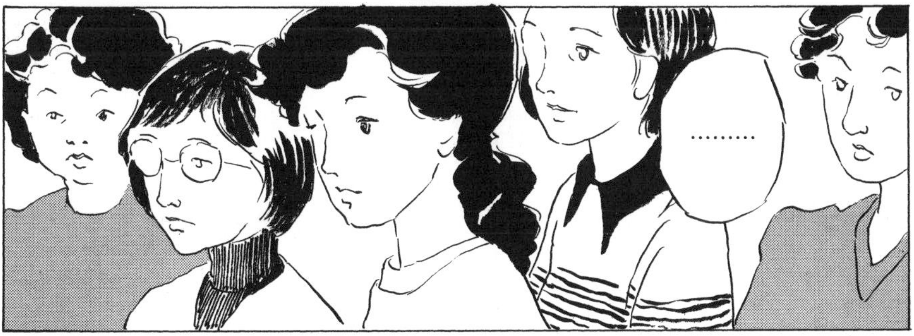
....

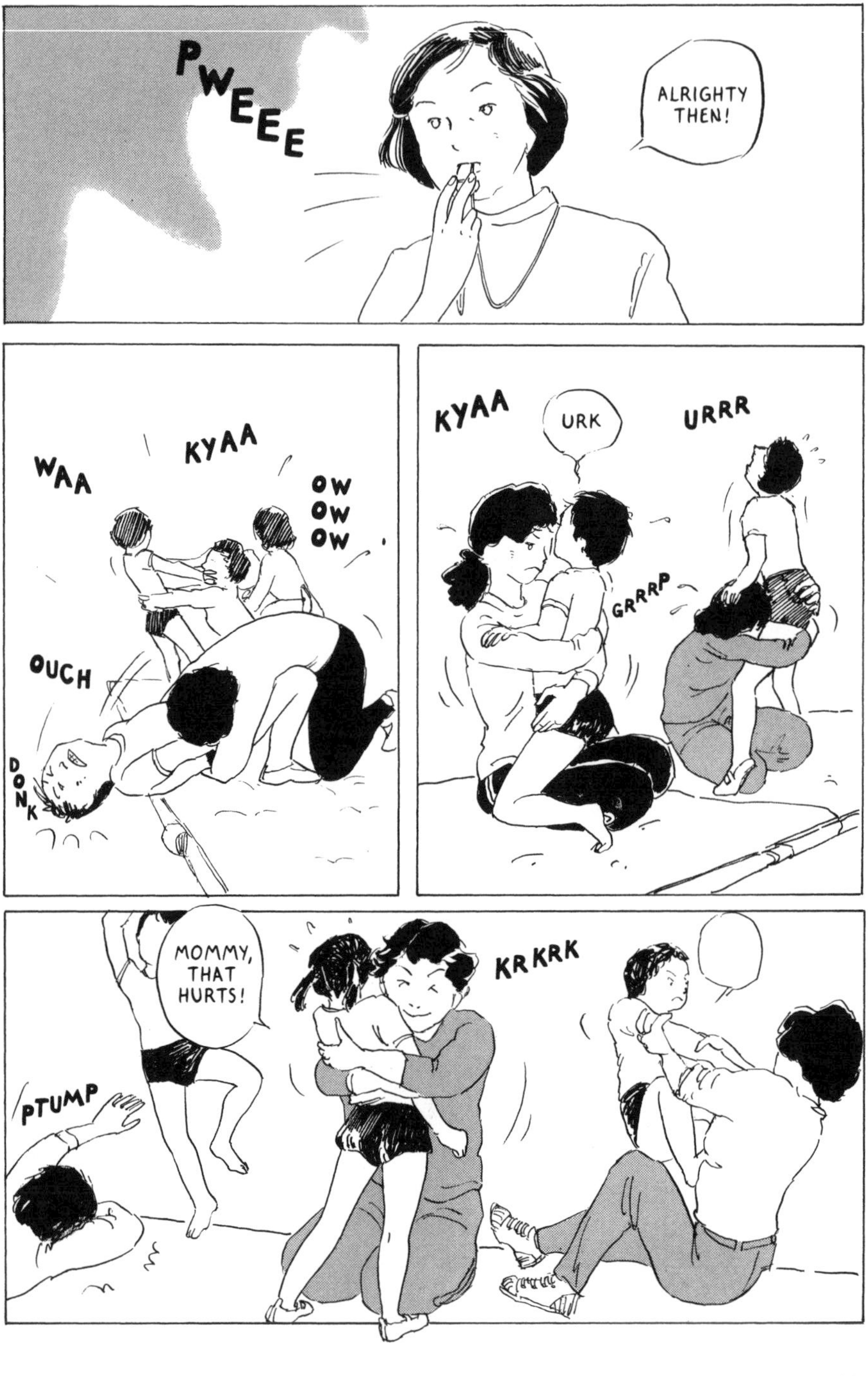
ALRIGHTY THEN!
PWEEE
URRR
URK
KYAA
GRRRP
OW OW OW
KYAA
WAA
OUCH
DONK
KRKRK
MOMMY, THAT HURTS!
PTUMP

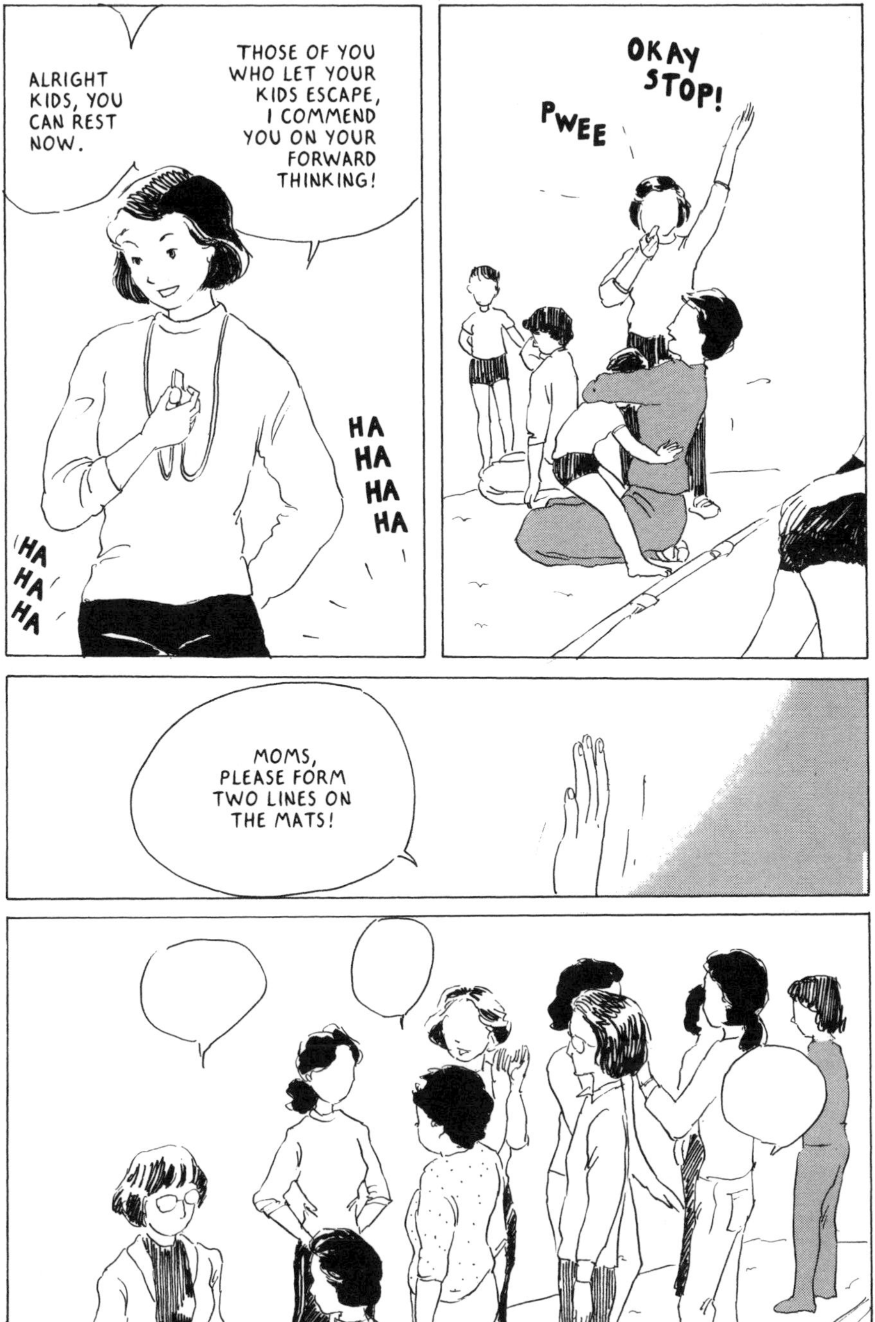
OKAY STOP!
PWEE
THOSE OF YOU WHO LET YOUR KIDS ESCAPE, I COMMEND YOU ON YOUR FORWARD THINKING!
ALRIGHT KIDS, YOU CAN REST NOW.
HA HA HA HA
HA HA HA
MOMS, PLEASE FORM TWO LINES ON THE MATS!

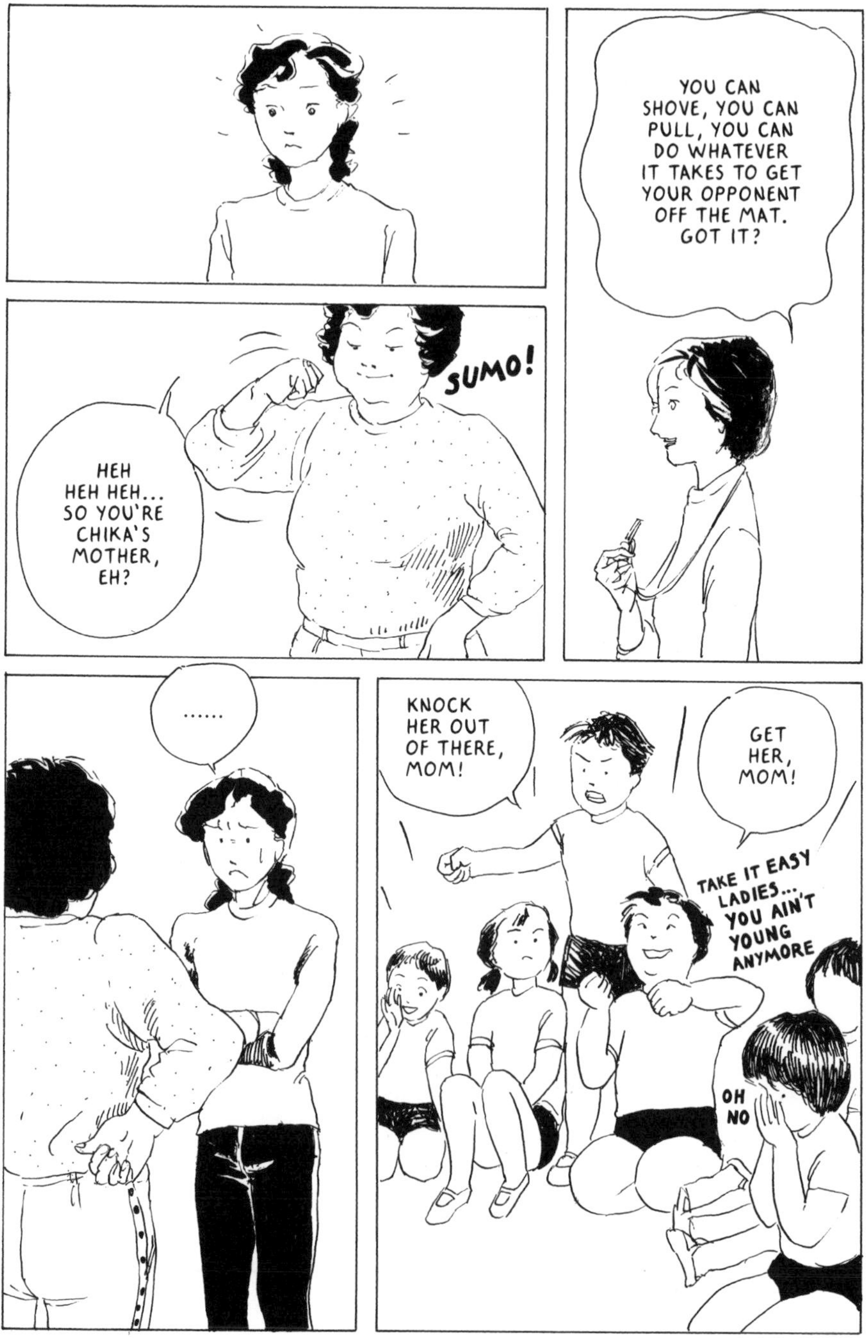
YOU CAN SHOVE, YOU CAN PULL, YOU CAN DO WHATEVER IT TAKES TO GET YOUR OPPONENT OFF THE MAT. GOT IT?
SUMO!
HEH HEH HEH... SO YOU'RE CHIKA'S MOTHER, EH?
GET HER, MOM!
KNOCK HER OUT OF THERE, MOM!
TAKE IT EASY LADIES... YOU AIN'T YOUNG ANYMORE
OH NO
......

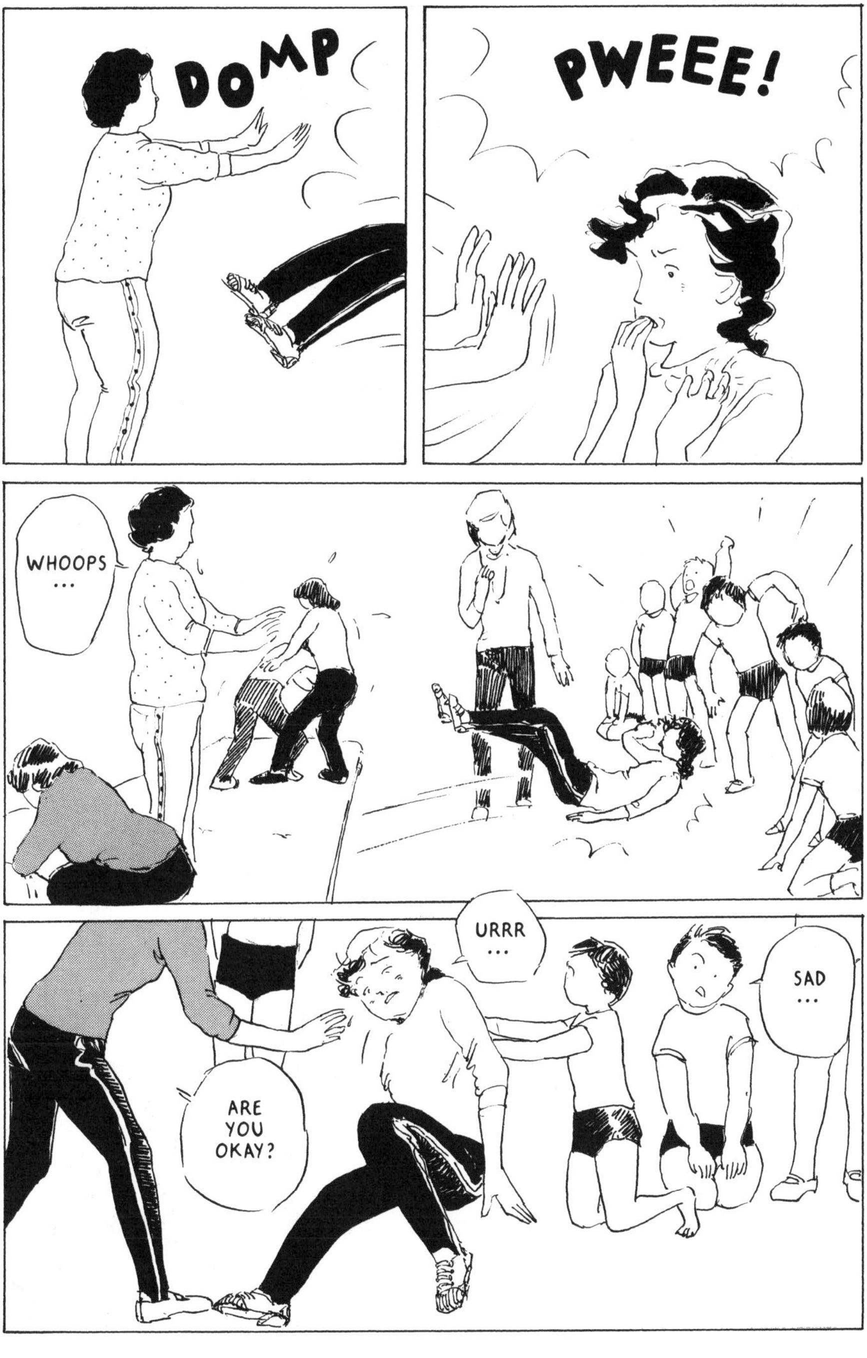
PWEEE!
DOMP
WHOOPS ...
SAD ...
URRR ...
ARE YOU OKAY?

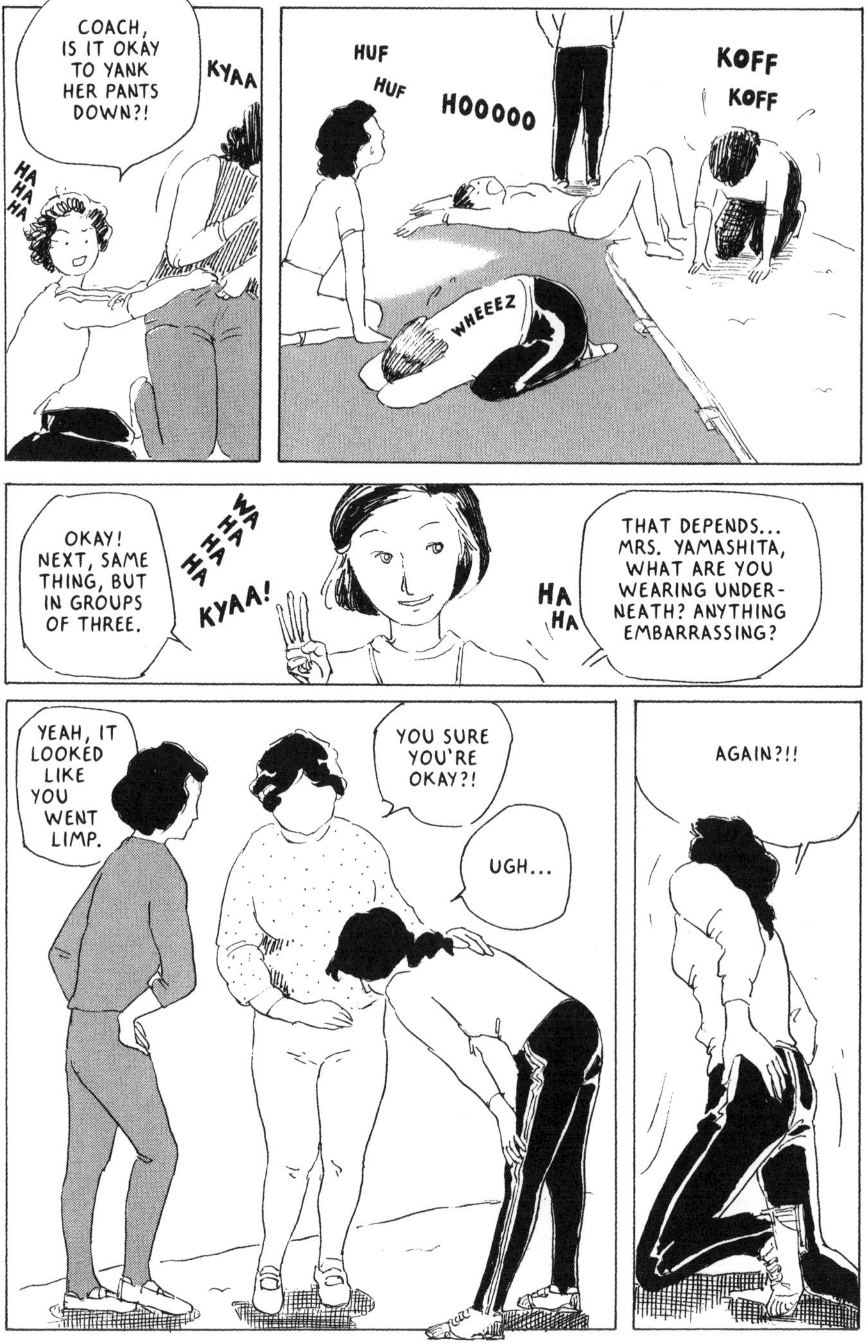
HUF
HUF
HOOOOO
KOFF
KOFF
WHEEEZ
KYAA
COACH, IS IT OKAY TO YANK HER PANTS DOWN?!
HA HA HA
THAT DEPENDS... MRS. YAMASHITA, WHAT ARE YOU WEARING UNDERNEATH? ANYTHING EMBARRASSING?
HA HA
WA HA HA HA HA
KYAA!
OKAY! NEXT, SAME THING, BUT IN GROUPS OF THREE.
AGAIN?!!
YOU SURE YOU'RE OKAY?!
UGH...
YEAH, IT LOOKED LIKE YOU WENT LIMP.

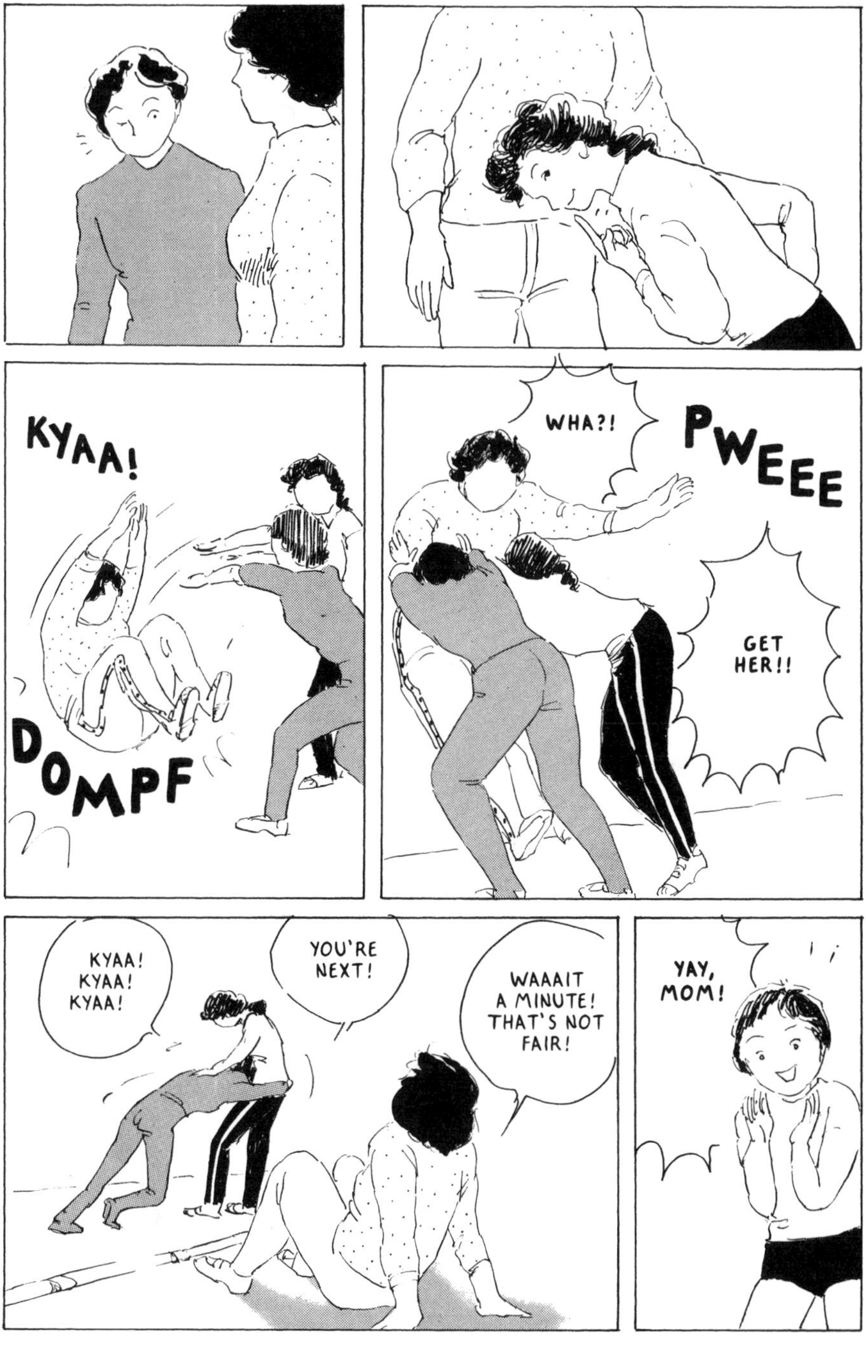
WHA?!
PWEEE
GET HER!!
KYAA!
DOMPF
YAY, MOM!
WAAAIT A MINUTE! THAT'S NOT FAIR!
YOU'RE NEXT!
KYAA! KYAA! KYAA!

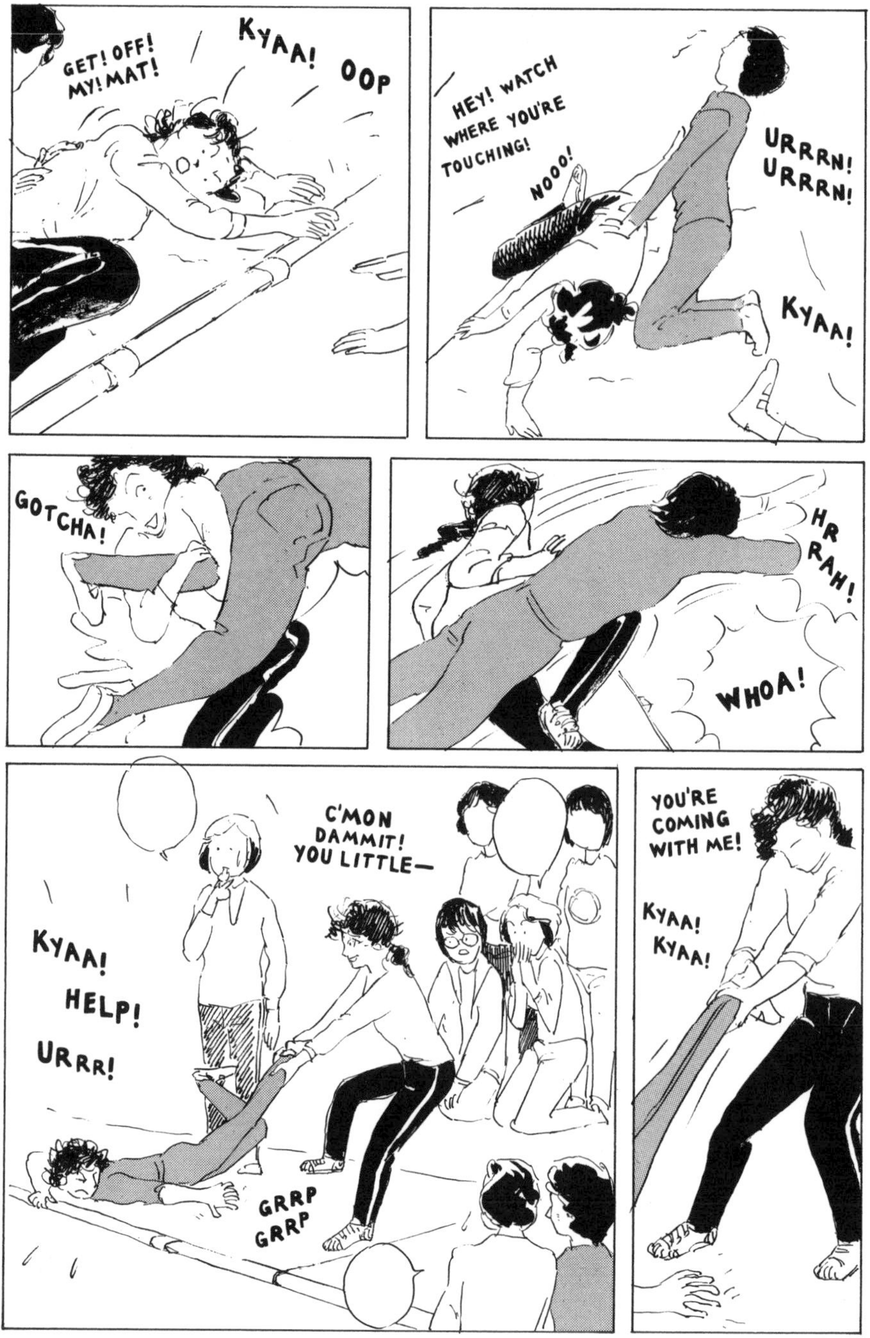
HEY! WATCH WHERE YOU'RE TOUCHING!
NOOO!
URRRN! URRRN!
KYAA!
GET! OFF! MY! MAT!
KYAA!
OOP
HR RAH!
WHOA!
GOTCHA!
YOU'RE COMING WITH ME!
KYAA! KYAA!
C'MON DAMMIT! YOU LITTLE—
KYAA!
HELP!
URRR!
GRRP GRRP

Banana Days

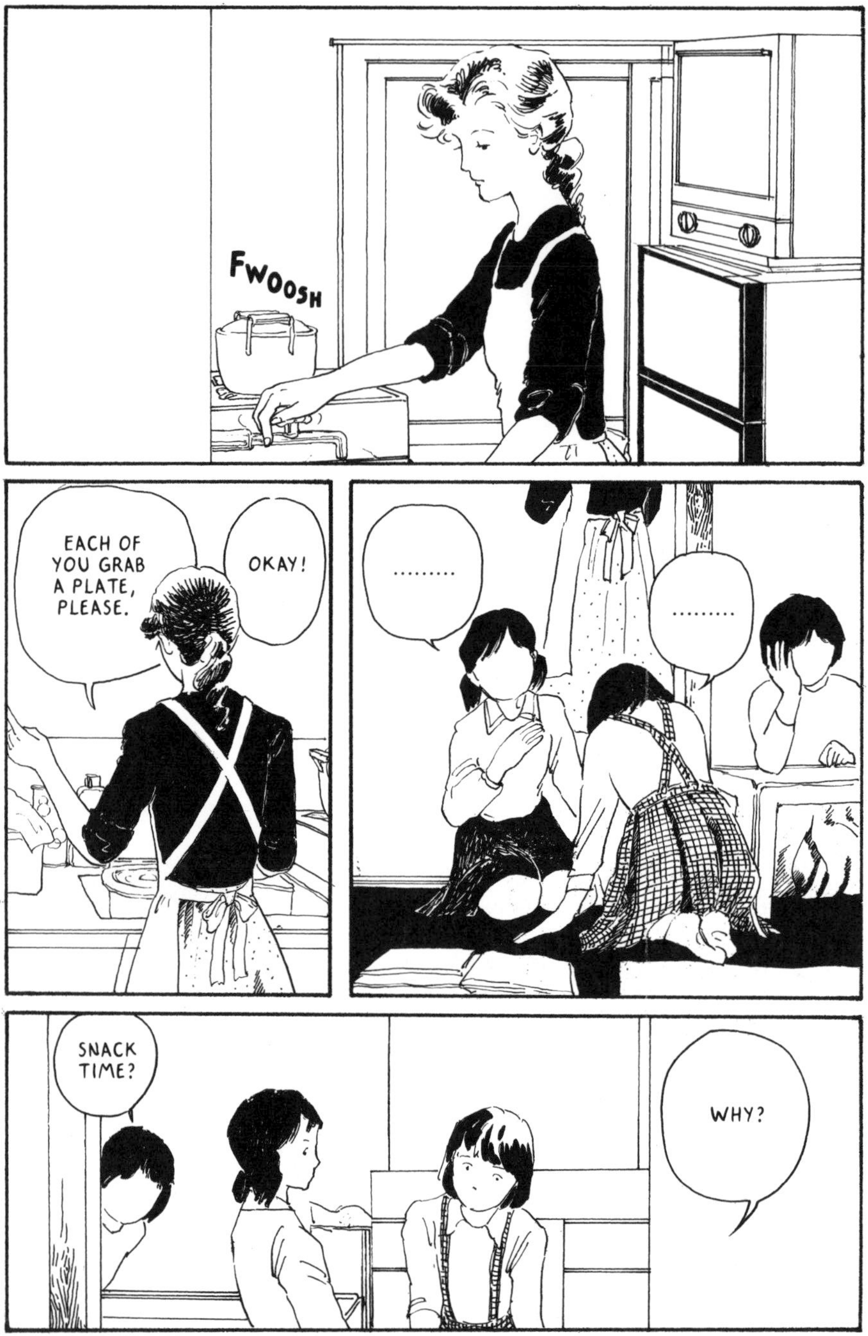
FWOOSH
....
....
OKAY!
EACH OF YOU GRAB A PLATE, PLEASE.
WHY?
SNACK TIME?

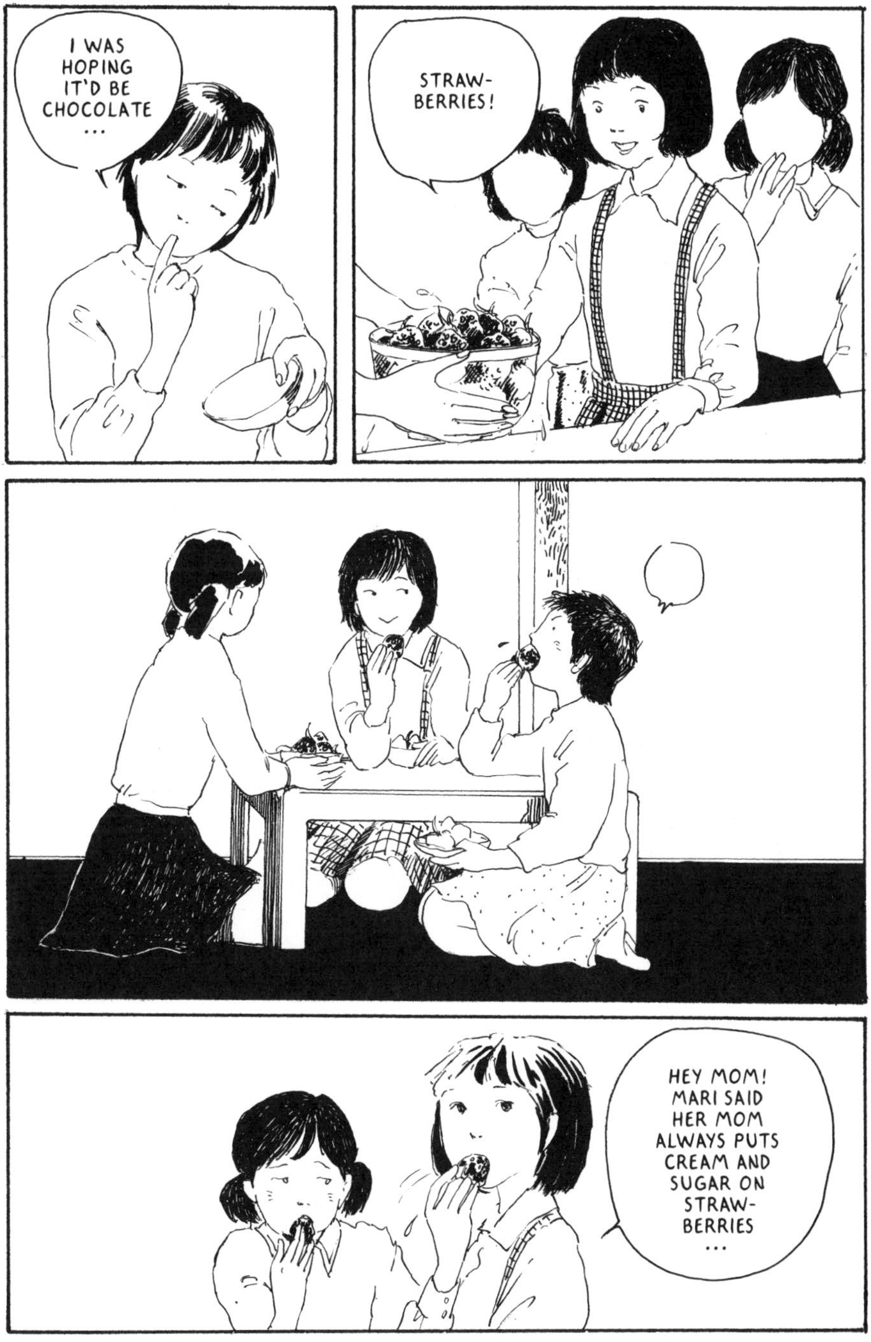
STRAW-BERRIES!
I WAS HOPING IT'D BE CHOCOLATE ...
HEY MOM! MARI SAID HER MOM ALWAYS PUTS CREAM AND SUGAR ON STRAW-BERRIES ...

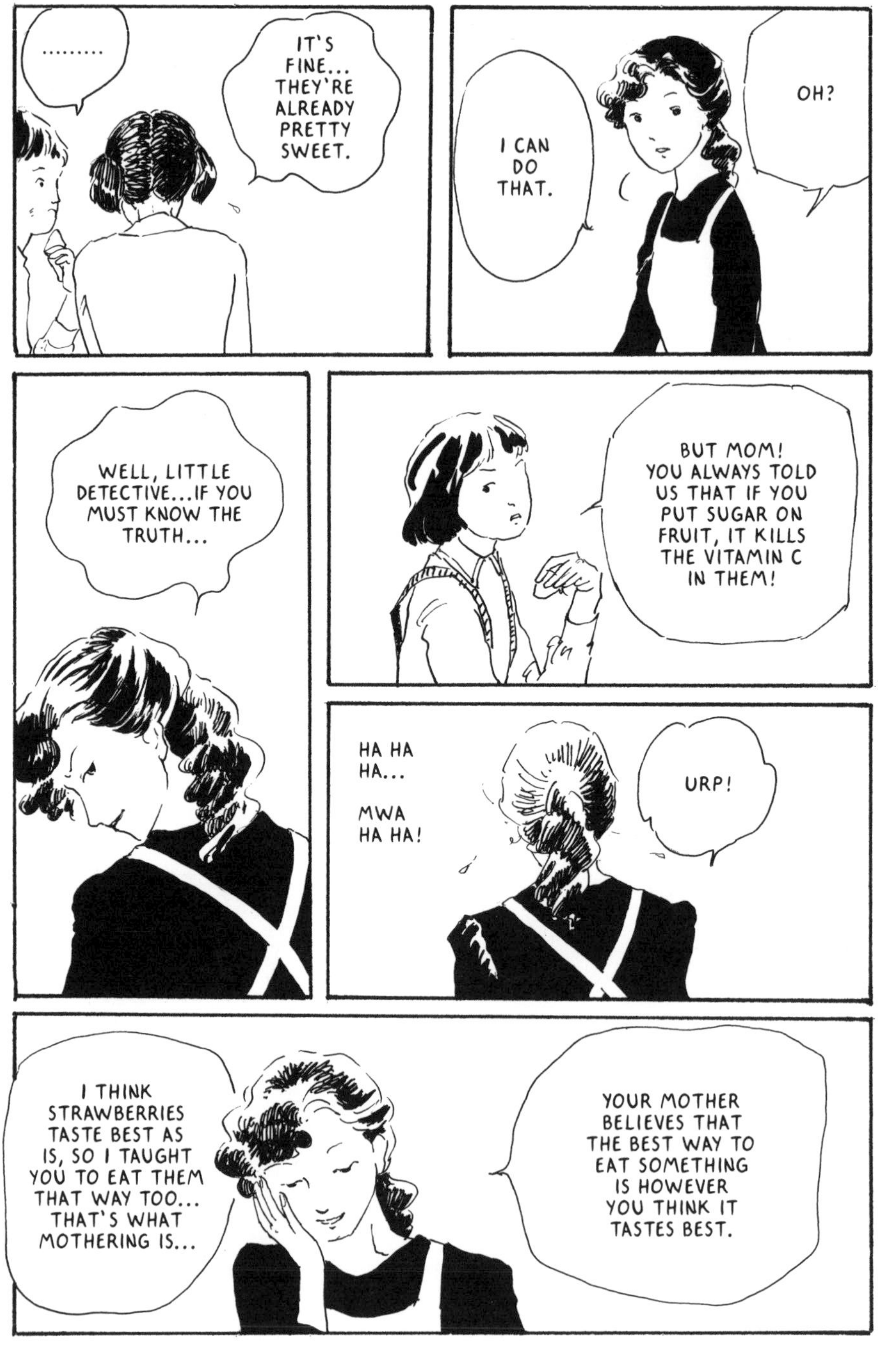
OH?
I CAN DO THAT.
IT'S FINE... THEY'RE ALREADY PRETTY SWEET.
....
BUT MOM! YOU ALWAYS TOLD US THAT IF YOU PUT SUGAR ON FRUIT, IT KILLS THE VITAMIN C IN THEM!
URP!
HA HA HA...
MWA HA HA!
WELL, LITTLE DETECTIVE...IF YOU MUST KNOW THE TRUTH...
YOUR MOTHER BELIEVES THAT THE BEST WAY TO EAT SOMETHING IS HOWEVER YOU THINK IT TASTES BEST.
I THINK STRAWBERRIES TASTE BEST AS IS, SO I TAUGHT YOU TO EAT THEM THAT WAY TOO... THAT'S WHAT MOTHERING IS...

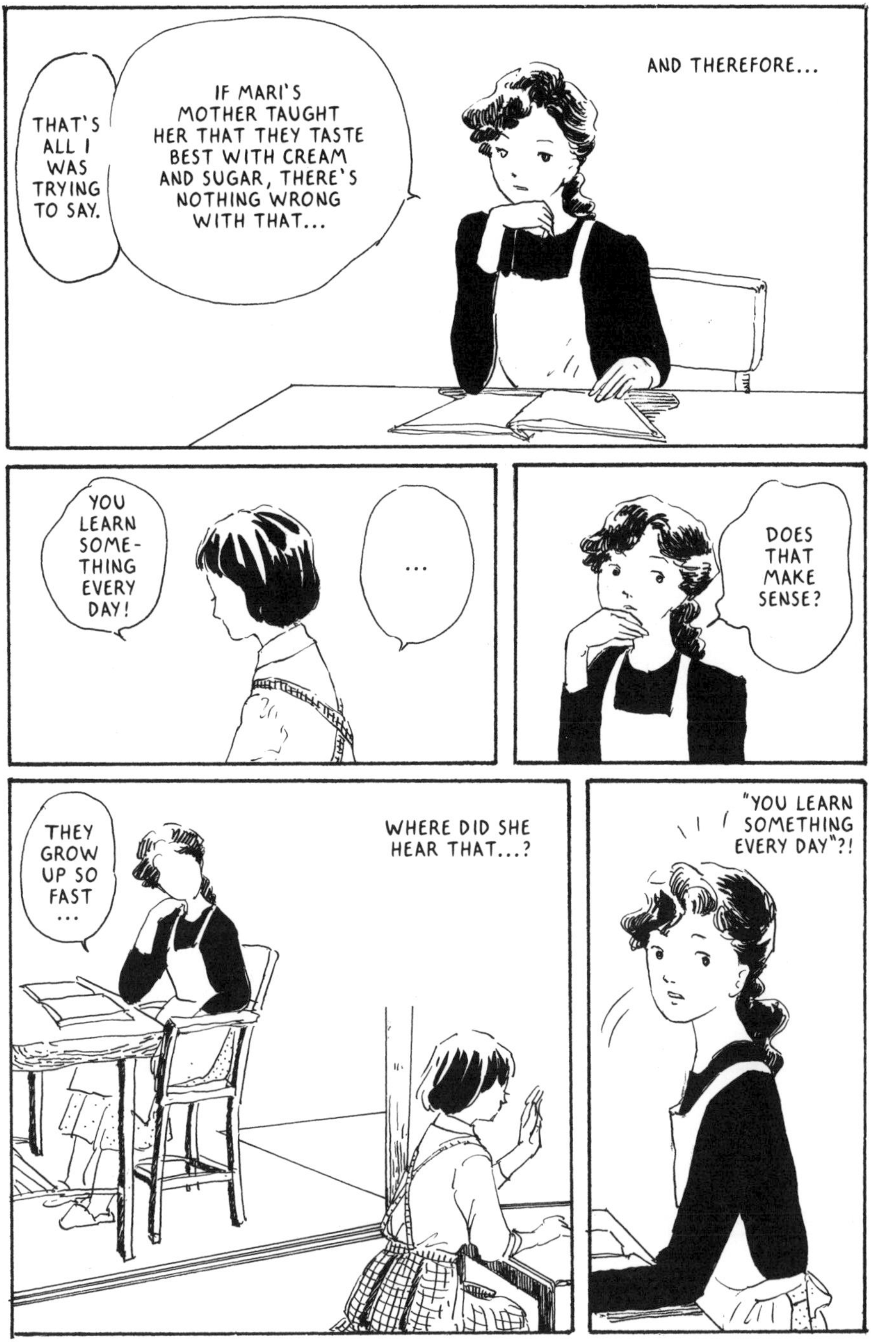
AND THEREFORE...
IF MARI'S MOTHER TAUGHT HER THAT THEY TASTE BEST WITH CREAM AND SUGAR, THERE'S NOTHING WRONG WITH THAT...
THAT'S ALL I WAS TRYING TO SAY.
DOES THAT MAKE SENSE?
...
YOU LEARN SOMETHING EVERY DAY!
"YOU LEARN SOMETHING EVERY DAY"?!
WHERE DID SHE HEAR THAT...?
THEY GROW UP SO FAST ...

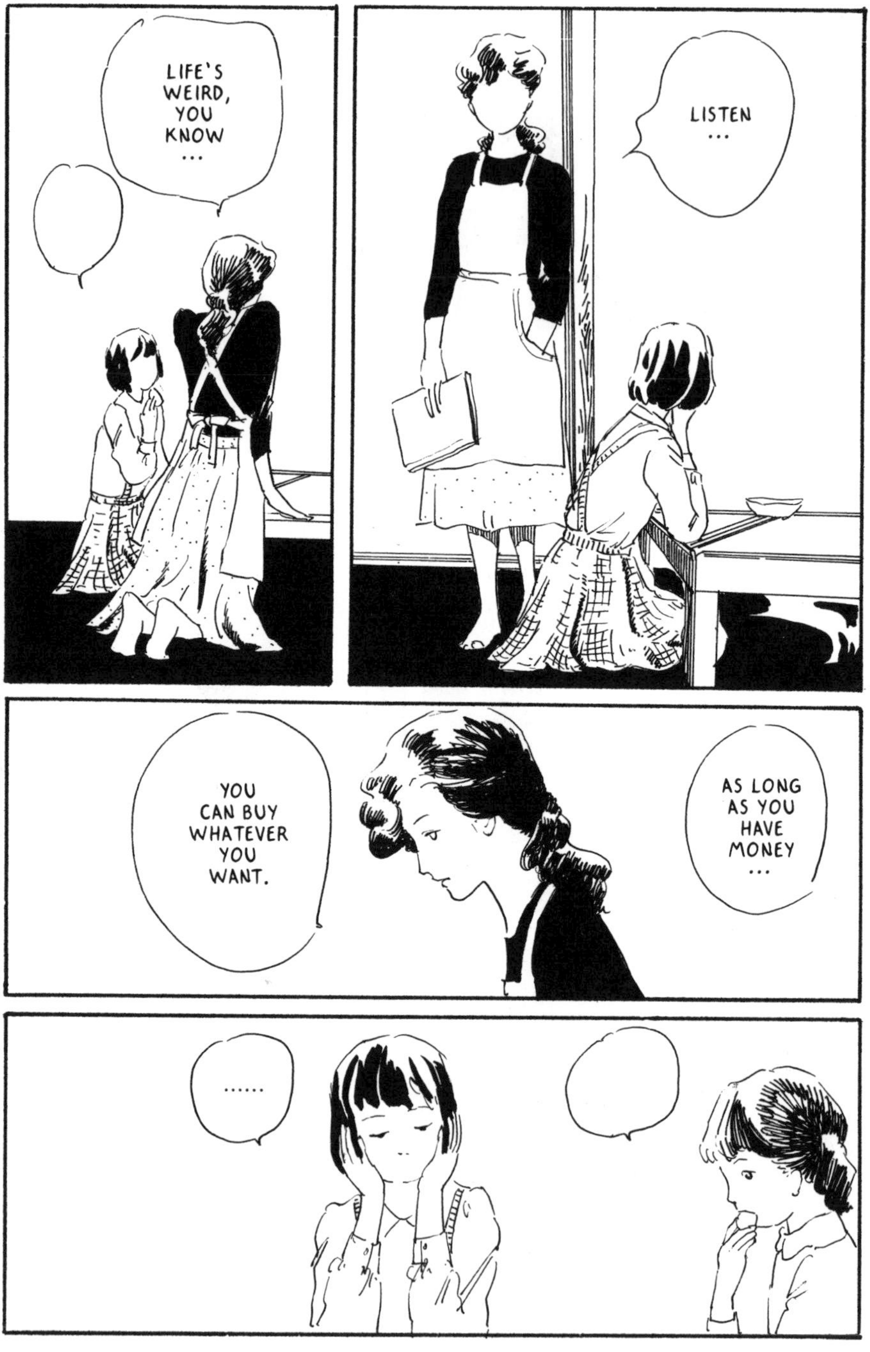
LISTEN ...
LIFE'S WEIRD, YOU KNOW ...
AS LONG AS YOU HAVE MONEY ...
YOU CAN BUY WHATEVER YOU WANT.
......

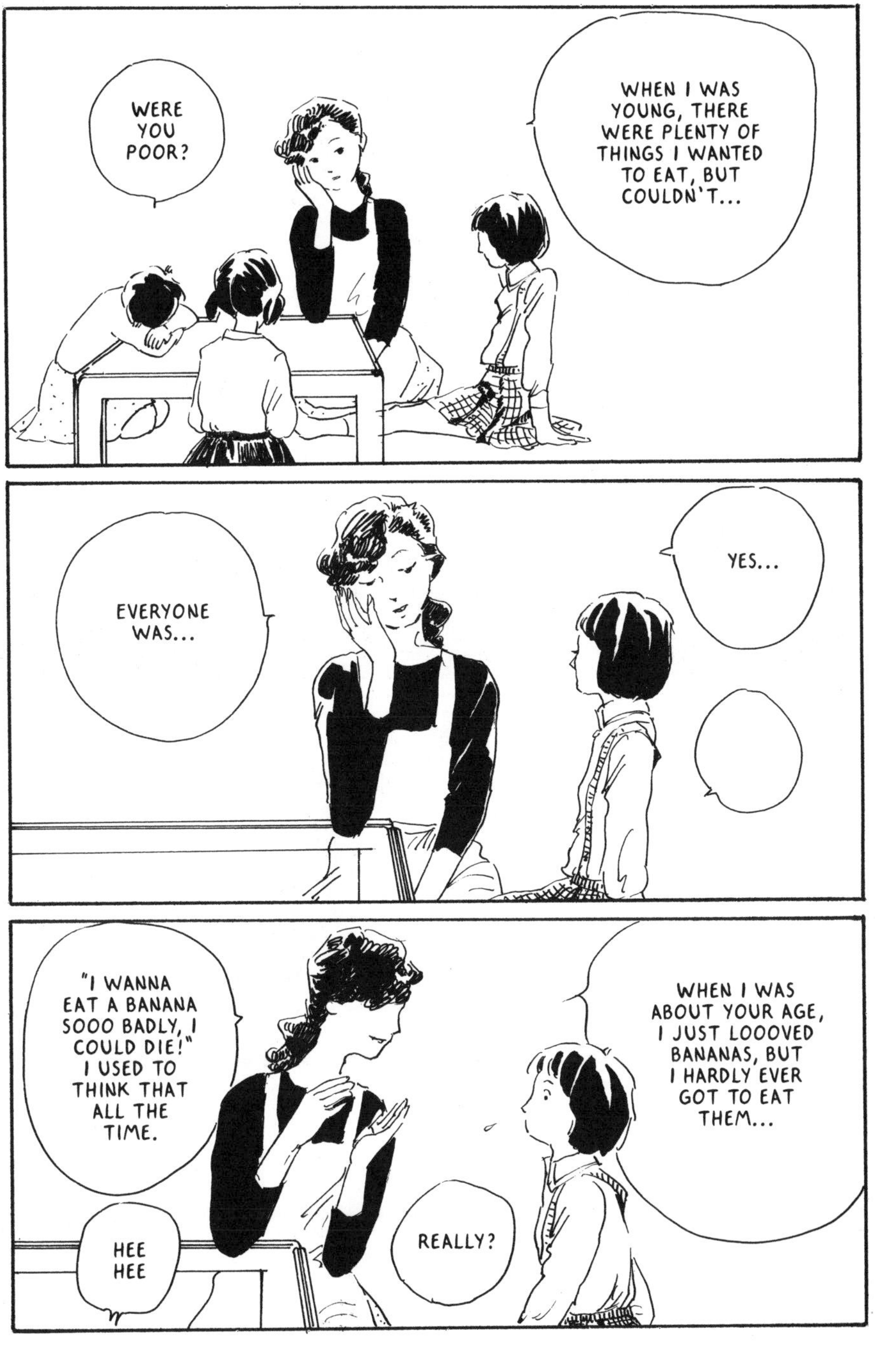
WHEN I WAS YOUNG, THERE WERE PLENTY OF THINGS I WANTED TO EAT, BUT COULDN'T...
WERE YOU POOR?
YES...
EVERYONE WAS...
WHEN I WAS ABOUT YOUR AGE, I JUST LOOOVED BANANAS, BUT I HARDLY EVER GOT TO EAT THEM...
"I WANNA EAT A BANANA SOOO BADLY, I COULD DIE!" I USED TO THINK THAT ALL THE TIME.
REALLY?
HEE HEE

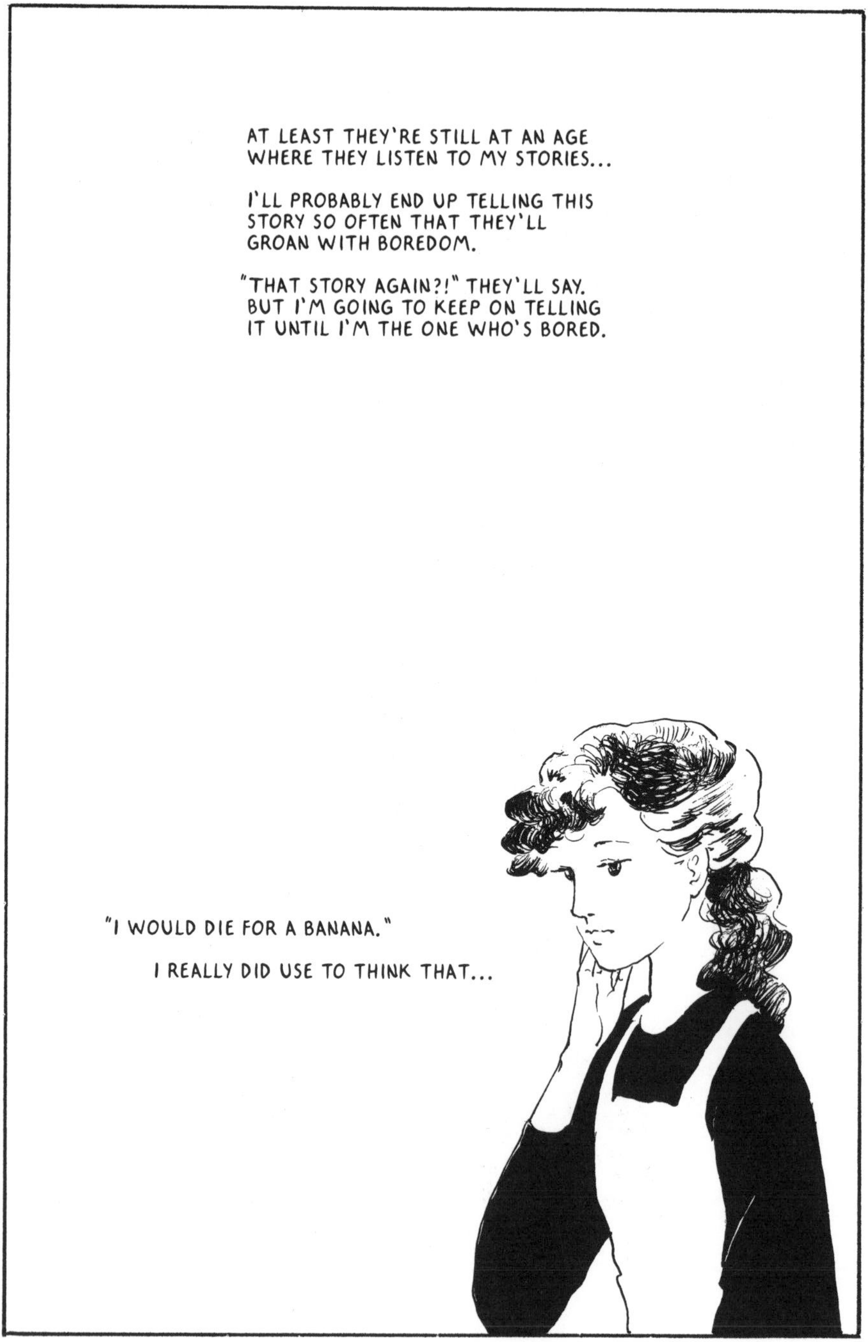
AT LEAST THEY'RE STILL AT AN AGE WHERE THEY LISTEN TO MY STORIES...
I'LL PROBABLY END UP TELLING THIS STORY SO OFTEN THAT THEY'LL GROAN WITH BOREDOM.
"THAT STORY AGAIN?!" THEY'LL SAY. BUT I'M GOING TO KEEP ON TELLING IT UNTIL I'M THE ONE WHO'S BORED.
"I WOULD DIE FOR A BANANA."
I REALLY DID USE TO THINK THAT...

Cool Kids

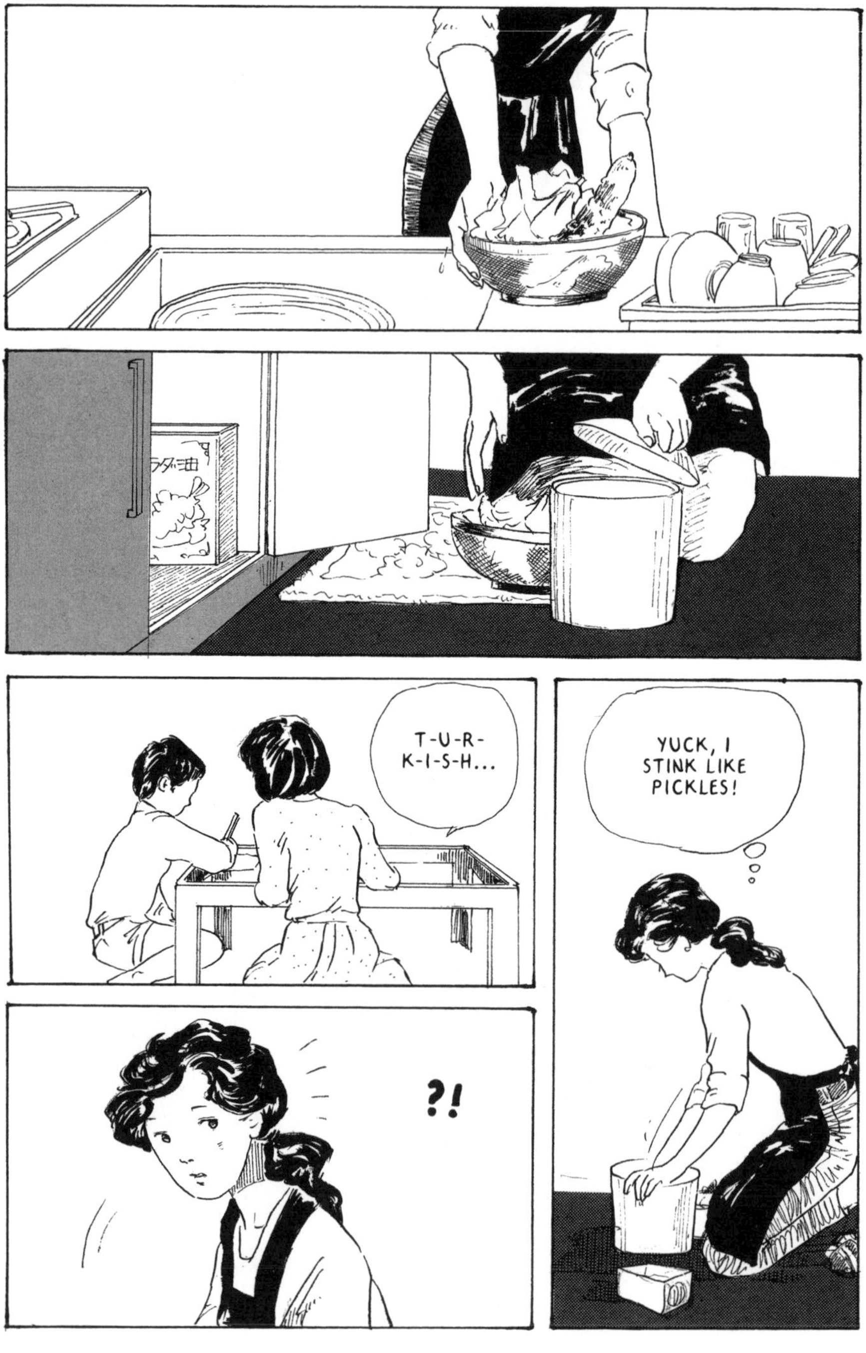
YUCK, I STINK LIKE PICKLES!
T-U-R-K-I-S-H...
?!

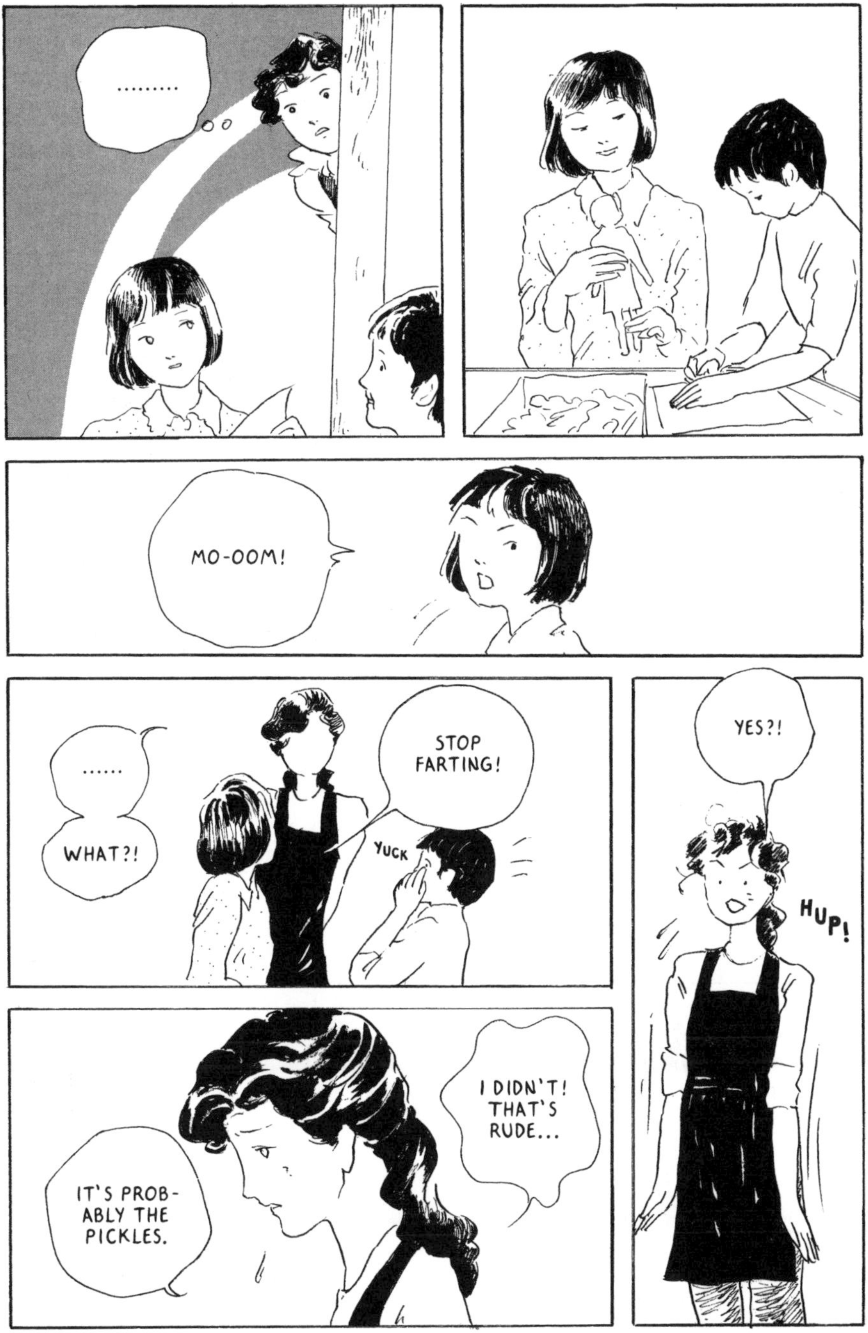
....
MO-OOM!
YES?!
HUP!
STOP FARTING!
YUCK
......
WHAT?!
I DIDN'T! THAT'S RUDE...
IT'S PROB-ABLY THE PICKLES.

OH...
IT STILL STINKS...
HEY, UM...
...
WHAT?
UM...DID I JUST HEAR YOU SPELL OUT THE WORD "TURKISH"?
FOOSH
YEAH, SO?
TURKISH FANNY?!
TURKISH FANNY.

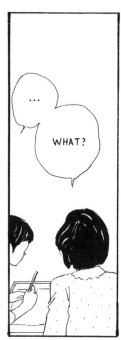

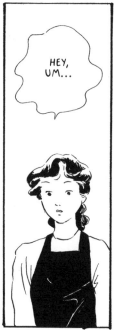

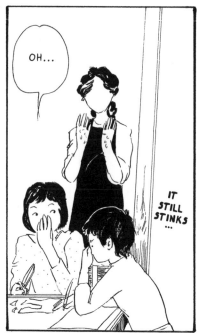

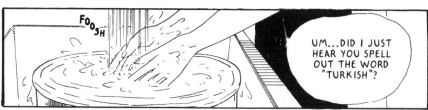

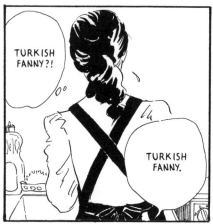

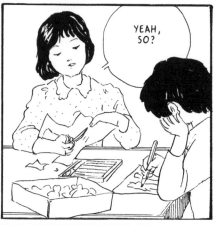

"TURKISH" (SHORT FOR "TURKISH BATH") USED TO REFER TO A KIND OF BATHING-BASED SEX ESTABLISHMENT IN JAPAN. NOW THEY ARE CALLED "SOAPLANDS."

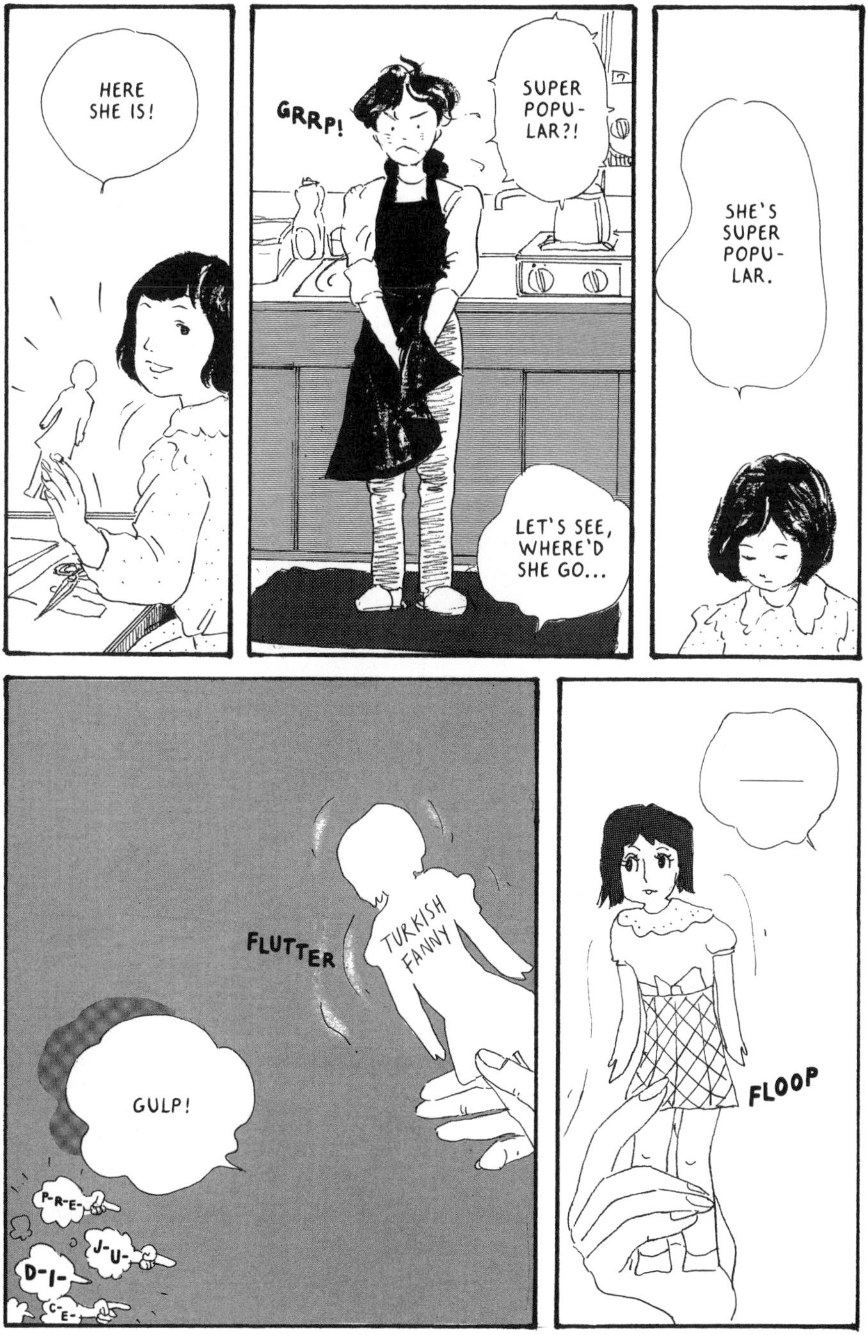
SHE'S SUPER POPULAR.
SUPER POPULAR?!
GRRP!
LET'S SEE, WHERE'D SHE GO...
HERE SHE IS!
——
FLOOP
FLUTTER
TURKISH FANNY
GULP!
P-R-E-
J-U-
D-I-
C-E-

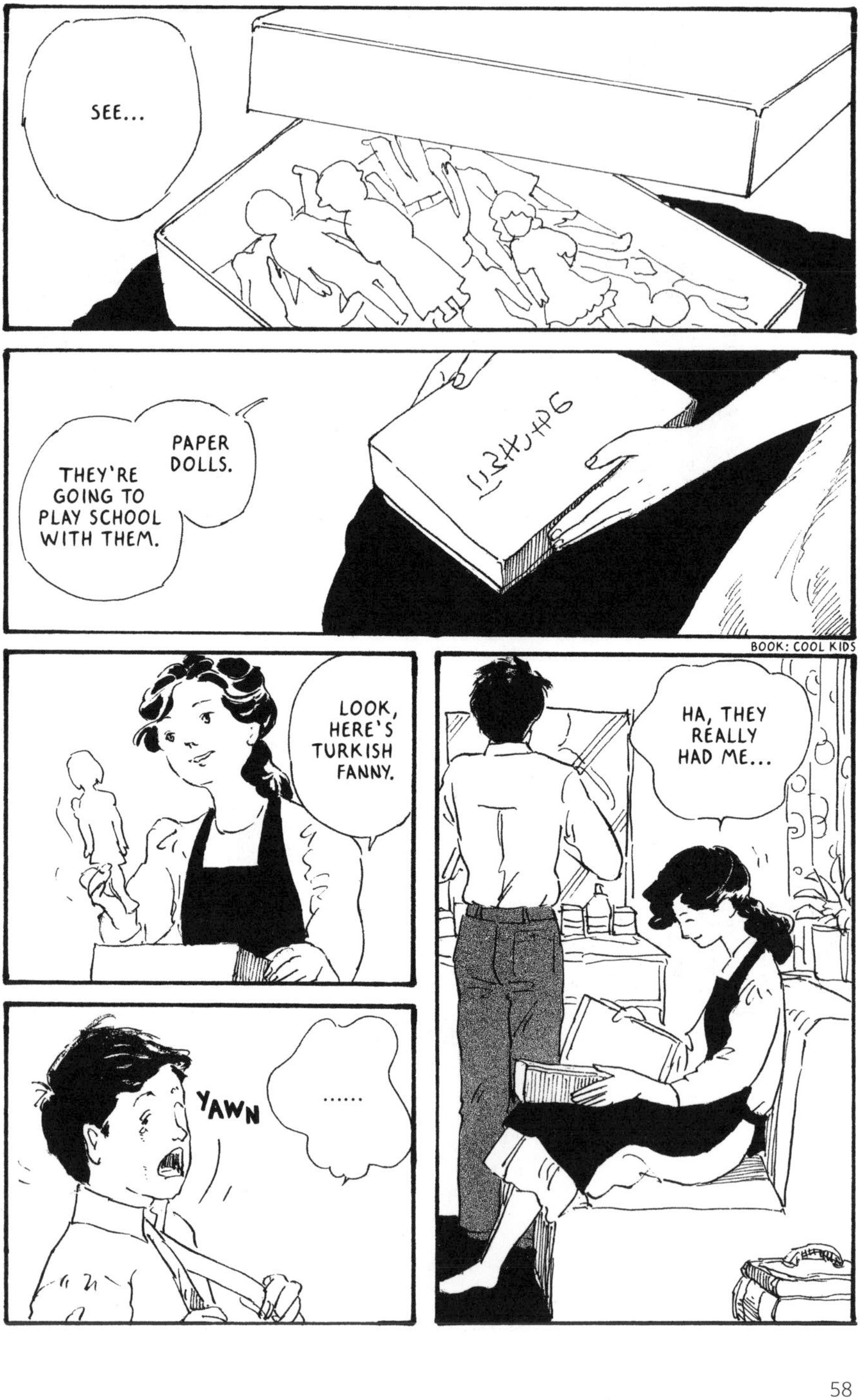
SEE...
PAPER DOLLS.
THEY'RE GOING TO PLAY SCHOOL WITH THEM.
BOOK: COOL KIDS
HA, THEY REALLY HAD ME...
LOOK, HERE'S TURKISH FANNY.
YAWN
......

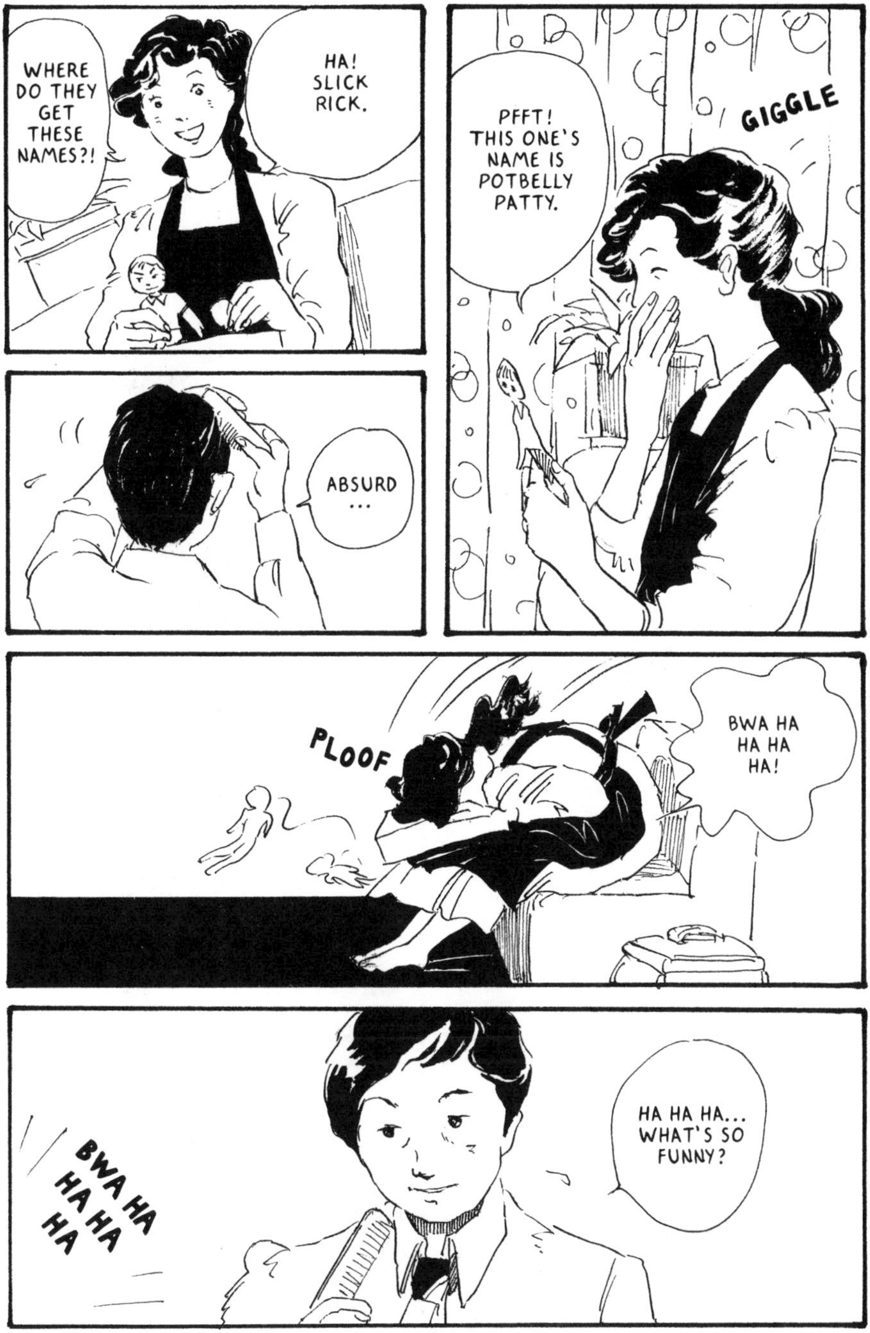
GIGGLE
PFFT! THIS ONE'S NAME IS POTBELLY PATTY.
HA! SLICK RICK.
WHERE DO THEY GET THESE NAMES?!
ABSURD ...
BWA HA HA HA HA!
PLOOF
HA HA HA... WHAT'S SO FUNNY?
BWA HA HA HA HA

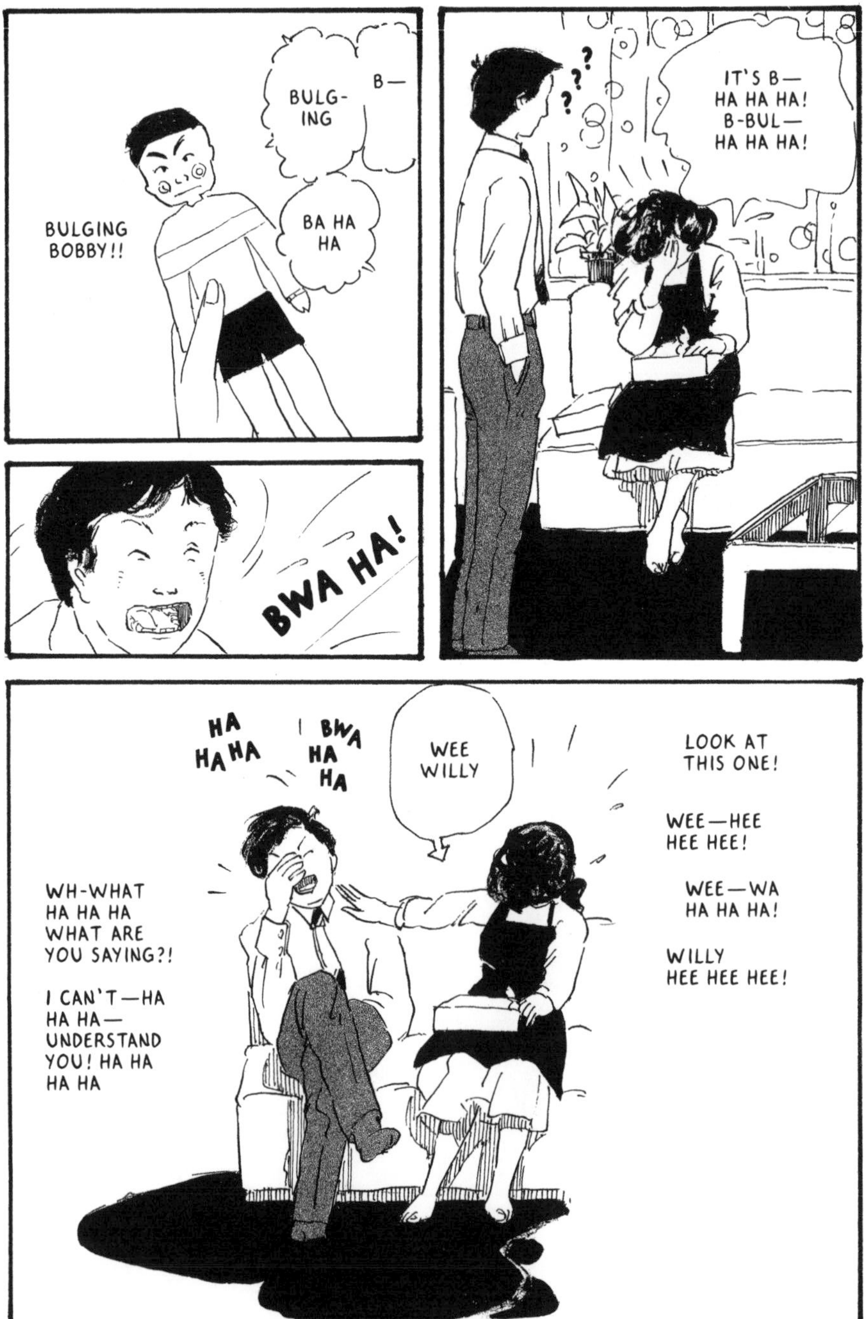
IT'S B— HA HA HA! B-BUL— HA HA HA!
B—
BULG- ING
BA HA HA
BULGING BOBBY!!
BWA HA!
LOOK AT THIS ONE!
WEE—HEE HEE HEE!
WEE—WA HA HA HA!
WILLY HEE HEE HEE!
WEE WILLY
BWA HA HA HA
HA HA HA
WH-WHAT HA HA HA WHAT ARE YOU SAYING?!
I CAN'T—HA HA HA— UNDERSTAND YOU! HA HA HA HA

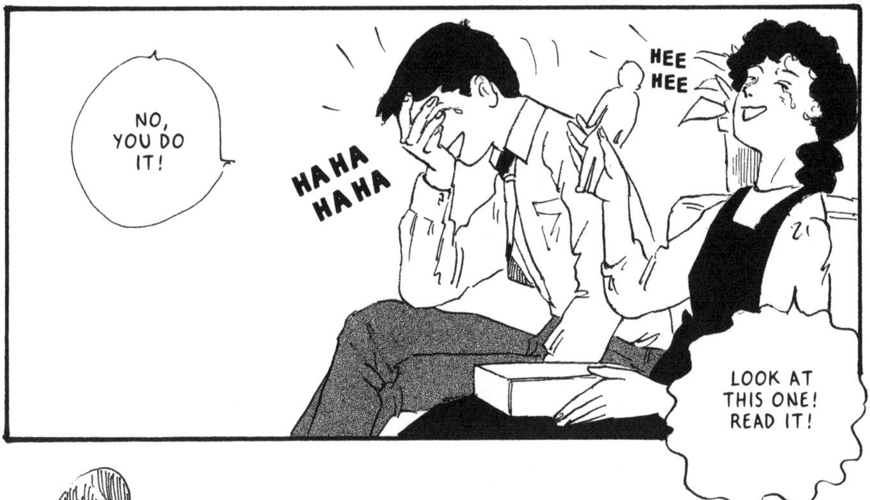
HEE HEE
LOOK AT THIS ONE! READ IT!
HAHA HAHA
NO, YOU DO IT!

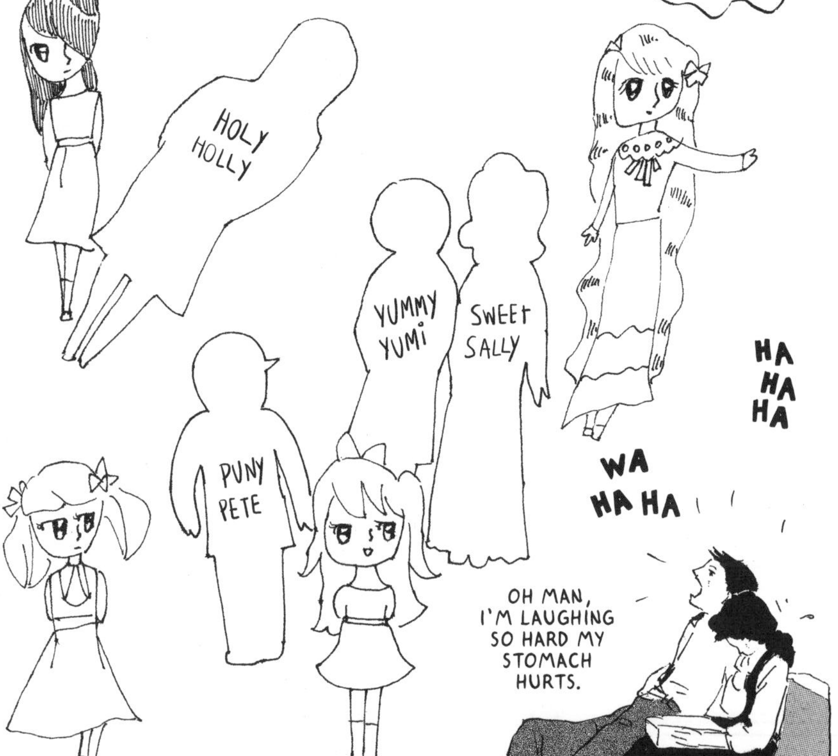
HA HA HA
WA HA HA
OH MAN, I'M LAUGHING SO HARD MY STOMACH HURTS.
HOLY HOLLY
SWEET SALLY
YUMMY YUMi
PUNY PETE

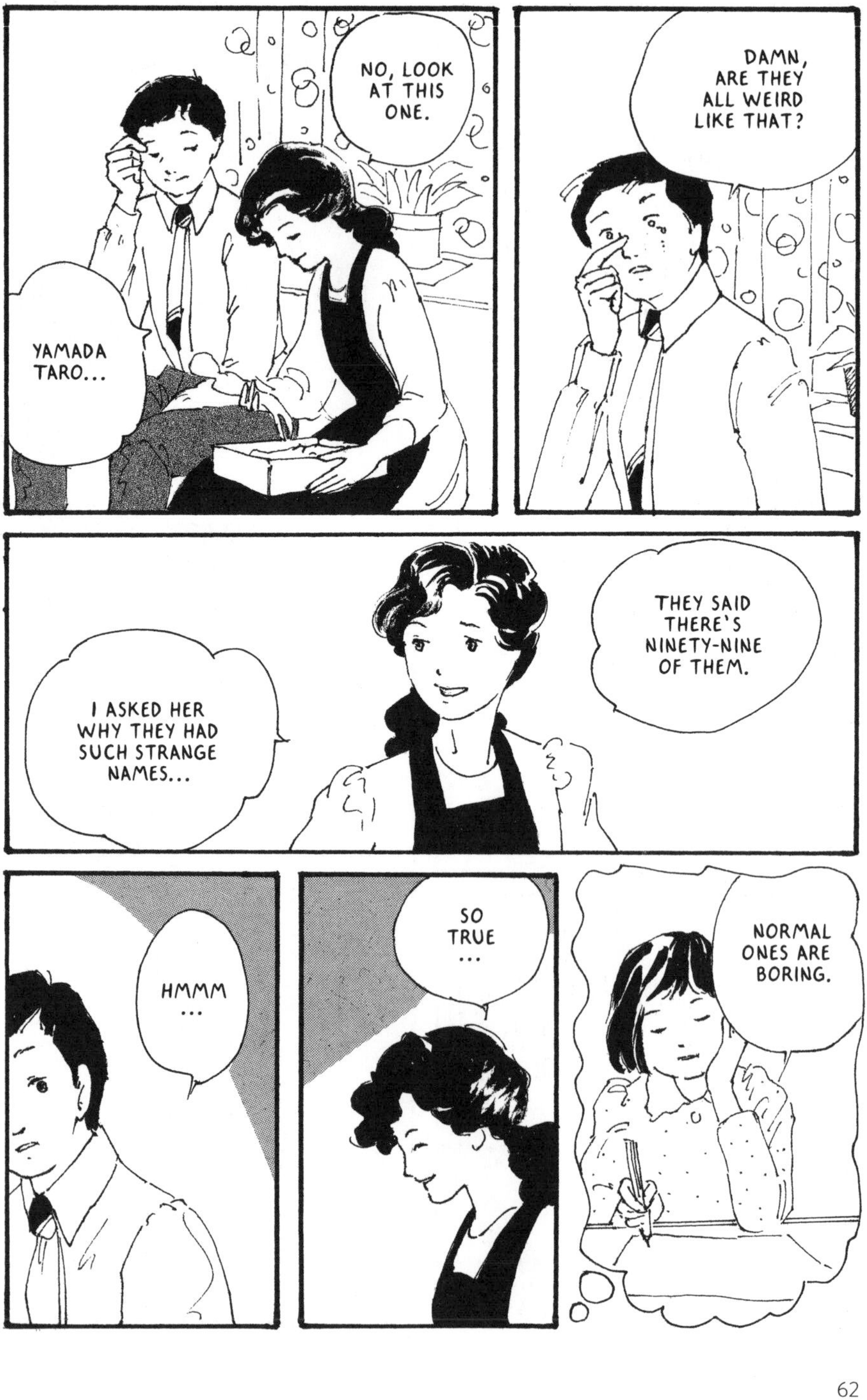
DAMN, ARE THEY ALL WEIRD LIKE THAT?
NO, LOOK AT THIS ONE.
YAMADA TARO...
THEY SAID THERE'S NINETY-NINE OF THEM.
I ASKED HER WHY THEY HAD SUCH STRANGE NAMES...
NORMAL ONES ARE BORING.
SO TRUE ...
HMMM ...

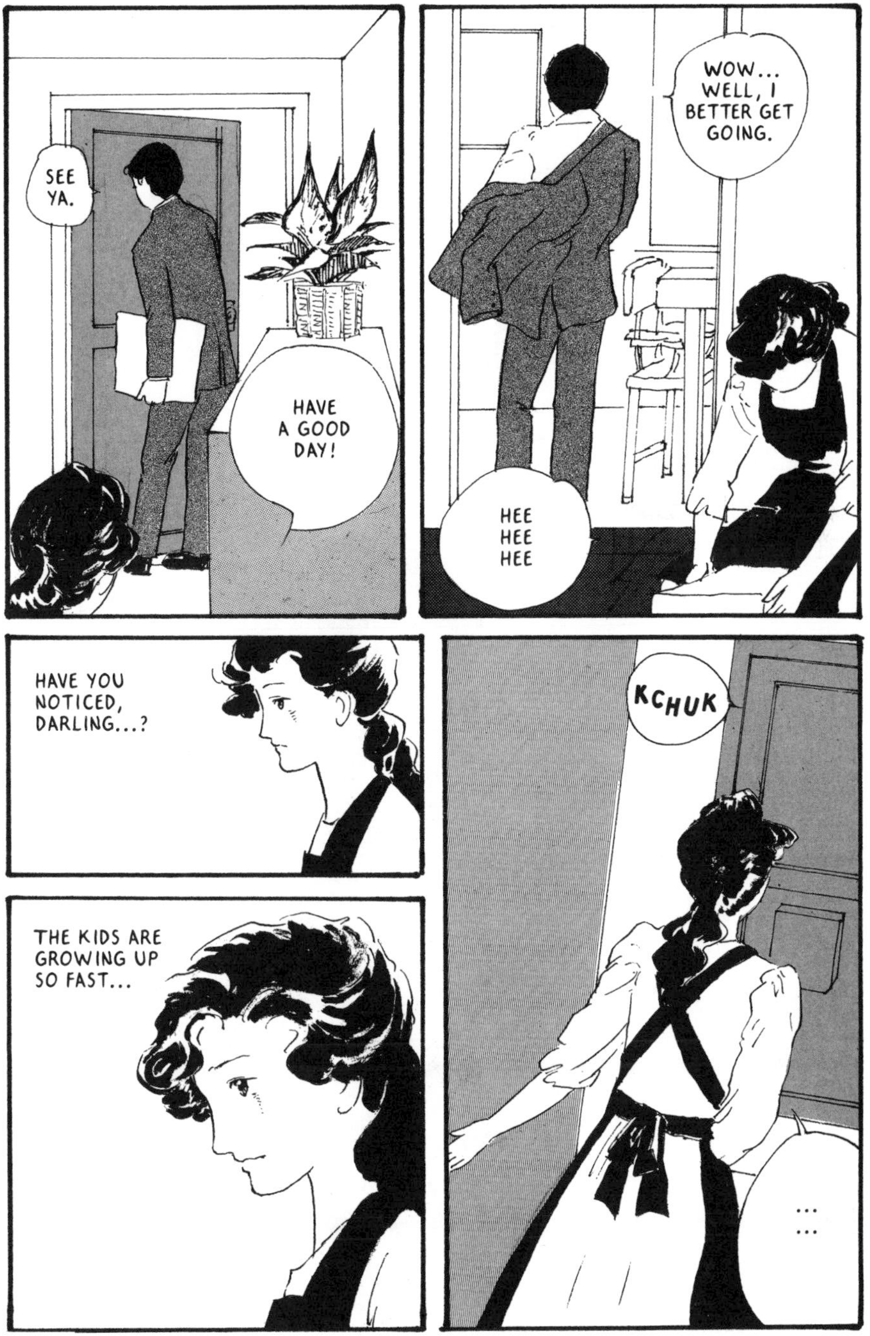
WOW... WELL, I BETTER GET GOING.
HEE HEE HEE
SEE YA.
HAVE A GOOD DAY!
KCHUK
... ...
HAVE YOU NOTICED, DARLING...?
THE KIDS ARE GROWING UP SO FAST...

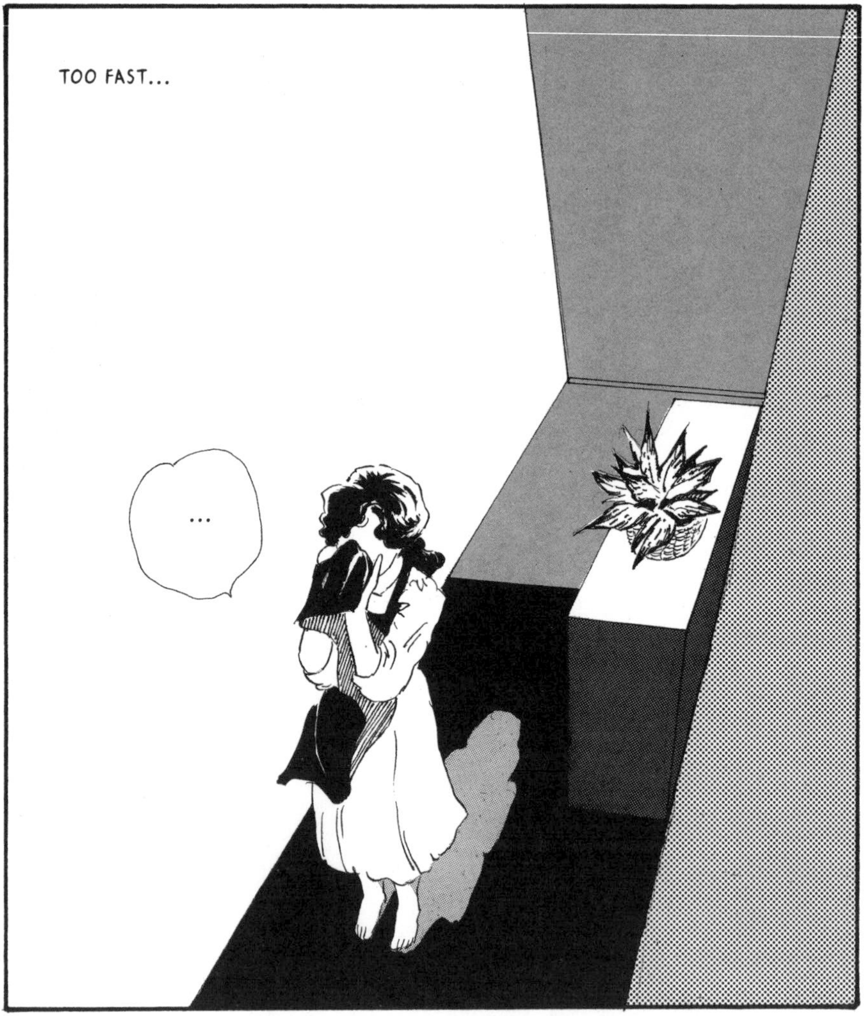
TOO FAST...
...

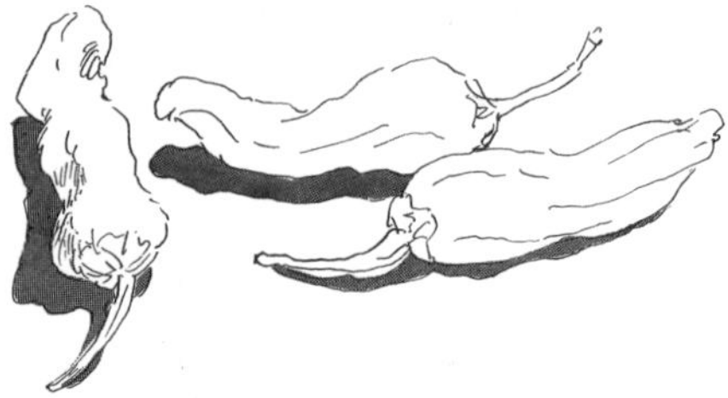

Every Time is a First Time

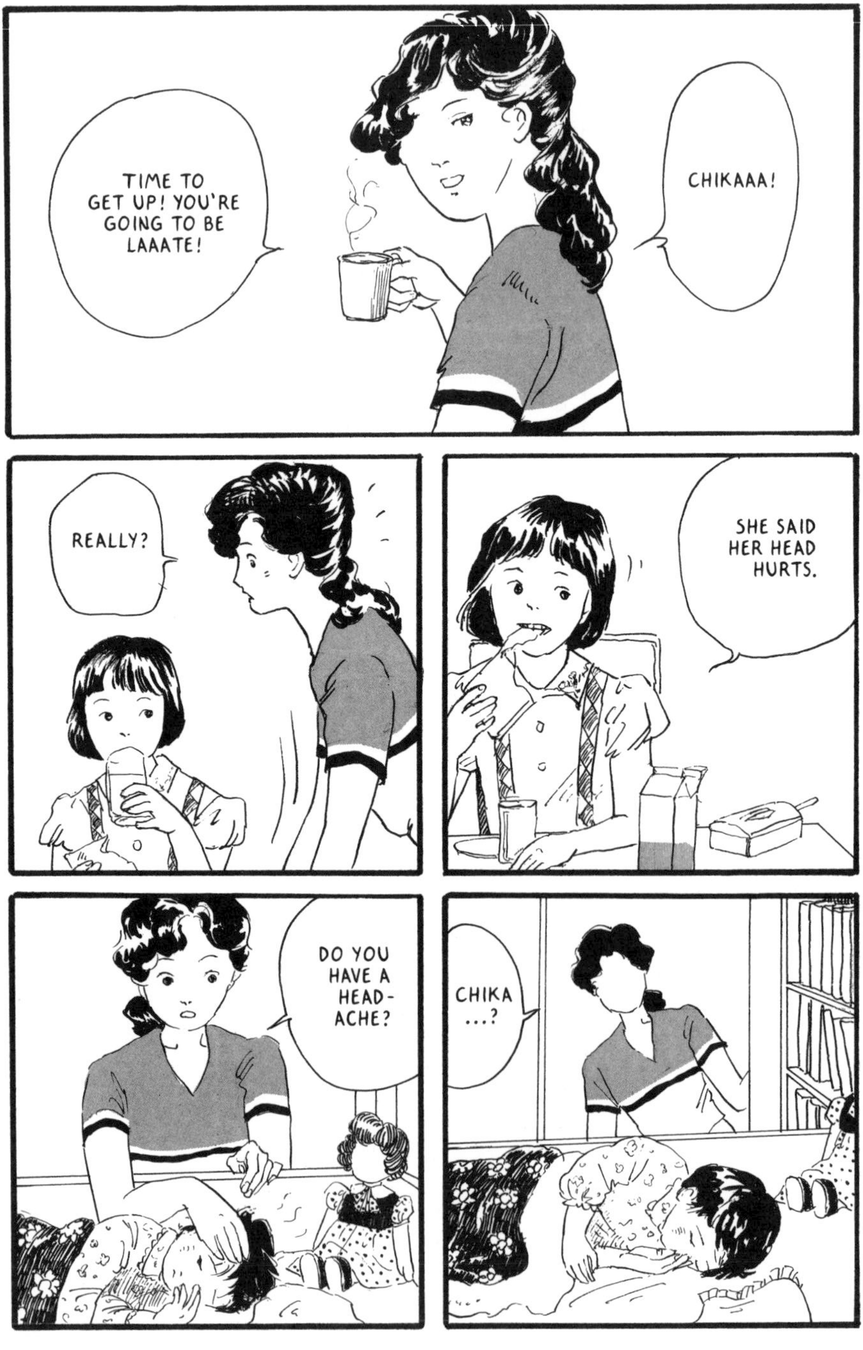
CHIKAAA!
TIME TO GET UP! YOU'RE GOING TO BE LAAATE!
SHE SAID HER HEAD HURTS.
REALLY?
CHIKA ...?
DO YOU HAVE A HEAD-ACHE?

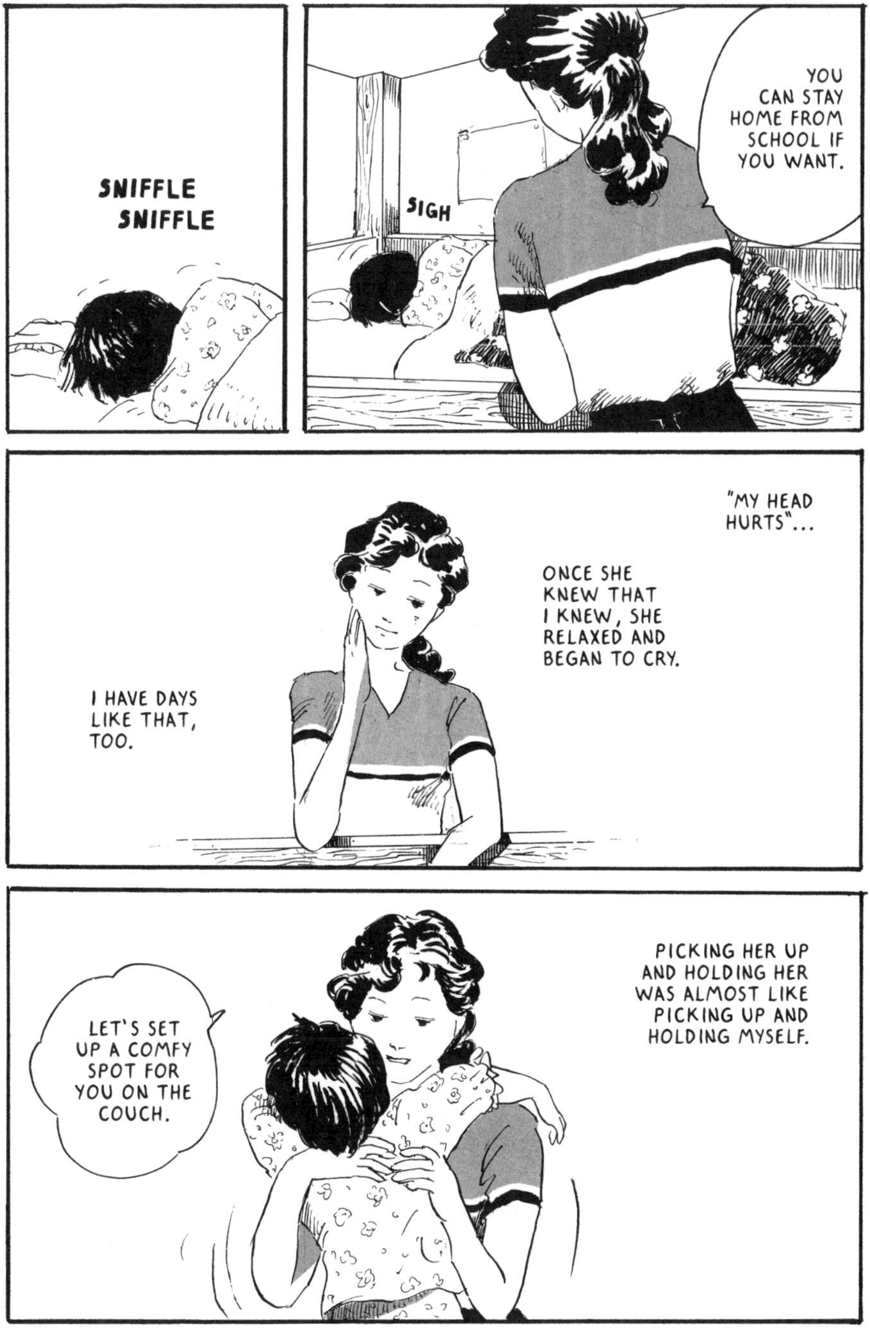
YOU CAN STAY HOME FROM SCHOOL IF YOU WANT.
SIGH
SNIFFLE SNIFFLE
"MY HEAD HURTS"...
ONCE SHE KNEW THAT I KNEW, SHE RELAXED AND BEGAN TO CRY.
I HAVE DAYS LIKE THAT, TOO.
PICKING HER UP AND HOLDING HER WAS ALMOST LIKE PICKING UP AND HOLDING MYSELF.
LET'S SET UP A COMFY SPOT FOR YOU ON THE COUCH.

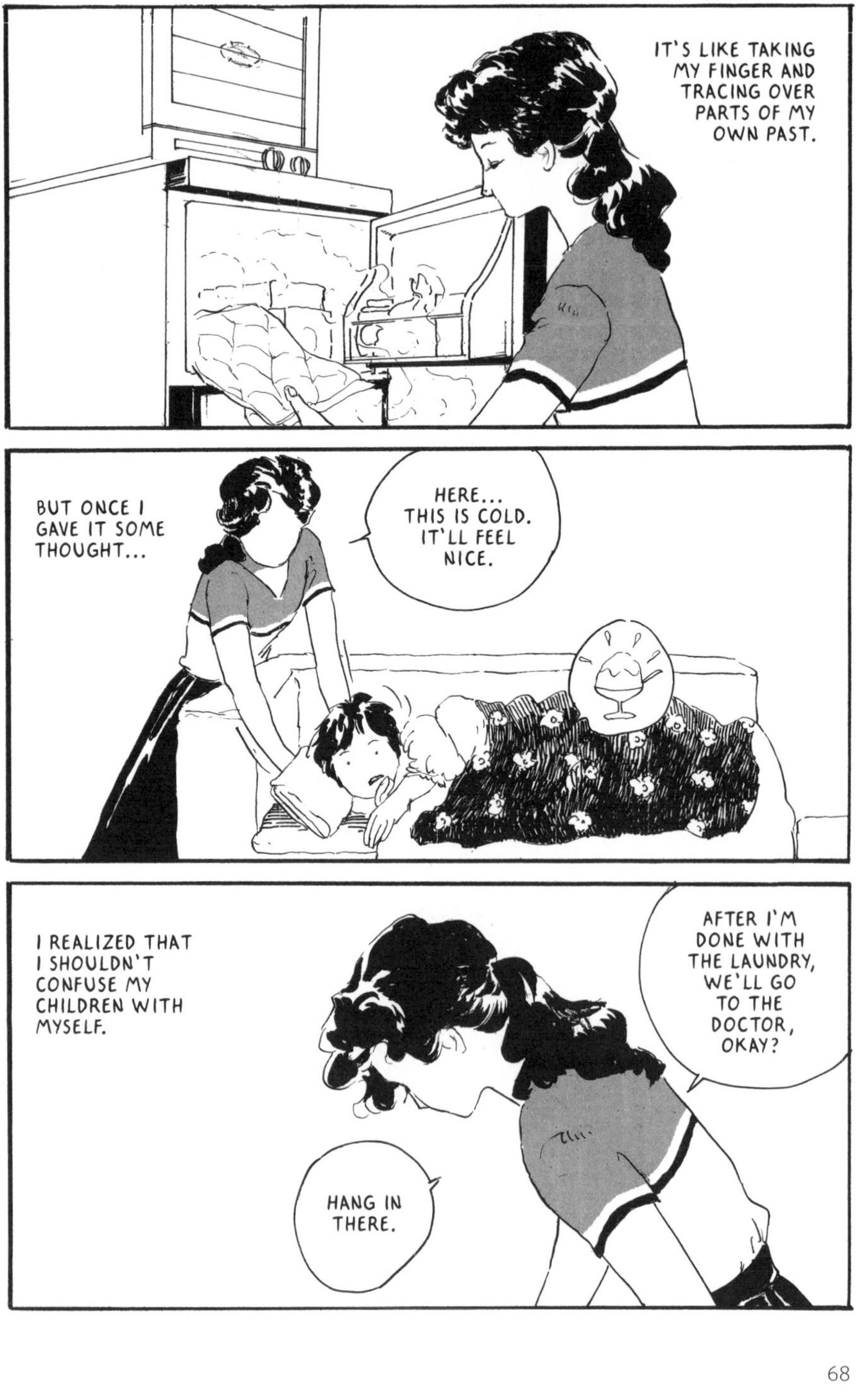
IT'S LIKE TAKING MY FINGER AND TRACING OVER PARTS OF MY OWN PAST.
HERE... THIS IS COLD. IT'LL FEEL NICE.
BUT ONCE I GAVE IT SOME THOUGHT...
AFTER I'M DONE WITH THE LAUNDRY, WE'LL GO TO THE DOCTOR, OKAY?
I REALIZED THAT I SHOULDN'T CONFUSE MY CHILDREN WITH MYSELF.
HANG IN THERE.

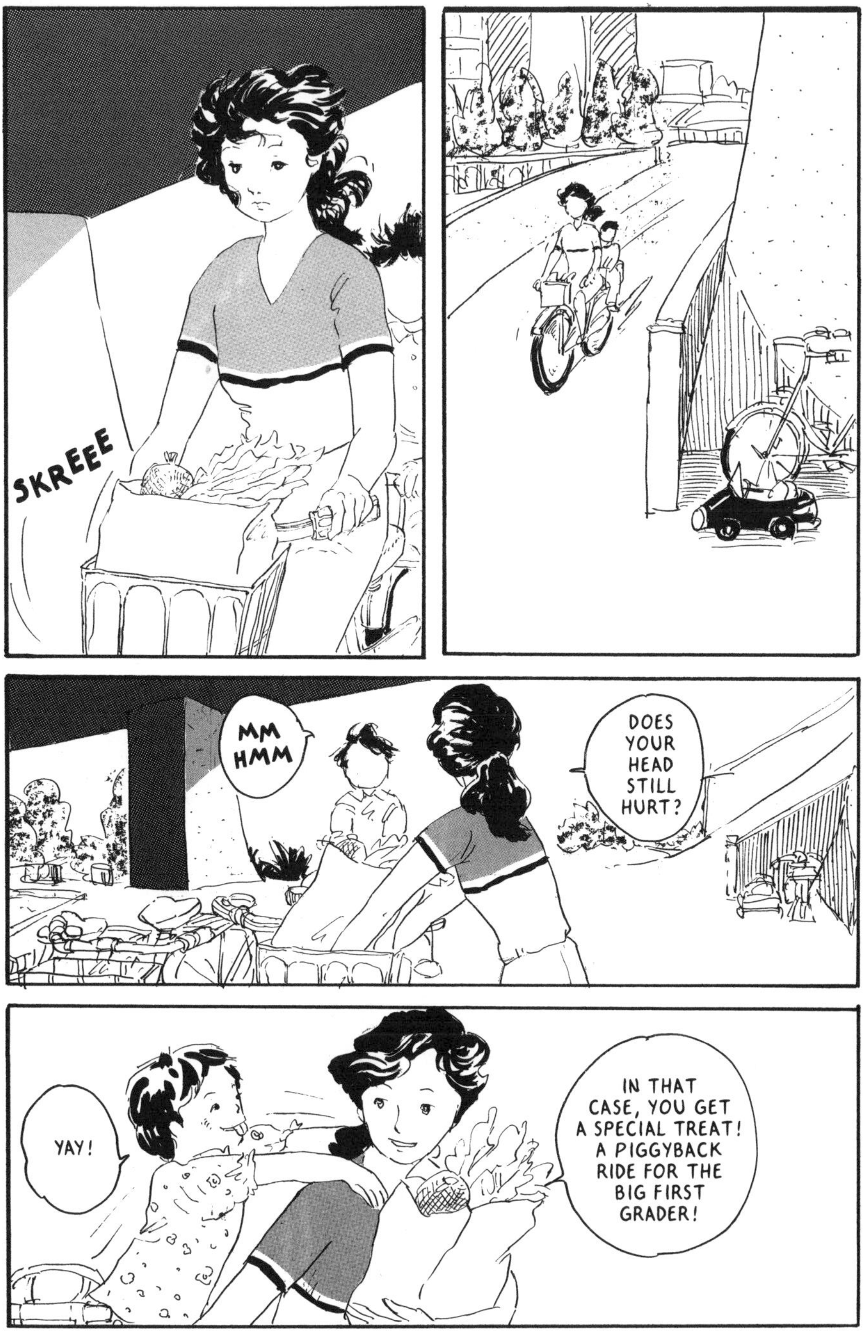
SKREEE
DOES YOUR HEAD STILL HURT?
MM HMM
IN THAT CASE, YOU GET A SPECIAL TREAT! A PIGGYBACK RIDE FOR THE BIG FIRST GRADER!
YAY!

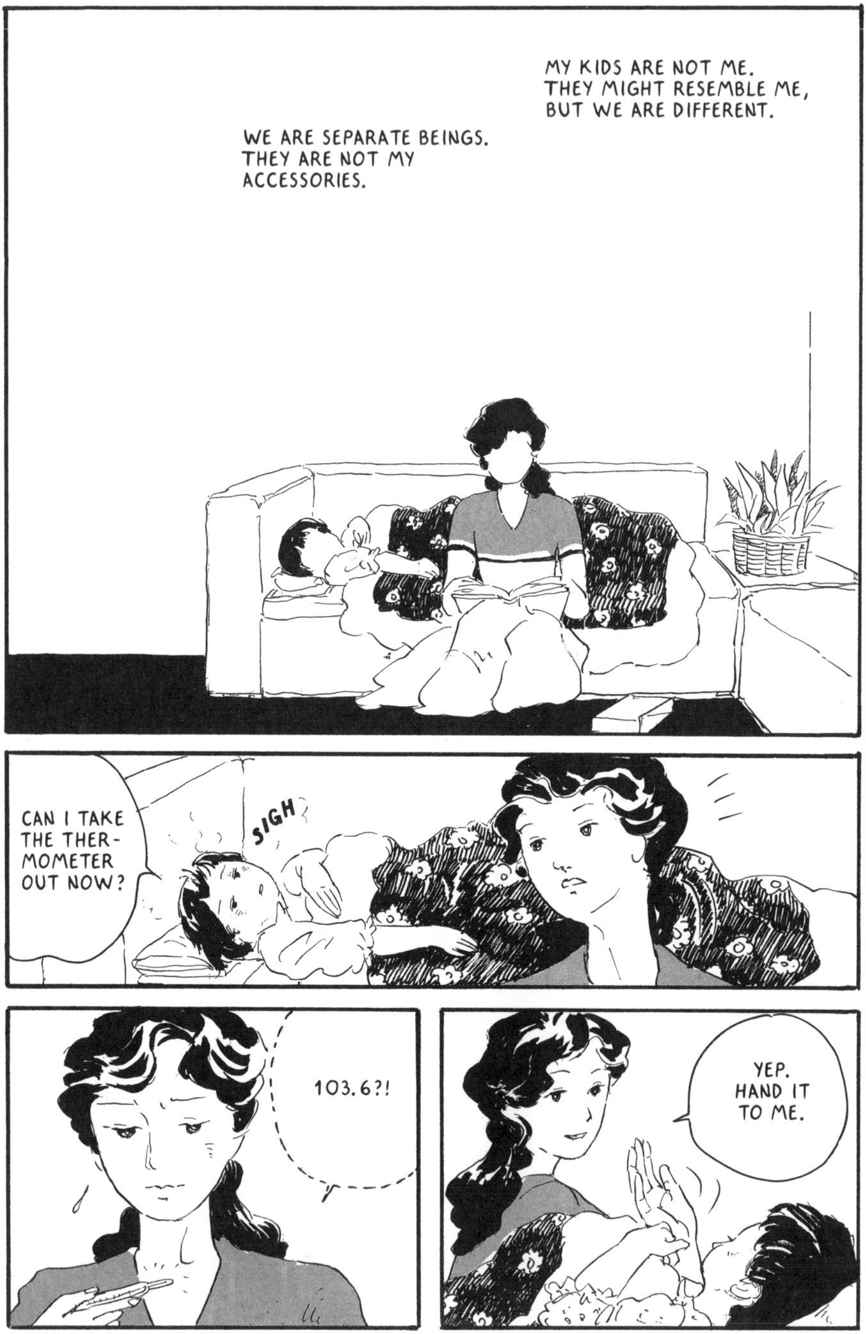
MY KIDS ARE NOT ME. THEY MIGHT RESEMBLE ME, BUT WE ARE DIFFERENT.
WE ARE SEPARATE BEINGS. THEY ARE NOT MY ACCESSORIES.
SIGH
CAN I TAKE THE THER-MOMETER OUT NOW?
YEP. HAND IT TO ME.
103.6?!

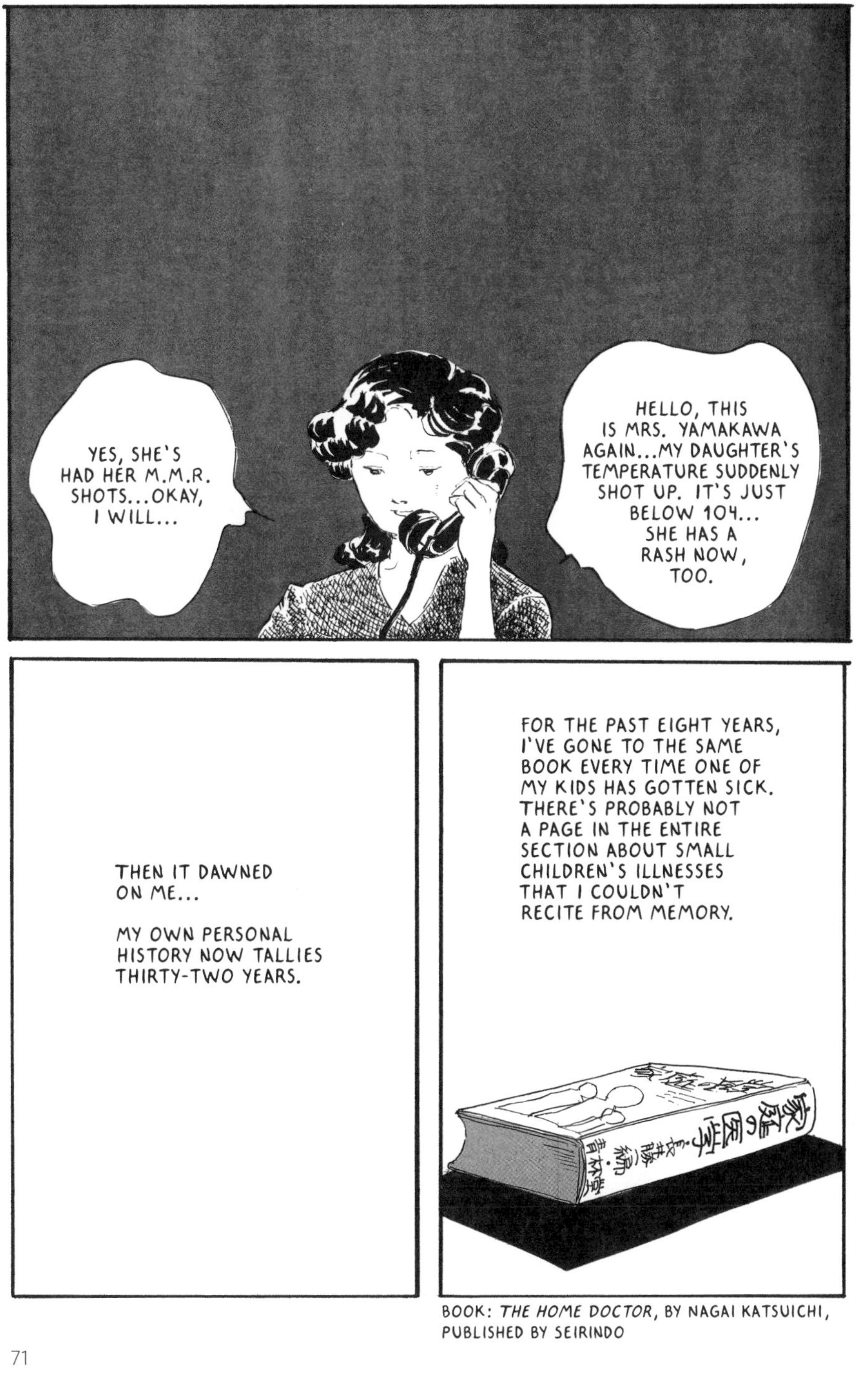
HELLO, THIS IS MRS. YAMAKAWA AGAIN...MY DAUGHTER'S TEMPERATURE SUDDENLY SHOT UP. IT'S JUST BELOW 104... SHE HAS A RASH NOW, TOO.
YES, SHE'S HAD HER M.M.R. SHOTS...OKAY, I WILL...
FOR THE PAST EIGHT YEARS, I'VE GONE TO THE SAME BOOK EVERY TIME ONE OF MY KIDS HAS GOTTEN SICK. THERE'S PROBABLY NOT A PAGE IN THE ENTIRE SECTION ABOUT SMALL CHILDREN'S ILLNESSES THAT I COULDN'T RECITE FROM MEMORY.
THEN IT DAWNED ON ME...
MY OWN PERSONAL HISTORY NOW TALLIES THIRTY-TWO YEARS.

BOOK: *THE HOME DOCTOR*, BY NAGAI KATSUICHI, PUBLISHED BY SEIRINDO

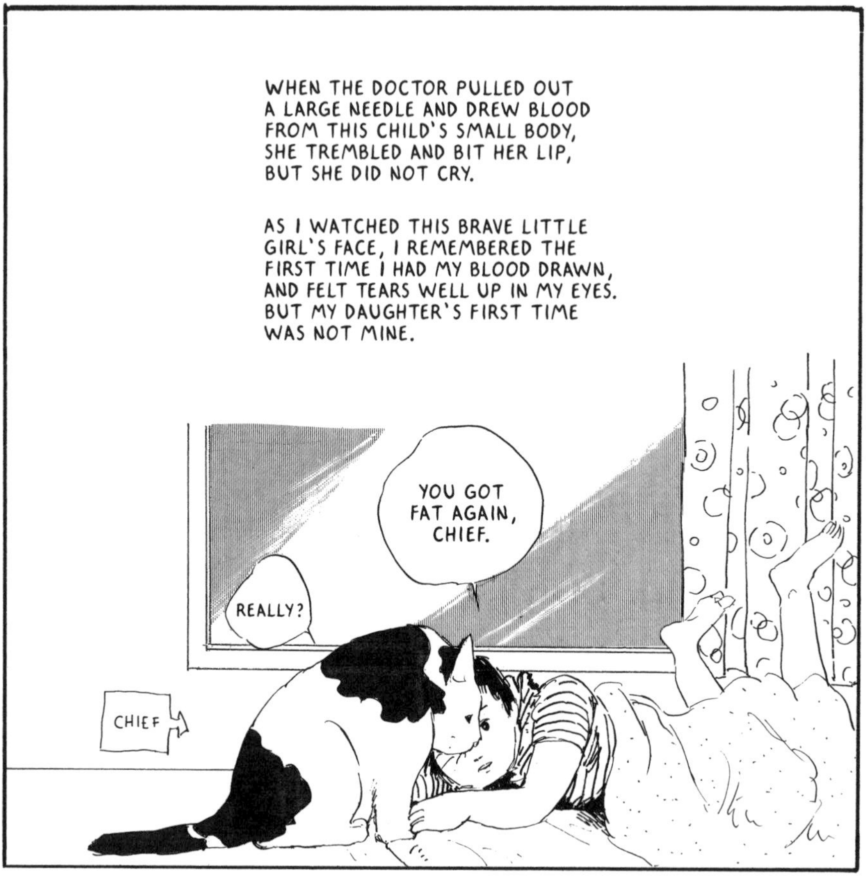
WHEN THE DOCTOR PULLED OUT A LARGE NEEDLE AND DREW BLOOD FROM THIS CHILD'S SMALL BODY, SHE TREMBLED AND BIT HER LIP, BUT SHE DID NOT CRY.
AS I WATCHED THIS BRAVE LITTLE GIRL'S FACE, I REMEMBERED THE FIRST TIME I HAD MY BLOOD DRAWN, AND FELT TEARS WELL UP IN MY EYES. BUT MY DAUGHTER'S FIRST TIME WAS NOT MINE.
YOU GOT FAT AGAIN, CHIEF.
REALLY?
CHIEF

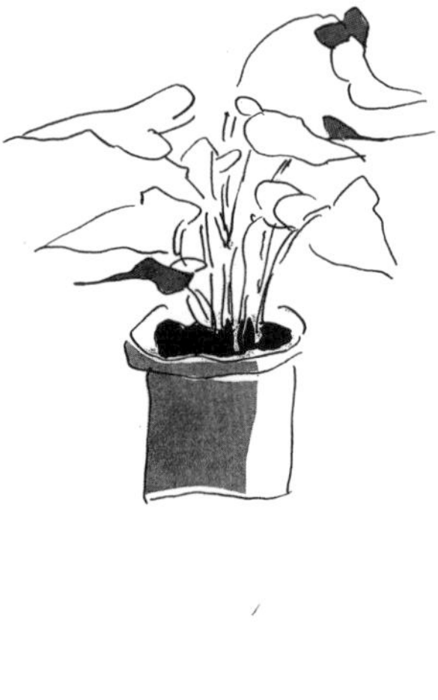

I Birthed a Human

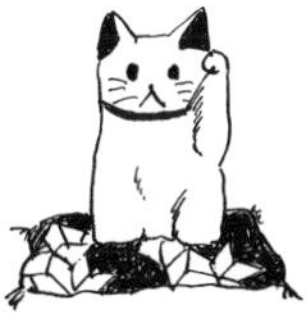

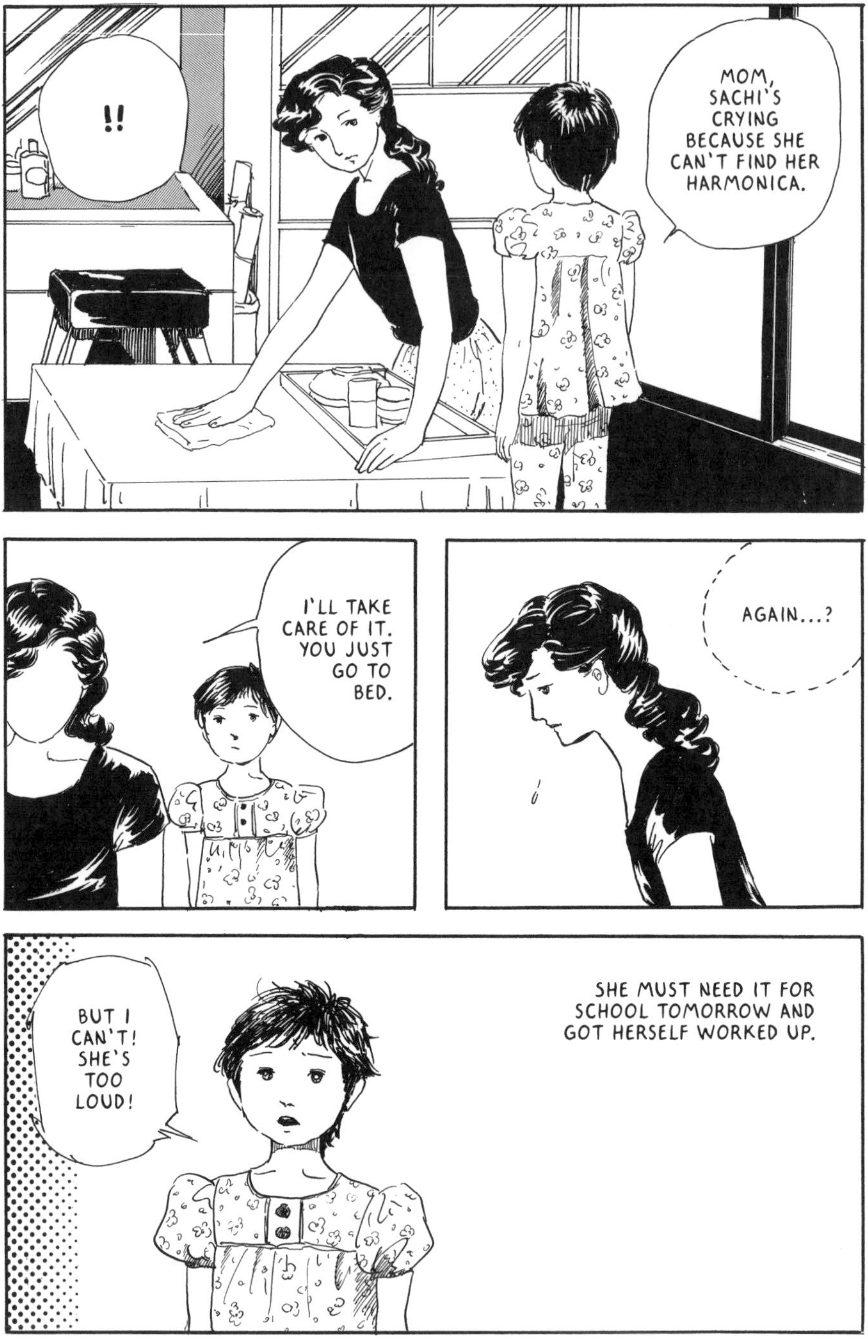
MOM, SACHI'S CRYING BECAUSE SHE CAN'T FIND HER HARMONICA.
!!
AGAIN...?
I'LL TAKE CARE OF IT. YOU JUST GO TO BED.
SHE MUST NEED IT FOR SCHOOL TOMORROW AND GOT HERSELF WORKED UP.
BUT I CAN'T! SHE'S TOO LOUD!

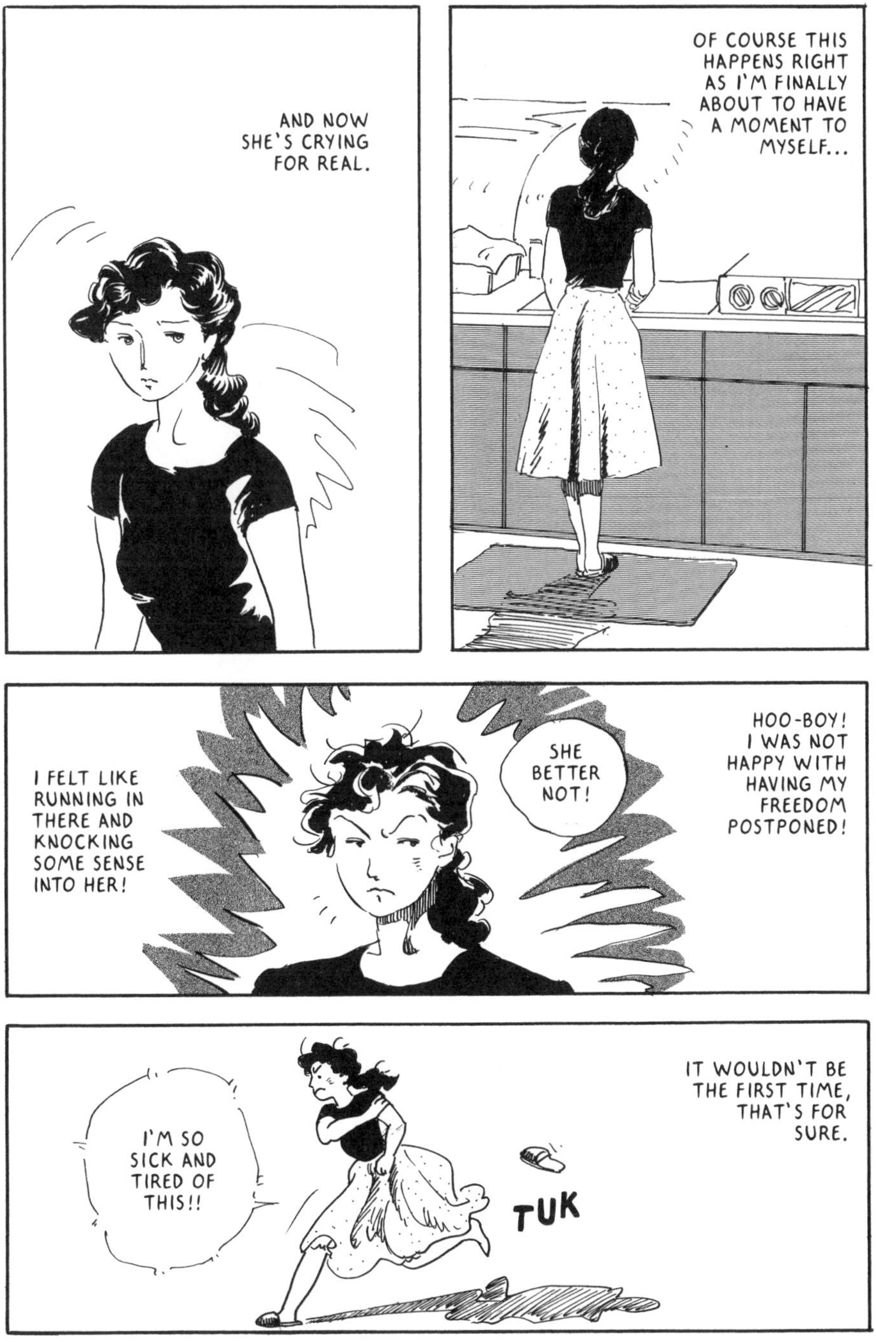
OF COURSE THIS HAPPENS RIGHT AS I'M FINALLY ABOUT TO HAVE A MOMENT TO MYSELF...
AND NOW SHE'S CRYING FOR REAL.
HOO-BOY! I WAS NOT HAPPY WITH HAVING MY FREEDOM POSTPONED!
SHE BETTER NOT!
I FELT LIKE RUNNING IN THERE AND KNOCKING SOME SENSE INTO HER!
IT WOULDN'T BE THE FIRST TIME, THAT'S FOR SURE.
TUK
I'M SO SICK AND TIRED OF THIS!!

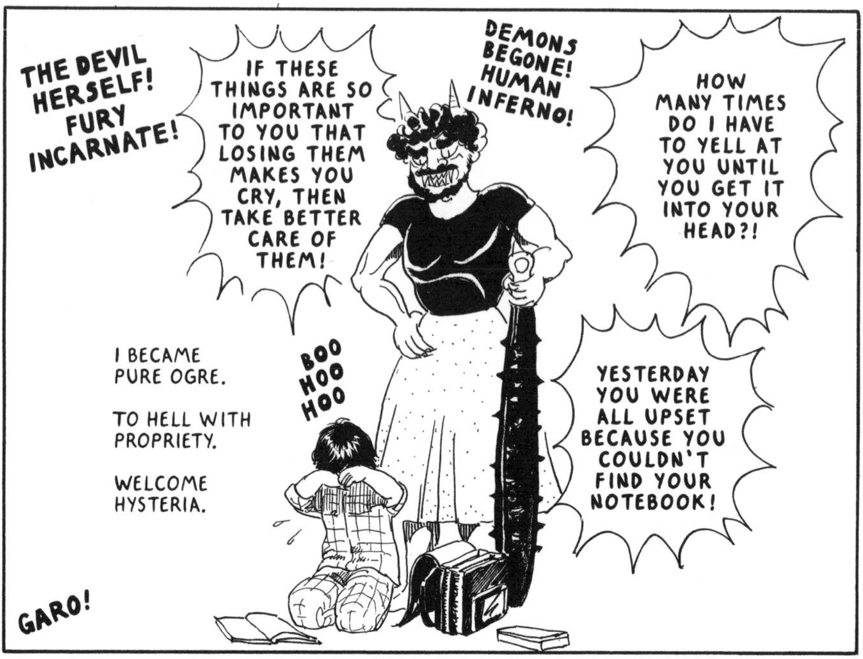
HOW MANY TIMES DO I HAVE TO YELL AT YOU UNTIL YOU GET IT INTO YOUR HEAD?!
DEMONS BEGONE! HUMAN INFERNO!
IF THESE THINGS ARE SO IMPORTANT TO YOU THAT LOSING THEM MAKES YOU CRY, THEN TAKE BETTER CARE OF THEM!
THE DEVIL HERSELF! FURY INCARNATE!
YESTERDAY YOU WERE ALL UPSET BECAUSE YOU COULDN'T FIND YOUR NOTEBOOK!
BOO HOO HOO
I BECAME PURE OGRE.
TO HELL WITH PROPRIETY.
WELCOME HYSTERIA.
GARO!

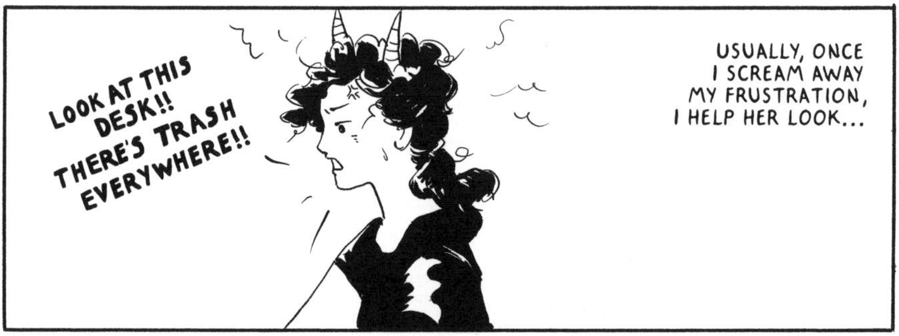
USUALLY, ONCE I SCREAM AWAY MY FRUSTRATION, I HELP HER LOOK...
LOOK AT THIS DESK!! THERE'S TRASH EVERYWHERE!!

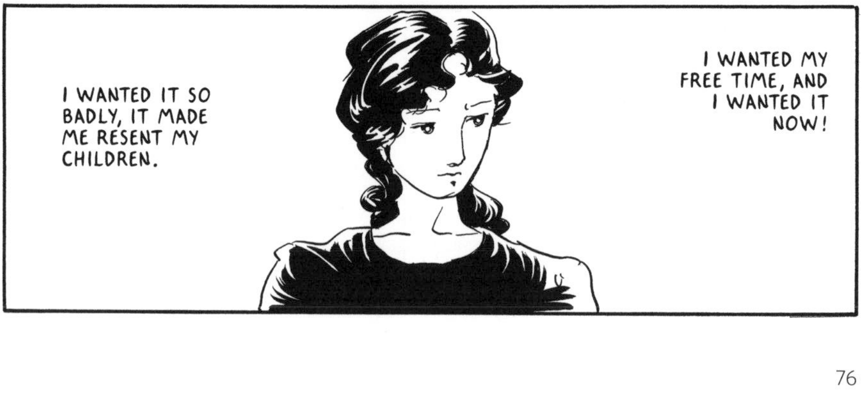
I WANTED MY FREE TIME, AND I WANTED IT NOW!
I WANTED IT SO BADLY, IT MADE ME RESENT MY CHILDREN.

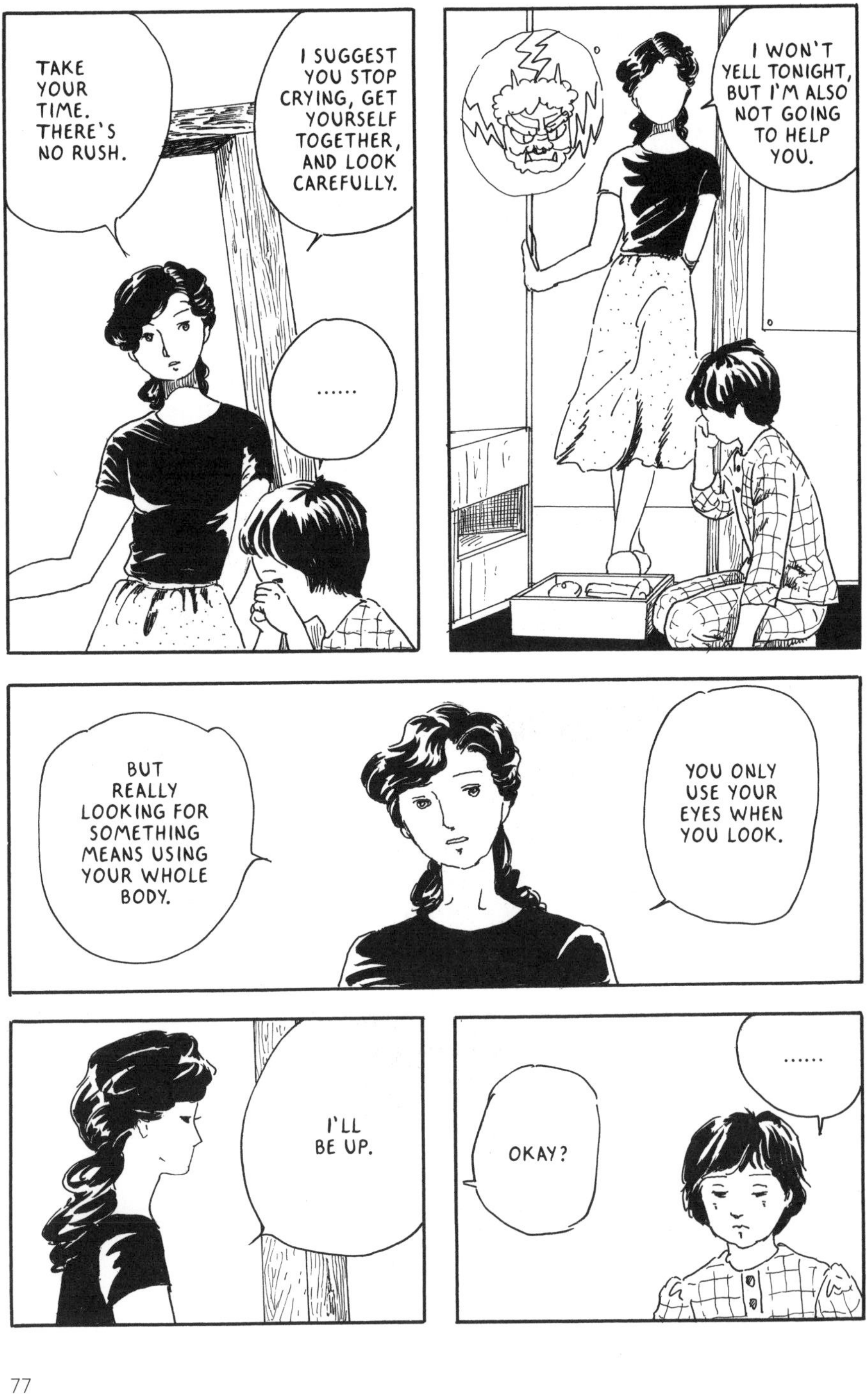
I WON'T YELL TONIGHT, BUT I'M ALSO NOT GOING TO HELP YOU.
I SUGGEST YOU STOP CRYING, GET YOURSELF TOGETHER, AND LOOK CAREFULLY.
TAKE YOUR TIME. THERE'S NO RUSH.
......
YOU ONLY USE YOUR EYES WHEN YOU LOOK.
BUT REALLY LOOKING FOR SOMETHING MEANS USING YOUR WHOLE BODY.
......
OKAY?
I'LL BE UP.

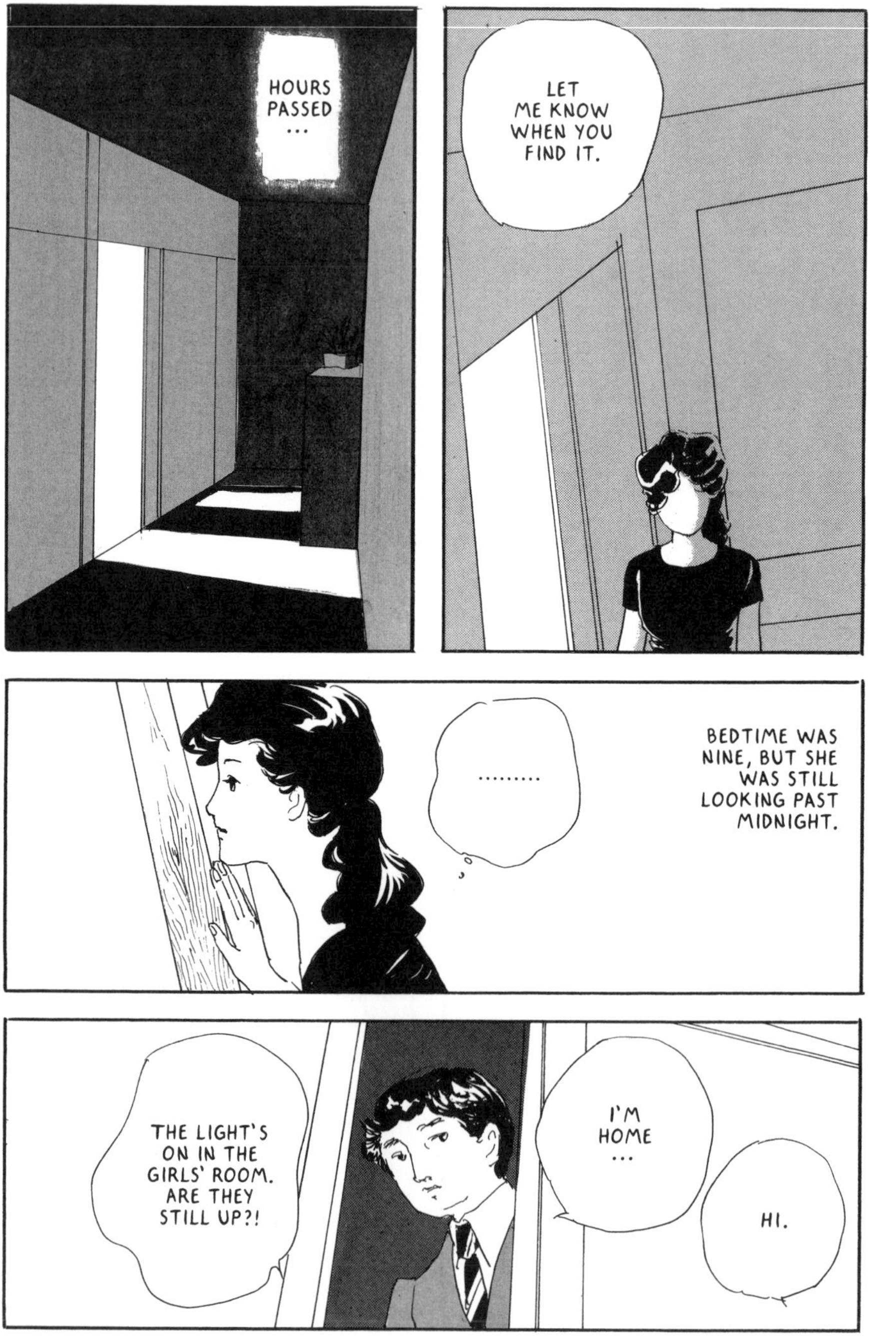
LET ME KNOW WHEN YOU FIND IT.
HOURS PASSED ...
BEDTIME WAS NINE, BUT SHE WAS STILL LOOKING PAST MIDNIGHT.
....
I'M HOME ...
HI.
THE LIGHT'S ON IN THE GIRLS' ROOM. ARE THEY STILL UP?!

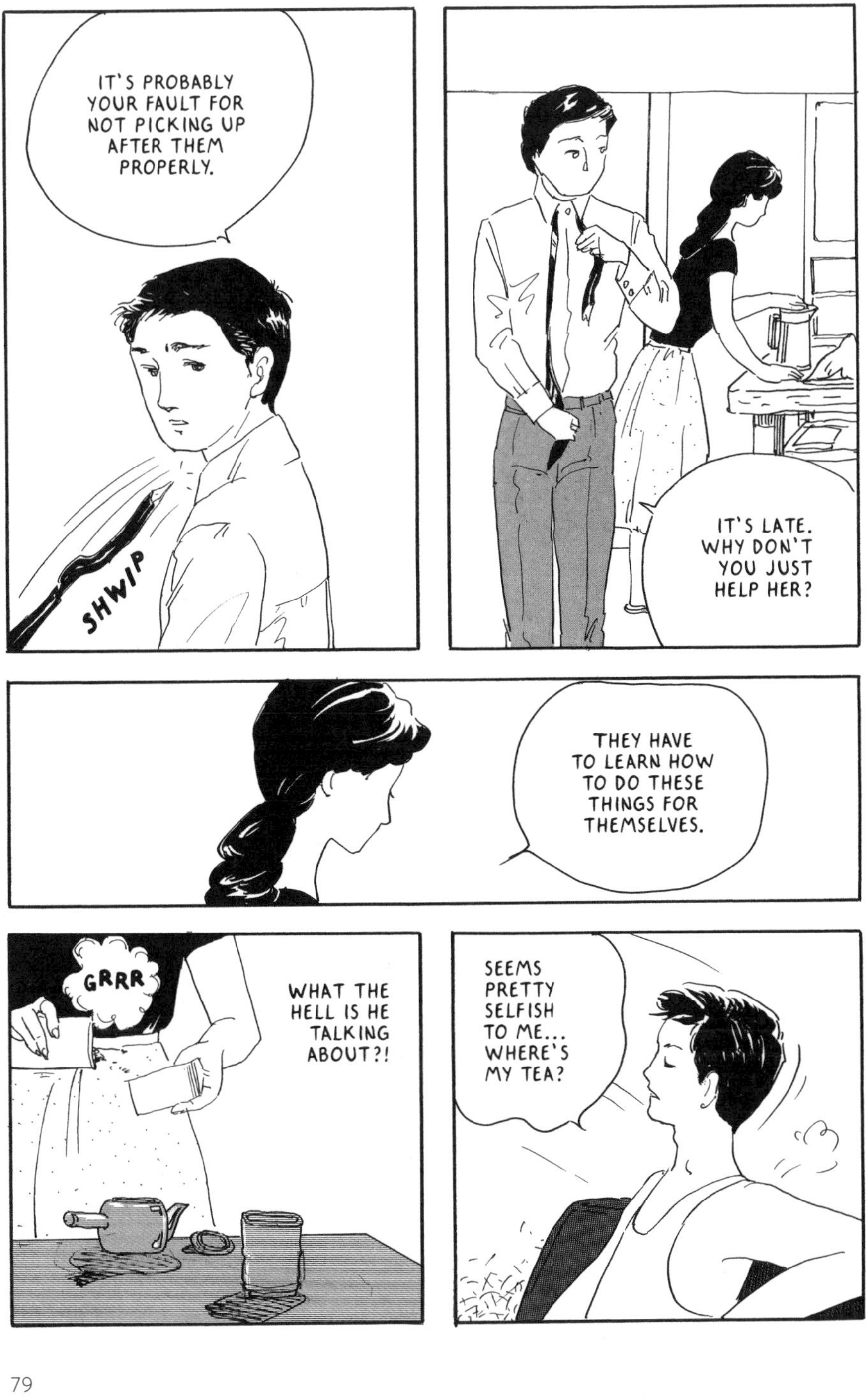
IT'S LATE. WHY DON'T YOU JUST HELP HER?
IT'S PROBABLY YOUR FAULT FOR NOT PICKING UP AFTER THEM PROPERLY.
SHWIP
THEY HAVE TO LEARN HOW TO DO THESE THINGS FOR THEMSELVES.
SEEMS PRETTY SELFISH TO ME... WHERE'S MY TEA?
GRRR
WHAT THE HELL IS HE TALKING ABOUT?!

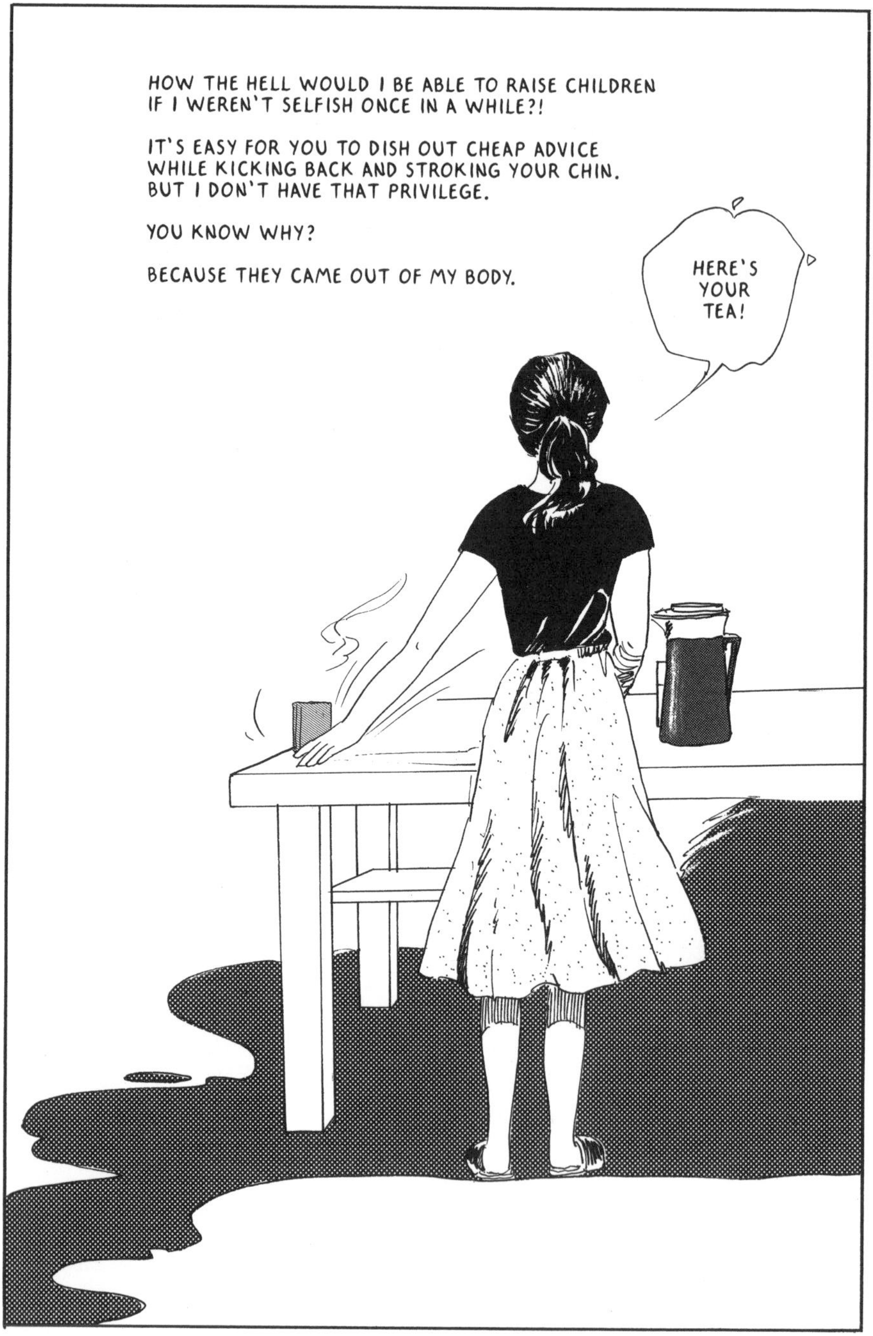
HOW THE HELL WOULD I BE ABLE TO RAISE CHILDREN IF I WEREN'T SELFISH ONCE IN A WHILE?!
IT'S EASY FOR YOU TO DISH OUT CHEAP ADVICE WHILE KICKING BACK AND STROKING YOUR CHIN. BUT I DON'T HAVE THAT PRIVILEGE.
YOU KNOW WHY?
BECAUSE THEY CAME OUT OF MY BODY.
HERE'S YOUR TEA!

Sometimes, Kids Drop

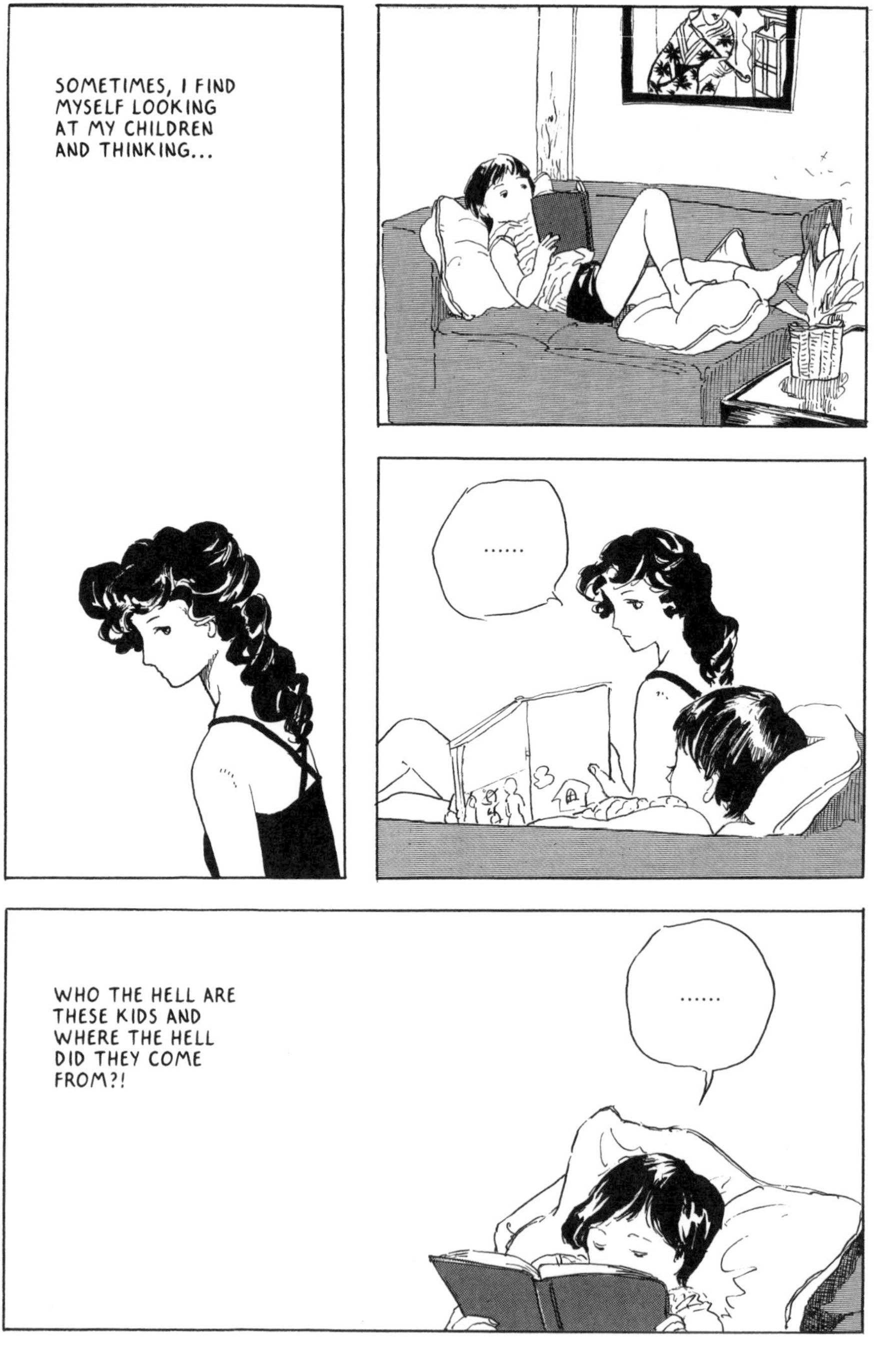
......
SOMETIMES, I FIND MYSELF LOOKING AT MY CHILDREN AND THINKING...
......
WHO THE HELL ARE THESE KIDS AND WHERE THE HELL DID THEY COME FROM?!

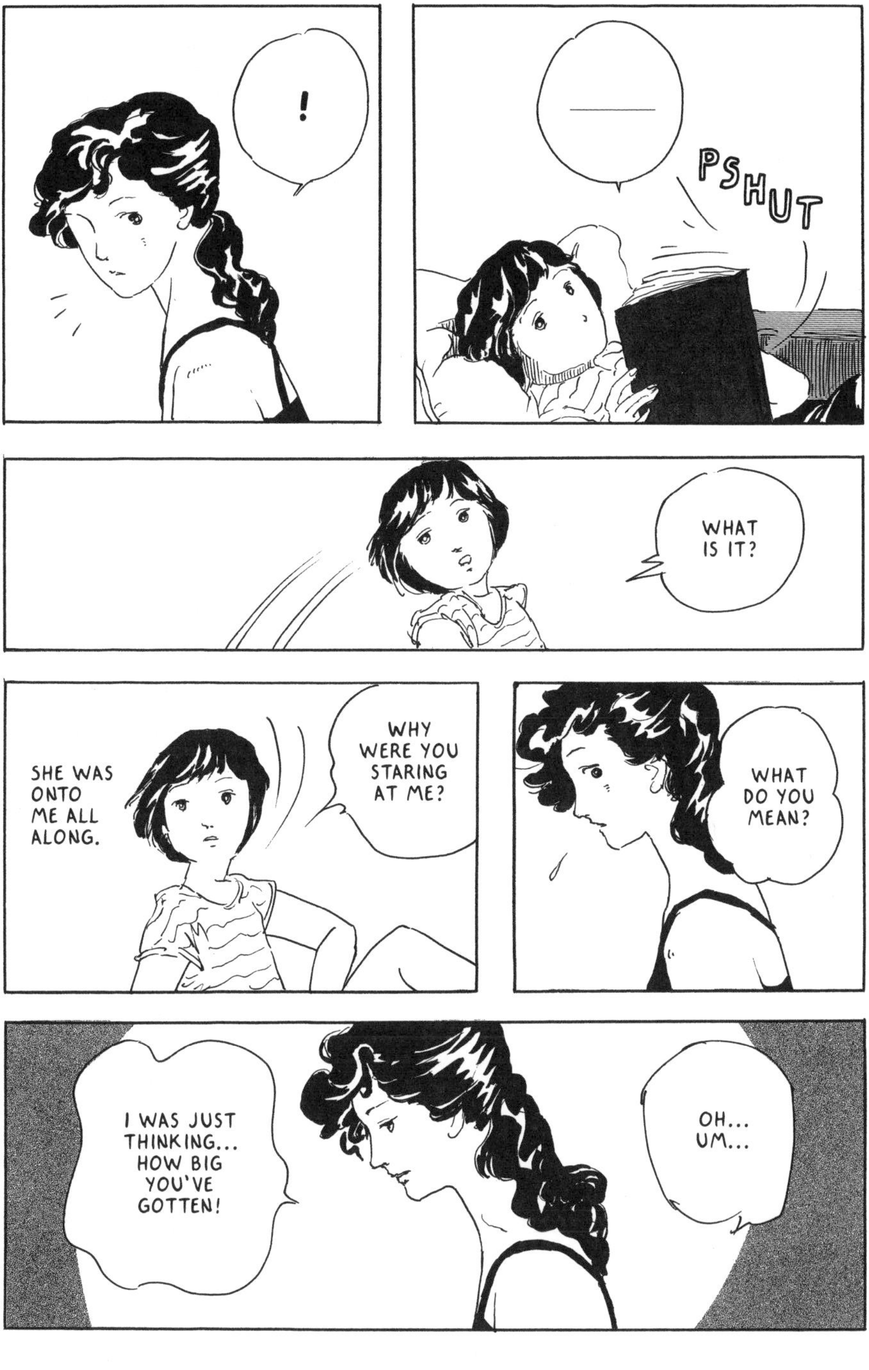
——
PSHUT
!
WHAT IS IT?
WHAT DO YOU MEAN?
WHY WERE YOU STARING AT ME?
SHE WAS ONTO ME ALL ALONG.
OH... UM...
I WAS JUST THINKING... HOW BIG YOU'VE GOTTEN!

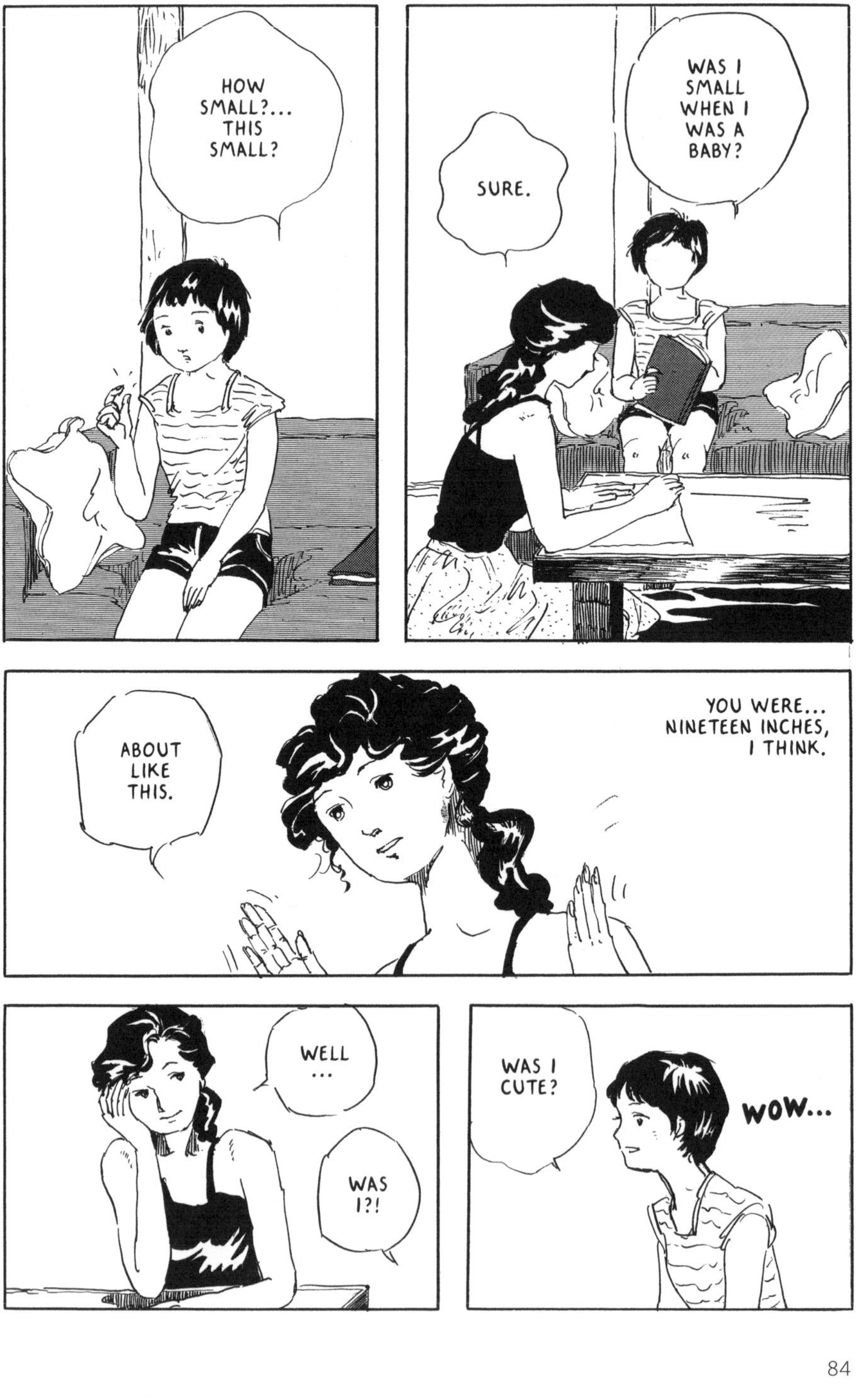
WAS I SMALL WHEN I WAS A BABY?
SURE.
HOW SMALL?... THIS SMALL?
YOU WERE... NINETEEN INCHES, I THINK.
ABOUT LIKE THIS.
WOW...
WAS I CUTE?
WELL ...
WAS I?!

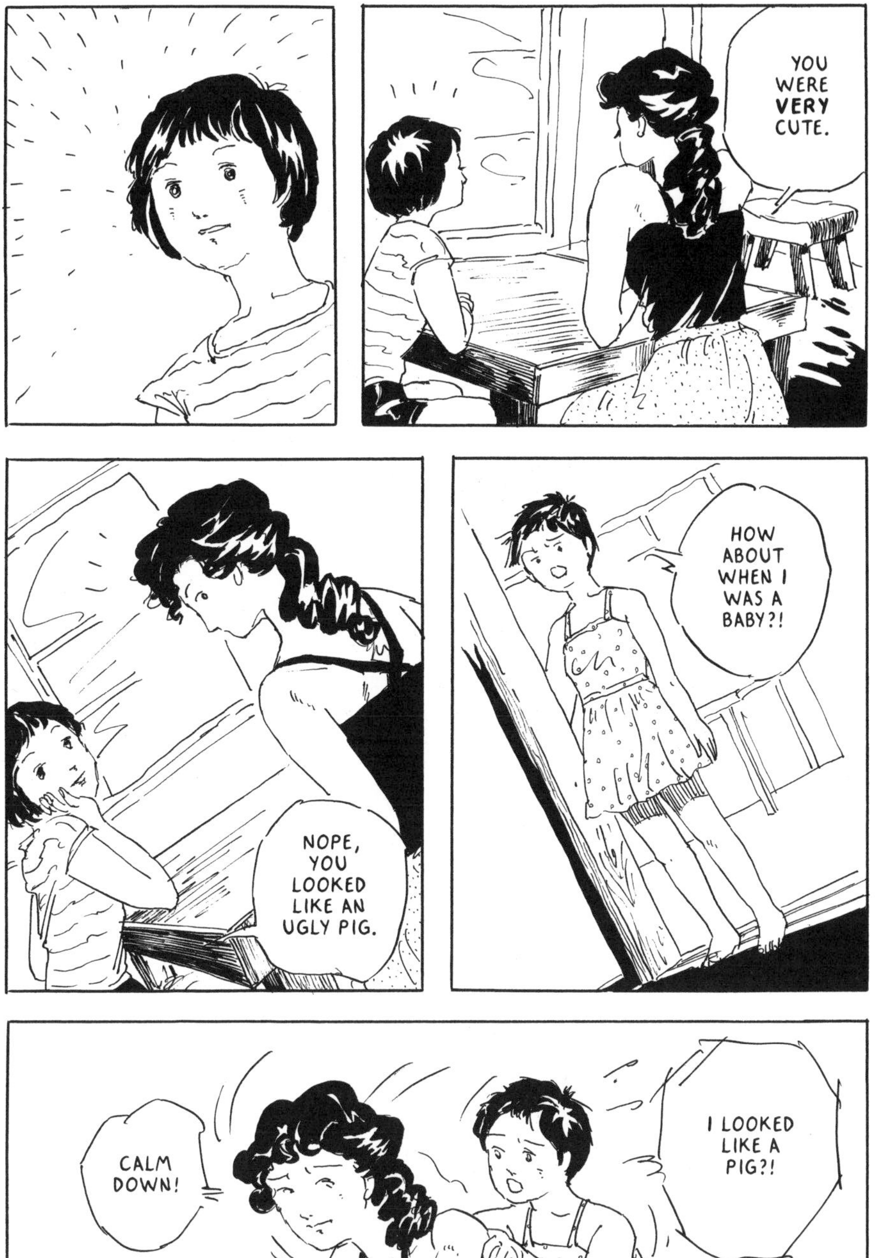
YOU WERE **VERY** CUTE.
HOW ABOUT WHEN I WAS A BABY?!
NOPE, YOU LOOKED LIKE AN UGLY PIG.
I LOOKED LIKE A PIG?!
CALM DOWN!

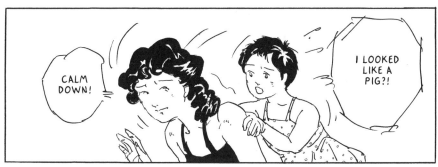

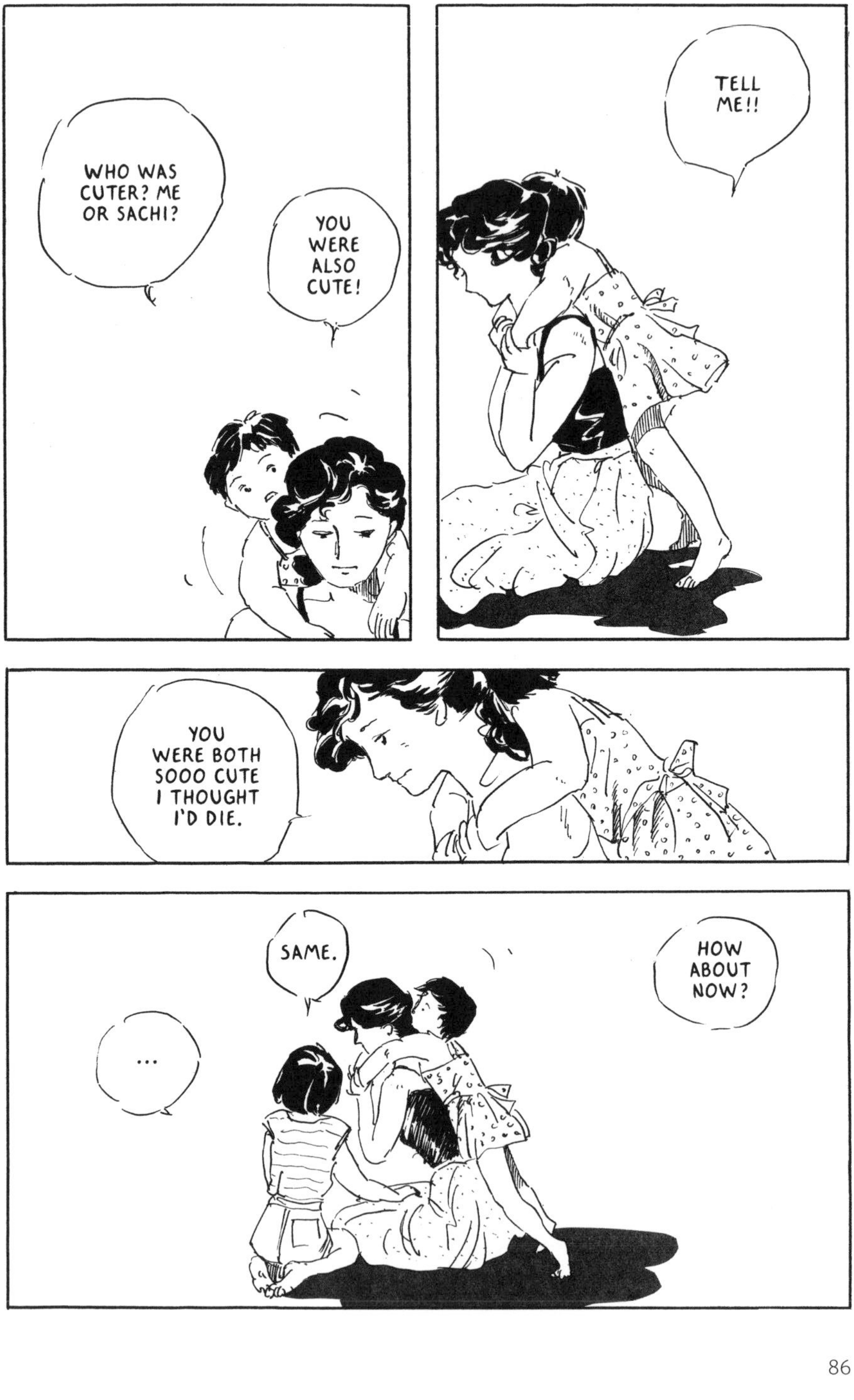
TELL ME!!
WHO WAS CUTER? ME OR SACHI?
YOU WERE ALSO CUTE!
YOU WERE BOTH SOOO CUTE I THOUGHT I'D DIE.
HOW ABOUT NOW?
SAME.
...

Even Little Ogres Cry

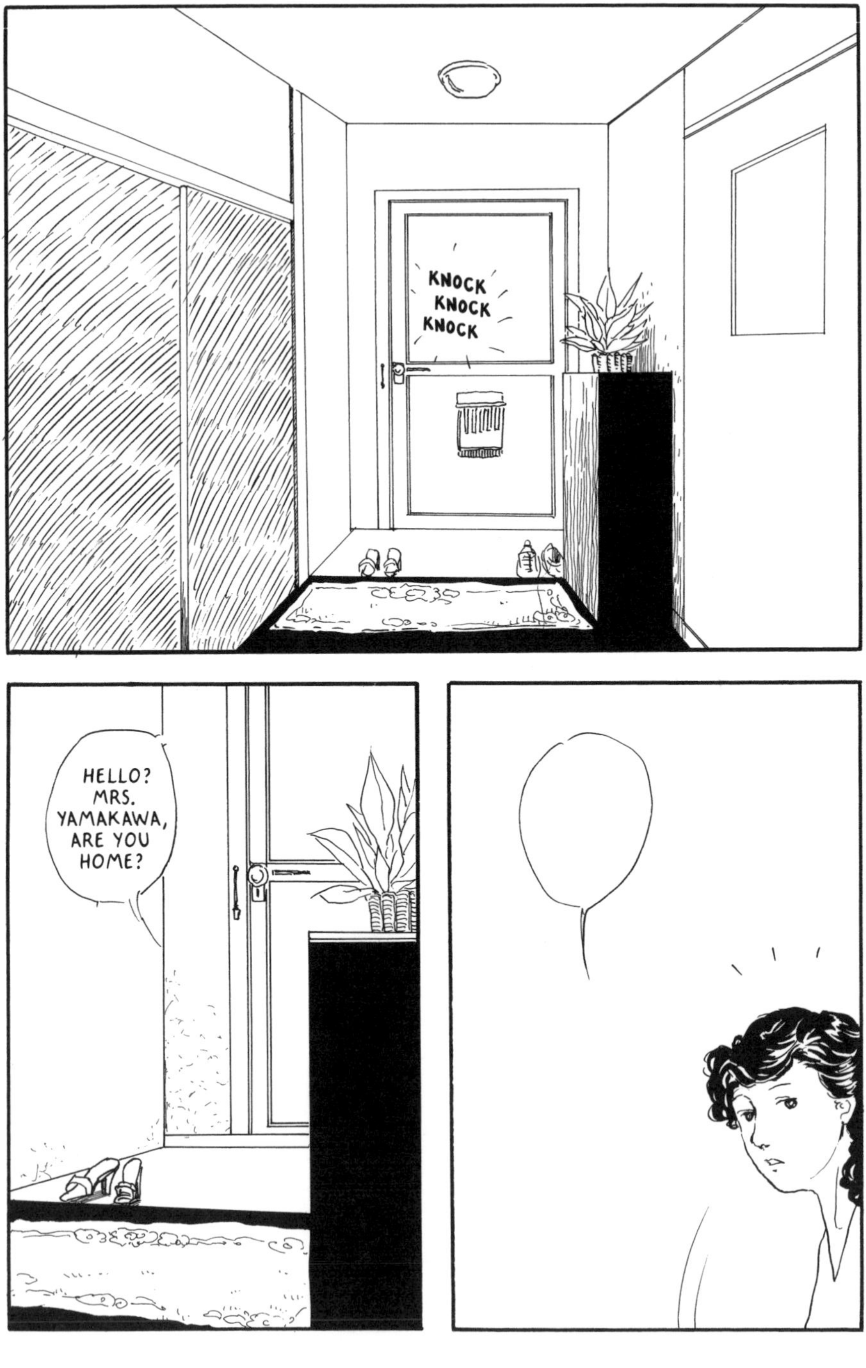
KNOCK KNOCK KNOCK
HELLO? MRS. YAMAKAWA, ARE YOU HOME?

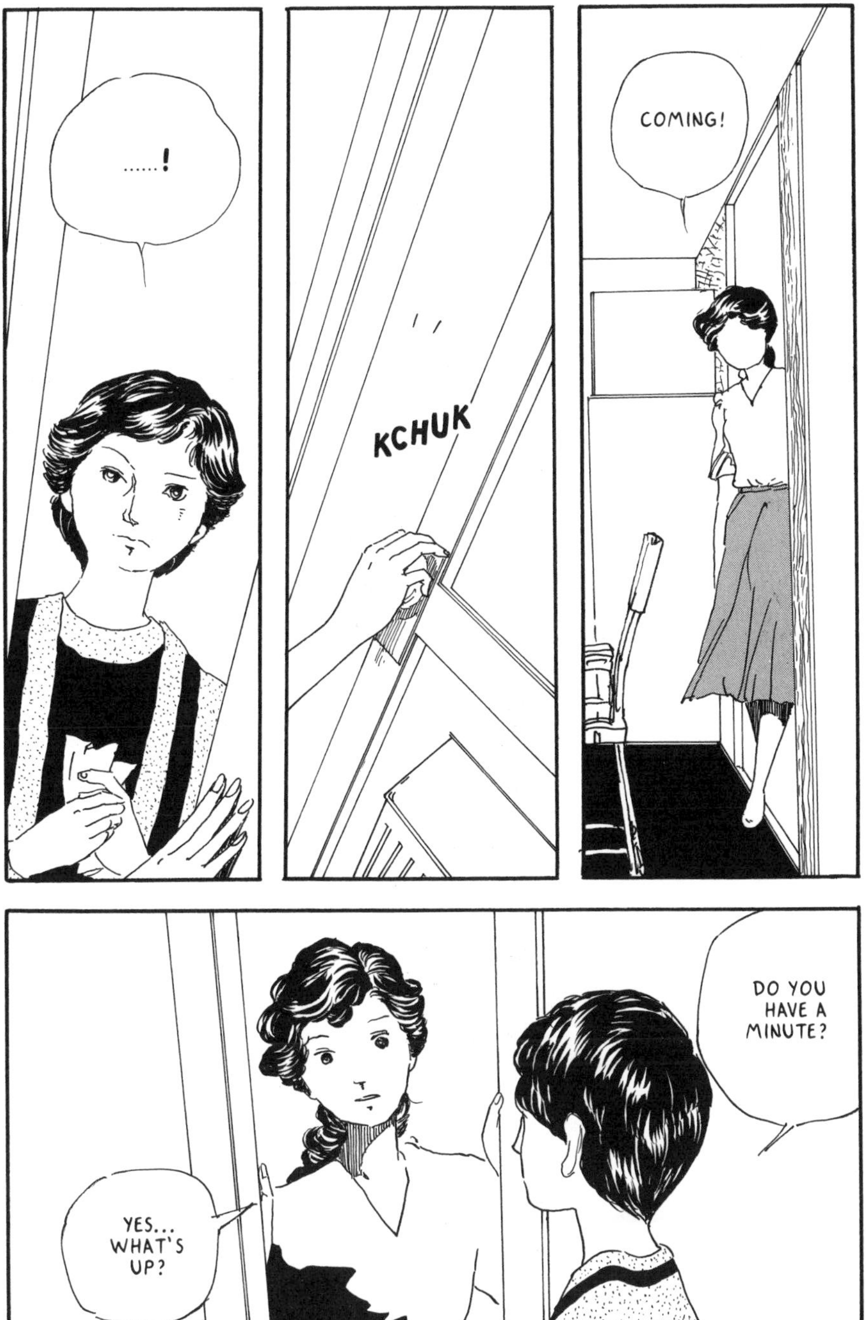
COMING!
KCHUK
......!
DO YOU HAVE A MINUTE?
YES... WHAT'S UP?

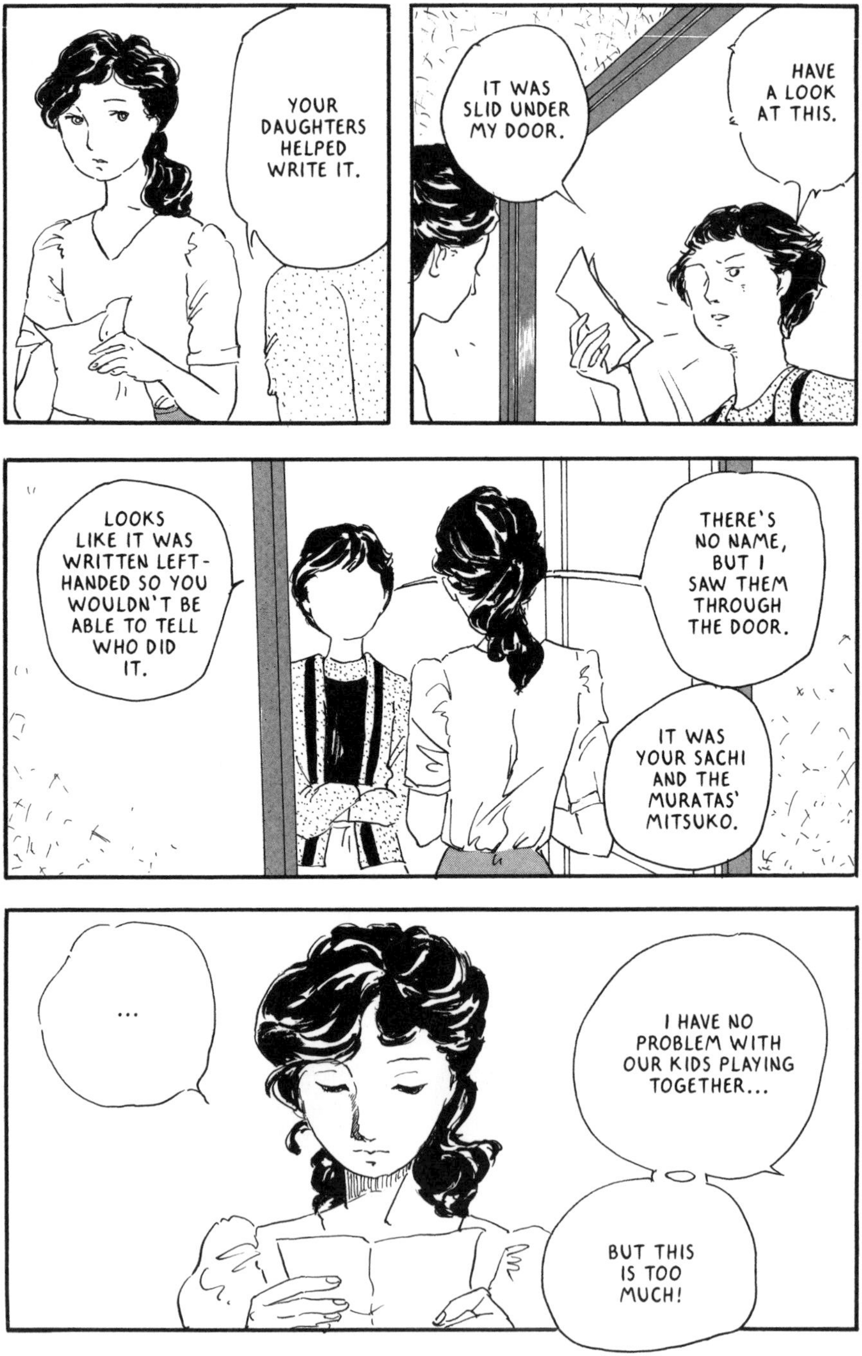
HAVE A LOOK AT THIS.
IT WAS SLID UNDER MY DOOR.
YOUR DAUGHTERS HELPED WRITE IT.
THERE'S NO NAME, BUT I SAW THEM THROUGH THE DOOR.
IT WAS YOUR SACHI AND THE MURATAS' MITSUKO.
LOOKS LIKE IT WAS WRITTEN LEFT-HANDED SO YOU WOULDN'T BE ABLE TO TELL WHO DID IT.
I HAVE NO PROBLEM WITH OUR KIDS PLAYING TOGETHER...
BUT THIS IS TOO MUCH!
...

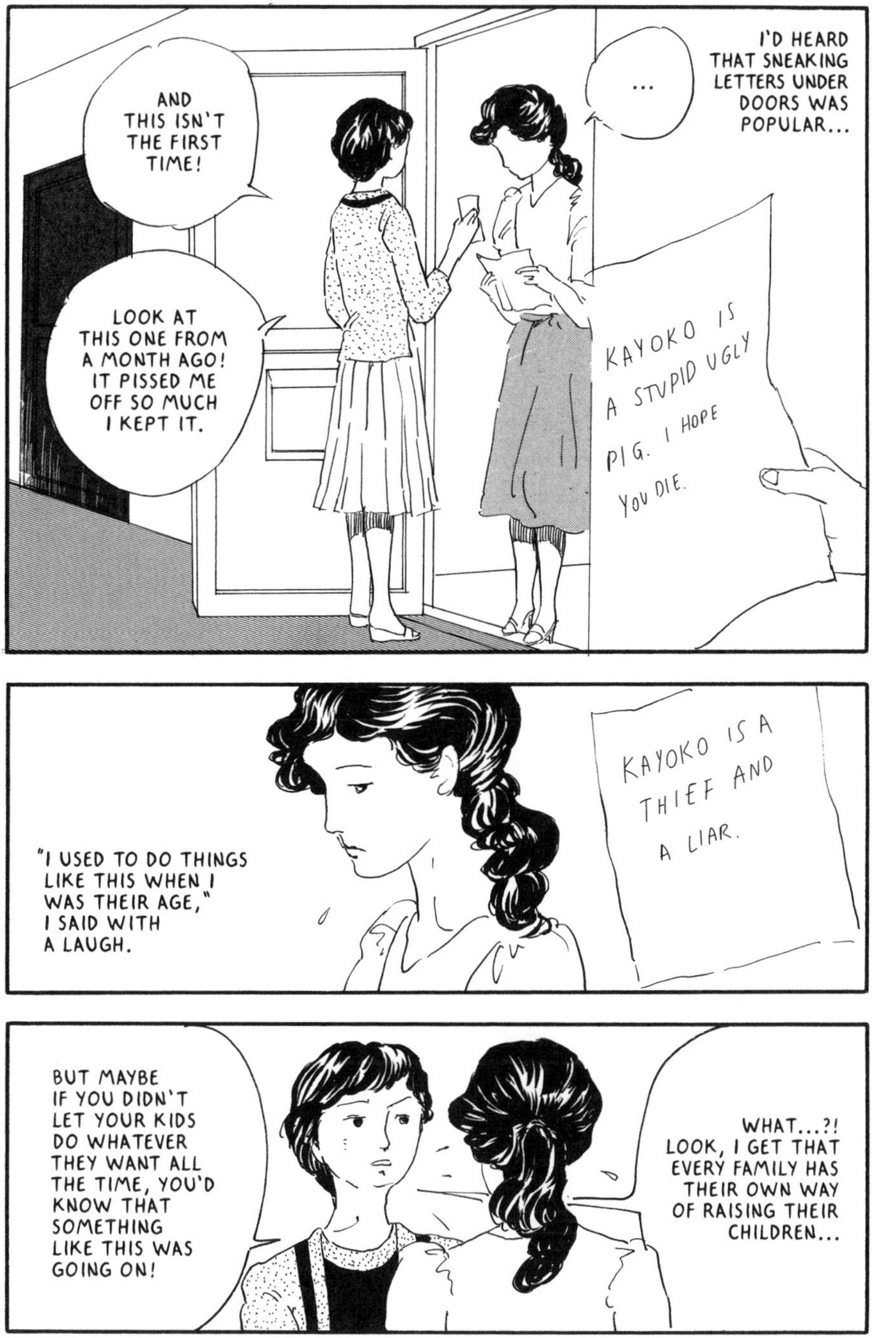
I'D HEARD THAT SNEAKING LETTERS UNDER DOORS WAS POPULAR...
...
KAYOKO IS A STUPID UGLY PIG. I HOPE YOU DIE.
AND THIS ISN'T THE FIRST TIME!
LOOK AT THIS ONE FROM A MONTH AGO! IT PISSED ME OFF SO MUCH I KEPT IT.
KAYOKO IS A THIEF AND A LIAR.
"I USED TO DO THINGS LIKE THIS WHEN I WAS THEIR AGE," I SAID WITH A LAUGH.
WHAT...?! LOOK, I GET THAT EVERY FAMILY HAS THEIR OWN WAY OF RAISING THEIR CHILDREN...
BUT MAYBE IF YOU DIDN'T LET YOUR KIDS DO WHATEVER THEY WANT ALL THE TIME, YOU'D KNOW THAT SOMETHING LIKE THIS WAS GOING ON!

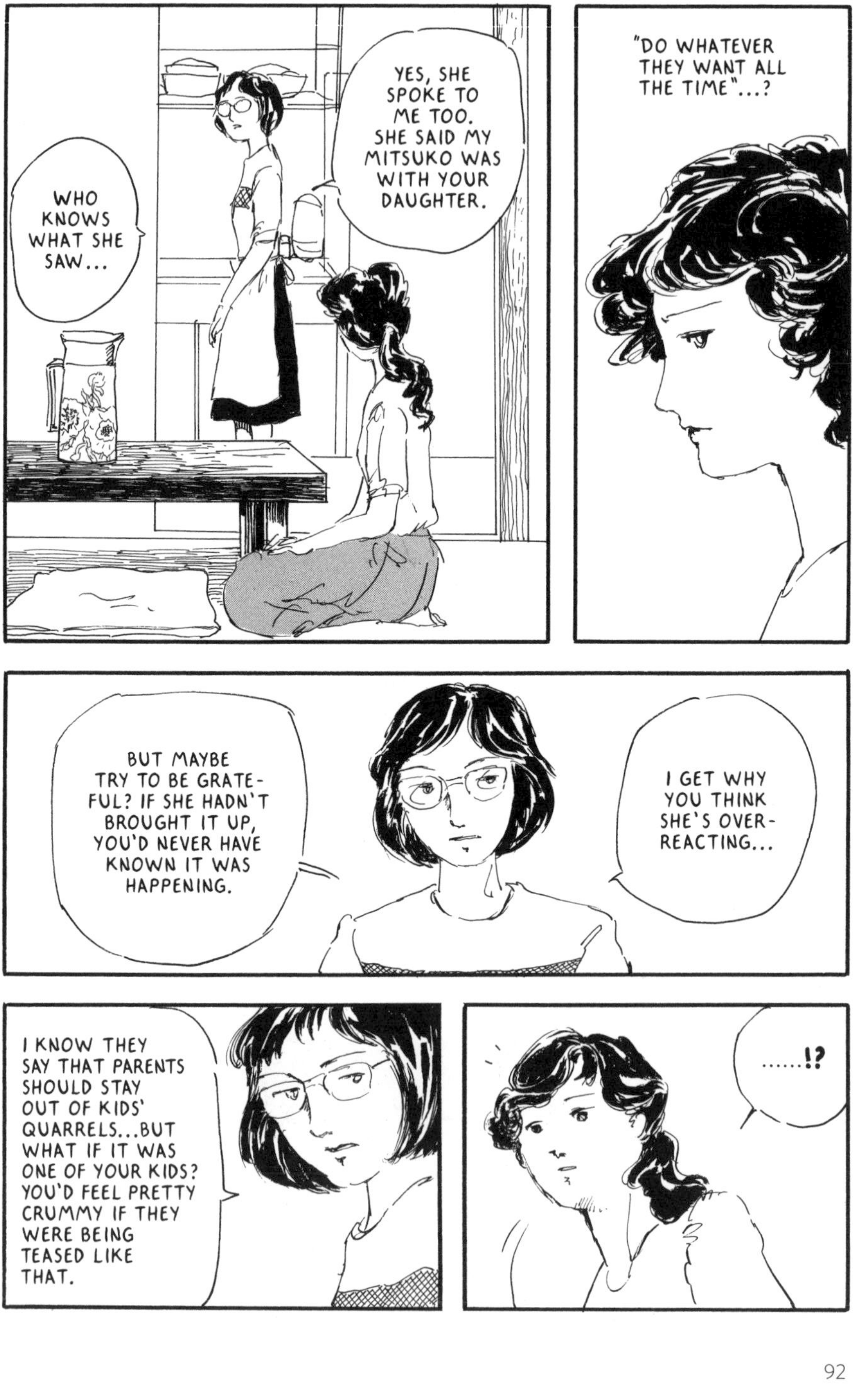
"DO WHATEVER THEY WANT ALL THE TIME"...?
YES, SHE SPOKE TO ME TOO. SHE SAID MY MITSUKO WAS WITH YOUR DAUGHTER.
WHO KNOWS WHAT SHE SAW...
I GET WHY YOU THINK SHE'S OVER-REACTING...
BUT MAYBE TRY TO BE GRATE-FUL? IF SHE HADN'T BROUGHT IT UP, YOU'D NEVER HAVE KNOWN IT WAS HAPPENING.
......!?
I KNOW THEY SAY THAT PARENTS SHOULD STAY OUT OF KIDS' QUARRELS...BUT WHAT IF IT WAS ONE OF YOUR KIDS? YOU'D FEEL PRETTY CRUMMY IF THEY WERE BEING TEASED LIKE THAT.

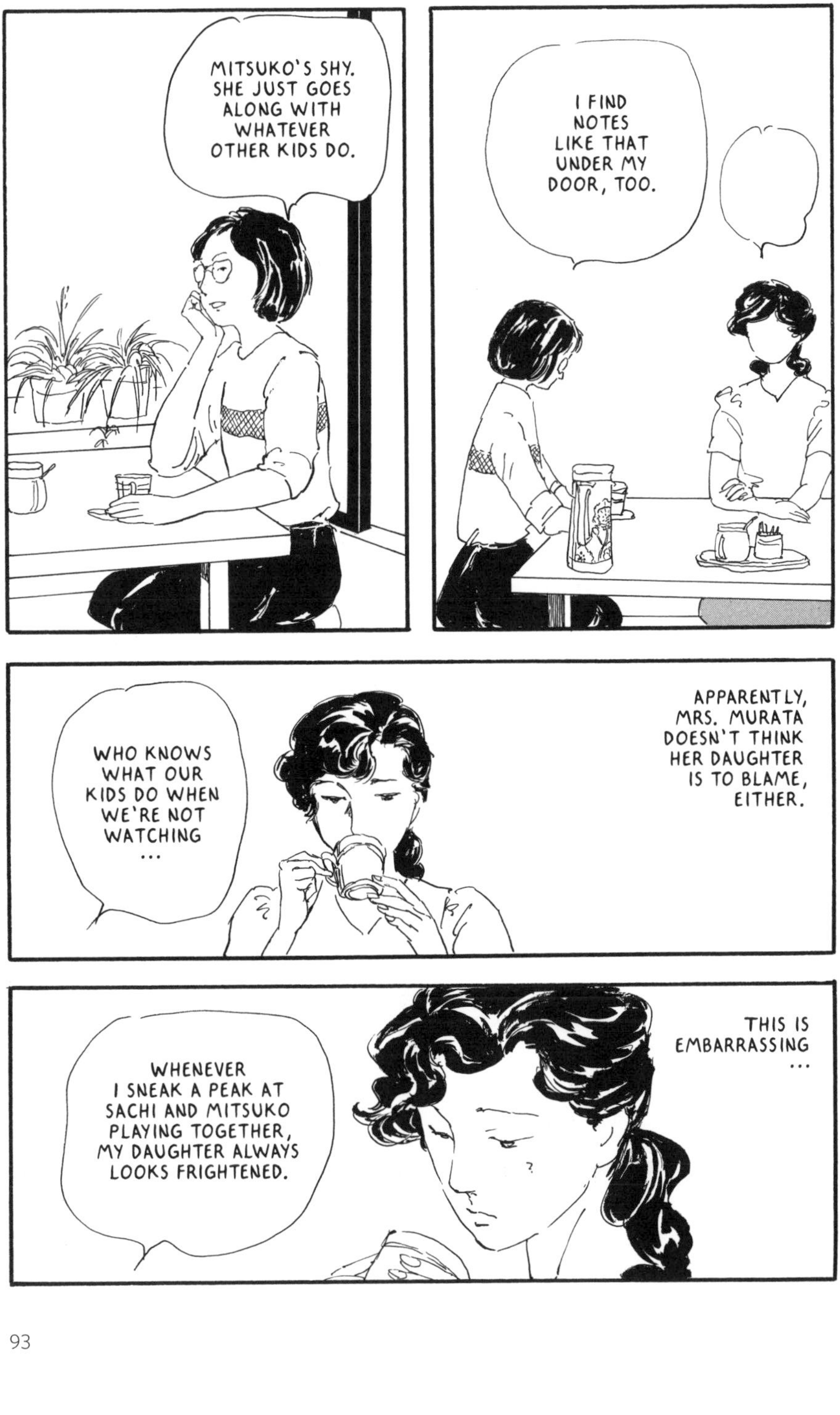
I FIND NOTES LIKE THAT UNDER MY DOOR, TOO.
MITSUKO'S SHY. SHE JUST GOES ALONG WITH WHATEVER OTHER KIDS DO.
APPARENTLY, MRS. MURATA DOESN'T THINK HER DAUGHTER IS TO BLAME, EITHER.
WHO KNOWS WHAT OUR KIDS DO WHEN WE'RE NOT WATCHING ...
THIS IS EMBARRASSING ...
WHENEVER I SNEAK A PEAK AT SACHI AND MITSUKO PLAYING TOGETHER, MY DAUGHTER ALWAYS LOOKS FRIGHTENED.

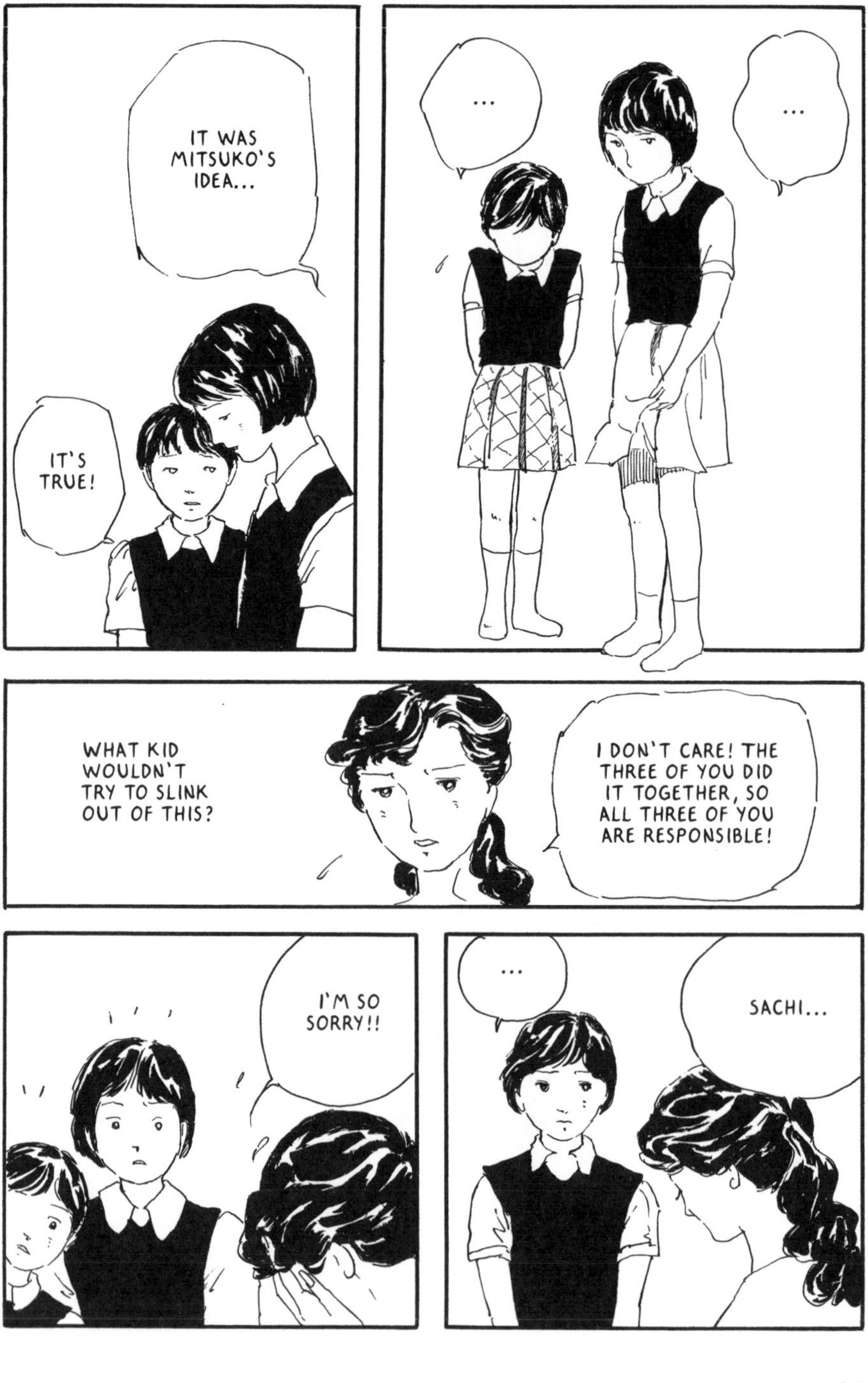
...
...
IT WAS MITSUKO'S IDEA...
IT'S TRUE!
I DON'T CARE! THE THREE OF YOU DID IT TOGETHER, SO ALL THREE OF YOU ARE RESPONSIBLE!
WHAT KID WOULDN'T TRY TO SLINK OUT OF THIS?
SACHI...
...
I'M SO SORRY!!

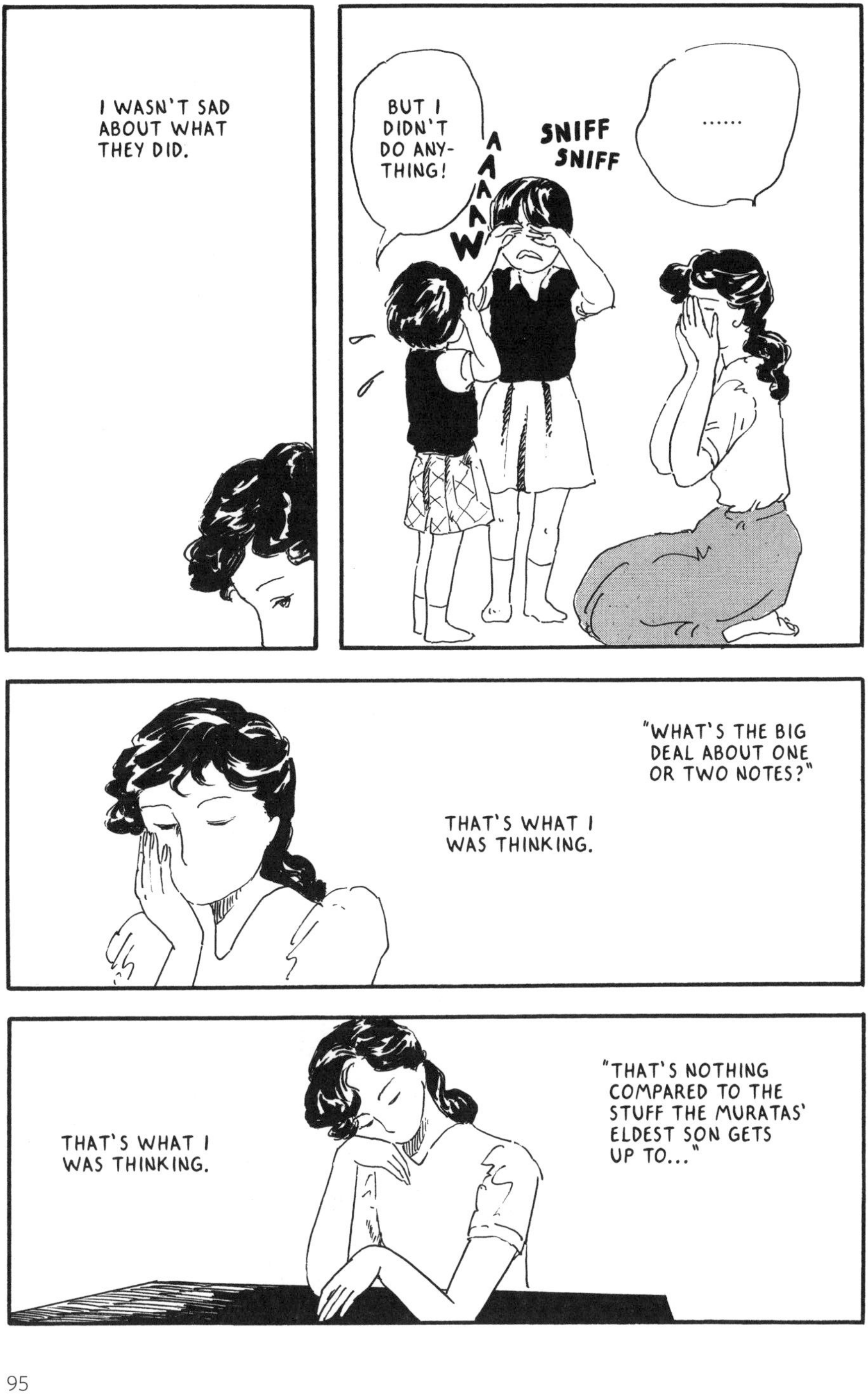
BUT I DIDN'T DO ANYTHING!
AAAAAW
SNIFF SNIFF
......
I WASN'T SAD ABOUT WHAT THEY DID.
"WHAT'S THE BIG DEAL ABOUT ONE OR TWO NOTES?"
THAT'S WHAT I WAS THINKING.
"THAT'S NOTHING COMPARED TO THE STUFF THE MURATAS' ELDEST SON GETS UP TO..."
THAT'S WHAT I WAS THINKING.

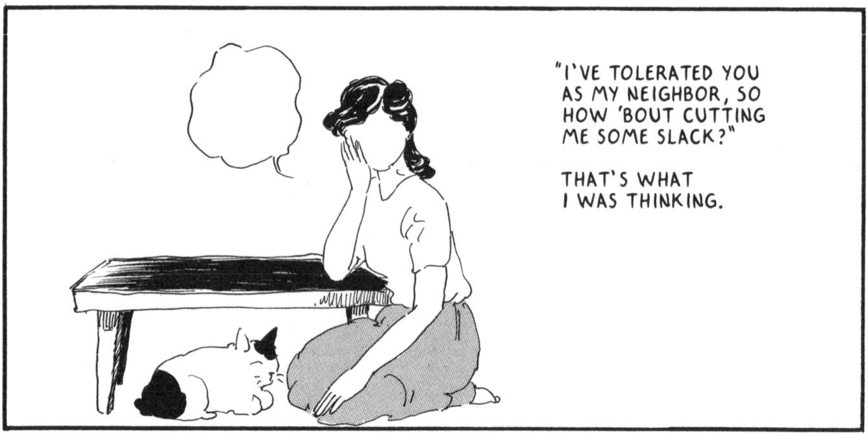
"I'VE TOLERATED YOU AS MY NEIGHBOR, SO HOW 'BOUT CUTTING ME SOME SLACK?"
THAT'S WHAT I WAS THINKING.

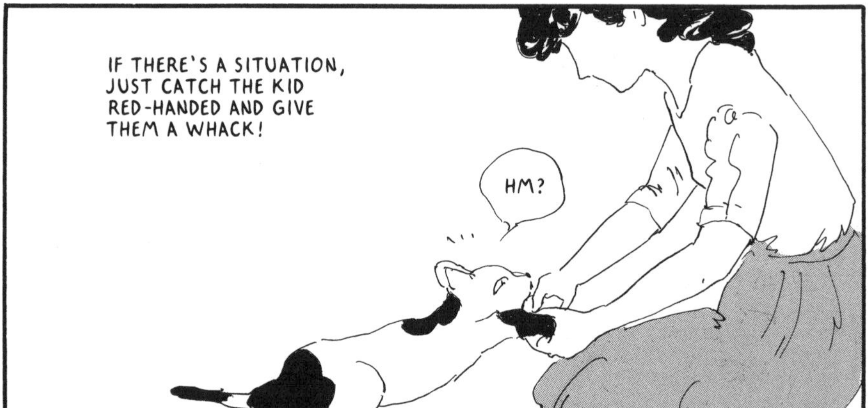
IF THERE'S A SITUATION, JUST CATCH THE KID RED-HANDED AND GIVE THEM A WHACK!
HM?

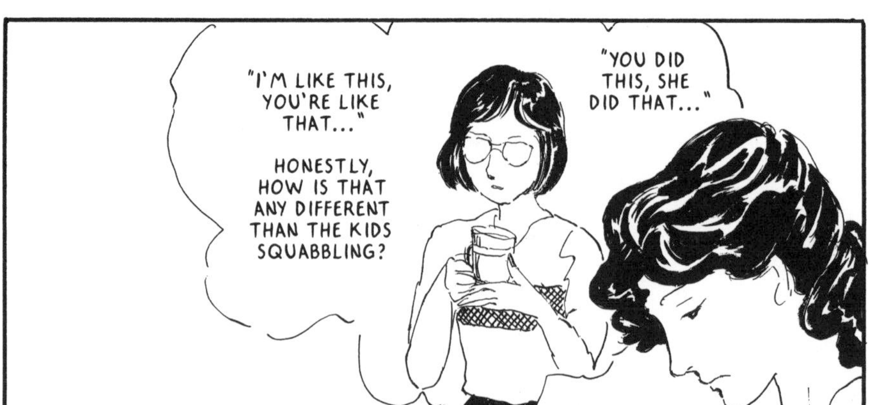
"YOU DID THIS, SHE DID THAT..."
"I'M LIKE THIS, YOU'RE LIKE THAT..."
HONESTLY, HOW IS THAT ANY DIFFERENT THAN THE KIDS SQUABBLING?

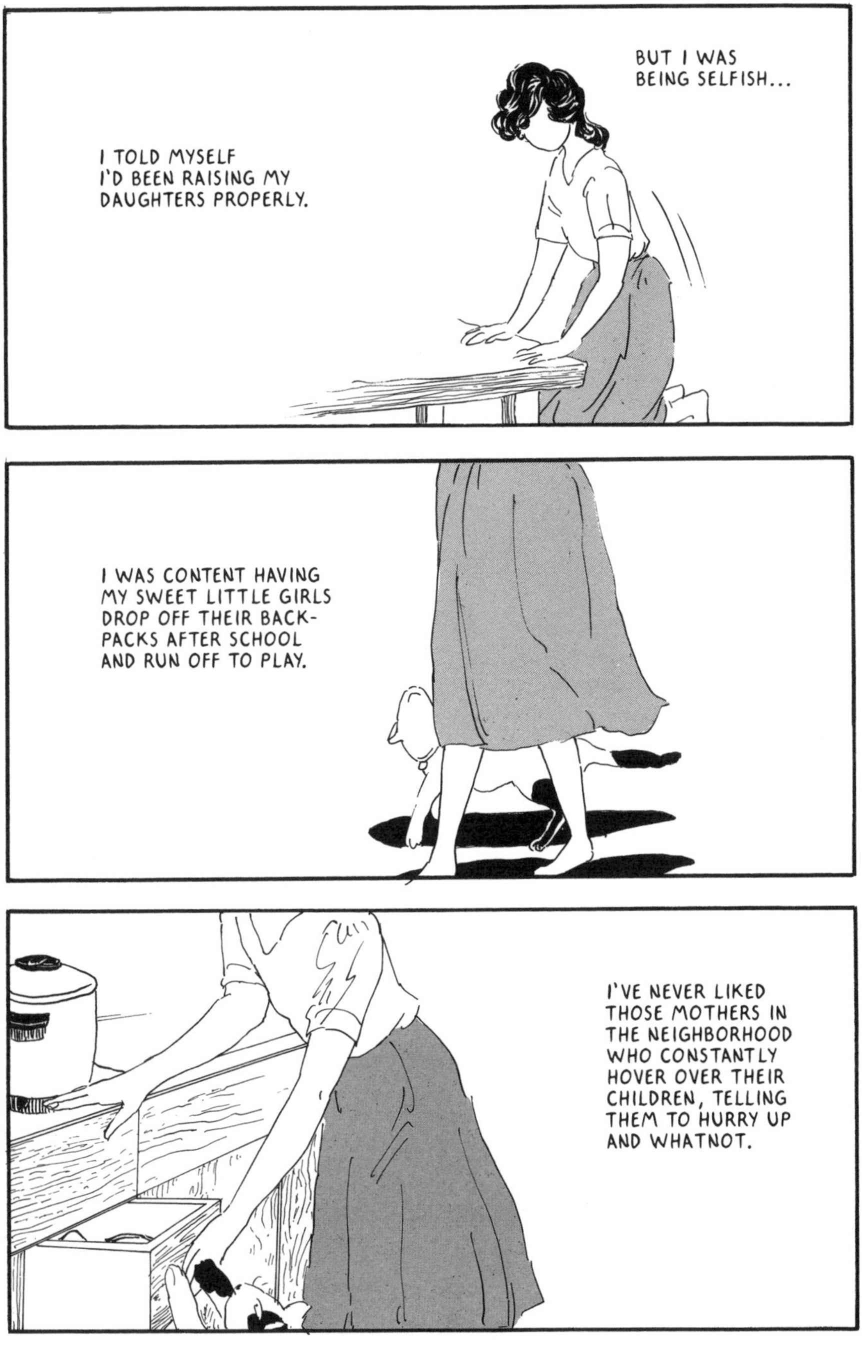
BUT I WAS BEING SELFISH...
I TOLD MYSELF I'D BEEN RAISING MY DAUGHTERS PROPERLY.
I WAS CONTENT HAVING MY SWEET LITTLE GIRLS DROP OFF THEIR BACK-PACKS AFTER SCHOOL AND RUN OFF TO PLAY.
I'VE NEVER LIKED THOSE MOTHERS IN THE NEIGHBORHOOD WHO CONSTANTLY HOVER OVER THEIR CHILDREN, TELLING THEM TO HURRY UP AND WHATNOT.

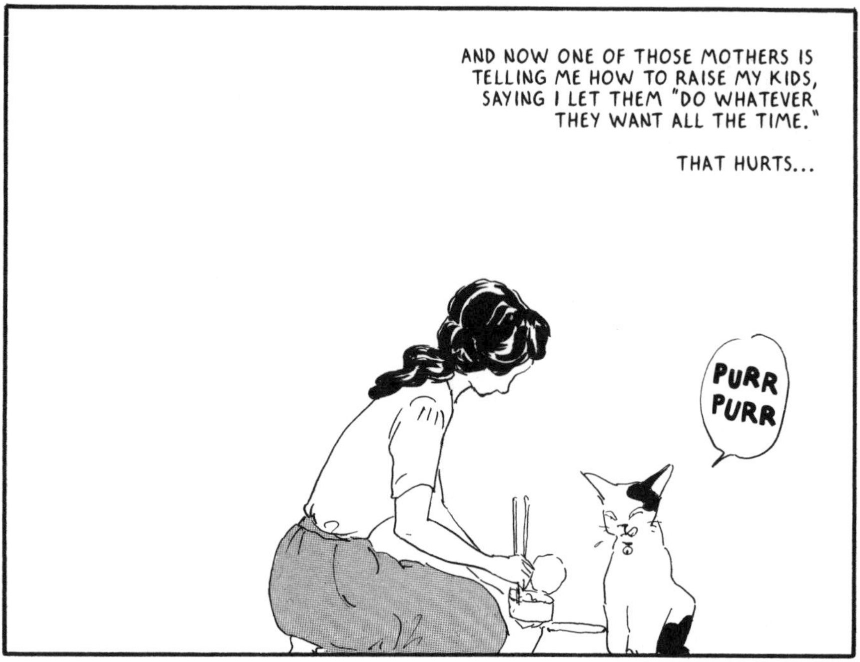
AND NOW ONE OF THOSE MOTHERS IS TELLING ME HOW TO RAISE MY KIDS, SAYING I LET THEM "DO WHATEVER THEY WANT ALL THE TIME."
THAT HURTS...
PURR PURR

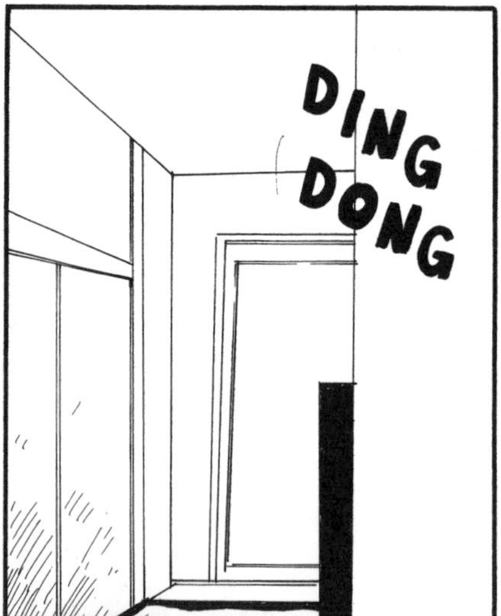
DING DONG

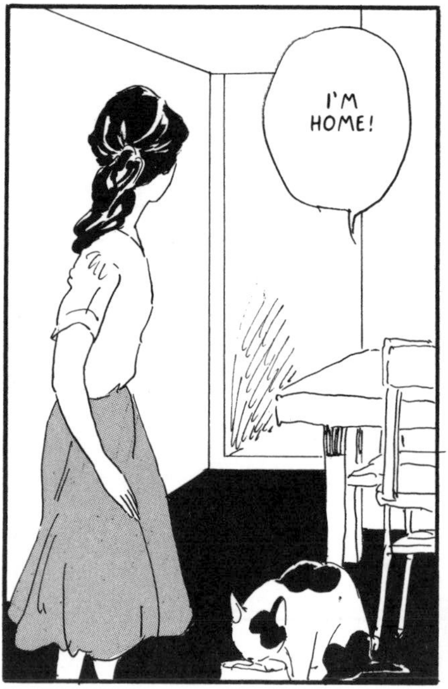
I'M HOME!

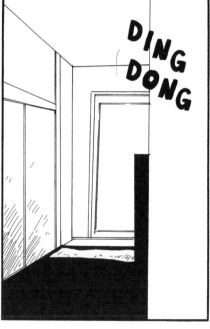

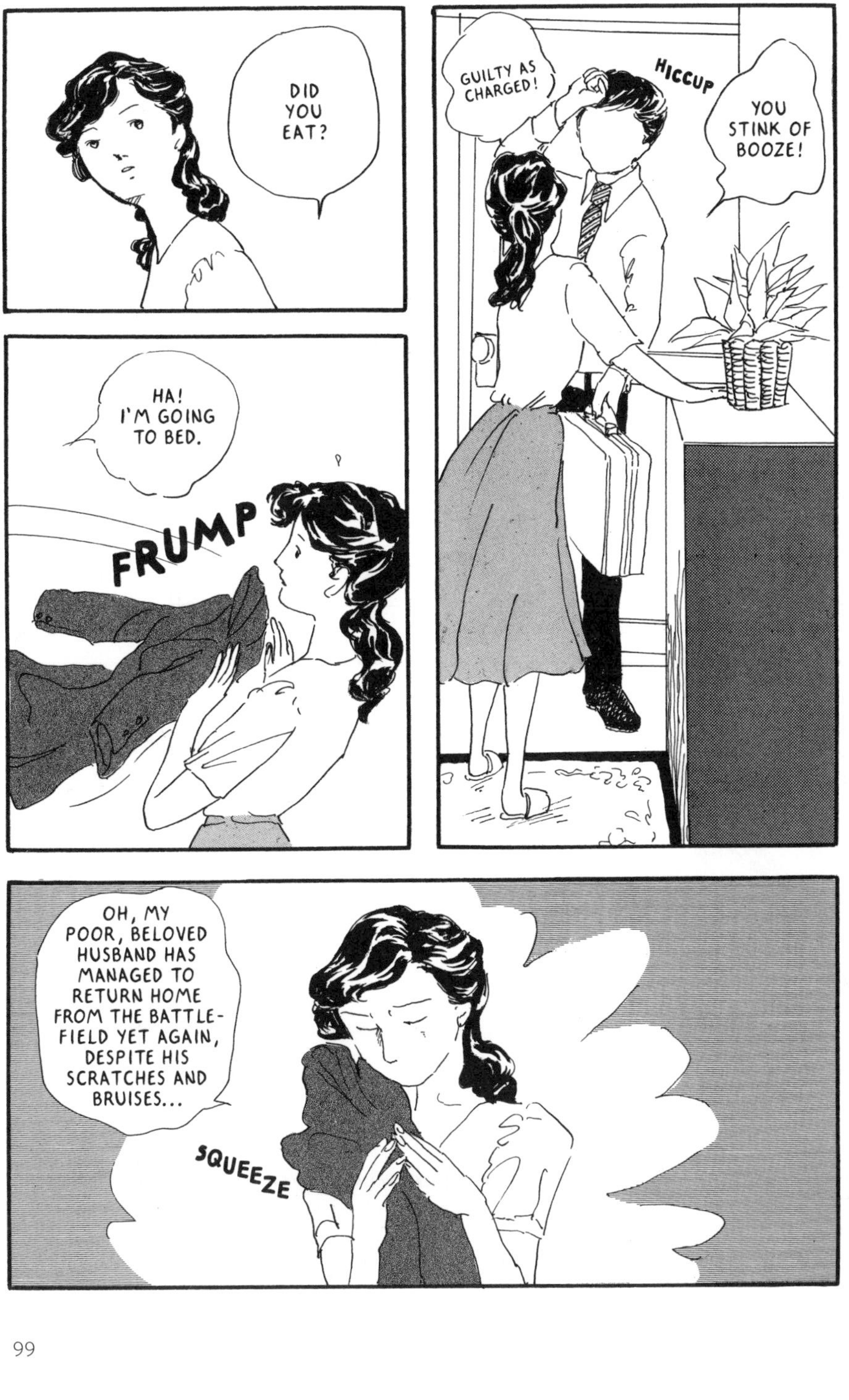
YOU STINK OF BOOZE!
HICCUP
GUILTY AS CHARGED!
DID YOU EAT?
HA! I'M GOING TO BED.
FRUMP
OH, MY POOR, BELOVED HUSBAND HAS MANAGED TO RETURN HOME FROM THE BATTLE-FIELD YET AGAIN, DESPITE HIS SCRATCHES AND BRUISES...
SQUEEZE

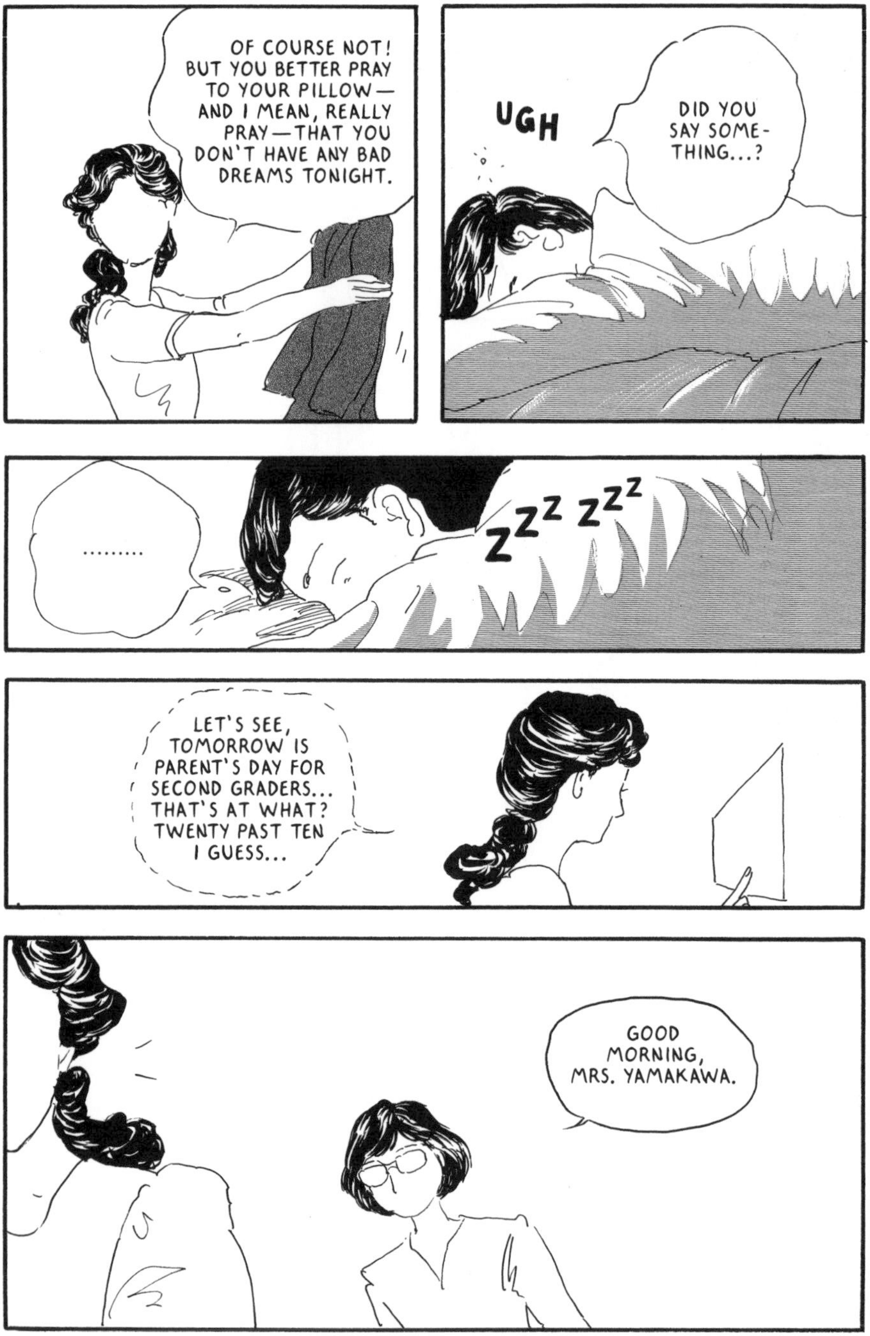
DID YOU SAY SOME-THING...?
UGH
OF COURSE NOT! BUT YOU BETTER PRAY TO YOUR PILLOW—AND I MEAN, REALLY PRAY—THAT YOU DON'T HAVE ANY BAD DREAMS TONIGHT.
ZZZ ZZZ
....
LET'S SEE, TOMORROW IS PARENT'S DAY FOR SECOND GRADERS... THAT'S AT WHAT? TWENTY PAST TEN I GUESS...
GOOD MORNING, MRS. YAMAKAWA.

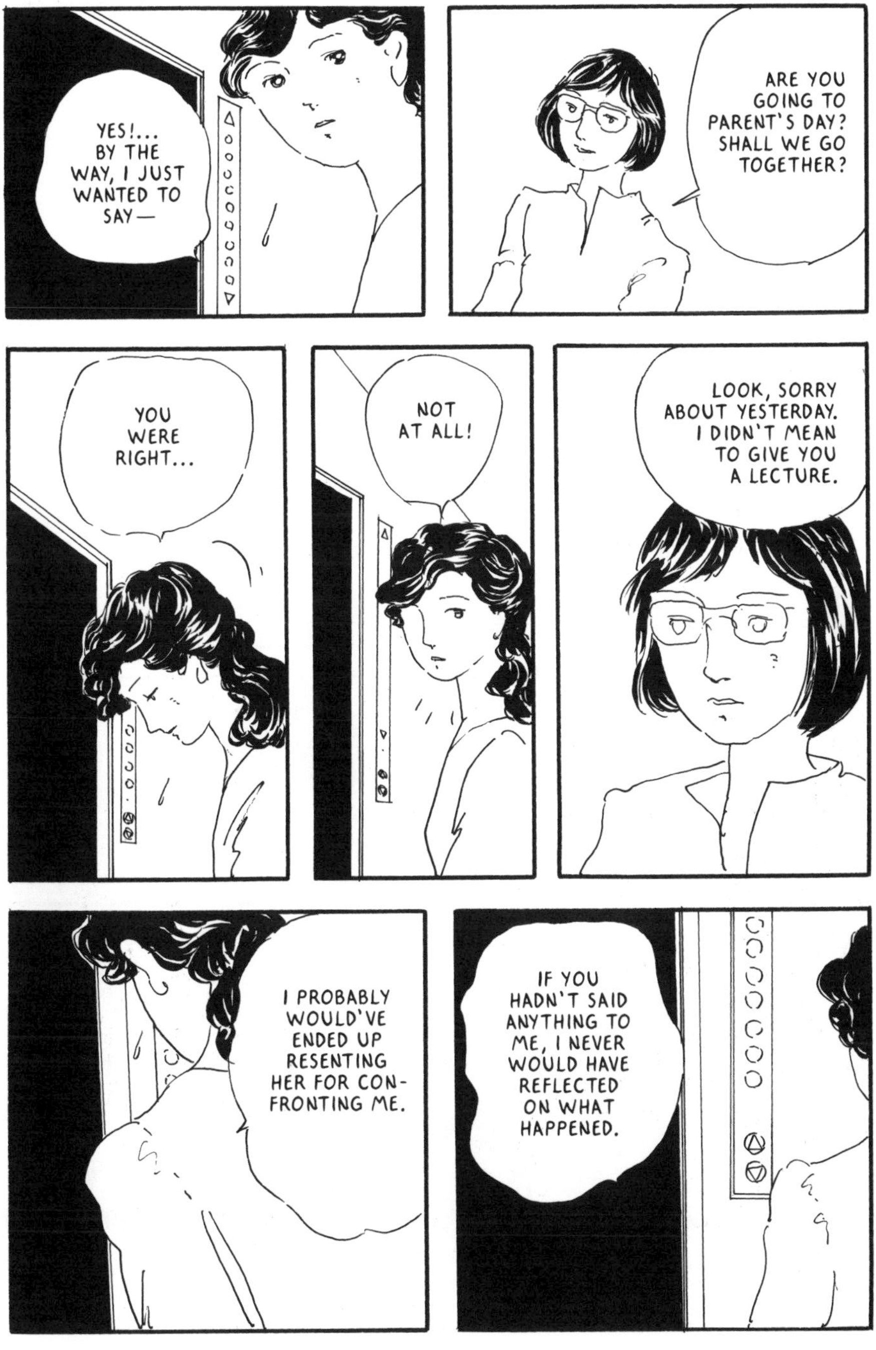
ARE YOU GOING TO PARENT'S DAY? SHALL WE GO TOGETHER?
YES!... BY THE WAY, I JUST WANTED TO SAY—
LOOK, SORRY ABOUT YESTERDAY. I DIDN'T MEAN TO GIVE YOU A LECTURE.
NOT AT ALL!
YOU WERE RIGHT...
IF YOU HADN'T SAID ANYTHING TO ME, I NEVER WOULD HAVE REFLECTED ON WHAT HAPPENED.
I PROBABLY WOULD'VE ENDED UP RESENTING HER FOR CON-FRONTING ME.

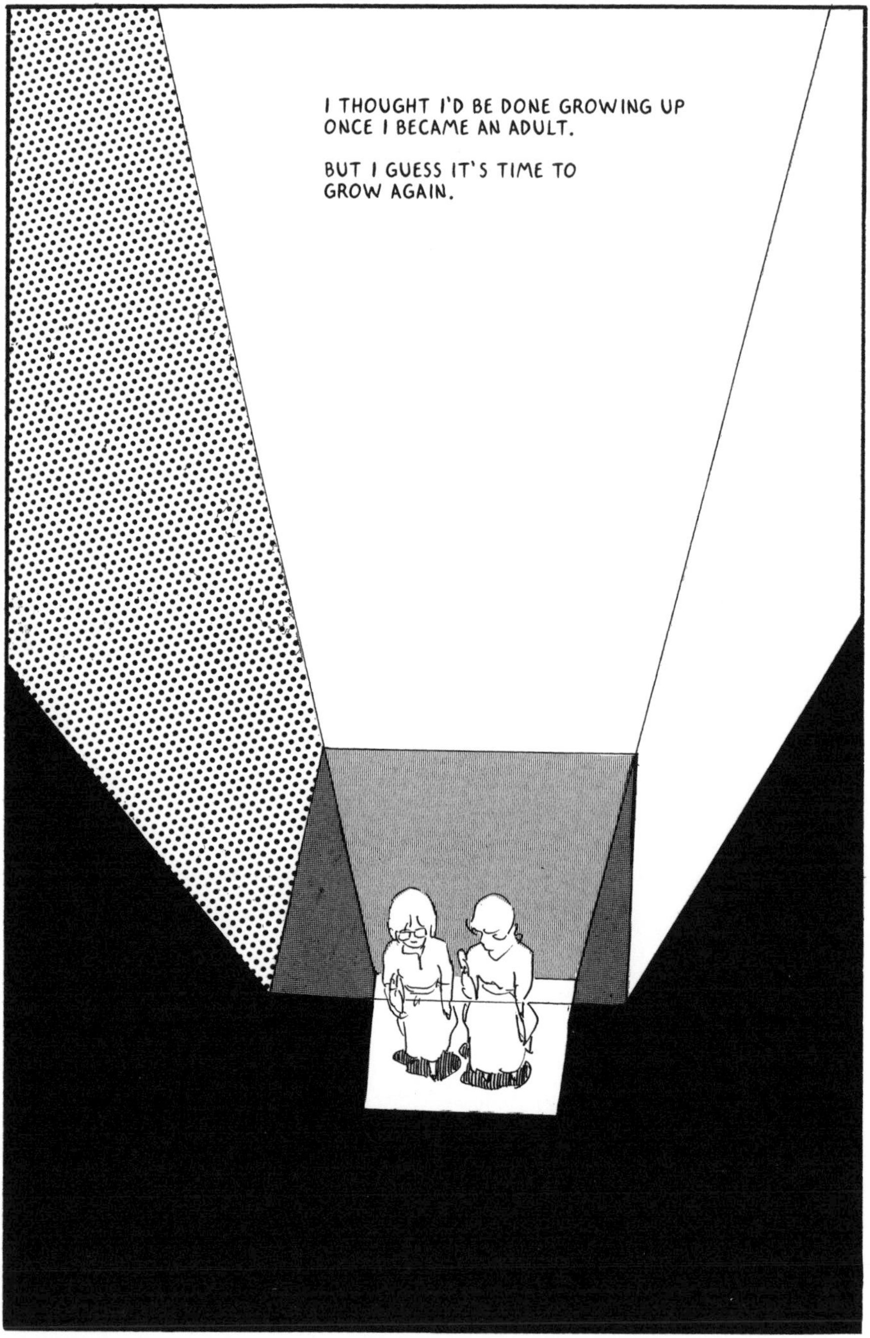
I THOUGHT I'D BE DONE GROWING UP ONCE I BECAME AN ADULT.
BUT I GUESS IT'S TIME TO GROW AGAIN.

Drops

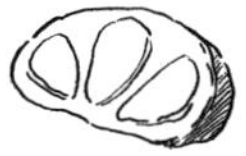

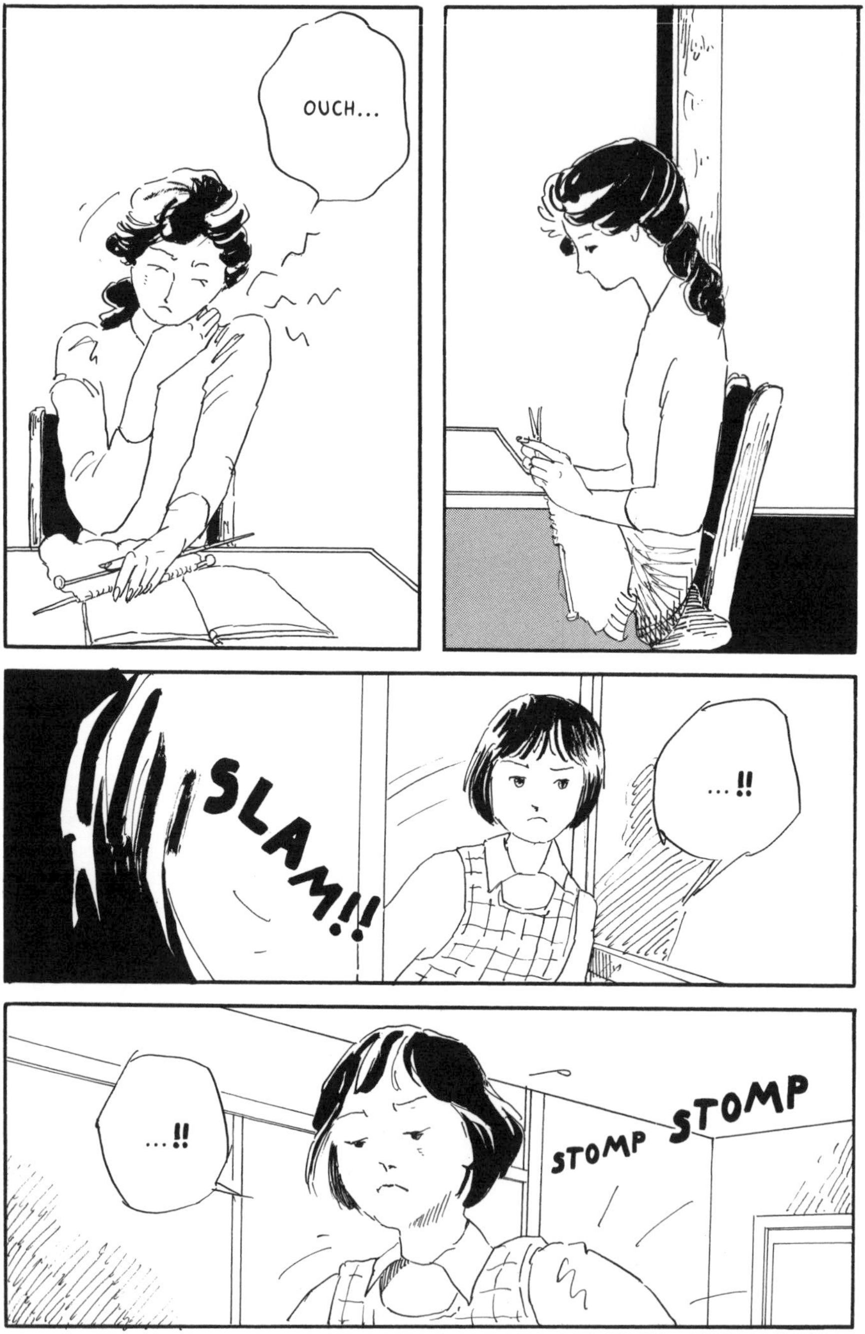
OUCH...
...!!
SLAM!!
STOMP STOMP
...!!

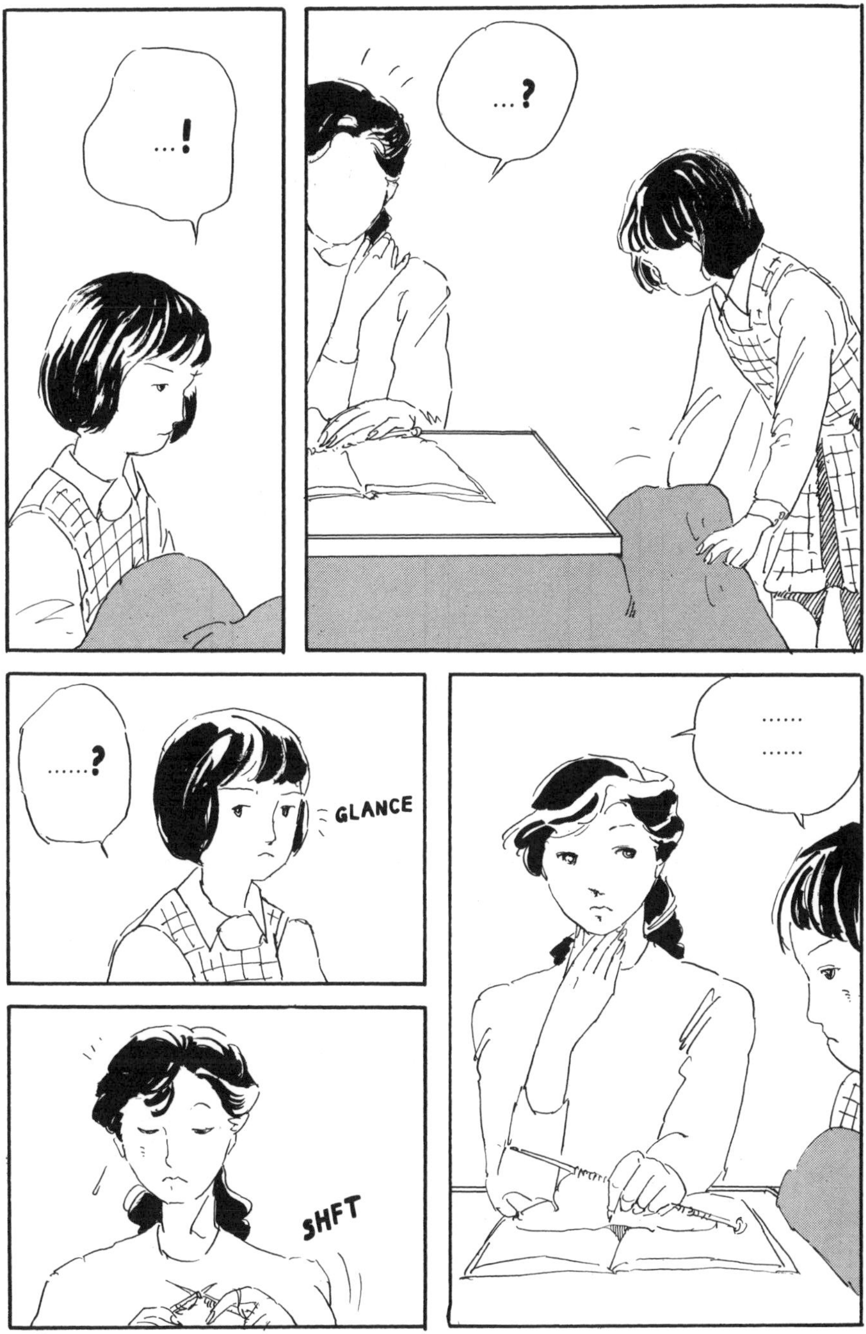
...?
...!
......
......
......?
GLANCE
SHFT

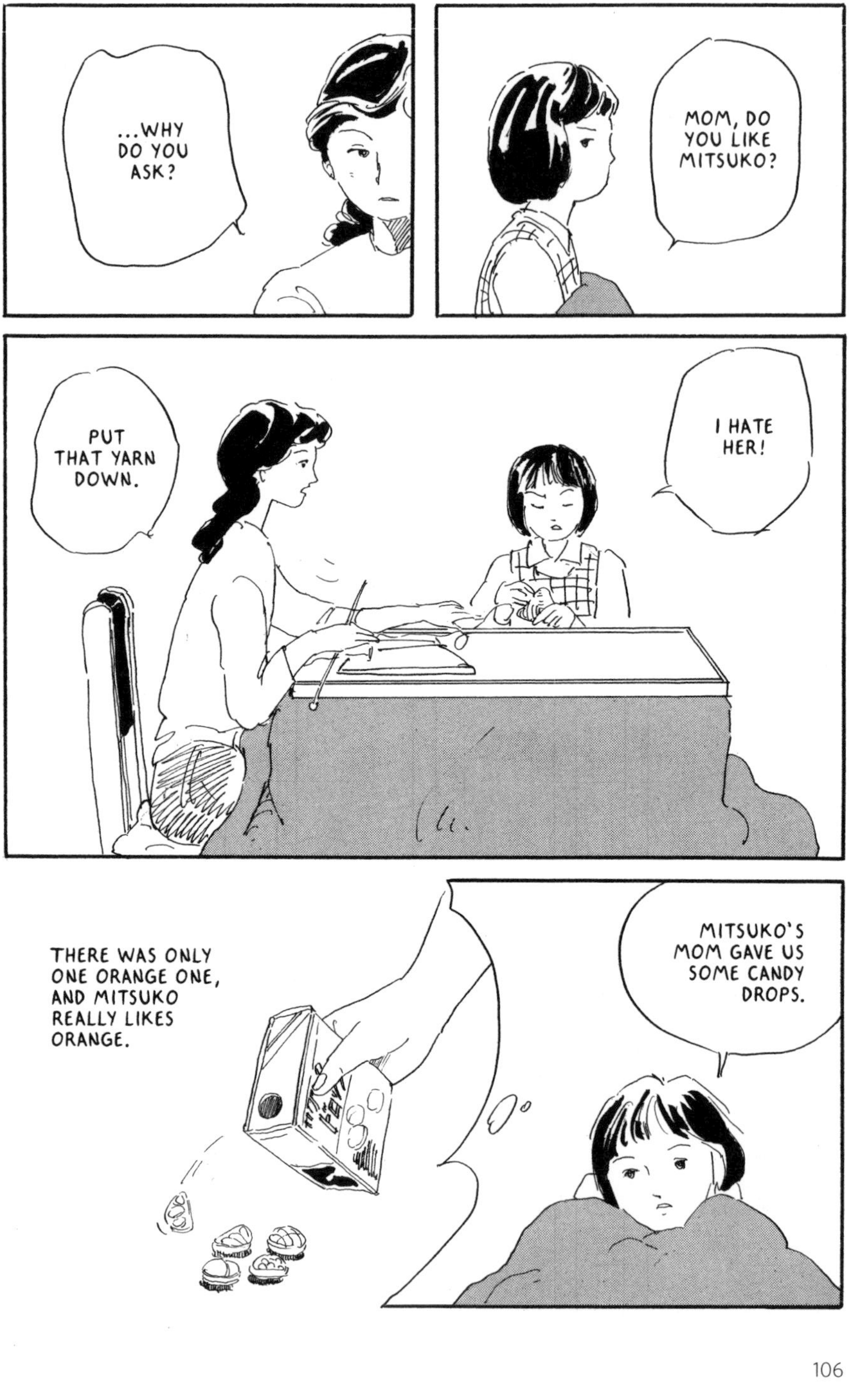
MOM, DO YOU LIKE MITSUKO?
...WHY DO YOU ASK?
I HATE HER!
PUT THAT YARN DOWN.
MITSUKO'S MOM GAVE US SOME CANDY DROPS.
THERE WAS ONLY ONE ORANGE ONE, AND MITSUKO REALLY LIKES ORANGE.

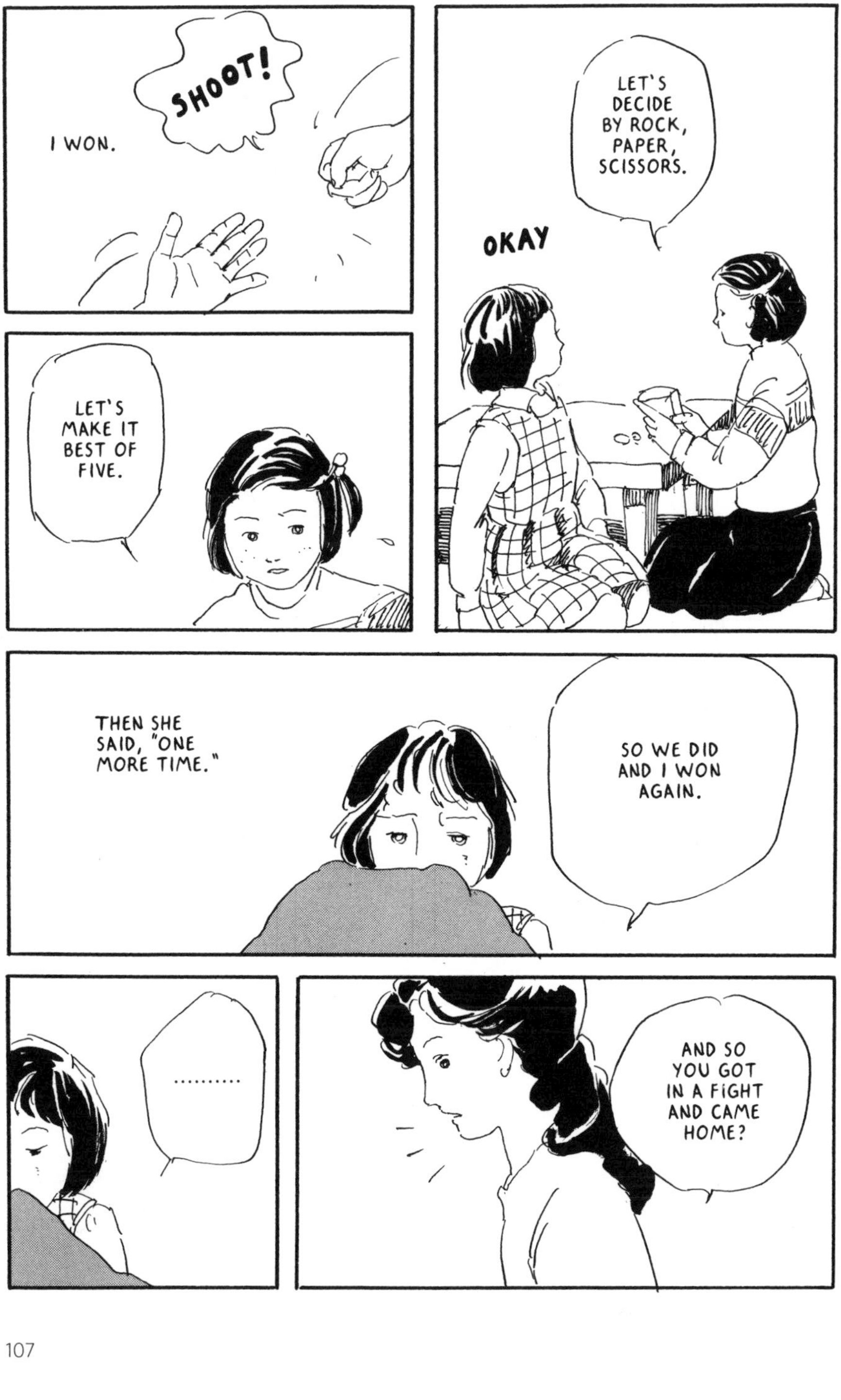
LET'S DECIDE BY ROCK, PAPER, SCISSORS.
OKAY
SHOOT!
I WON.
LET'S MAKE IT BEST OF FIVE.
THEN SHE SAID, "ONE MORE TIME."
SO WE DID AND I WON AGAIN.
AND SO YOU GOT IN A FIGHT AND CAME HOME?
....

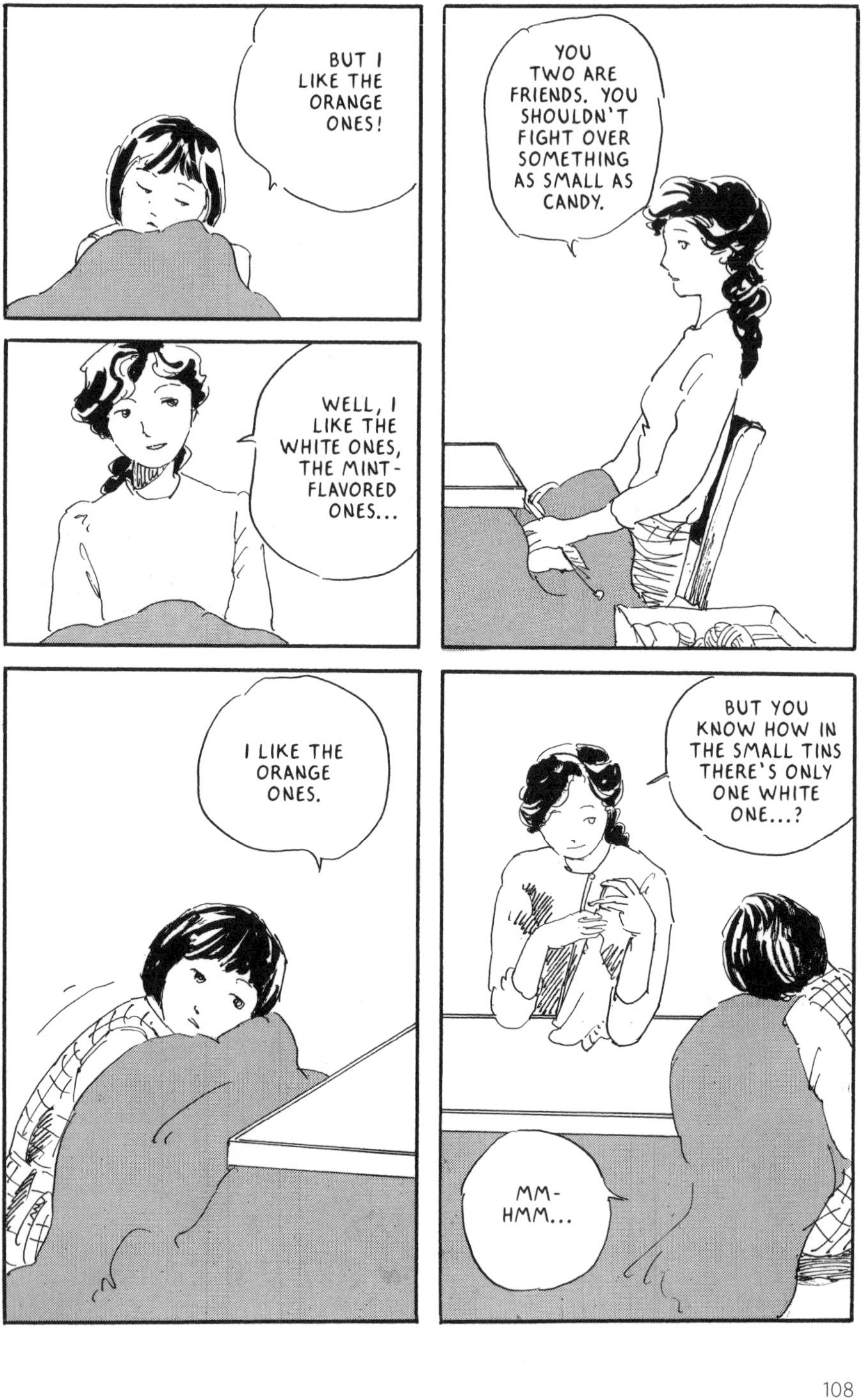
YOU TWO ARE FRIENDS. YOU SHOULDN'T FIGHT OVER SOMETHING AS SMALL AS CANDY.
BUT I LIKE THE ORANGE ONES!
WELL, I LIKE THE WHITE ONES, THE MINT-FLAVORED ONES...
BUT YOU KNOW HOW IN THE SMALL TINS THERE'S ONLY ONE WHITE ONE...?
MM-HMM...
I LIKE THE ORANGE ONES.

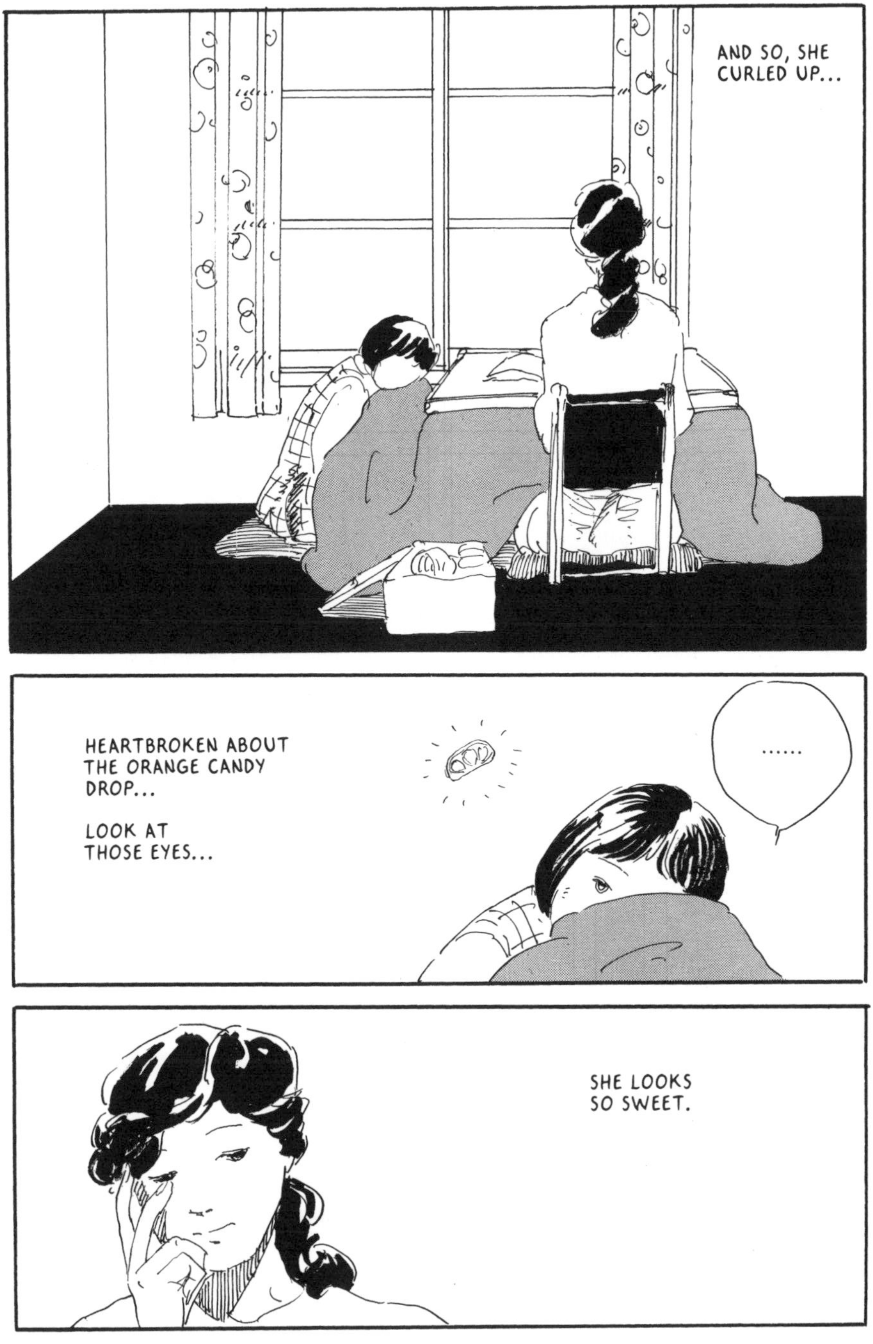
AND SO, SHE CURLED UP...
......
HEARTBROKEN ABOUT THE ORANGE CANDY DROP...
LOOK AT THOSE EYES...
SHE LOOKS SO SWEET.

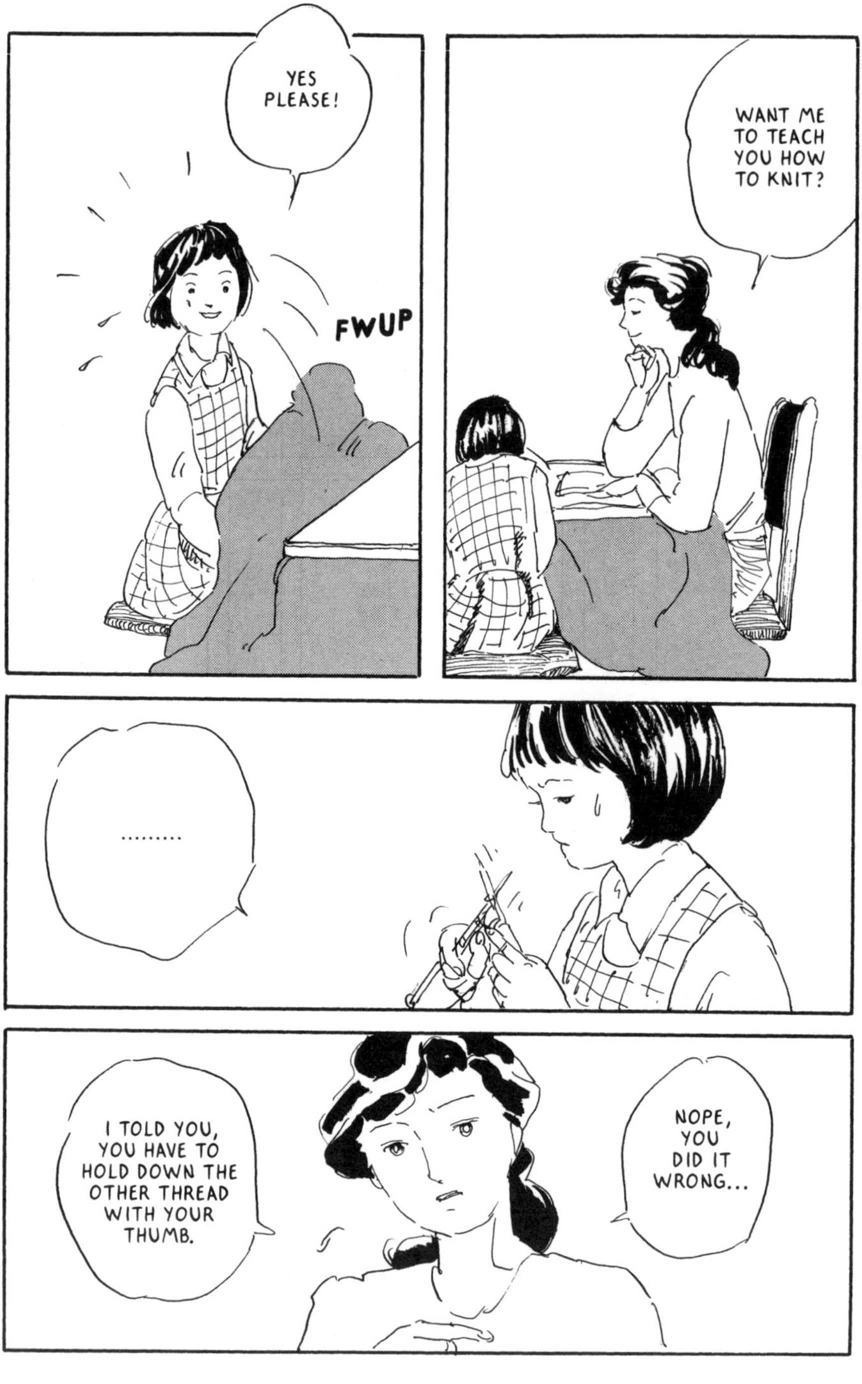
WANT ME TO TEACH YOU HOW TO KNIT?
YES PLEASE!
FWUP
....
NOPE, YOU DID IT WRONG...
I TOLD YOU, YOU HAVE TO HOLD DOWN THE OTHER THREAD WITH YOUR THUMB.

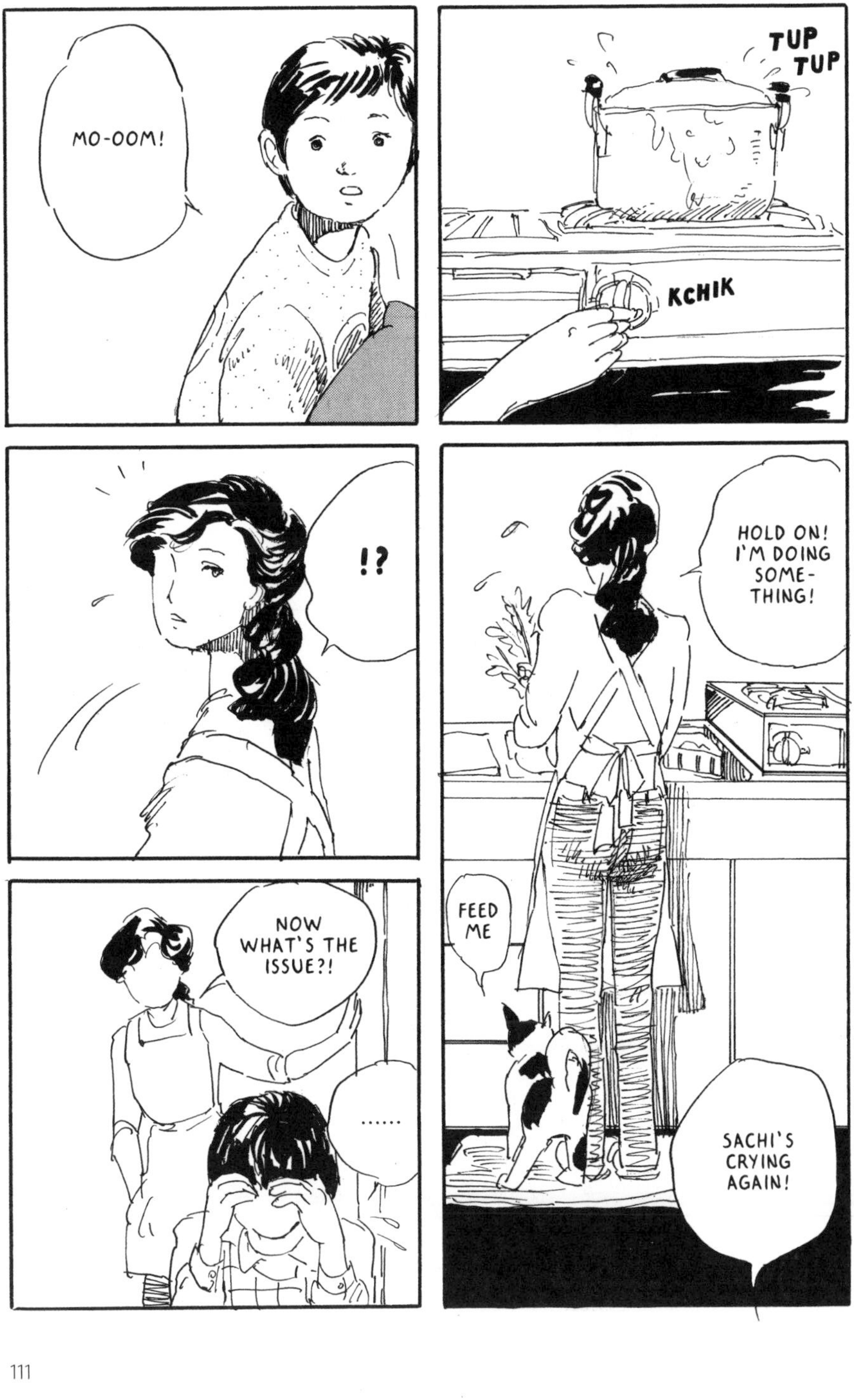
TUP
TUP
KCHIK
MO-OOM!
HOLD ON! I'M DOING SOME-THING!
FEED ME
SACHI'S CRYING AGAIN!
!?
NOW WHAT'S THE ISSUE?!
......

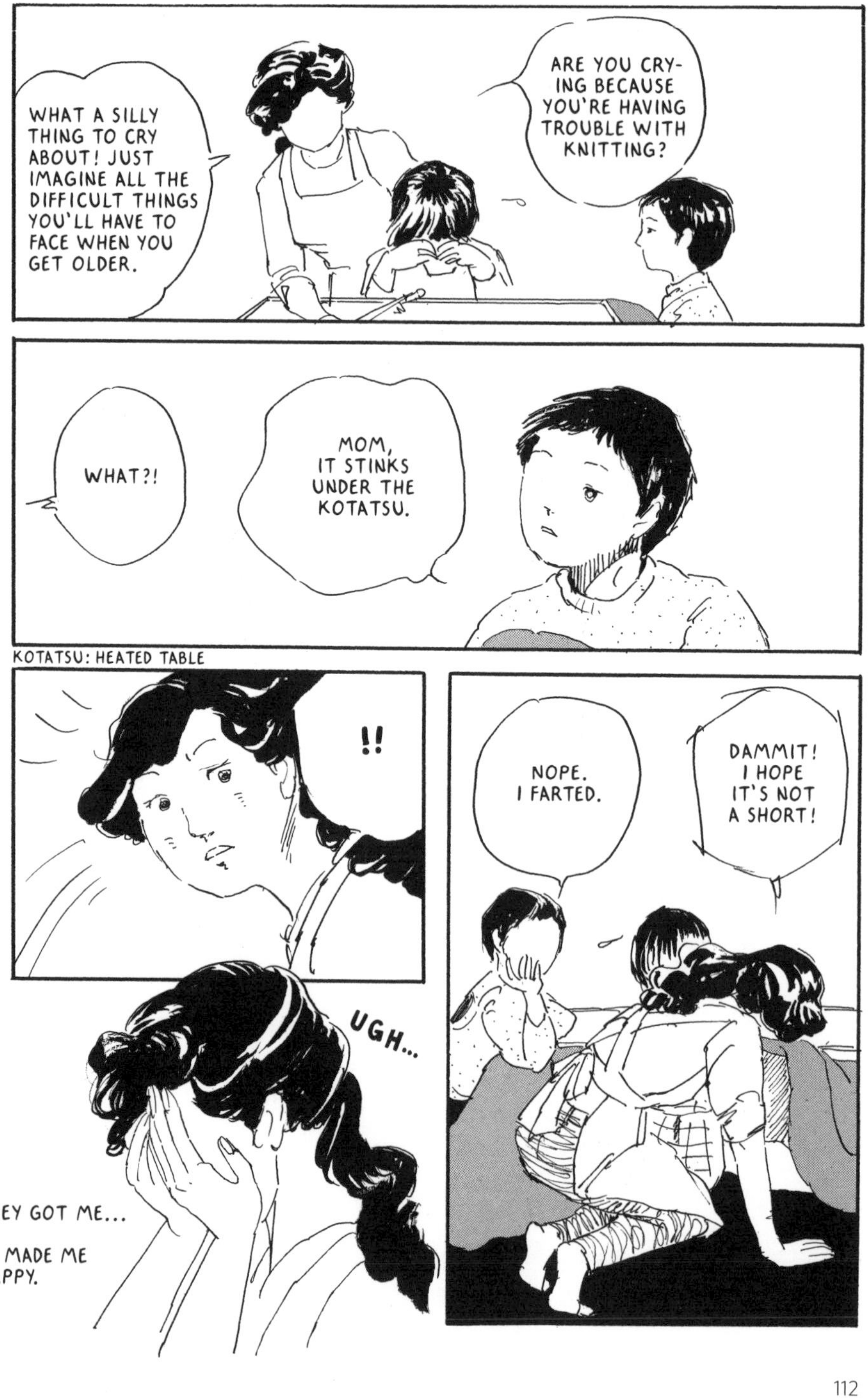
ARE YOU CRYING BECAUSE YOU'RE HAVING TROUBLE WITH KNITTING?
WHAT A SILLY THING TO CRY ABOUT! JUST IMAGINE ALL THE DIFFICULT THINGS YOU'LL HAVE TO FACE WHEN YOU GET OLDER.
MOM, IT STINKS UNDER THE KOTATSU.
WHAT?!
KOTATSU: HEATED TABLE
DAMMIT! I HOPE IT'S NOT A SHORT!
NOPE. I FARTED.
!!
UGH...
THEY GOT ME...
IT MADE ME HAPPY.

Peace and Stability

I'M NOT
SLEEPY.

NOT EVEN A
LITTLE BIT.

BUT IF I GET
INTO BED, I'M
SURE I'LL FALL
ASLEEP PRETTY
QUICK.

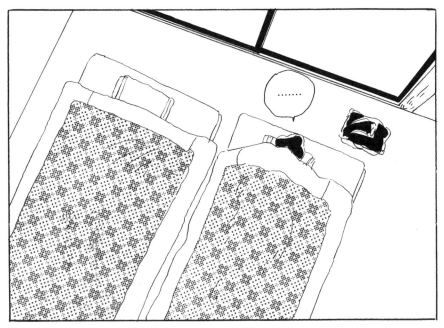

I'LL JUST TOSS ABOUT UNTIL I DO.

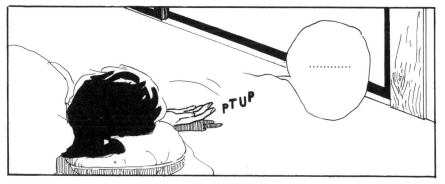

PTUP

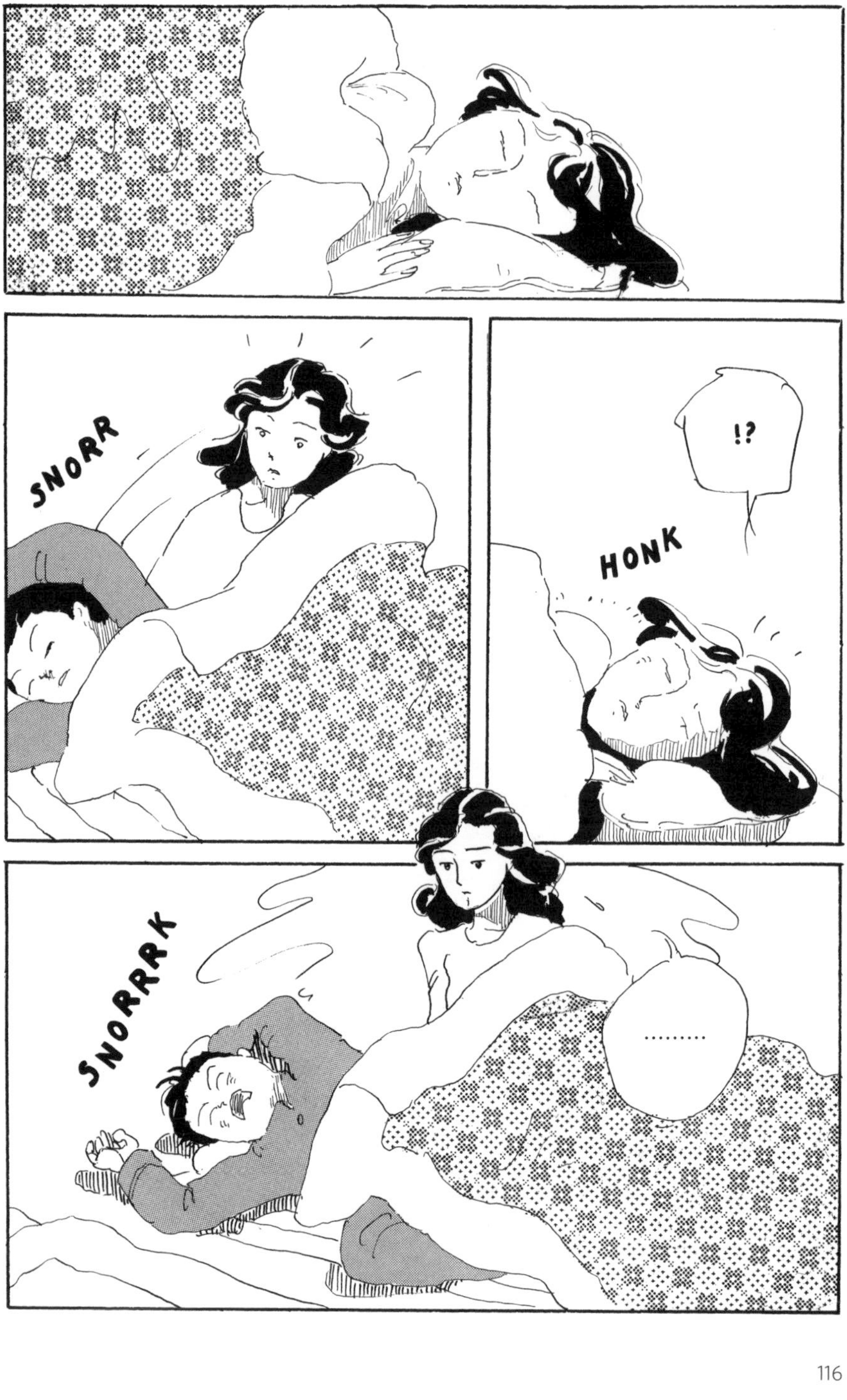
!?
HONK
SNORR
....
SNORRRK

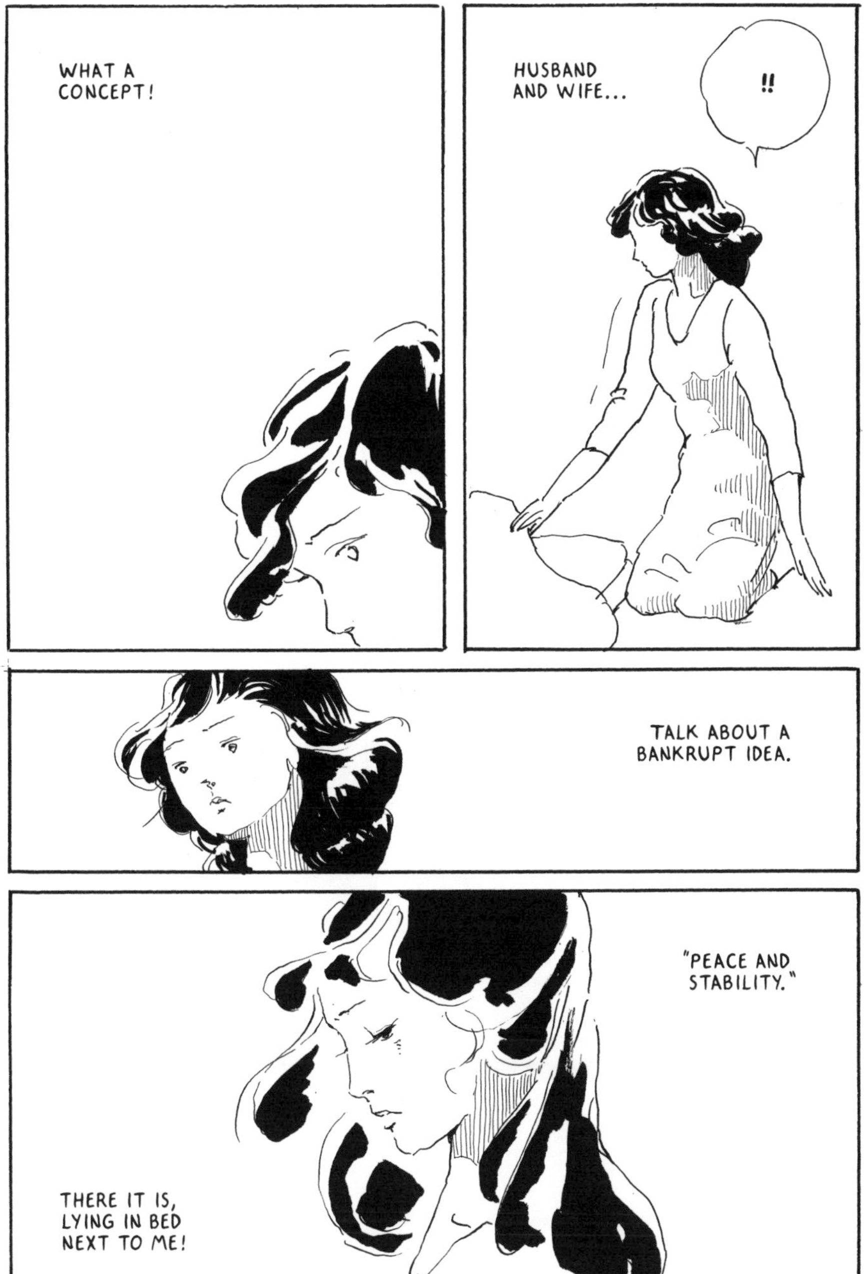
HUSBAND AND WIFE...
!!
WHAT A CONCEPT!
TALK ABOUT A BANKRUPT IDEA.
"PEACE AND STABILITY."
THERE IT IS, LYING IN BED NEXT TO ME!

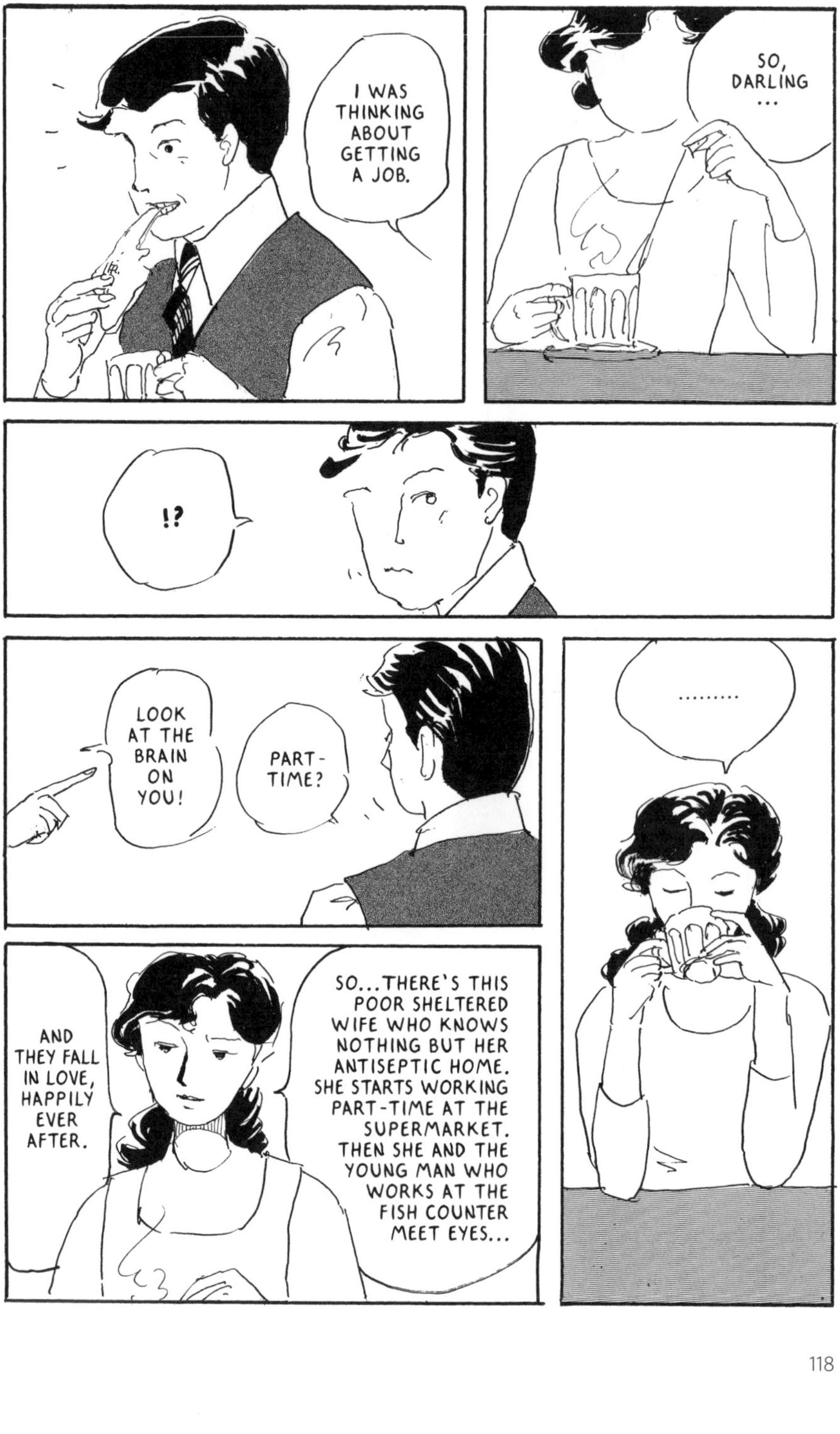
SO, DARLING ...
I WAS THINKING ABOUT GETTING A JOB.
!?
....
PART-TIME?
LOOK AT THE BRAIN ON YOU!
SO...THERE'S THIS POOR SHELTERED WIFE WHO KNOWS NOTHING BUT HER ANTISEPTIC HOME. SHE STARTS WORKING PART-TIME AT THE SUPERMARKET. THEN SHE AND THE YOUNG MAN WHO WORKS AT THE FISH COUNTER MEET EYES...
AND THEY FALL IN LOVE, HAPPILY EVER AFTER.

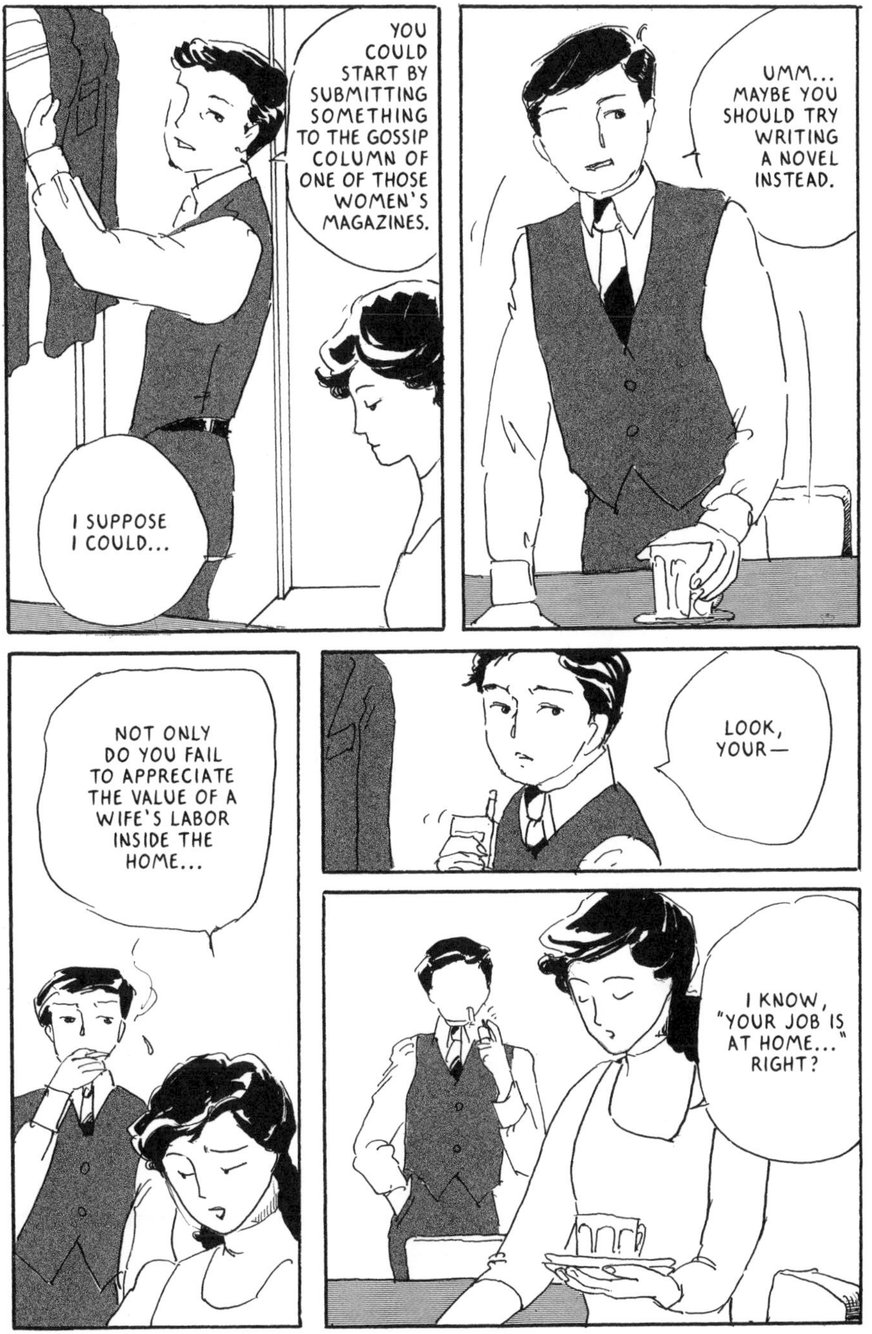
UMM... MAYBE YOU SHOULD TRY WRITING A NOVEL INSTEAD.
YOU COULD START BY SUBMITTING SOMETHING TO THE GOSSIP COLUMN OF ONE OF THOSE WOMEN'S MAGAZINES.
I SUPPOSE I COULD...
LOOK, YOUR—
I KNOW, "YOUR JOB IS AT HOME..." RIGHT?
NOT ONLY DO YOU FAIL TO APPRECIATE THE VALUE OF A WIFE'S LABOR INSIDE THE HOME...

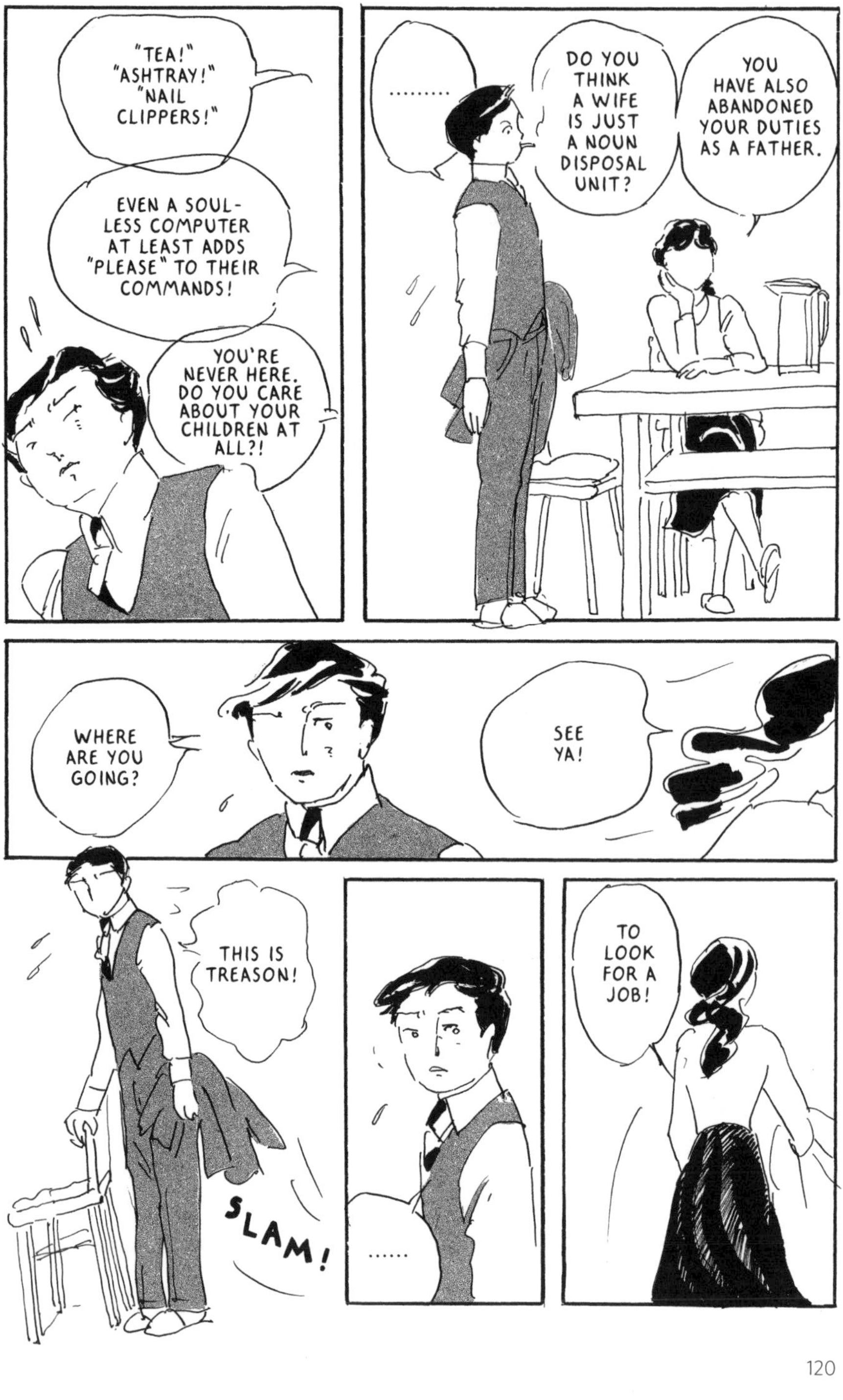
YOU HAVE ALSO ABANDONED YOUR DUTIES AS A FATHER.
DO YOU THINK A WIFE IS JUST A NOUN DISPOSAL UNIT?
....
"TEA!" "ASHTRAY!" "NAIL CLIPPERS!"
EVEN A SOUL-LESS COMPUTER AT LEAST ADDS "PLEASE" TO THEIR COMMANDS!
YOU'RE NEVER HERE. DO YOU CARE ABOUT YOUR CHILDREN AT ALL?!
SEE YA!
WHERE ARE YOU GOING?
TO LOOK FOR A JOB!
......
THIS IS TREASON!
SLAM!

Who Am I?

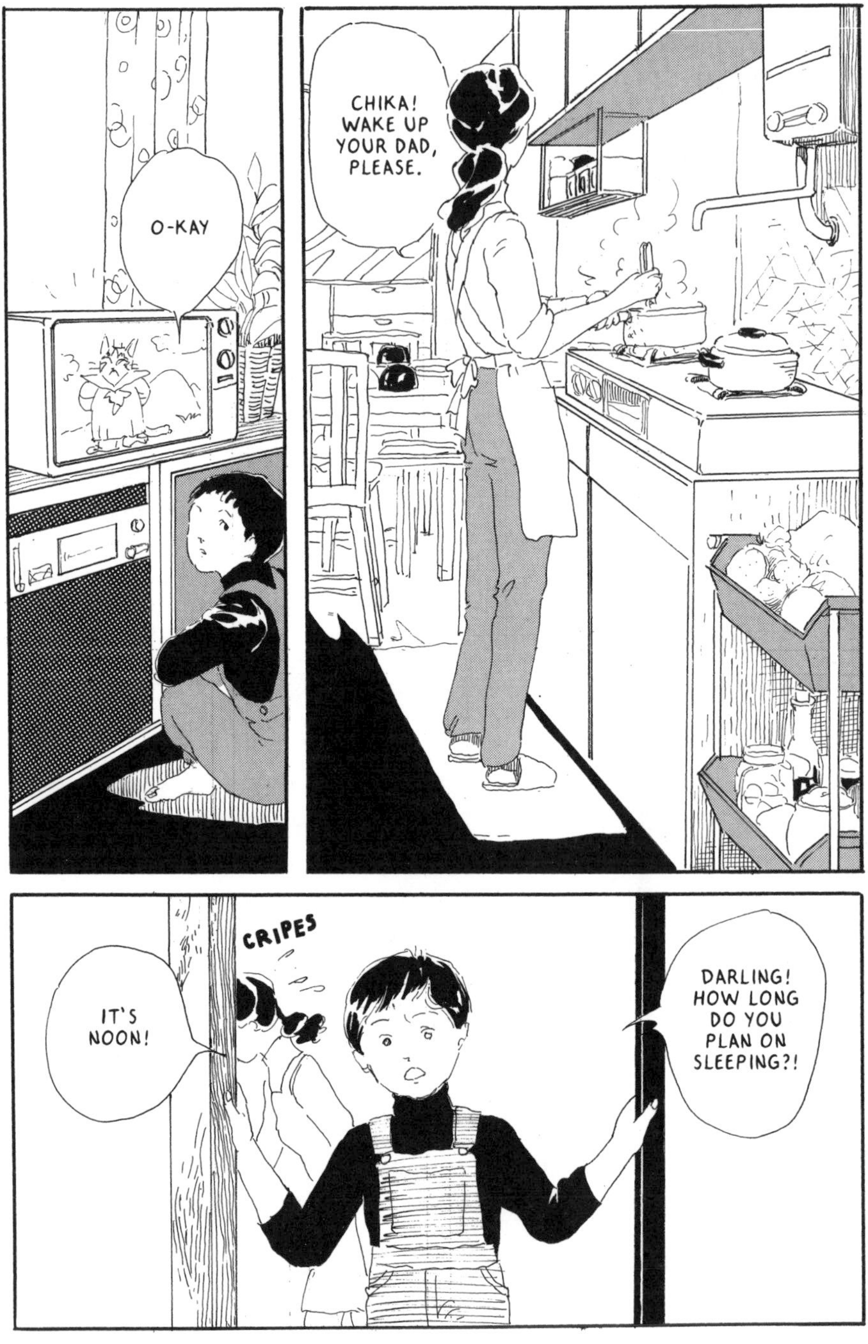
CHIKA! WAKE UP YOUR DAD, PLEASE.
O-KAY
DARLING! HOW LONG DO YOU PLAN ON SLEEPING?!
CRIPES
IT'S NOON!

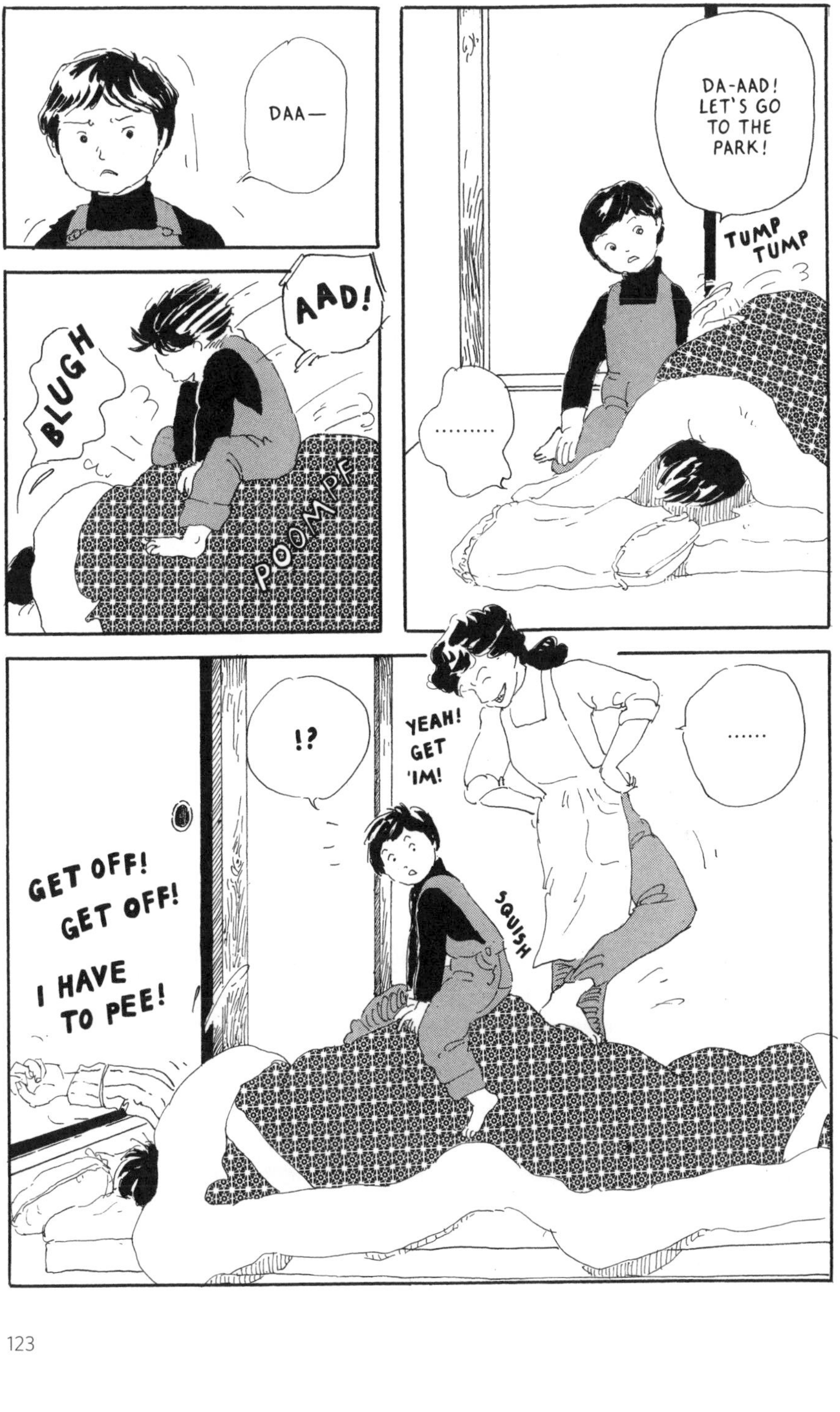
DA-AAD! LET'S GO TO THE PARK!
TUMP TUMP
....
DAA—
AAD!
BLUGH
POOMPF
......
YEAH! GET 'IM!
!?
SQUISH
GET OFF! GET OFF!
I HAVE TO PEE!

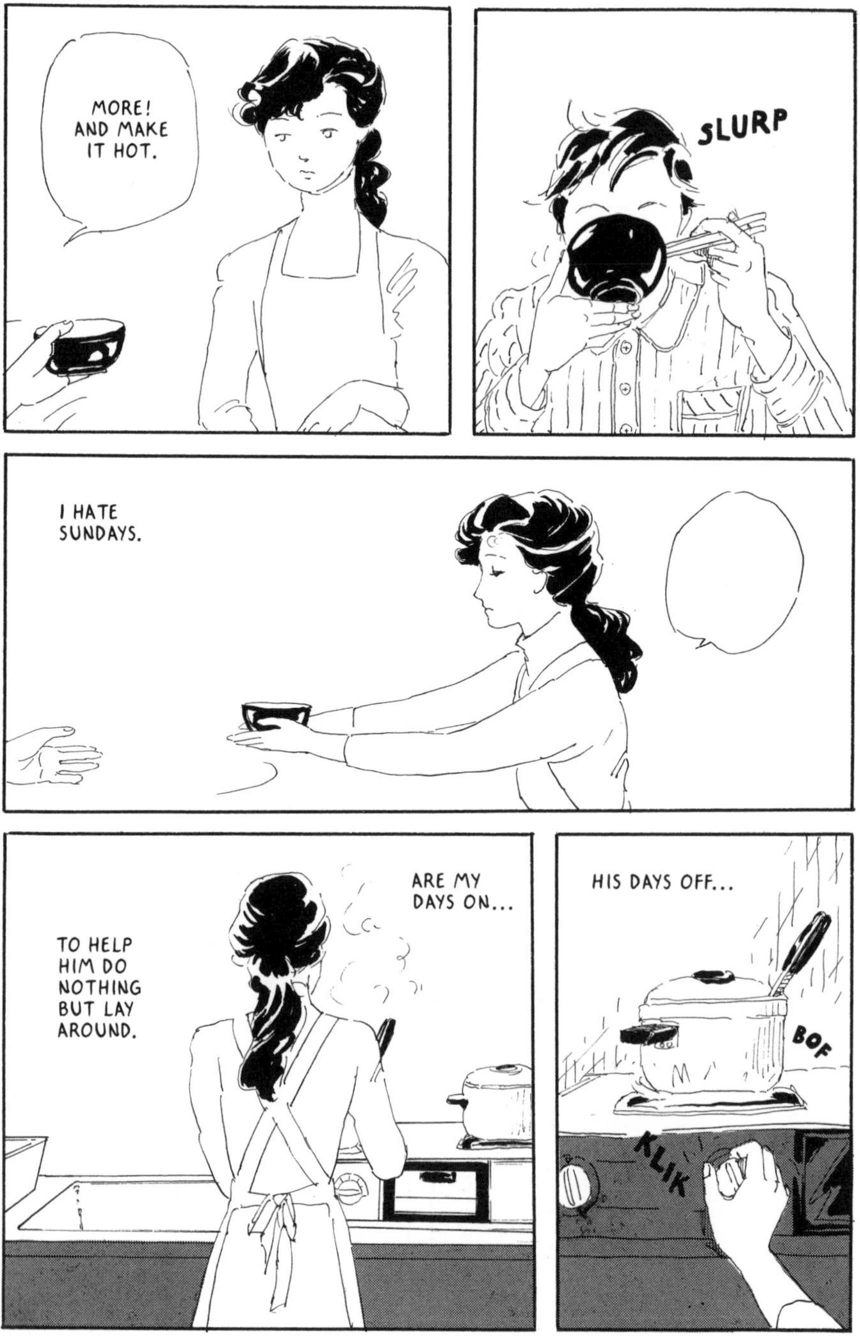
SLURP
MORE! AND MAKE IT HOT.
I HATE SUNDAYS.
HIS DAYS OFF...
BOF
KLIK
ARE MY DAYS ON...
TO HELP HIM DO NOTHING BUT LAY AROUND.

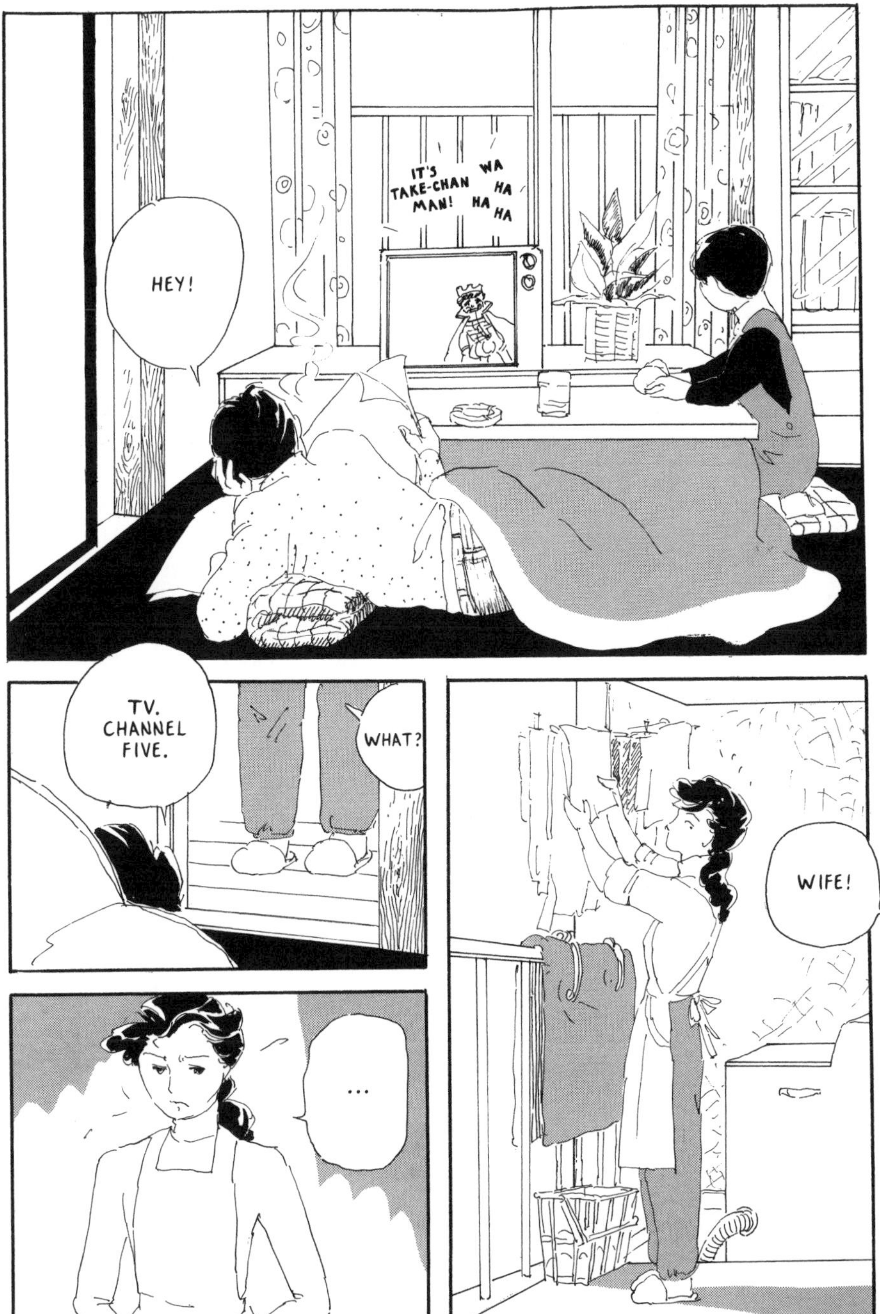
IT'S TAKE-CHAN MAN!
WA HA HA HA HA
HEY!
WIFE!
WHAT?
TV. CHANNEL FIVE.
...

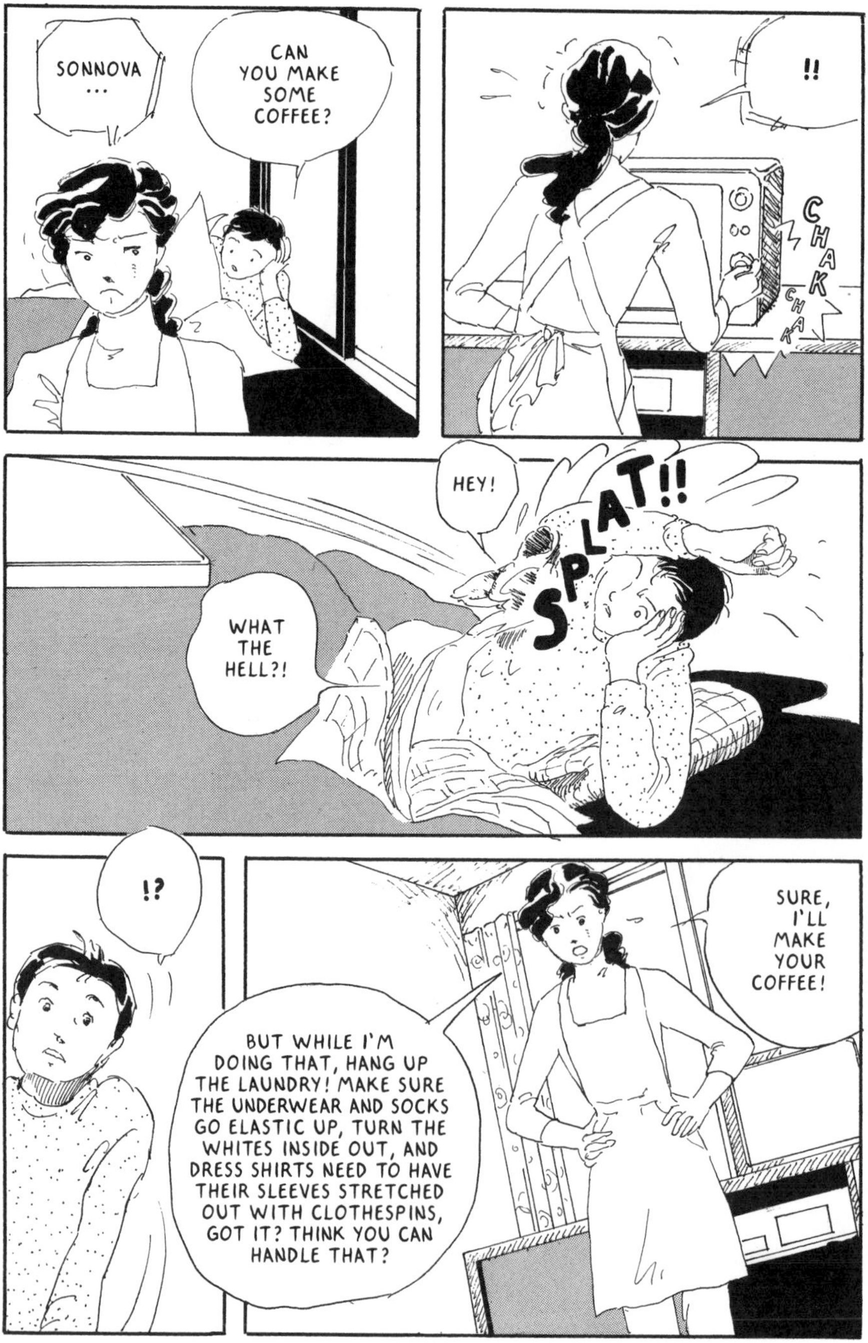
!!
CHAK
CHAKA
CAN YOU MAKE SOME COFFEE?
SONNOVA ...
HEY!
SPLAT!!
WHAT THE HELL?!
SURE, I'LL MAKE YOUR COFFEE!
BUT WHILE I'M DOING THAT, HANG UP THE LAUNDRY! MAKE SURE THE UNDERWEAR AND SOCKS GO ELASTIC UP, TURN THE WHITES INSIDE OUT, AND DRESS SHIRTS NEED TO HAVE THEIR SLEEVES STRETCHED OUT WITH CLOTHESPINS, GOT IT? THINK YOU CAN HANDLE THAT?
!?

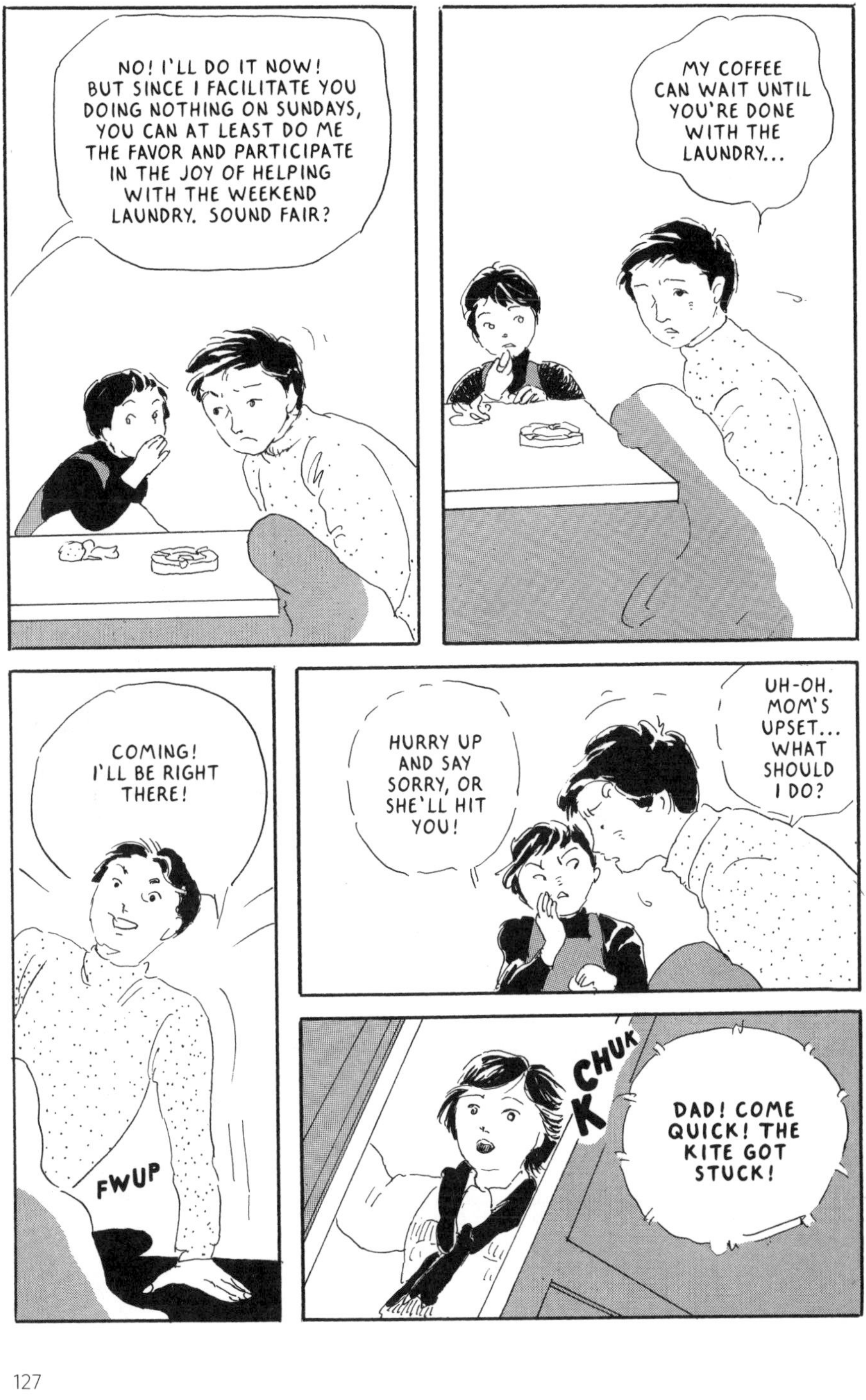

MY COFFEE CAN WAIT UNTIL YOU'RE DONE WITH THE LAUNDRY...
NO! I'LL DO IT NOW! BUT SINCE I FACILITATE YOU DOING NOTHING ON SUNDAYS, YOU CAN AT LEAST DO ME THE FAVOR AND PARTICIPATE IN THE JOY OF HELPING WITH THE WEEKEND LAUNDRY. SOUND FAIR?
UH-OH. MOM'S UPSET... WHAT SHOULD I DO?
HURRY UP AND SAY SORRY, OR SHE'LL HIT YOU!
DAD! COME QUICK! THE KITE GOT STUCK!
KCHUK
COMING! I'LL BE RIGHT THERE!
FWUP

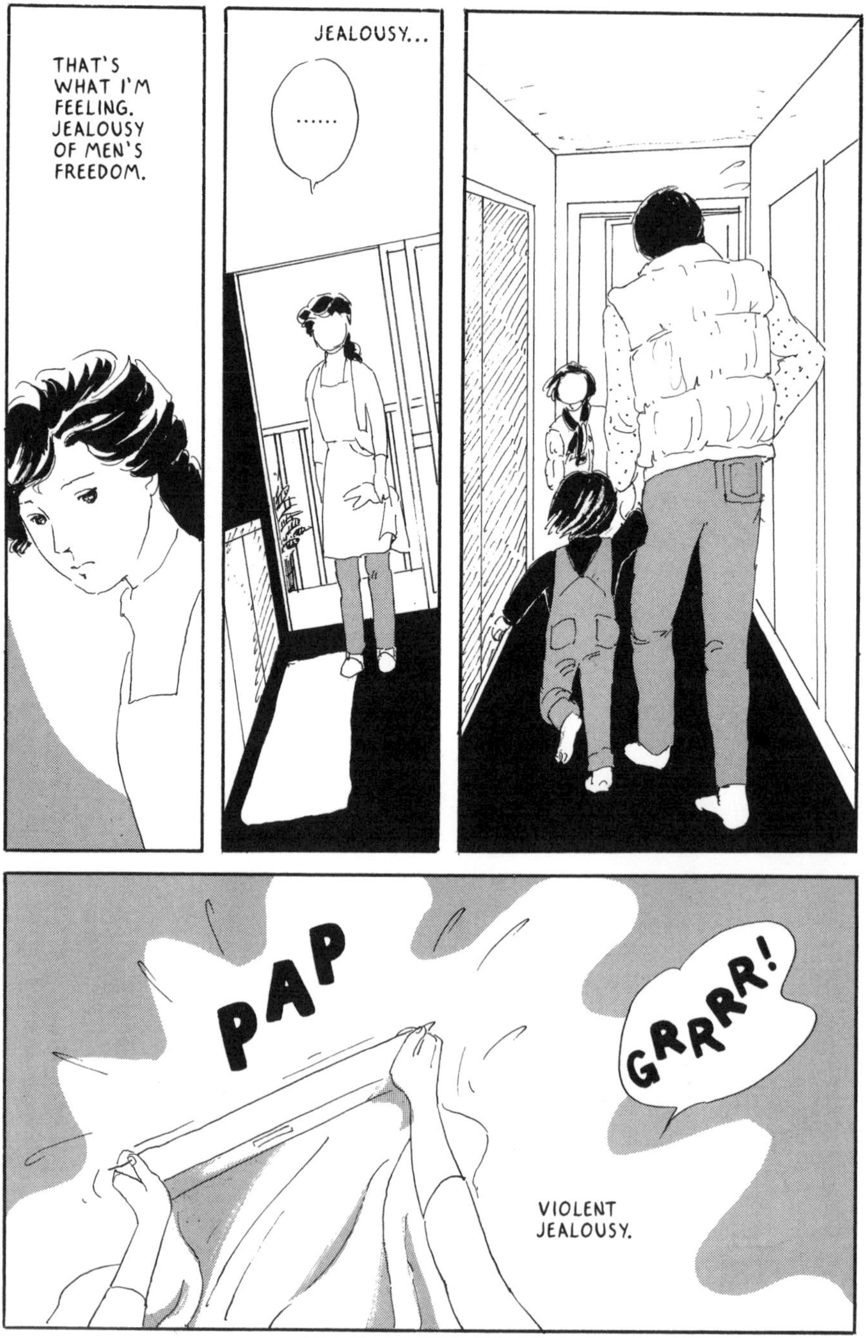
JEALOUSY...
......
THAT'S WHAT I'M FEELING. JEALOUSY OF MEN'S FREEDOM.
GRRRR!
PAP
VIOLENT JEALOUSY.

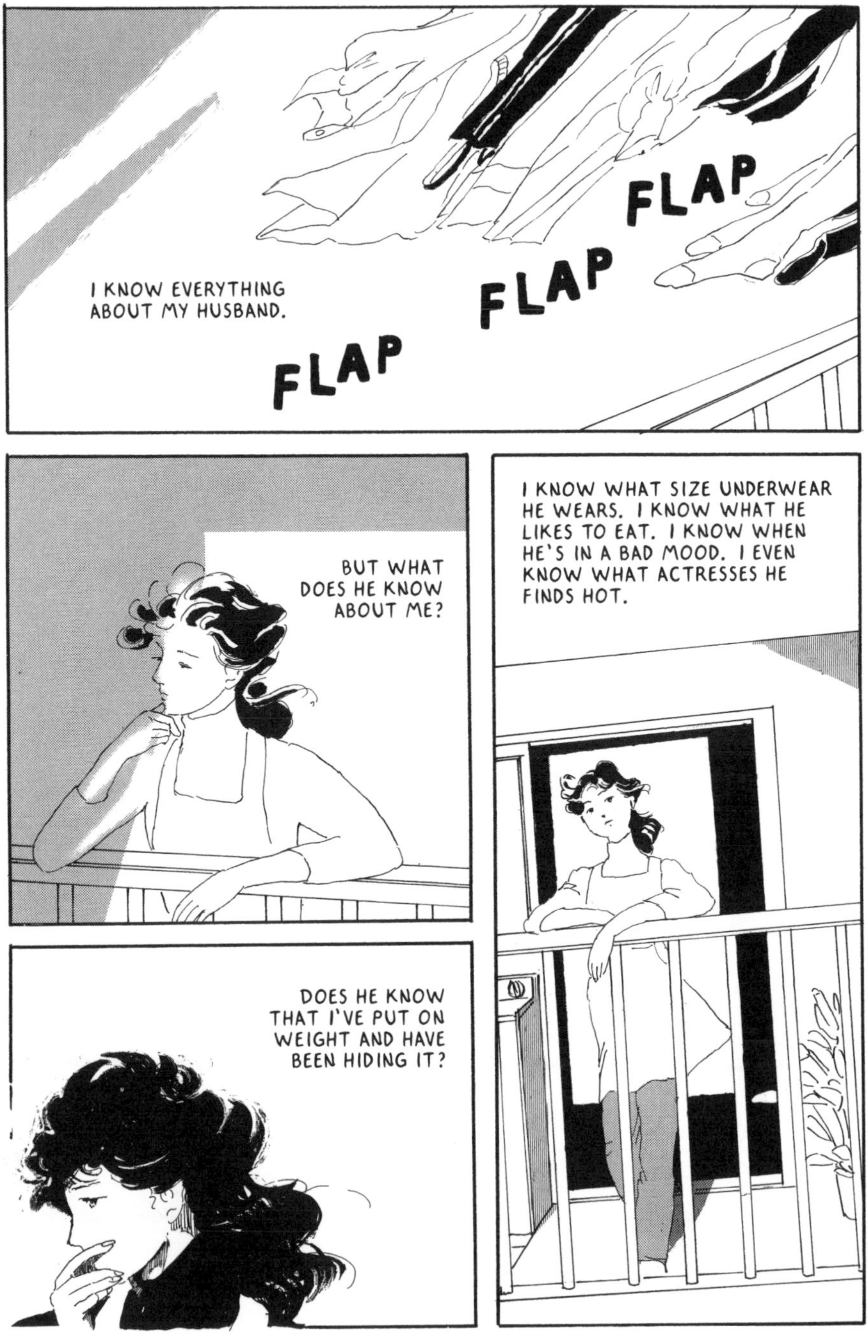
I KNOW EVERYTHING ABOUT MY HUSBAND.
FLAP
FLAP
FLAP
I KNOW WHAT SIZE UNDERWEAR HE WEARS. I KNOW WHAT HE LIKES TO EAT. I KNOW WHEN HE'S IN A BAD MOOD. I EVEN KNOW WHAT ACTRESSES HE FINDS HOT.
BUT WHAT DOES HE KNOW ABOUT ME?
DOES HE KNOW THAT I'VE PUT ON WEIGHT AND HAVE BEEN HIDING IT?

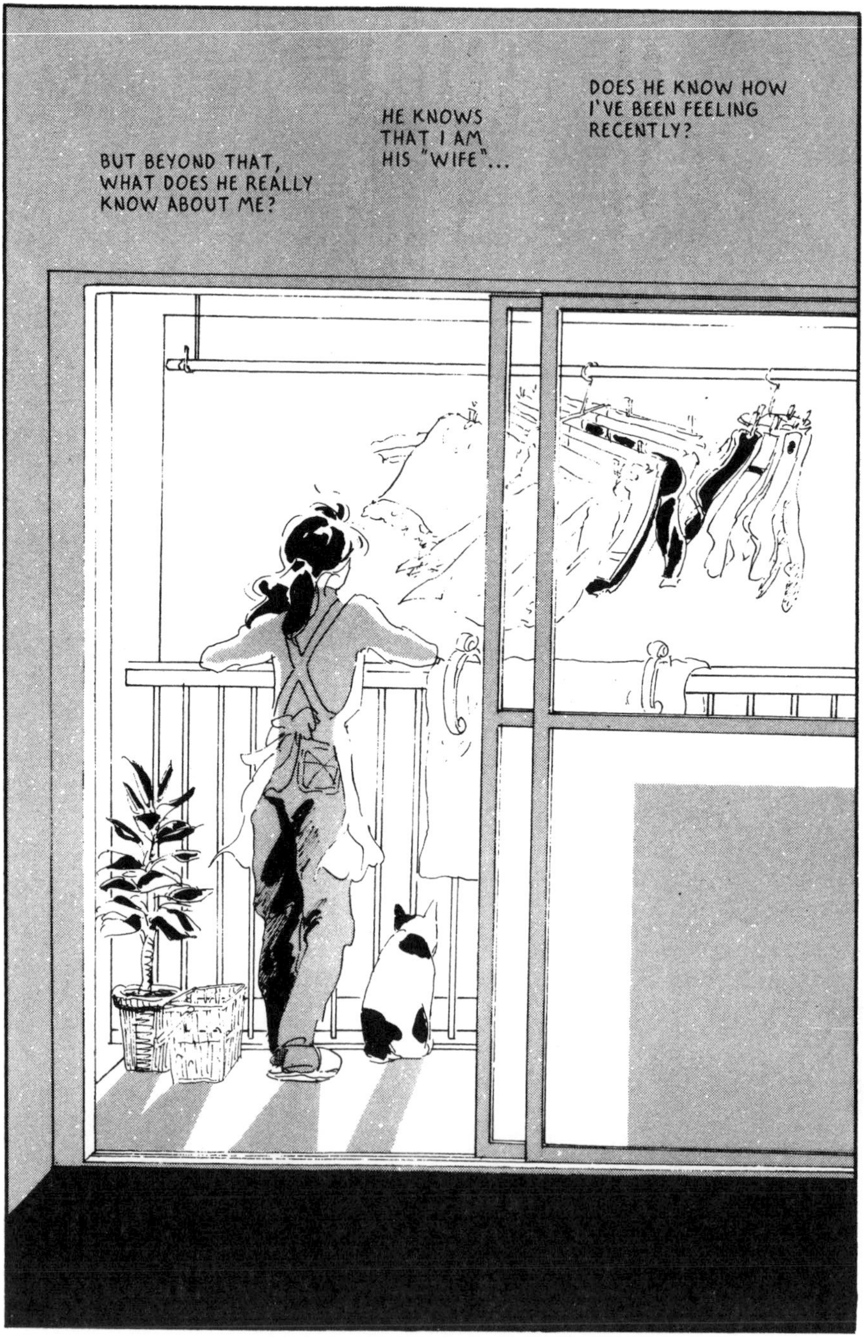
DOES HE KNOW HOW I'VE BEEN FEELING RECENTLY?
HE KNOWS THAT I AM HIS "WIFE"...
BUT BEYOND THAT, WHAT DOES HE REALLY KNOW ABOUT ME?

Spring Again

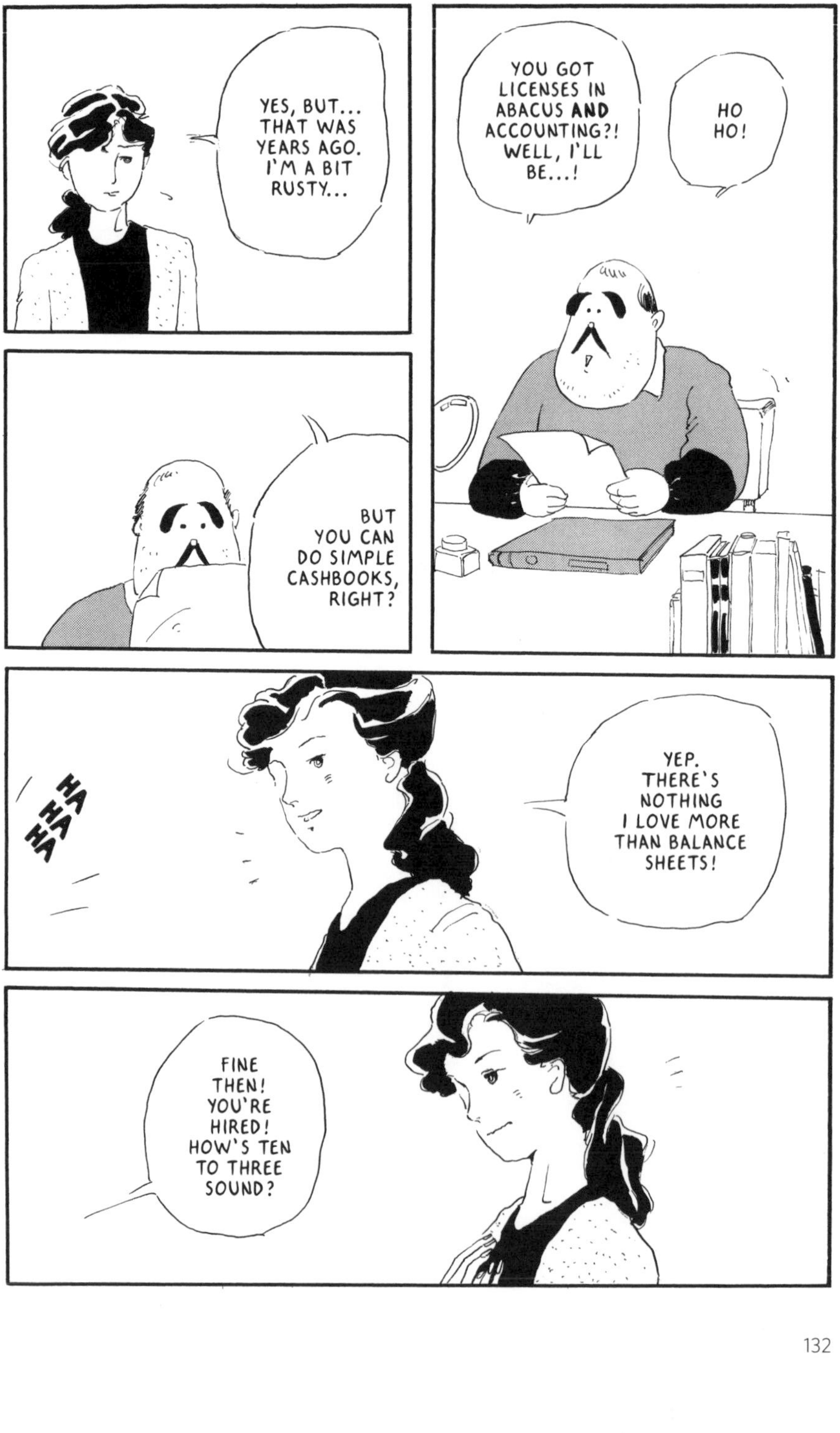
HO HO!
YOU GOT LICENSES IN ABACUS **AND** ACCOUNTING?! WELL, I'LL BE...!
YES, BUT... THAT WAS YEARS AGO. I'M A BIT RUSTY...
BUT YOU CAN DO SIMPLE CASHBOOKS, RIGHT?
YEP. THERE'S NOTHING I LOVE MORE THAN BALANCE SHEETS!
HA HA HA
FINE THEN! YOU'RE HIRED! HOW'S TEN TO THREE SOUND?

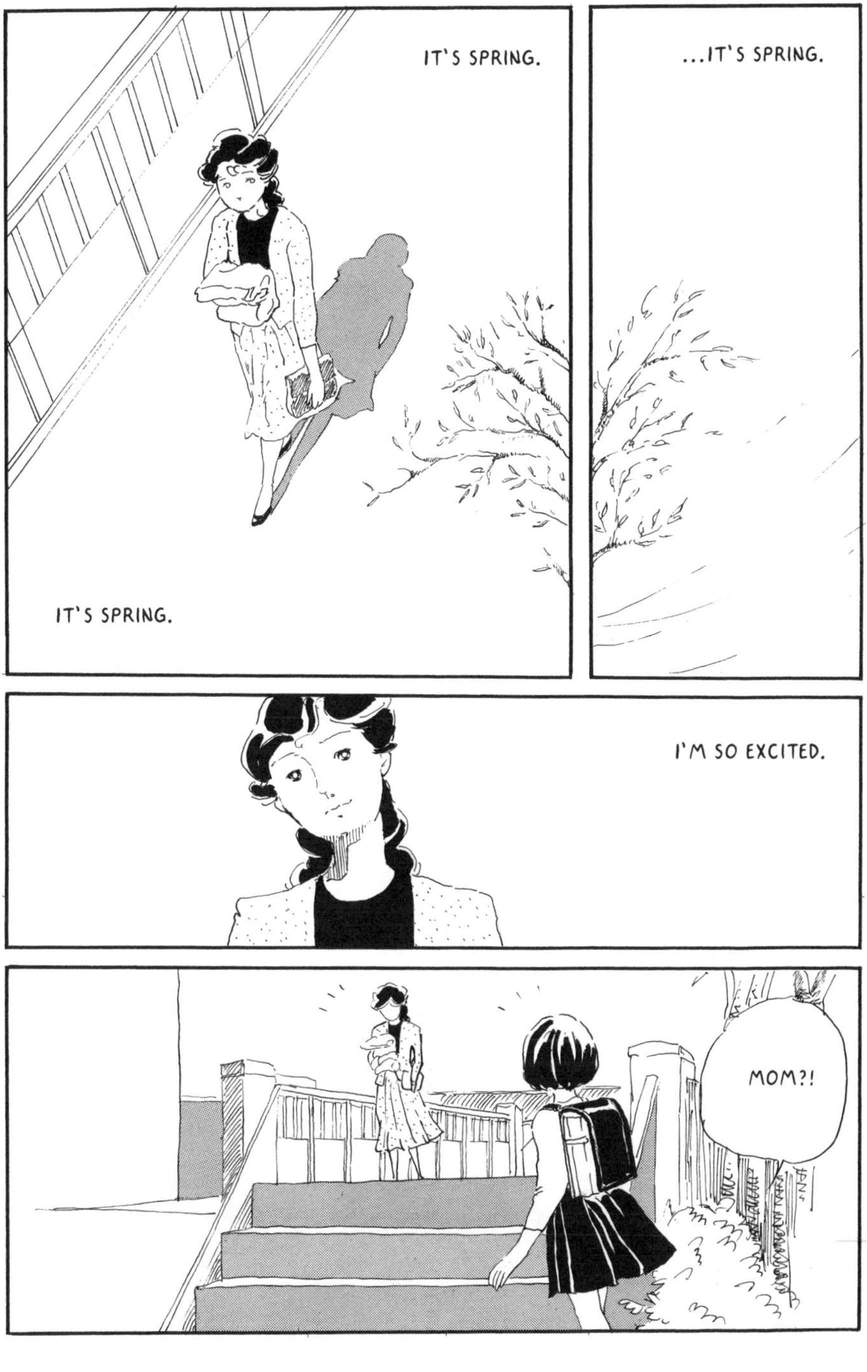
...IT'S SPRING.
IT'S SPRING.
IT'S SPRING.
I'M SO EXCITED.
MOM?!

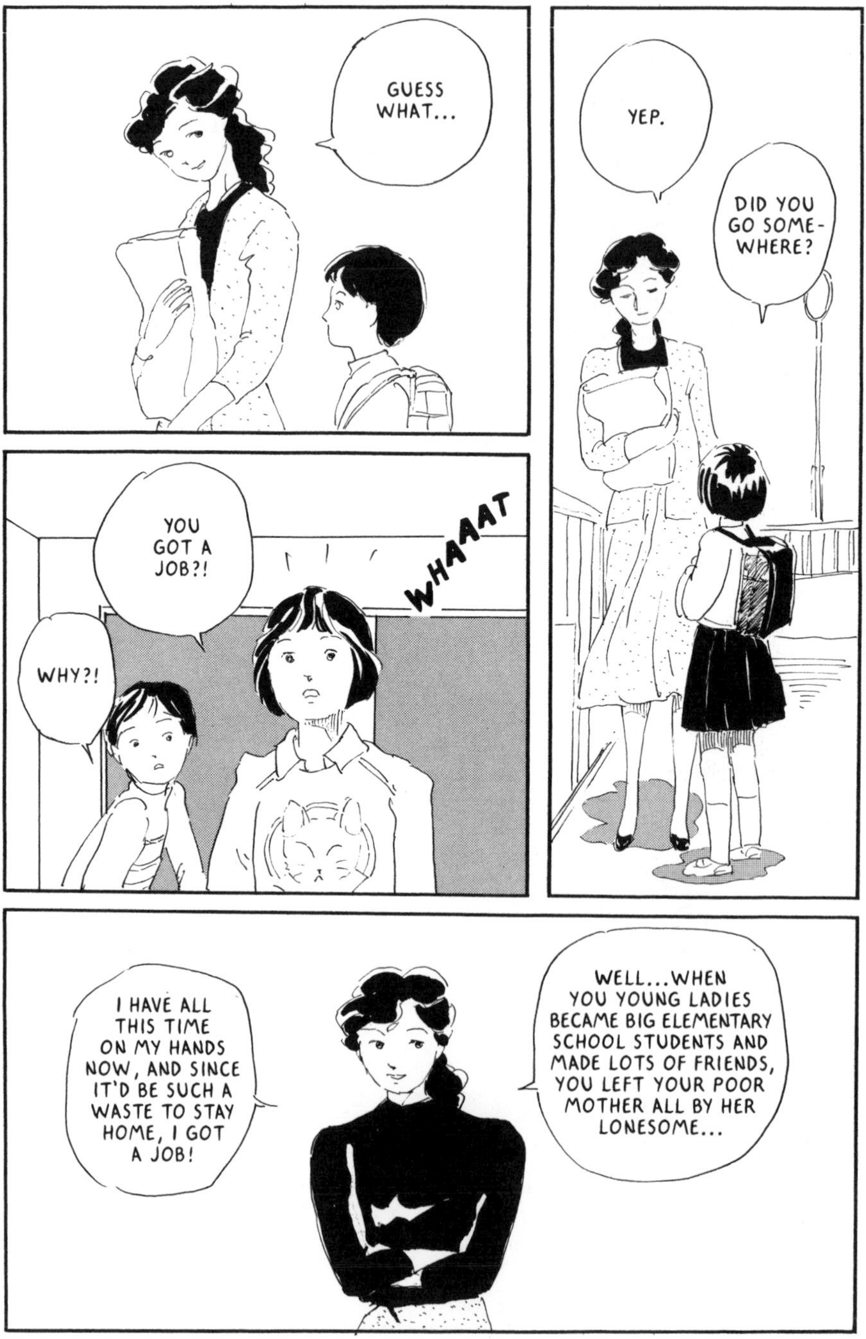
YEP.
DID YOU GO SOME-WHERE?
GUESS WHAT...
YOU GOT A JOB?!
WHY?!
WHAAAT
WELL...WHEN YOU YOUNG LADIES BECAME BIG ELEMENTARY SCHOOL STUDENTS AND MADE LOTS OF FRIENDS, YOU LEFT YOUR POOR MOTHER ALL BY HER LONESOME...
I HAVE ALL THIS TIME ON MY HANDS NOW, AND SINCE IT'D BE SUCH A WASTE TO STAY HOME, I GOT A JOB!

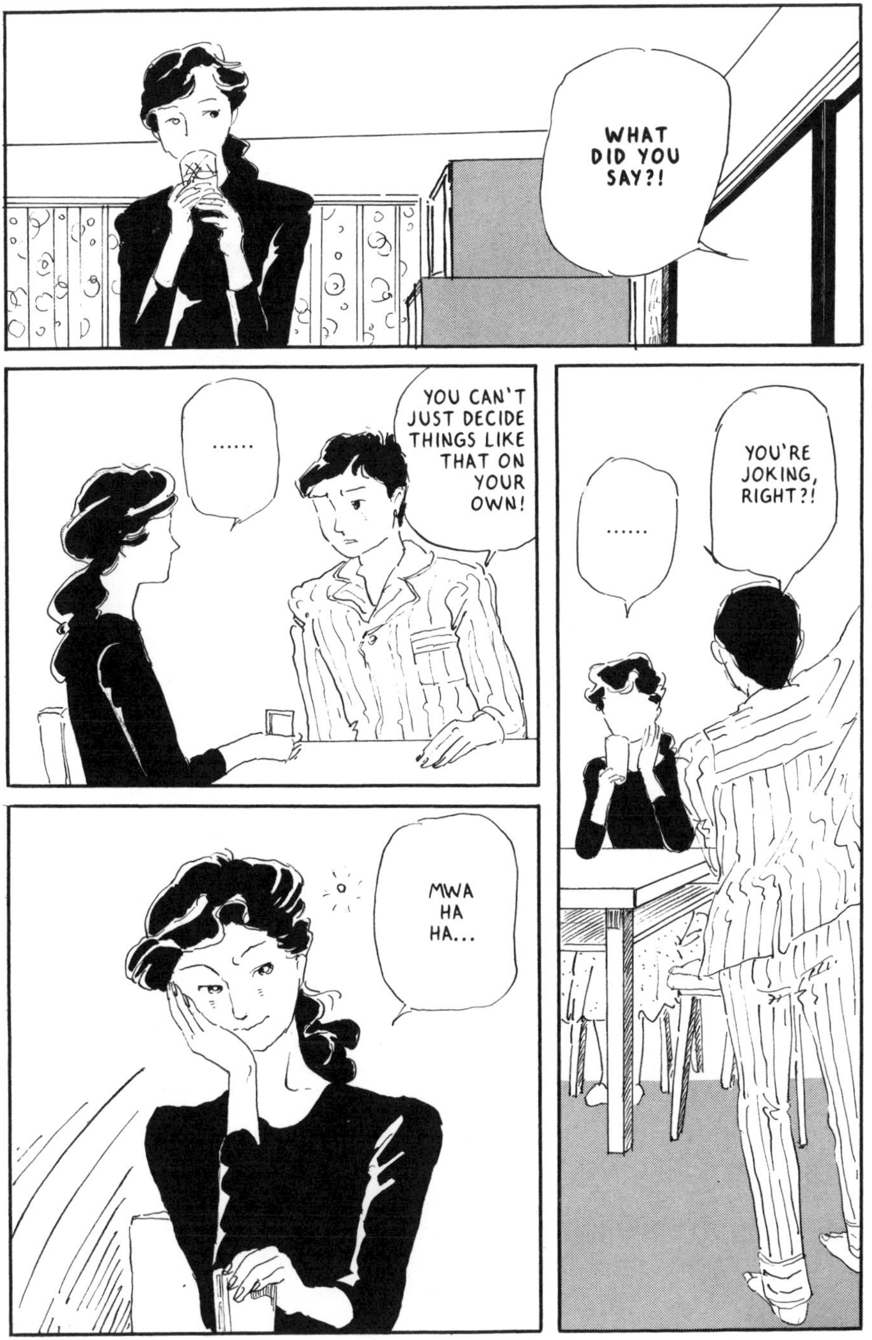
WHAT DID YOU SAY?!
YOU'RE JOKING, RIGHT?!
......
YOU CAN'T JUST DECIDE THINGS LIKE THAT ON YOUR OWN!
......
MWA HA HA...

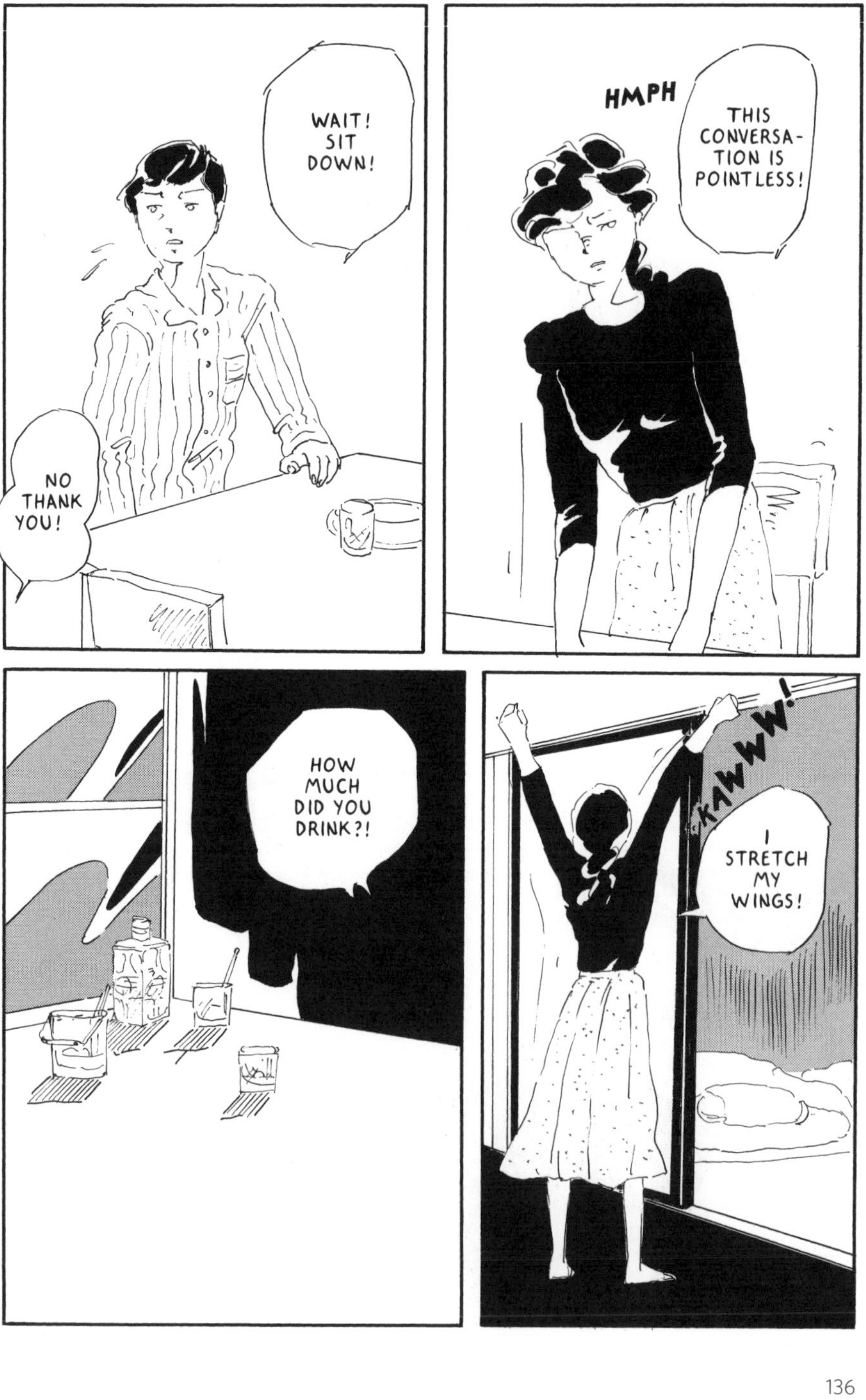
HMPH
THIS CONVERSA- TION IS POINTLESS!
WAIT! SIT DOWN!
NO THANK YOU!
KAWWW!
I STRETCH MY WINGS!
HOW MUCH DID YOU DRINK?!

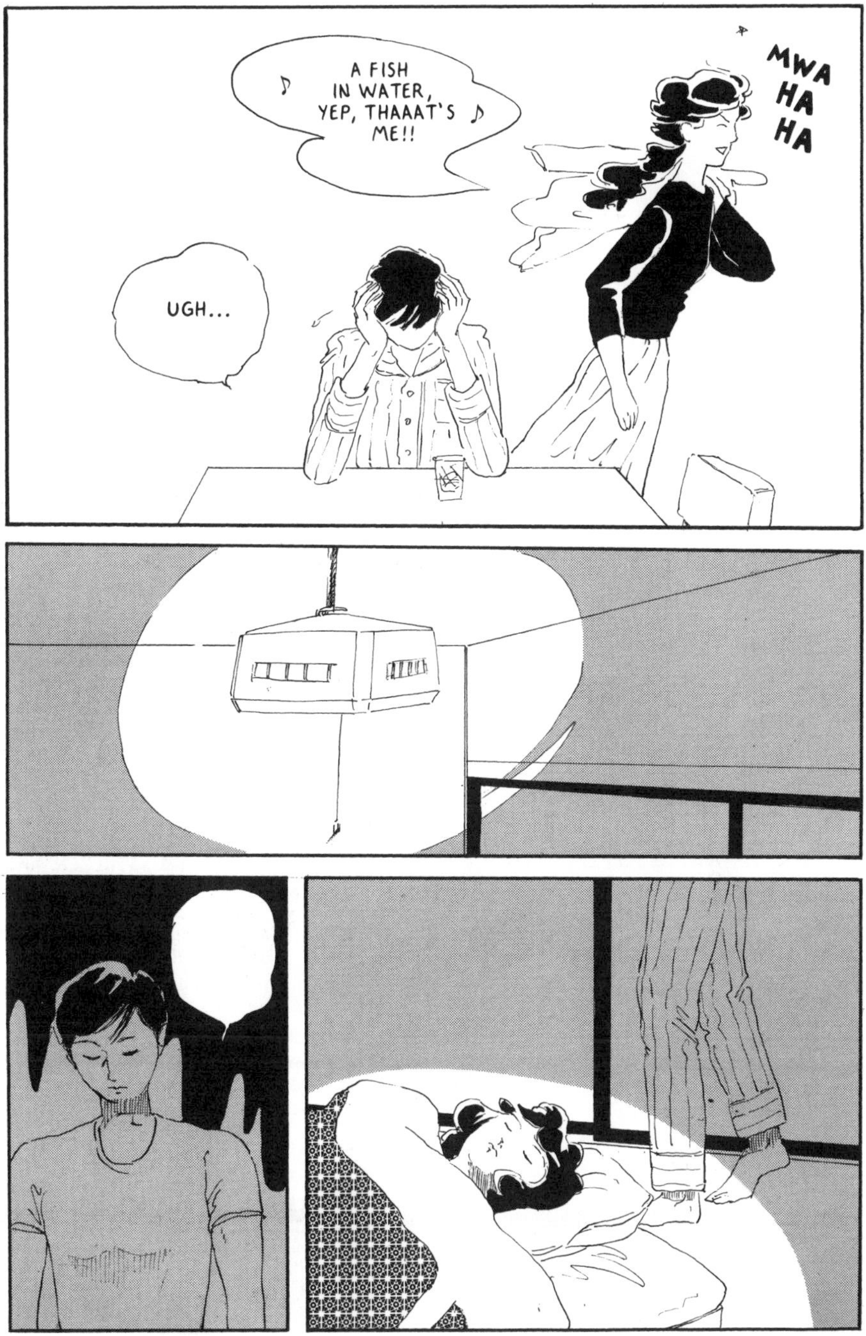
MWA HA HA
♪ A FISH IN WATER, YEP, THAAAT'S ME!! ♪
UGH...

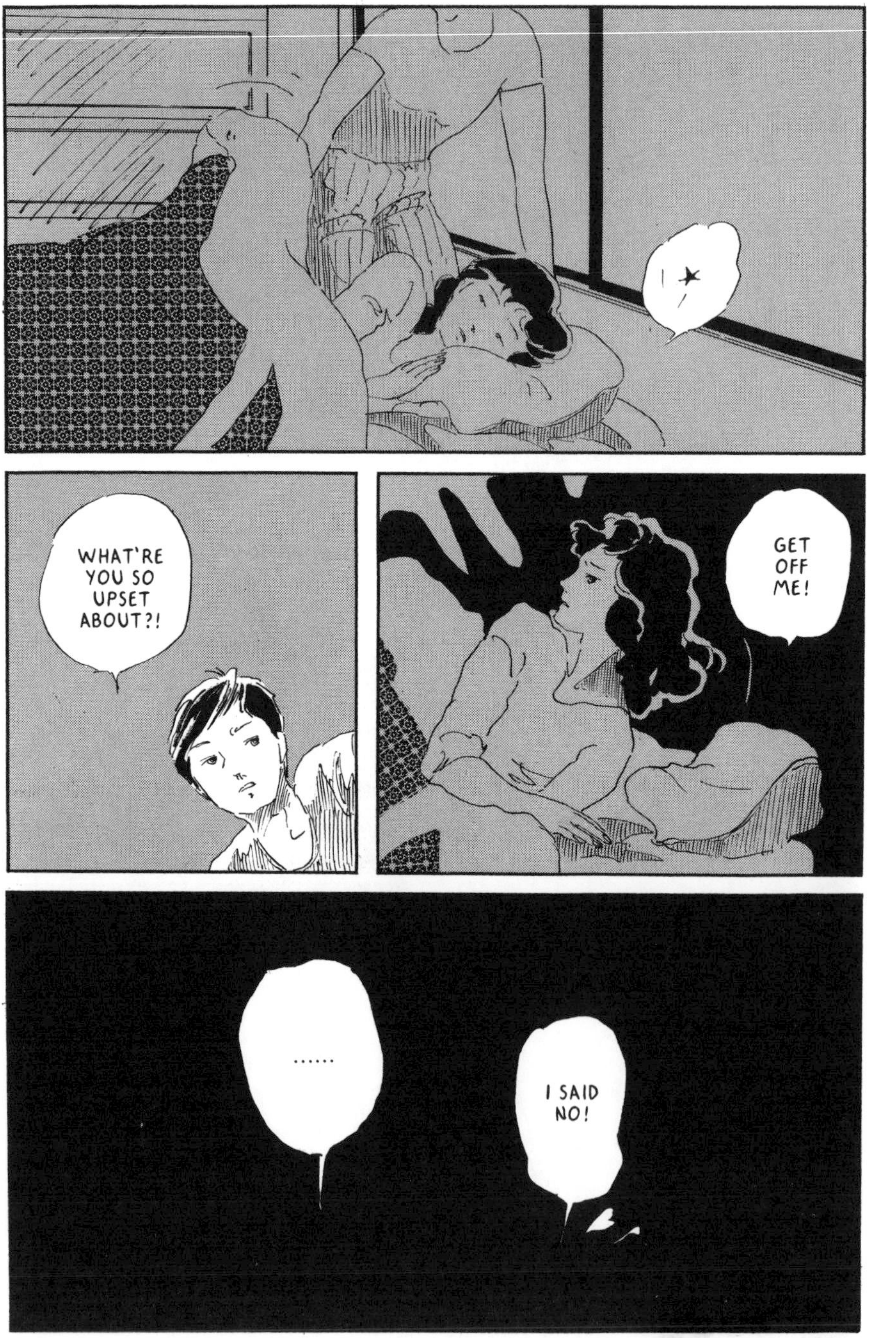
!
GET OFF ME!
WHAT'RE YOU SO UPSET ABOUT?!
I SAID NO!
......

Home Sun

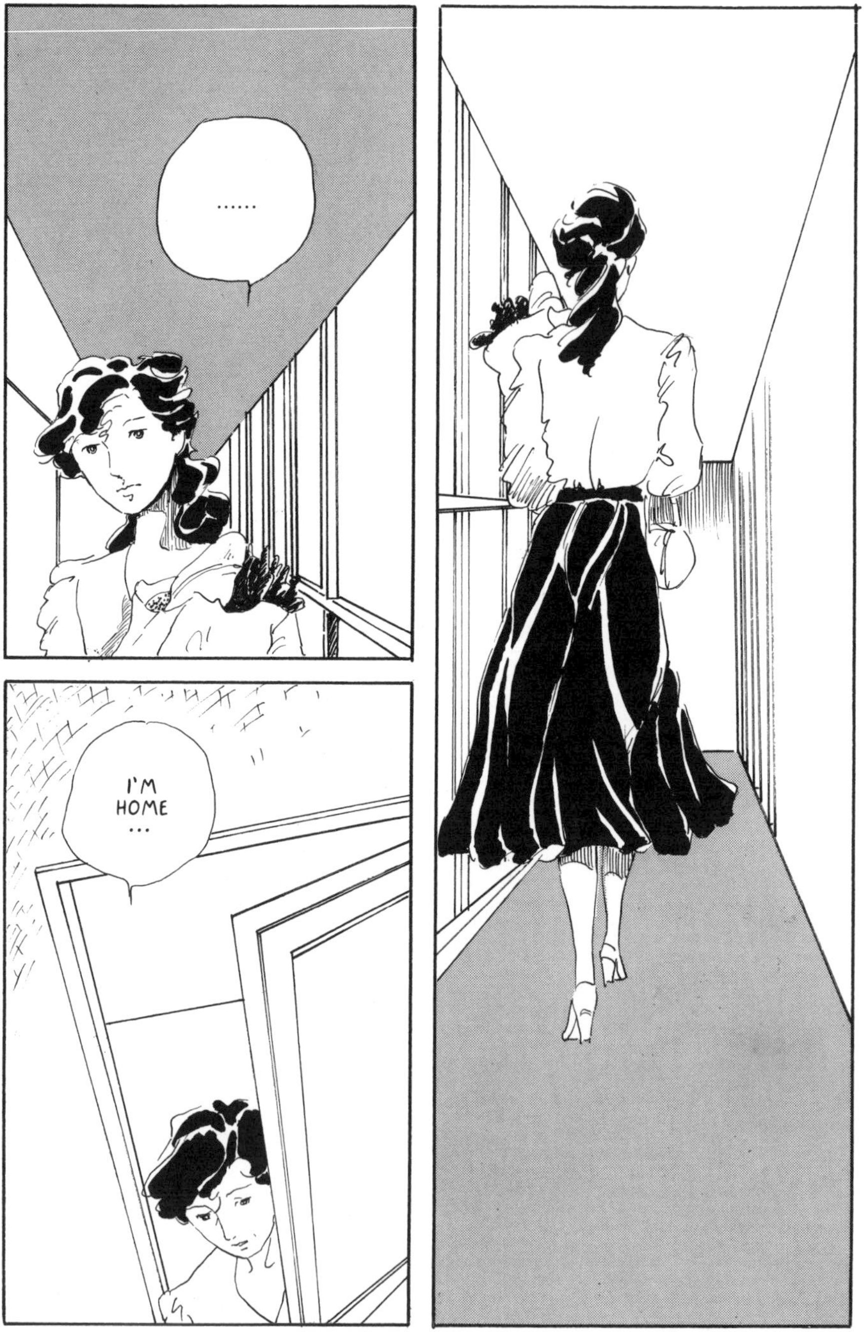
......
I'M HOME ...

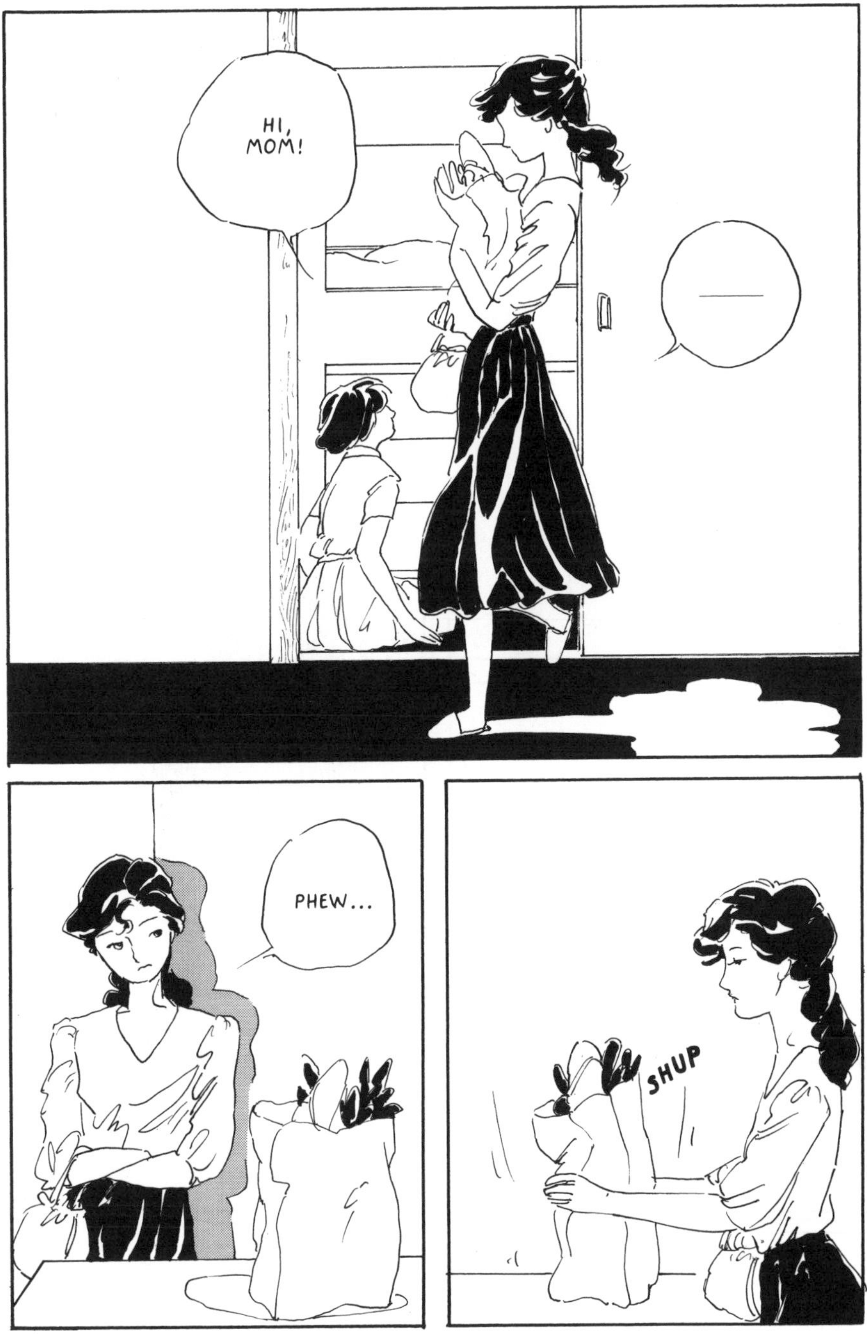
HI, MOM!
——
SHUP
PHEW...

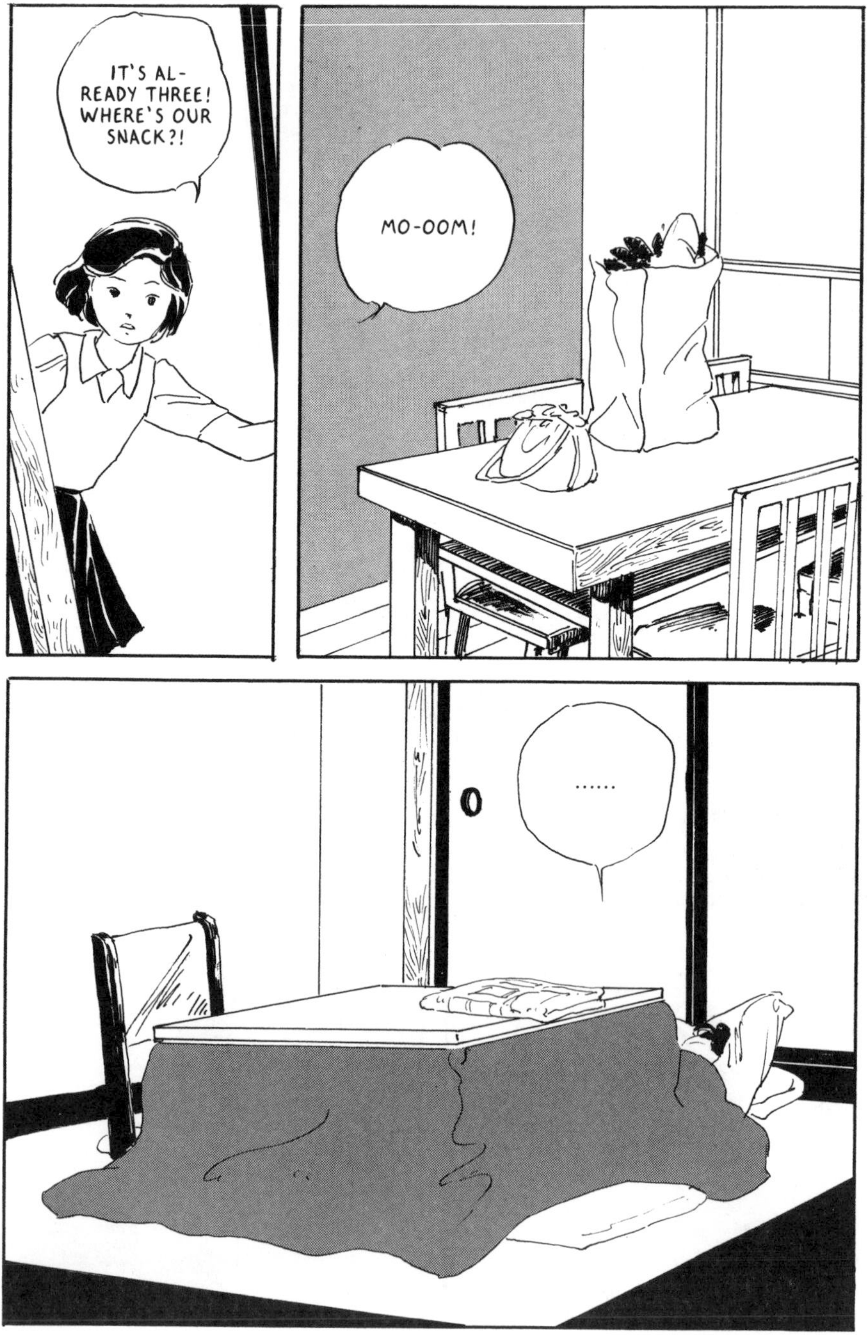
MO-OOM!
IT'S AL-READY THREE! WHERE'S OUR SNACK?!
......

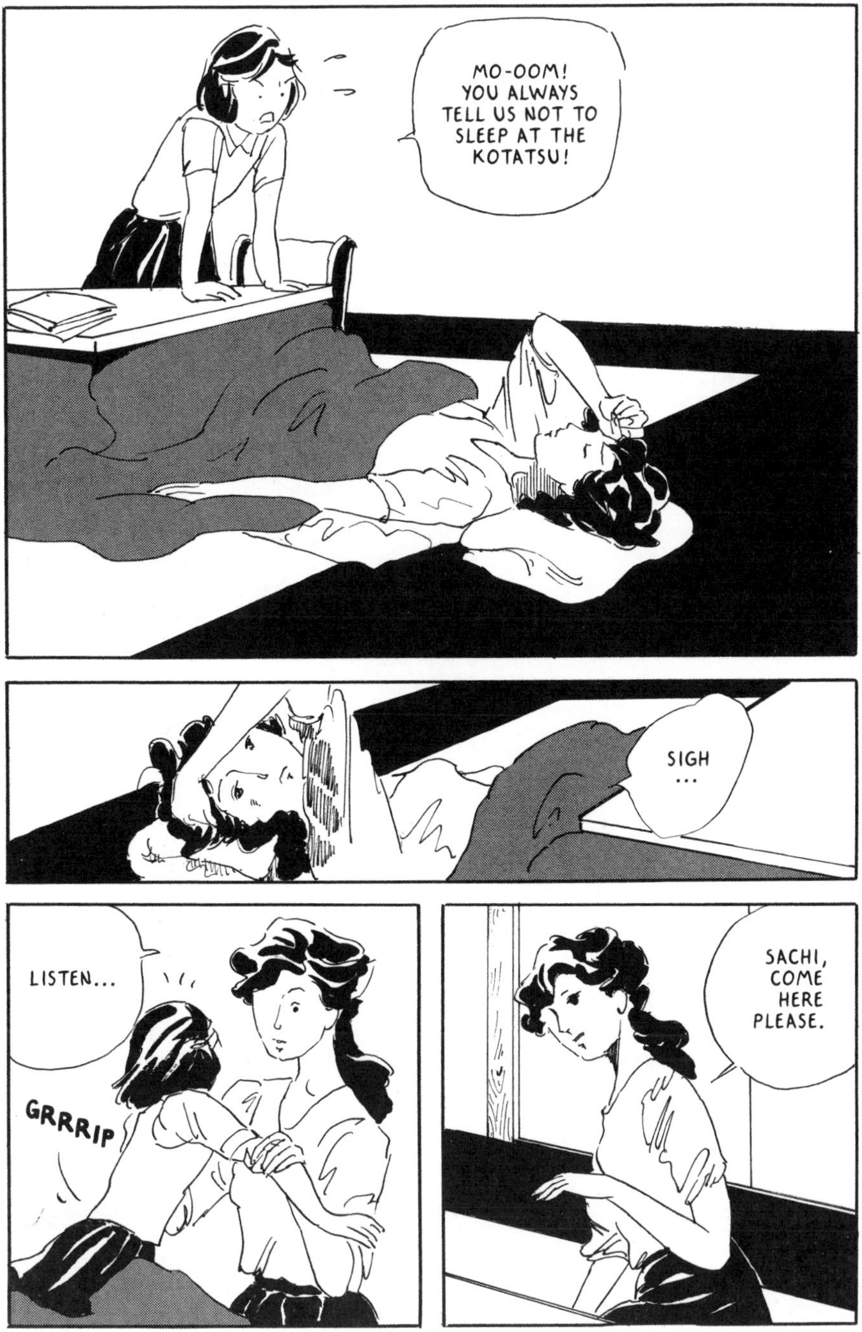
MO-OOM! YOU ALWAYS TELL US NOT TO SLEEP AT THE KOTATSU!
SIGH ...
SACHI, COME HERE PLEASE.
LISTEN...
GRRRIP

MOMMY'S GOT A JOB NOW...AND IT'S REALLY TIRING.
WORKING TAKES A LOT OF ENERGY...
HEE HEE HEE...
"HEE HEE" WHAT?
HEE HEE HEE
SMIRK SMIRK
WHERE'S OUR SNACK— HEY, WHAT'S GOING ON?!

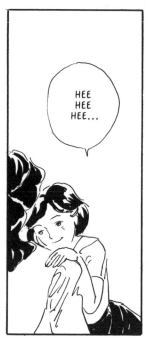

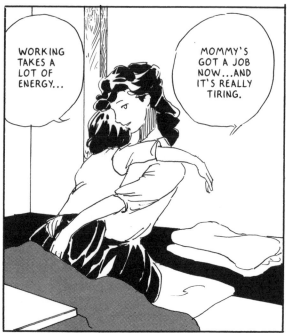

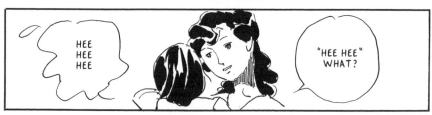

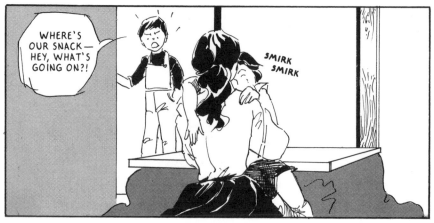

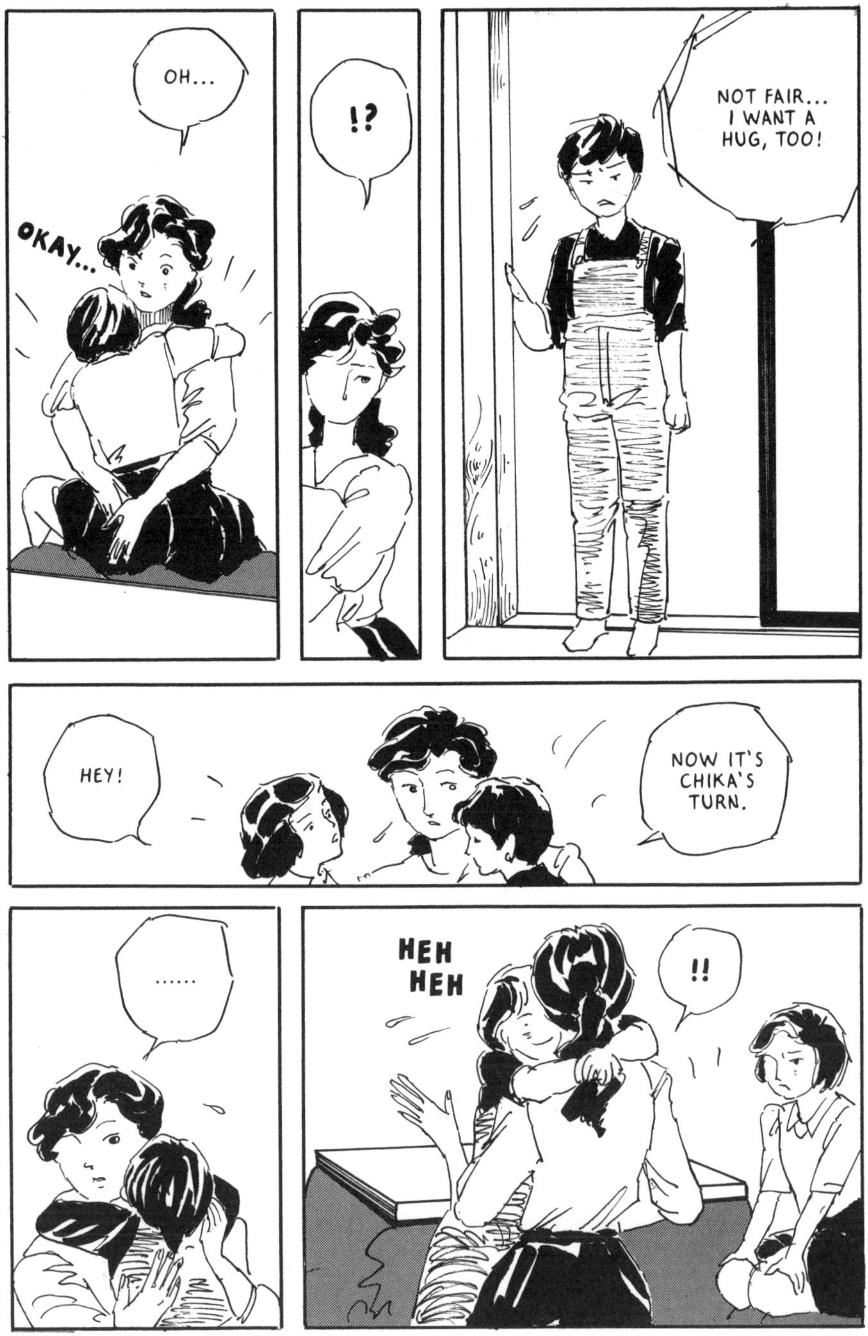
NOT FAIR... I WANT A HUG, TOO!
!?
OH...
OKAY...
NOW IT'S CHIKA'S TURN.
HEY!
!!
HEH HEH
......

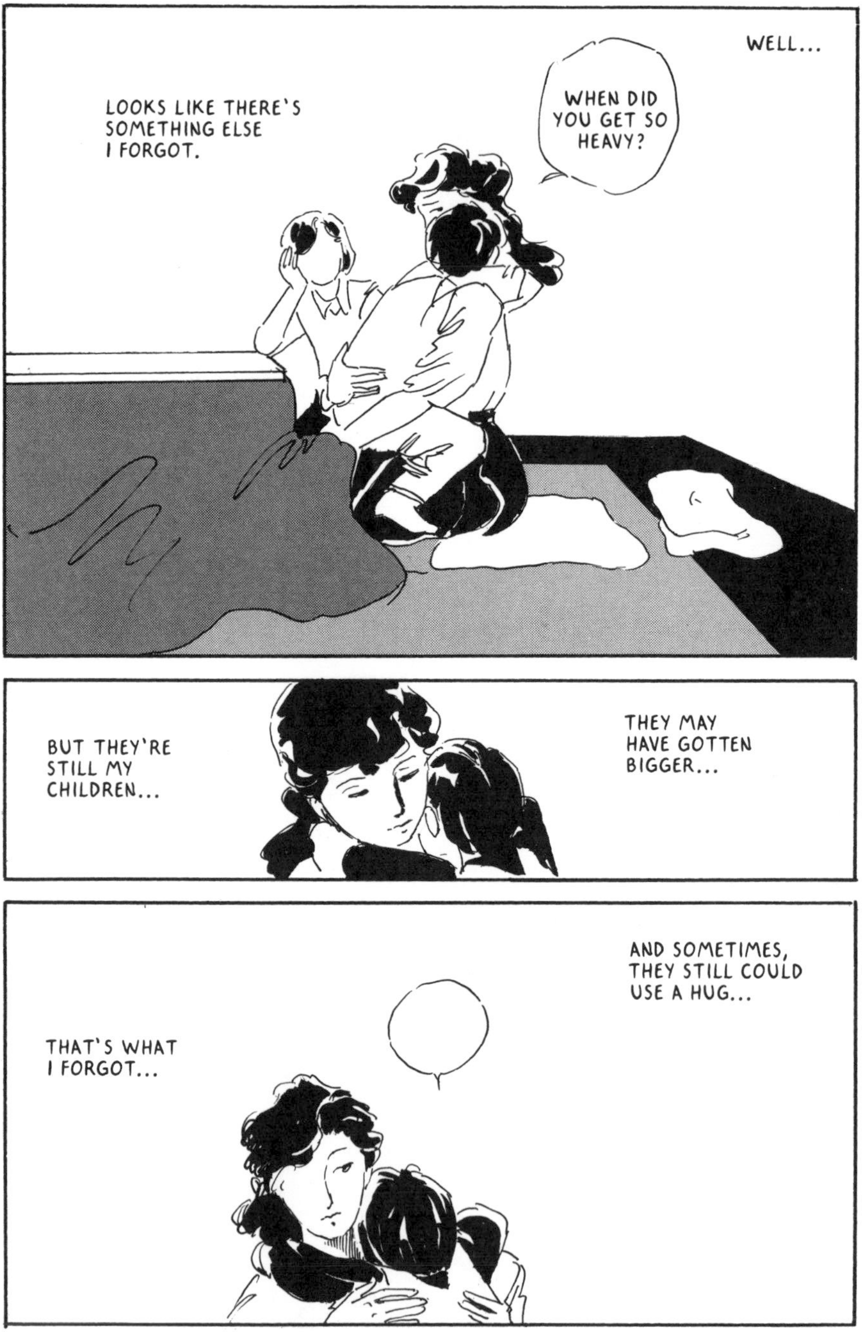
WELL...
WHEN DID YOU GET SO HEAVY?
LOOKS LIKE THERE'S SOMETHING ELSE I FORGOT.
THEY MAY HAVE GOTTEN BIGGER...
BUT THEY'RE STILL MY CHILDREN...
AND SOMETIMES, THEY STILL COULD USE A HUG...
THAT'S WHAT I FORGOT...

PSSSH
WELL...?
WHAT'S IT LIKE BEING A PART-TIME BREADWINNER?
......
I'LL PROBABLY BE WIPED OUT EVERY DAY UNTIL I GET USED TO IT...
BUT IT'S NICE TO DO SOME-THING NEW.
HUH...

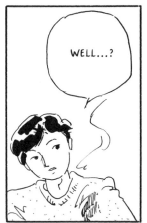

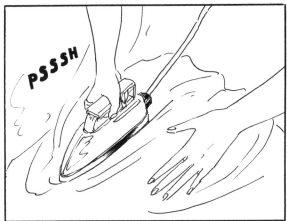

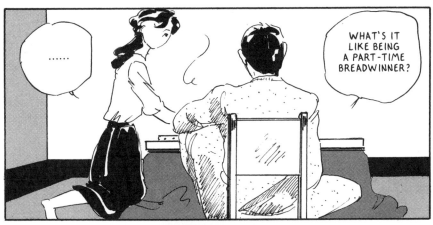

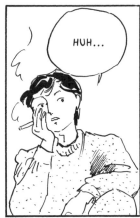

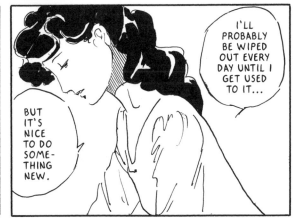

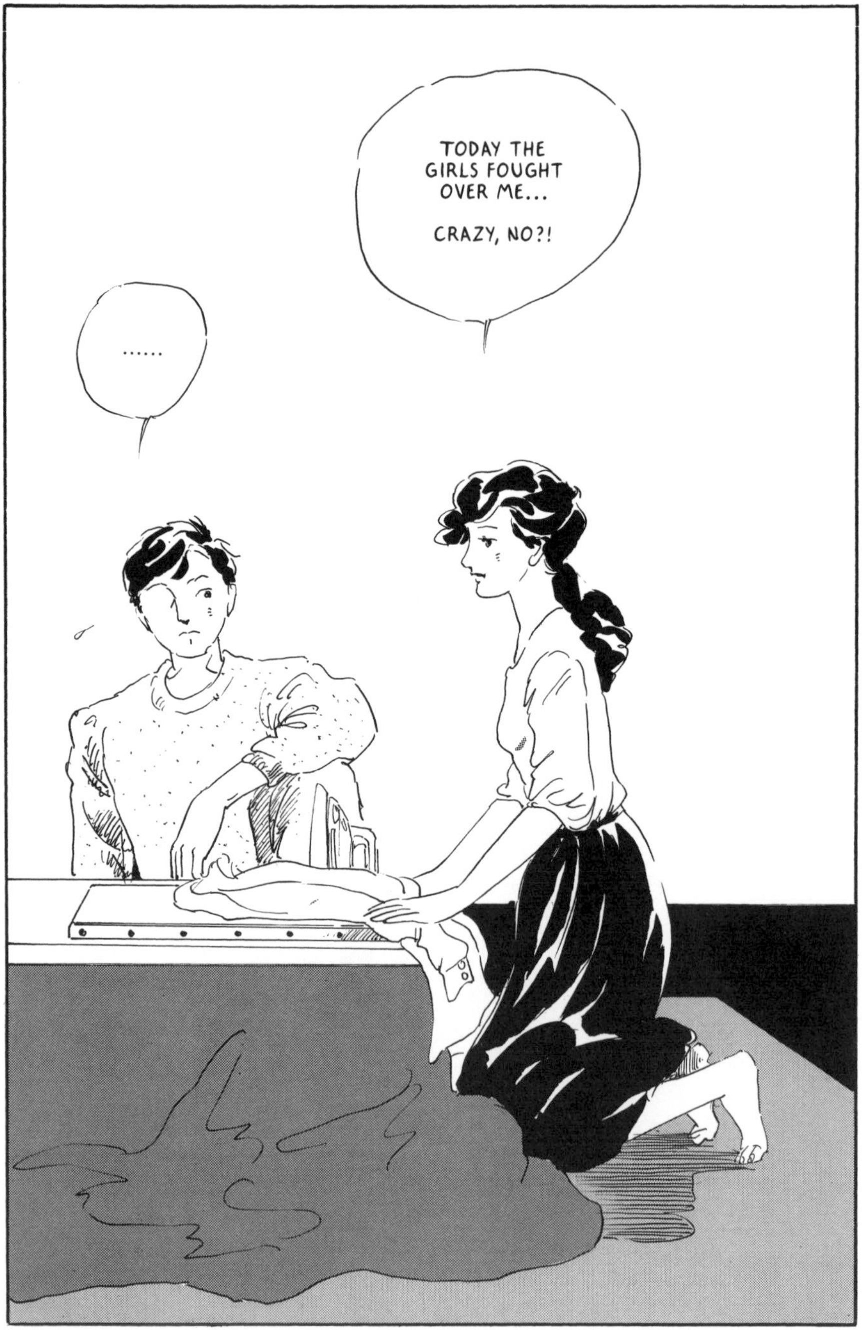
TODAY THE GIRLS FOUGHT OVER ME...
CRAZY, NO?!
......

Downpour

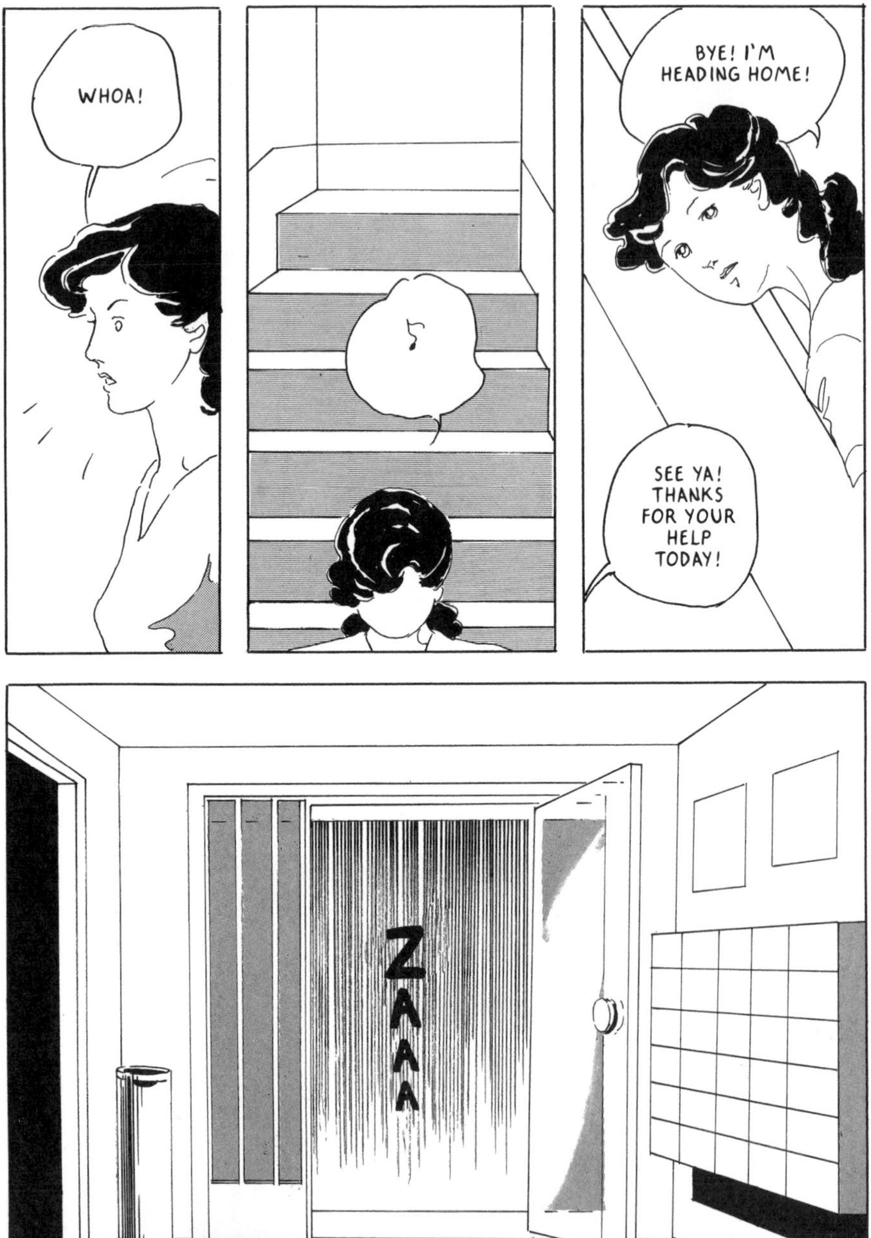
BYE! I'M HEADING HOME!
SEE YA! THANKS FOR YOUR HELP TODAY!
WHOA!
ZAAA

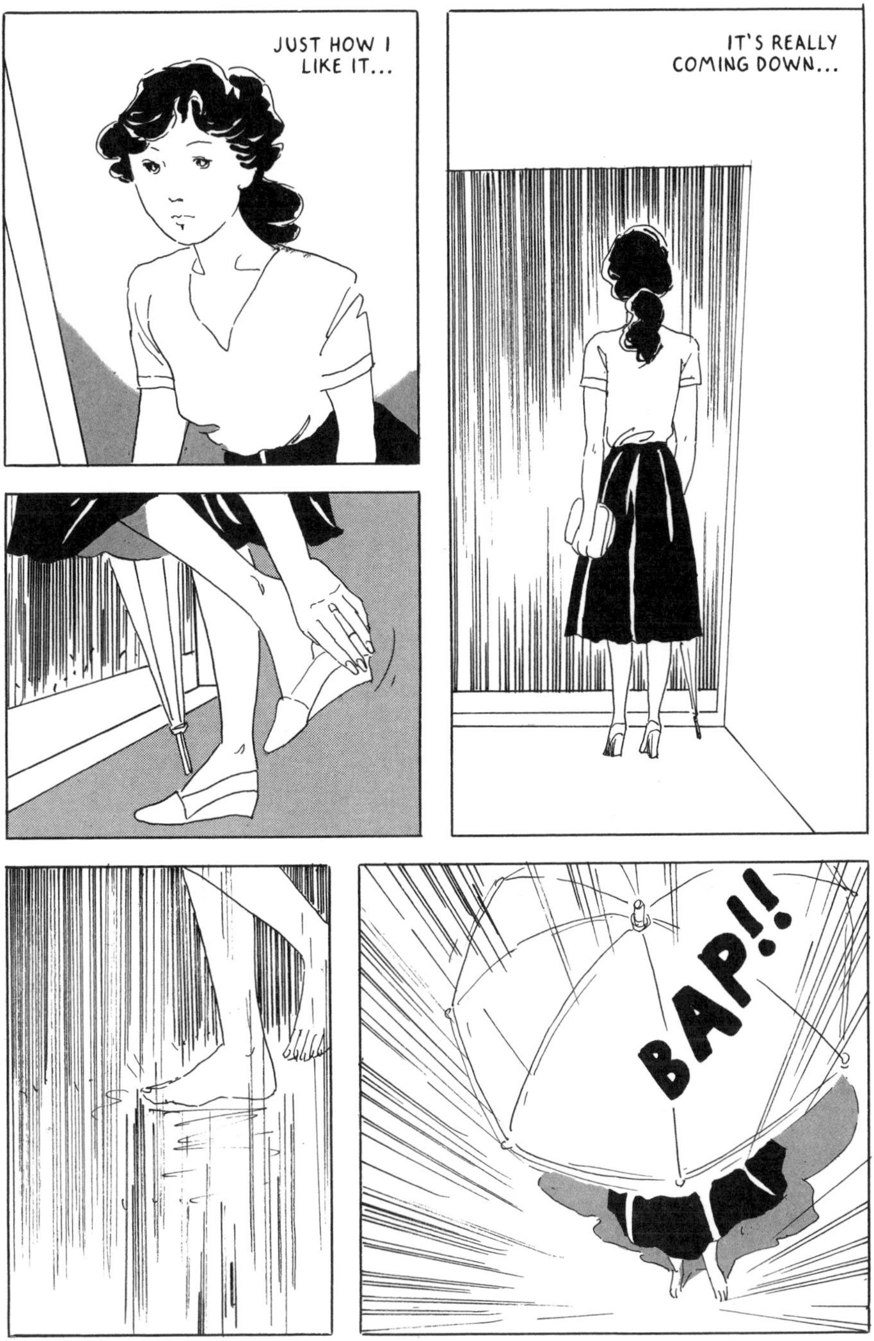
IT'S REALLY COMING DOWN...
JUST HOW I LIKE IT...
BAP!!

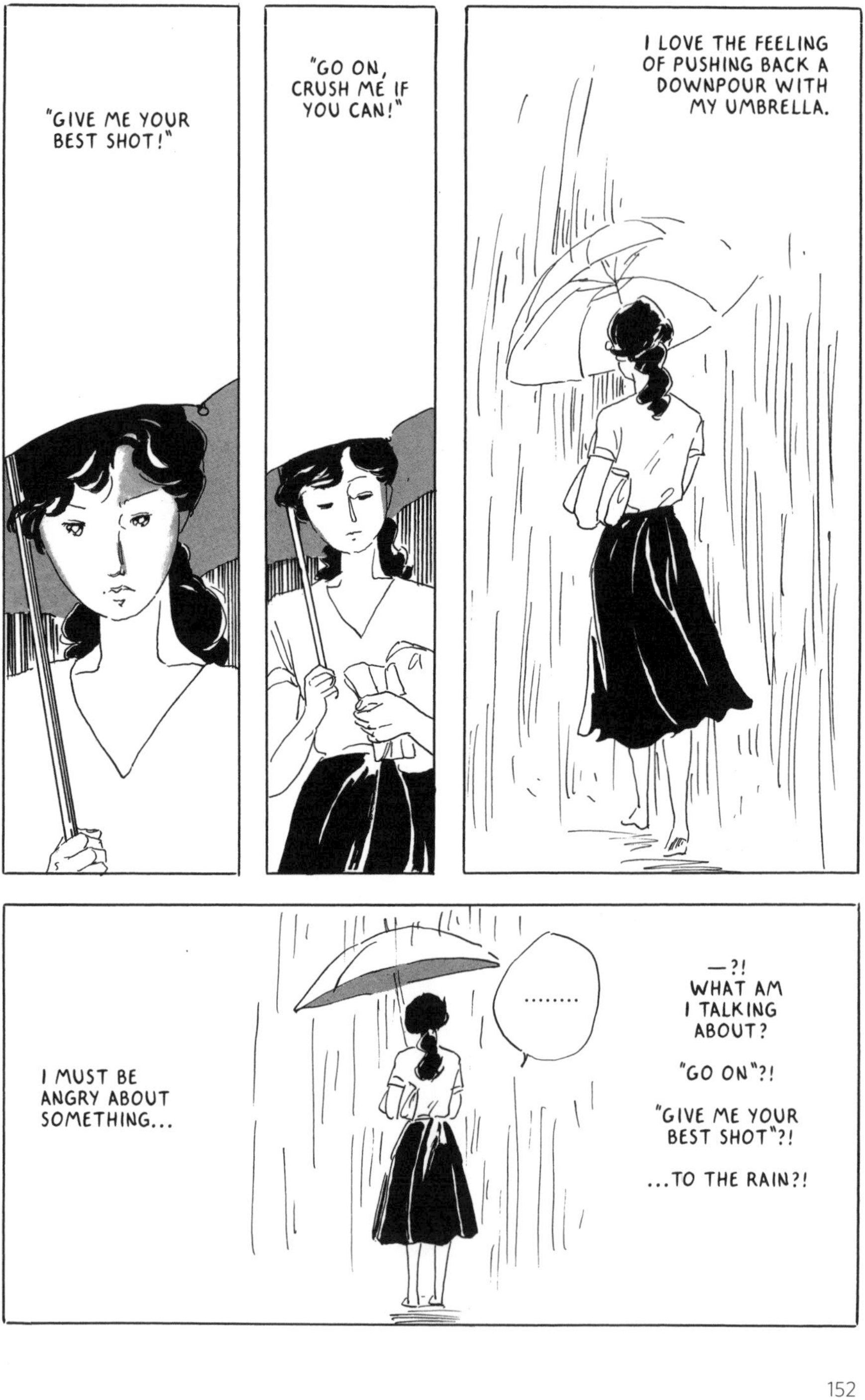
I LOVE THE FEELING OF PUSHING BACK A DOWNPOUR WITH MY UMBRELLA.
"GO ON, CRUSH ME IF YOU CAN!"
"GIVE ME YOUR BEST SHOT!"
—?! WHAT AM I TALKING ABOUT?
"GO ON"?!
"GIVE ME YOUR BEST SHOT"?!
...TO THE RAIN?!
....
I MUST BE ANGRY ABOUT SOMETHING...

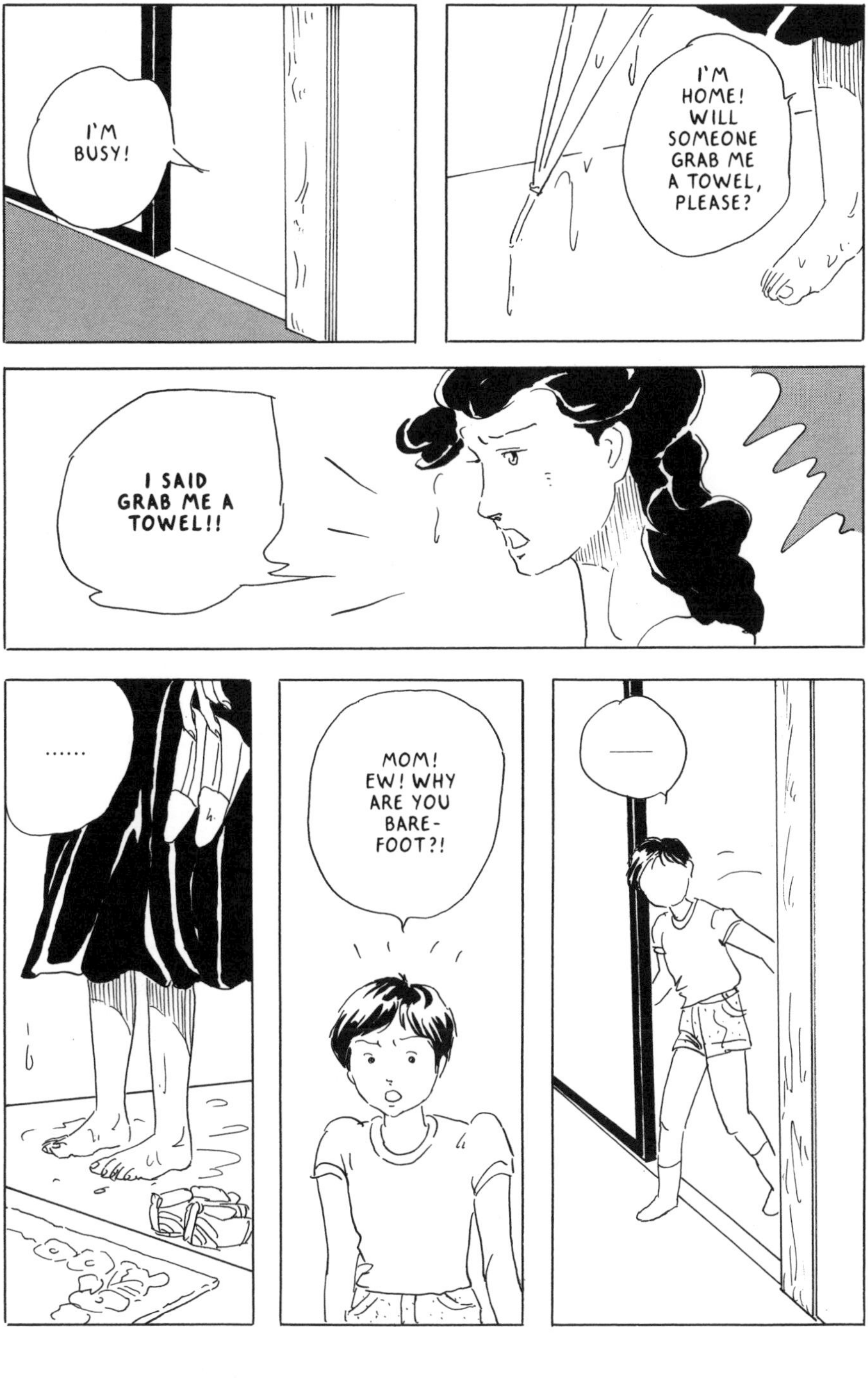
I'M HOME! WILL SOMEONE GRAB ME A TOWEL, PLEASE?
I'M BUSY!
I SAID GRAB ME A TOWEL!!
——
MOM! EW! WHY ARE YOU BARE-FOOT?!
......

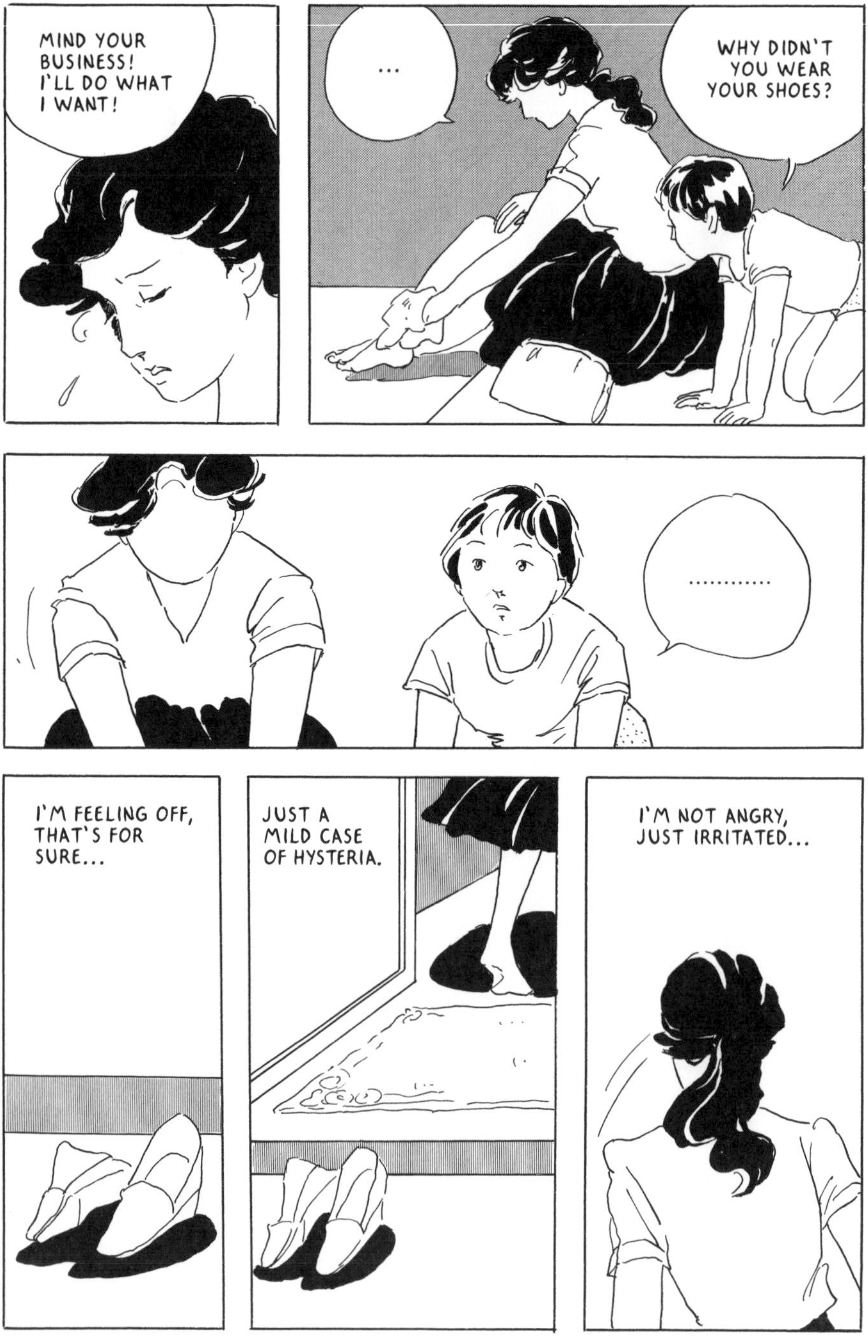
WHY DIDN'T YOU WEAR YOUR SHOES?
...
MIND YOUR BUSINESS! I'LL DO WHAT I WANT!
....
I'M NOT ANGRY, JUST IRRITATED...
JUST A MILD CASE OF HYSTERIA.
I'M FEELING OFF, THAT'S FOR SURE...

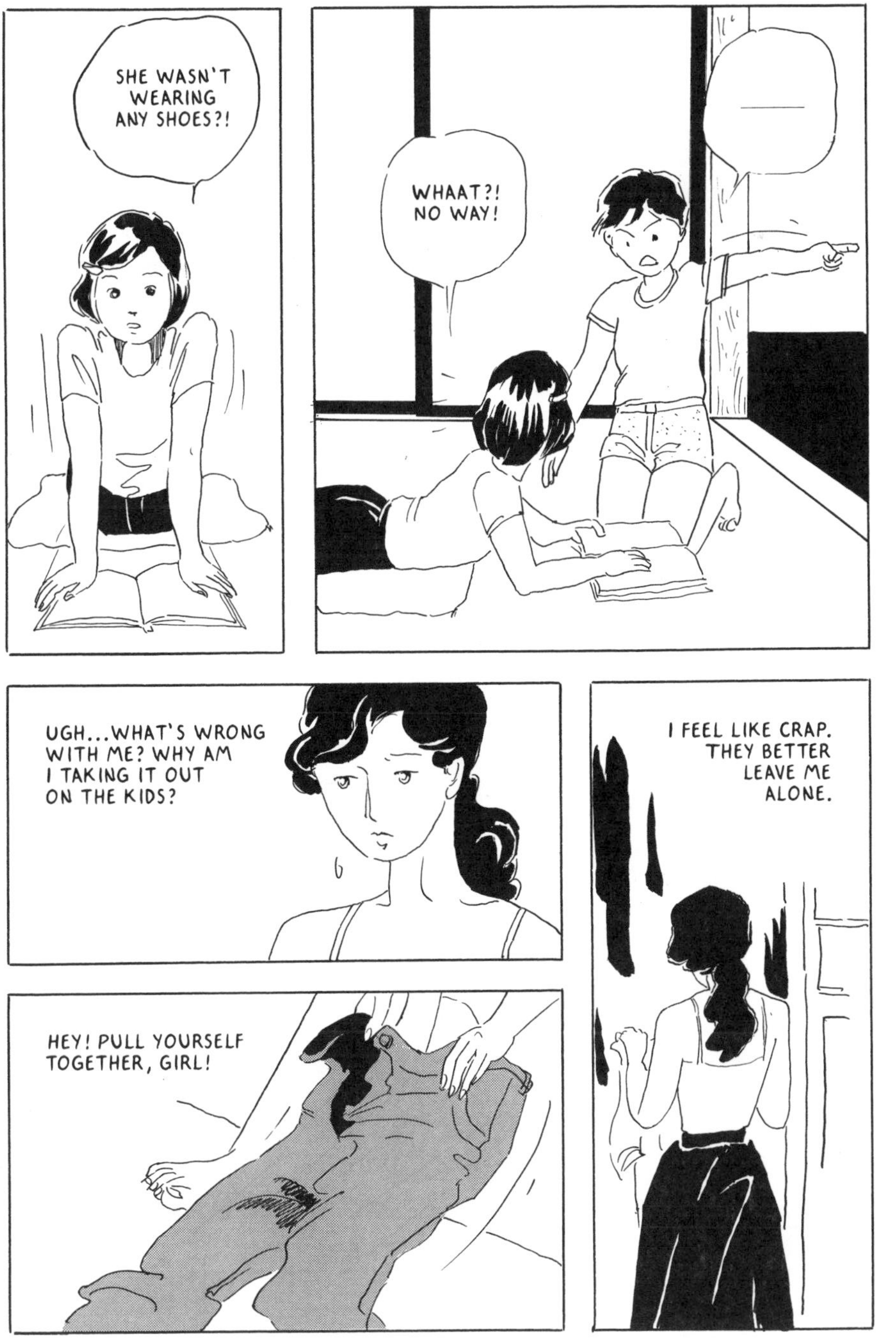
——
WHAAT?! NO WAY!
SHE WASN'T WEARING ANY SHOES?!
I FEEL LIKE CRAP. THEY BETTER LEAVE ME ALONE.
UGH...WHAT'S WRONG WITH ME? WHY AM I TAKING IT OUT ON THE KIDS?
HEY! PULL YOURSELF TOGETHER, GIRL!

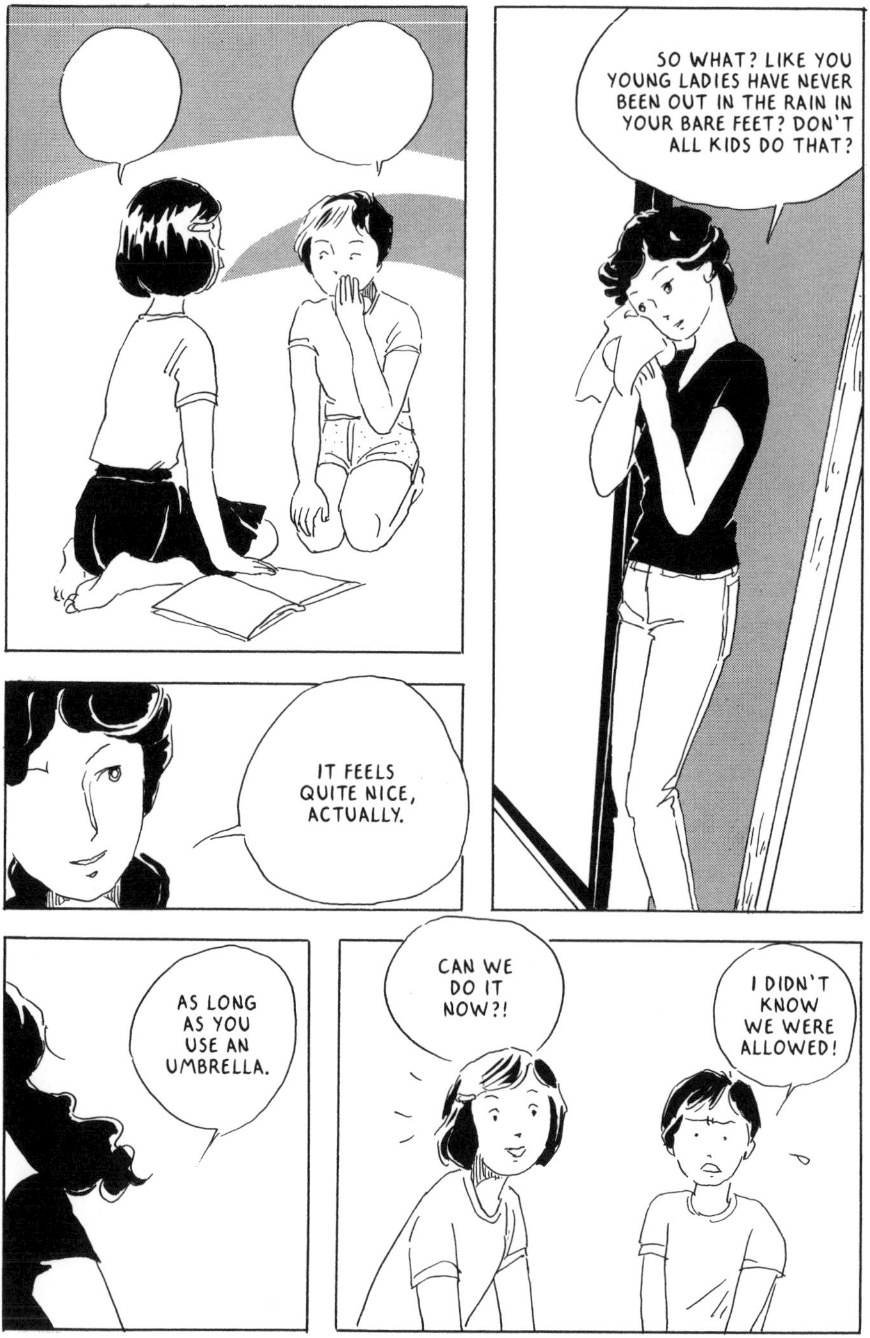
SO WHAT? LIKE YOU YOUNG LADIES HAVE NEVER BEEN OUT IN THE RAIN IN YOUR BARE FEET? DON'T ALL KIDS DO THAT?
IT FEELS QUITE NICE, ACTUALLY.
I DIDN'T KNOW WE WERE ALLOWED!
CAN WE DO IT NOW?!
AS LONG AS YOU USE AN UMBRELLA.

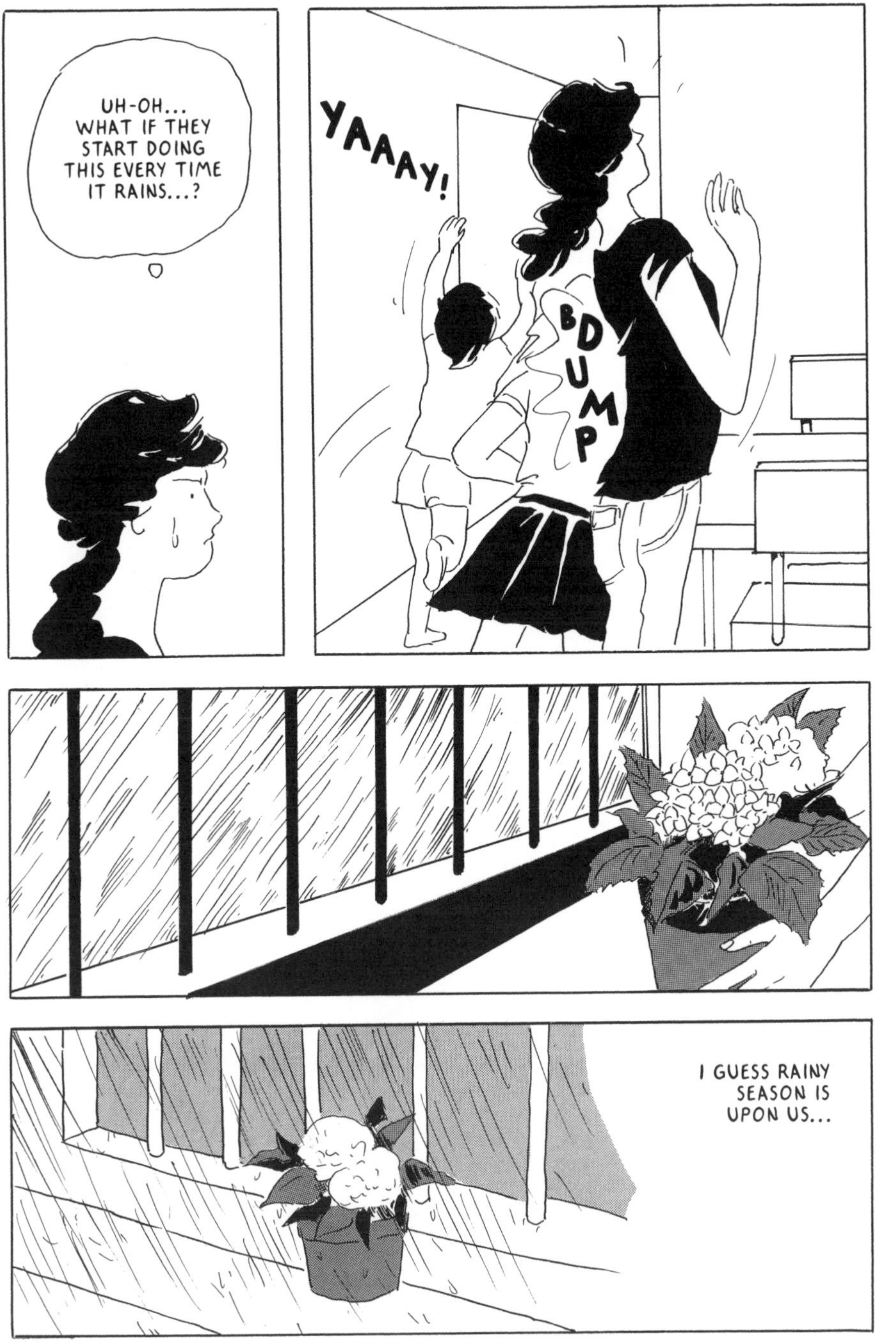
YAAAY!
BDUMP
UH-OH... WHAT IF THEY START DOING THIS EVERY TIME IT RAINS...?
I GUESS RAINY SEASON IS UPON US...

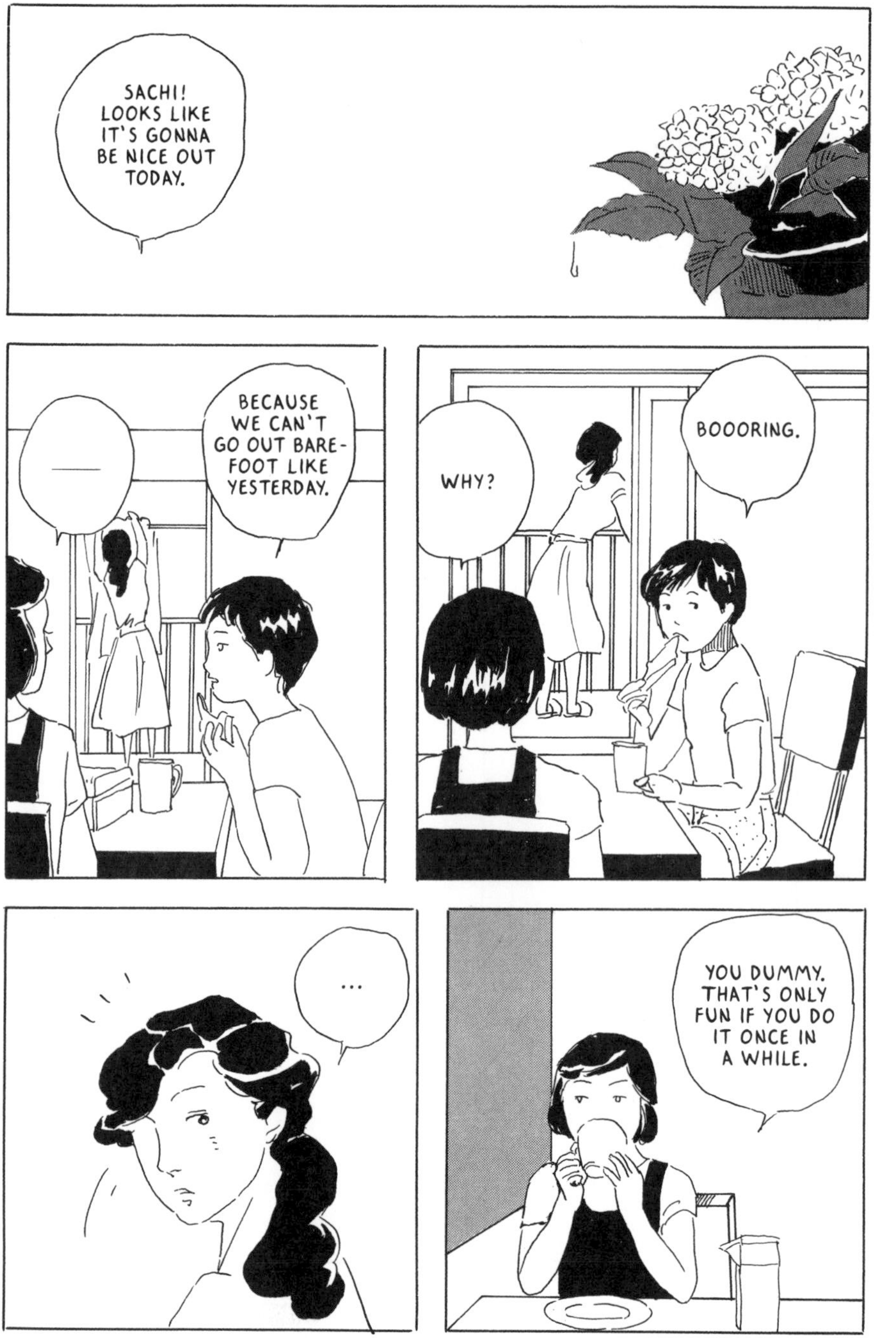
SACHI! LOOKS LIKE IT'S GONNA BE NICE OUT TODAY.
BOOORING.
WHY?
BECAUSE WE CAN'T GO OUT BARE-FOOT LIKE YESTERDAY.
——
YOU DUMMY. THAT'S ONLY FUN IF YOU DO IT ONCE IN A WHILE.
...

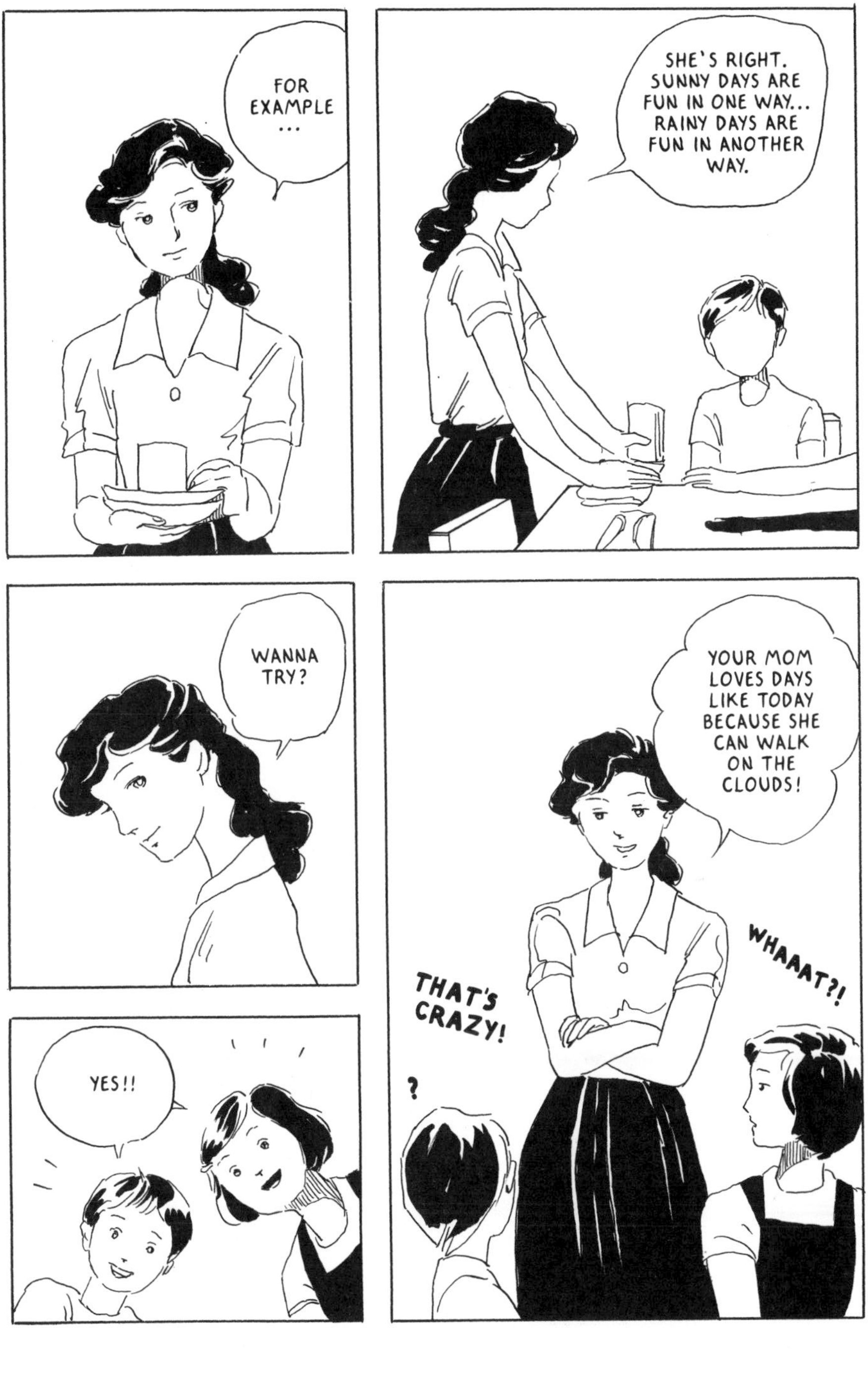
SHE'S RIGHT. SUNNY DAYS ARE FUN IN ONE WAY... RAINY DAYS ARE FUN IN ANOTHER WAY.
FOR EXAMPLE ...
YOUR MOM LOVES DAYS LIKE TODAY BECAUSE SHE CAN WALK ON THE CLOUDS!
WHAAAT?!
THAT'S CRAZY!
?
WANNA TRY?
YES!!

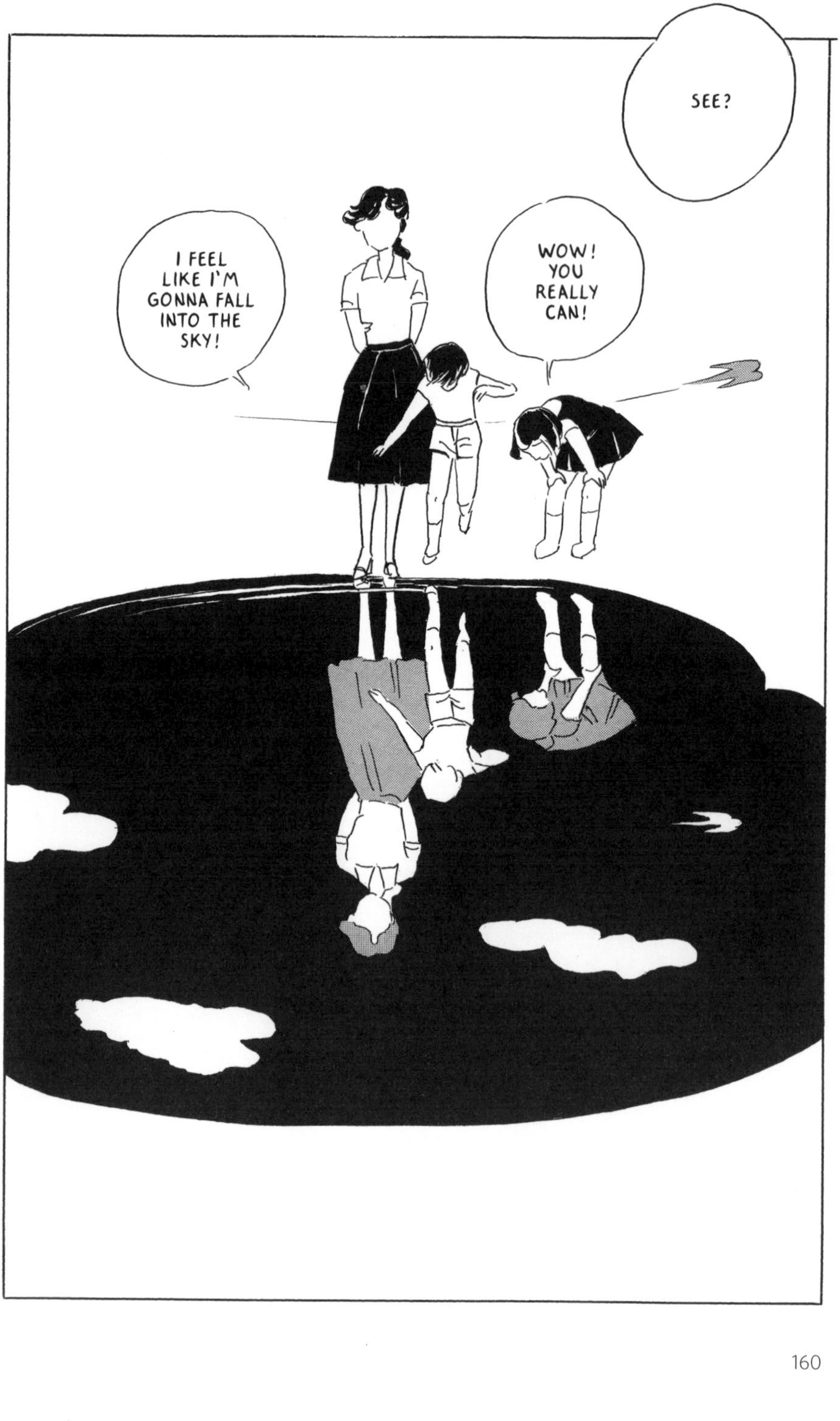
SEE?
WOW! YOU REALLY CAN!
I FEEL LIKE I'M GONNA FALL INTO THE SKY!

Waking from the Dream

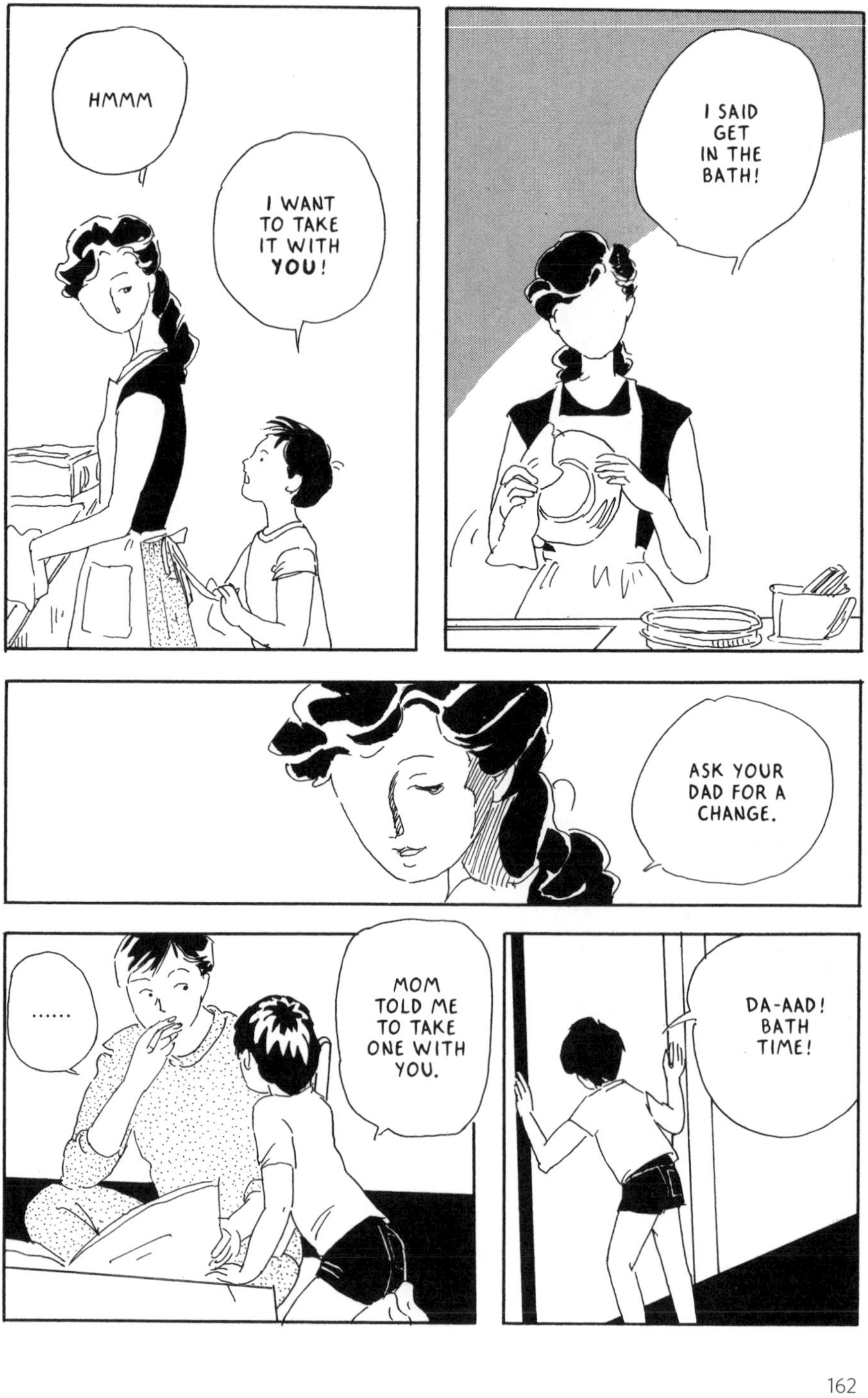
I SAID GET IN THE BATH!
I WANT TO TAKE IT WITH YOU!
HMMM
ASK YOUR DAD FOR A CHANGE.
DA-AAD! BATH TIME!
MOM TOLD ME TO TAKE ONE WITH YOU.
......

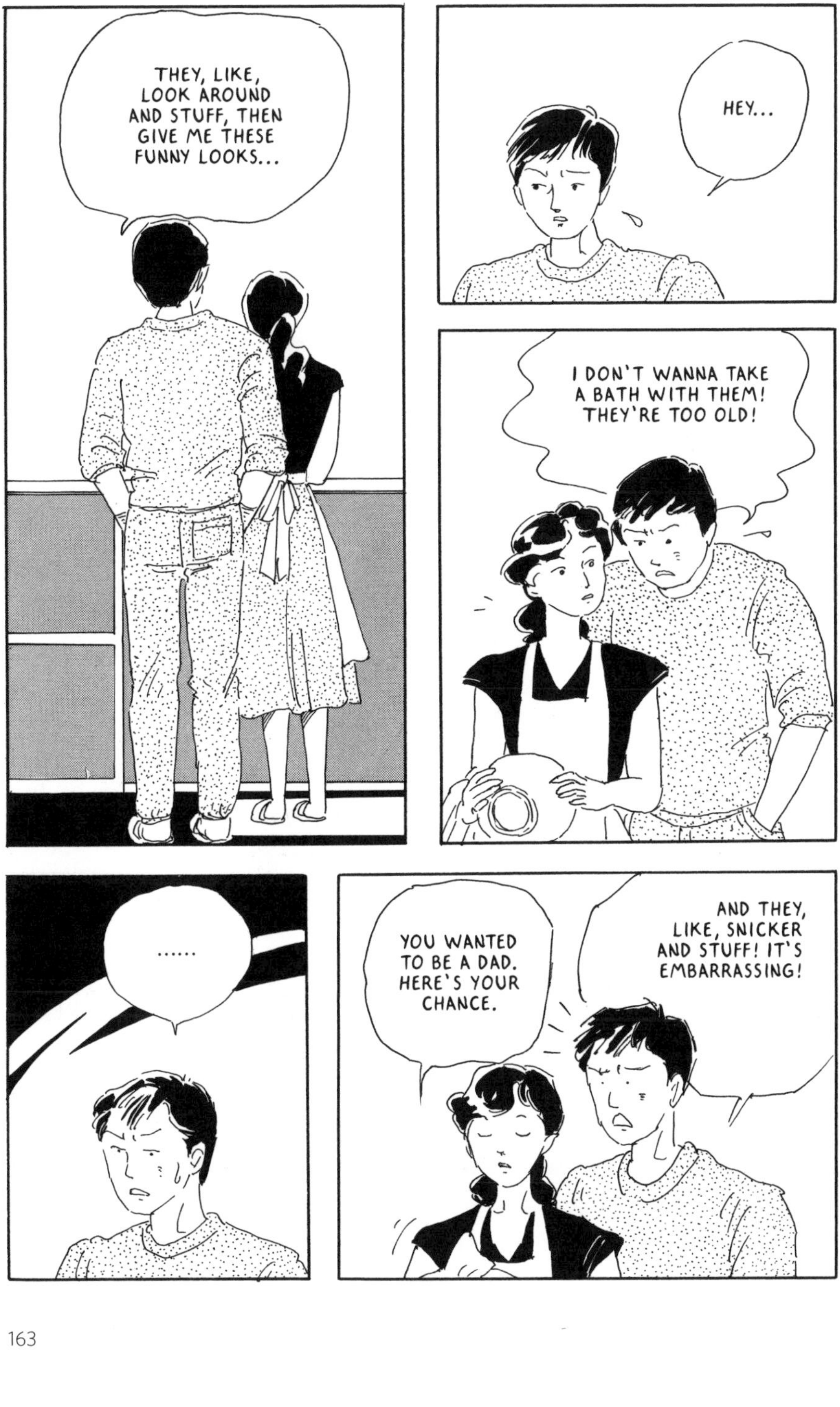
HEY...
I DON'T WANNA TAKE A BATH WITH THEM! THEY'RE TOO OLD!
THEY, LIKE, LOOK AROUND AND STUFF, THEN GIVE ME THESE FUNNY LOOKS...
AND THEY, LIKE, SNICKER AND STUFF! IT'S EMBARRASSING!
YOU WANTED TO BE A DAD. HERE'S YOUR CHANCE.
......

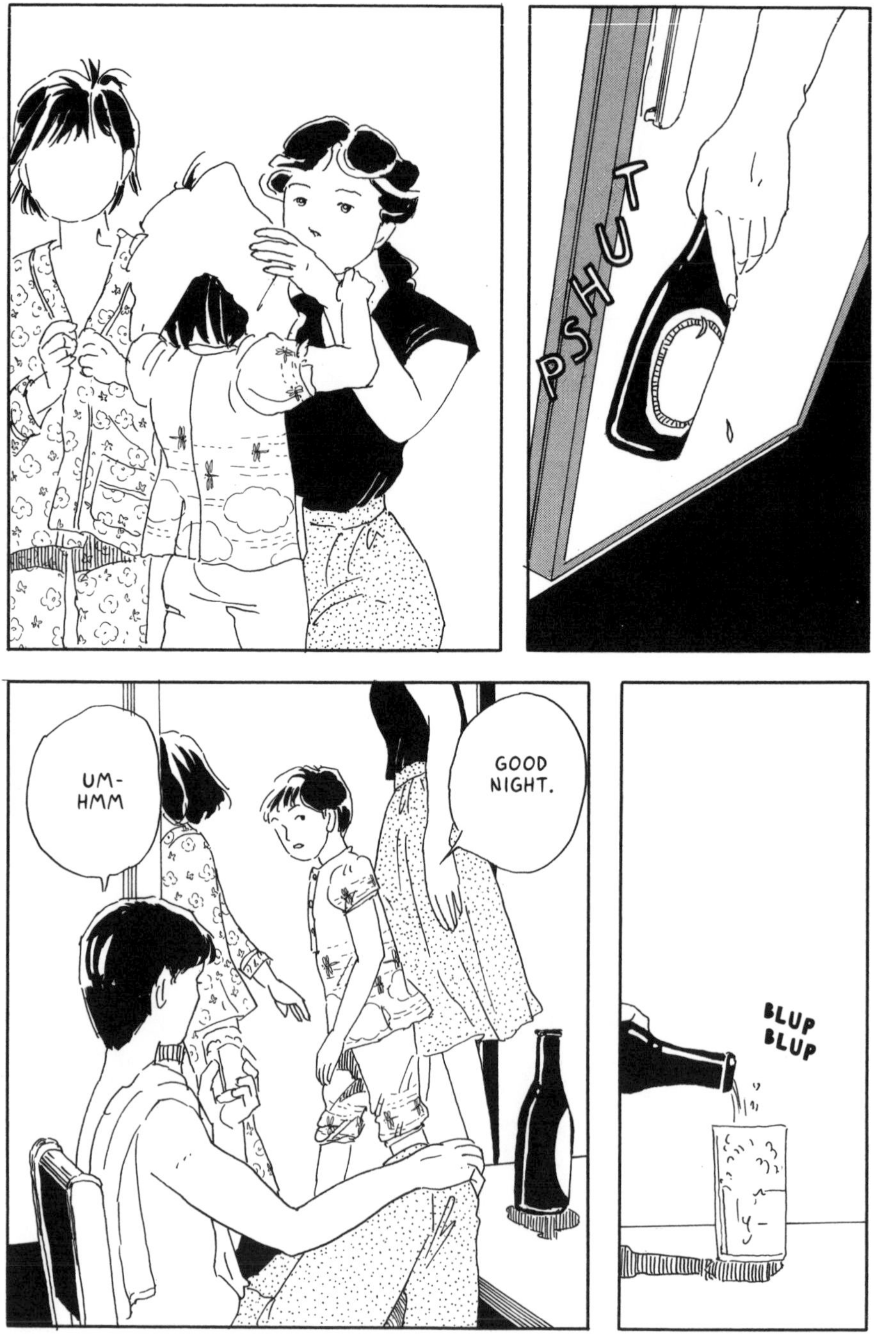
PSHUT
BLUP BLUP
GOOD NIGHT.
UM-HMM

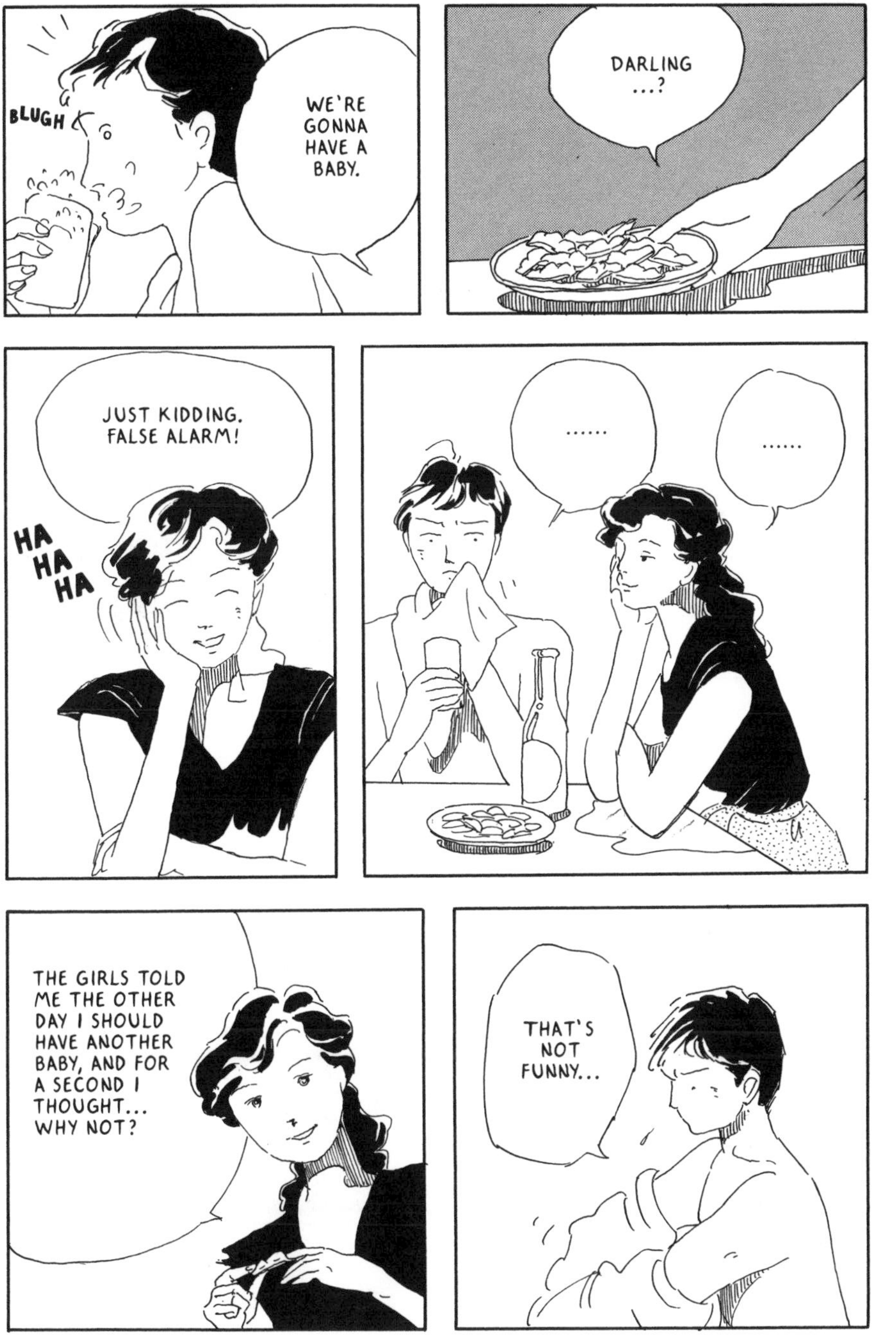
DARLING ...?
BLUGH
WE'RE GONNA HAVE A BABY.
......
......
JUST KIDDING. FALSE ALARM!
HA HA HA
THAT'S NOT FUNNY...
THE GIRLS TOLD ME THE OTHER DAY I SHOULD HAVE ANOTHER BABY, AND FOR A SECOND I THOUGHT... WHY NOT?

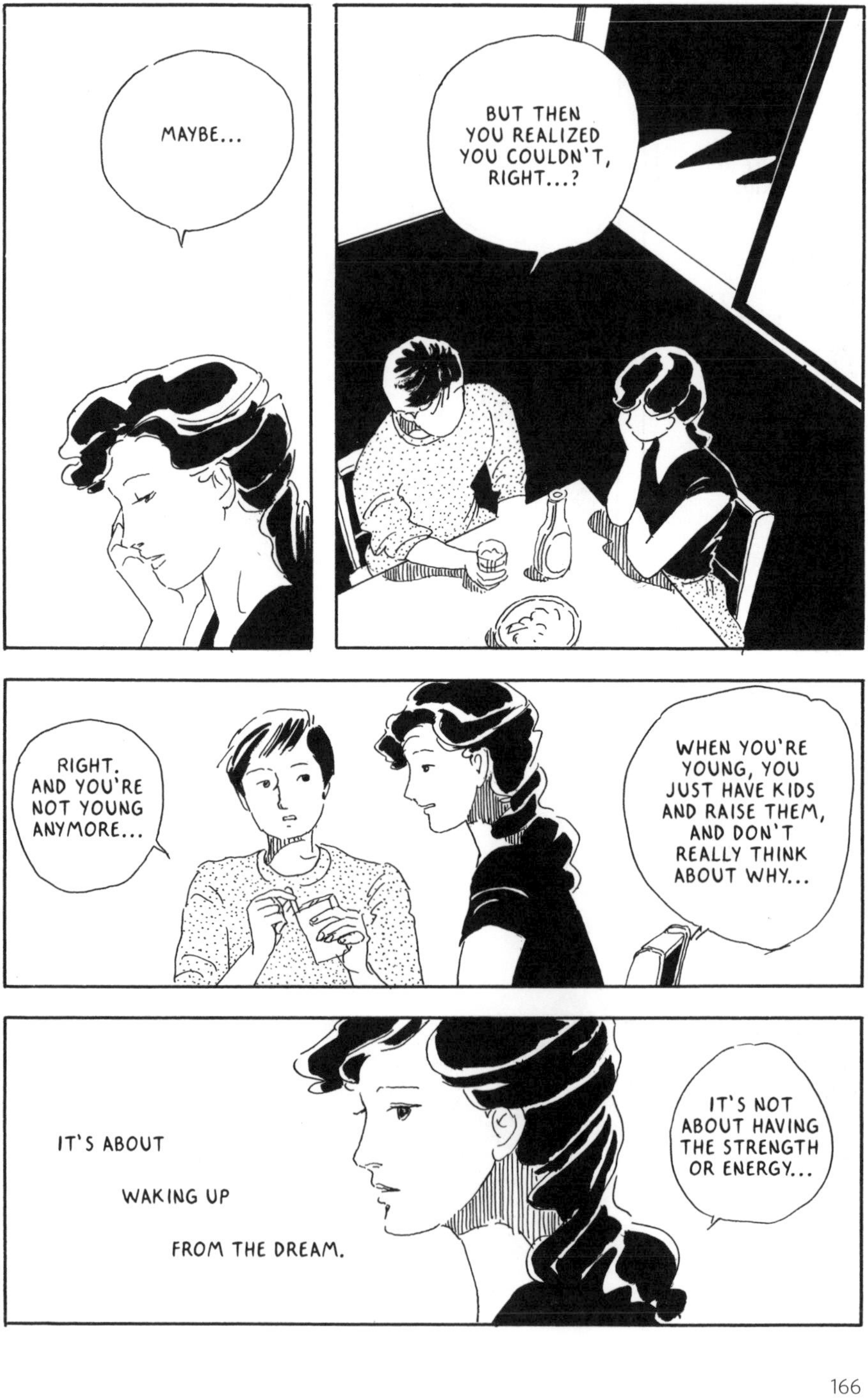
BUT THEN YOU REALIZED YOU COULDN'T, RIGHT...?
MAYBE...
WHEN YOU'RE YOUNG, YOU JUST HAVE KIDS AND RAISE THEM, AND DON'T REALLY THINK ABOUT WHY...
RIGHT. AND YOU'RE NOT YOUNG ANYMORE...
IT'S NOT ABOUT HAVING THE STRENGTH OR ENERGY...
IT'S ABOUT
WAKING UP
FROM THE DREAM.

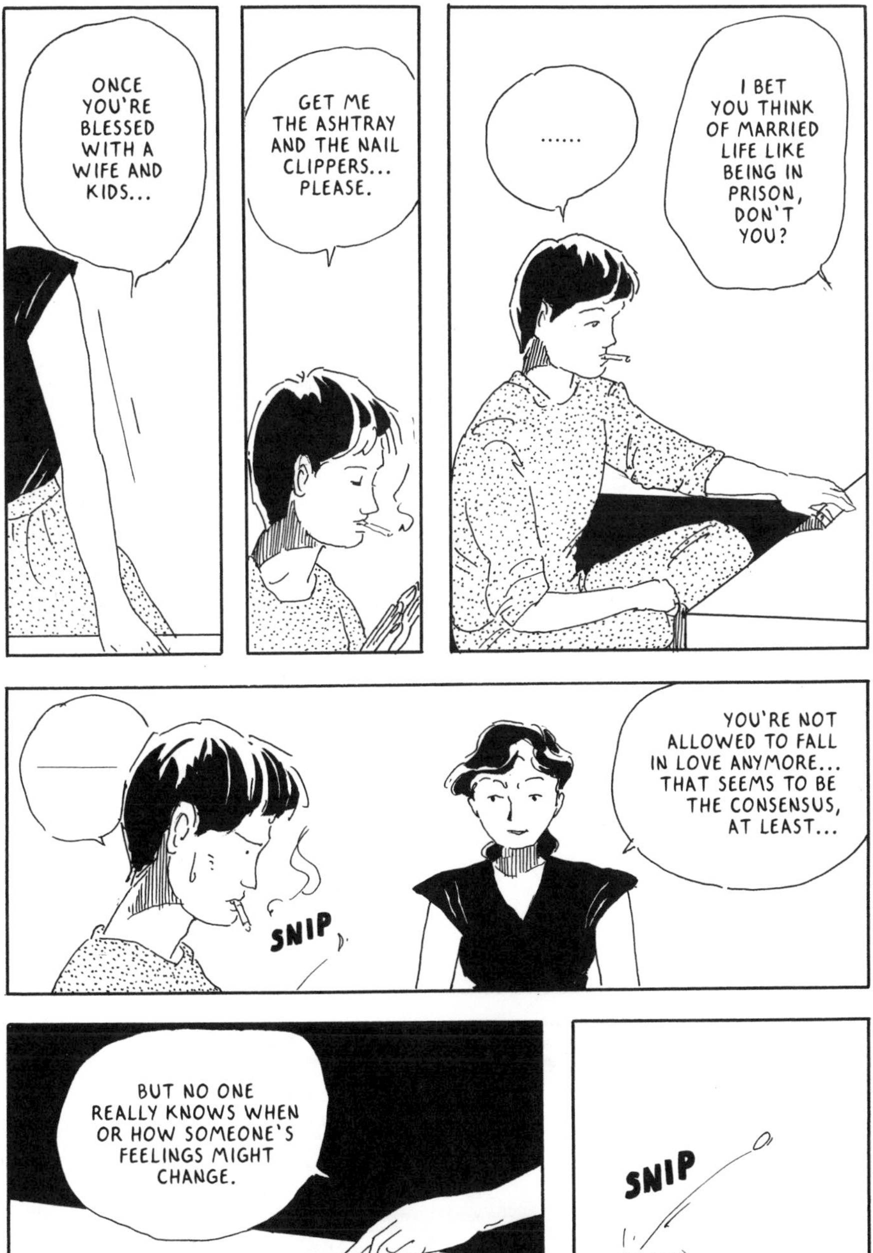
I BET YOU THINK OF MARRIED LIFE LIKE BEING IN PRISON, DON'T YOU?
......
GET ME THE ASHTRAY AND THE NAIL CLIPPERS... PLEASE.
ONCE YOU'RE BLESSED WITH A WIFE AND KIDS...
YOU'RE NOT ALLOWED TO FALL IN LOVE ANYMORE... THAT SEEMS TO BE THE CONSENSUS, AT LEAST...
SNIP
——
SNIP
BUT NO ONE REALLY KNOWS WHEN OR HOW SOMEONE'S FEELINGS MIGHT CHANGE.

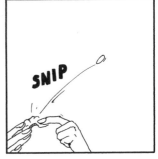

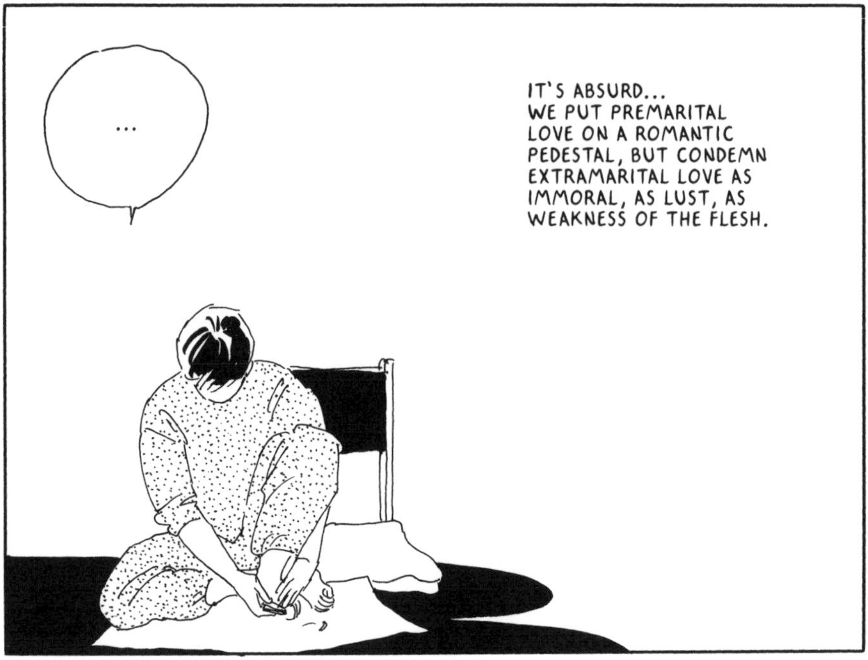
IT'S ABSURD... WE PUT PREMARITAL LOVE ON A ROMANTIC PEDESTAL, BUT CONDEMN EXTRAMARITAL LOVE AS IMMORAL, AS LUST, AS WEAKNESS OF THE FLESH.
...

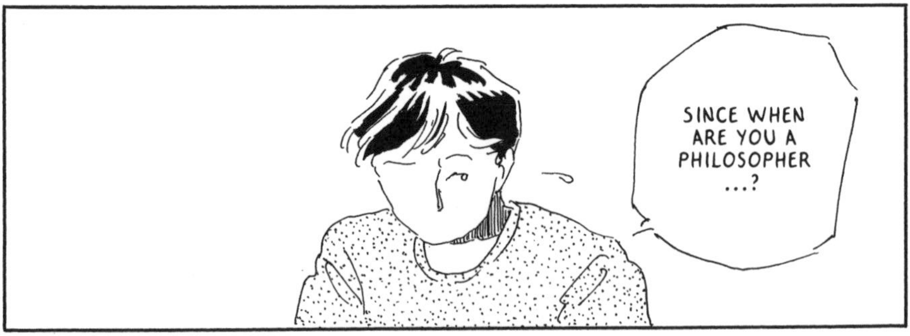
SINCE WHEN ARE YOU A PHILOSOPHER ...?

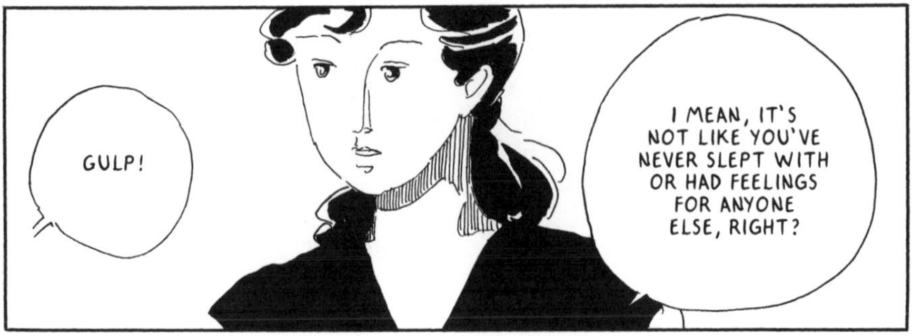
I MEAN, IT'S NOT LIKE YOU'VE NEVER SLEPT WITH OR HAD FEELINGS FOR ANYONE ELSE, RIGHT?
GULP!

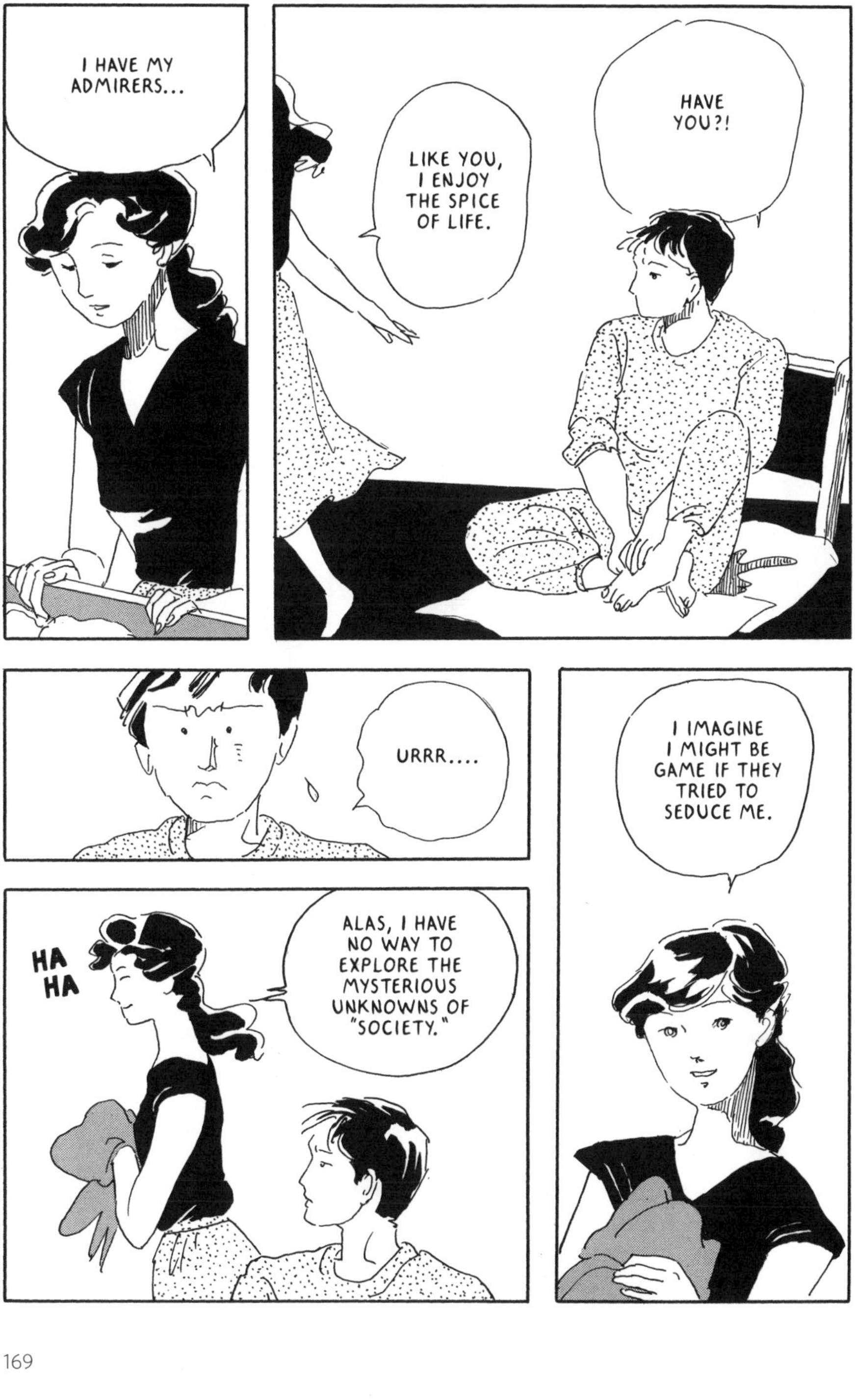
I HAVE MY ADMIRERS...
LIKE YOU, I ENJOY THE SPICE OF LIFE.
HAVE YOU?!
URRR....
I IMAGINE I MIGHT BE GAME IF THEY TRIED TO SEDUCE ME.
HA HA
ALAS, I HAVE NO WAY TO EXPLORE THE MYSTERIOUS UNKNOWNS OF "SOCIETY."

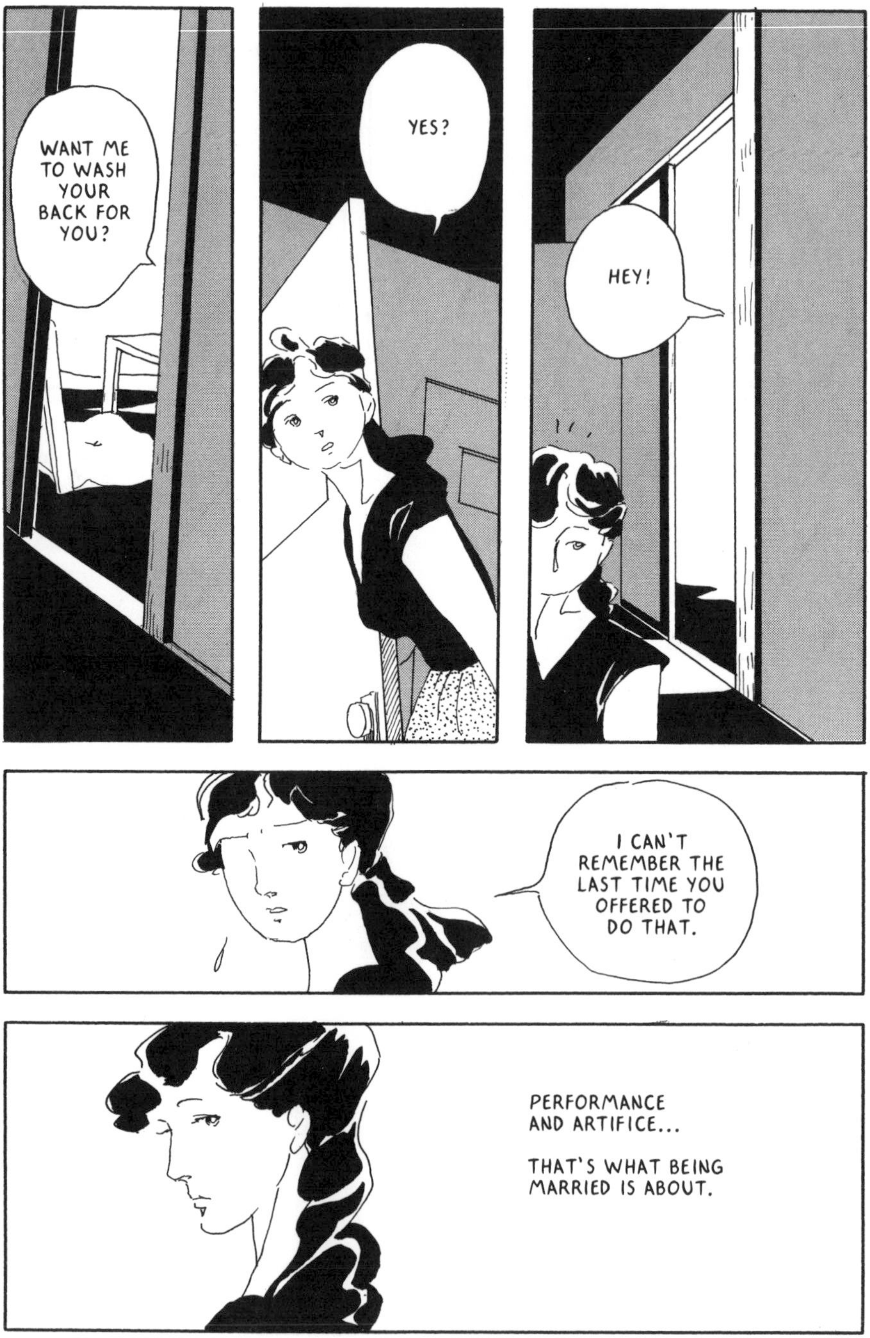
HEY!
YES?
WANT ME TO WASH YOUR BACK FOR YOU?
I CAN'T REMEMBER THE LAST TIME YOU OFFERED TO DO THAT.
PERFORMANCE AND ARTIFICE...
THAT'S WHAT BEING MARRIED IS ABOUT.

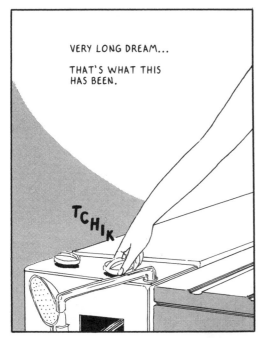

VERY LONG DREAM...

THAT'S WHAT THIS
HAS BEEN.

TCHIK

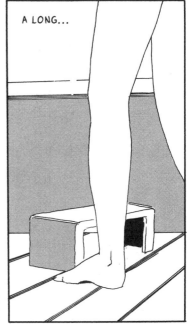

A LONG...

WE DATED FOR
SIX YEARS...

WE'VE BEEN
MARRIED TEN...

A SIXTEEN-YEAR
DREAM.

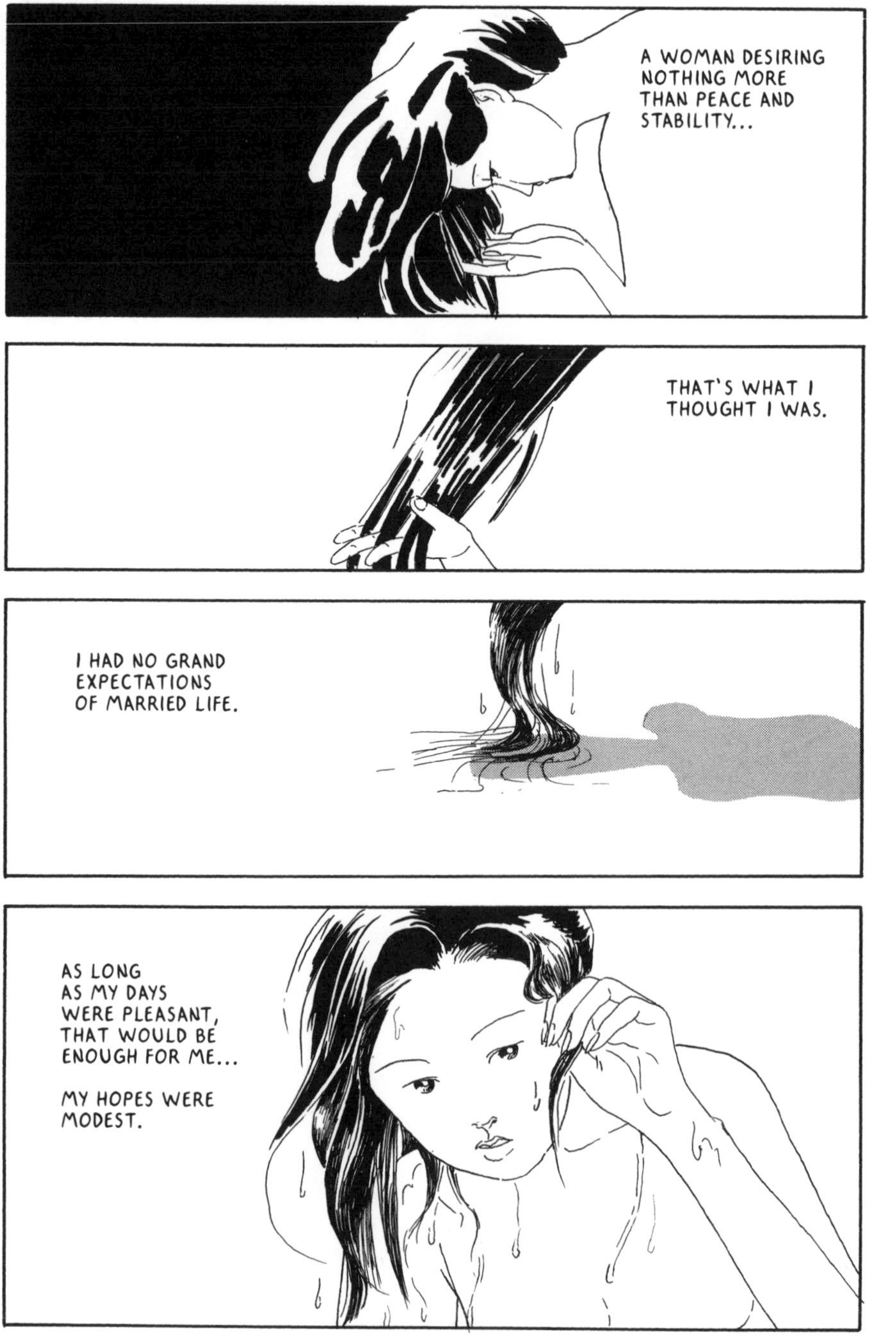
A WOMAN DESIRING NOTHING MORE THAN PEACE AND STABILITY...
THAT'S WHAT I THOUGHT I WAS.
I HAD NO GRAND EXPECTATIONS OF MARRIED LIFE.
AS LONG AS MY DAYS WERE PLEASANT, THAT WOULD BE ENOUGH FOR ME...
MY HOPES WERE MODEST.

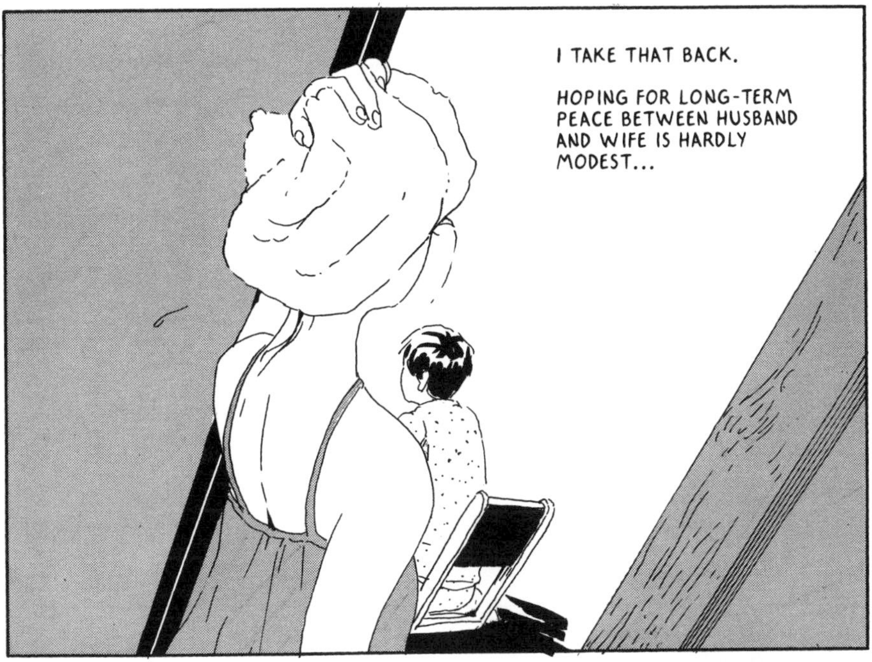
I TAKE THAT BACK.
HOPING FOR LONG-TERM PEACE BETWEEN HUSBAND AND WIFE IS HARDLY MODEST...
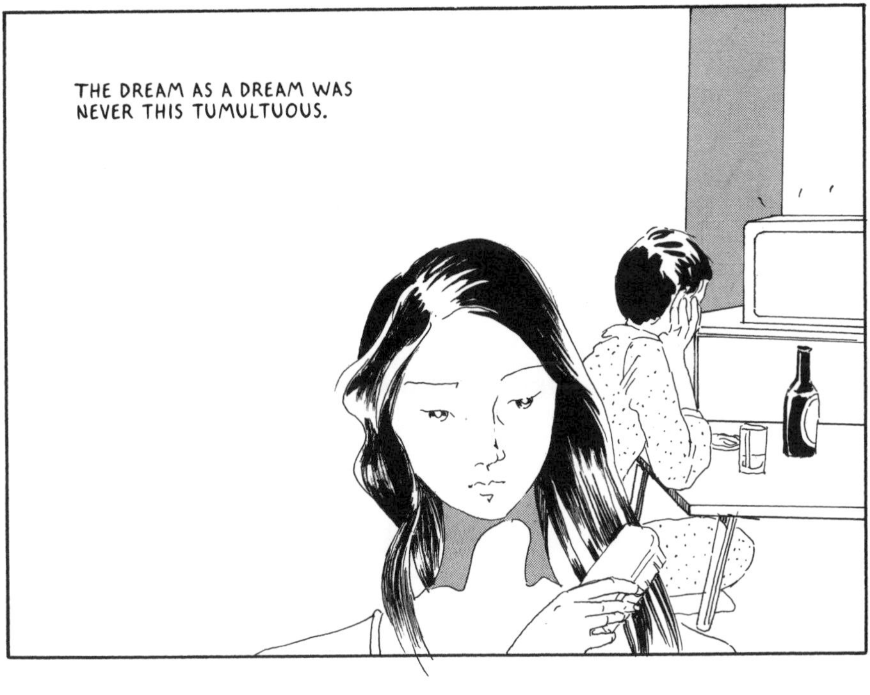
THE DREAM AS A DREAM WAS NEVER THIS TUMULTUOUS.

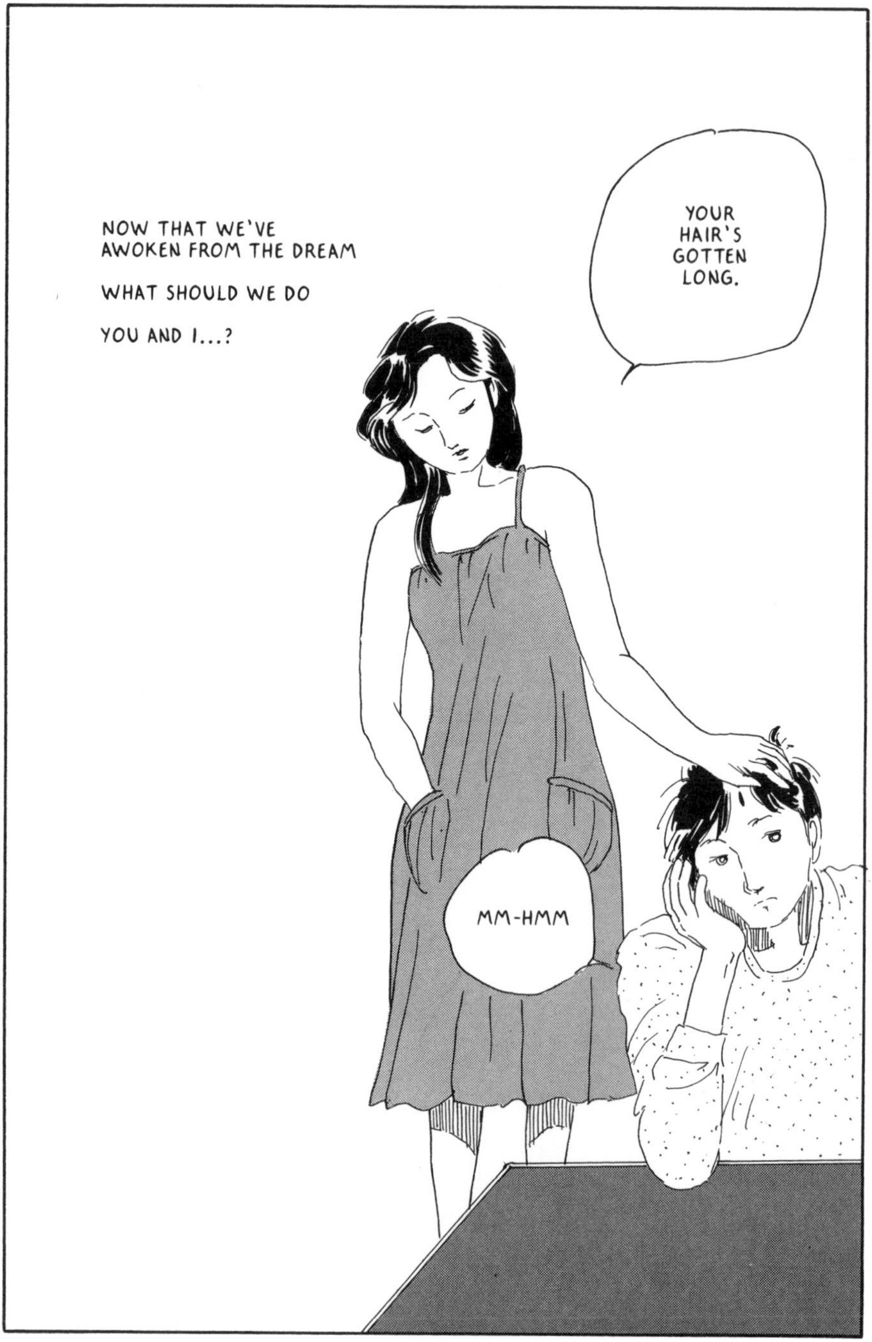
YOUR HAIR'S GOTTEN LONG.
NOW THAT WE'VE AWOKEN FROM THE DREAM
WHAT SHOULD WE DO
YOU AND I...?
MM-HMM

Cat-in-Chief

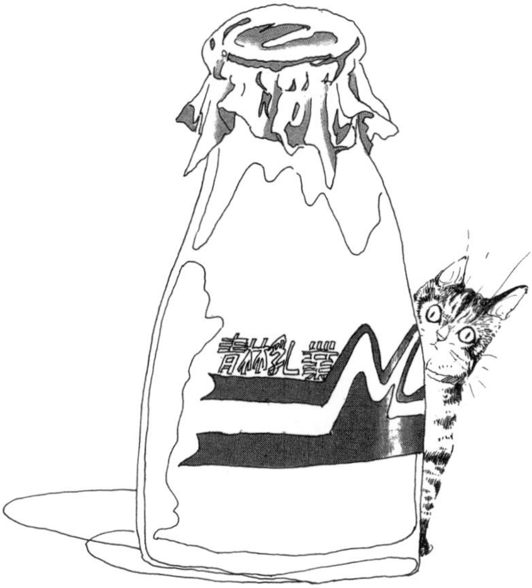
青林乳業

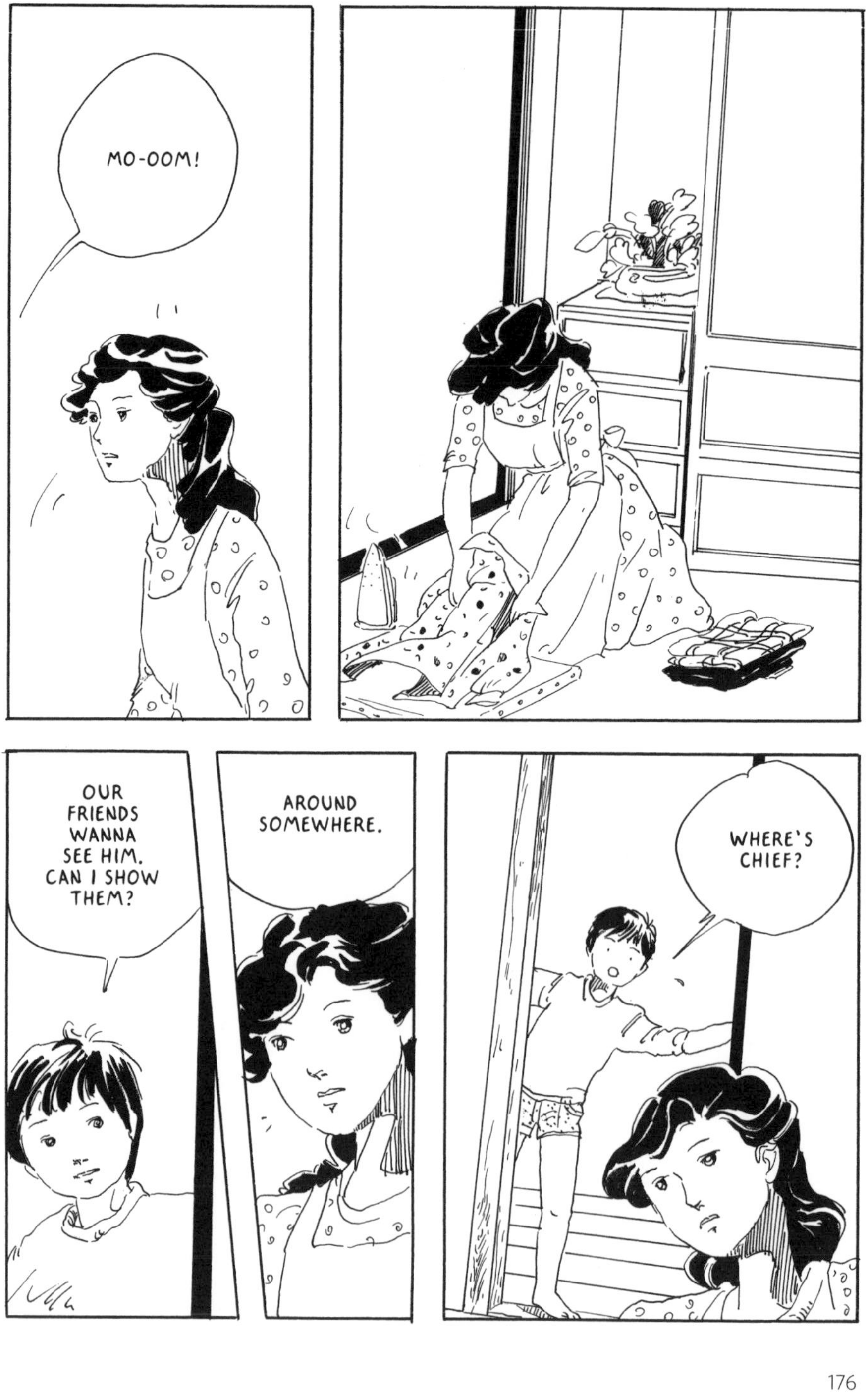
MO-OOM!
WHERE'S CHIEF?
AROUND SOMEWHERE.
OUR FRIENDS WANNA SEE HIM. CAN I SHOW THEM?

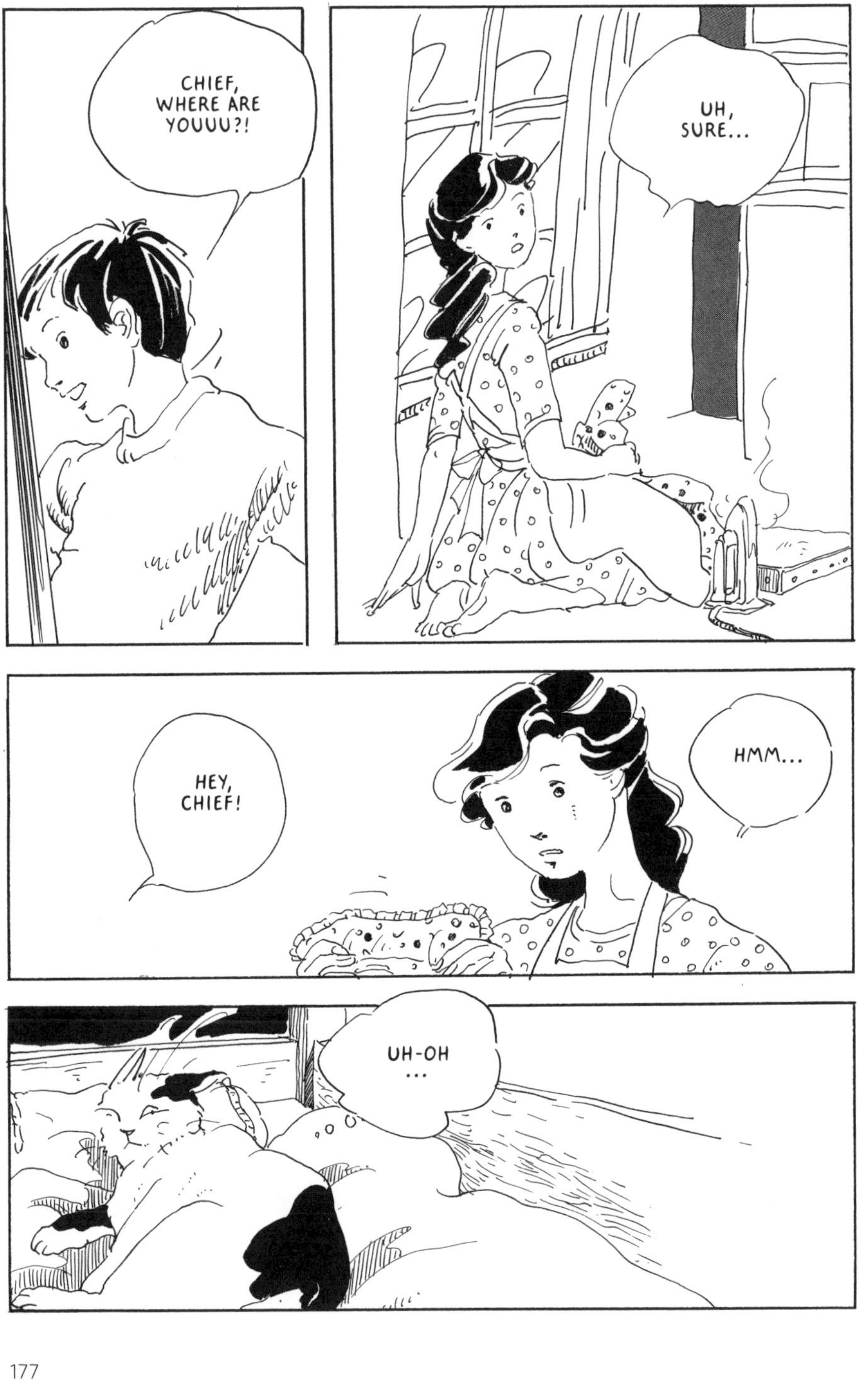
UH, SURE...
CHIEF, WHERE ARE YOUUU?!
HMM...
HEY, CHIEF!
UH-OH ...

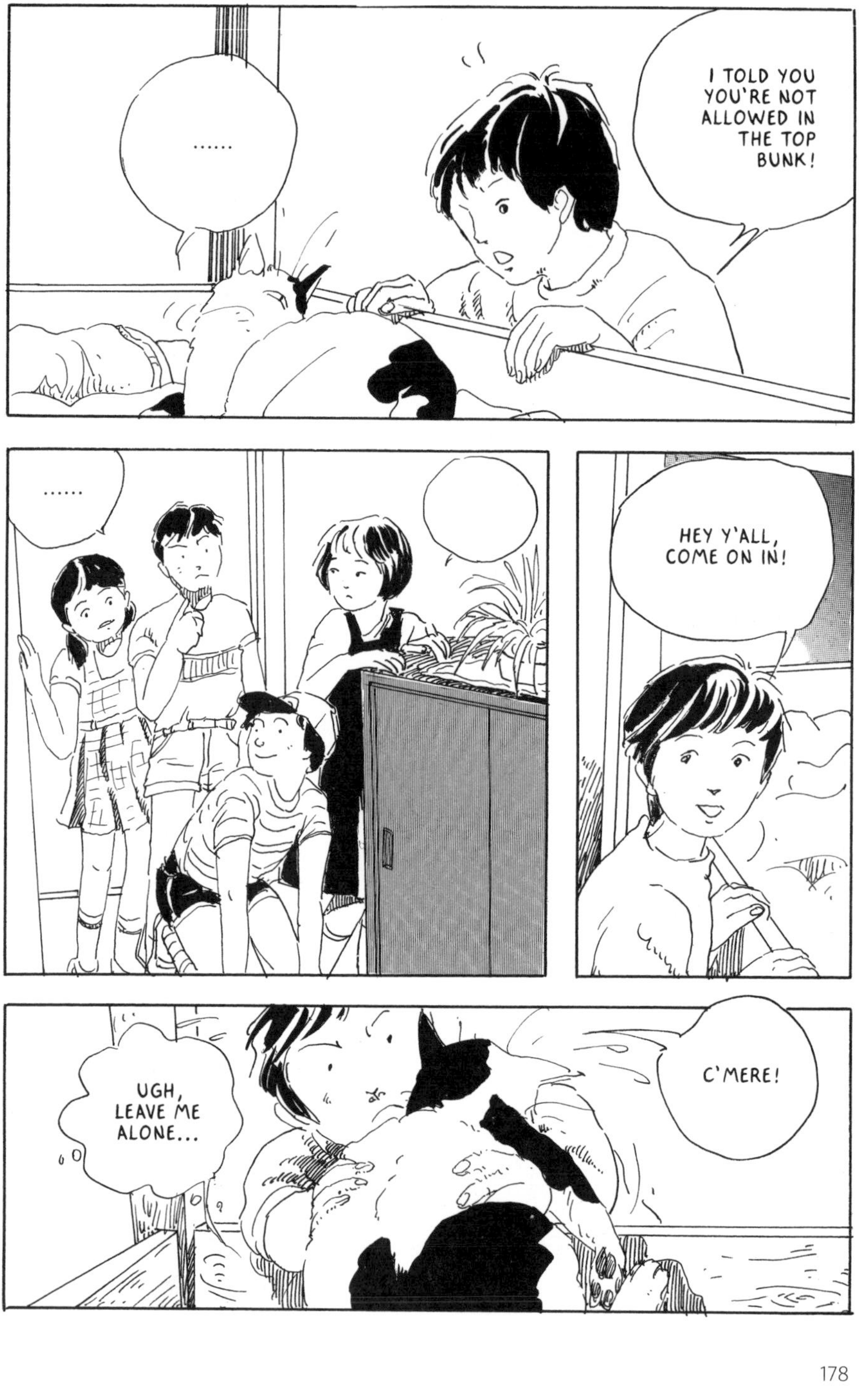
I TOLD YOU YOU'RE NOT ALLOWED IN THE TOP BUNK!
......
HEY Y'ALL, COME ON IN!
......
C'MERE!
UGH, LEAVE ME ALONE...

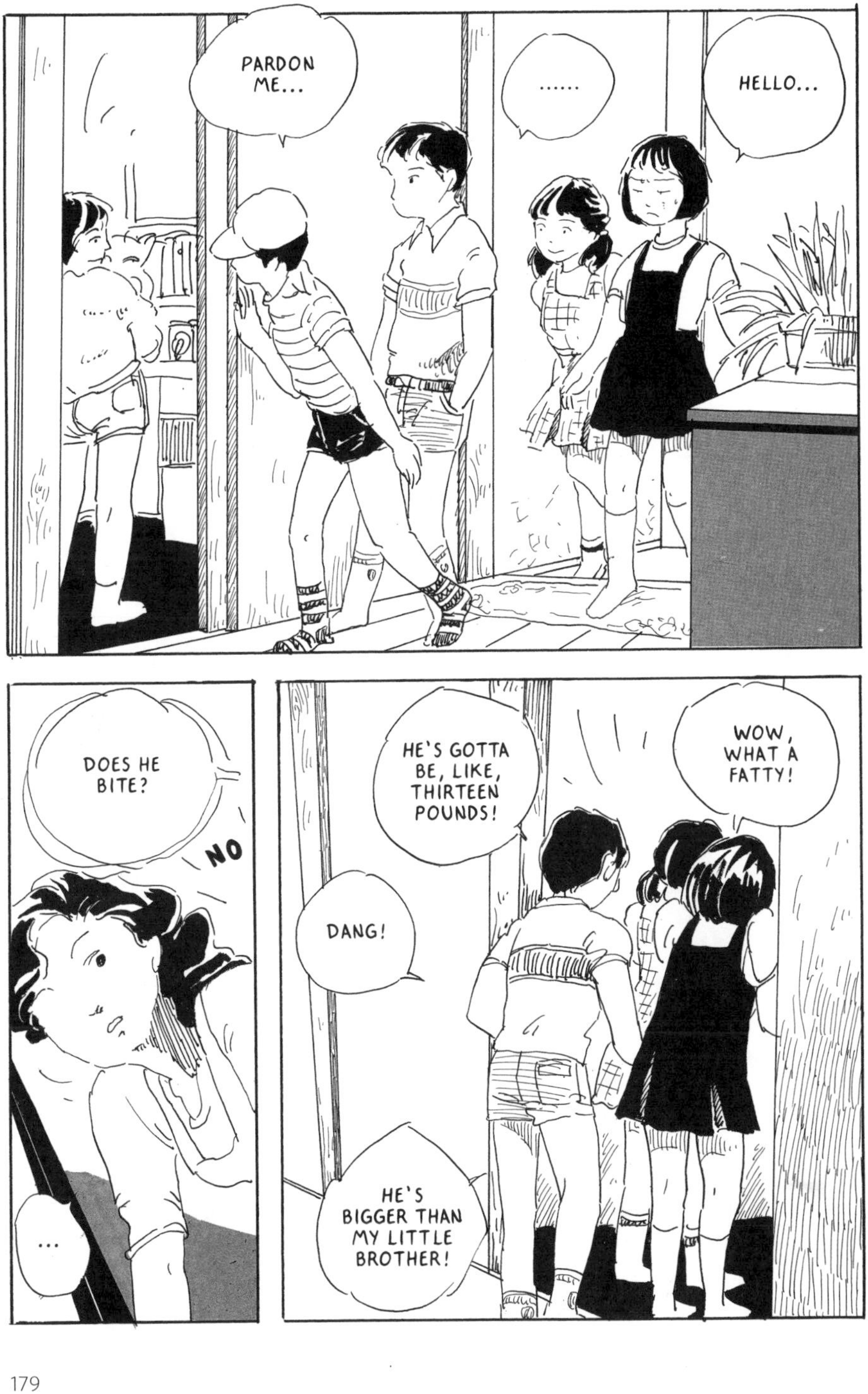
HELLO...
......
PARDON ME...
WOW, WHAT A FATTY!
HE'S GOTTA BE, LIKE, THIRTEEN POUNDS!
DANG!
HE'S BIGGER THAN MY LITTLE BROTHER!
DOES HE BITE?
NO
...

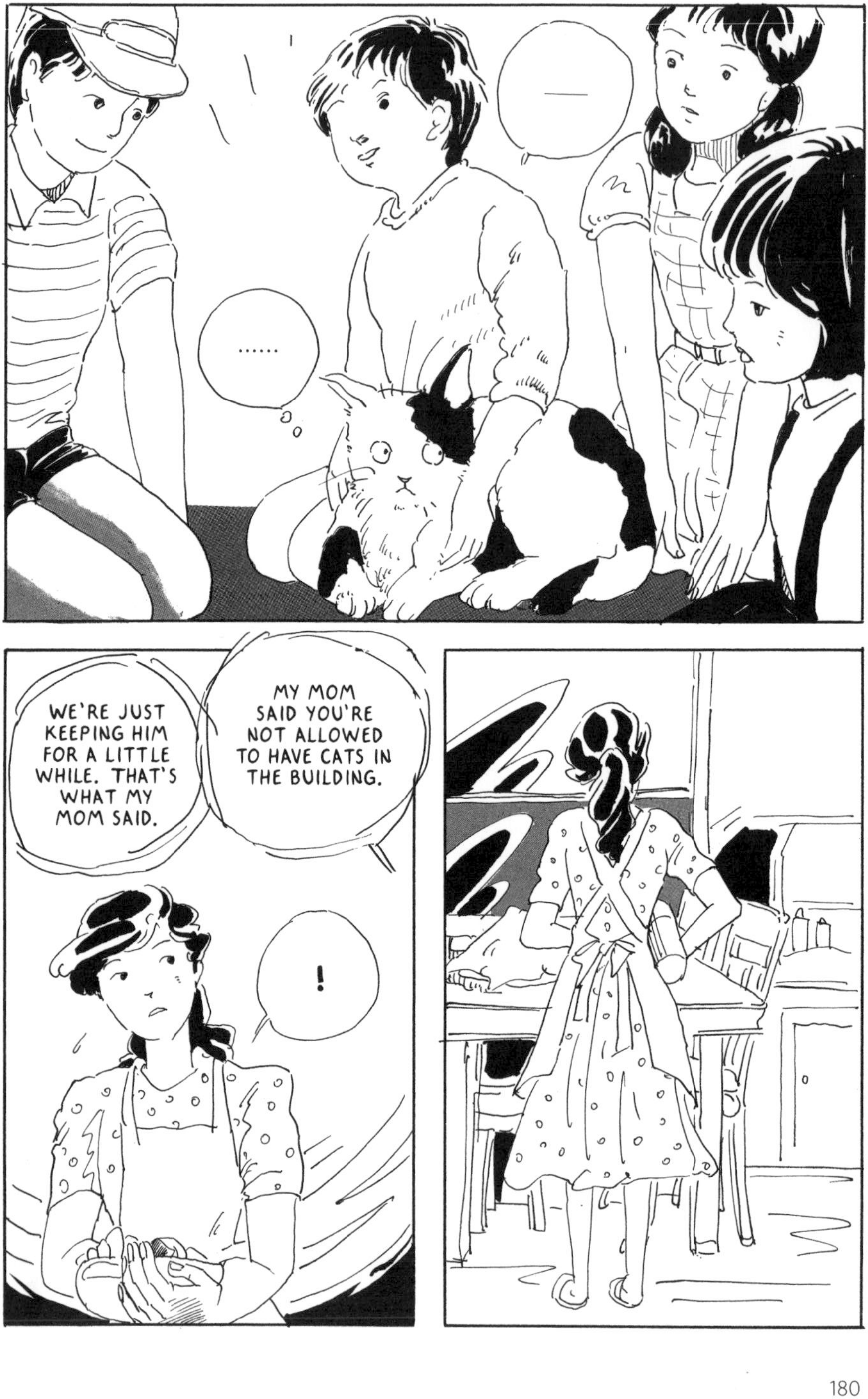
—
......
MY MOM SAID YOU'RE NOT ALLOWED TO HAVE CATS IN THE BUILDING.
WE'RE JUST KEEPING HIM FOR A LITTLE WHILE. THAT'S WHAT MY MOM SAID.
!

KYAAA!!

RICE CRACKERS, ANYONE?

WHAT HAPPENED?!

WHAT WAS THAT?!

OH...

CHIEF WENT OVER TO HER AND SHE FREAKED OUT.

NOOO!

HE'S SCARY

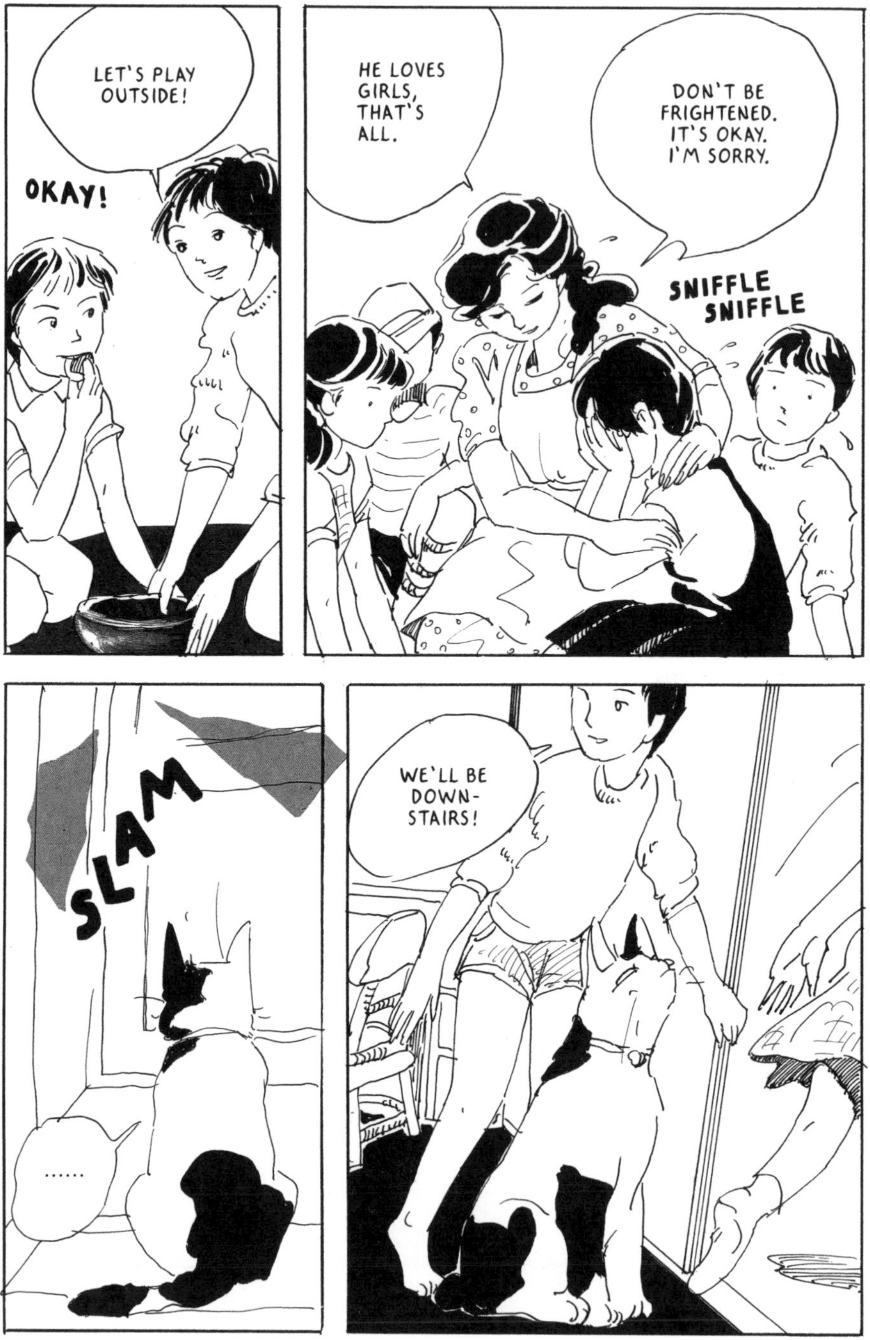
DON'T BE FRIGHTENED. IT'S OKAY. I'M SORRY.
HE LOVES GIRLS, THAT'S ALL.
SNIFFLE SNIFFLE
LET'S PLAY OUTSIDE!
OKAY!
WE'LL BE DOWN-STAIRS!
SLAM
......

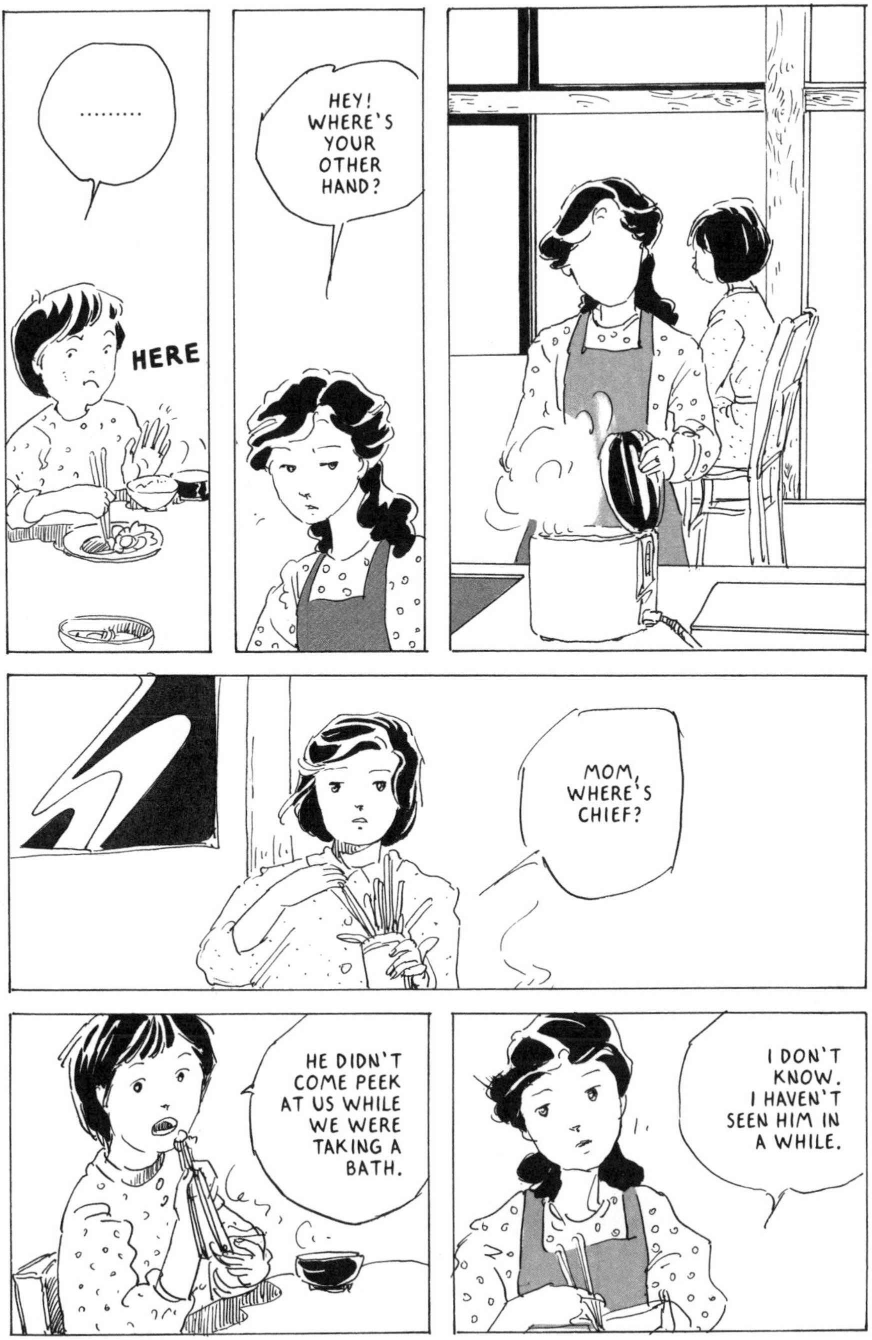
HEY! WHERE'S YOUR OTHER HAND?
....
HERE
MOM, WHERE'S CHIEF?
I DON'T KNOW. I HAVEN'T SEEN HIM IN A WHILE.
HE DIDN'T COME PEEK AT US WHILE WE WERE TAKING A BATH.

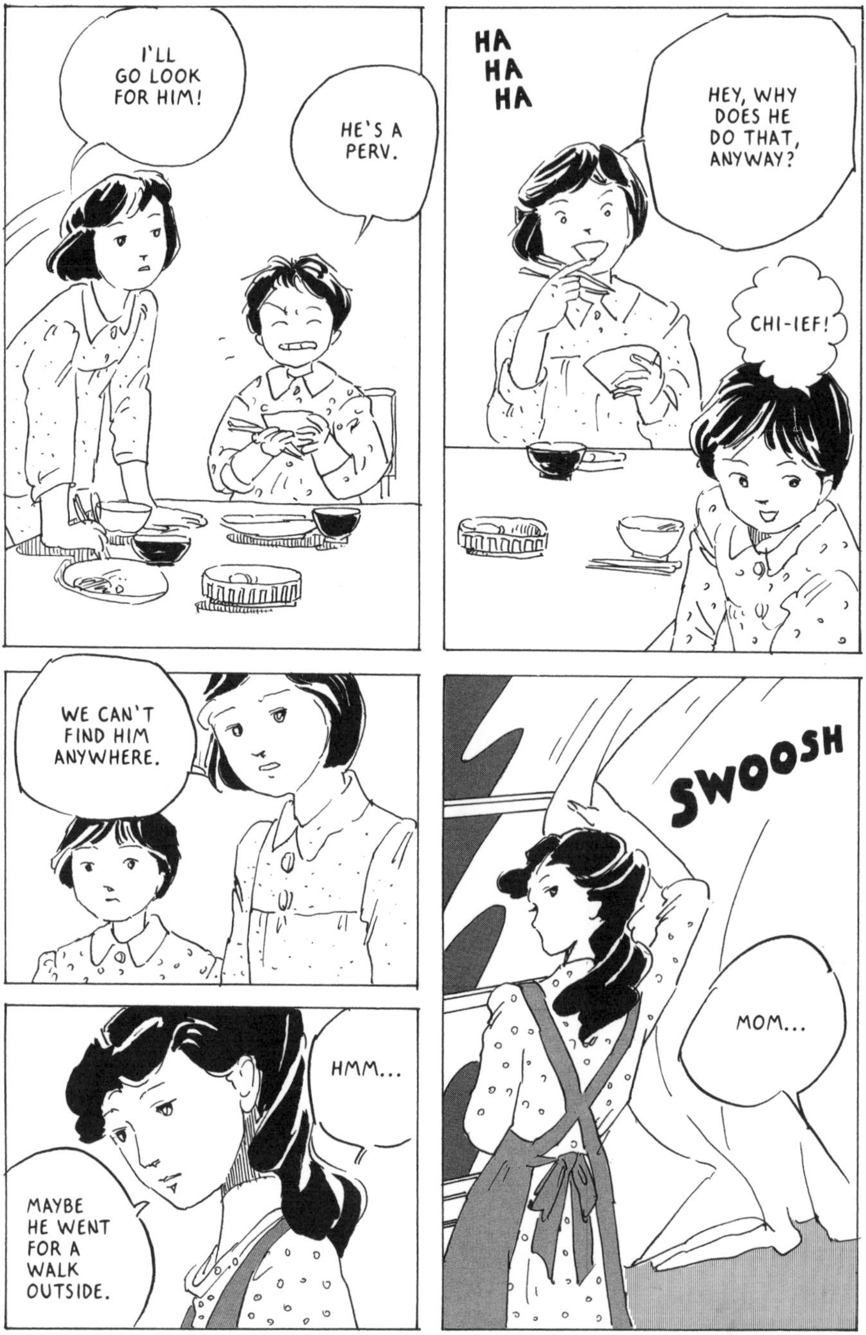
HA
HA
HA
HEY, WHY DOES HE DO THAT, ANYWAY?
CHI-IEF!
HE'S A PERV.
I'LL GO LOOK FOR HIM!
SWOOSH
MOM...
WE CAN'T FIND HIM ANYWHERE.
HMM...
MAYBE HE WENT FOR A WALK OUTSIDE.

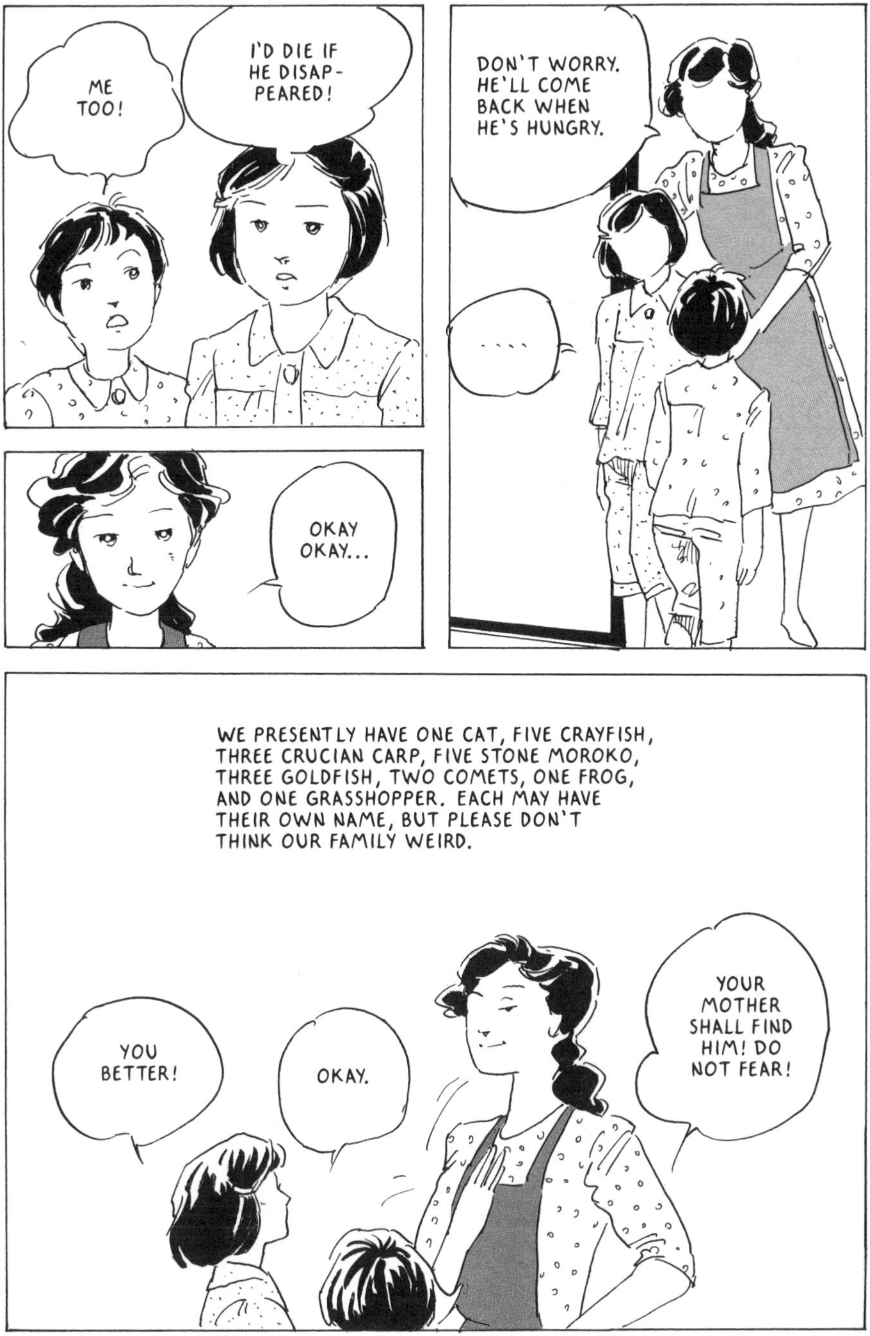

DON'T WORRY. HE'LL COME BACK WHEN HE'S HUNGRY.
....
I'D DIE IF HE DISAP-PEARED!
ME TOO!
OKAY OKAY...
WE PRESENTLY HAVE ONE CAT, FIVE CRAYFISH, THREE CRUCIAN CARP, FIVE STONE MOROKO, THREE GOLDFISH, TWO COMETS, ONE FROG, AND ONE GRASSHOPPER. EACH MAY HAVE THEIR OWN NAME, BUT PLEASE DON'T THINK OUR FAMILY WEIRD.
YOUR MOTHER SHALL FIND HIM! DO NOT FEAR!
OKAY.
YOU BETTER!

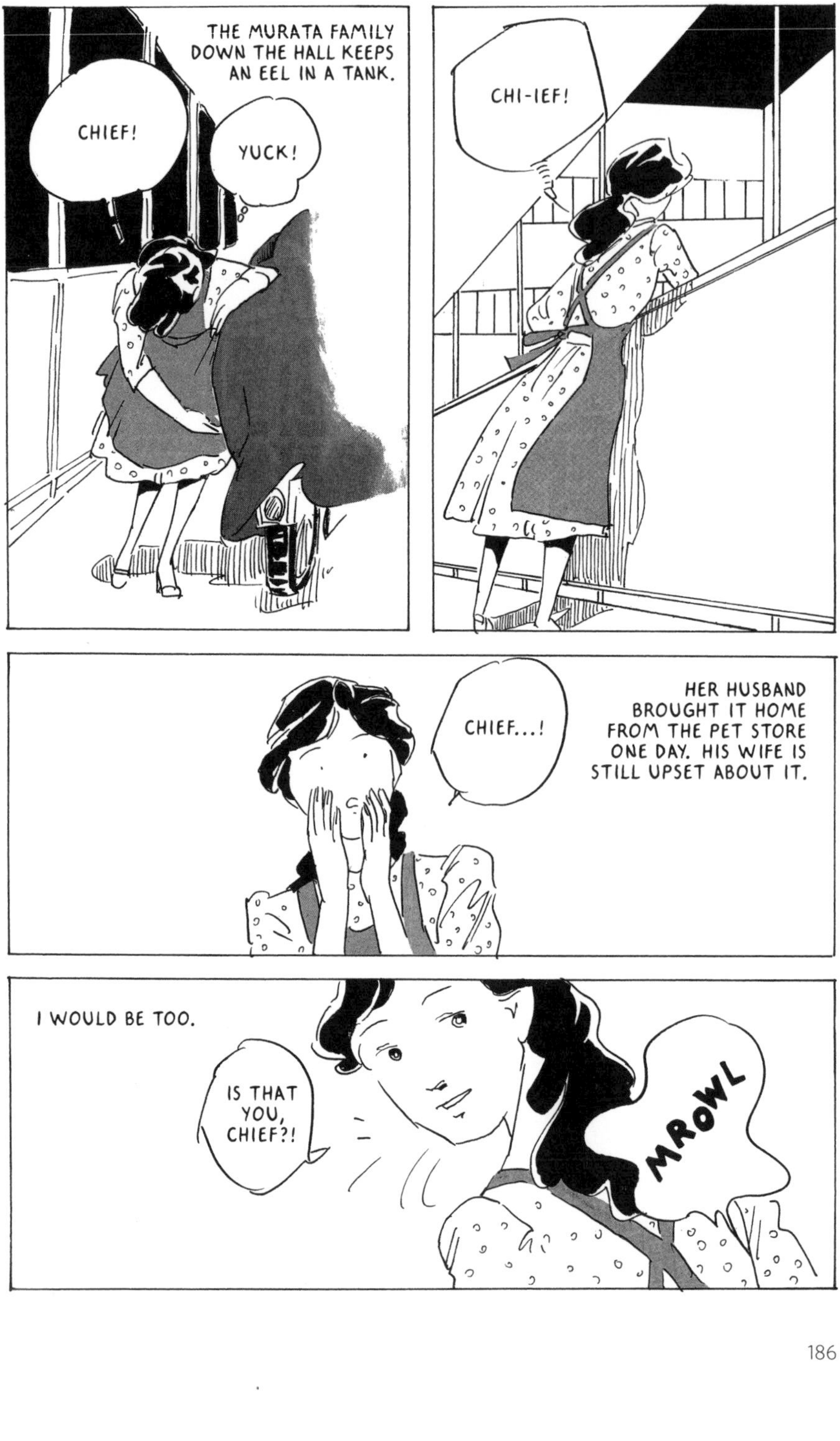
CHI-IEF!
THE MURATA FAMILY DOWN THE HALL KEEPS AN EEL IN A TANK.
YUCK!
CHIEF!
HER HUSBAND BROUGHT IT HOME FROM THE PET STORE ONE DAY. HIS WIFE IS STILL UPSET ABOUT IT.
CHIEF...!
I WOULD BE TOO.
MROWL
IS THAT YOU, CHIEF?!

Freedom's Curtain

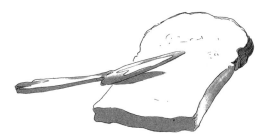

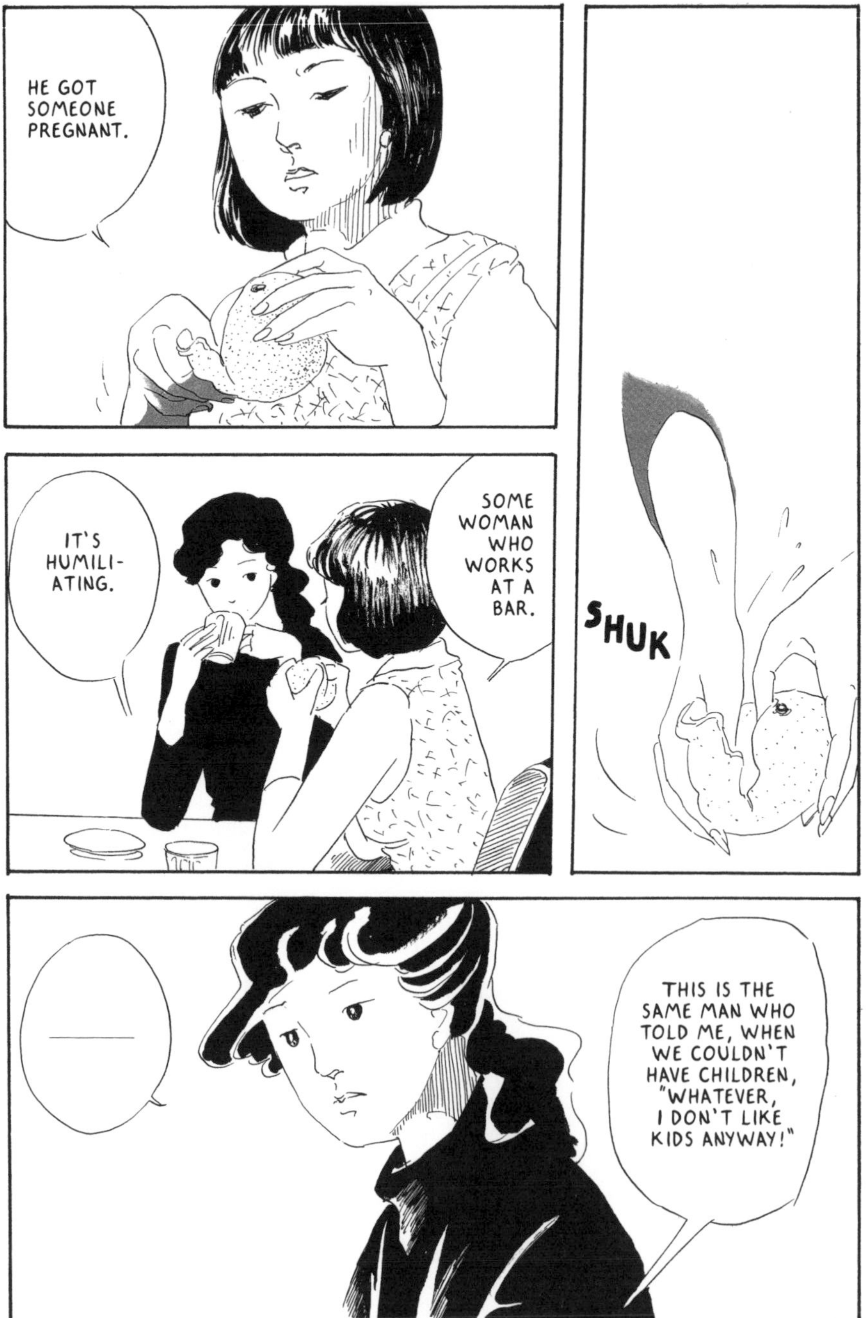
SHUK
HE GOT SOMEONE PREGNANT.
SOME WOMAN WHO WORKS AT A BAR.
IT'S HUMILI-ATING.
THIS IS THE SAME MAN WHO TOLD ME, WHEN WE COULDN'T HAVE CHILDREN, "WHATEVER, I DON'T LIKE KIDS ANYWAY!"
——

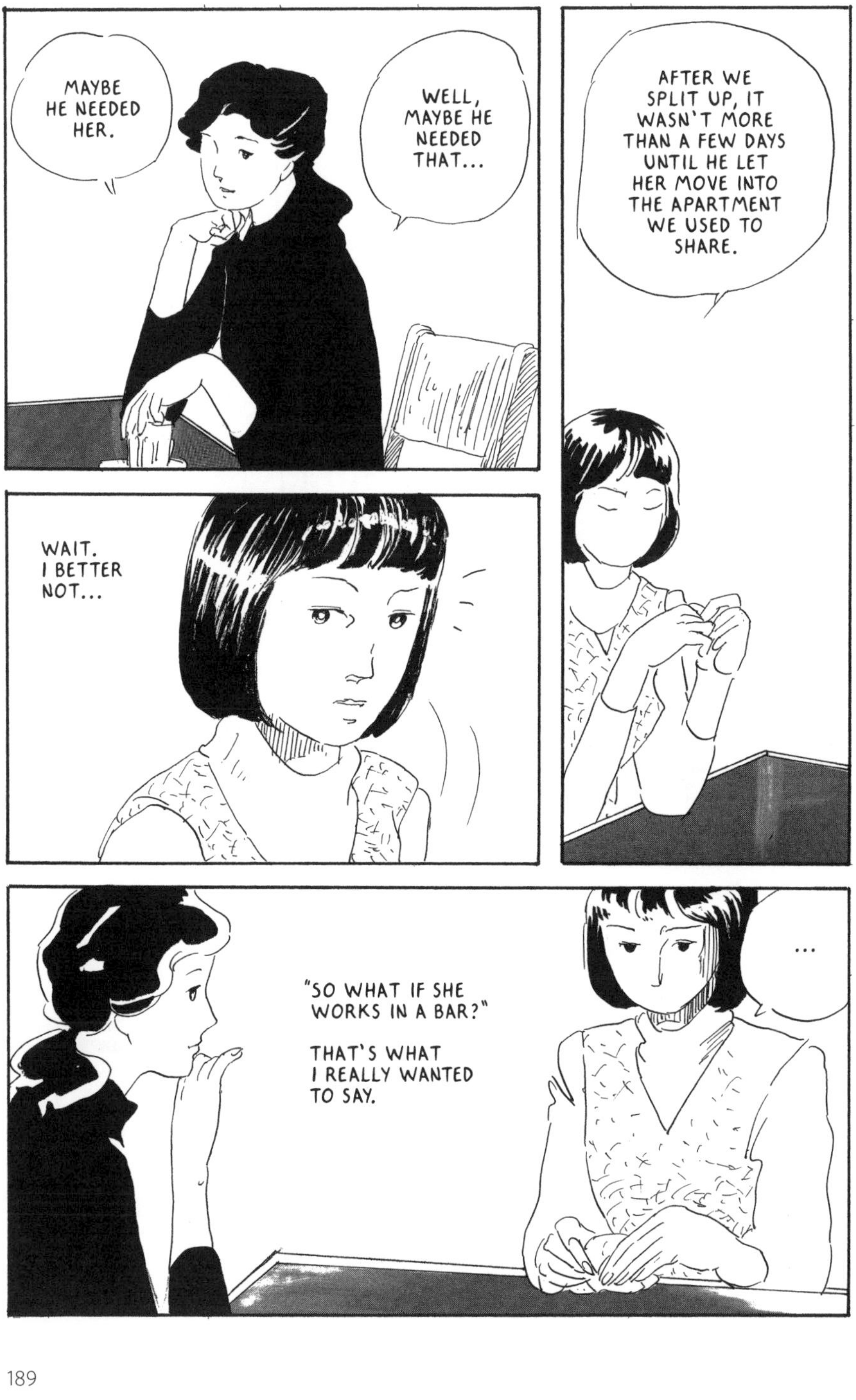
AFTER WE SPLIT UP, IT WASN'T MORE THAN A FEW DAYS UNTIL HE LET HER MOVE INTO THE APARTMENT WE USED TO SHARE.
WELL, MAYBE HE NEEDED THAT...
MAYBE HE NEEDED HER.
WAIT. I BETTER NOT...
...
"SO WHAT IF SHE WORKS IN A BAR?"
THAT'S WHAT I REALLY WANTED TO SAY.

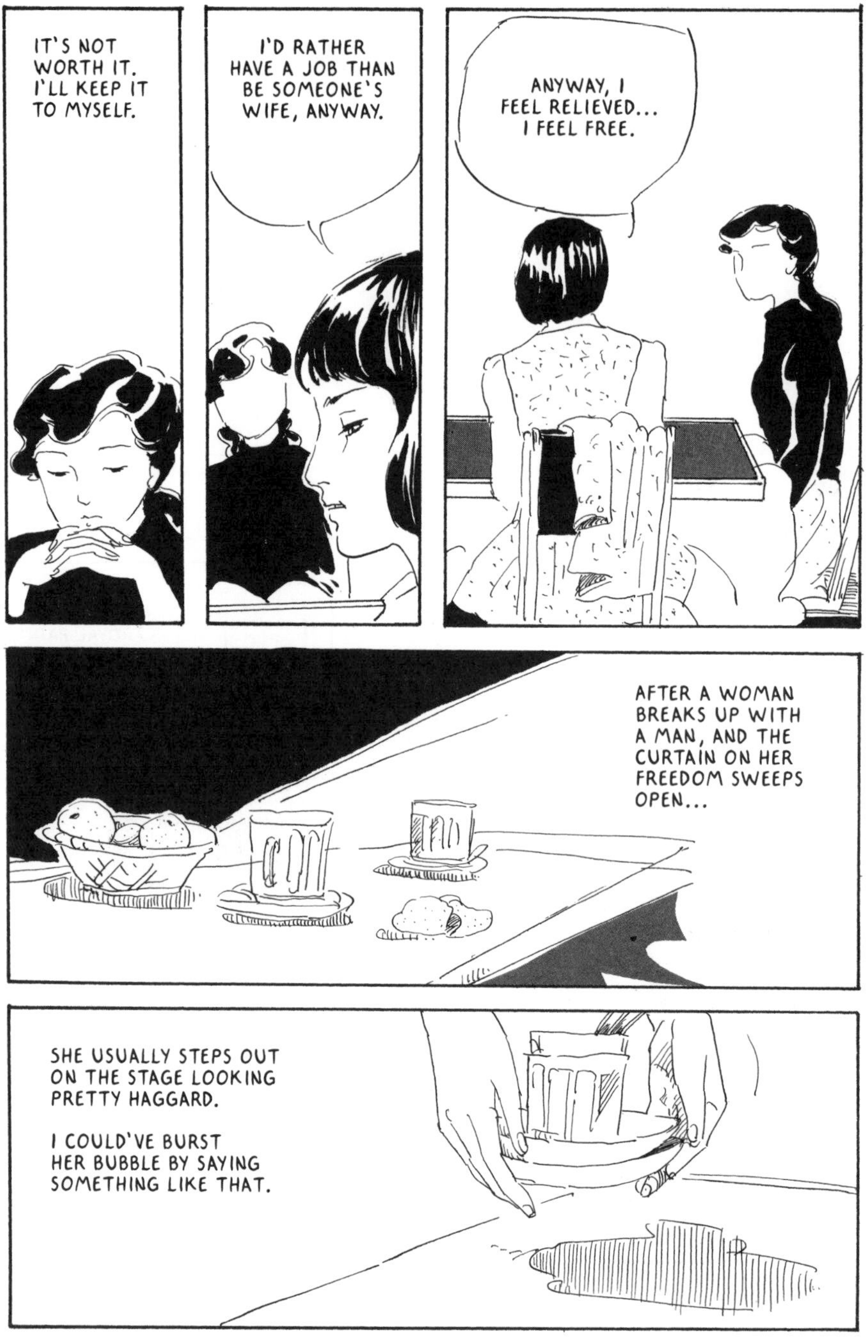
ANYWAY, I FEEL RELIEVED... I FEEL FREE.
I'D RATHER HAVE A JOB THAN BE SOMEONE'S WIFE, ANYWAY.
IT'S NOT WORTH IT. I'LL KEEP IT TO MYSELF.
AFTER A WOMAN BREAKS UP WITH A MAN, AND THE CURTAIN ON HER FREEDOM SWEEPS OPEN...
SHE USUALLY STEPS OUT ON THE STAGE LOOKING PRETTY HAGGARD.
I COULD'VE BURST HER BUBBLE BY SAYING SOMETHING LIKE THAT.

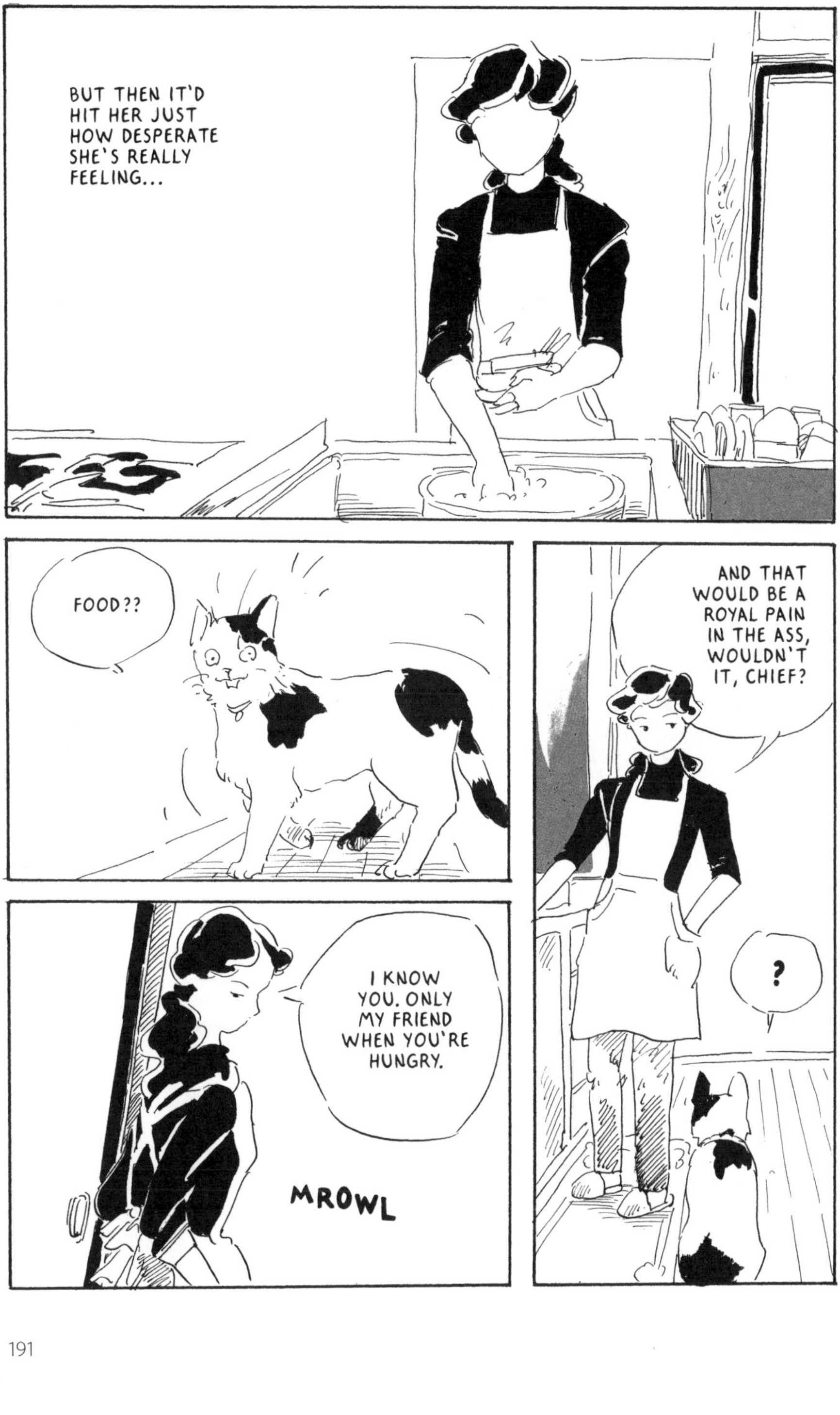
BUT THEN IT'D HIT HER JUST HOW DESPERATE SHE'S REALLY FEELING...
AND THAT WOULD BE A ROYAL PAIN IN THE ASS, WOULDN'T IT, CHIEF?
?
FOOD??
I KNOW YOU. ONLY MY FRIEND WHEN YOU'RE HUNGRY.
MROWL

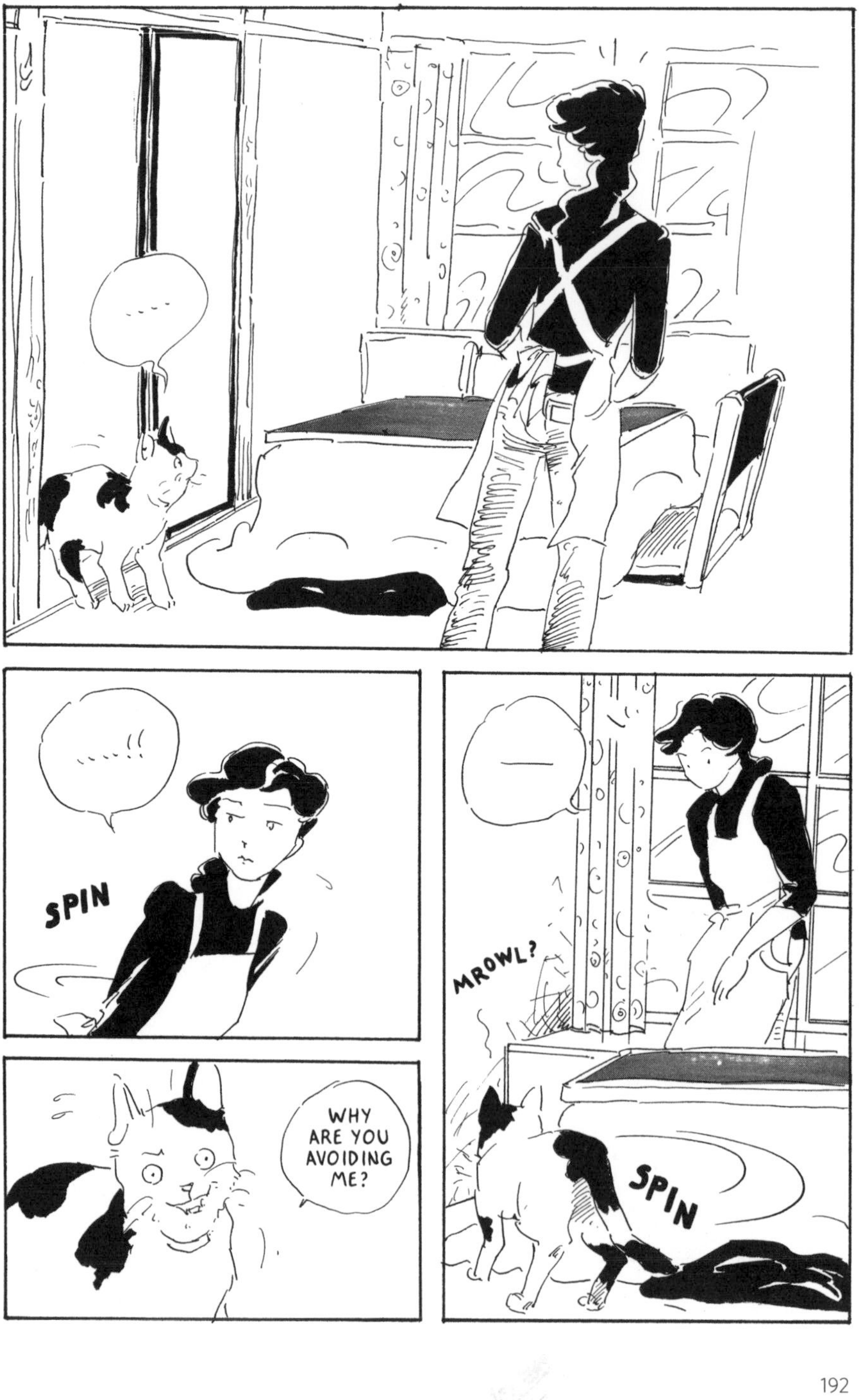
MROWL?
SPIN
SPIN
WHY ARE YOU AVOIDING ME?

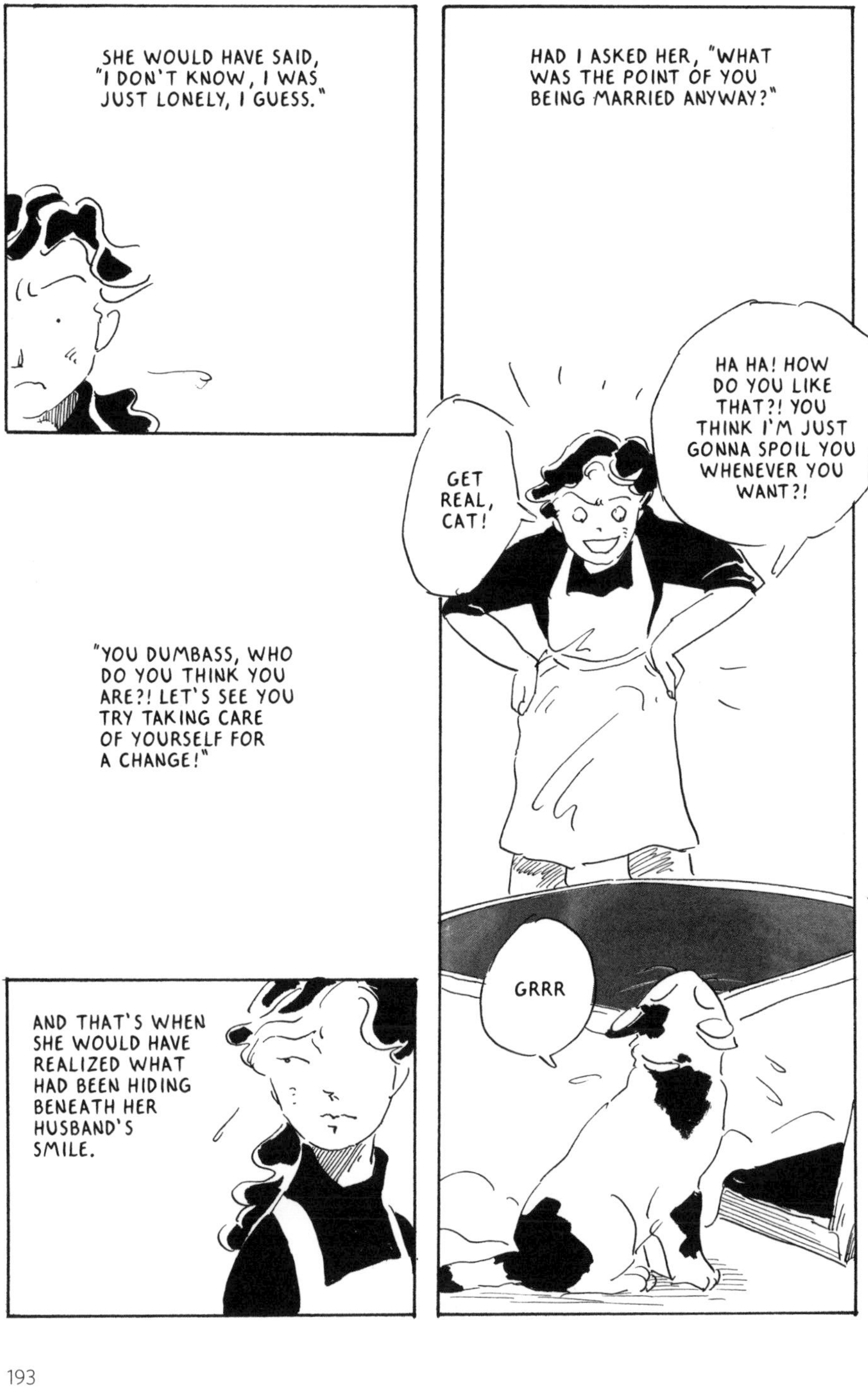
HAD I ASKED HER, "WHAT WAS THE POINT OF YOU BEING MARRIED ANYWAY?"
HA HA! HOW DO YOU LIKE THAT?! YOU THINK I'M JUST GONNA SPOIL YOU WHENEVER YOU WANT?!
GET REAL, CAT!
SHE WOULD HAVE SAID, "I DON'T KNOW, I WAS JUST LONELY, I GUESS."
"YOU DUMBASS, WHO DO YOU THINK YOU ARE?! LET'S SEE YOU TRY TAKING CARE OF YOURSELF FOR A CHANGE!"
GRRR
AND THAT'S WHEN SHE WOULD HAVE REALIZED WHAT HAD BEEN HIDING BENEATH HER HUSBAND'S SMILE.

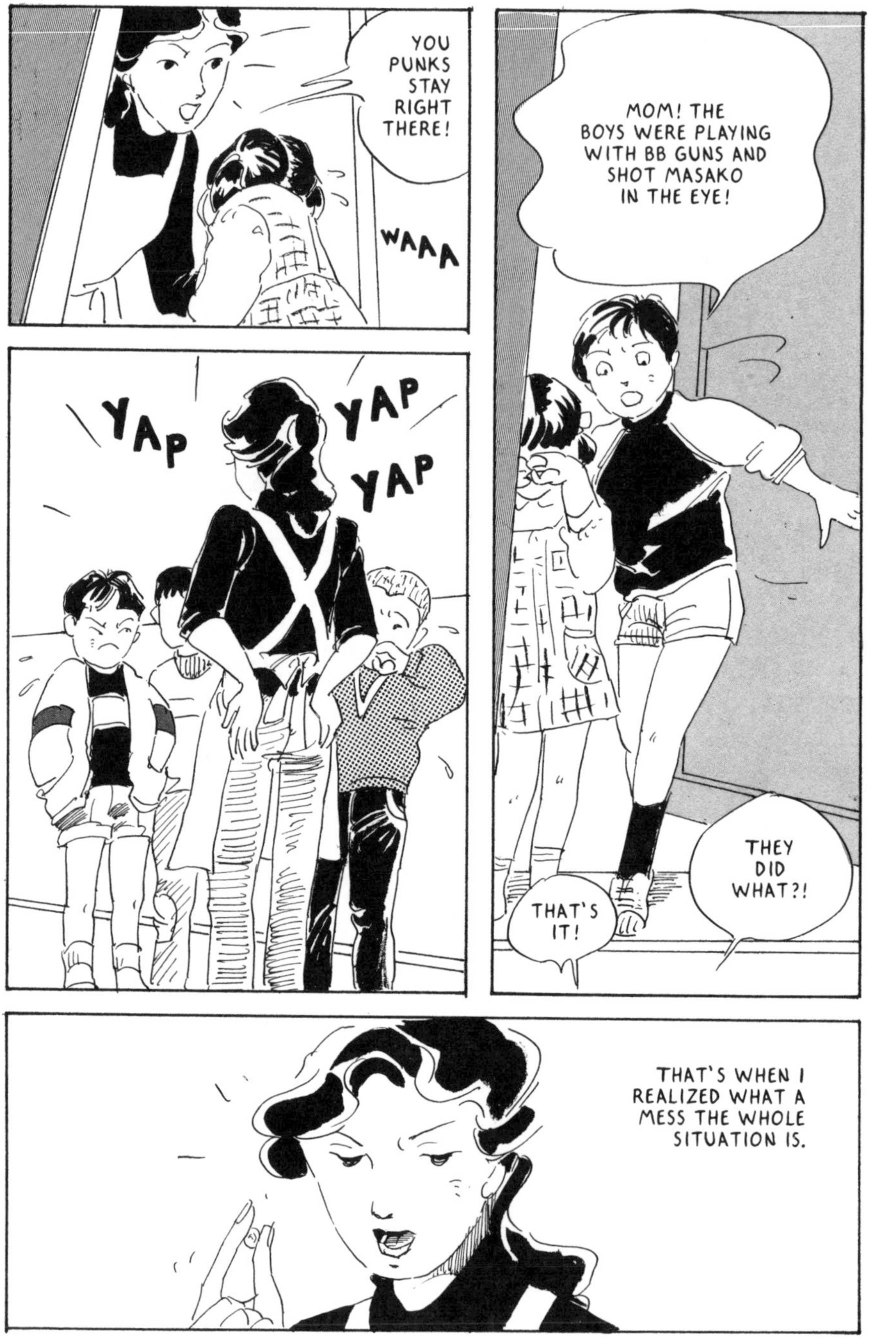
MOM! THE BOYS WERE PLAYING WITH BB GUNS AND SHOT MASAKO IN THE EYE!
THEY DID WHAT?!
THAT'S IT!
YOU PUNKS STAY RIGHT THERE!
WAAA
YAP
YAP
YAP
THAT'S WHEN I REALIZED WHAT A MESS THE WHOLE SITUATION IS.

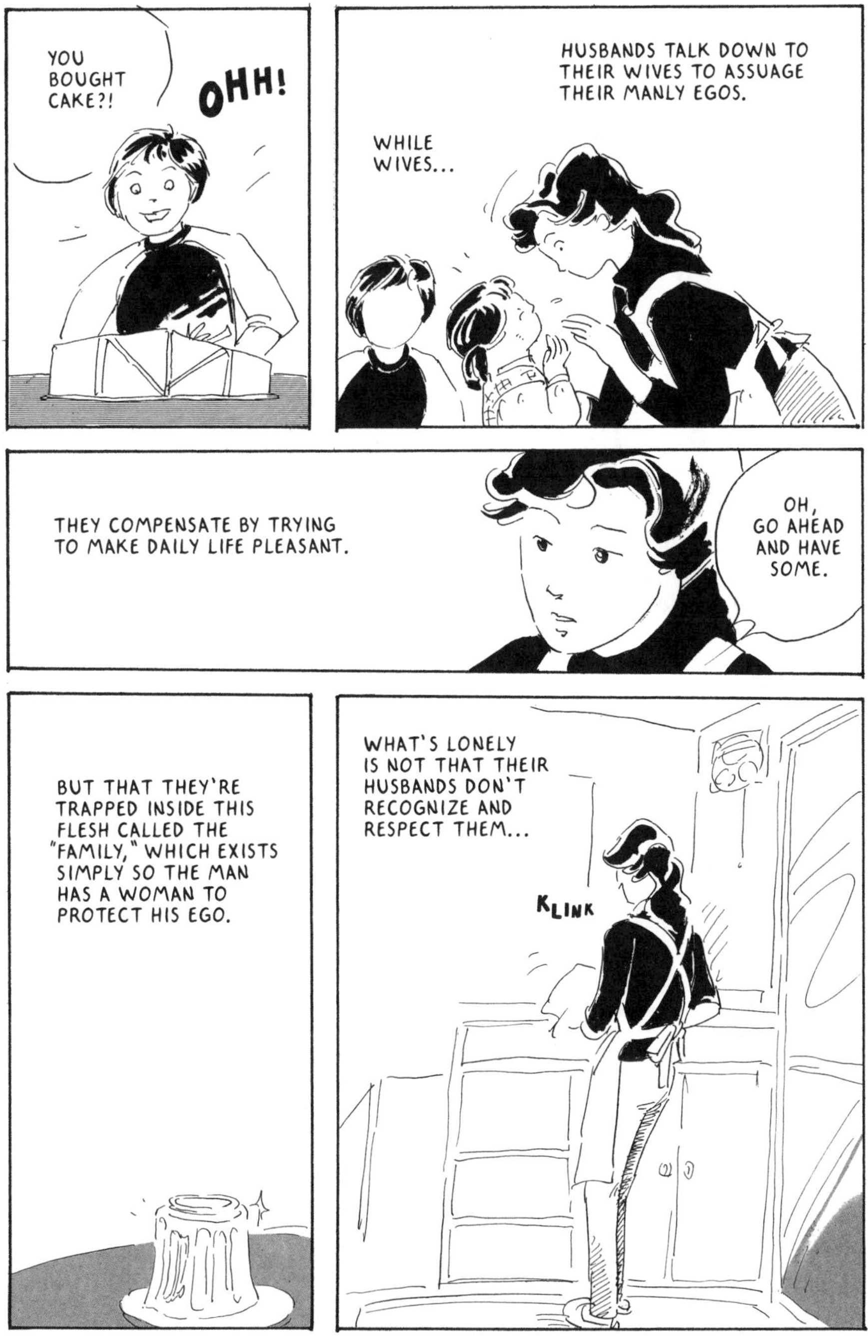
HUSBANDS TALK DOWN TO THEIR WIVES TO ASSUAGE THEIR MANLY EGOS.
WHILE WIVES...
OHH!
YOU BOUGHT CAKE?!
OH, GO AHEAD AND HAVE SOME.
THEY COMPENSATE BY TRYING TO MAKE DAILY LIFE PLEASANT.
WHAT'S LONELY IS NOT THAT THEIR HUSBANDS DON'T RECOGNIZE AND RESPECT THEM...
KLINK
BUT THAT THEY'RE TRAPPED INSIDE THIS FLESH CALLED THE "FAMILY," WHICH EXISTS SIMPLY SO THE MAN HAS A WOMAN TO PROTECT HIS EGO.

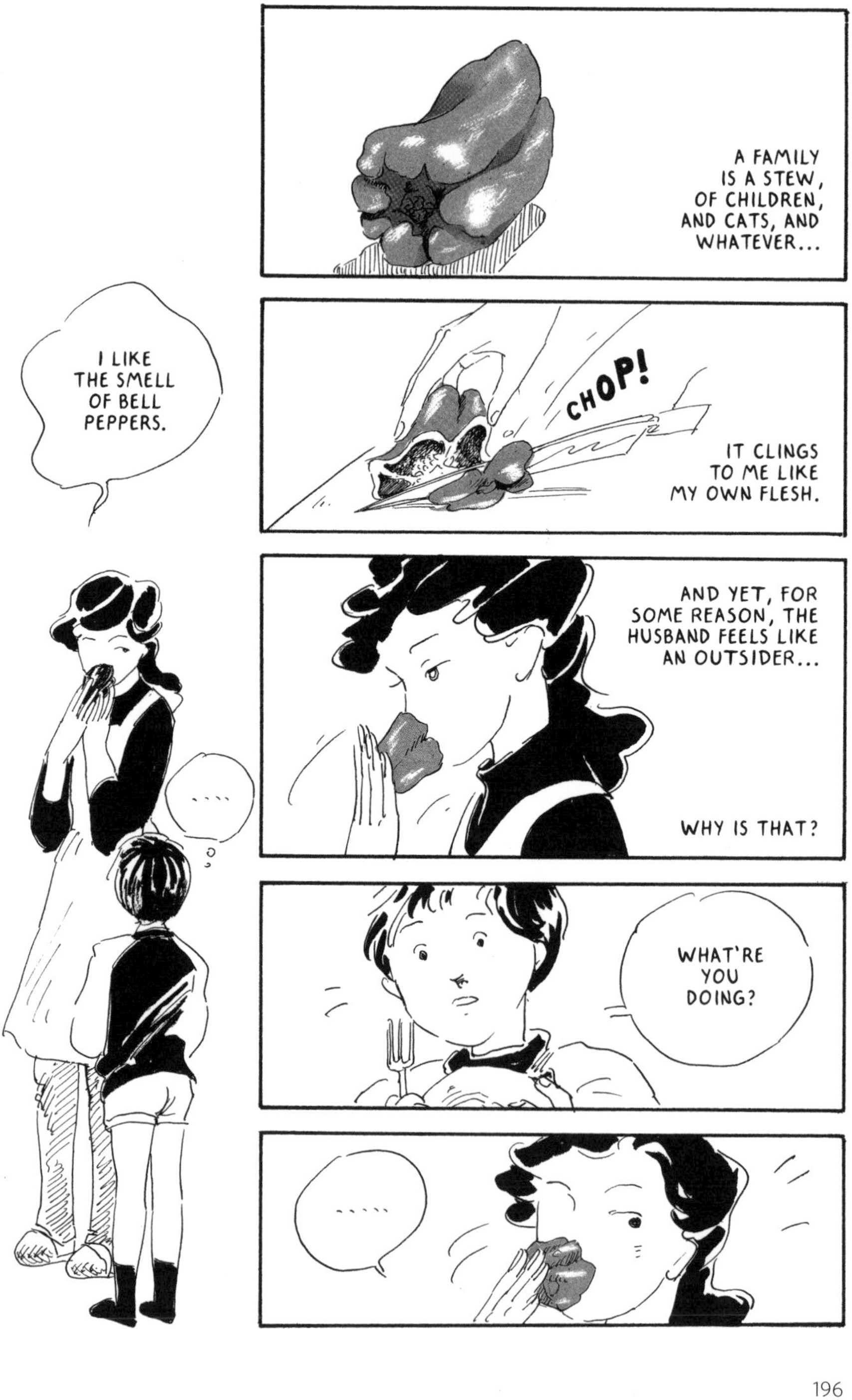
A FAMILY IS A STEW, OF CHILDREN, AND CATS, AND WHATEVER...
CHOP!
IT CLINGS TO ME LIKE MY OWN FLESH.
AND YET, FOR SOME REASON, THE HUSBAND FEELS LIKE AN OUTSIDER...
WHY IS THAT?
WHAT'RE YOU DOING?
.....
I LIKE THE SMELL OF BELL PEPPERS.
....

Santa Claus

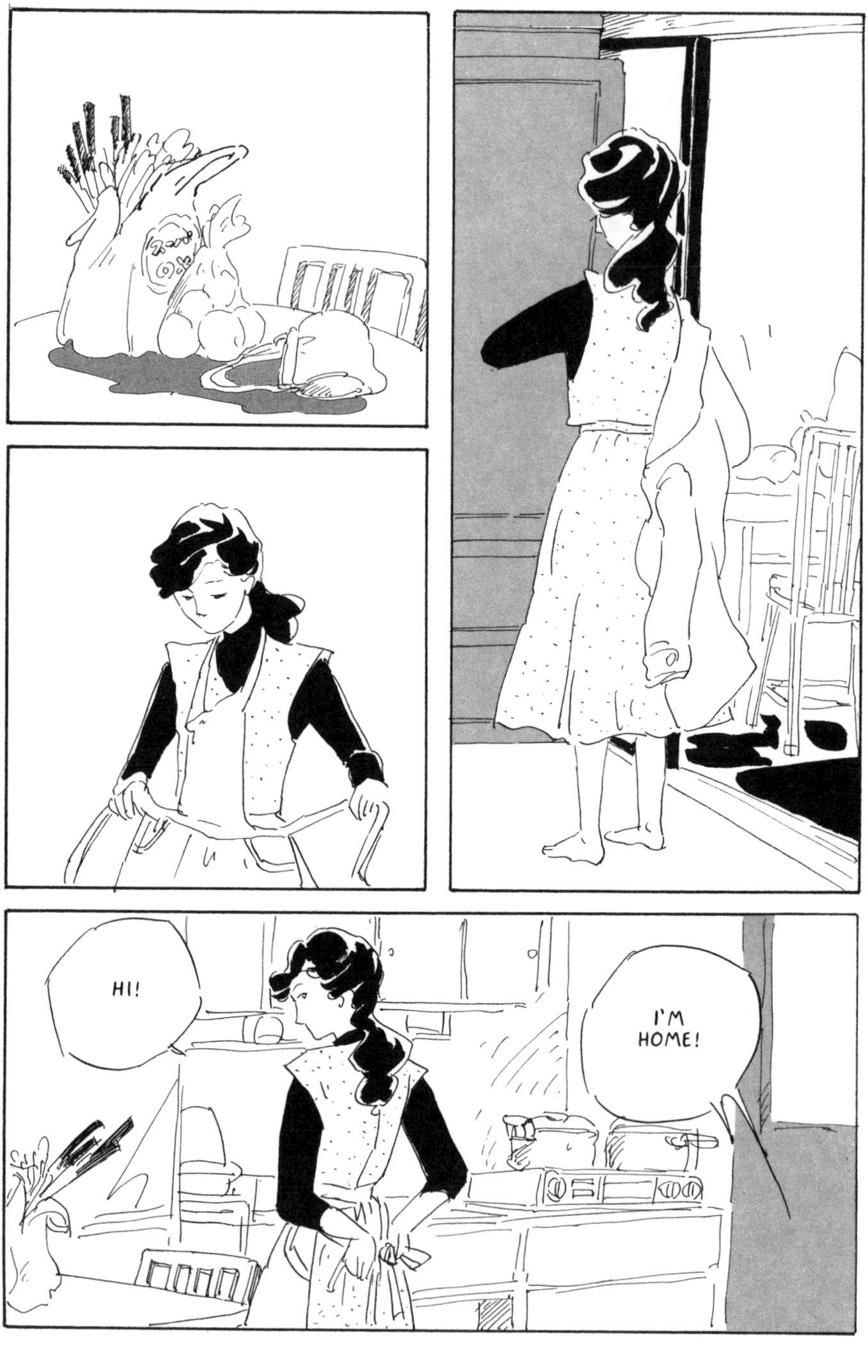
I'M HOME!
HI!

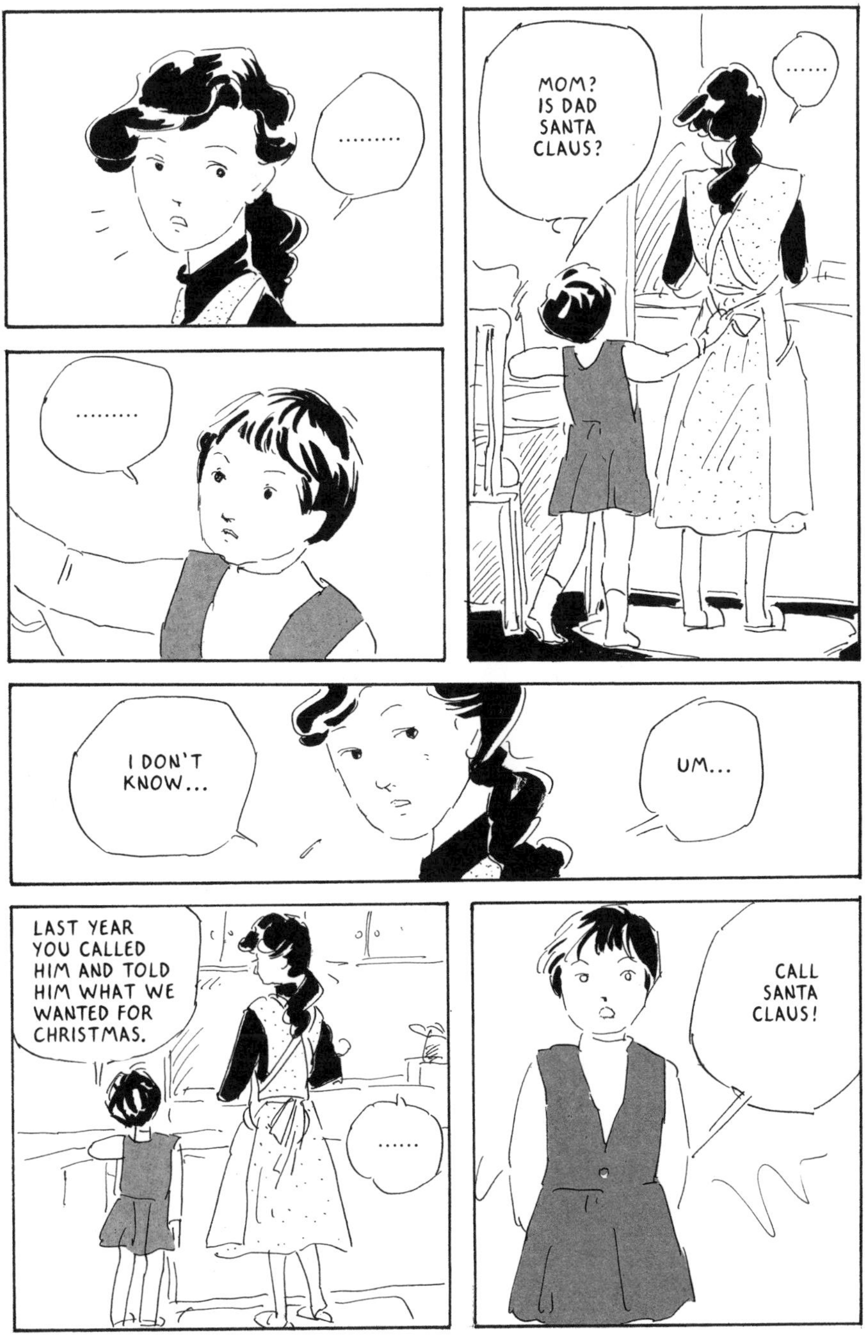

......
MOM? IS DAD SANTA CLAUS?
....
....
UM...
I DON'T KNOW...
CALL SANTA CLAUS!
LAST YEAR YOU CALLED HIM AND TOLD HIM WHAT WE WANTED FOR CHRISTMAS.
......

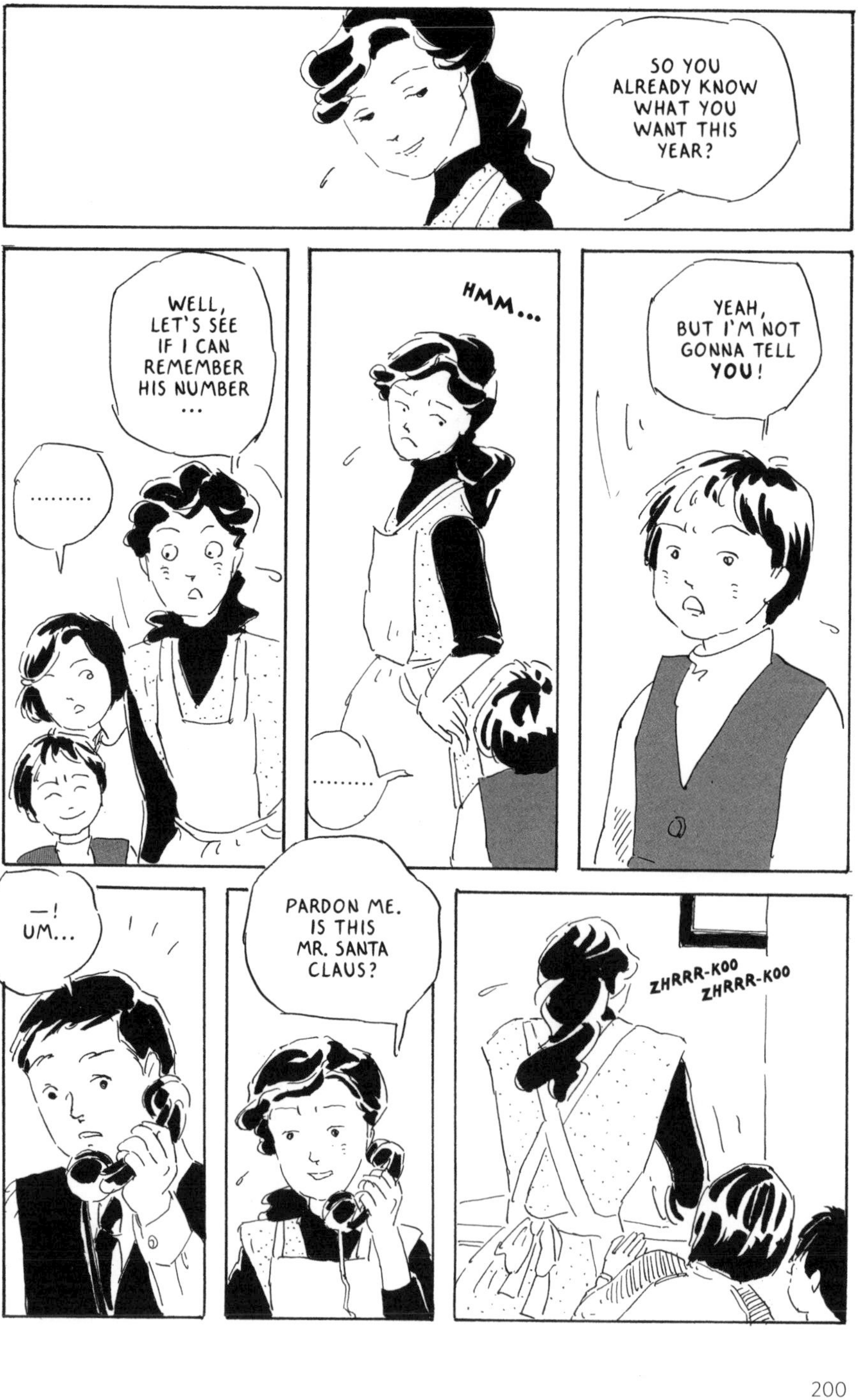
SO YOU ALREADY KNOW WHAT YOU WANT THIS YEAR?
YEAH, BUT I'M NOT GONNA TELL **YOU**!
HMM...
....
WELL, LET'S SEE IF I CAN REMEMBER HIS NUMBER ...
....
ZHRRR-KOO
ZHRRR-KOO
PARDON ME. IS THIS MR. SANTA CLAUS?
—! UM...

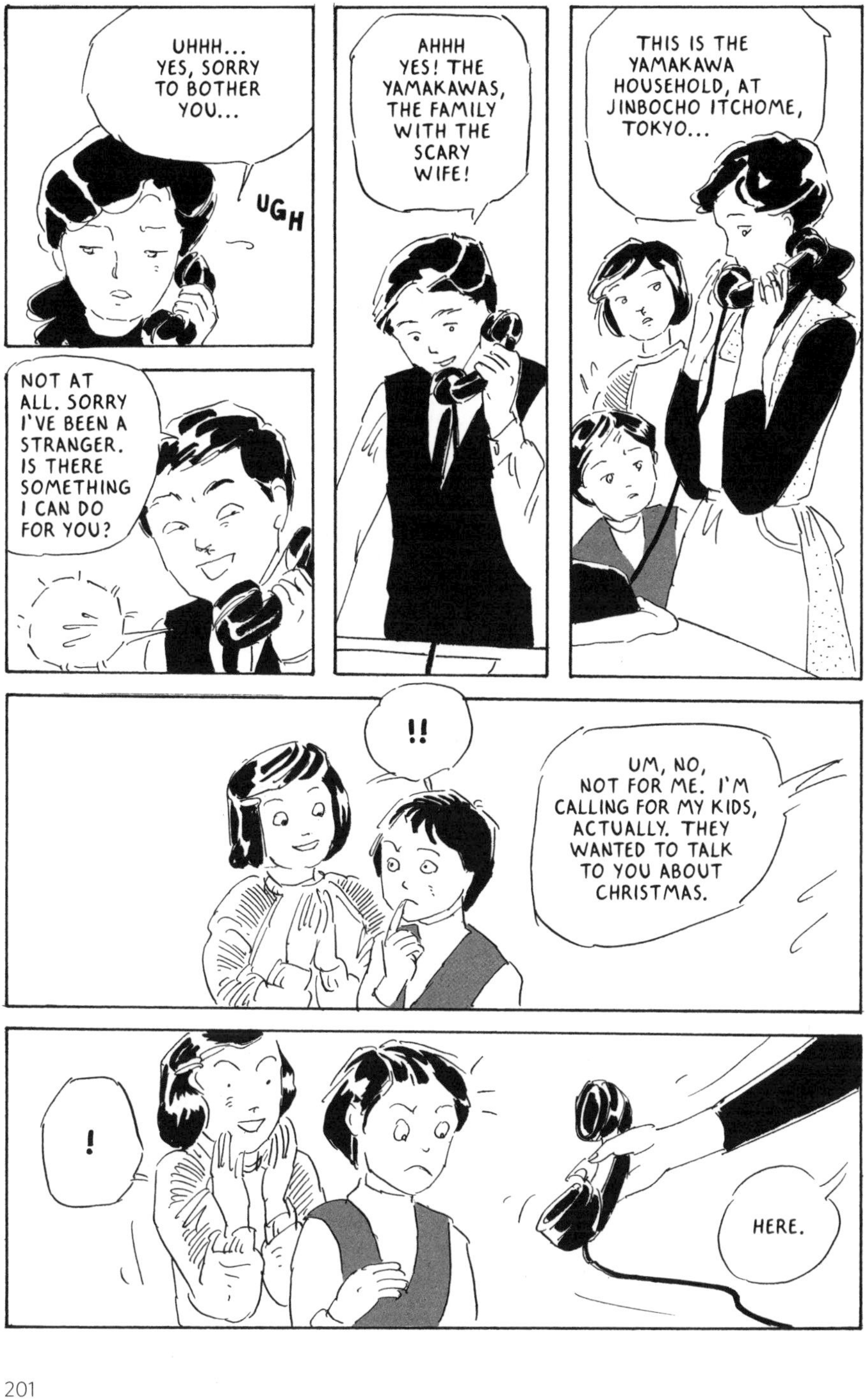
THIS IS THE YAMAKAWA HOUSEHOLD, AT JINBOCHO ITCHOME, TOKYO...
AHHH YES! THE YAMAKAWAS, THE FAMILY WITH THE SCARY WIFE!
UHHH... YES, SORRY TO BOTHER YOU...
UGH
NOT AT ALL. SORRY I'VE BEEN A STRANGER. IS THERE SOMETHING I CAN DO FOR YOU?
UM, NO, NOT FOR ME. I'M CALLING FOR MY KIDS, ACTUALLY. THEY WANTED TO TALK TO YOU ABOUT CHRISTMAS.
!!
HERE.
!

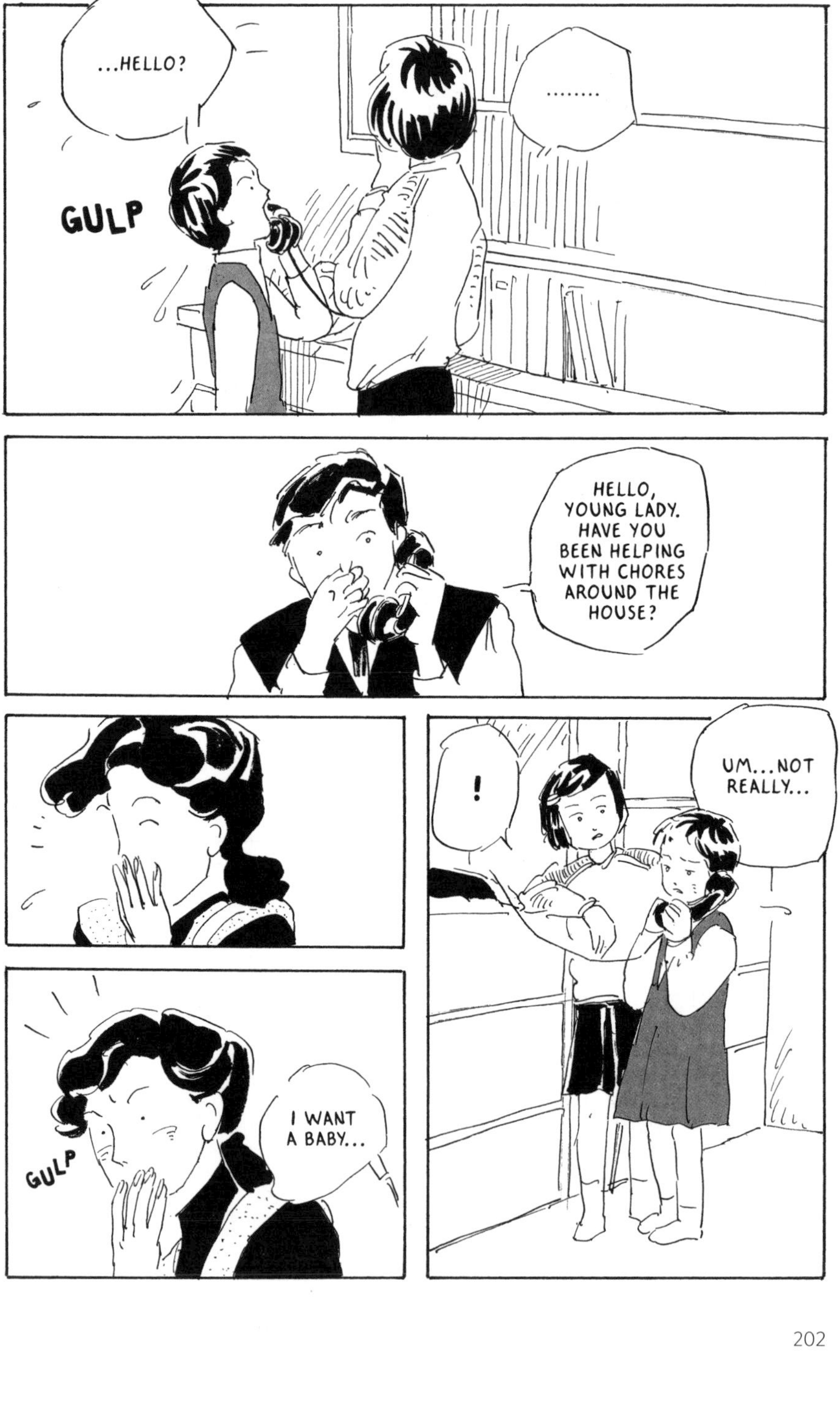
....
...HELLO?
GULP
HELLO, YOUNG LADY. HAVE YOU BEEN HELPING WITH CHORES AROUND THE HOUSE?
UM...NOT REALLY...
!
I WANT A BABY...
GULP

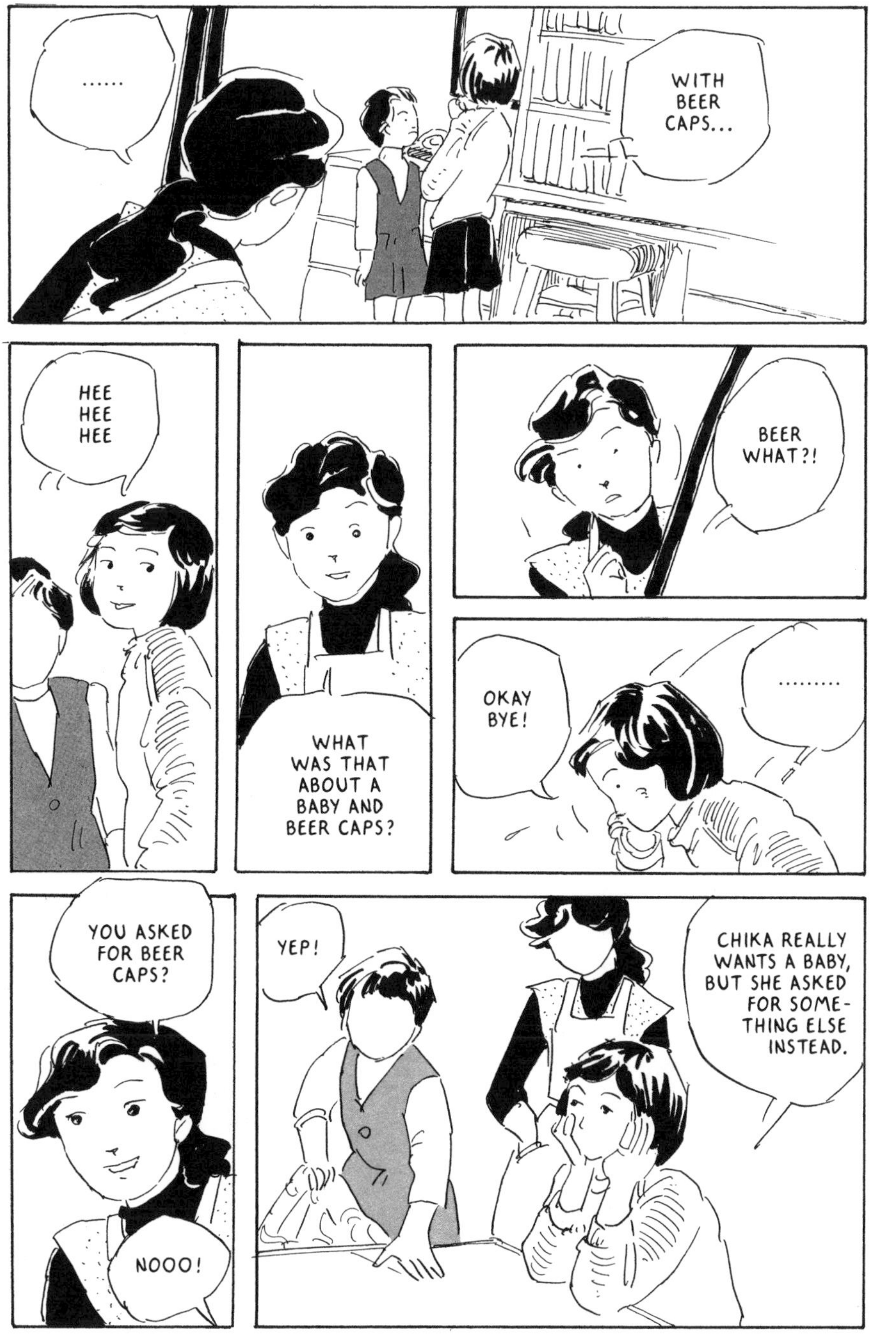
WITH BEER CAPS...
......
BEER WHAT?!
....
OKAY BYE!
WHAT WAS THAT ABOUT A BABY AND BEER CAPS?
HEE HEE HEE
CHIKA REALLY WANTS A BABY, BUT SHE ASKED FOR SOMETHING ELSE INSTEAD.
YEP!
YOU ASKED FOR BEER CAPS?
NOOO!

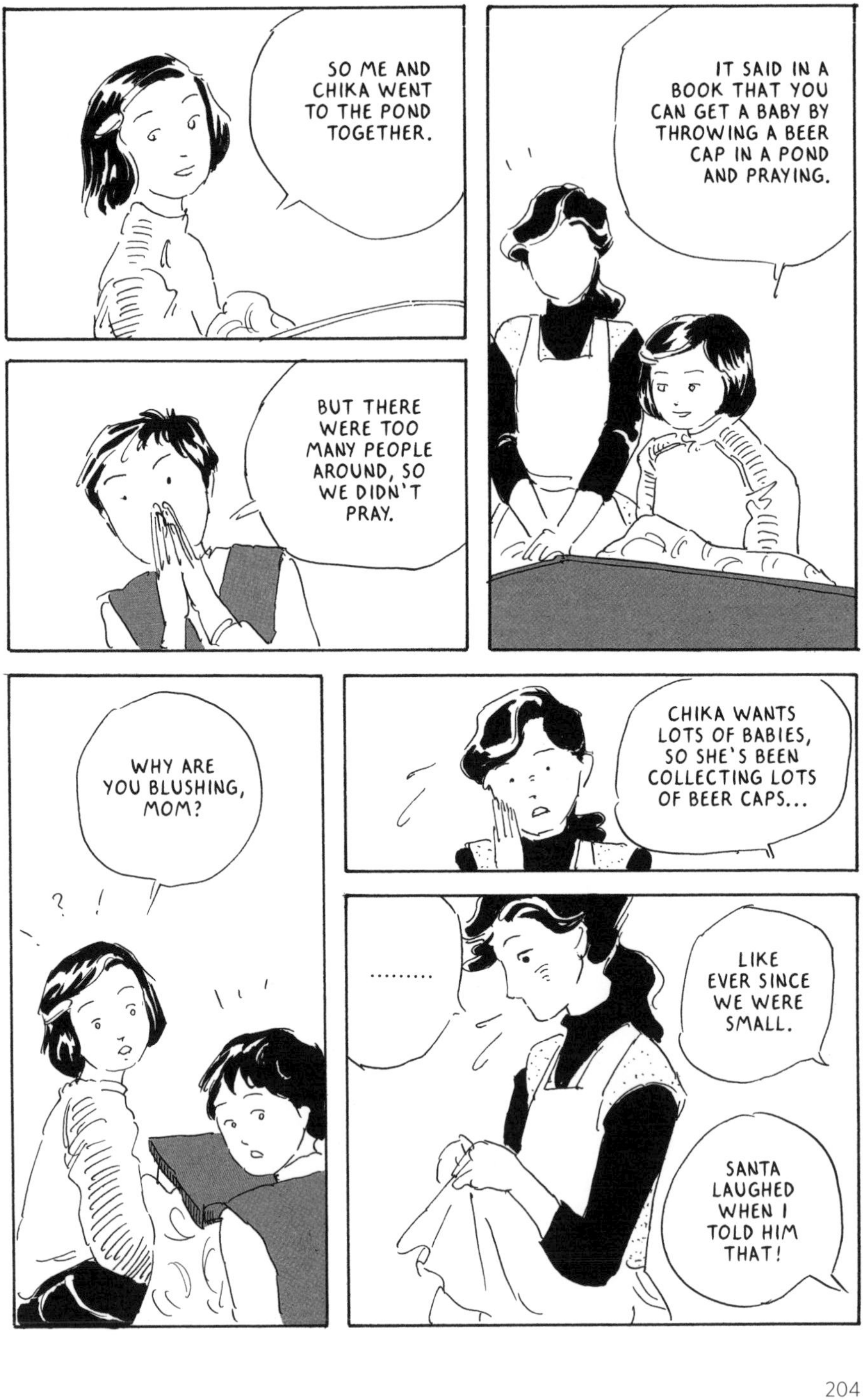
IT SAID IN A BOOK THAT YOU CAN GET A BABY BY THROWING A BEER CAP IN A POND AND PRAYING.
SO ME AND CHIKA WENT TO THE POND TOGETHER.
BUT THERE WERE TOO MANY PEOPLE AROUND, SO WE DIDN'T PRAY.
CHIKA WANTS LOTS OF BABIES, SO SHE'S BEEN COLLECTING LOTS OF BEER CAPS...
LIKE EVER SINCE WE WERE SMALL.
....
SANTA LAUGHED WHEN I TOLD HIM THAT!
WHY ARE YOU BLUSHING, MOM?
? !

Snowy Day

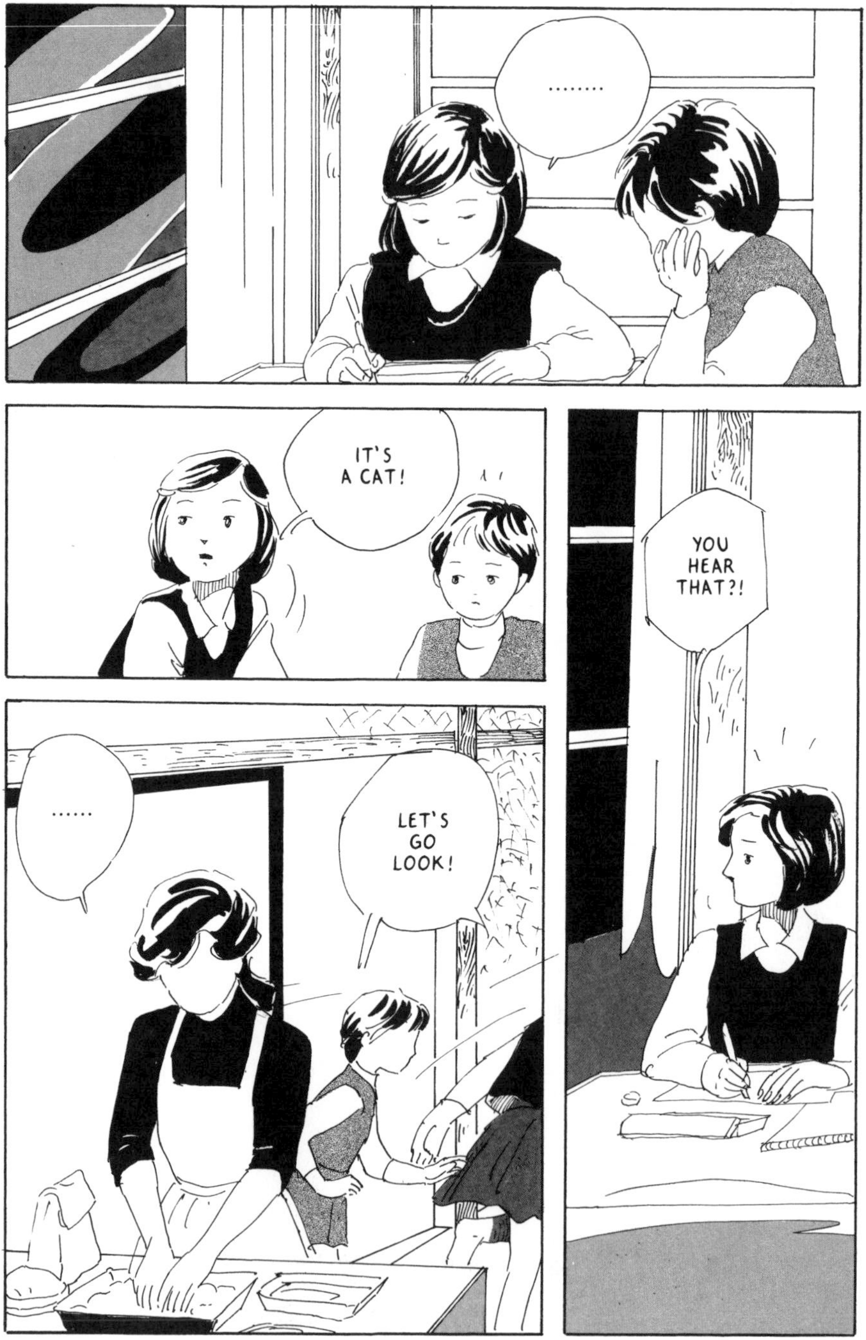
....
YOU HEAR THAT?!
IT'S A CAT!
LET'S GO LOOK!
......

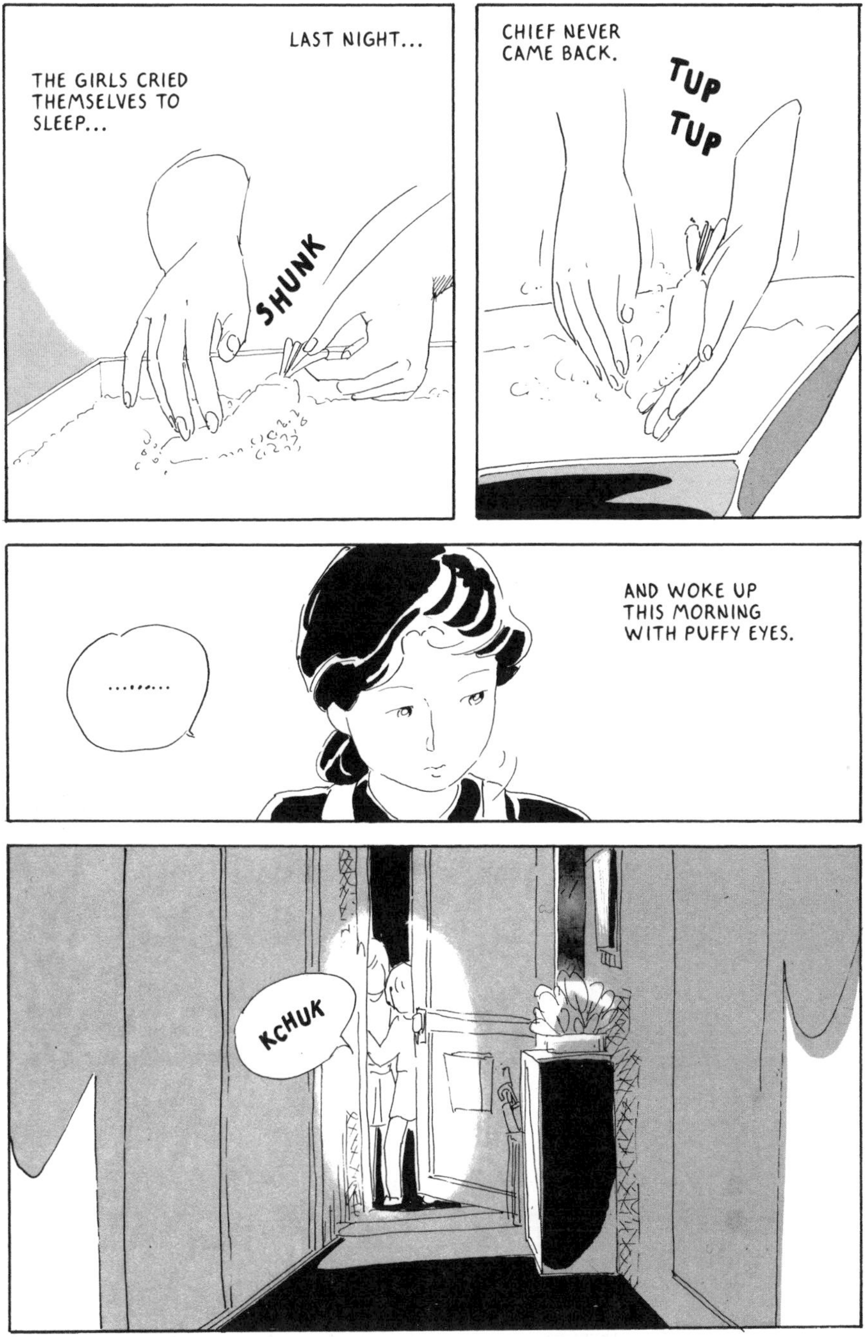
CHIEF NEVER CAME BACK.
TUP TUP
LAST NIGHT...
THE GIRLS CRIED THEMSELVES TO SLEEP...
SHUNK
AND WOKE UP THIS MORNING WITH PUFFY EYES.
....
KCHUK

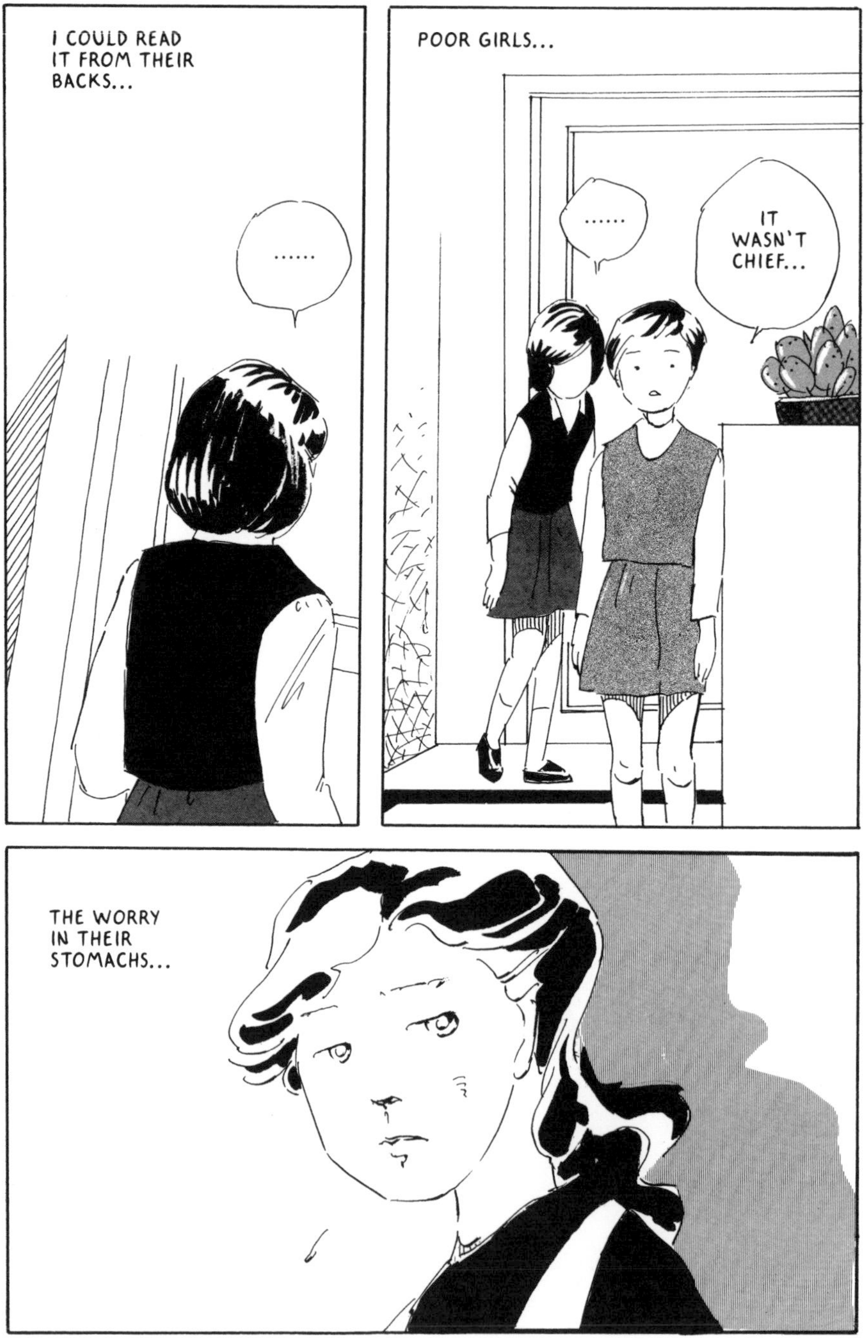
POOR GIRLS...
IT WASN'T CHIEF...
......
I COULD READ IT FROM THEIR BACKS...
......
THE WORRY IN THEIR STOMACHS...

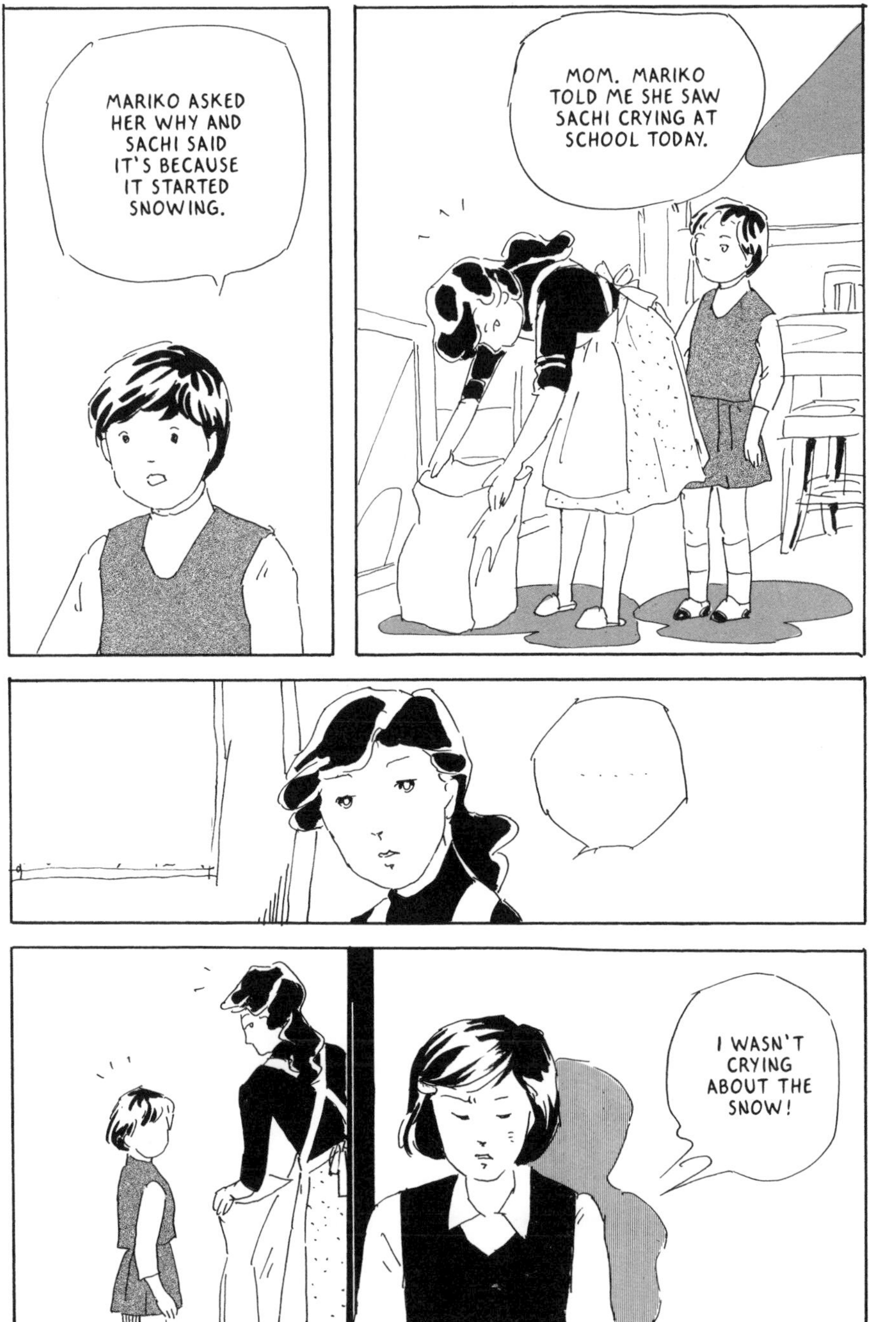
MOM. MARIKO TOLD ME SHE SAW SACHI CRYING AT SCHOOL TODAY.
MARIKO ASKED HER WHY AND SACHI SAID IT'S BECAUSE IT STARTED SNOWING.
.....
I WASN'T CRYING ABOUT THE SNOW!

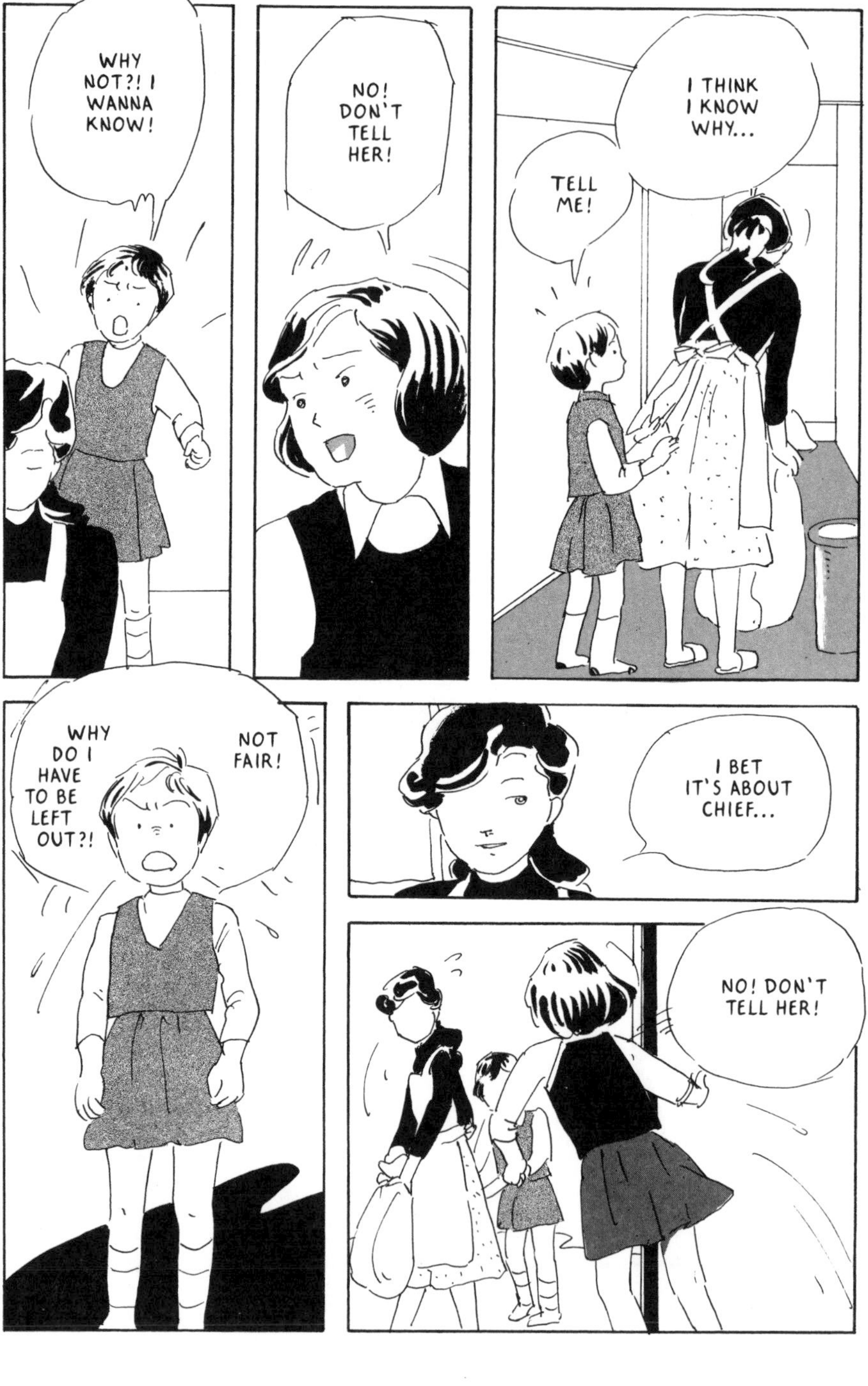
I THINK I KNOW WHY...
TELL ME!
NO! DON'T TELL HER!
WHY NOT?! I WANNA KNOW!
I BET IT'S ABOUT CHIEF...
NO! DON'T TELL HER!
NOT FAIR!
WHY DO I HAVE TO BE LEFT OUT?!

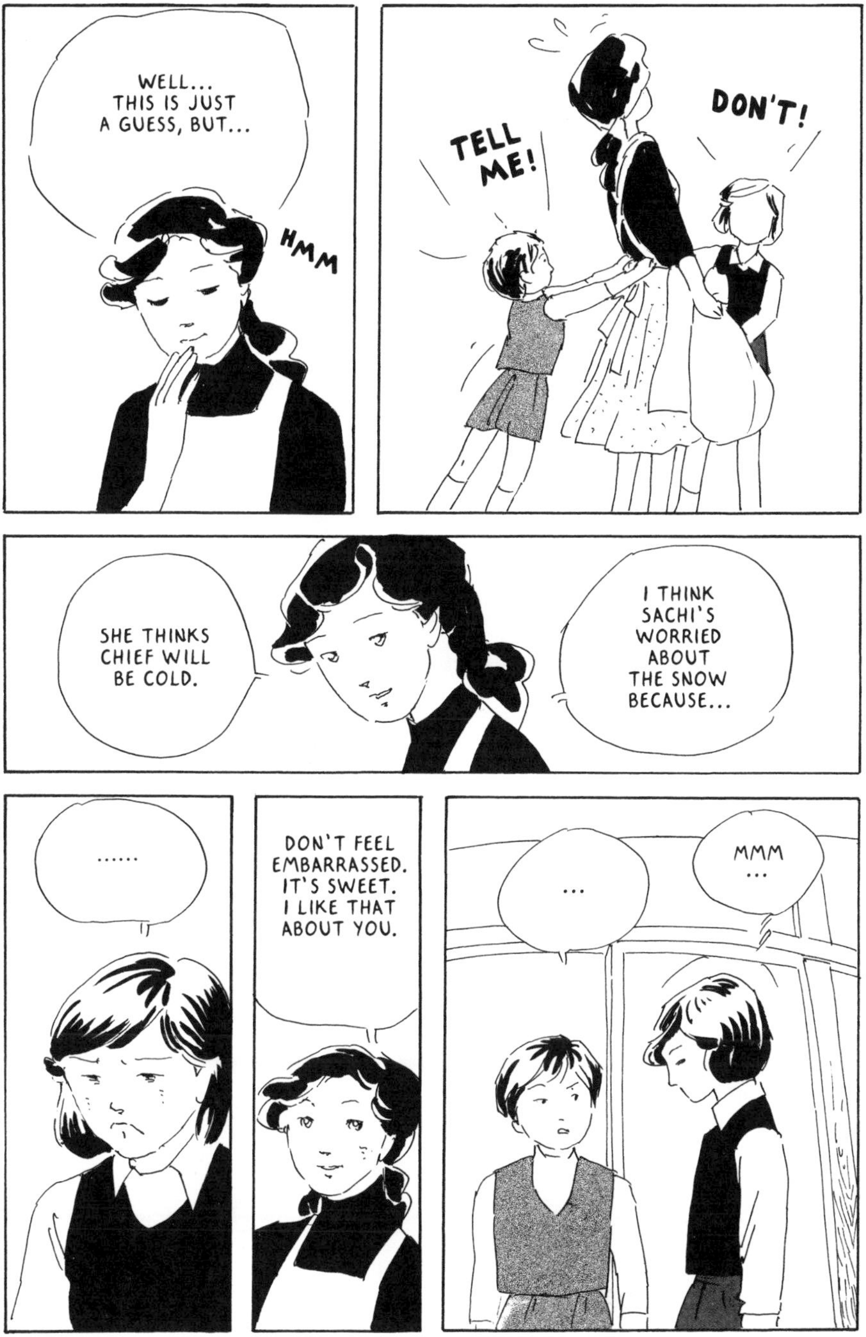
DON'T!
TELL ME!
WELL... THIS IS JUST A GUESS, BUT...
HMM
I THINK SACHI'S WORRIED ABOUT THE SNOW BECAUSE...
SHE THINKS CHIEF WILL BE COLD.
MMM ...
...
DON'T FEEL EMBARRASSED. IT'S SWEET. I LIKE THAT ABOUT YOU.
......

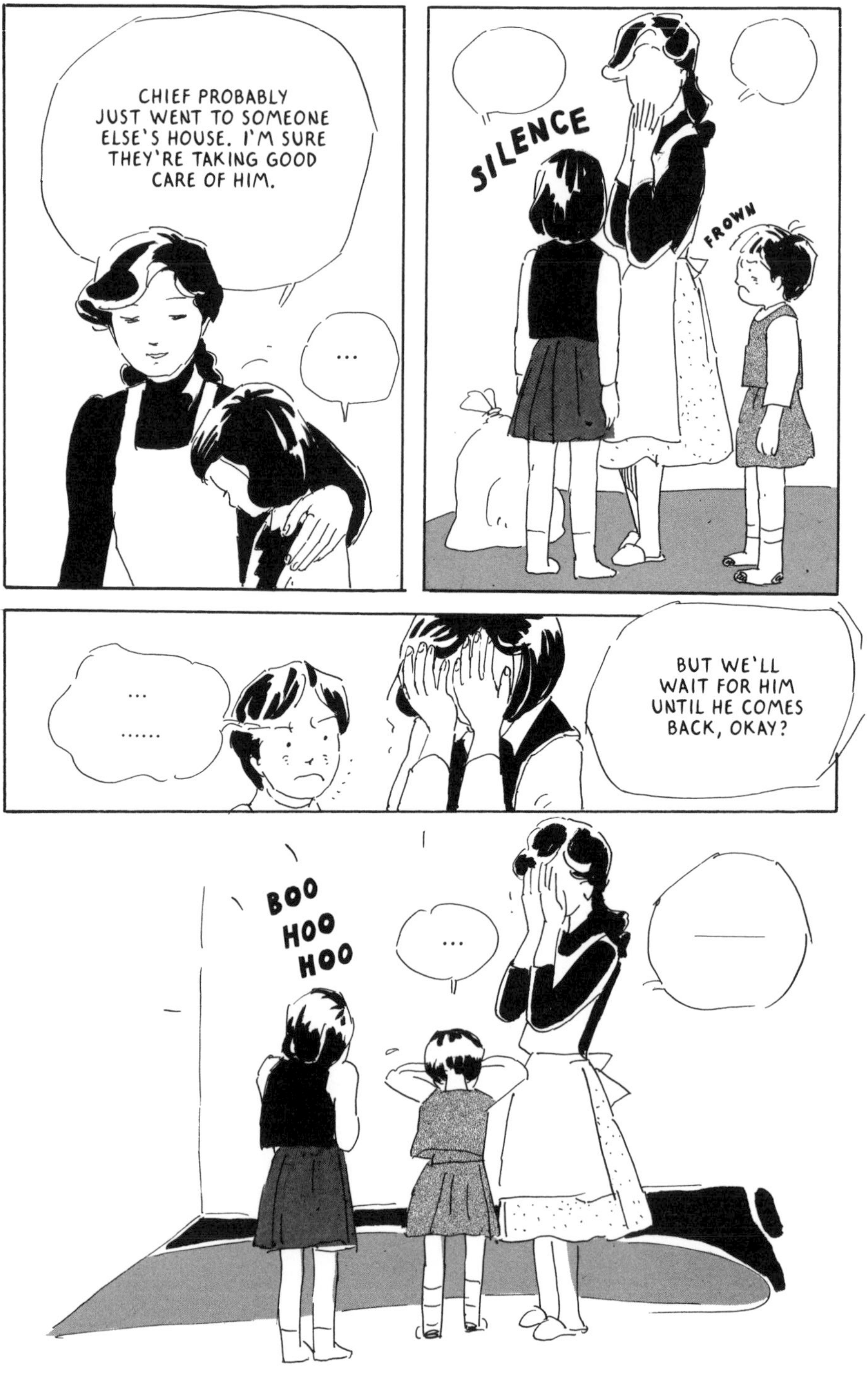
SILENCE
FROWN
CHIEF PROBABLY JUST WENT TO SOMEONE ELSE'S HOUSE. I'M SURE THEY'RE TAKING GOOD CARE OF HIM.
...
BUT WE'LL WAIT FOR HIM UNTIL HE COMES BACK, OKAY?
... .
——
...
BOO HOO HOO

A Slight Fever

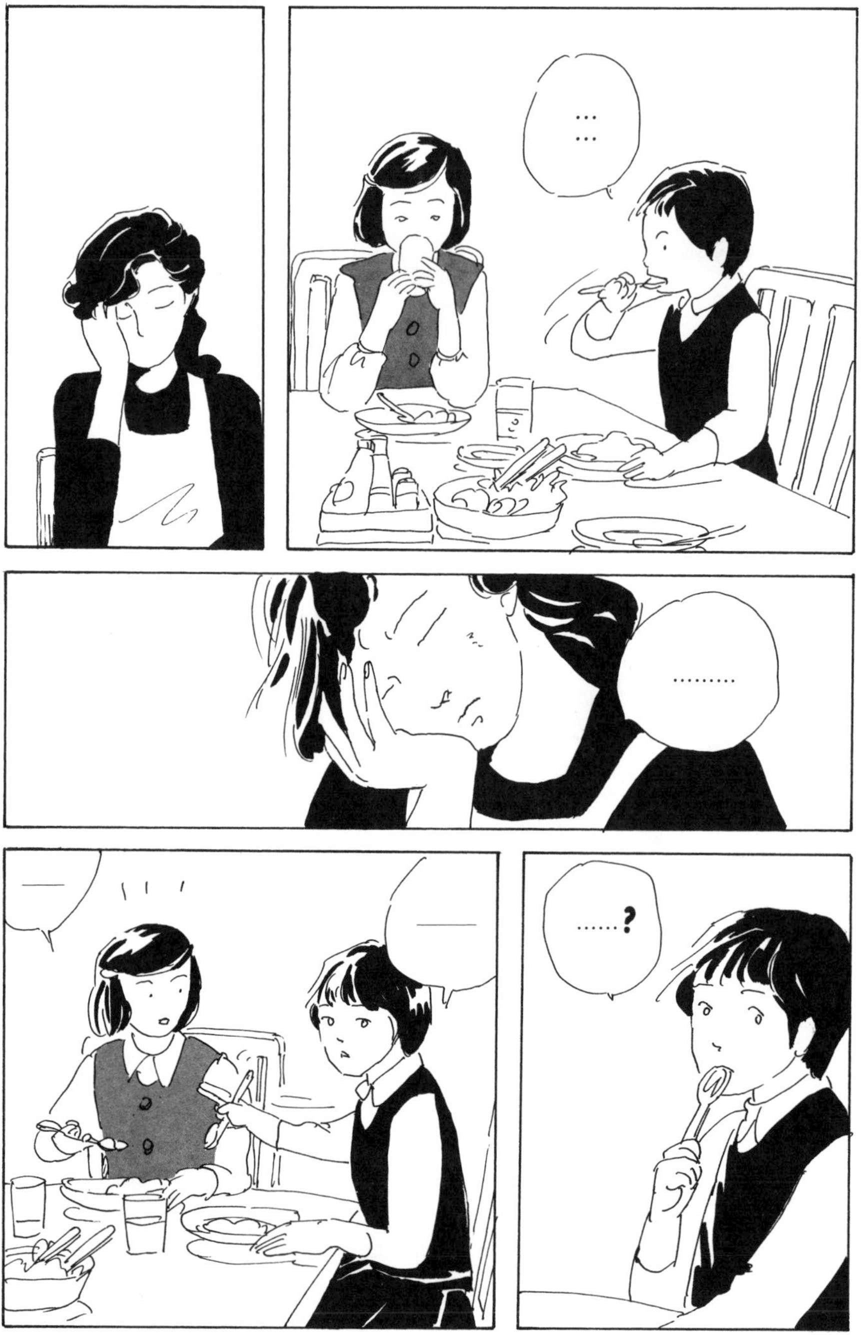
……
………
……?
——
——

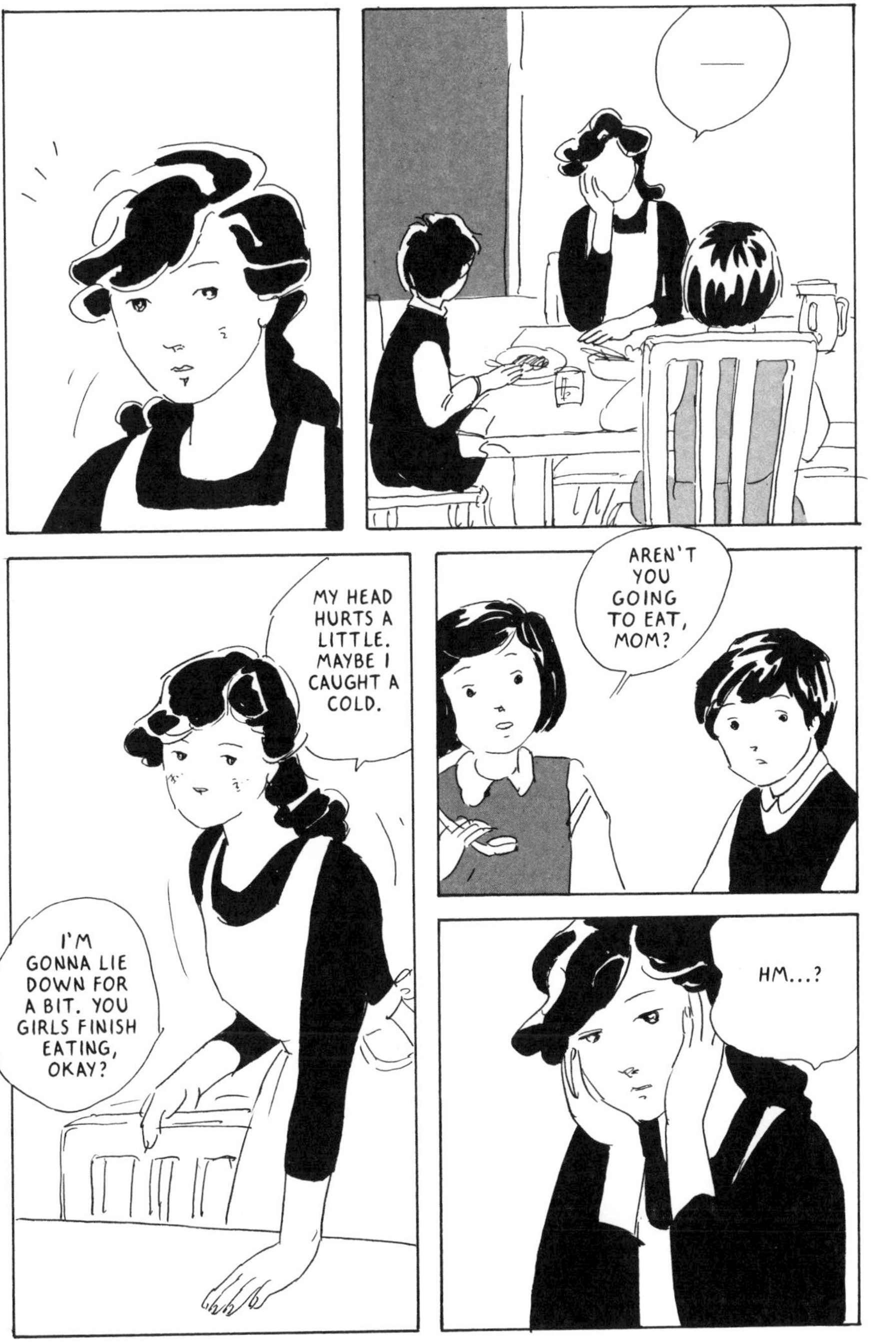
—
AREN'T YOU GOING TO EAT, MOM?
HM...?
MY HEAD HURTS A LITTLE. MAYBE I CAUGHT A COLD.
I'M GONNA LIE DOWN FOR A BIT. YOU GIRLS FINISH EATING, OKAY?

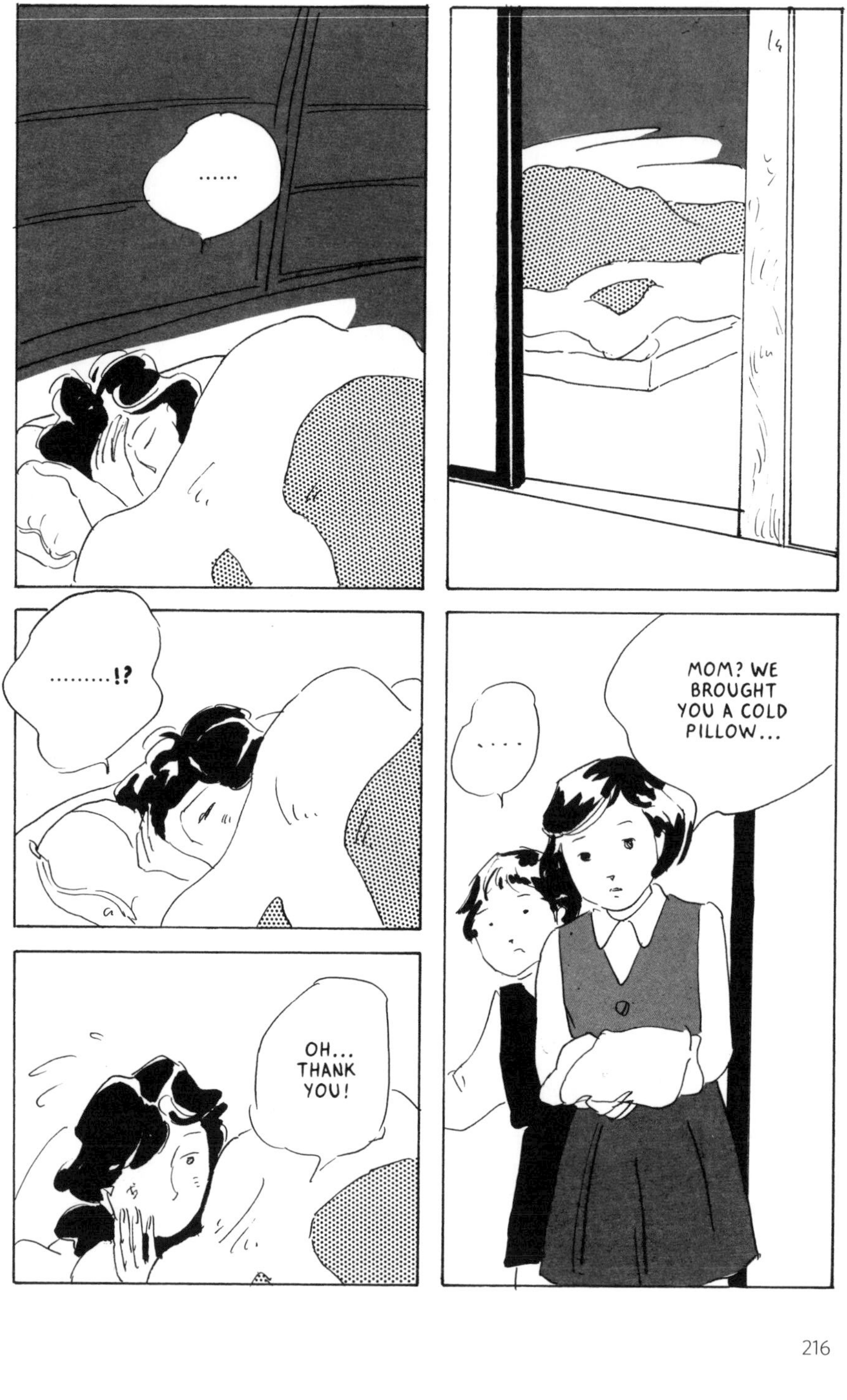
......
MOM? WE BROUGHT YOU A COLD PILLOW...
....
.........!?
OH... THANK YOU!

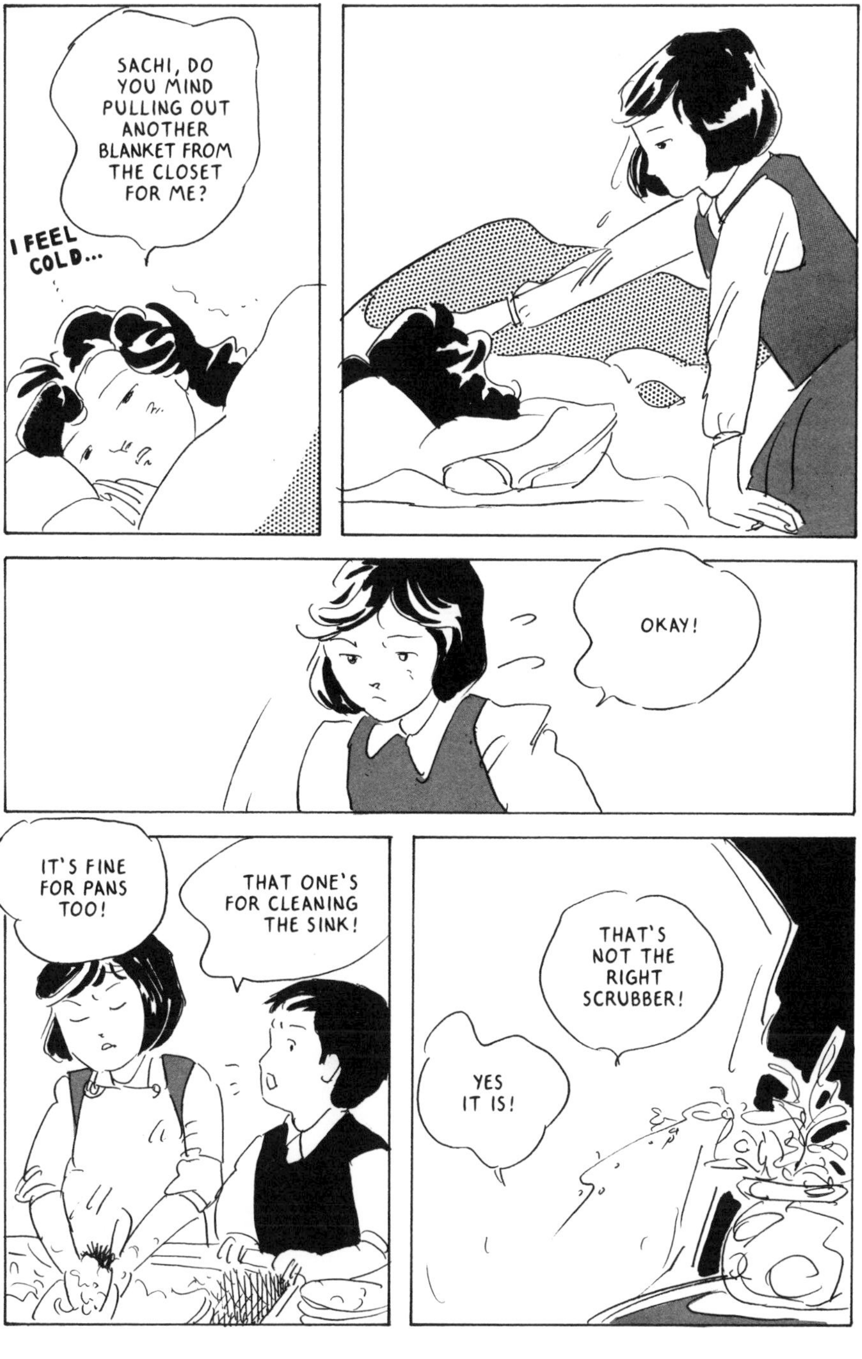
SACHI, DO YOU MIND PULLING OUT ANOTHER BLANKET FROM THE CLOSET FOR ME?
I FEEL COLD...
OKAY!
THAT'S NOT THE RIGHT SCRUBBER!
YES IT IS!
THAT ONE'S FOR CLEANING THE SINK!
IT'S FINE FOR PANS TOO!

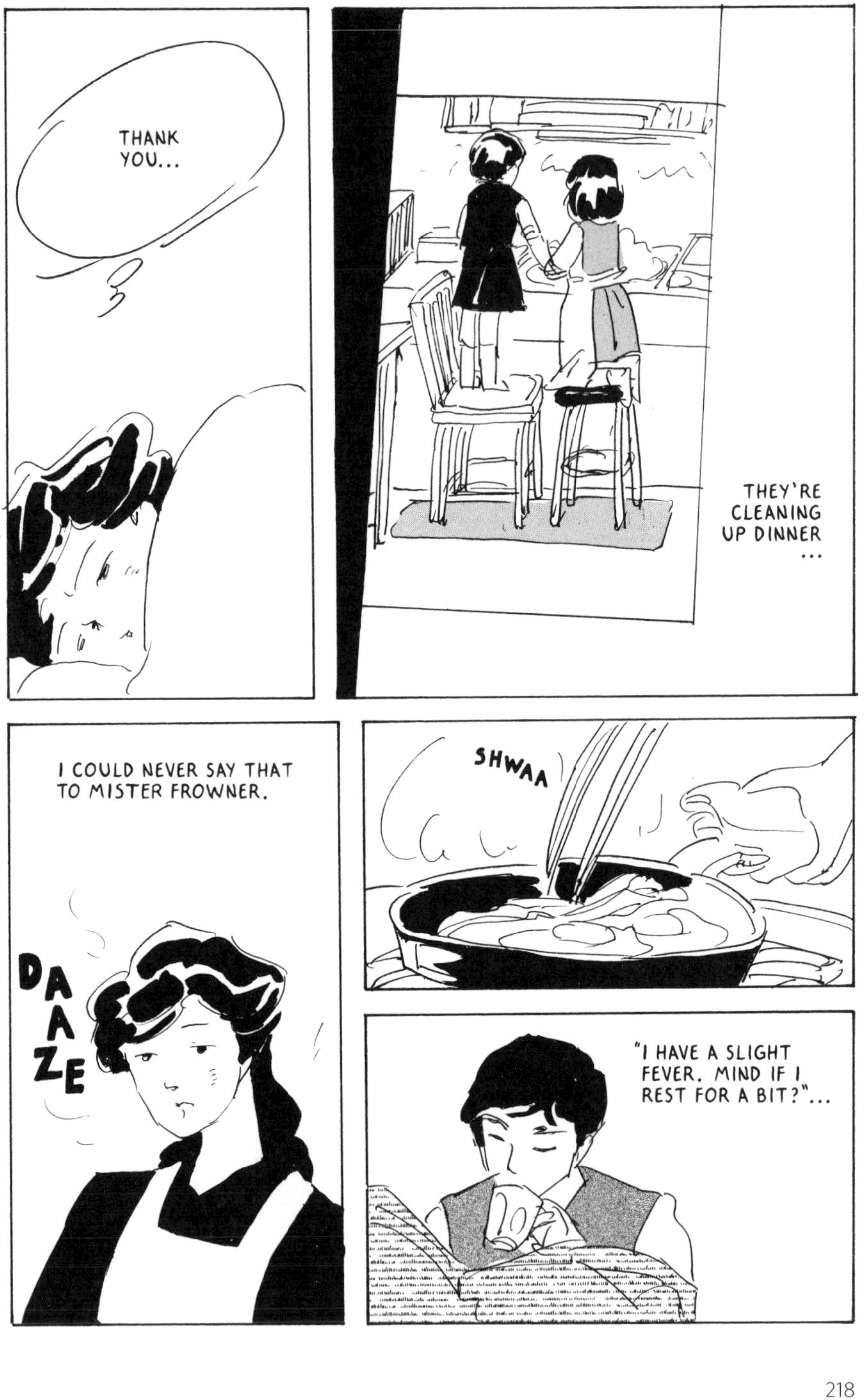
THEY'RE CLEANING UP DINNER ...
THANK YOU...
SHWAA
"I HAVE A SLIGHT FEVER. MIND IF I REST FOR A BIT?"...
I COULD NEVER SAY THAT TO MISTER FROWNER.
DAAZE

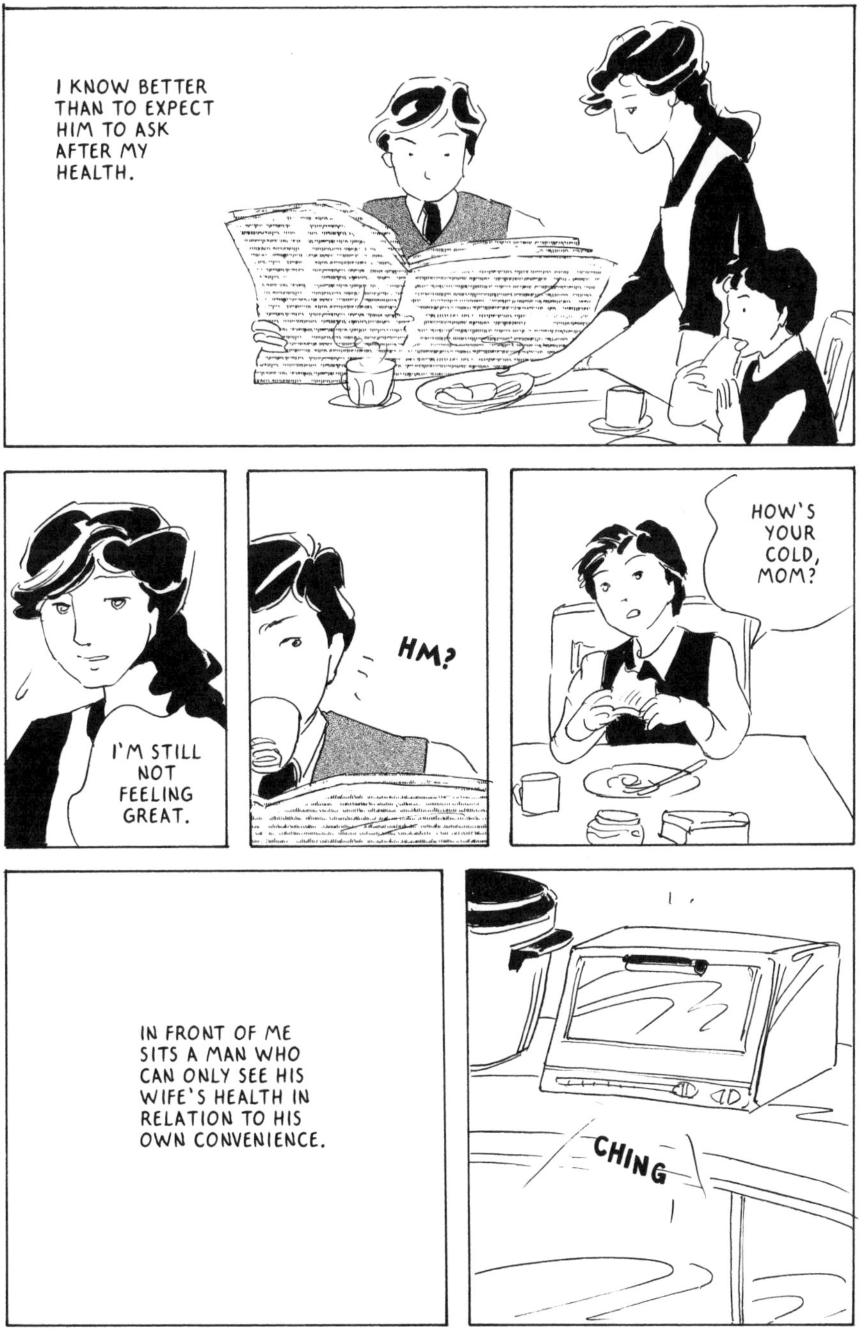
I KNOW BETTER THAN TO EXPECT HIM TO ASK AFTER MY HEALTH.
HOW'S YOUR COLD, MOM?
HM?
I'M STILL NOT FEELING GREAT.
CHING
IN FRONT OF ME SITS A MAN WHO CAN ONLY SEE HIS WIFE'S HEALTH IN RELATION TO HIS OWN CONVENIENCE.

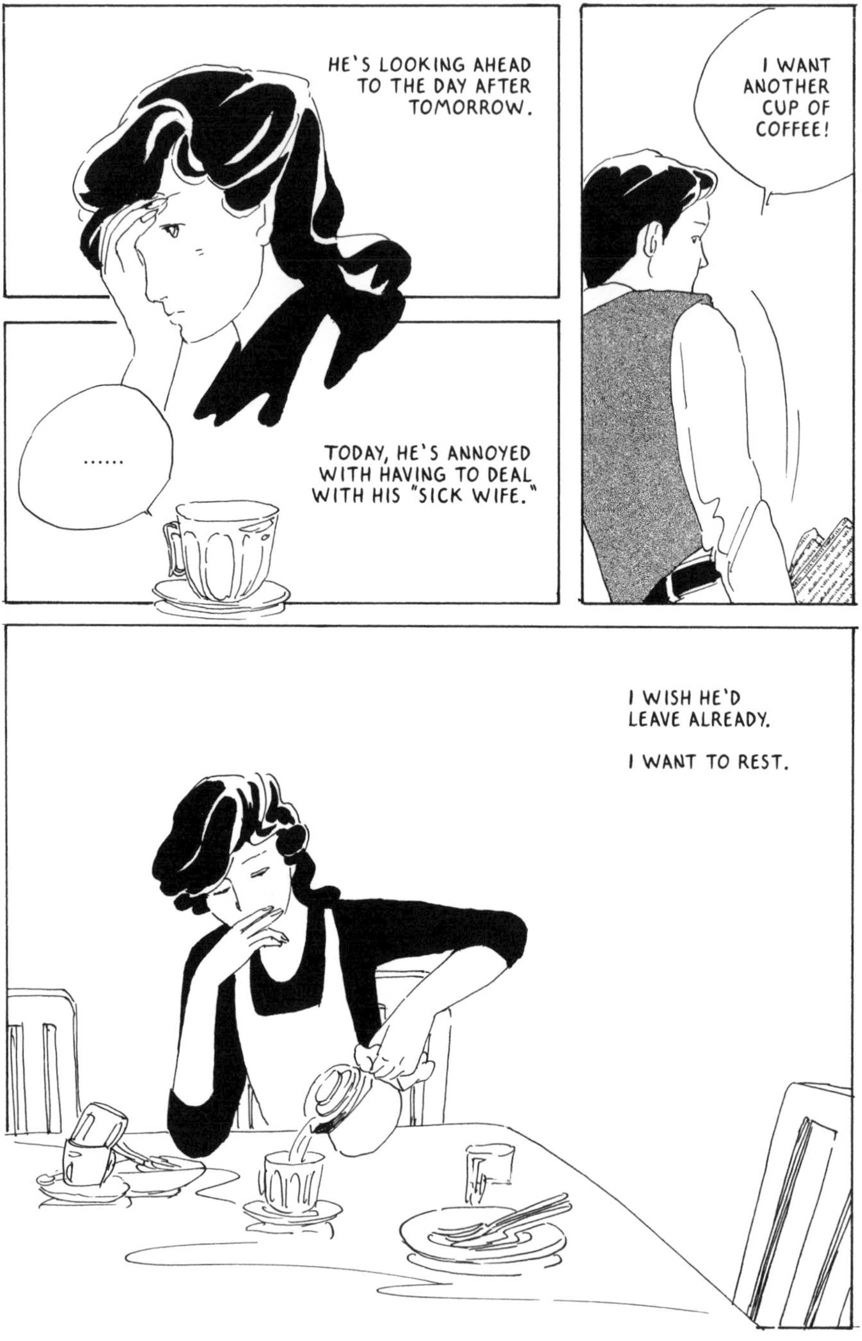
I WANT ANOTHER CUP OF COFFEE!
HE'S LOOKING AHEAD TO THE DAY AFTER TOMORROW.
TODAY, HE'S ANNOYED WITH HAVING TO DEAL WITH HIS "SICK WIFE."
......
I WISH HE'D LEAVE ALREADY.
I WANT TO REST.

Stray Dog

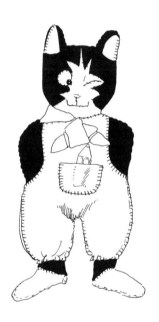

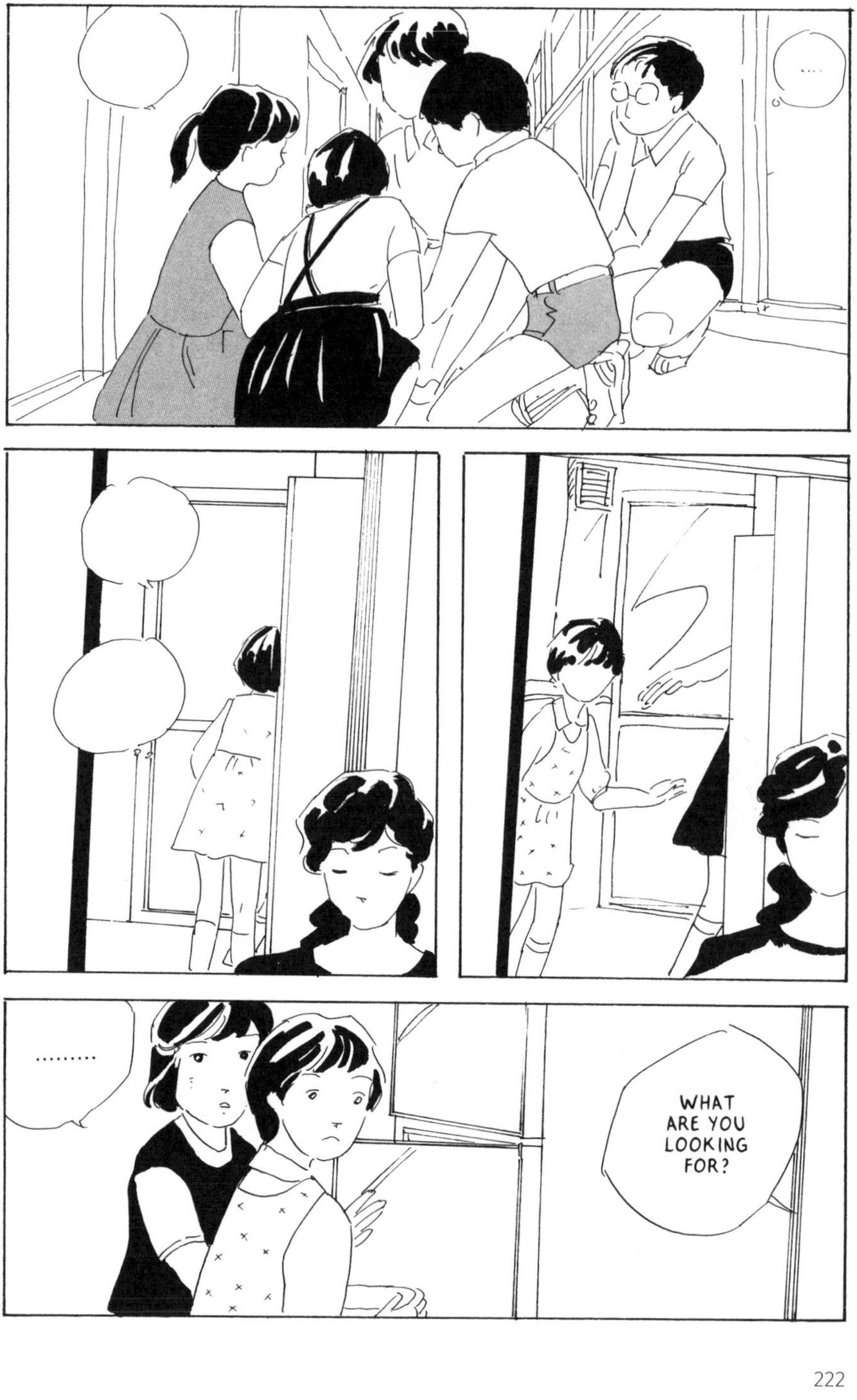
....
WHAT ARE YOU LOOKING FOR?
....

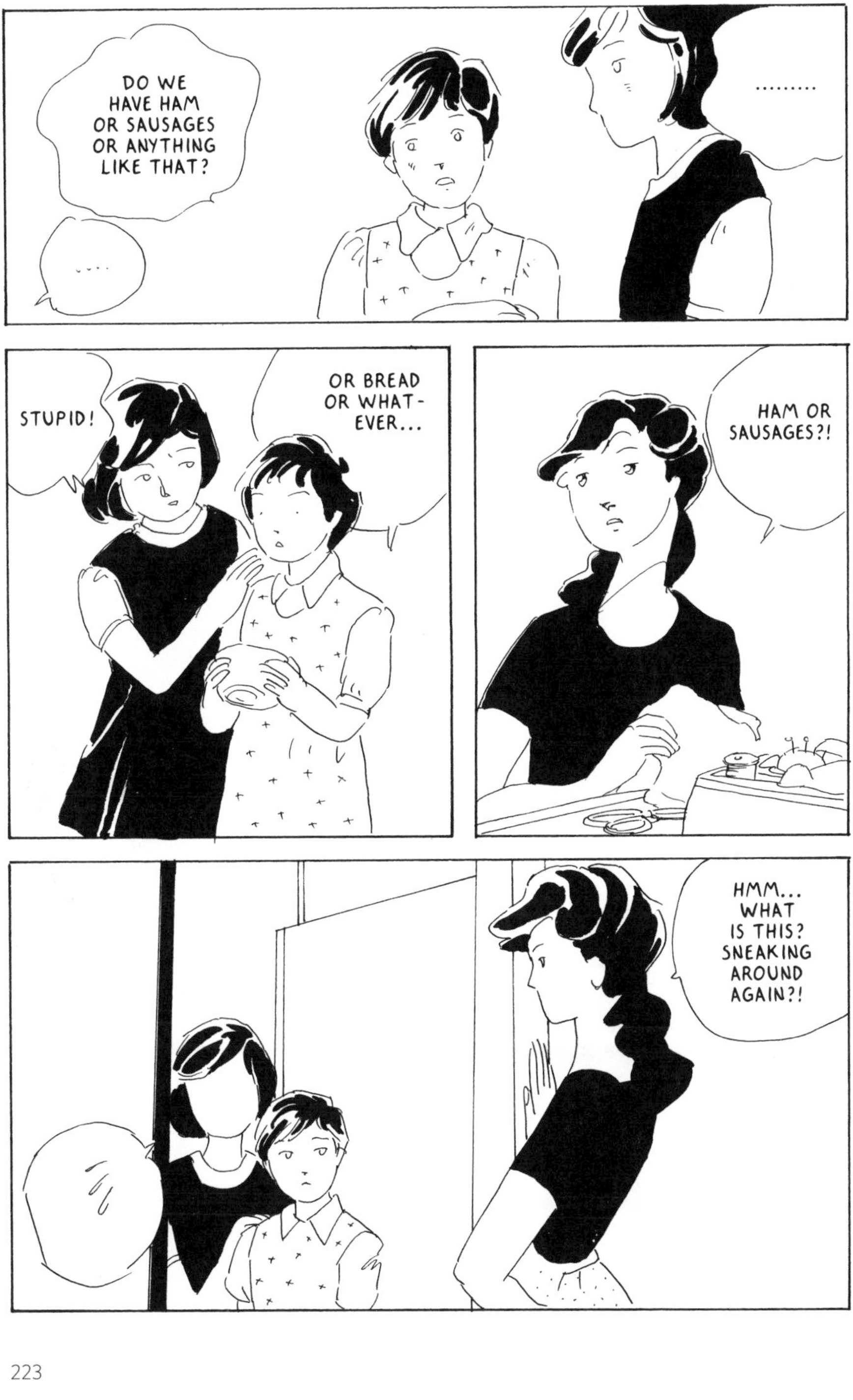
....
DO WE HAVE HAM OR SAUSAGES OR ANYTHING LIKE THAT?
....
HAM OR SAUSAGES?!
OR BREAD OR WHAT-EVER...
STUPID!
HMM... WHAT IS THIS? SNEAKING AROUND AGAIN?!

A-HA! JUST AS I THOUGHT!
THE BOYS WERE TORTURING HIM! THEY TIED HIM UP AND WERE DRAGGING HIM AROUND!
YEAH, AND HE WAS CRYING REALLY LOUDLY!
NO! NO WAY! WE ARE NOT KEEPING A DOG!
TAKE HIM BACK TO WHERE YOU FOUND HIM RIGHT NOW!

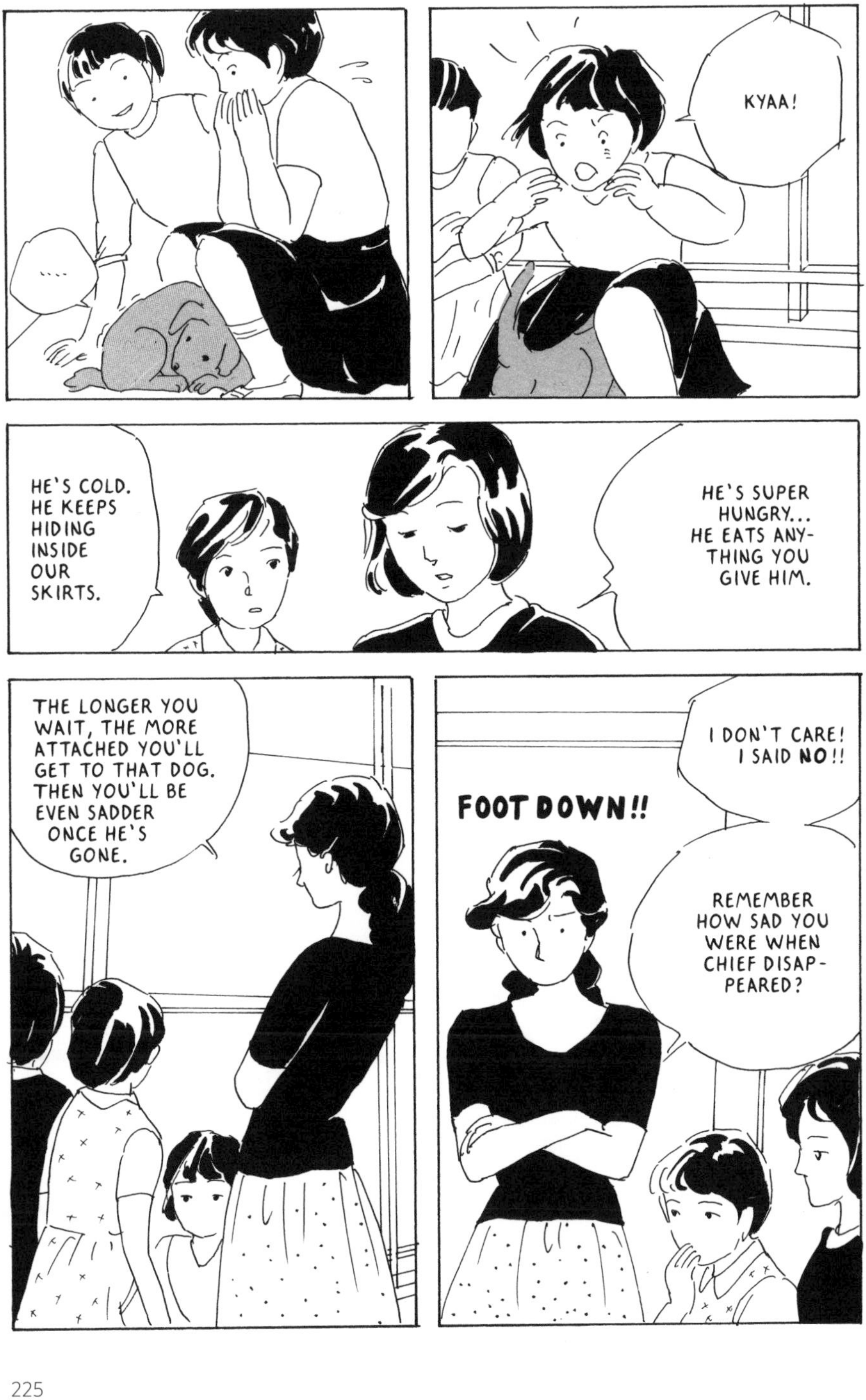
KYAA!
....
HE'S SUPER HUNGRY... HE EATS ANYTHING YOU GIVE HIM.
HE'S COLD. HE KEEPS HIDING INSIDE OUR SKIRTS.
I DON'T CARE! I SAID NO!!
FOOT DOWN!!
REMEMBER HOW SAD YOU WERE WHEN CHIEF DISAPPEARED?
THE LONGER YOU WAIT, THE MORE ATTACHED YOU'LL GET TO THAT DOG. THEN YOU'LL BE EVEN SADDER ONCE HE'S GONE.

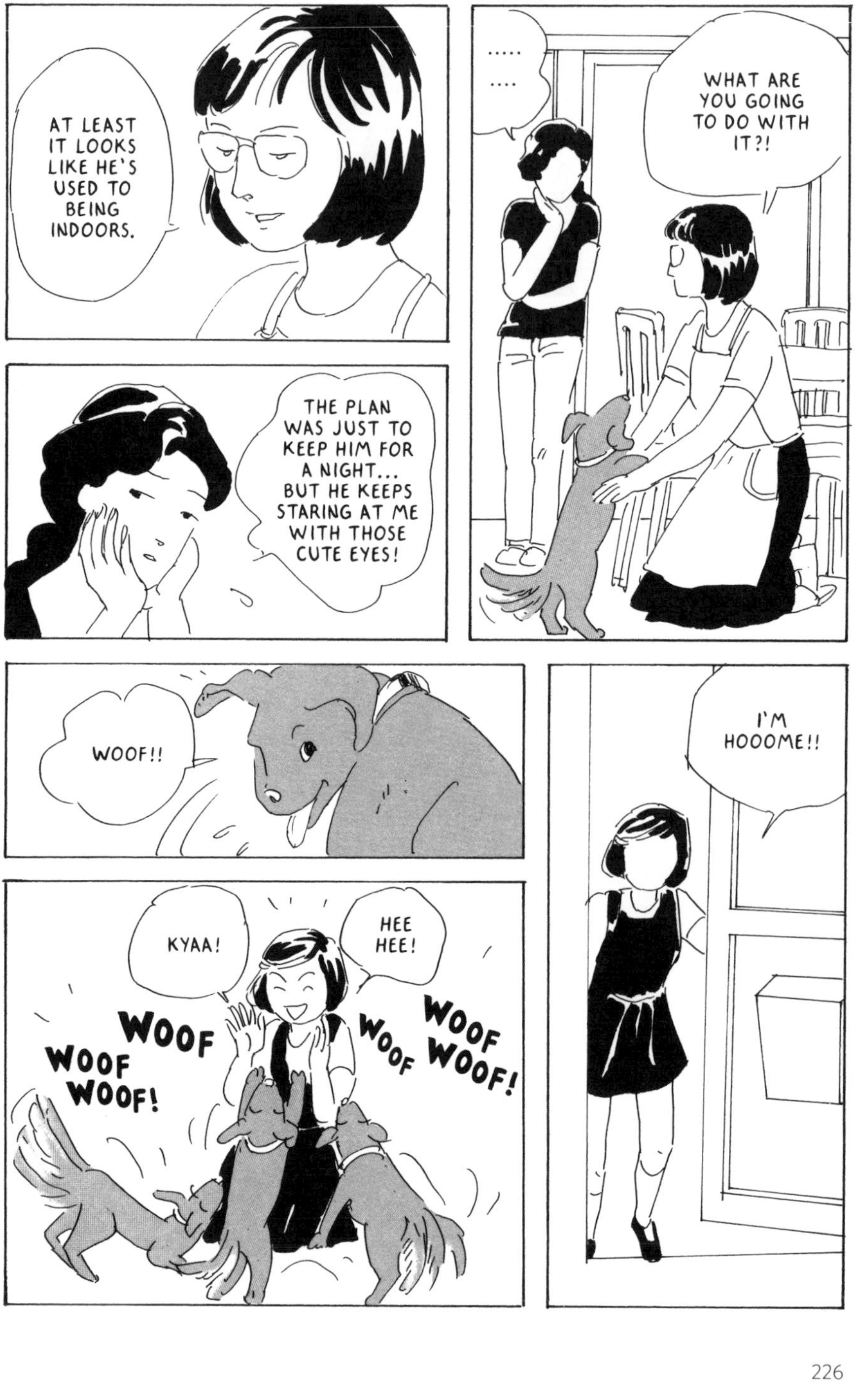
WHAT ARE YOU GOING TO DO WITH IT?!
....
AT LEAST IT LOOKS LIKE HE'S USED TO BEING INDOORS.
THE PLAN WAS JUST TO KEEP HIM FOR A NIGHT... BUT HE KEEPS STARING AT ME WITH THOSE CUTE EYES!
I'M HOOOME!!
WOOF!!
HEE HEE!
KYAA!
WOOF WOOF!
WOOF WOOF
WOOF
WOOF WOOF!

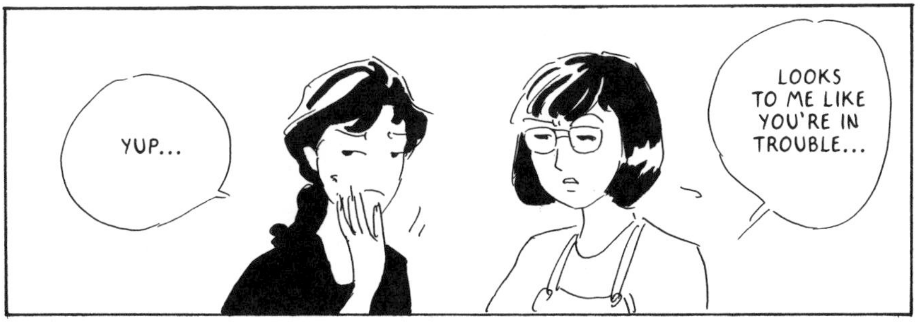
LOOKS TO ME LIKE YOU'RE IN TROUBLE...
YUP...

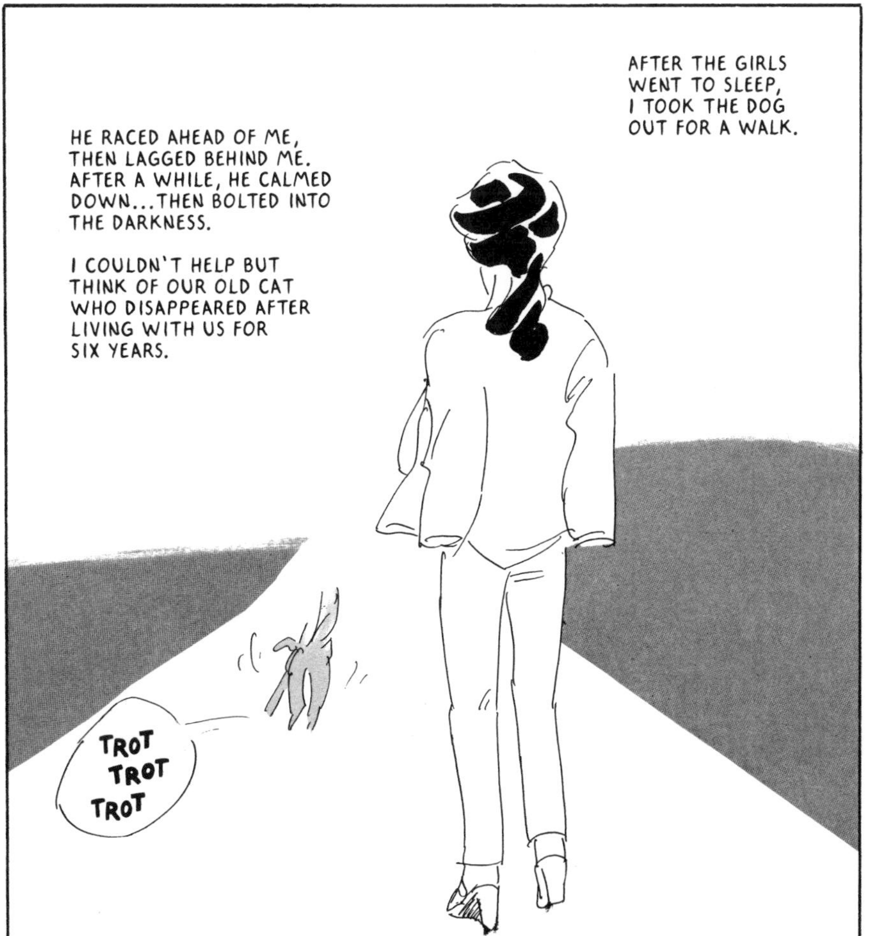
AFTER THE GIRLS WENT TO SLEEP, I TOOK THE DOG OUT FOR A WALK.
HE RACED AHEAD OF ME, THEN LAGGED BEHIND ME. AFTER A WHILE, HE CALMED DOWN...THEN BOLTED INTO THE DARKNESS.
I COULDN'T HELP BUT THINK OF OUR OLD CAT WHO DISAPPEARED AFTER LIVING WITH US FOR SIX YEARS.
TROT TROT TROT

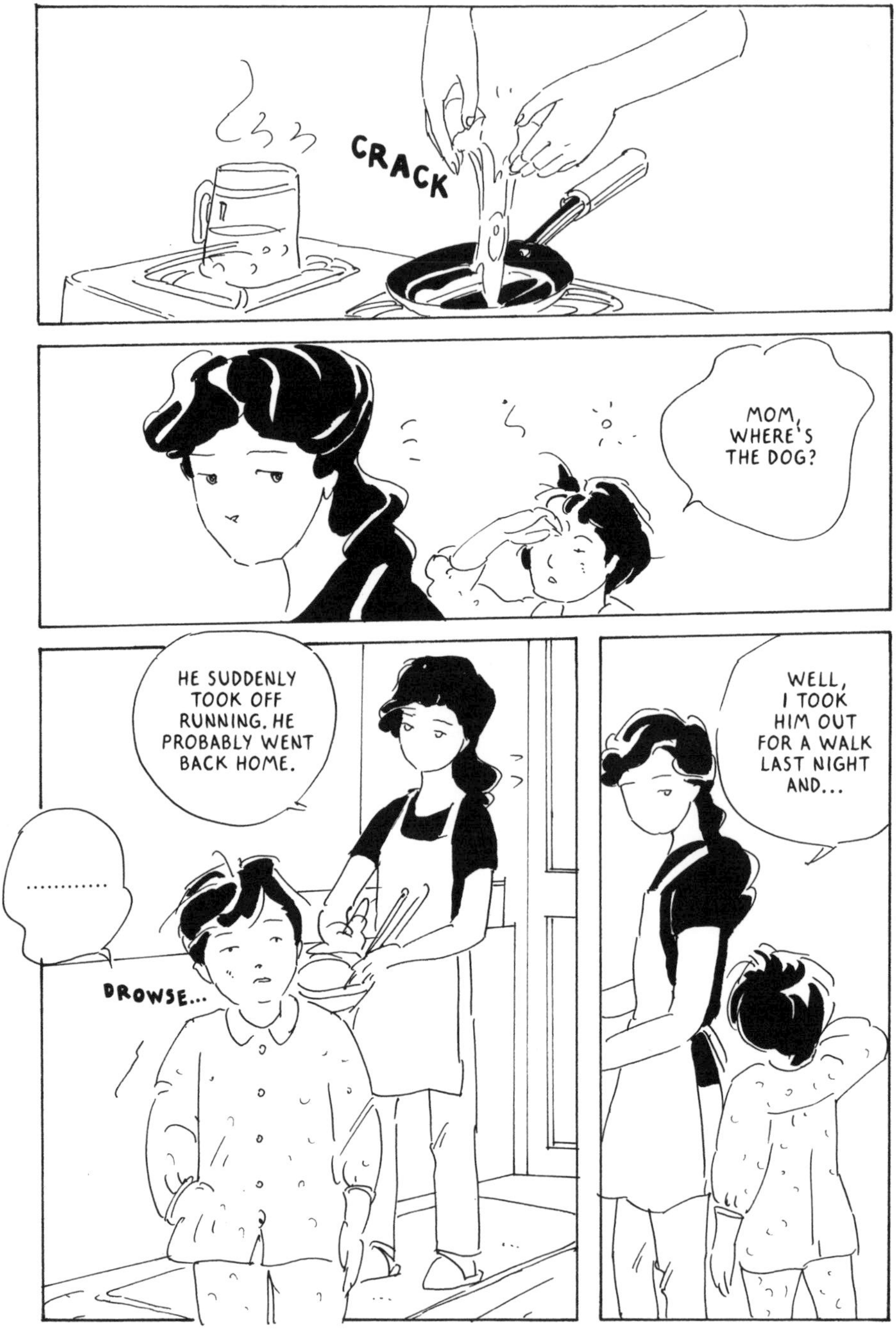
CRACK
MOM, WHERE'S THE DOG?
WELL, I TOOK HIM OUT FOR A WALK LAST NIGHT AND...
HE SUDDENLY TOOK OFF RUNNING. HE PROBABLY WENT BACK HOME.
....
DROWSE...

A Mother's Pride

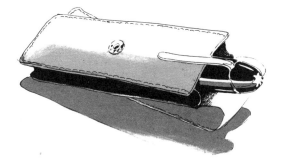

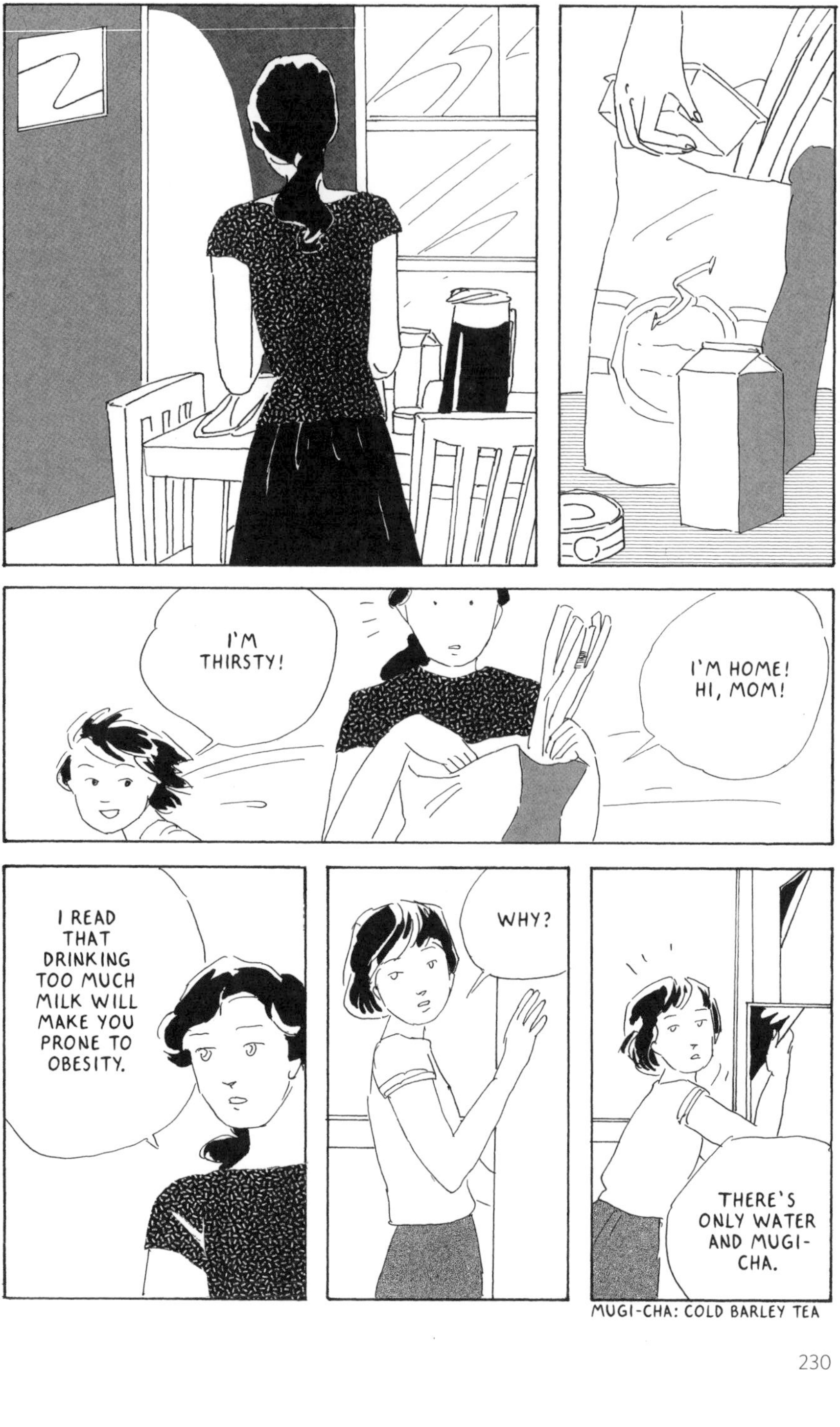
I'M HOME! HI, MOM!
I'M THIRSTY!
THERE'S ONLY WATER AND MUGI-CHA.
WHY?
I READ THAT DRINKING TOO MUCH MILK WILL MAKE YOU PRONE TO OBESITY.

MUGI-CHA: COLD BARLEY TEA

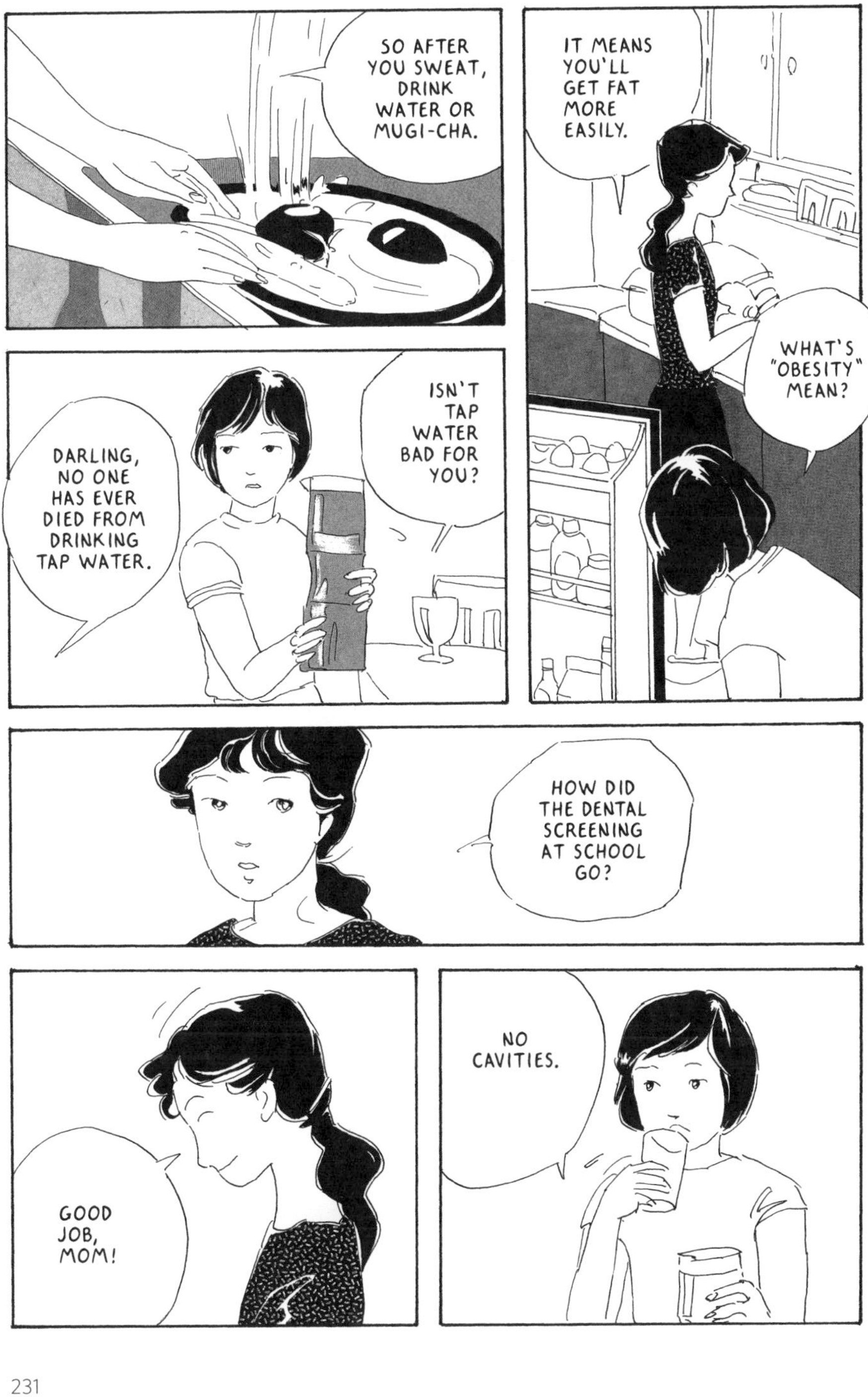
IT MEANS YOU'LL GET FAT MORE EASILY.
WHAT'S "OBESITY" MEAN?
SO AFTER YOU SWEAT, DRINK WATER OR MUGI-CHA.
ISN'T TAP WATER BAD FOR YOU?
DARLING, NO ONE HAS EVER DIED FROM DRINKING TAP WATER.
HOW DID THE DENTAL SCREENING AT SCHOOL GO?
NO CAVITIES.
GOOD JOB, MOM!

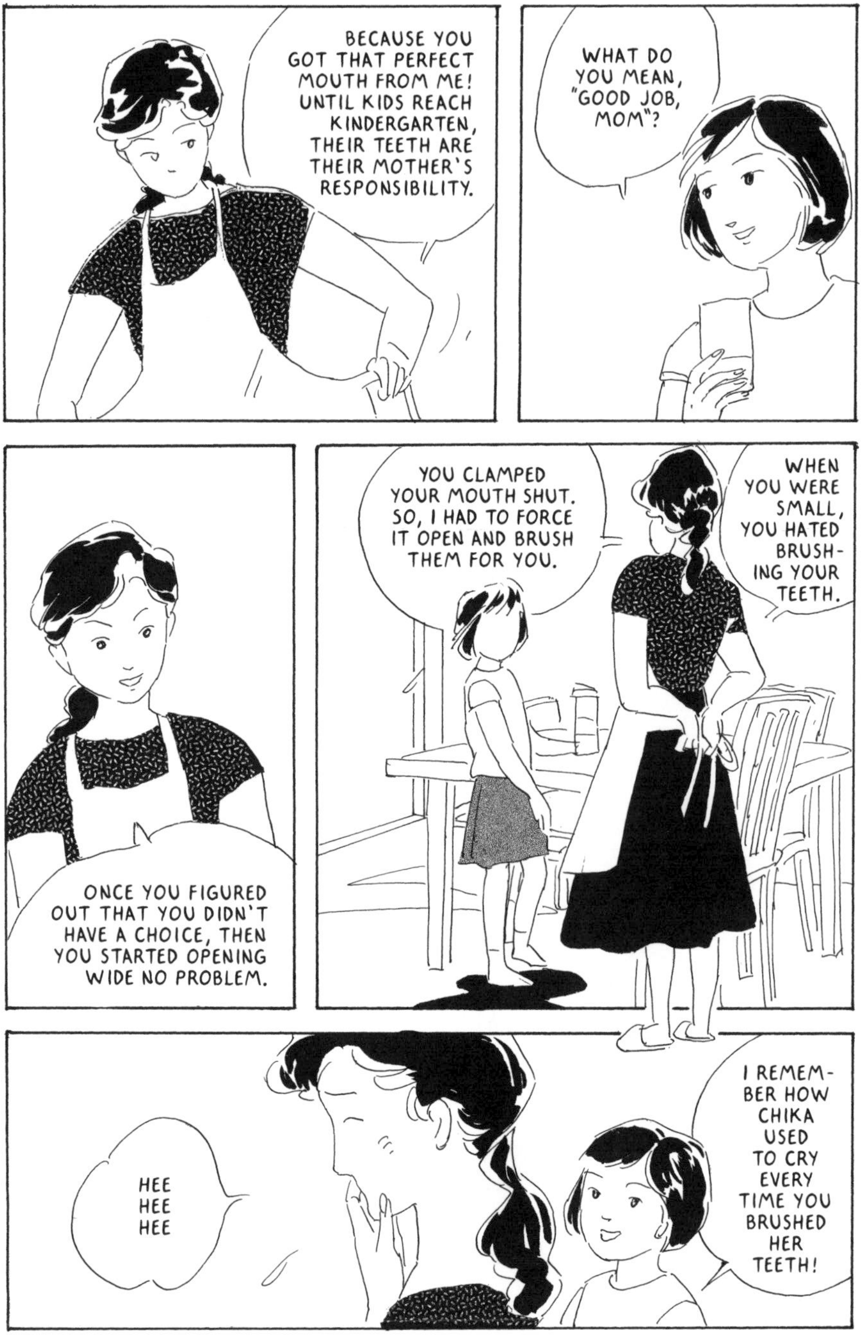
WHAT DO YOU MEAN, "GOOD JOB, MOM"?
BECAUSE YOU GOT THAT PERFECT MOUTH FROM ME! UNTIL KIDS REACH KINDERGARTEN, THEIR TEETH ARE THEIR MOTHER'S RESPONSIBILITY.
WHEN YOU WERE SMALL, YOU HATED BRUSH-ING YOUR TEETH.
YOU CLAMPED YOUR MOUTH SHUT. SO, I HAD TO FORCE IT OPEN AND BRUSH THEM FOR YOU.
ONCE YOU FIGURED OUT THAT YOU DIDN'T HAVE A CHOICE, THEN YOU STARTED OPENING WIDE NO PROBLEM.
I REMEM-BER HOW CHIKA USED TO CRY EVERY TIME YOU BRUSHED HER TEETH!
HEE HEE HEE

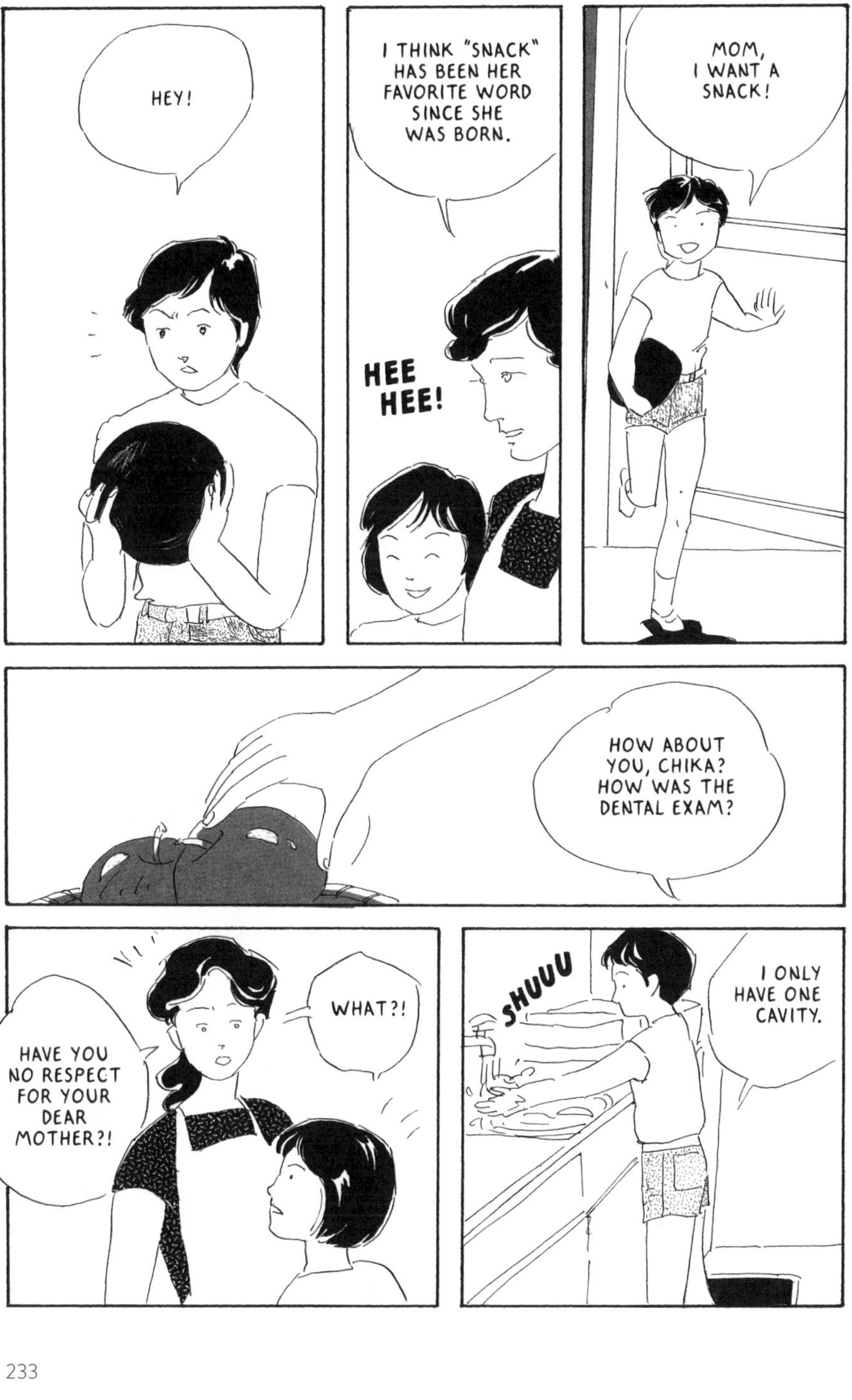
MOM, I WANT A SNACK!
I THINK "SNACK" HAS BEEN HER FAVORITE WORD SINCE SHE WAS BORN.
HEE HEE!
HEY!
HOW ABOUT YOU, CHIKA? HOW WAS THE DENTAL EXAM?
I ONLY HAVE ONE CAVITY.
SHUUU
WHAT?!
HAVE YOU NO RESPECT FOR YOUR DEAR MOTHER?!

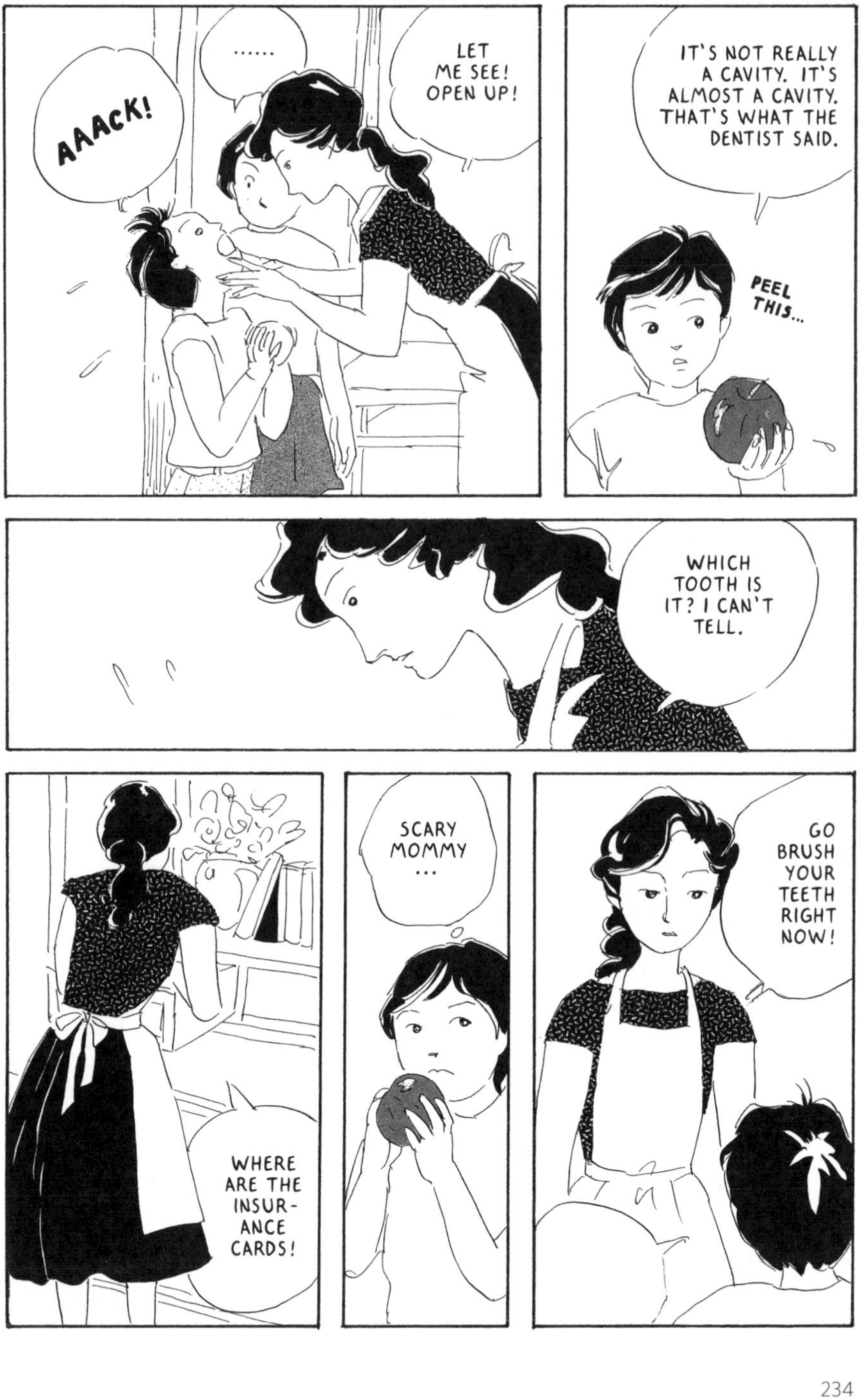
IT'S NOT REALLY A CAVITY. IT'S ALMOST A CAVITY. THAT'S WHAT THE DENTIST SAID.
PEEL THIS...
LET ME SEE! OPEN UP!
......
AAACK!
WHICH TOOTH IS IT? I CAN'T TELL.
GO BRUSH YOUR TEETH RIGHT NOW!
SCARY MOMMY ...
WHERE ARE THE INSUR-ANCE CARDS!

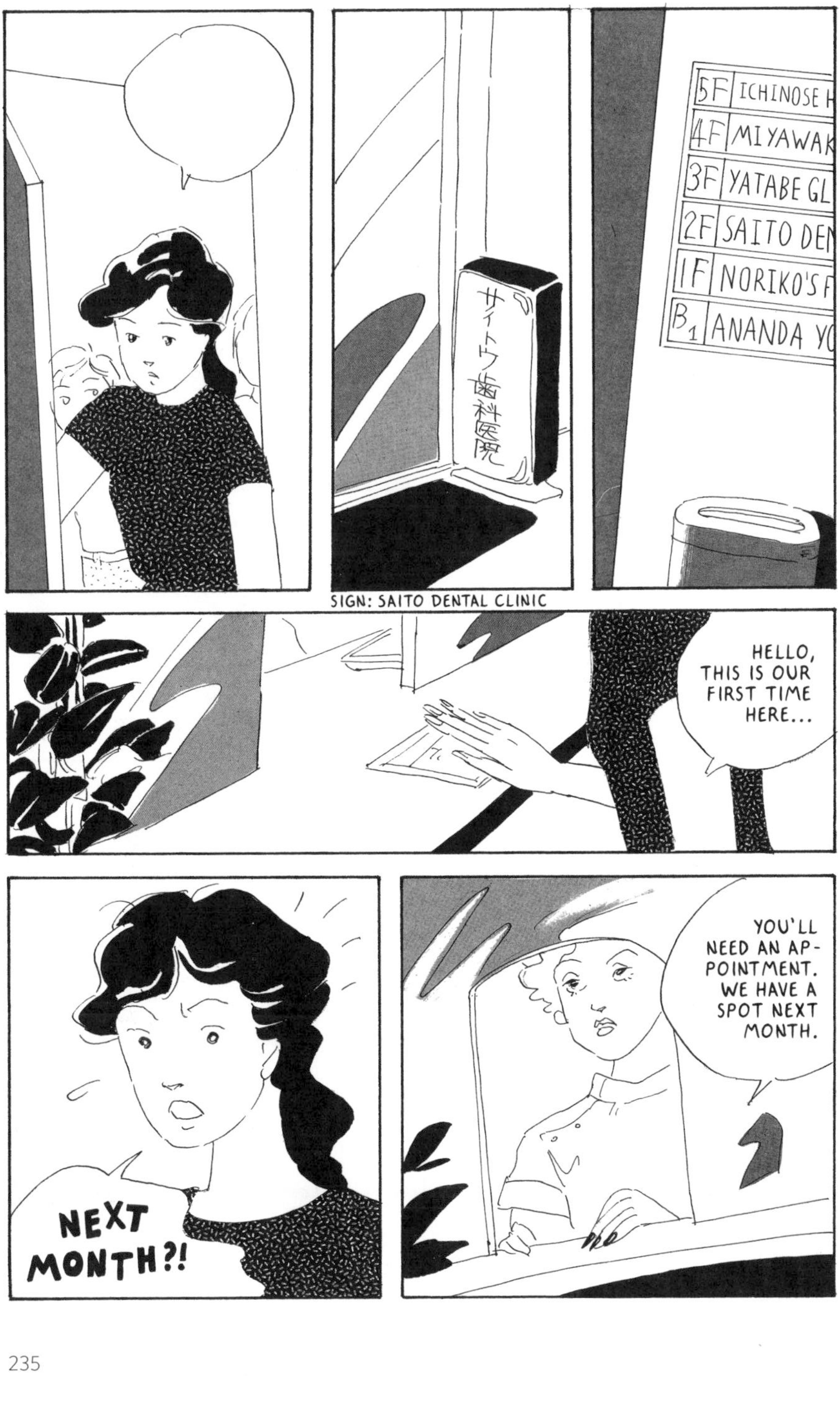
5F ICHINOSE
4F MIYAWA
3F YATABE G
2F SAITO DE
1F NORIKO'S
B1 ANANDA
サイトウ歯科医院
SIGN: SAITO DENTAL CLINIC
HELLO, THIS IS OUR FIRST TIME HERE...
YOU'LL NEED AN AP-POINTMENT. WE HAVE A SPOT NEXT MONTH.
NEXT MONTH?!

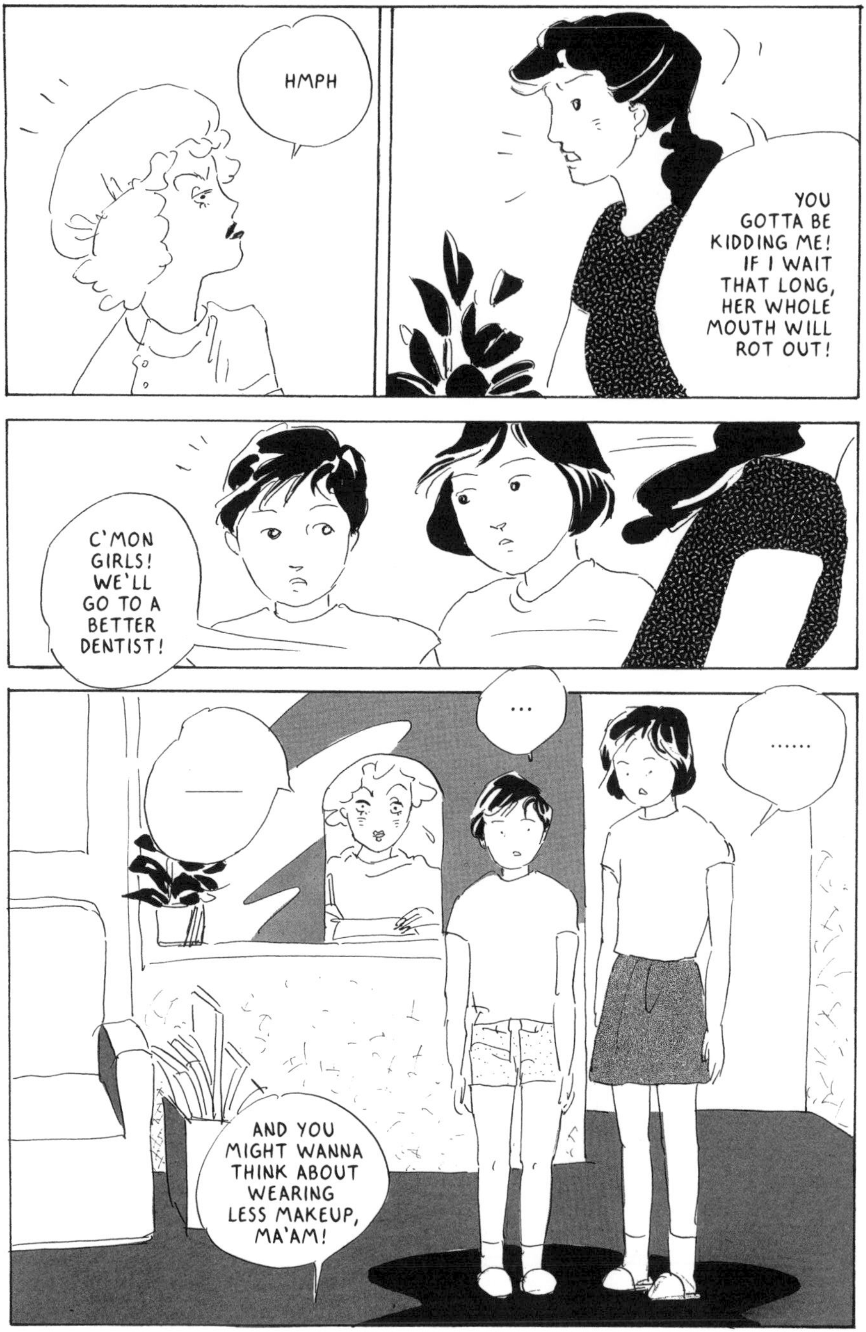
YOU GOTTA BE KIDDING ME! IF I WAIT THAT LONG, HER WHOLE MOUTH WILL ROT OUT!
HMPH
C'MON GIRLS! WE'LL GO TO A BETTER DENTIST!
......
...
AND YOU MIGHT WANNA THINK ABOUT WEARING LESS MAKEUP, MA'AM!

Now I'm Angry

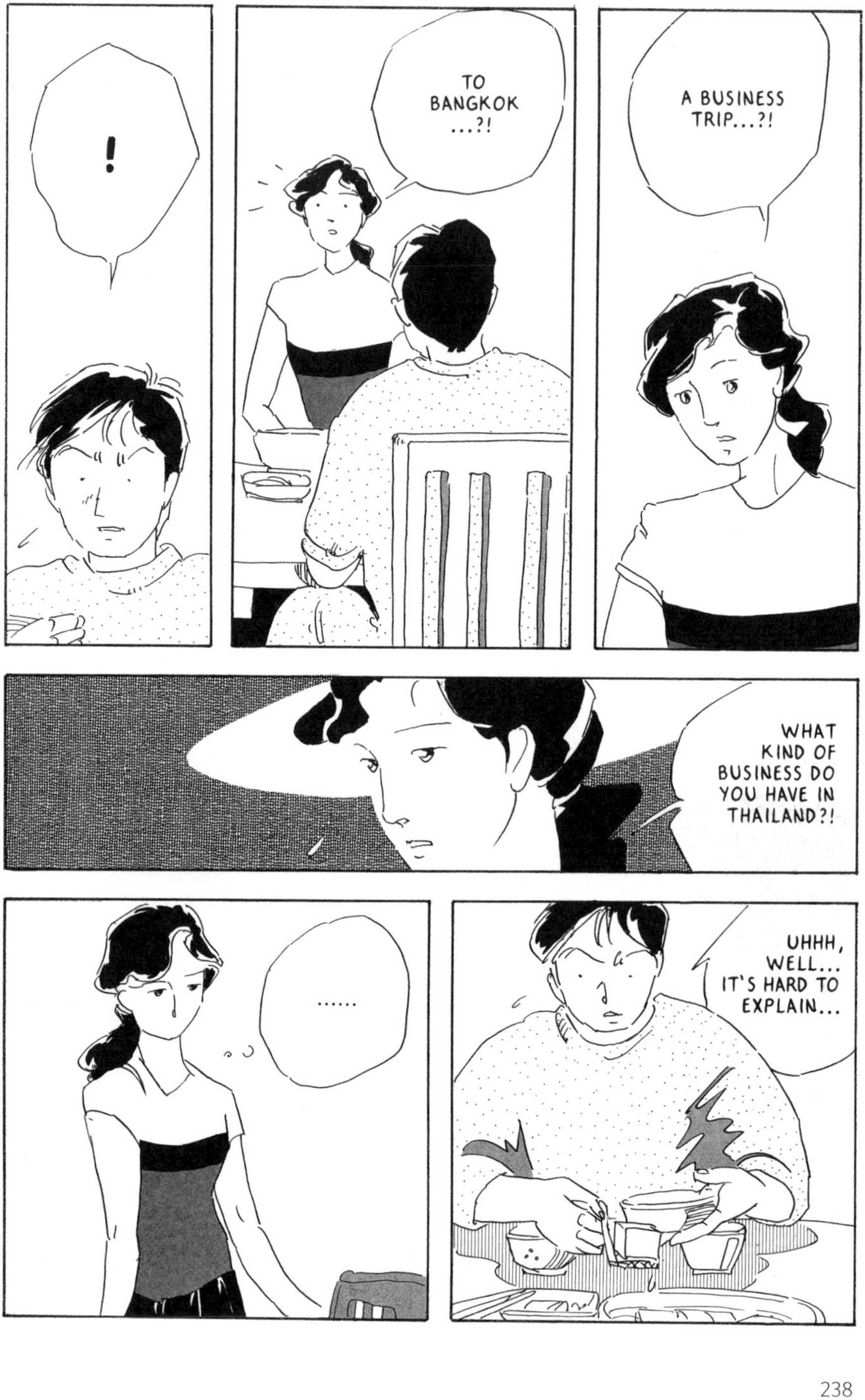
A BUSINESS TRIP...?!
TO BANGKOK ...?!
!
WHAT KIND OF BUSINESS DO YOU HAVE IN THAILAND?!
UHHH, WELL... IT'S HARD TO EXPLAIN...
......

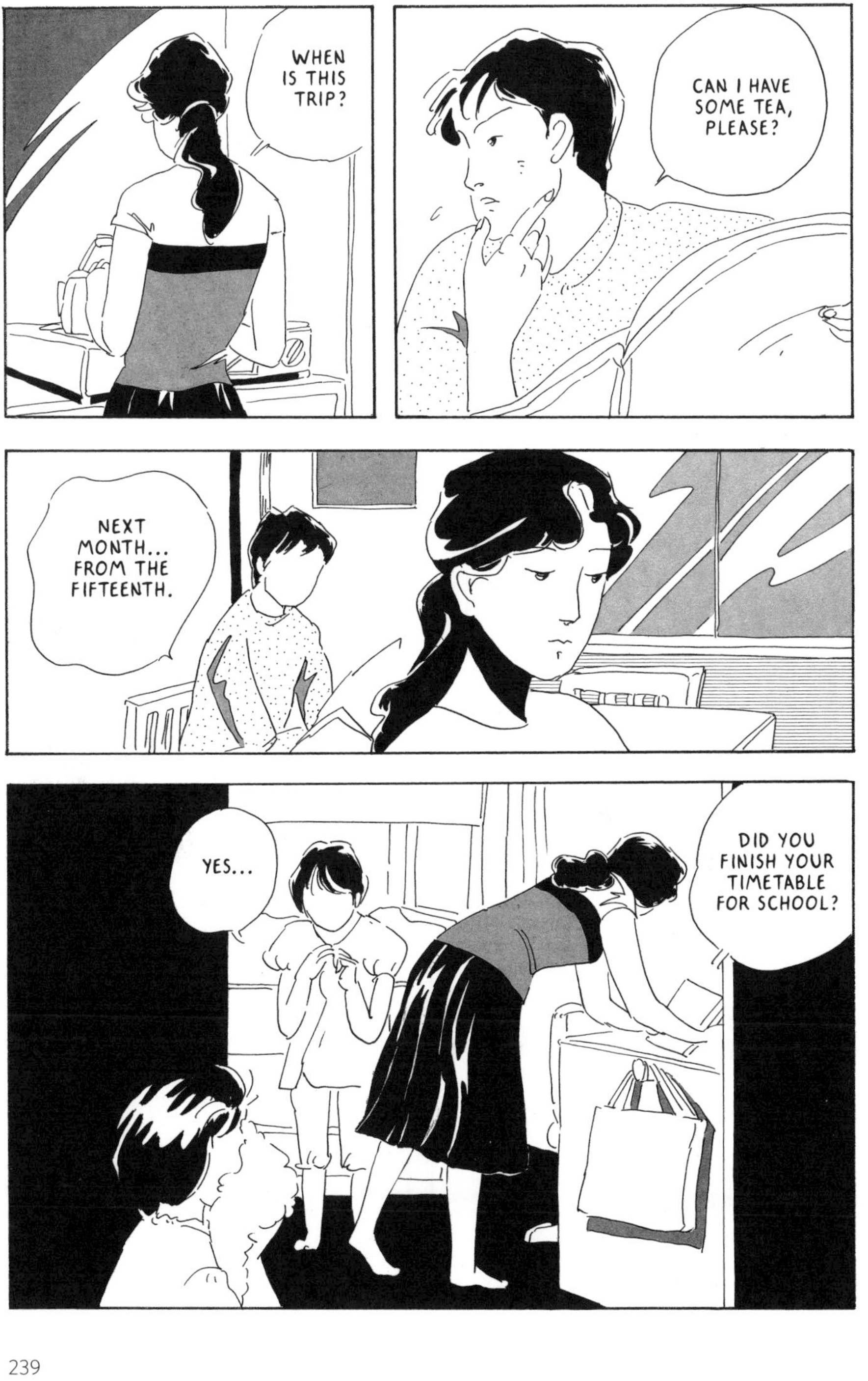
CAN I HAVE SOME TEA, PLEASE?
WHEN IS THIS TRIP?
NEXT MONTH... FROM THE FIFTEENTH.
DID YOU FINISH YOUR TIMETABLE FOR SCHOOL?
YES...

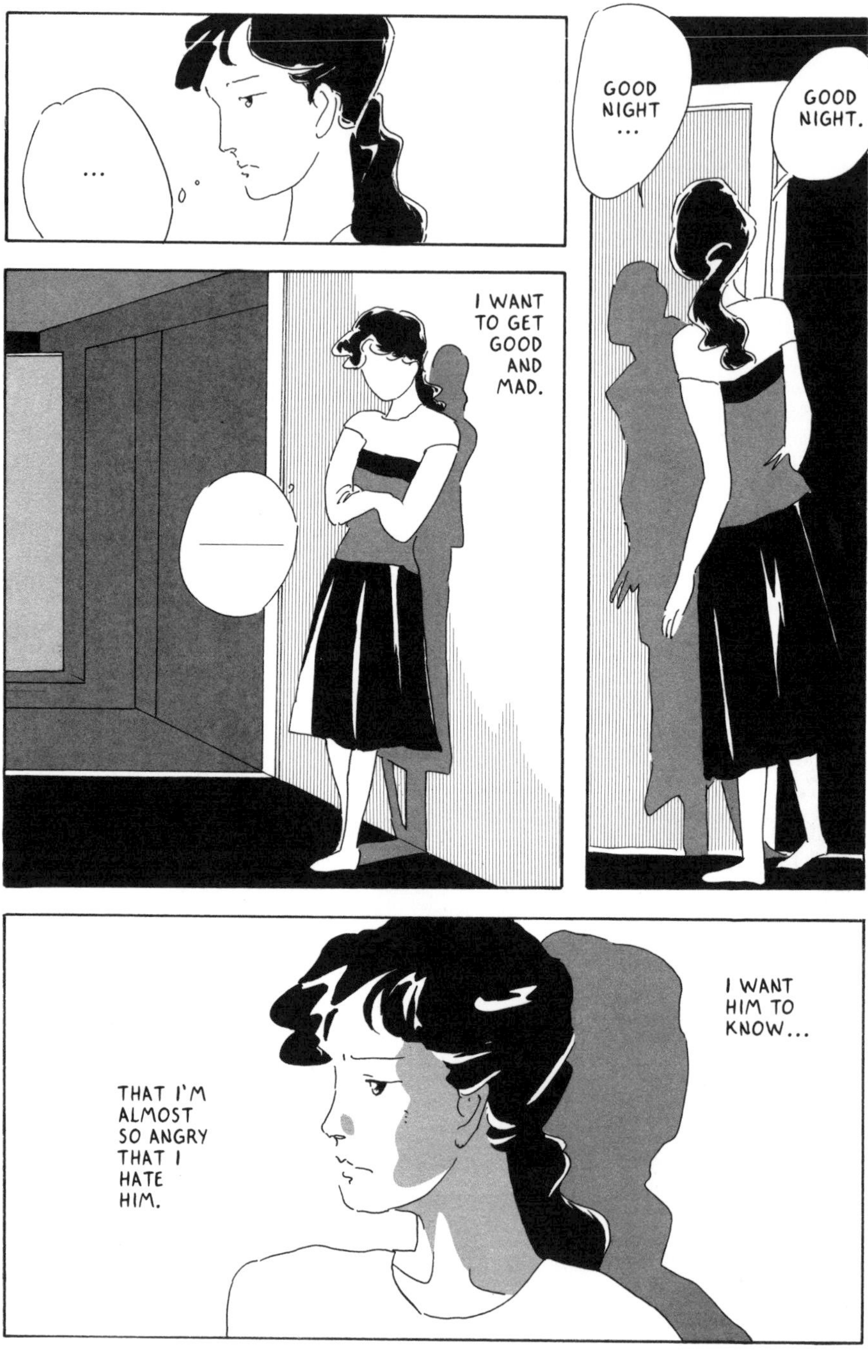
GOOD NIGHT.
GOOD NIGHT ...
...
I WANT TO GET GOOD AND MAD.
I WANT HIM TO KNOW...
THAT I'M ALMOST SO ANGRY THAT I HATE HIM.

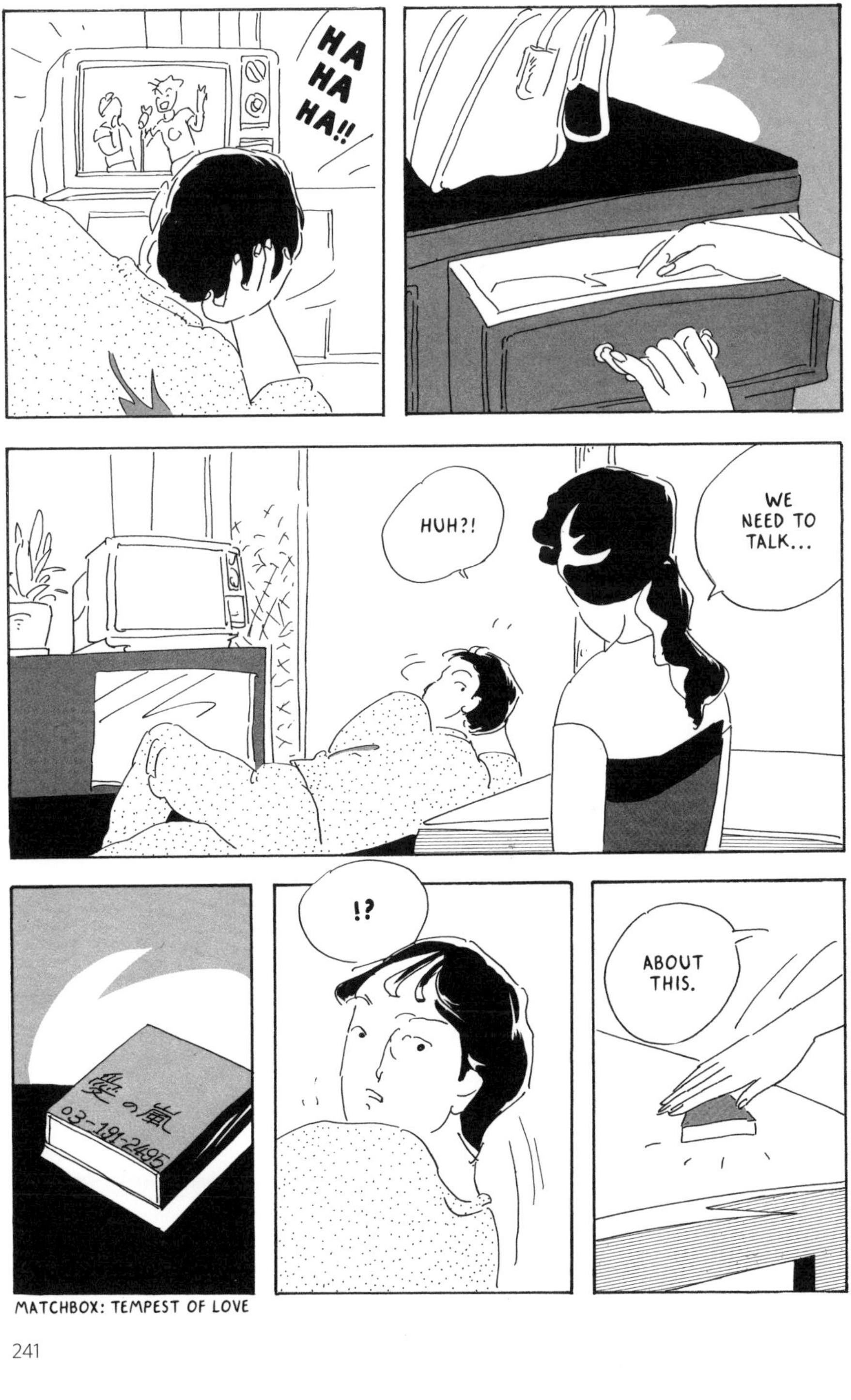
HA HA HA!!
WE NEED TO TALK...
HUH?!
ABOUT THIS.
!?
愛の嵐
03-191-2495

MATCHBOX: TEMPEST OF LOVE

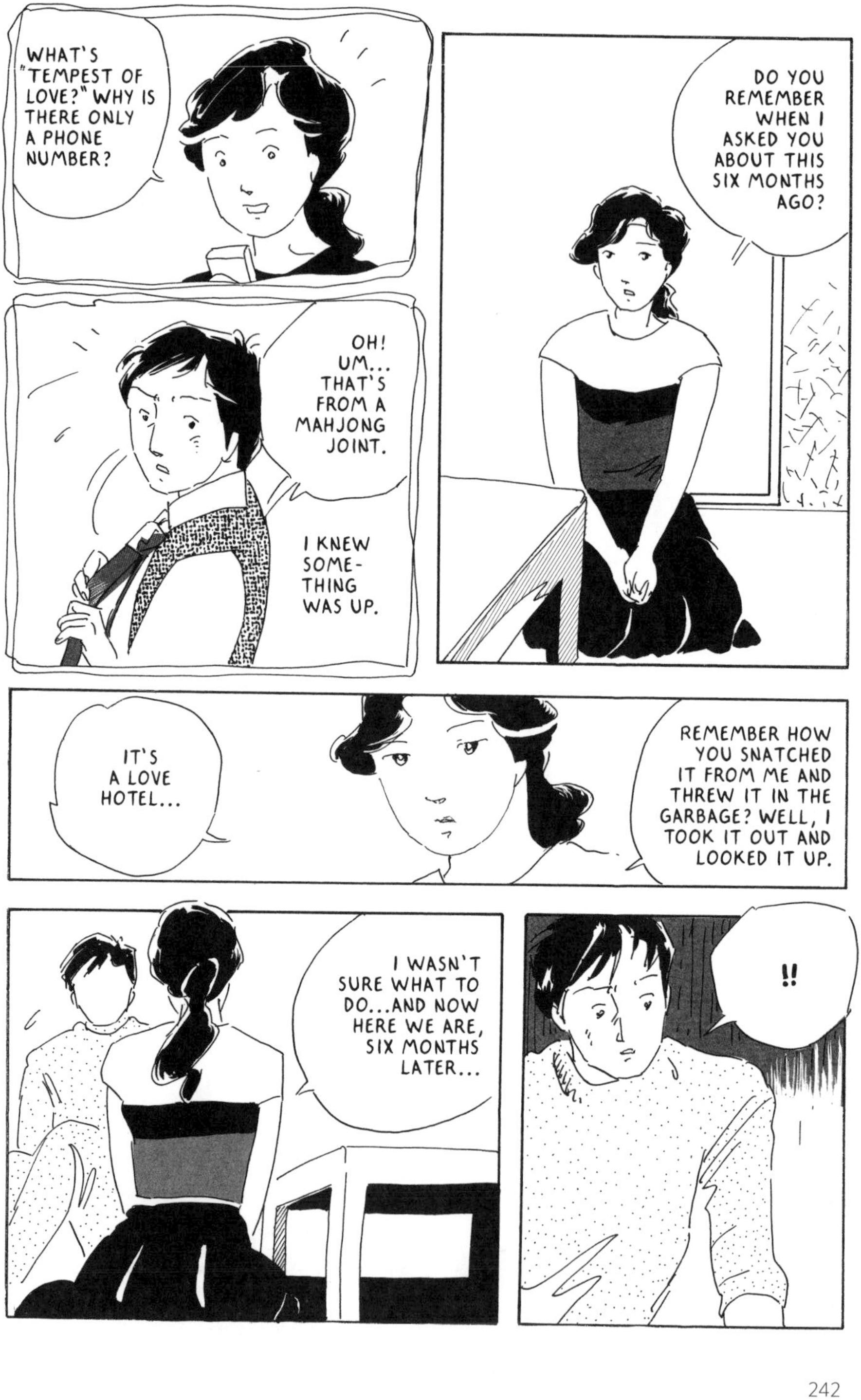
DO YOU REMEMBER WHEN I ASKED YOU ABOUT THIS SIX MONTHS AGO?
WHAT'S "TEMPEST OF LOVE?" WHY IS THERE ONLY A PHONE NUMBER?
OH! UM... THAT'S FROM A MAHJONG JOINT.
I KNEW SOME-THING WAS UP.
REMEMBER HOW YOU SNATCHED IT FROM ME AND THREW IT IN THE GARBAGE? WELL, I TOOK IT OUT AND LOOKED IT UP.
IT'S A LOVE HOTEL...
!!
I WASN'T SURE WHAT TO DO...AND NOW HERE WE ARE, SIX MONTHS LATER...

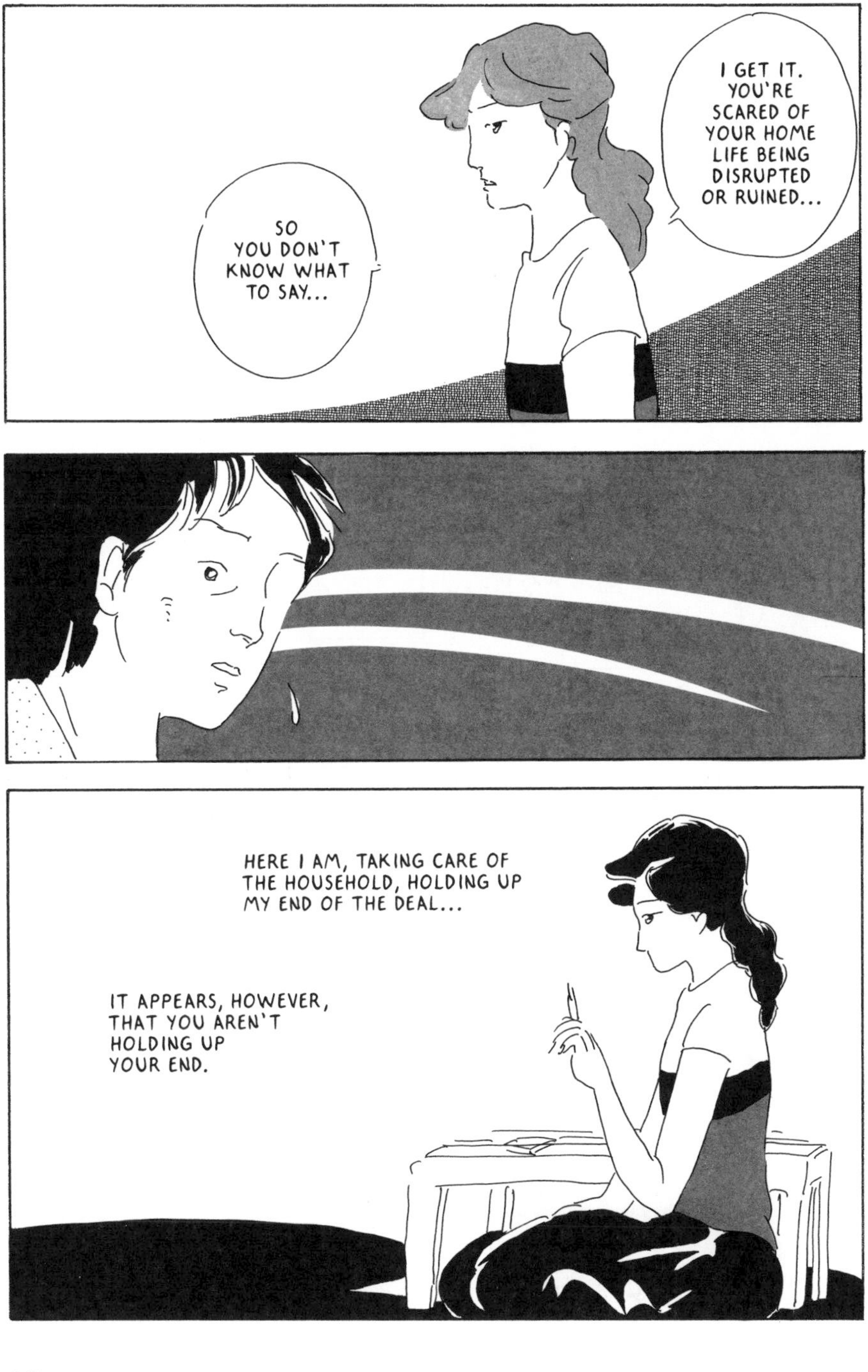
I GET IT. YOU'RE SCARED OF YOUR HOME LIFE BEING DISRUPTED OR RUINED...
SO YOU DON'T KNOW WHAT TO SAY...
HERE I AM, TAKING CARE OF THE HOUSEHOLD, HOLDING UP MY END OF THE DEAL...
IT APPEARS, HOWEVER, THAT YOU AREN'T HOLDING UP YOUR END.

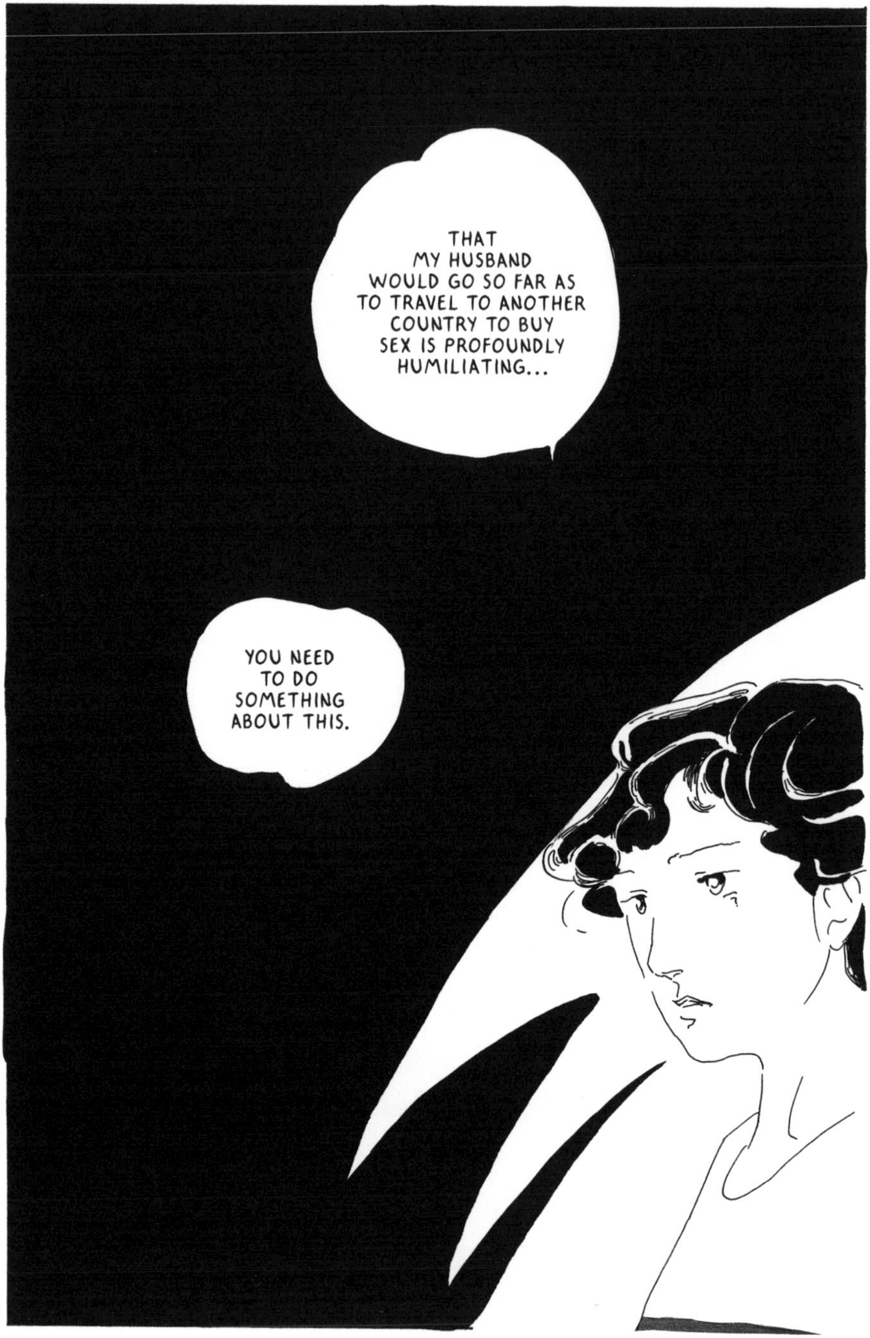
THAT MY HUSBAND WOULD GO SO FAR AS TO TRAVEL TO ANOTHER COUNTRY TO BUY SEX IS PROFOUNDLY HUMILIATING...
YOU NEED TO DO SOMETHING ABOUT THIS.

Talk To My Back

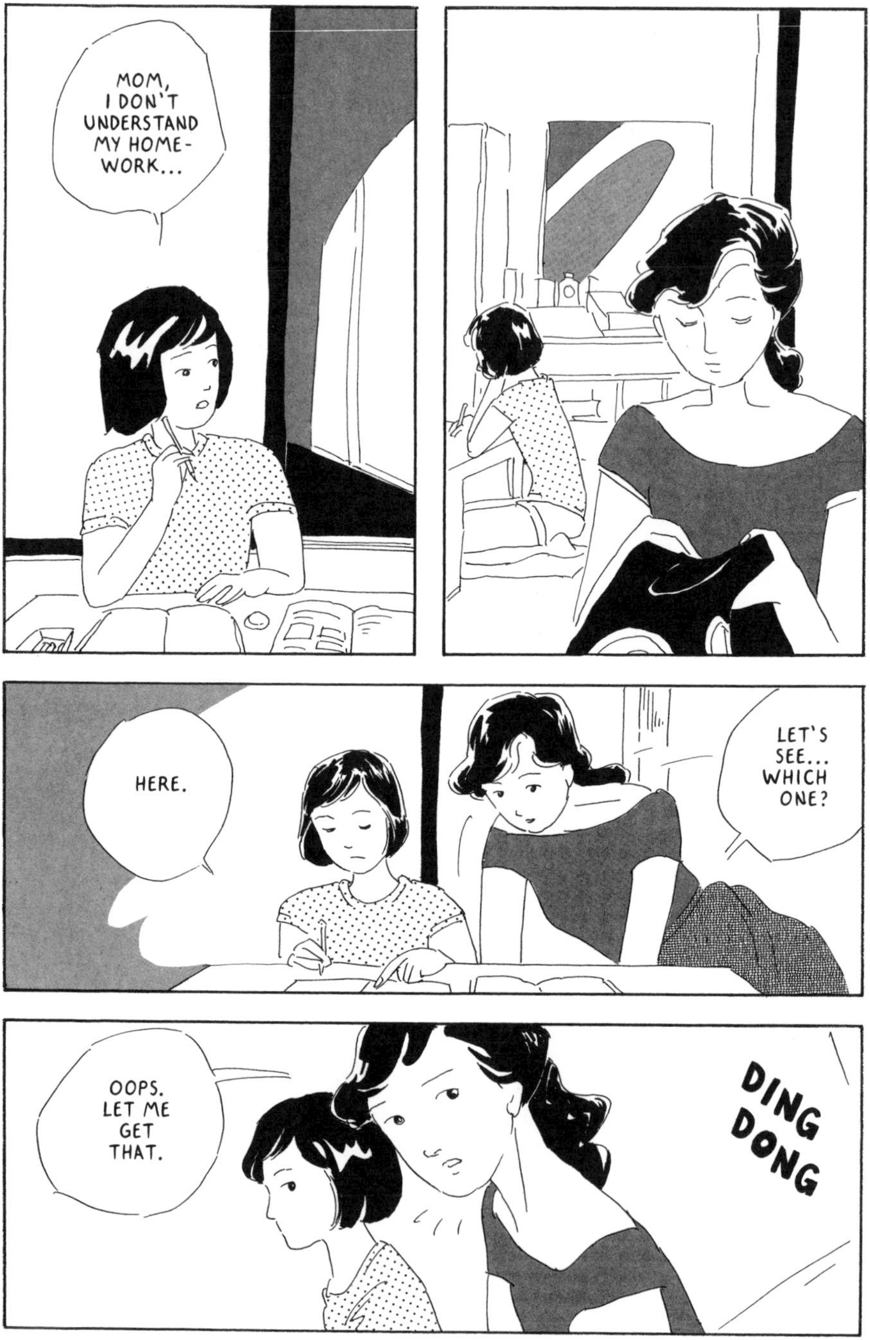
MOM, I DON'T UNDERSTAND MY HOME-WORK...
LET'S SEE... WHICH ONE?
HERE.
DING DONG
OOPS. LET ME GET THAT.

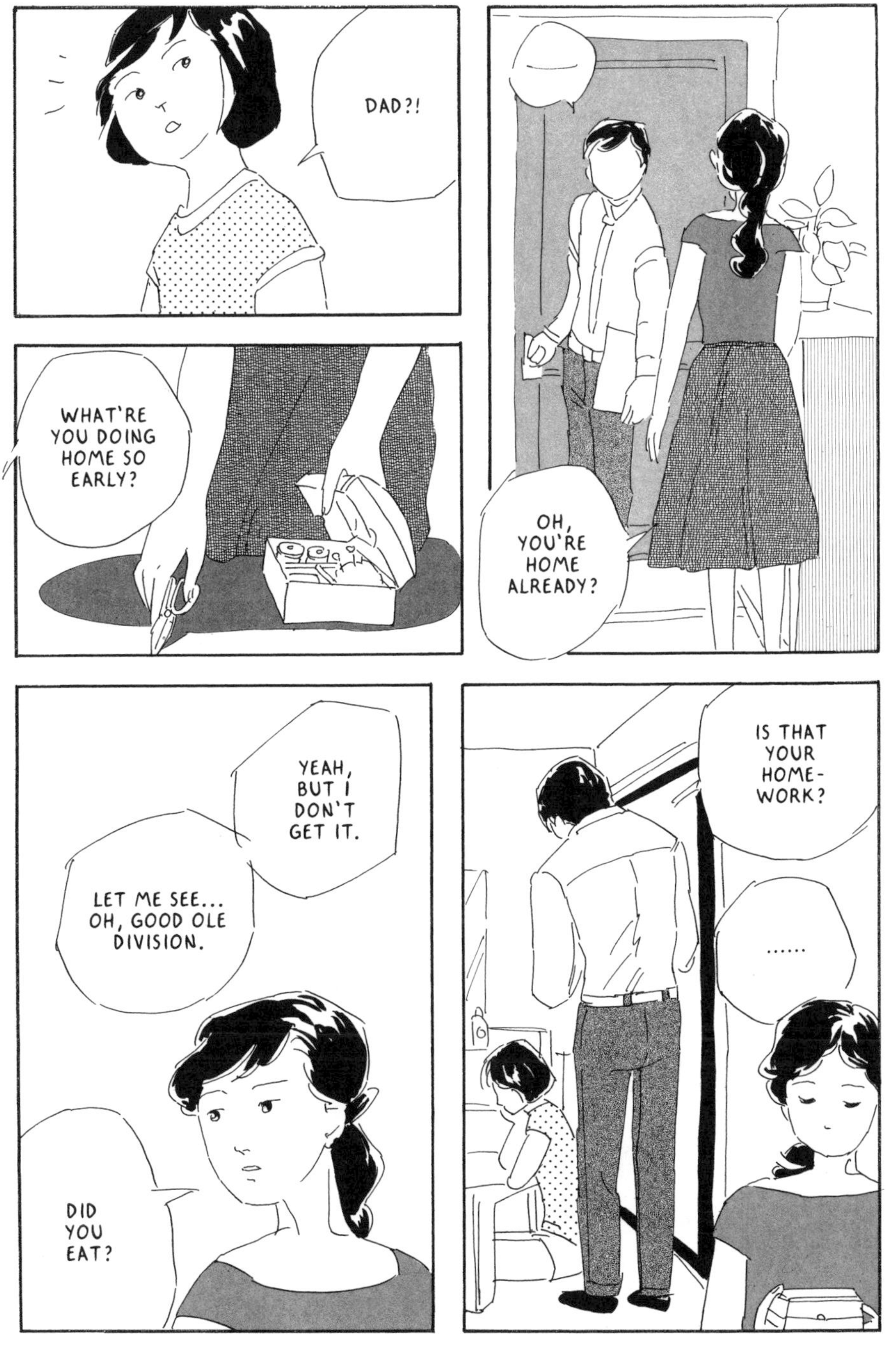
OH, YOU'RE HOME ALREADY?
DAD?!
WHAT'RE YOU DOING HOME SO EARLY?
IS THAT YOUR HOME-WORK?
......
YEAH, BUT I DON'T GET IT.
LET ME SEE... OH, GOOD OLE DIVISION.
DID YOU EAT?

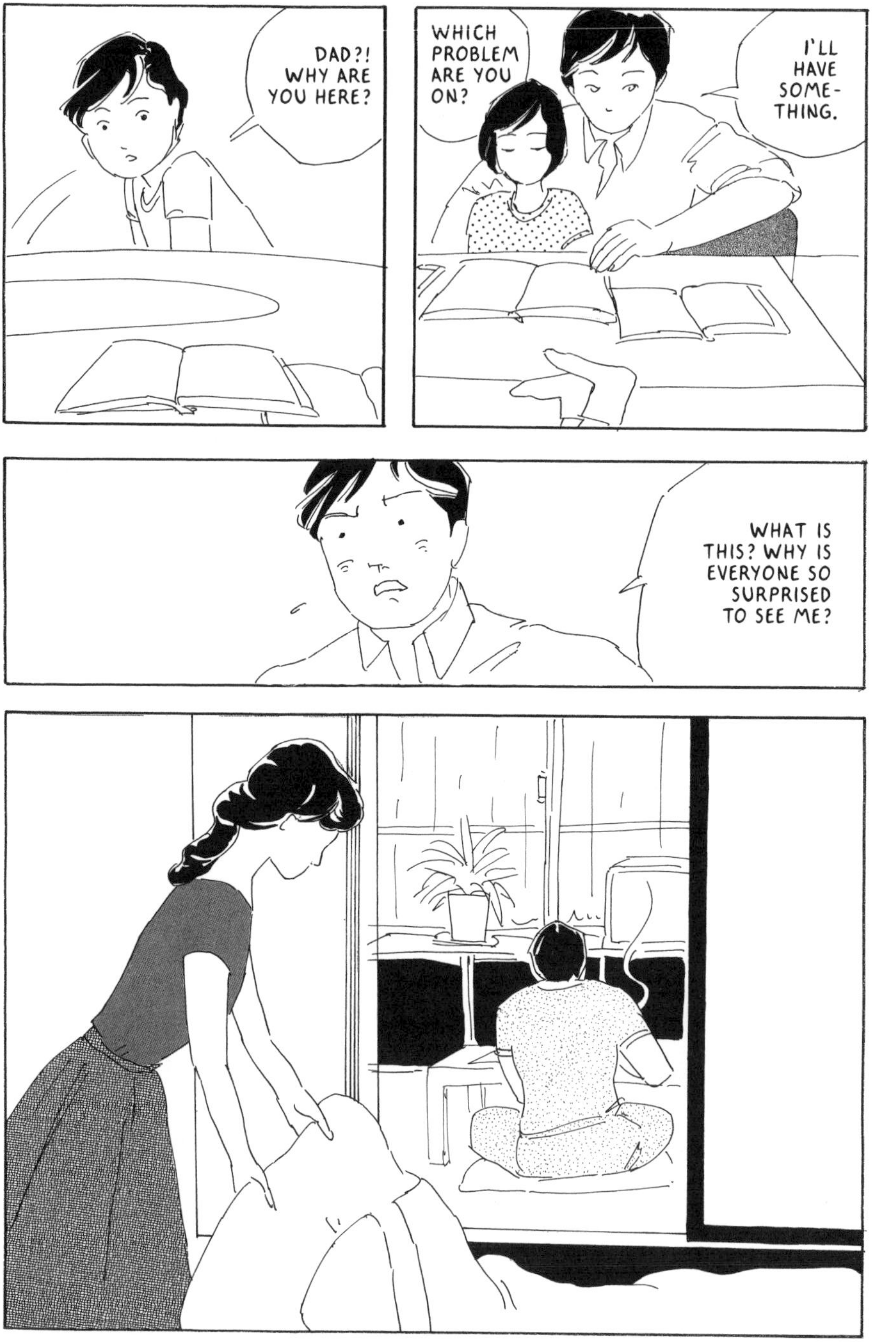
I'LL HAVE SOME-THING.
WHICH PROBLEM ARE YOU ON?
DAD?! WHY ARE YOU HERE?
WHAT IS THIS? WHY IS EVERYONE SO SURPRISED TO SEE ME?

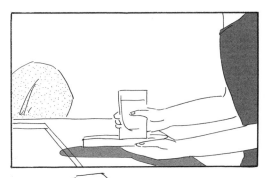

CAN I HAVE SOME MUGI-CHA?

THE TRIP GOT CANCELLED... THE ONE TO BANGKOK.

......

THEY COULDN'T GET ENOUGH PEOPLE TOGETHER...

....

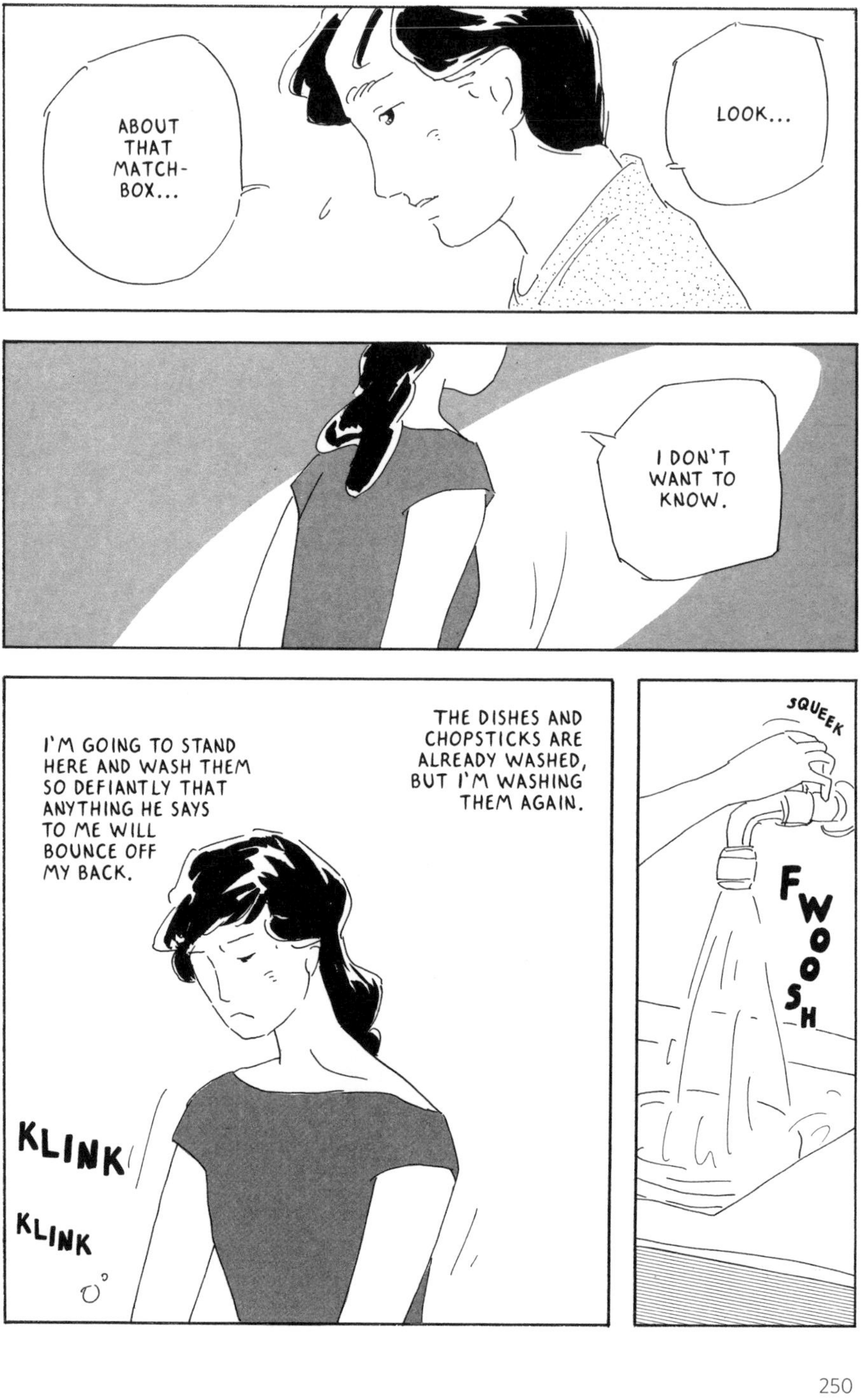
LOOK...
ABOUT THAT MATCH-BOX...
I DON'T WANT TO KNOW.
SQUEEK
FWOOSH
THE DISHES AND CHOPSTICKS ARE ALREADY WASHED, BUT I'M WASHING THEM AGAIN.
I'M GOING TO STAND HERE AND WASH THEM SO DEFIANTLY THAT ANYTHING HE SAYS TO ME WILL BOUNCE OFF MY BACK.
KLINK
KLINK

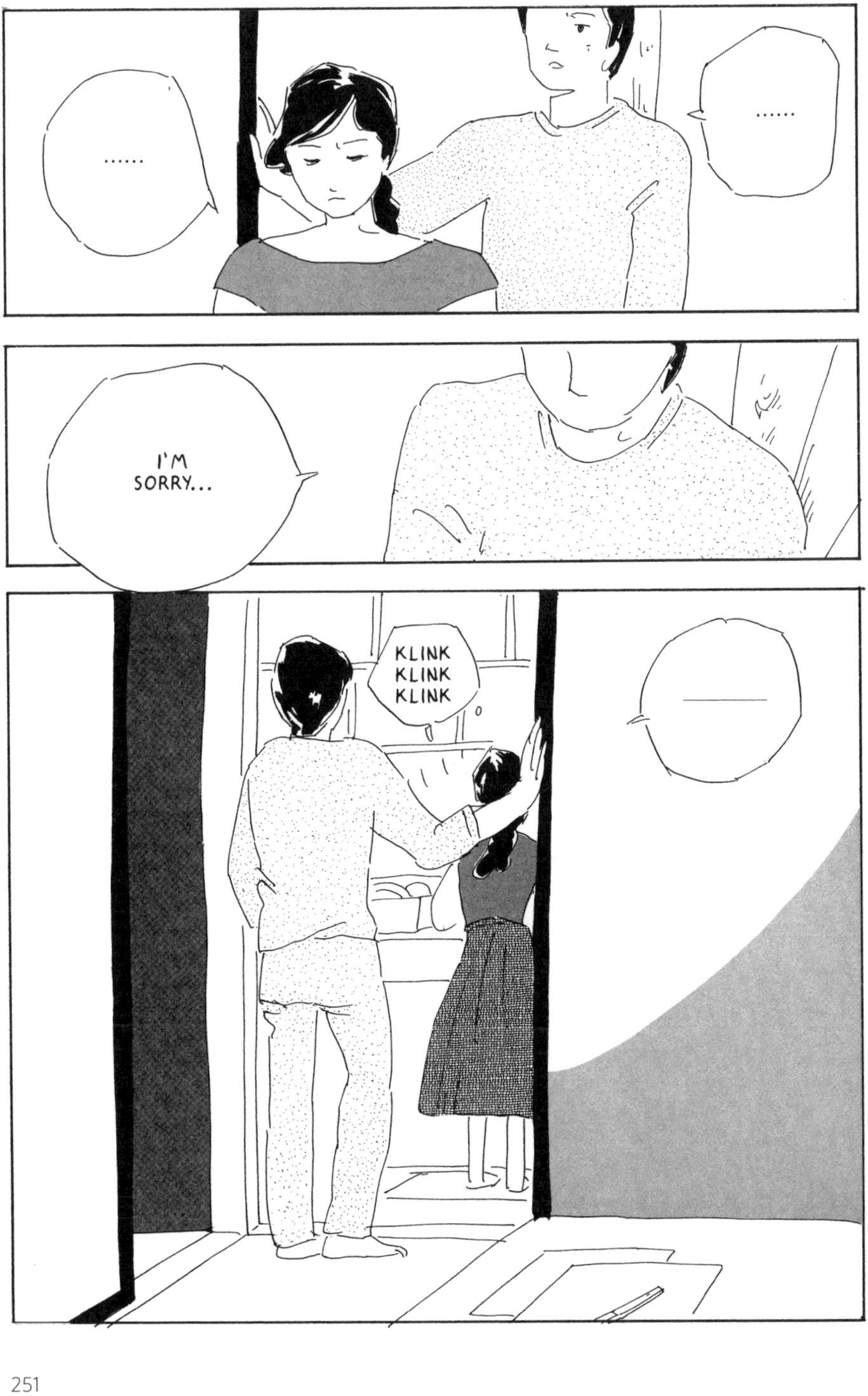
......
......
I'M SORRY...
————
KLINK KLINK KLINK

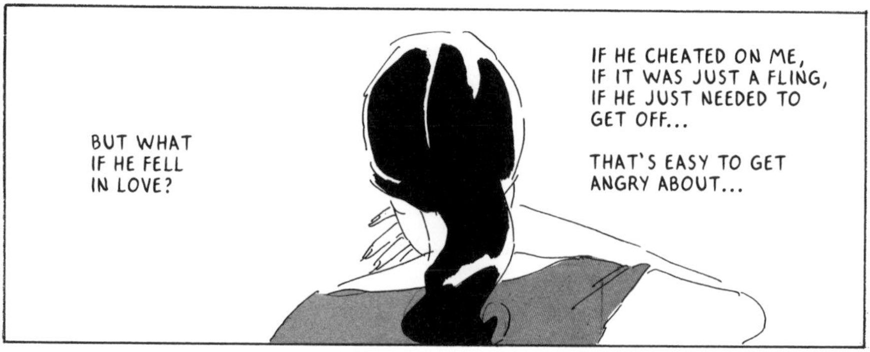
IF HE CHEATED ON ME, IF IT WAS JUST A FLING, IF HE JUST NEEDED TO GET OFF...
THAT'S EASY TO GET ANGRY ABOUT...
BUT WHAT IF HE FELL IN LOVE?

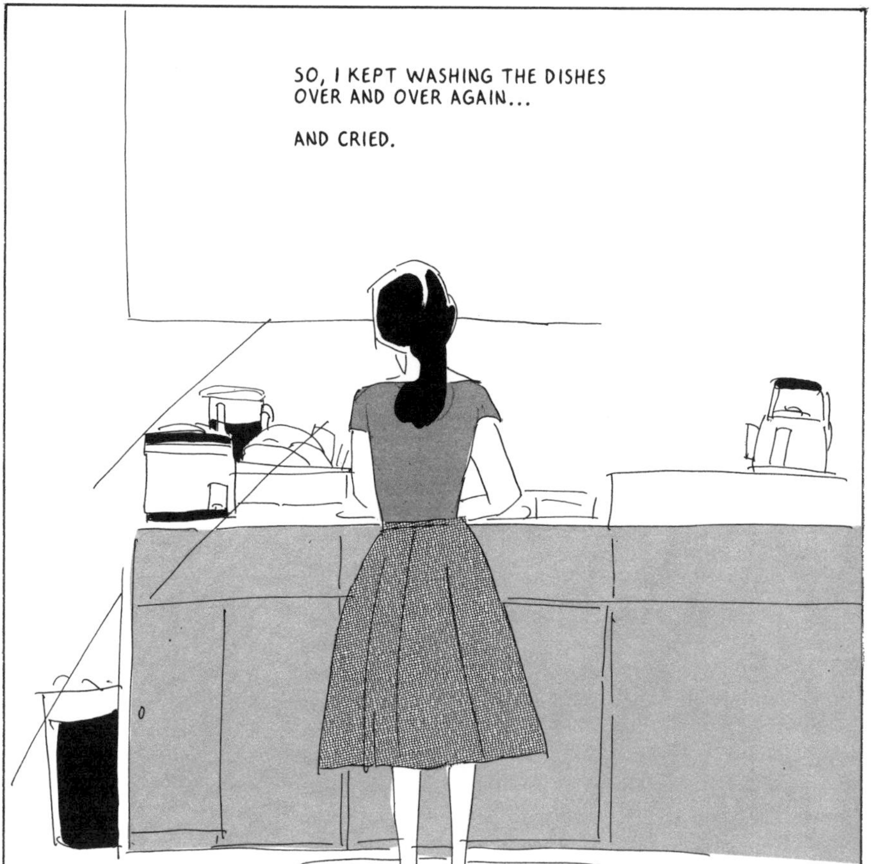
SO, I KEPT WASHING THE DISHES OVER AND OVER AGAIN...
AND CRIED.

Emancipation Day

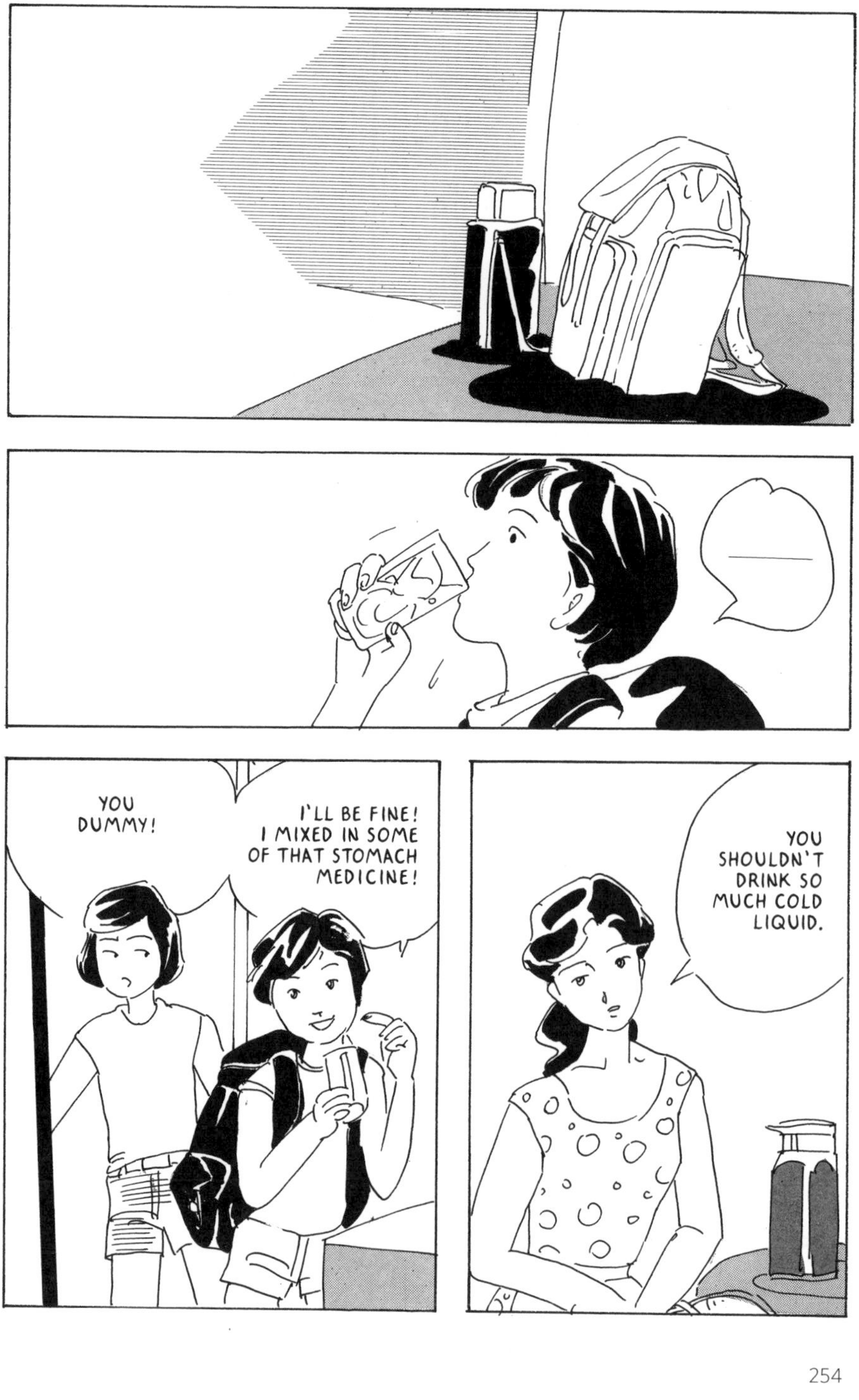
—
YOU SHOULDN'T DRINK SO MUCH COLD LIQUID.
I'LL BE FINE! I MIXED IN SOME OF THAT STOMACH MEDICINE!
YOU DUMMY!

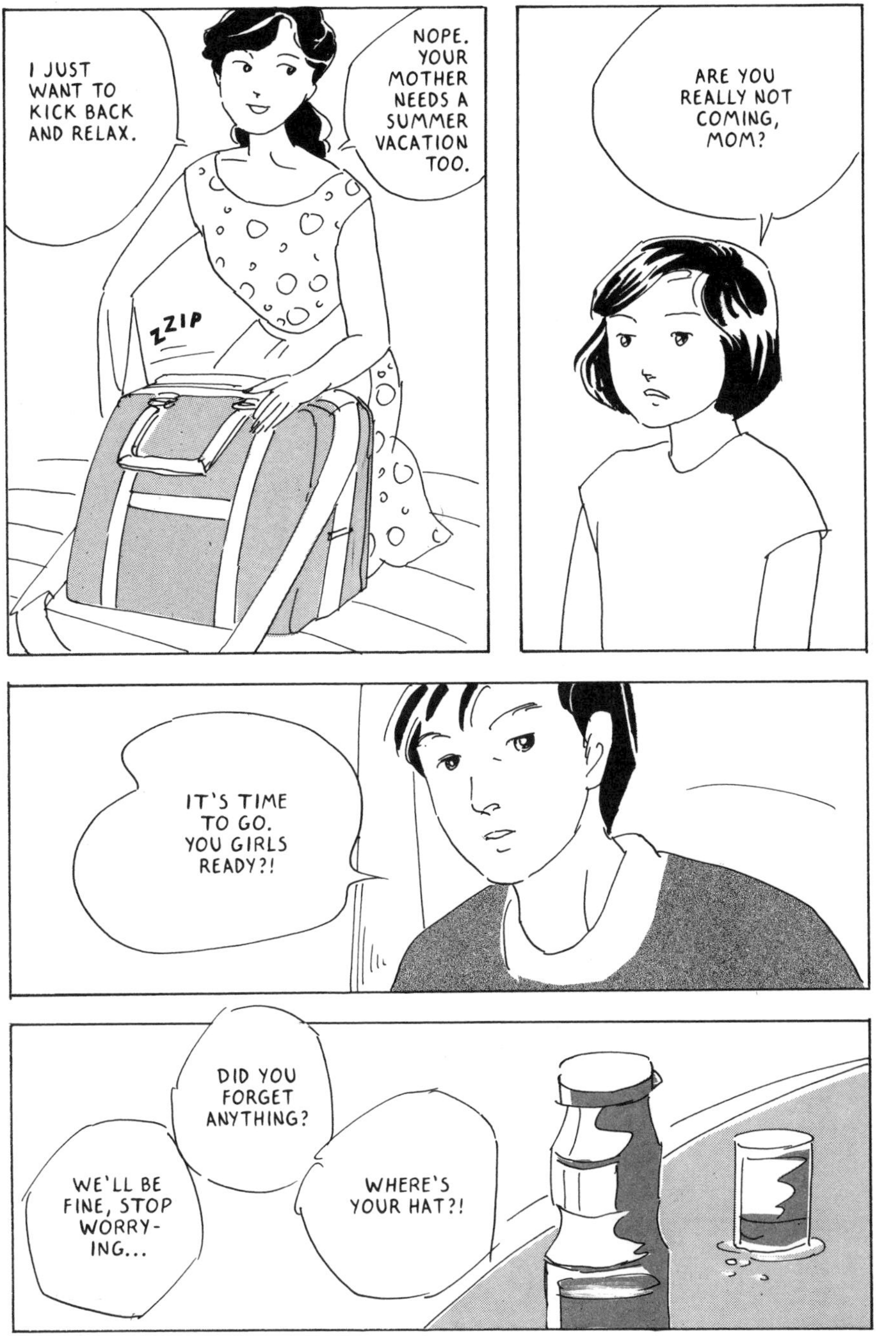
ARE YOU REALLY NOT COMING, MOM?
NOPE. YOUR MOTHER NEEDS A SUMMER VACATION TOO.
I JUST WANT TO KICK BACK AND RELAX.
ZZIP
IT'S TIME TO GO. YOU GIRLS READY?!
DID YOU FORGET ANYTHING?
WHERE'S YOUR HAT?!
WE'LL BE FINE, STOP WORRY-ING...

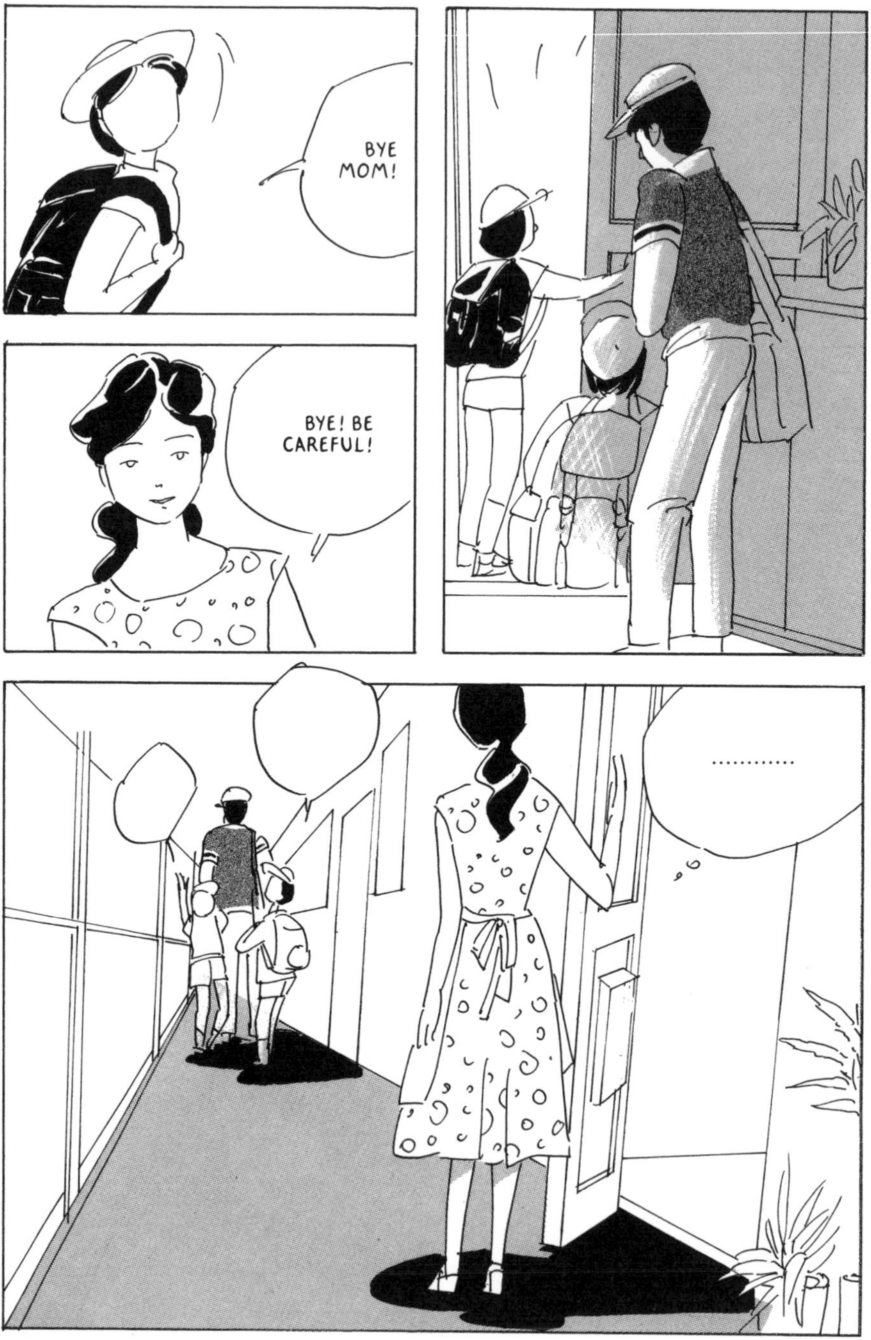
BYE MOM!
BYE! BE CAREFUL!
....

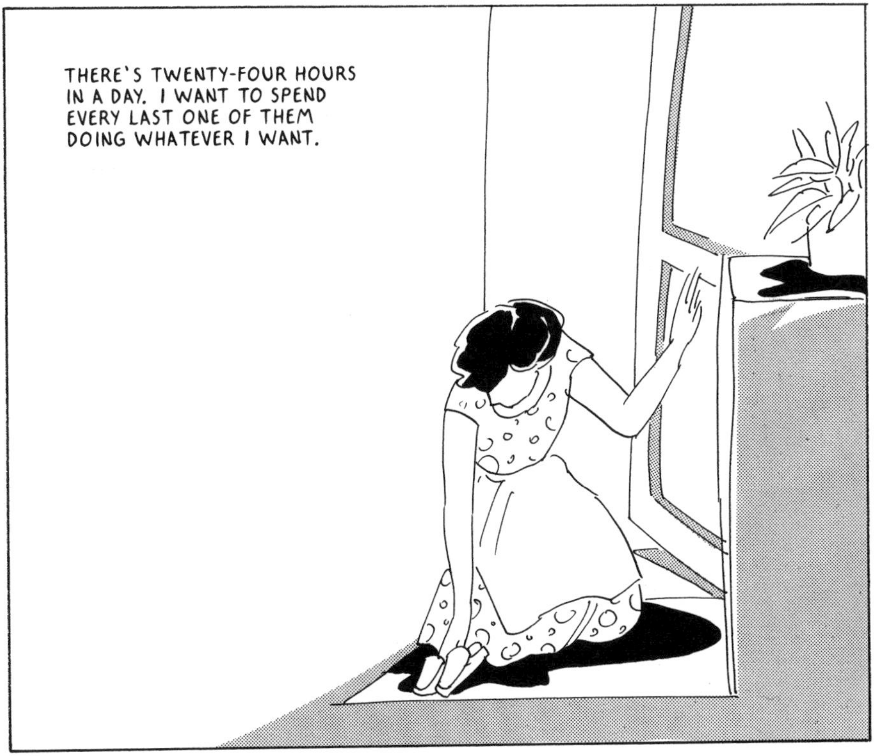
THERE'S TWENTY-FOUR HOURS IN A DAY. I WANT TO SPEND EVERY LAST ONE OF THEM DOING WHATEVER I WANT.

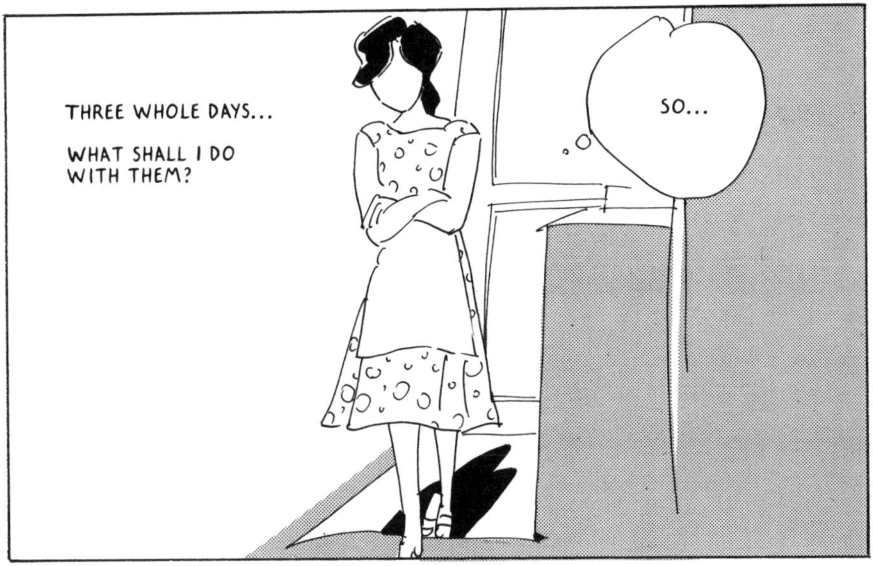
SO...
THREE WHOLE DAYS...
WHAT SHALL I DO WITH THEM?

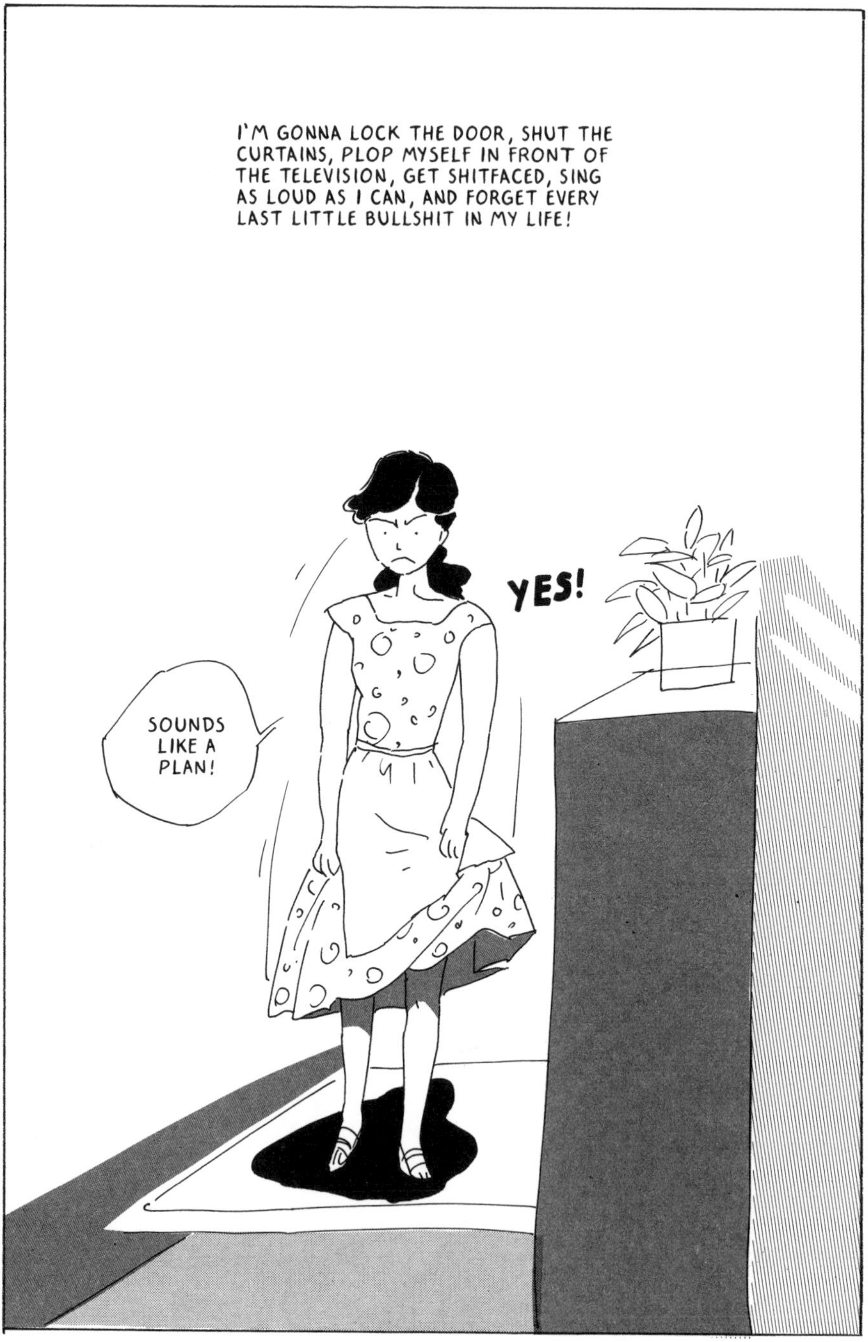
I'M GONNA LOCK THE DOOR, SHUT THE CURTAINS, PLOP MYSELF IN FRONT OF THE TELEVISION, GET SHITFACED, SING AS LOUD AS I CAN, AND FORGET EVERY LAST LITTLE BULLSHIT IN MY LIFE!
YES!
SOUNDS LIKE A PLAN!

Part-time Job

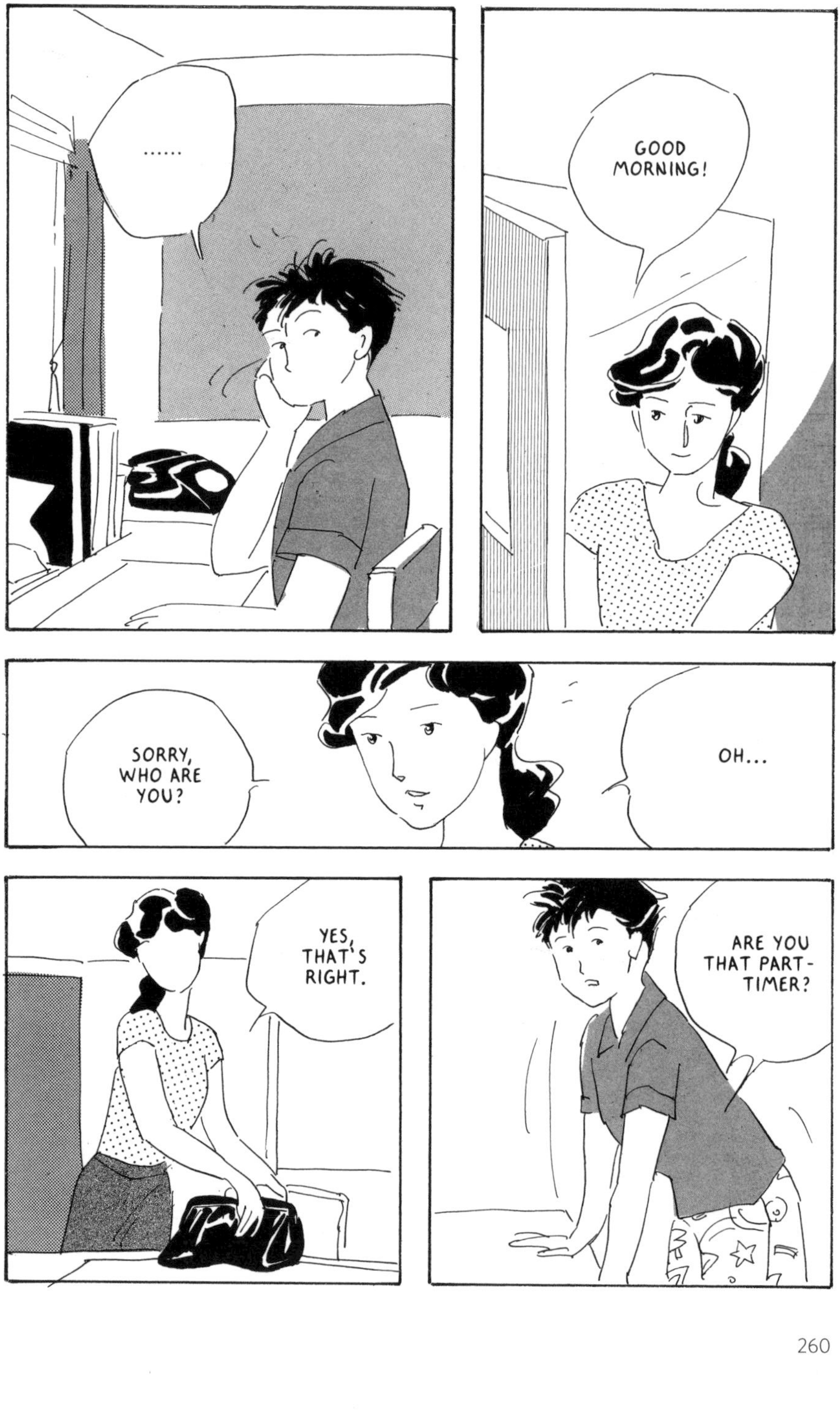
GOOD MORNING!
......
OH...
SORRY, WHO ARE YOU?
ARE YOU THAT PART-TIMER?
YES, THAT'S RIGHT.

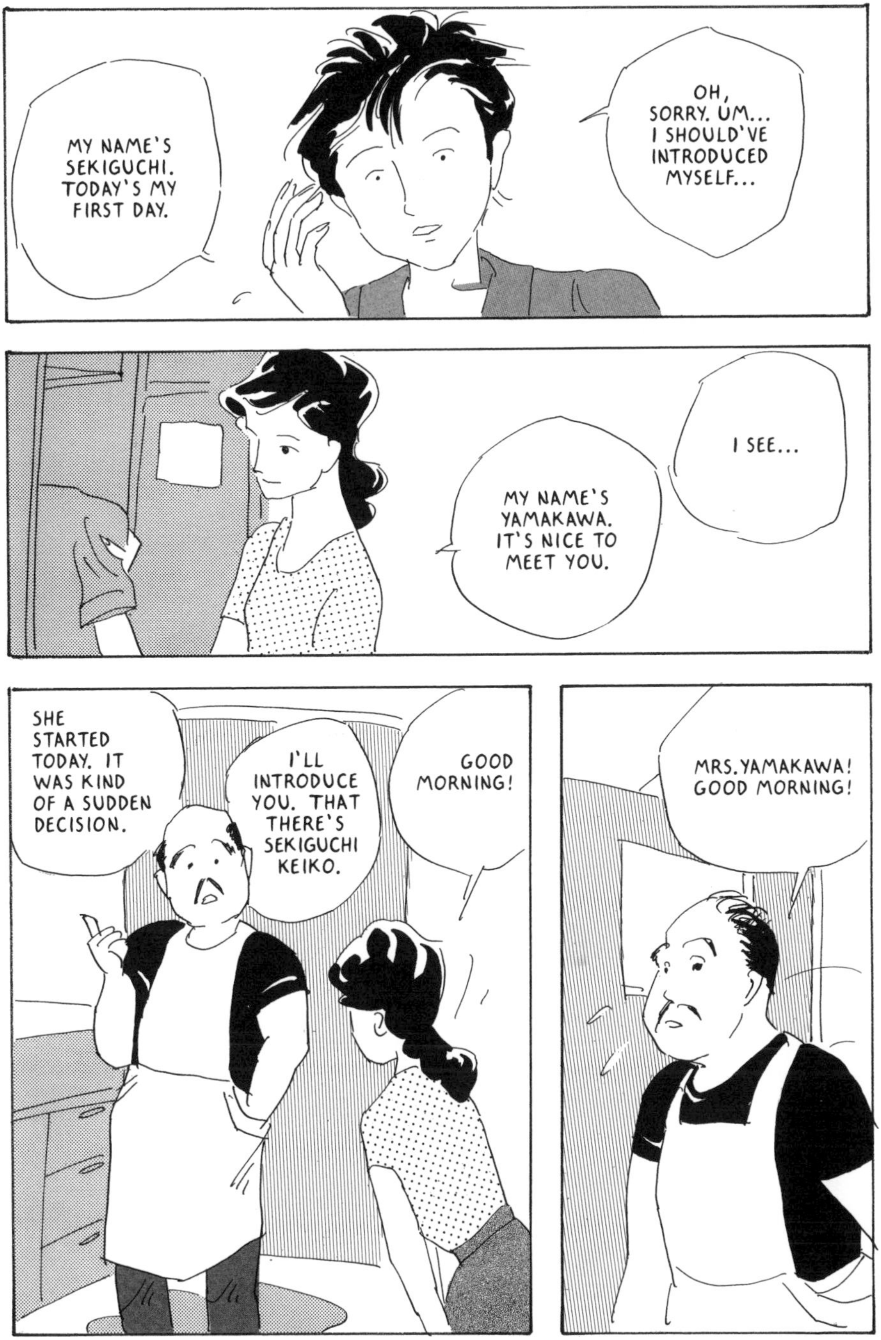
OH, SORRY. UM... I SHOULD'VE INTRODUCED MYSELF...
MY NAME'S SEKIGUCHI. TODAY'S MY FIRST DAY.
I SEE...
MY NAME'S YAMAKAWA. IT'S NICE TO MEET YOU.
MRS.YAMAKAWA! GOOD MORNING!
GOOD MORNING!
I'LL INTRODUCE YOU. THAT THERE'S SEKIGUCHI KEIKO.
SHE STARTED TODAY. IT WAS KIND OF A SUDDEN DECISION.

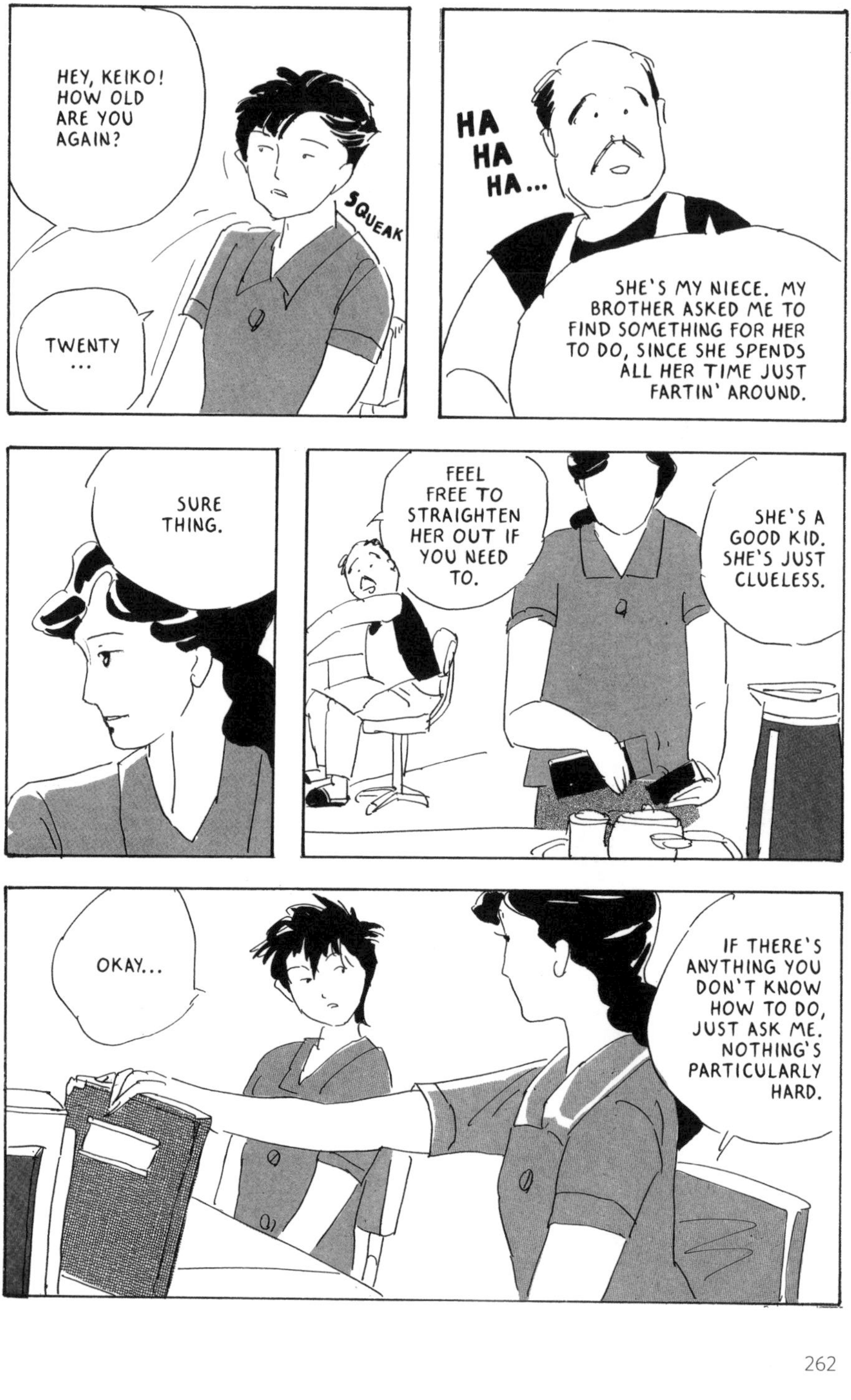
HA HA HA...
SHE'S MY NIECE. MY BROTHER ASKED ME TO FIND SOMETHING FOR HER TO DO, SINCE SHE SPENDS ALL HER TIME JUST FARTIN' AROUND.
HEY, KEIKO! HOW OLD ARE YOU AGAIN?
SQUEAK
TWENTY ...
SHE'S A GOOD KID. SHE'S JUST CLUELESS.
FEEL FREE TO STRAIGHTEN HER OUT IF YOU NEED TO.
SURE THING.
IF THERE'S ANYTHING YOU DON'T KNOW HOW TO DO, JUST ASK ME. NOTHING'S PARTICULARLY HARD.
OKAY...

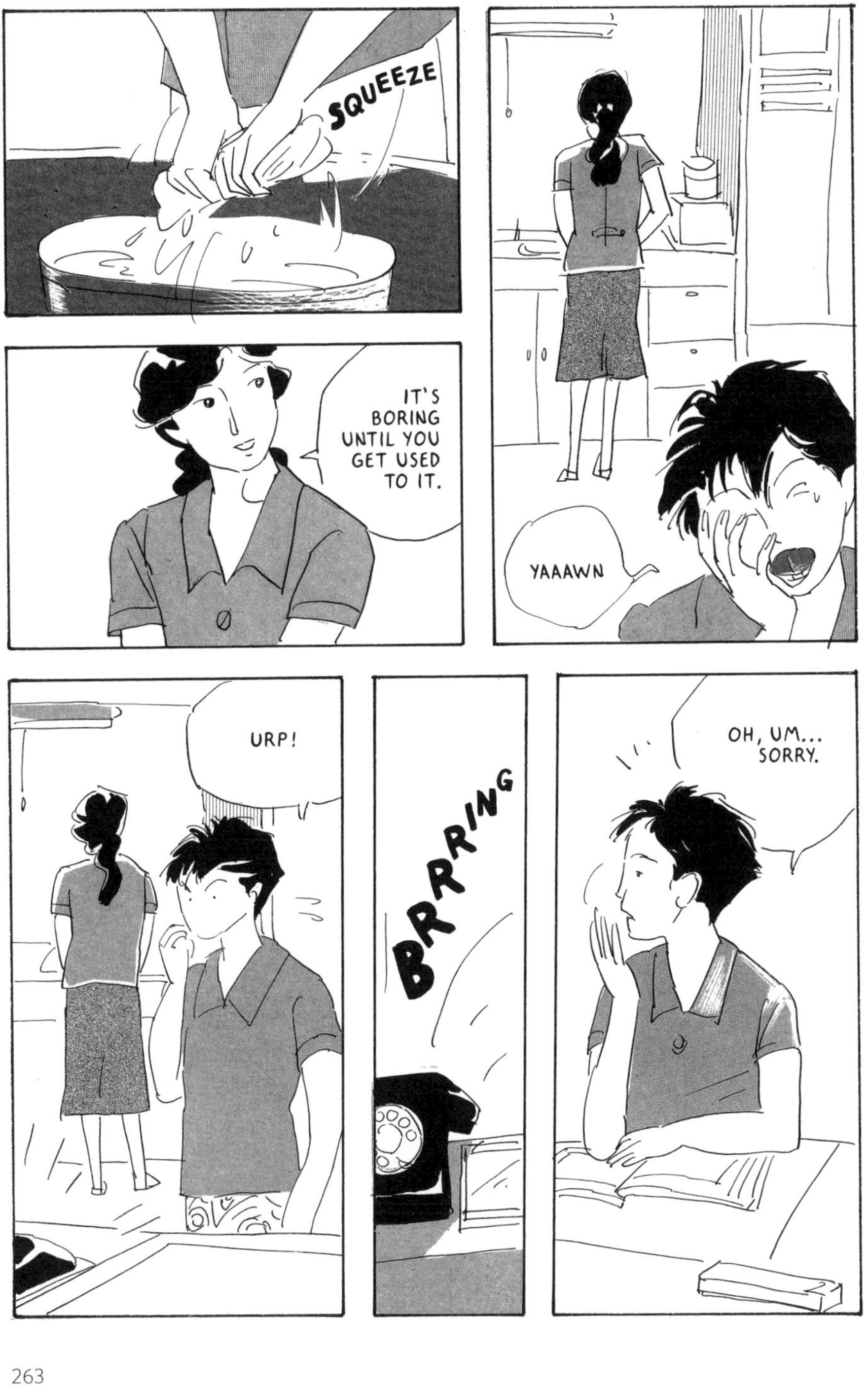
YAAAWN
SQUEEZE
IT'S BORING UNTIL YOU GET USED TO IT.
OH, UM... SORRY.
BRRRING
URP!

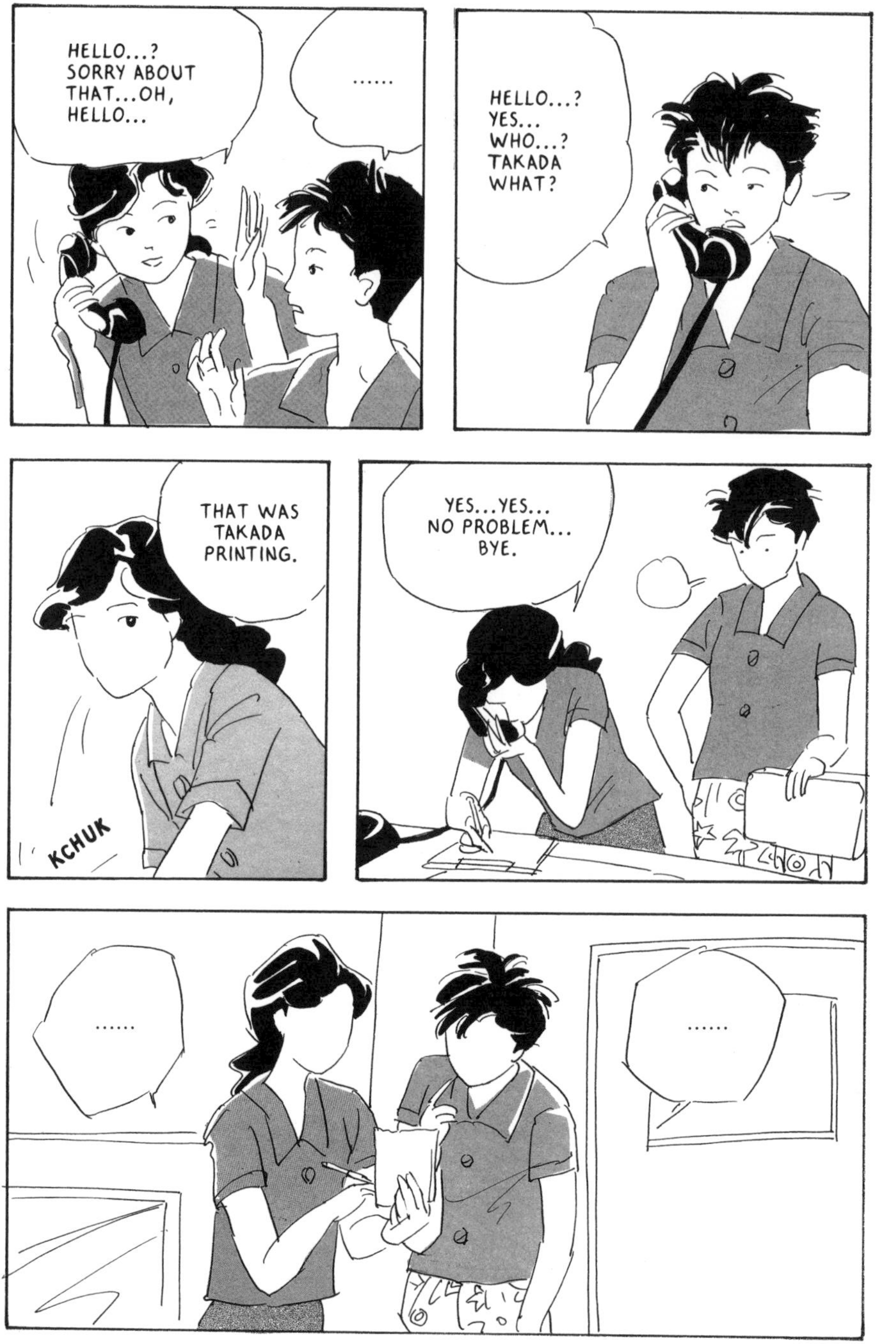
HELLO...? YES... WHO...? TAKADA WHAT?
......
HELLO...? SORRY ABOUT THAT...OH, HELLO...
YES...YES... NO PROBLEM... BYE.
THAT WAS TAKADA PRINTING.
KCHUK
......
......

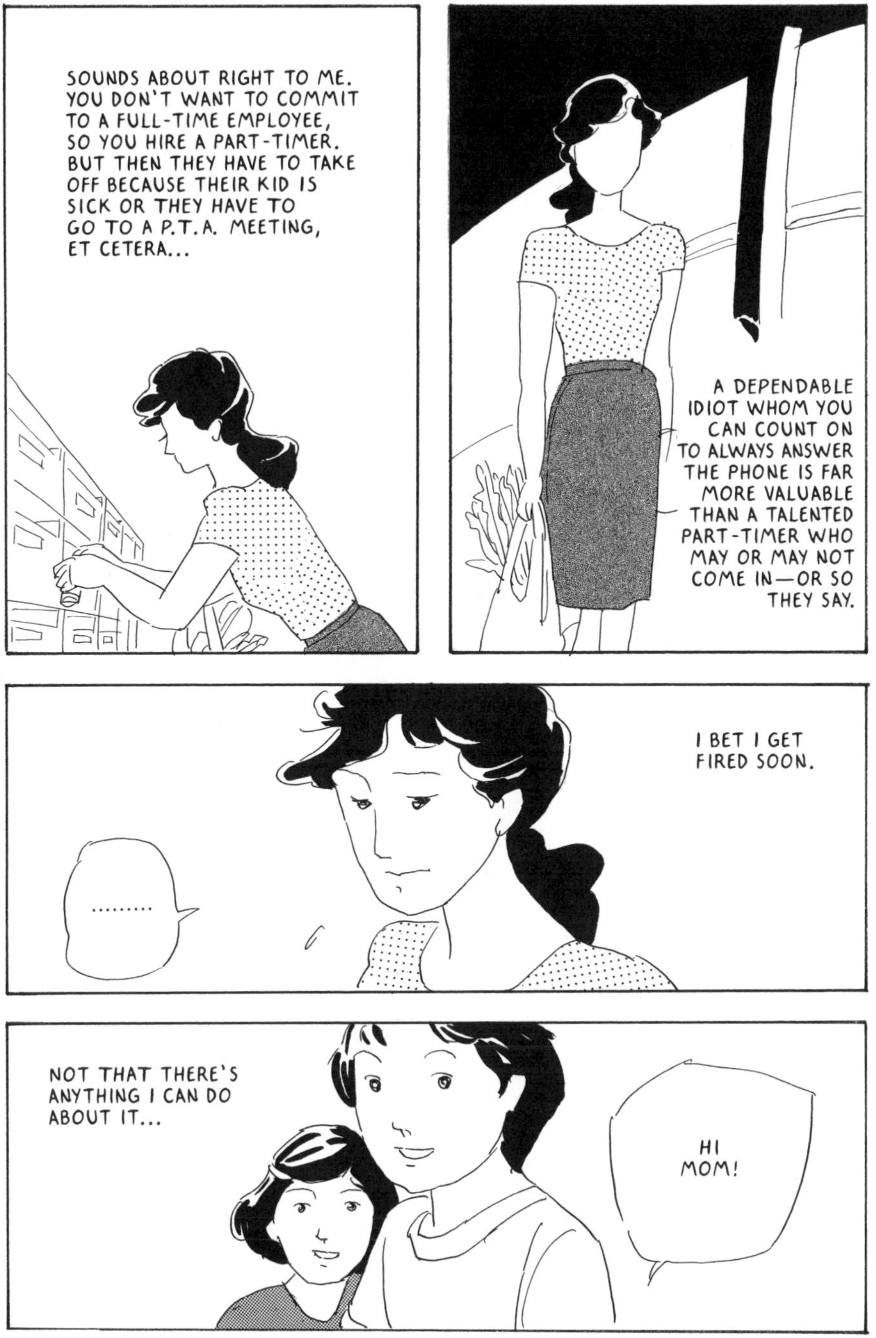
SOUNDS ABOUT RIGHT TO ME. YOU DON'T WANT TO COMMIT TO A FULL-TIME EMPLOYEE, SO YOU HIRE A PART-TIMER. BUT THEN THEY HAVE TO TAKE OFF BECAUSE THEIR KID IS SICK OR THEY HAVE TO GO TO A P.T.A. MEETING, ET CETERA...
A DEPENDABLE IDIOT WHOM YOU CAN COUNT ON TO ALWAYS ANSWER THE PHONE IS FAR MORE VALUABLE THAN A TALENTED PART-TIMER WHO MAY OR MAY NOT COME IN—OR SO THEY SAY.
I BET I GET FIRED SOON.
....
NOT THAT THERE'S ANYTHING I CAN DO ABOUT IT...
HI MOM!

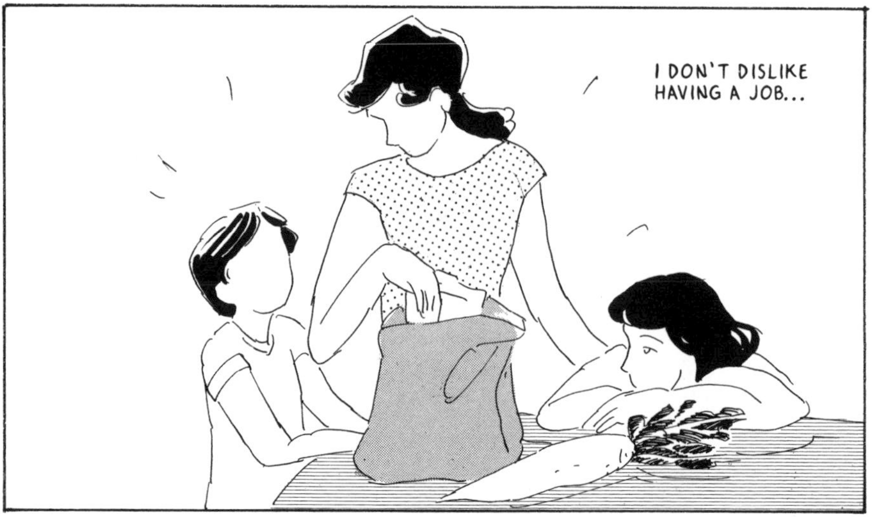
I DON'T DISLIKE
HAVING A JOB...
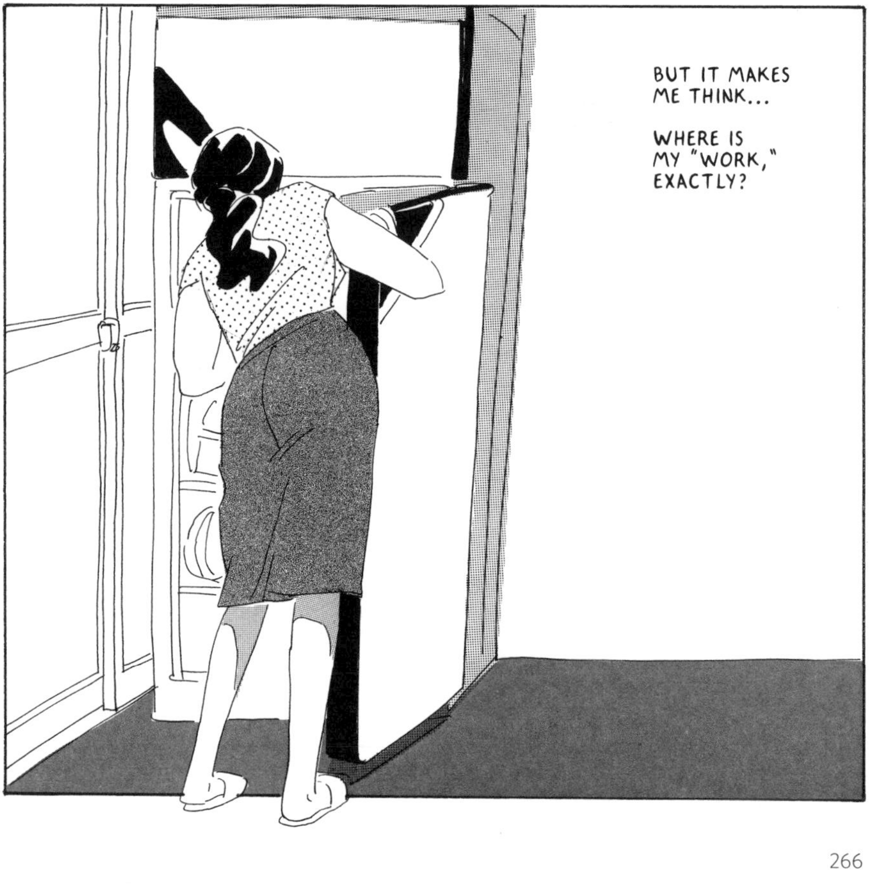
BUT IT MAKES
ME THINK...
WHERE IS
MY "WORK,"
EXACTLY?

Eggs

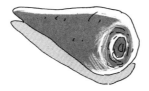

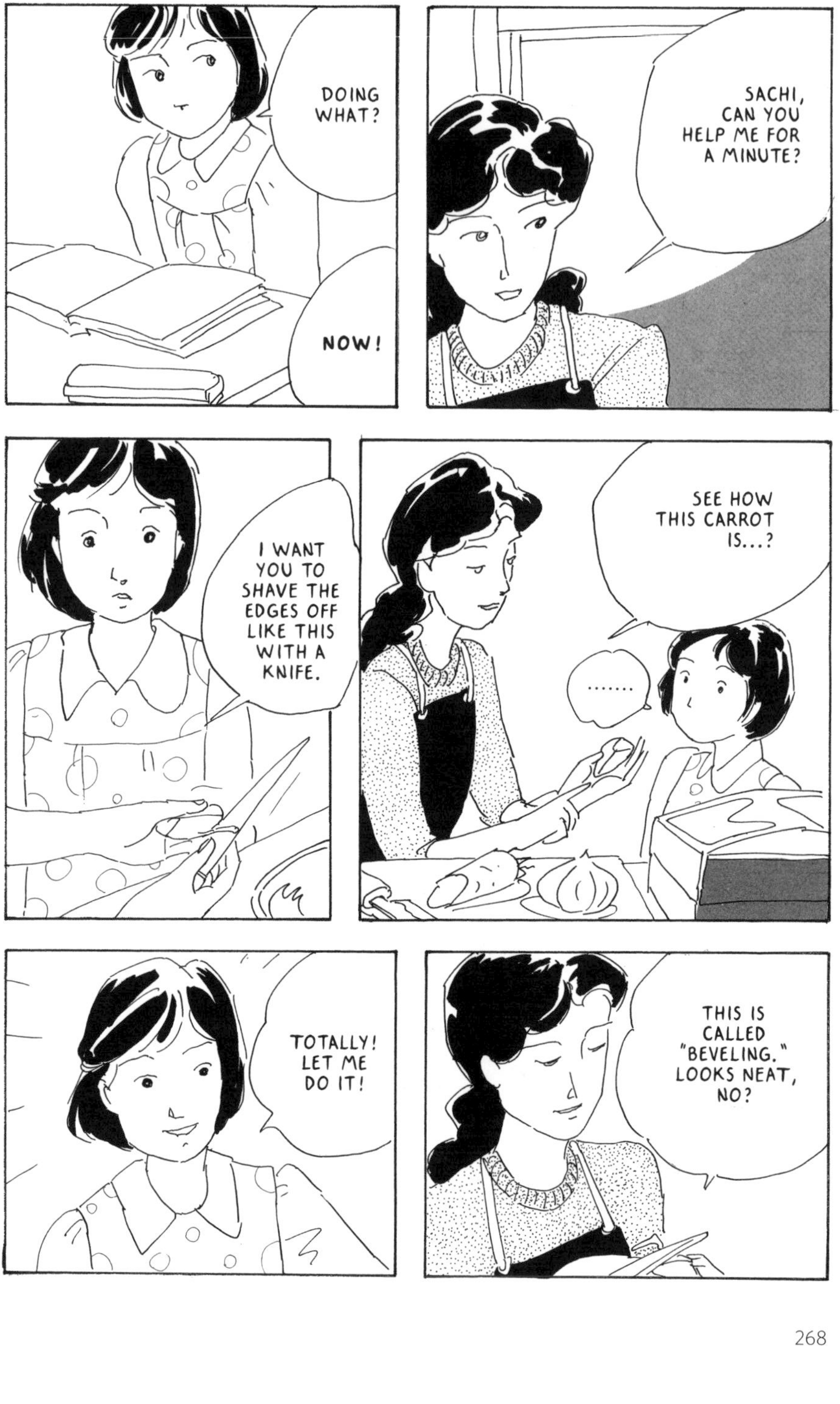
SACHI, CAN YOU HELP ME FOR A MINUTE?
DOING WHAT?
NOW!
SEE HOW THIS CARROT IS...?
....
I WANT YOU TO SHAVE THE EDGES OFF LIKE THIS WITH A KNIFE.
THIS IS CALLED "BEVELING." LOOKS NEAT, NO?
TOTALLY! LET ME DO IT!

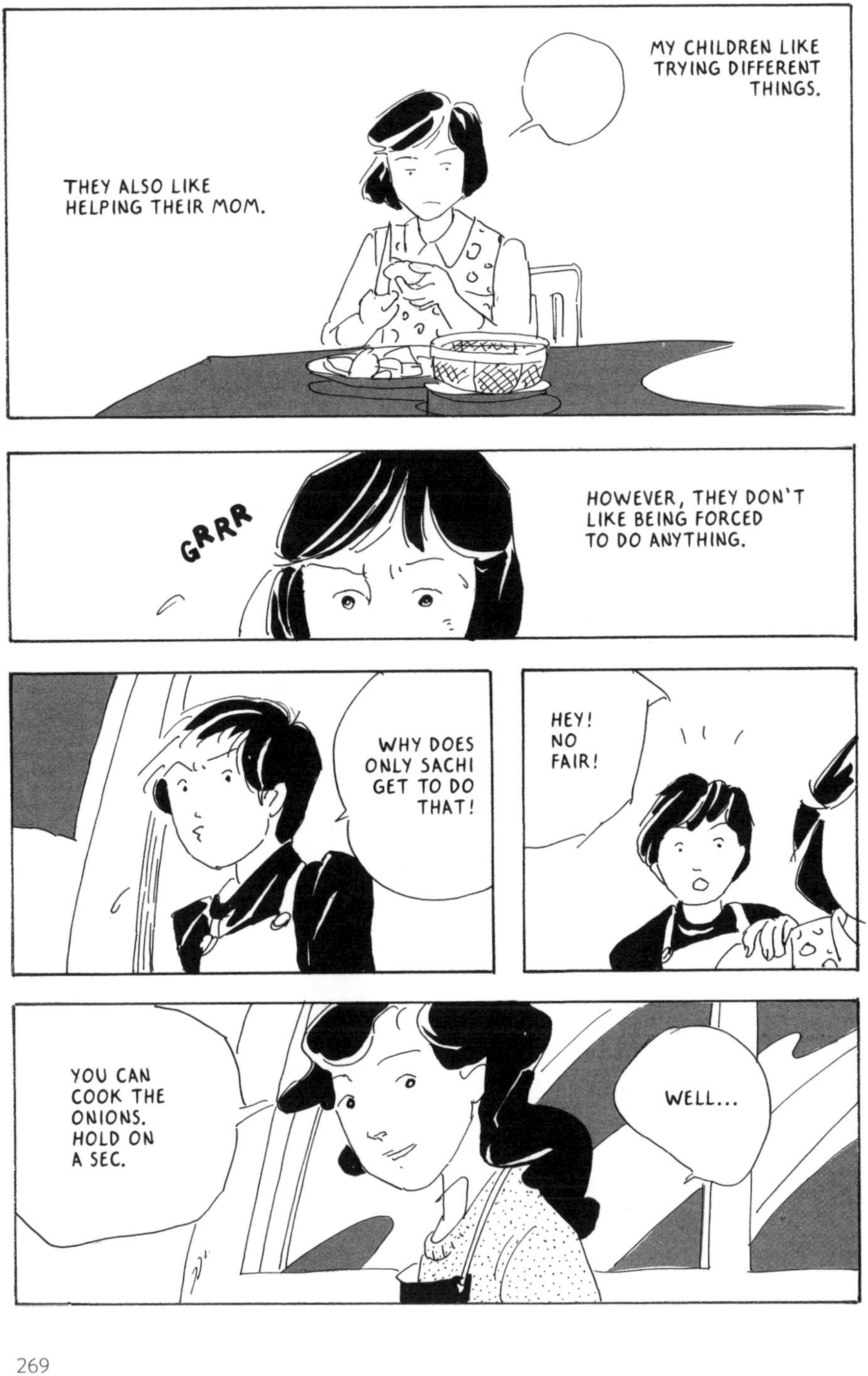
MY CHILDREN LIKE TRYING DIFFERENT THINGS.
THEY ALSO LIKE HELPING THEIR MOM.
HOWEVER, THEY DON'T LIKE BEING FORCED TO DO ANYTHING.
GRRR
HEY! NO FAIR!
WHY DOES ONLY SACHI GET TO DO THAT!
WELL...
YOU CAN COOK THE ONIONS. HOLD ON A SEC.

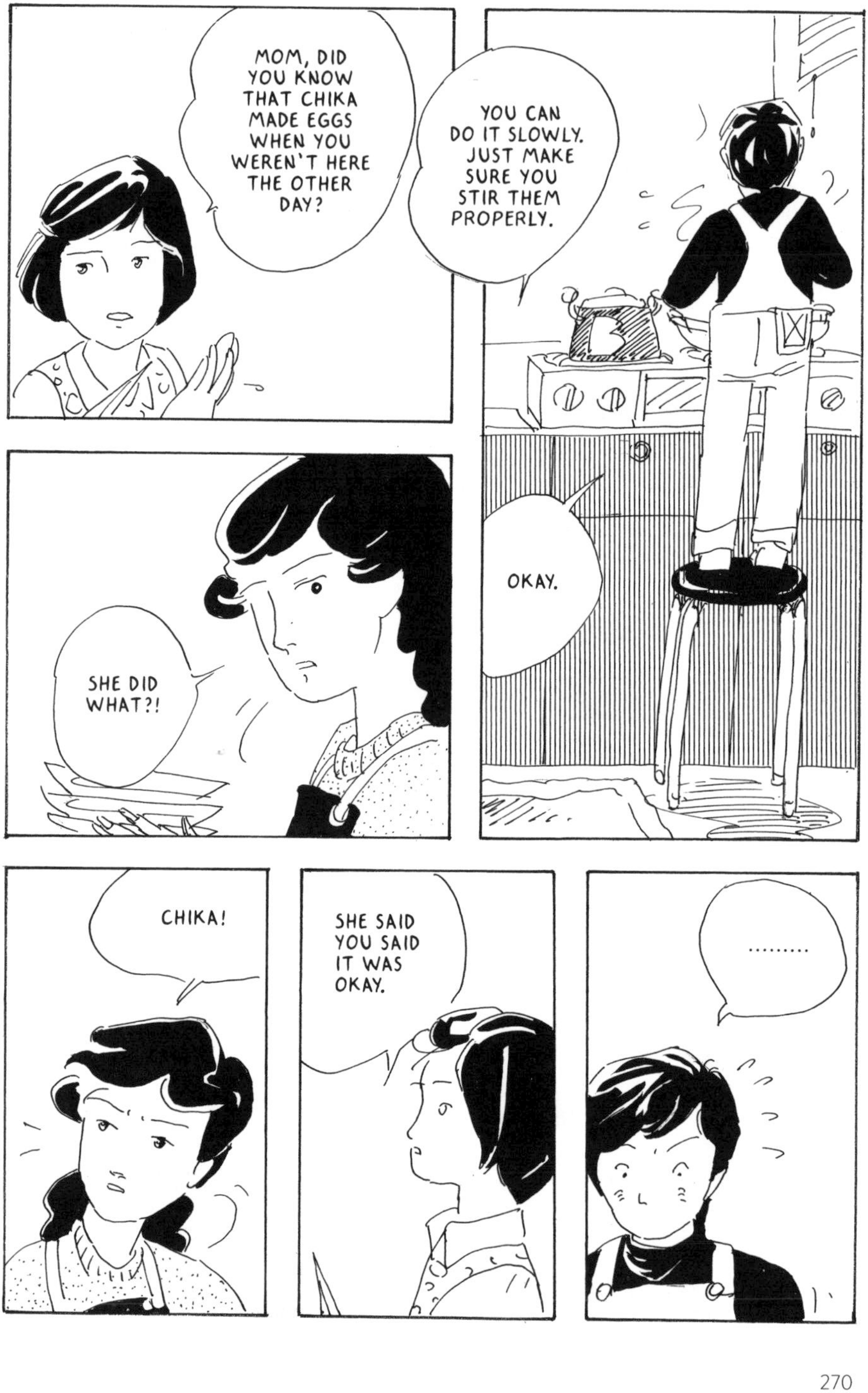
YOU CAN DO IT SLOWLY. JUST MAKE SURE YOU STIR THEM PROPERLY.
OKAY.
MOM, DID YOU KNOW THAT CHIKA MADE EGGS WHEN YOU WEREN'T HERE THE OTHER DAY?
SHE DID WHAT?!
....
SHE SAID YOU SAID IT WAS OKAY.
CHIKA!

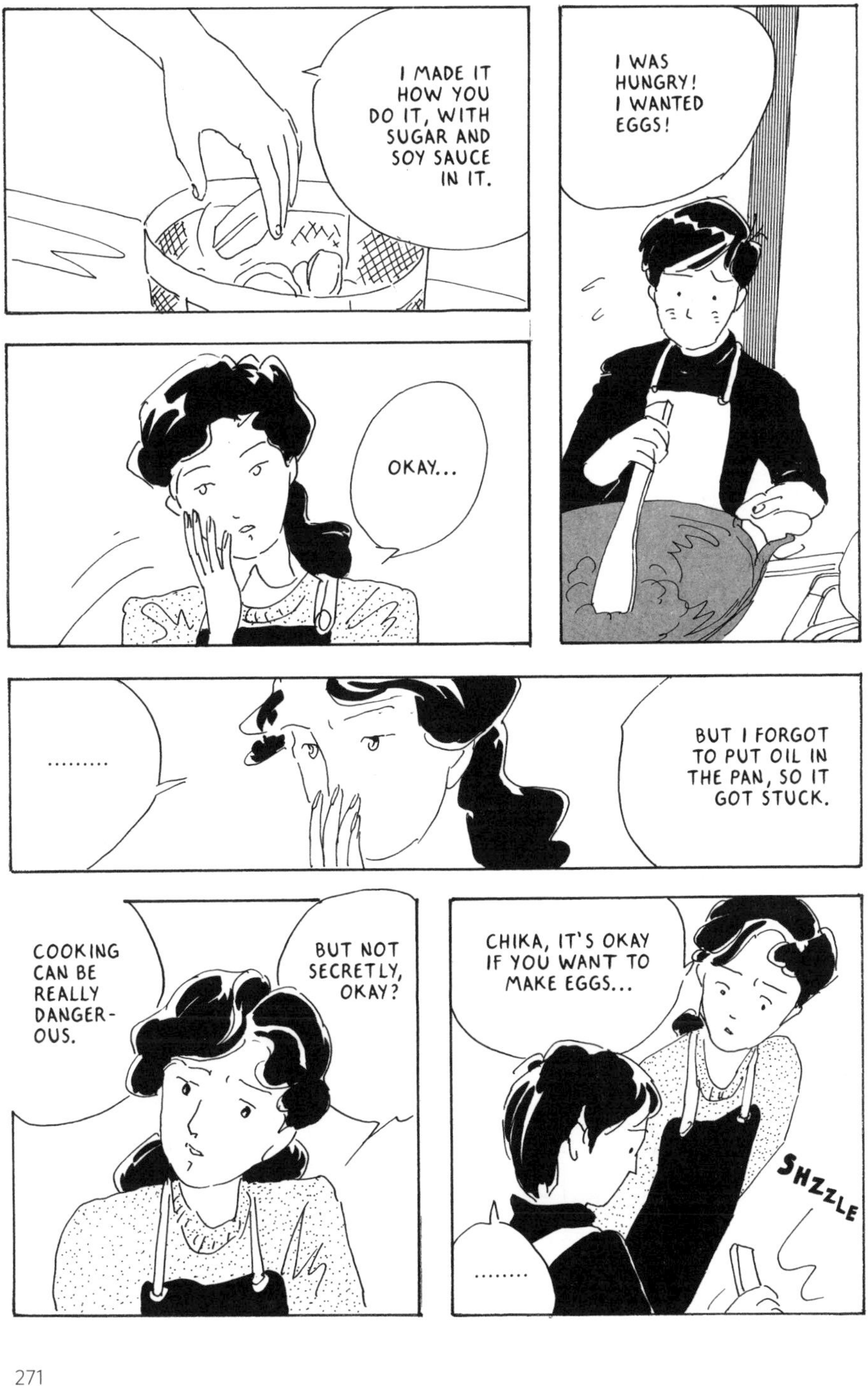
I WAS HUNGRY! I WANTED EGGS!
I MADE IT HOW YOU DO IT, WITH SUGAR AND SOY SAUCE IN IT.
OKAY...
BUT I FORGOT TO PUT OIL IN THE PAN, SO IT GOT STUCK.
....
CHIKA, IT'S OKAY IF YOU WANT TO MAKE EGGS...
SHZZLE
....
BUT NOT SECRETLY, OKAY?
COOKING CAN BE REALLY DANGER-OUS.

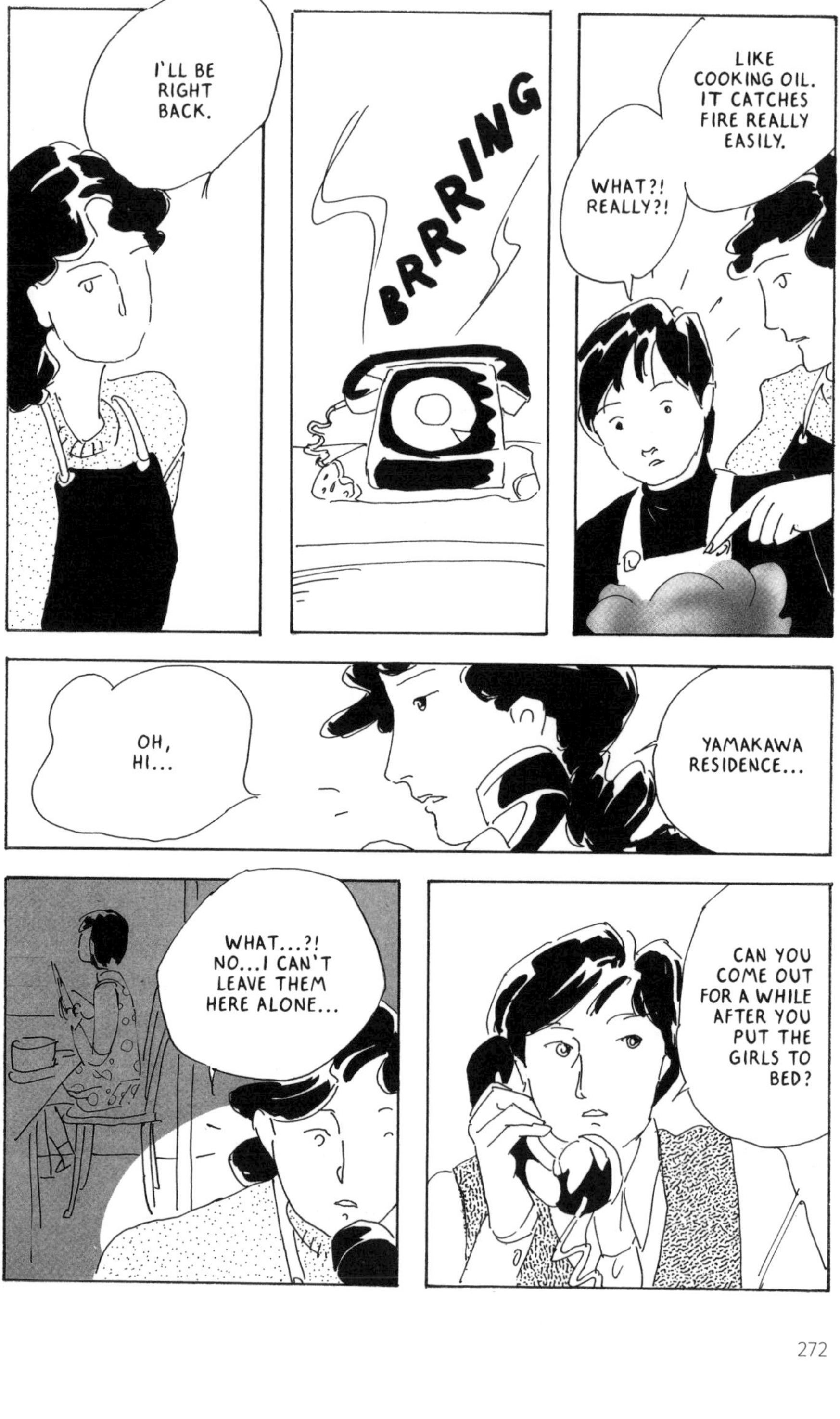
LIKE COOKING OIL. IT CATCHES FIRE REALLY EASILY.
WHAT?! REALLY?!
BRRRING
I'LL BE RIGHT BACK.
YAMAKAWA RESIDENCE...
OH, HI...
CAN YOU COME OUT FOR A WHILE AFTER YOU PUT THE GIRLS TO BED?
WHAT...?! NO...I CAN'T LEAVE THEM HERE ALONE...

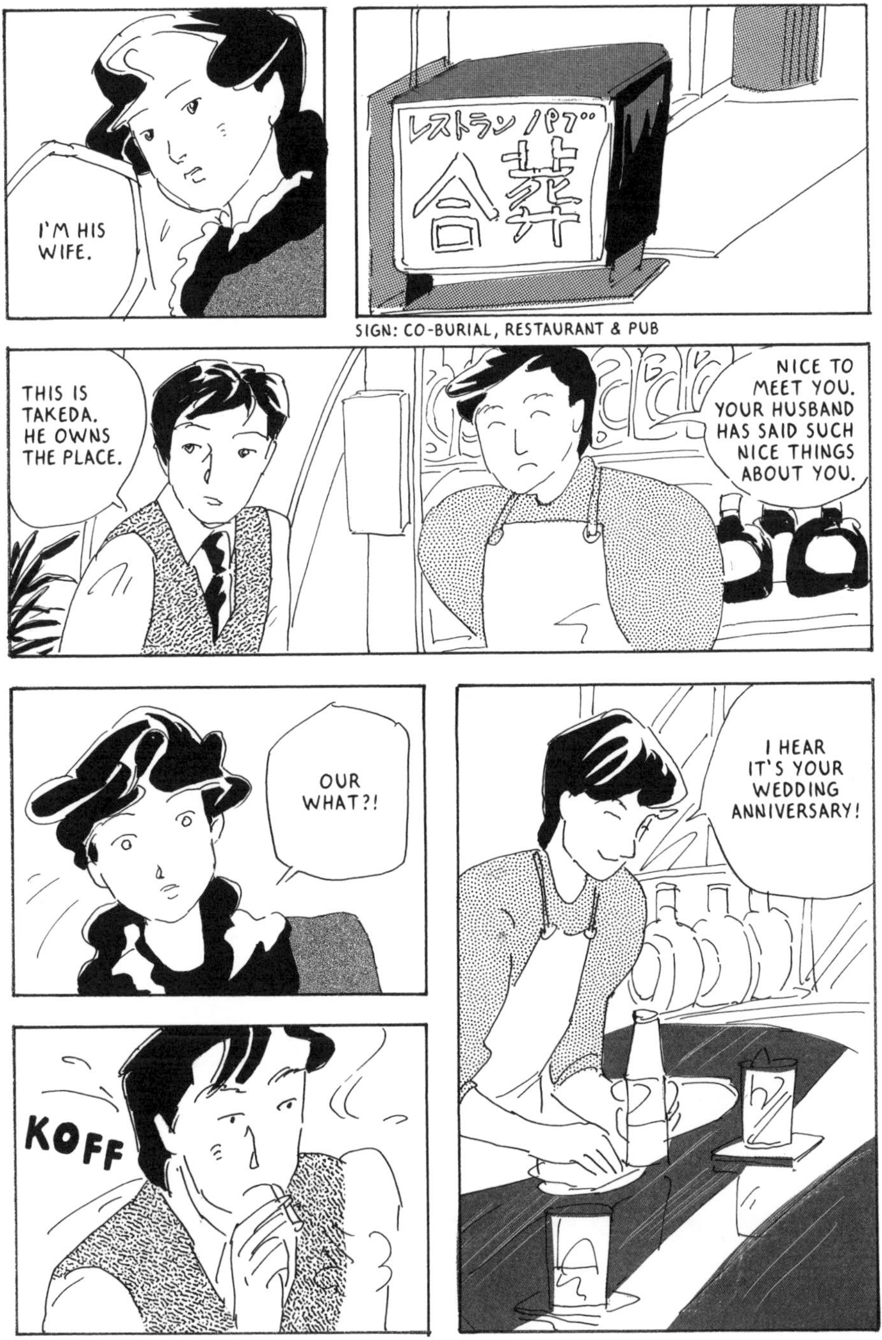
レストラン パブ
合葬
SIGN: CO-BURIAL, RESTAURANT & PUB
I'M HIS WIFE.
NICE TO MEET YOU. YOUR HUSBAND HAS SAID SUCH NICE THINGS ABOUT YOU.
THIS IS TAKEDA. HE OWNS THE PLACE.
I HEAR IT'S YOUR WEDDING ANNIVERSARY!
OUR WHAT?!
KOFF

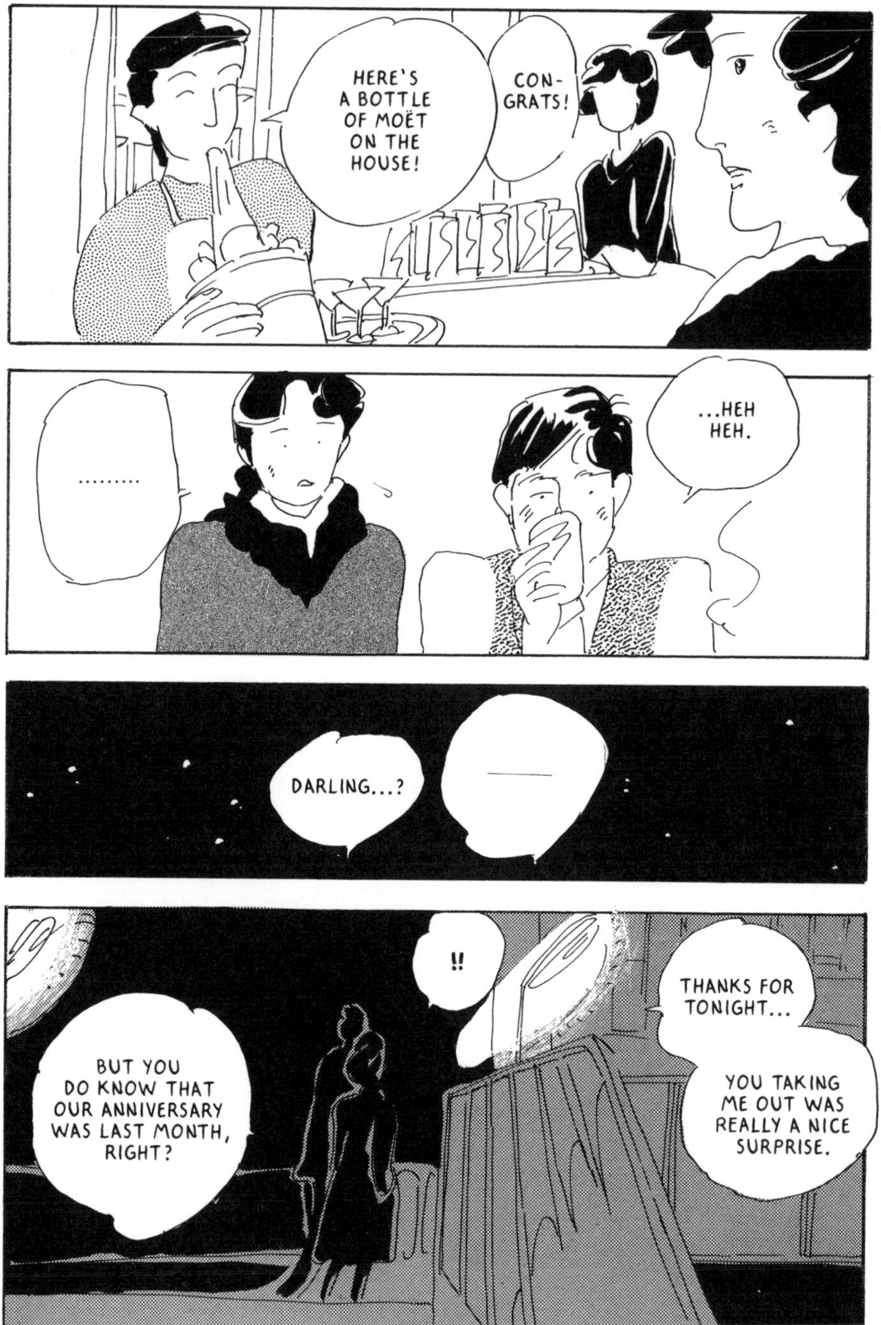
CON-GRATS!
HERE'S A BOTTLE OF MOËT ON THE HOUSE!
...HEH HEH.
....
—
DARLING...?
THANKS FOR TONIGHT...
YOU TAKING ME OUT WAS REALLY A NICE SURPRISE.
!!
BUT YOU DO KNOW THAT OUR ANNIVERSARY WAS LAST MONTH, RIGHT?

Leaving the Nest

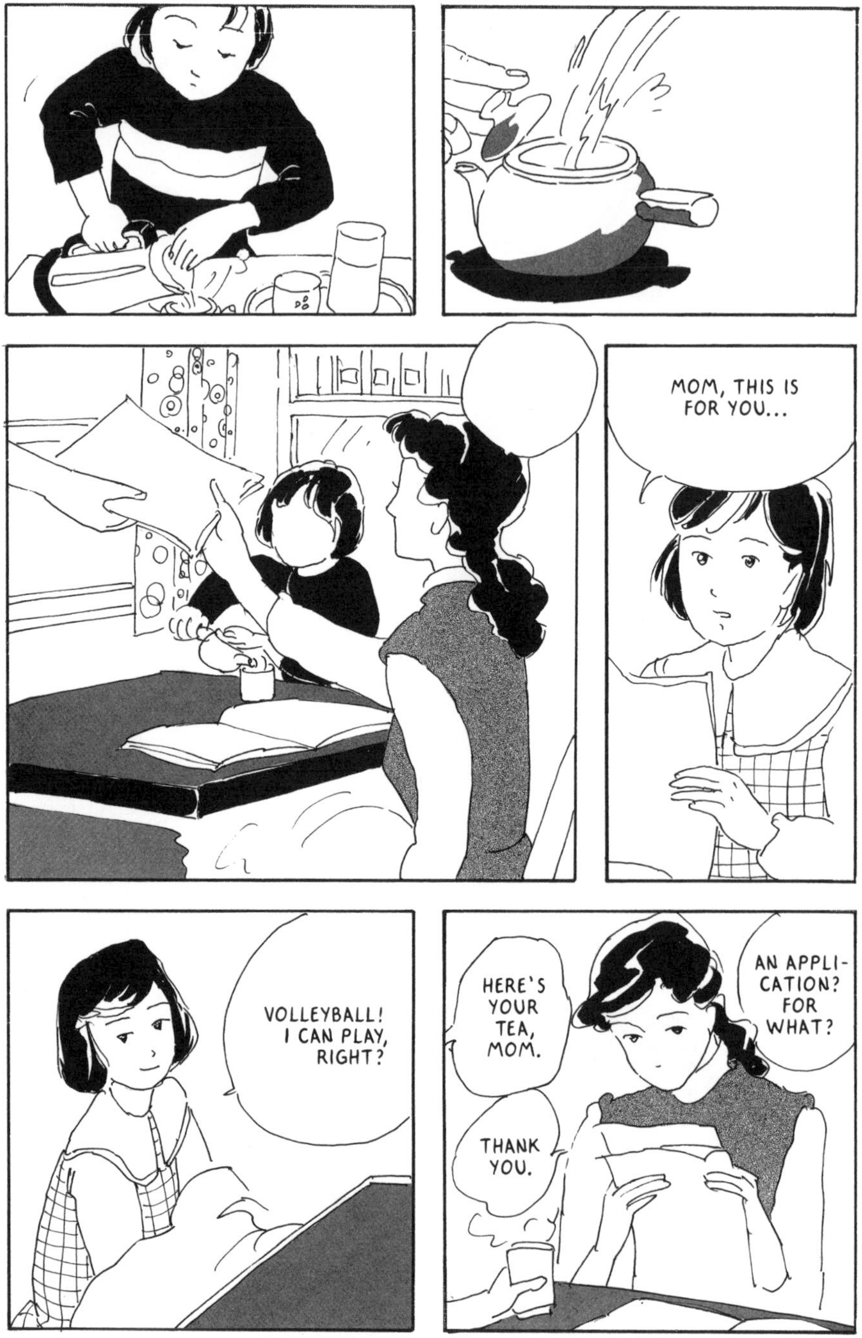
MOM, THIS IS FOR YOU...
AN APPLICATION? FOR WHAT?
HERE'S YOUR TEA, MOM.
THANK YOU.
VOLLEYBALL! I CAN PLAY, RIGHT?

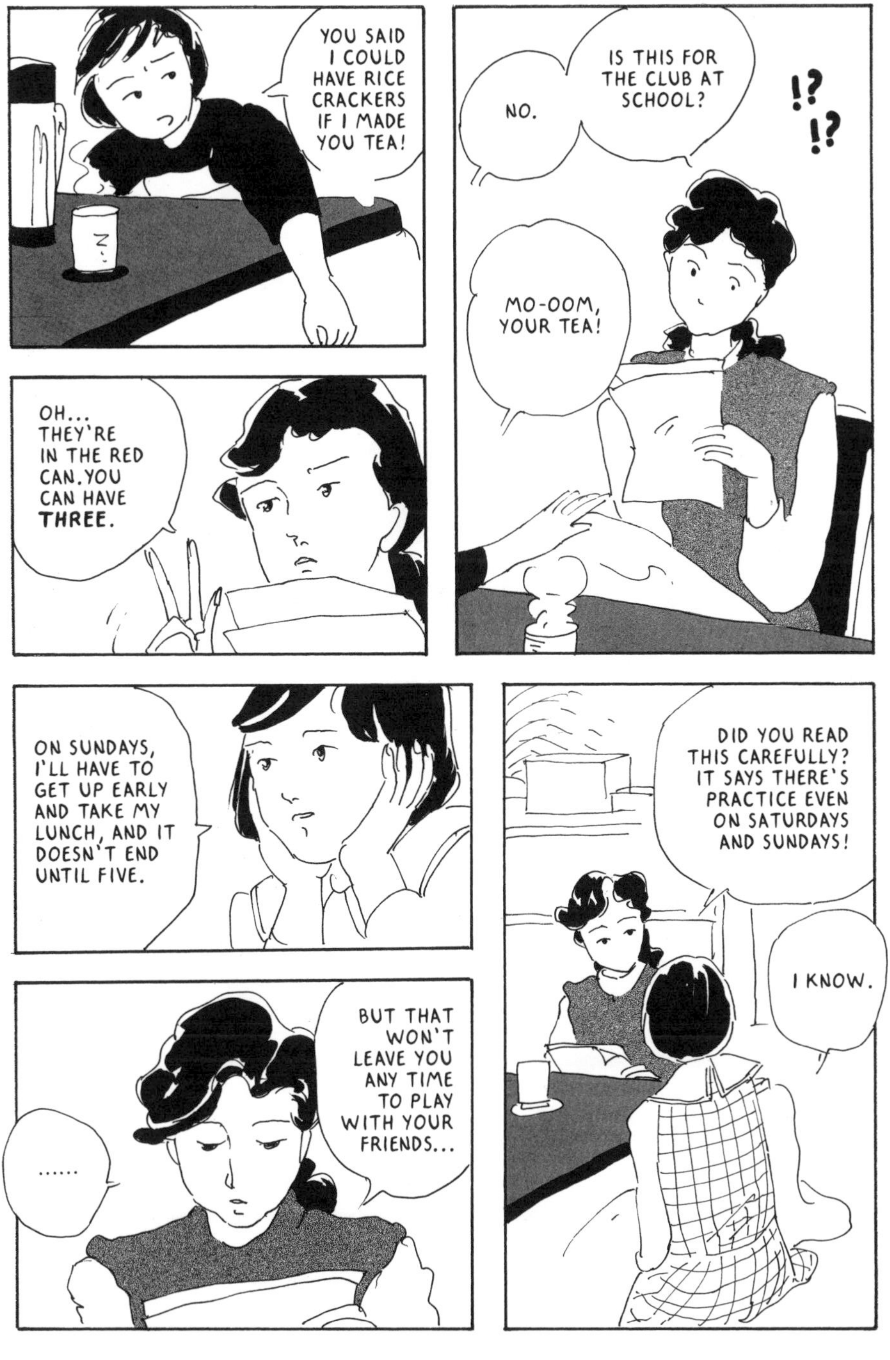
!?
!?
IS THIS FOR THE CLUB AT SCHOOL?
NO.
MO-OOM, YOUR TEA!
YOU SAID I COULD HAVE RICE CRACKERS IF I MADE YOU TEA!
OH... THEY'RE IN THE RED CAN. YOU CAN HAVE **THREE**.
DID YOU READ THIS CAREFULLY? IT SAYS THERE'S PRACTICE EVEN ON SATURDAYS AND SUNDAYS!
I KNOW.
ON SUNDAYS, I'LL HAVE TO GET UP EARLY AND TAKE MY LUNCH, AND IT DOESN'T END UNTIL FIVE.
BUT THAT WON'T LEAVE YOU ANY TIME TO PLAY WITH YOUR FRIENDS...
......

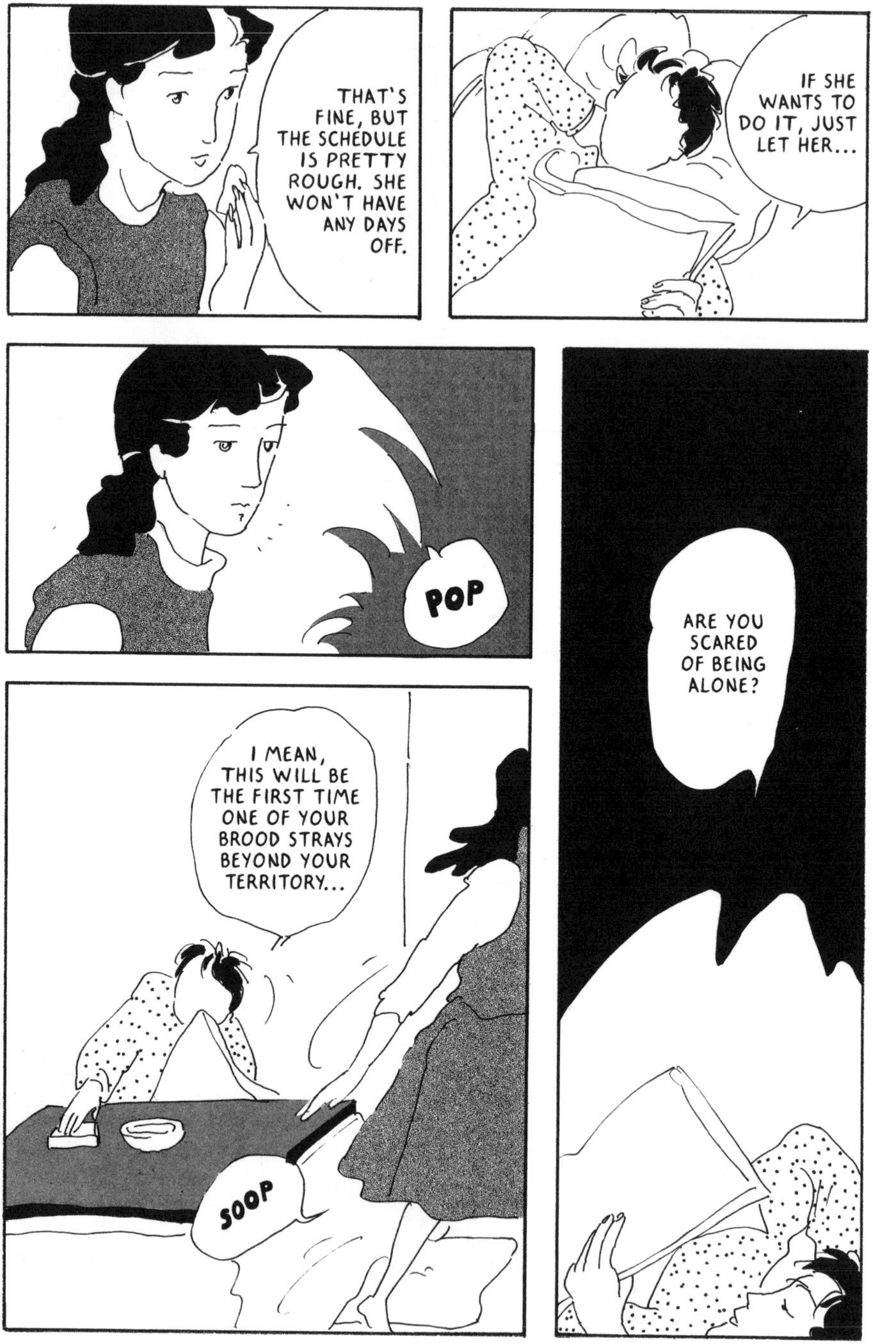
IF SHE WANTS TO DO IT, JUST LET HER...
THAT'S FINE, BUT THE SCHEDULE IS PRETTY ROUGH. SHE WON'T HAVE ANY DAYS OFF.
ARE YOU SCARED OF BEING ALONE?
POP
I MEAN, THIS WILL BE THE FIRST TIME ONE OF YOUR BROOD STRAYS BEYOND YOUR TERRITORY...
SOOP

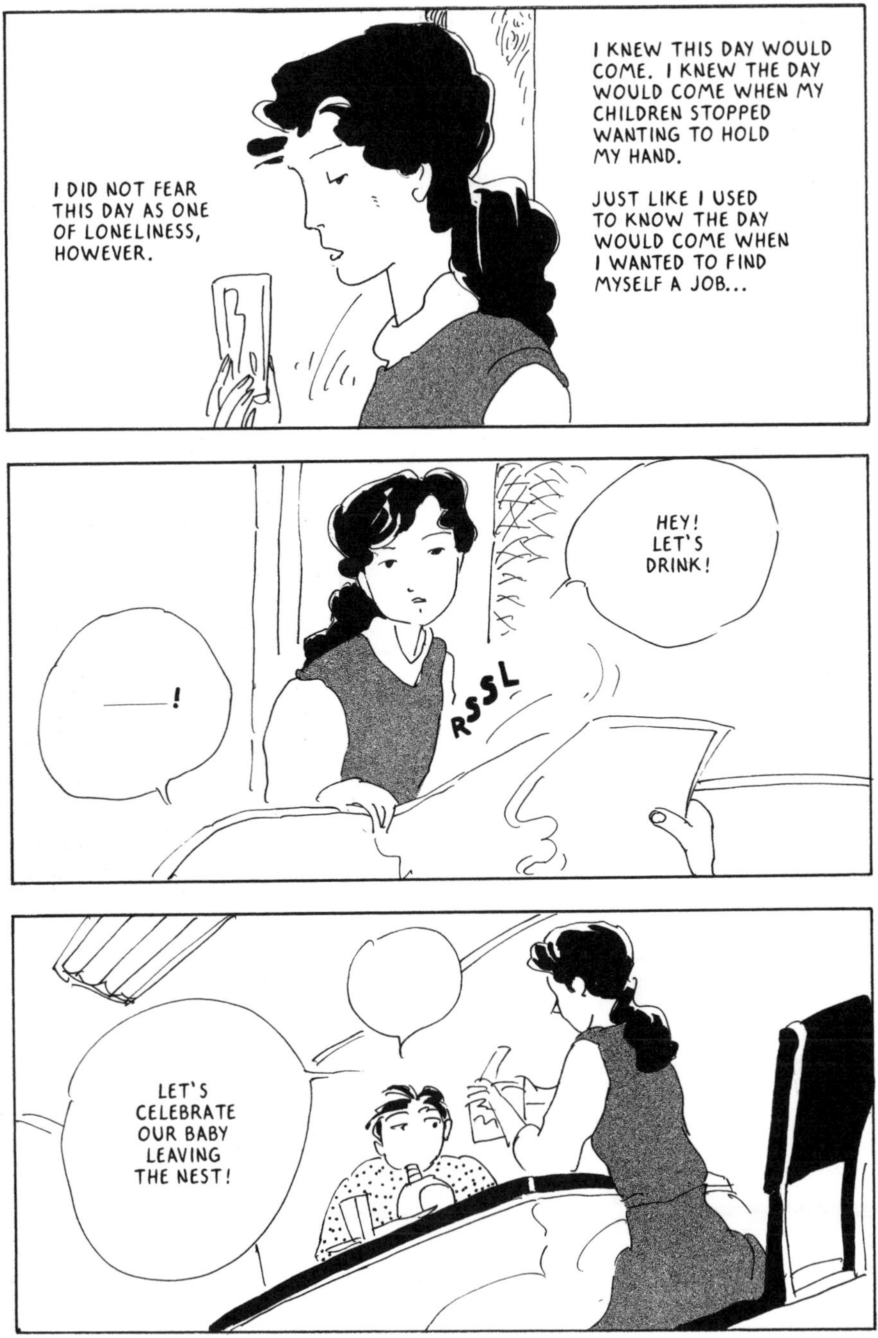
I KNEW THIS DAY WOULD COME. I KNEW THE DAY WOULD COME WHEN MY CHILDREN STOPPED WANTING TO HOLD MY HAND.
JUST LIKE I USED TO KNOW THE DAY WOULD COME WHEN I WANTED TO FIND MYSELF A JOB...
I DID NOT FEAR THIS DAY AS ONE OF LONELINESS, HOWEVER.
HEY! LET'S DRINK!
RSSL
——!
LET'S CELEBRATE OUR BABY LEAVING THE NEST!

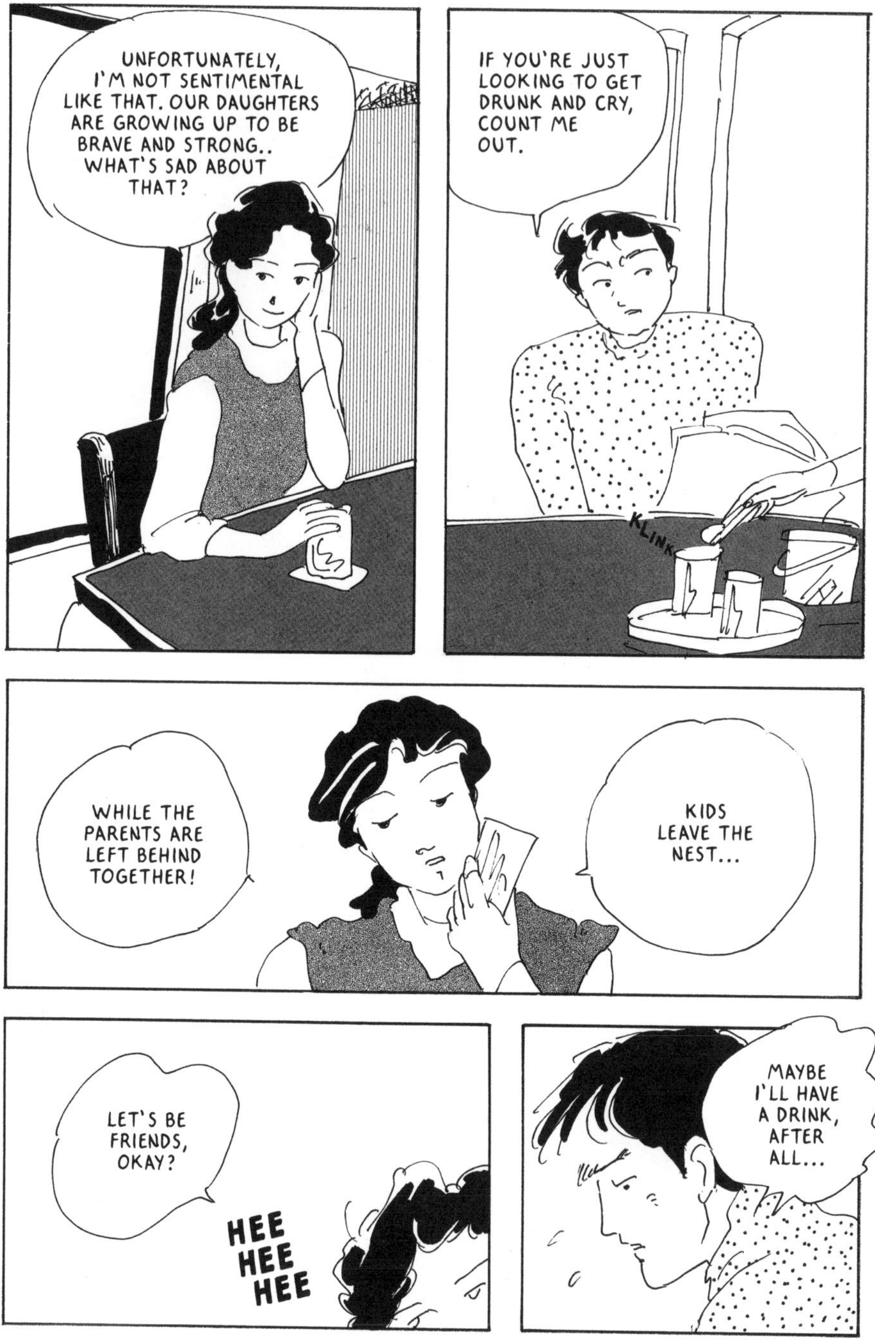
IF YOU'RE JUST LOOKING TO GET DRUNK AND CRY, COUNT ME OUT.
KLINK
UNFORTUNATELY, I'M NOT SENTIMENTAL LIKE THAT. OUR DAUGHTERS ARE GROWING UP TO BE BRAVE AND STRONG.. WHAT'S SAD ABOUT THAT?
KIDS LEAVE THE NEST...
WHILE THE PARENTS ARE LEFT BEHIND TOGETHER!
MAYBE I'LL HAVE A DRINK, AFTER ALL...
LET'S BE FRIENDS, OKAY?
HEE HEE HEE

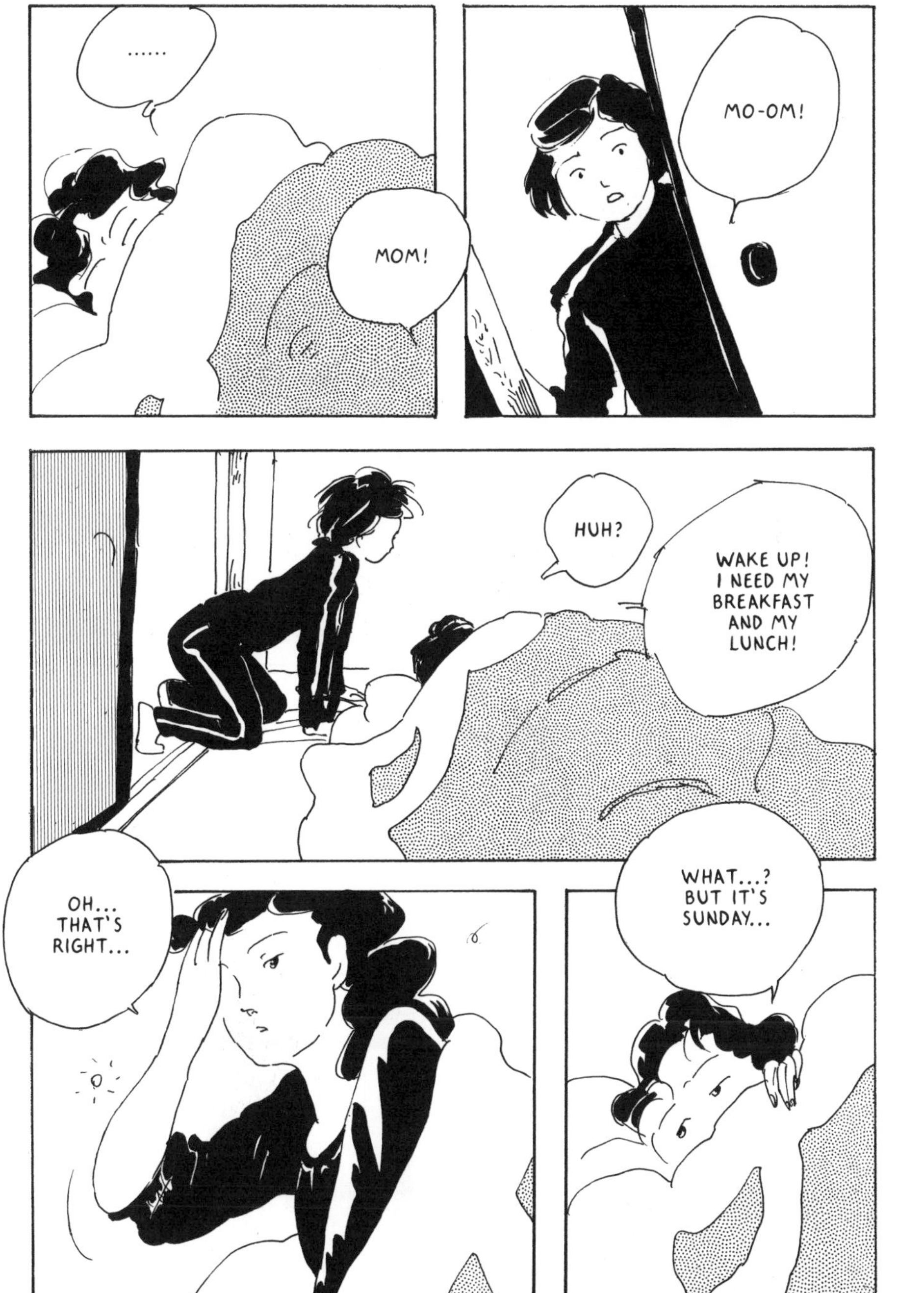
MO-OM!
......
MOM!
HUH?
WAKE UP! I NEED MY BREAKFAST AND MY LUNCH!
WHAT...? BUT IT'S SUNDAY...
OH... THAT'S RIGHT...

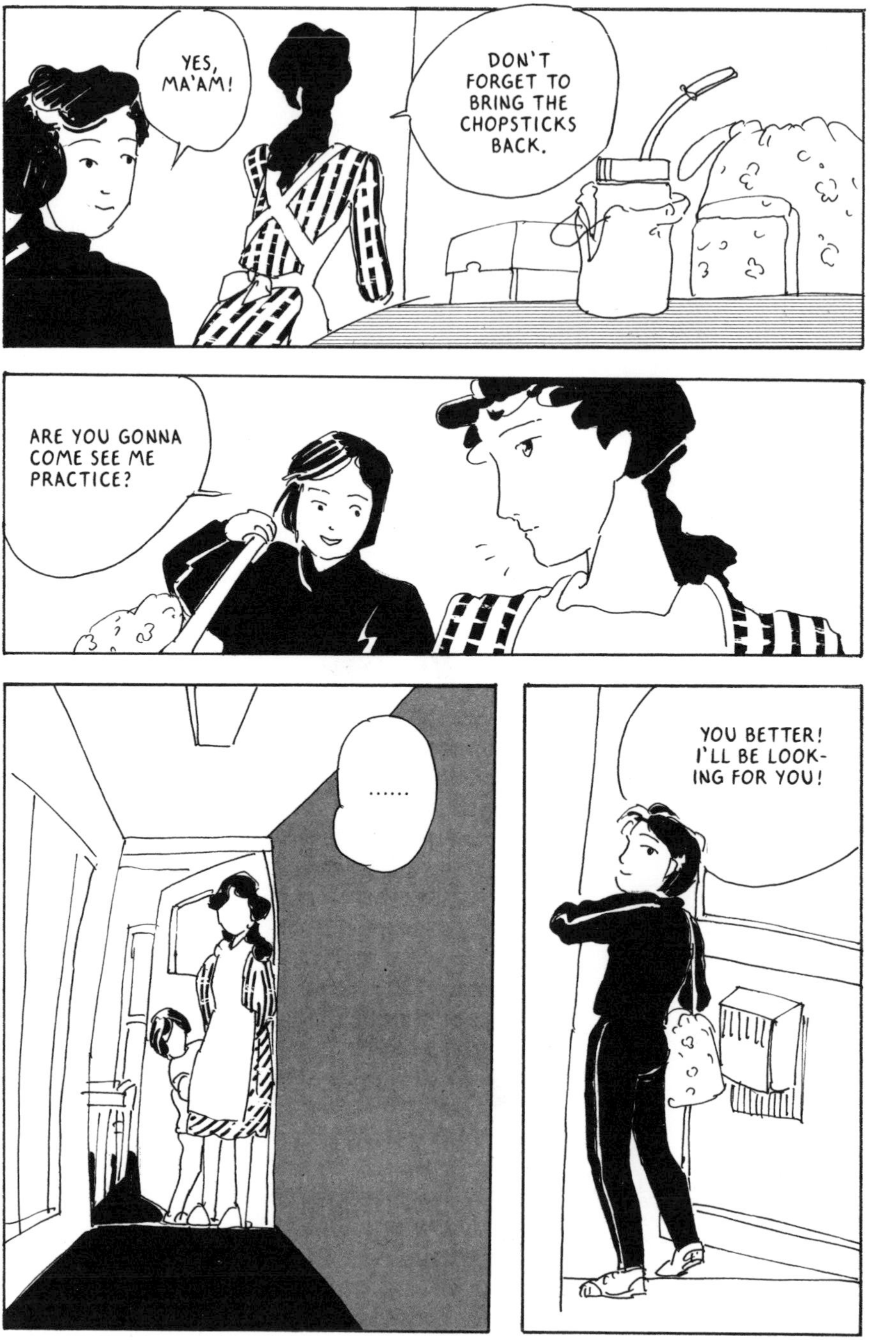
DON'T FORGET TO BRING THE CHOPSTICKS BACK.
YES, MA'AM!
ARE YOU GONNA COME SEE ME PRACTICE?
YOU BETTER! I'LL BE LOOKING FOR YOU!
......

Playing Cockroach

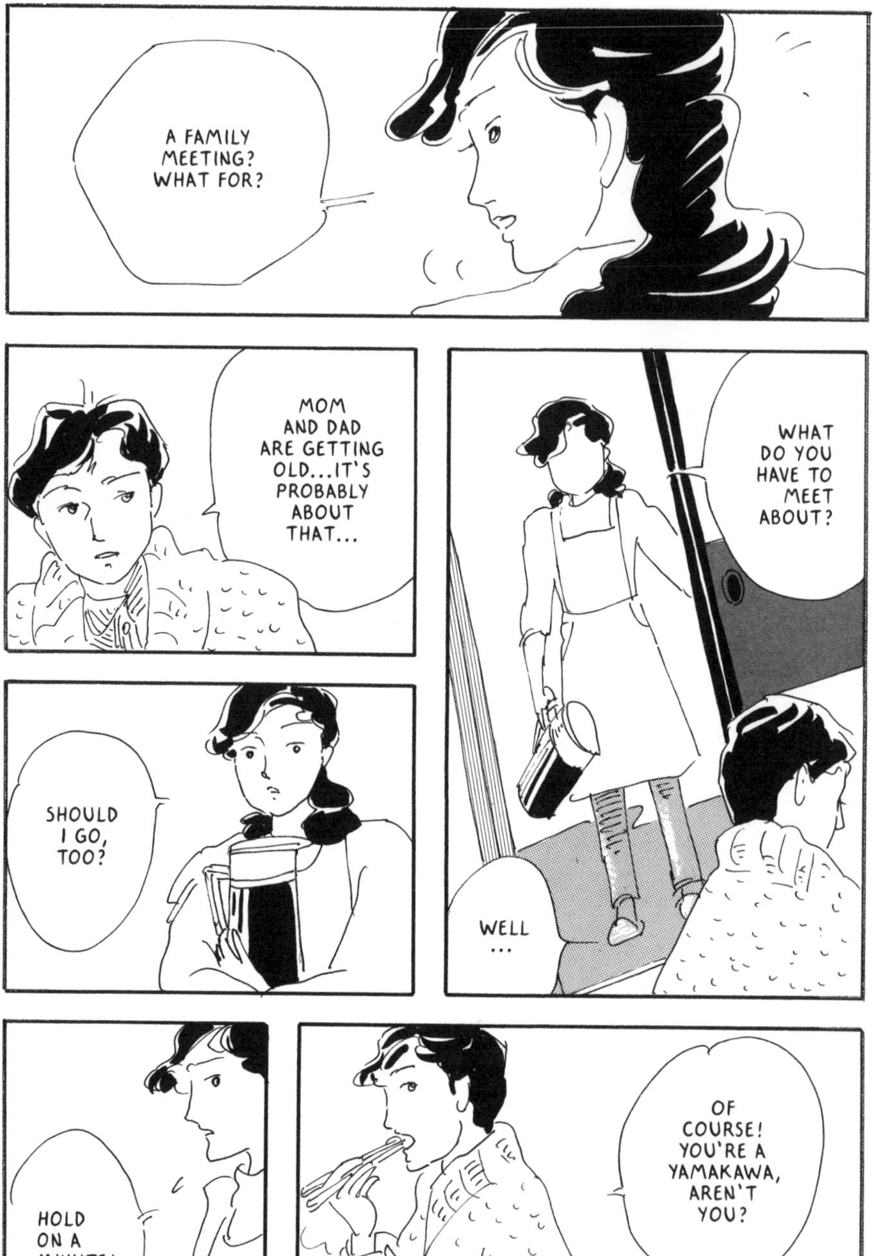
A FAMILY MEETING? WHAT FOR?
WHAT DO YOU HAVE TO MEET ABOUT?
WELL...
MOM AND DAD ARE GETTING OLD...IT'S PROBABLY ABOUT THAT...
SHOULD I GO, TOO?
OF COURSE! YOU'RE A YAMAKAWA, AREN'T YOU?
HOLD ON A MINUTE!

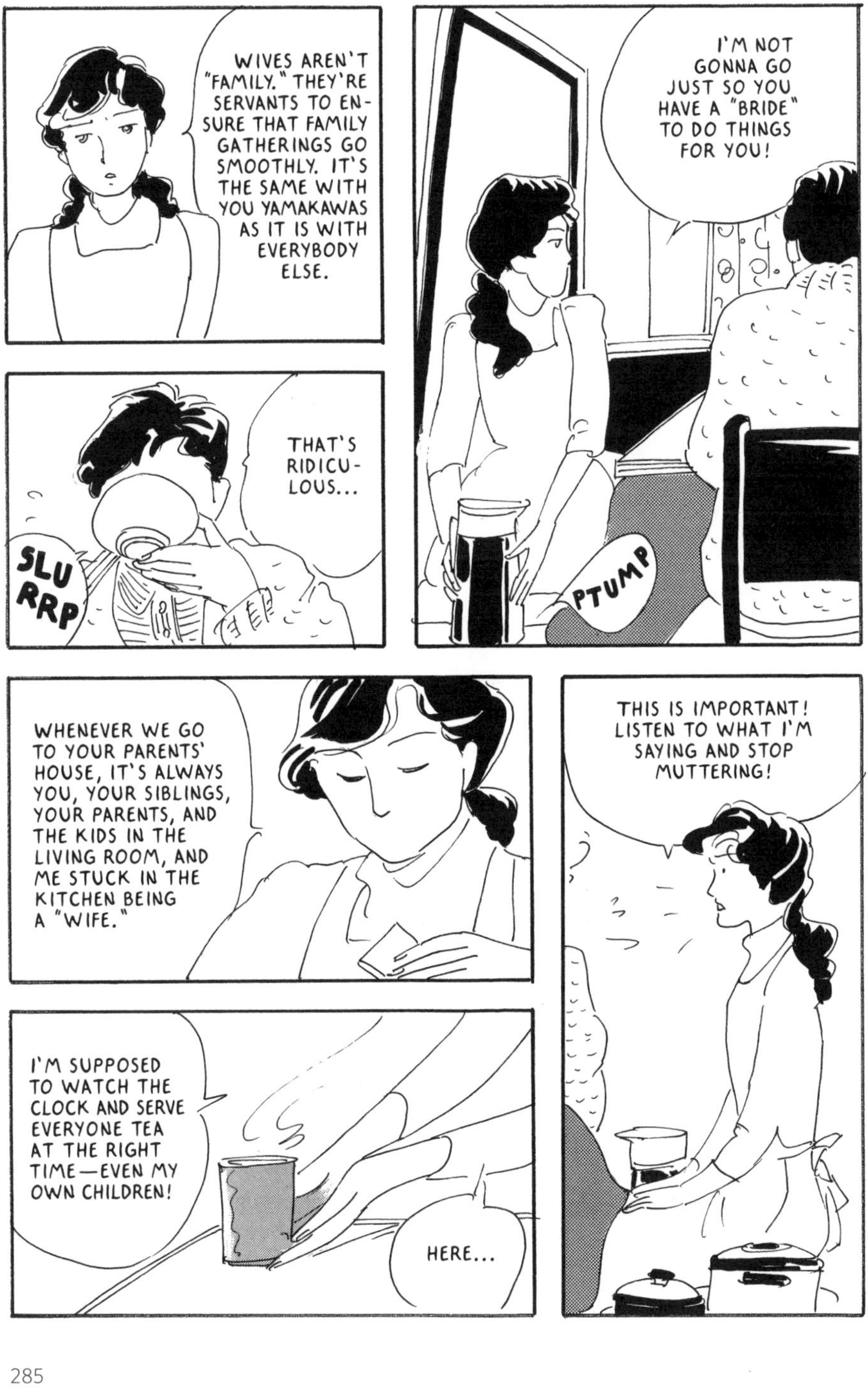
I'M NOT GONNA GO JUST SO YOU HAVE A "BRIDE" TO DO THINGS FOR YOU!
PTUMP
WIVES AREN'T "FAMILY." THEY'RE SERVANTS TO EN-SURE THAT FAMILY GATHERINGS GO SMOOTHLY. IT'S THE SAME WITH YOU YAMAKAWAS AS IT IS WITH EVERYBODY ELSE.
THAT'S RIDICU-LOUS...
SLURRP
THIS IS IMPORTANT! LISTEN TO WHAT I'M SAYING AND STOP MUTTERING!
WHENEVER WE GO TO YOUR PARENTS' HOUSE, IT'S ALWAYS YOU, YOUR SIBLINGS, YOUR PARENTS, AND THE KIDS IN THE LIVING ROOM, AND ME STUCK IN THE KITCHEN BEING A "WIFE."
I'M SUPPOSED TO WATCH THE CLOCK AND SERVE EVERYONE TEA AT THE RIGHT TIME—EVEN MY OWN CHILDREN!
HERE...

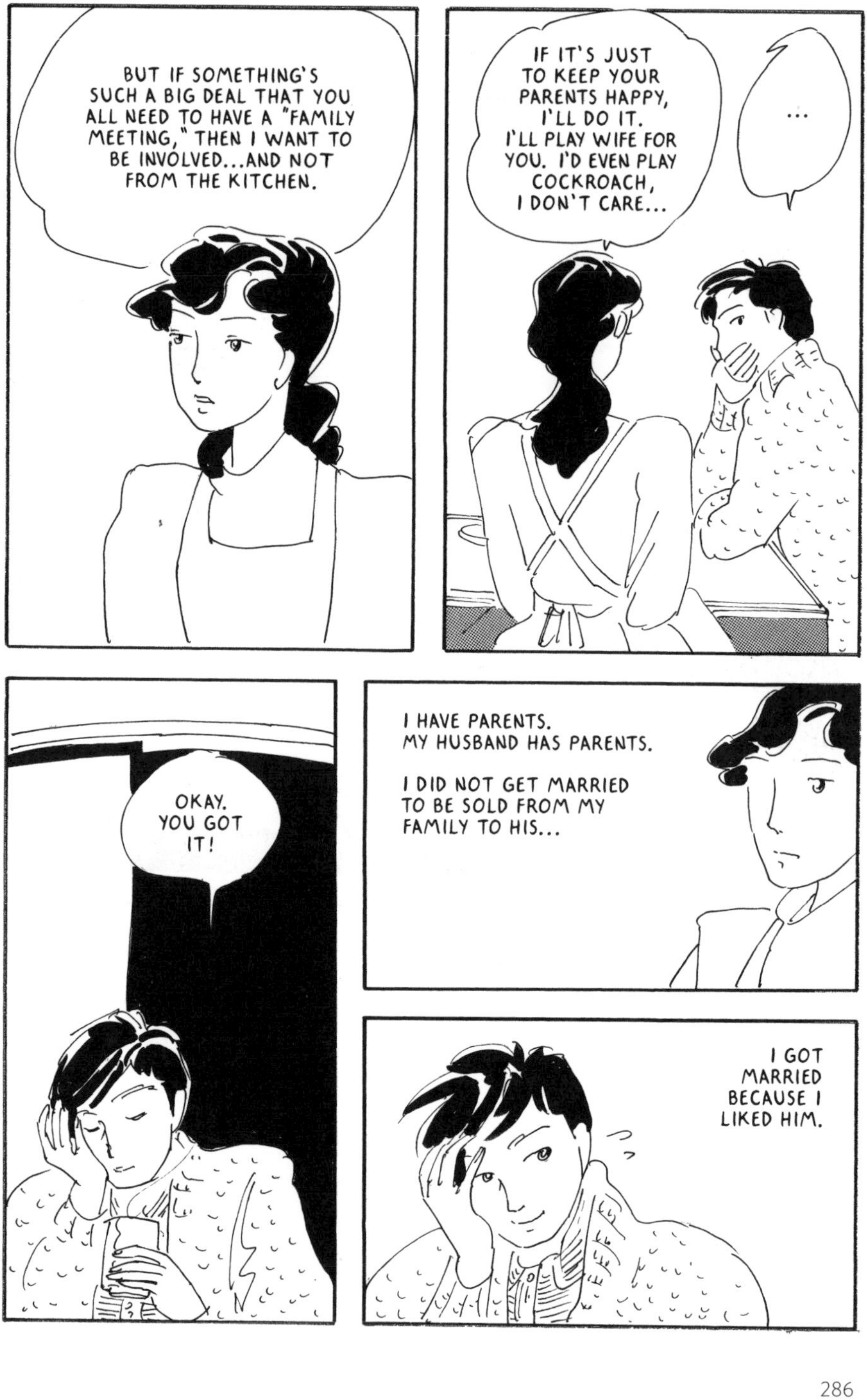
IF IT'S JUST TO KEEP YOUR PARENTS HAPPY, I'LL DO IT. I'LL PLAY WIFE FOR YOU. I'D EVEN PLAY COCKROACH, I DON'T CARE...
...
BUT IF SOMETHING'S SUCH A BIG DEAL THAT YOU ALL NEED TO HAVE A "FAMILY MEETING," THEN I WANT TO BE INVOLVED...AND NOT FROM THE KITCHEN.
I HAVE PARENTS. MY HUSBAND HAS PARENTS.
I DID NOT GET MARRIED TO BE SOLD FROM MY FAMILY TO HIS...
I GOT MARRIED BECAUSE I LIKED HIM.
OKAY. YOU GOT IT!

ONCE IN A WHILE, HE MAKES ME HAPPY AS A PARTNER.

?

DARLING ...?

DO YOU WANT SOME STRAWBER- RIES?

SURE.

JUST HIM SAYING "OKAY" AT TIMES LIKE THIS MEANS THE WORLD TO ME.

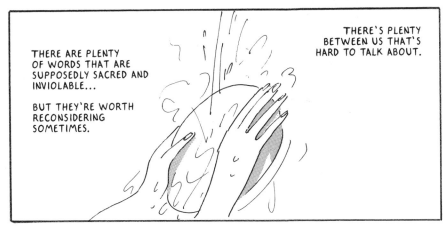

THERE'S PLENTY BETWEEN US THAT'S HARD TO TALK ABOUT.

THERE ARE PLENTY OF WORDS THAT ARE SUPPOSEDLY SACRED AND INVIOLABLE...

BUT THEY'RE WORTH RECONSIDERING SOMETIMES.

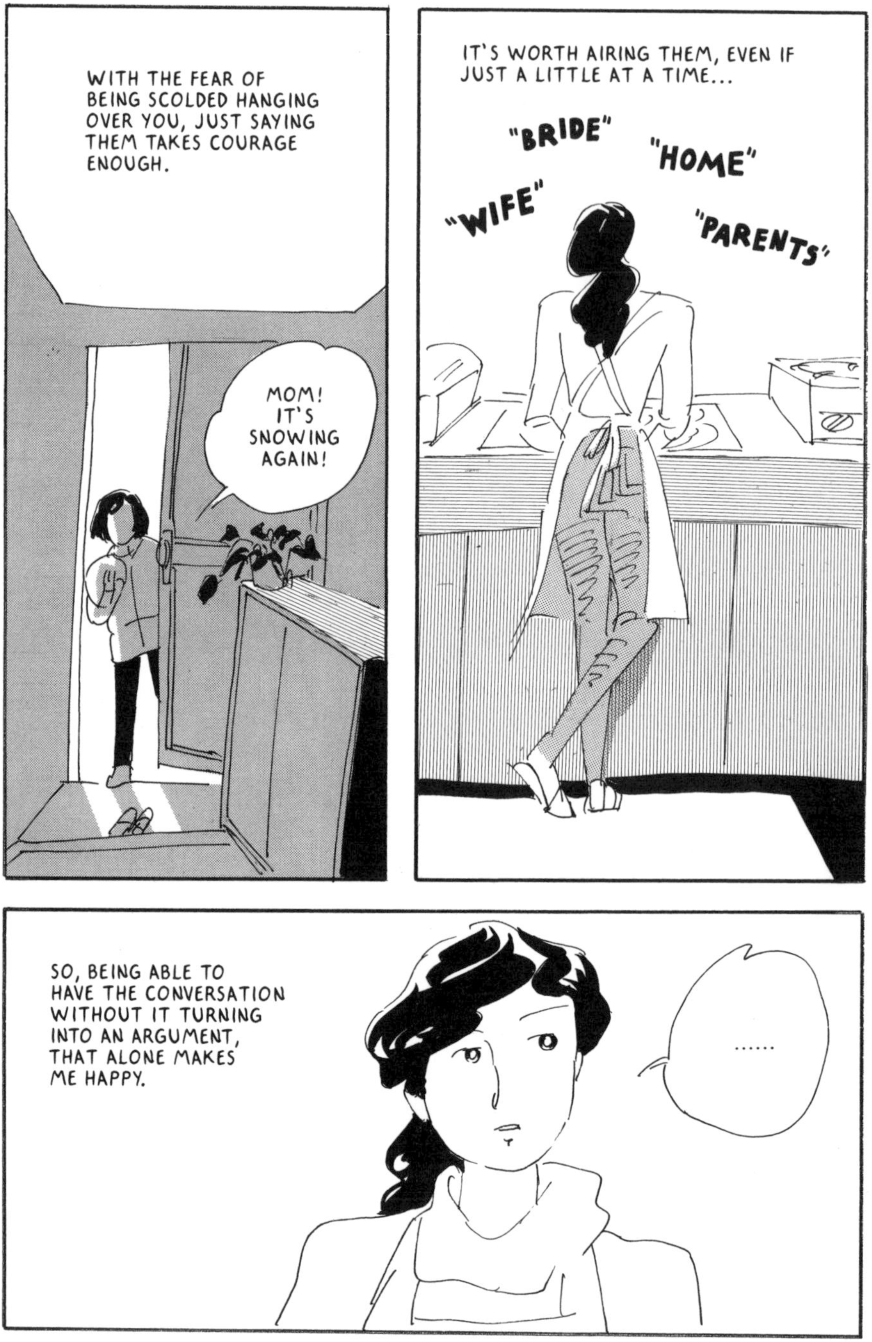
IT'S WORTH AIRING THEM, EVEN IF JUST A LITTLE AT A TIME...
"BRIDE"
"HOME"
"WIFE"
"PARENTS"
WITH THE FEAR OF BEING SCOLDED HANGING OVER YOU, JUST SAYING THEM TAKES COURAGE ENOUGH.
MOM! IT'S SNOWING AGAIN!
SO, BEING ABLE TO HAVE THE CONVERSATION WITHOUT IT TURNING INTO AN ARGUMENT, THAT ALONE MAKES ME HAPPY.
......

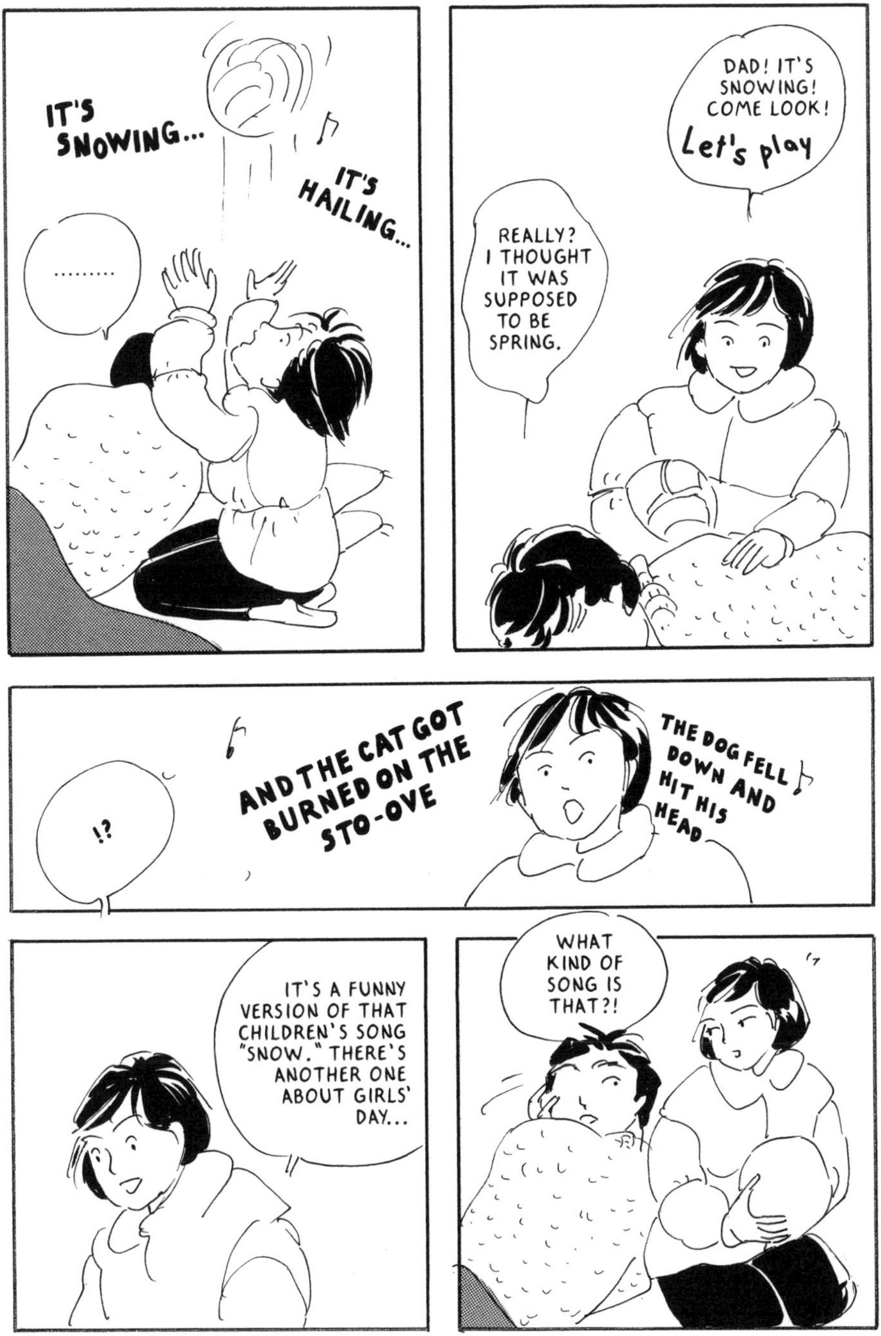
DAD! IT'S SNOWING! COME LOOK!
Let's play
REALLY? I THOUGHT IT WAS SUPPOSED TO BE SPRING.
IT'S SNOWING...
IT'S HAILING...
....
THE DOG FELL DOWN AND HIT HIS HEAD
AND THE CAT GOT BURNED ON THE STO-OVE
!?
WHAT KIND OF SONG IS THAT?!
IT'S A FUNNY VERSION OF THAT CHILDREN'S SONG "SNOW." THERE'S ANOTHER ONE ABOUT GIRLS' DAY...

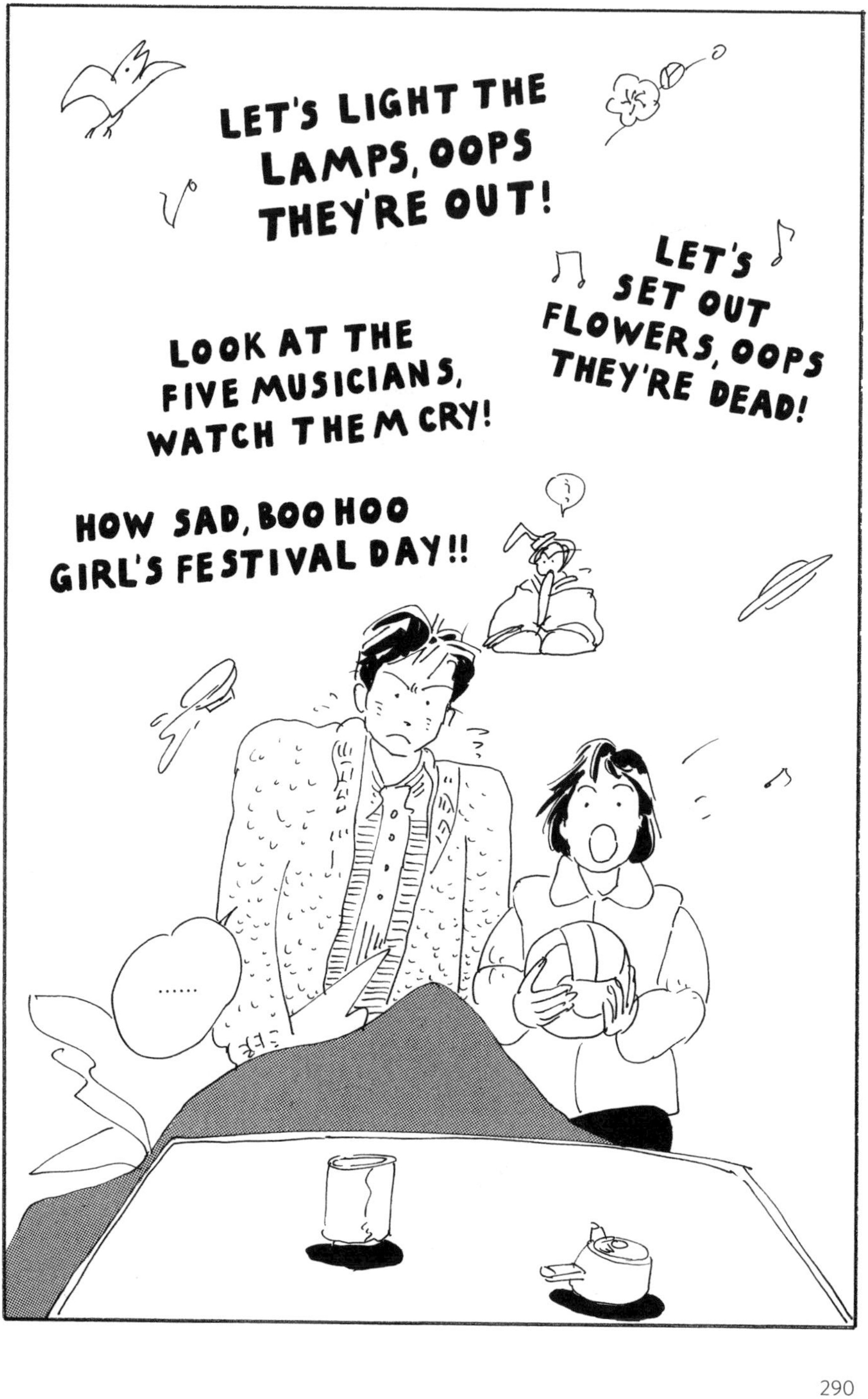
LET'S LIGHT THE LAMPS, OOPS THEY'RE OUT!
LET'S SET OUT FLOWERS, OOPS THEY'RE DEAD!
LOOK AT THE FIVE MUSICIANS, WATCH THEM CRY!
HOW SAD, BOO HOO GIRL'S FESTIVAL DAY!!
……

Passing Through

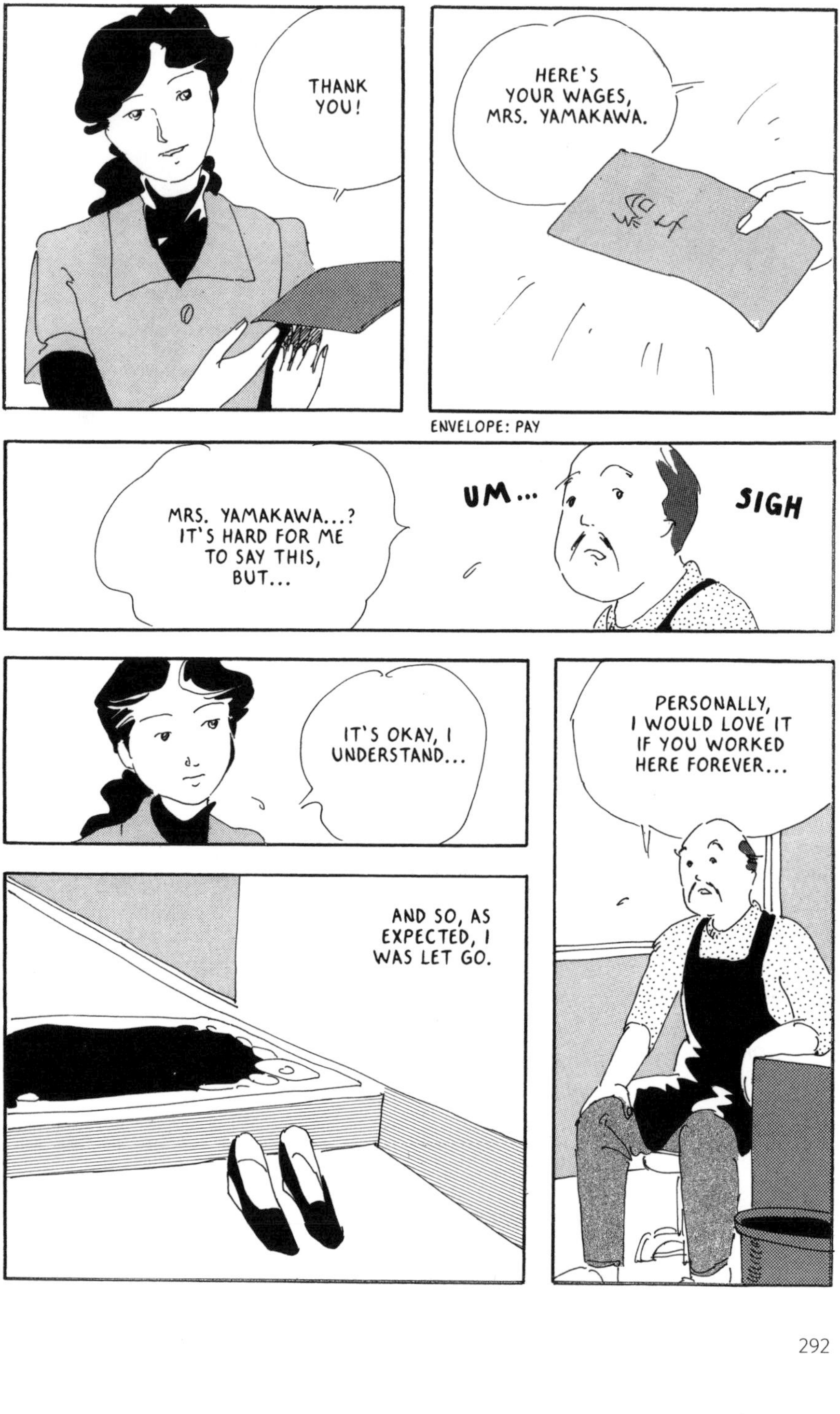
HERE'S YOUR WAGES, MRS. YAMAKAWA.
ENVELOPE: PAY
THANK YOU!
SIGH
UM...
MRS. YAMAKAWA...? IT'S HARD FOR ME TO SAY THIS, BUT...
PERSONALLY, I WOULD LOVE IT IF YOU WORKED HERE FOREVER...
IT'S OKAY, I UNDERSTAND...
AND SO, AS EXPECTED, I WAS LET GO.

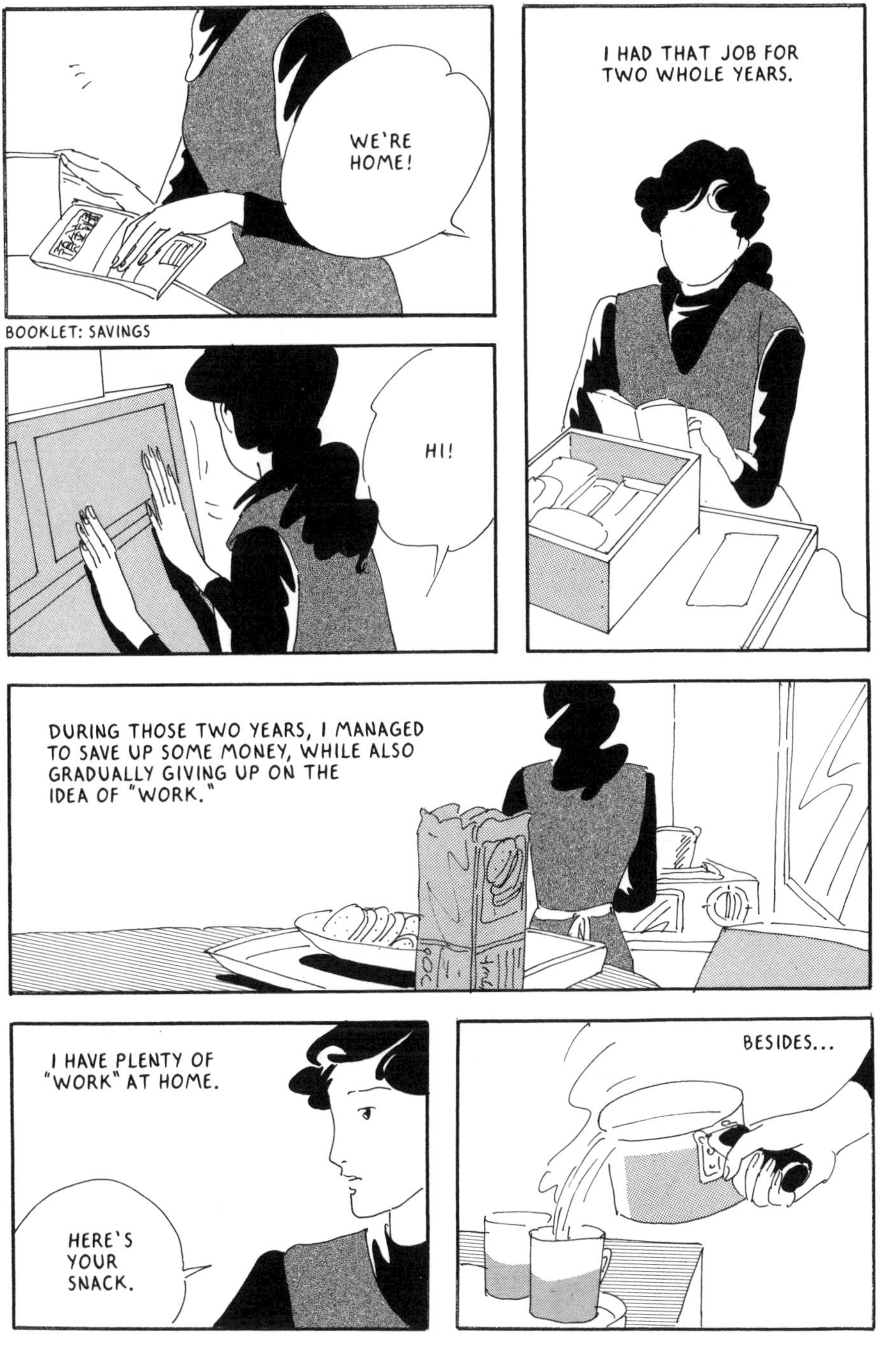
I HAD THAT JOB FOR TWO WHOLE YEARS.
WE'RE HOME!
BOOKLET: SAVINGS
HI!
DURING THOSE TWO YEARS, I MANAGED TO SAVE UP SOME MONEY, WHILE ALSO GRADUALLY GIVING UP ON THE IDEA OF "WORK."
BESIDES...
I HAVE PLENTY OF "WORK" AT HOME.
HERE'S YOUR SNACK.

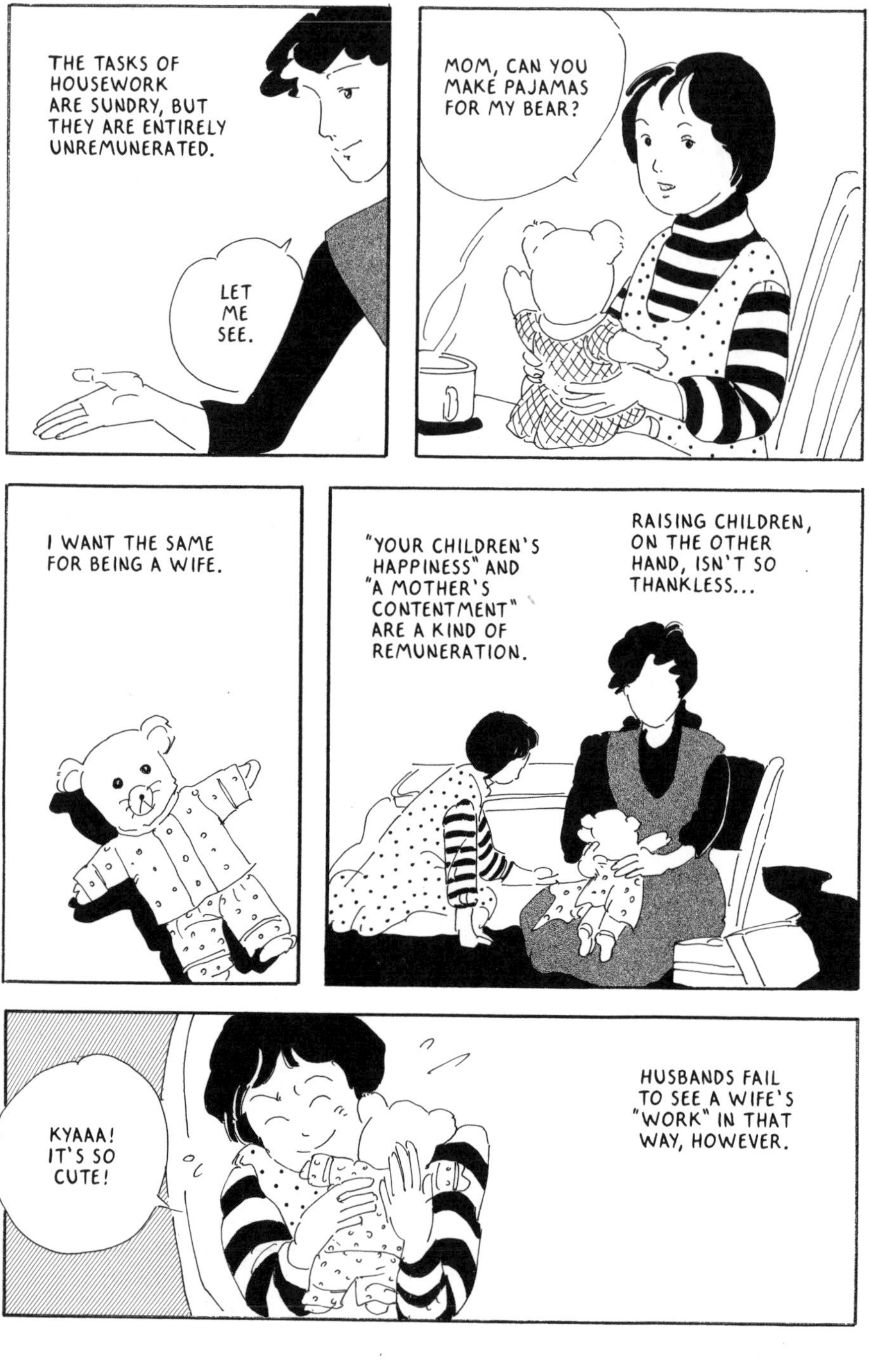

MOM, CAN YOU MAKE PAJAMAS FOR MY BEAR?
THE TASKS OF HOUSEWORK ARE SUNDRY, BUT THEY ARE ENTIRELY UNREMUNERATED.
LET ME SEE.
RAISING CHILDREN, ON THE OTHER HAND, ISN'T SO THANKLESS...
"YOUR CHILDREN'S HAPPINESS" AND "A MOTHER'S CONTENTMENT" ARE A KIND OF REMUNERATION.
I WANT THE SAME FOR BEING A WIFE.
HUSBANDS FAIL TO SEE A WIFE'S "WORK" IN THAT WAY, HOWEVER.
KYAAA! IT'S SO CUTE!

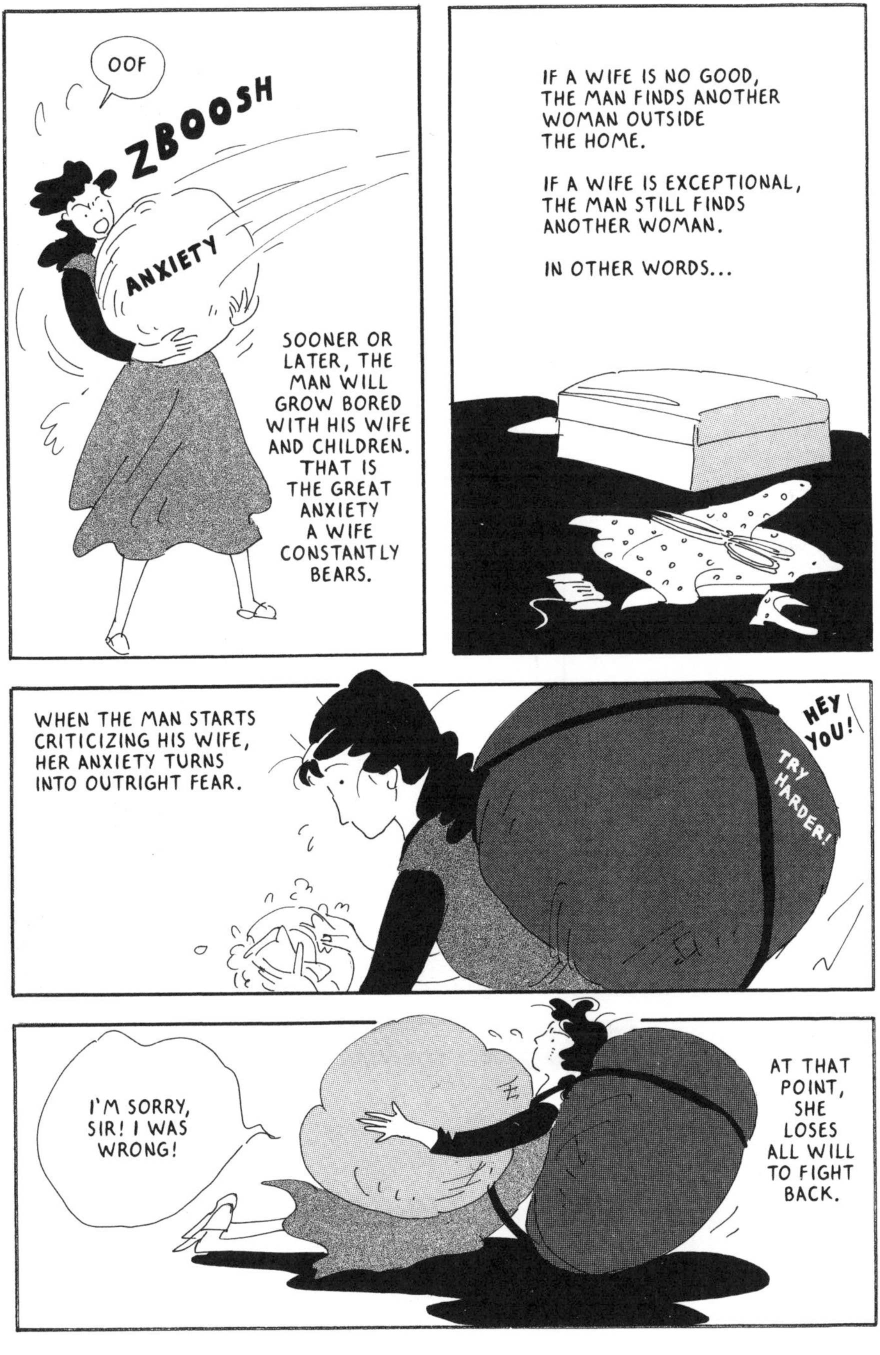
IF A WIFE IS NO GOOD, THE MAN FINDS ANOTHER WOMAN OUTSIDE THE HOME.
IF A WIFE IS EXCEPTIONAL, THE MAN STILL FINDS ANOTHER WOMAN.
IN OTHER WORDS...
OOF
ZBOOSH
ANXIETY
SOONER OR LATER, THE MAN WILL GROW BORED WITH HIS WIFE AND CHILDREN. THAT IS THE GREAT ANXIETY A WIFE CONSTANTLY BEARS.
HEY YOU!
TRY HARDER!
WHEN THE MAN STARTS CRITICIZING HIS WIFE, HER ANXIETY TURNS INTO OUTRIGHT FEAR.
AT THAT POINT, SHE LOSES ALL WILL TO FIGHT BACK.
I'M SORRY, SIR! I WAS WRONG!

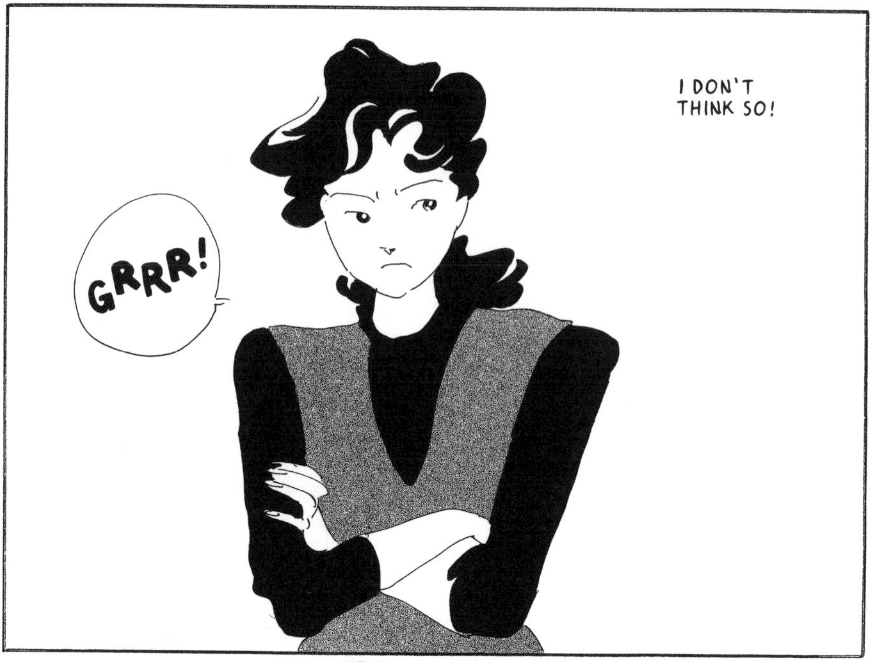
I DON'T THINK SO!
GRRR!

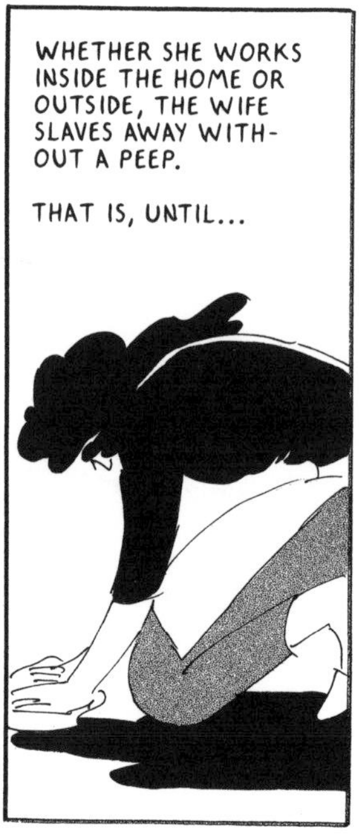
WHETHER SHE WORKS INSIDE THE HOME OR OUTSIDE, THE WIFE SLAVES AWAY WITH-OUT A PEEP.
THAT IS, UNTIL...

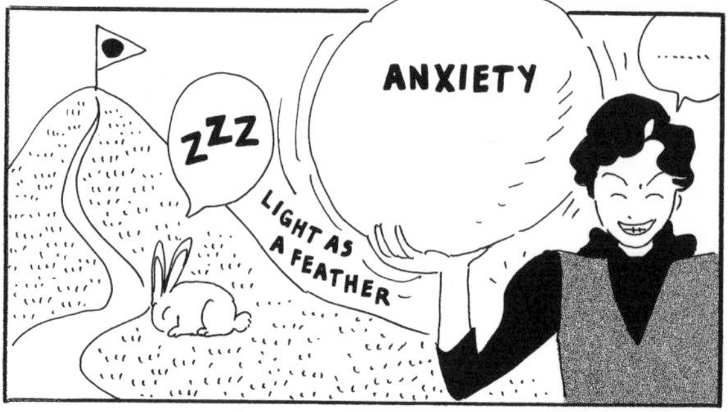
......
ANXIETY
ZZZ
LIGHT AS A FEATHER

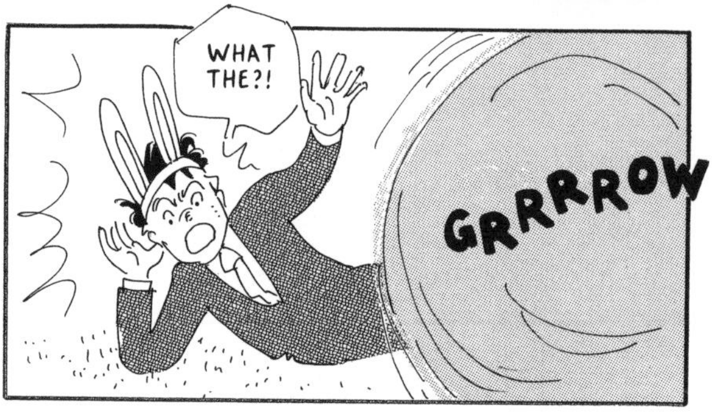
GRRRROW
WHAT THE?!

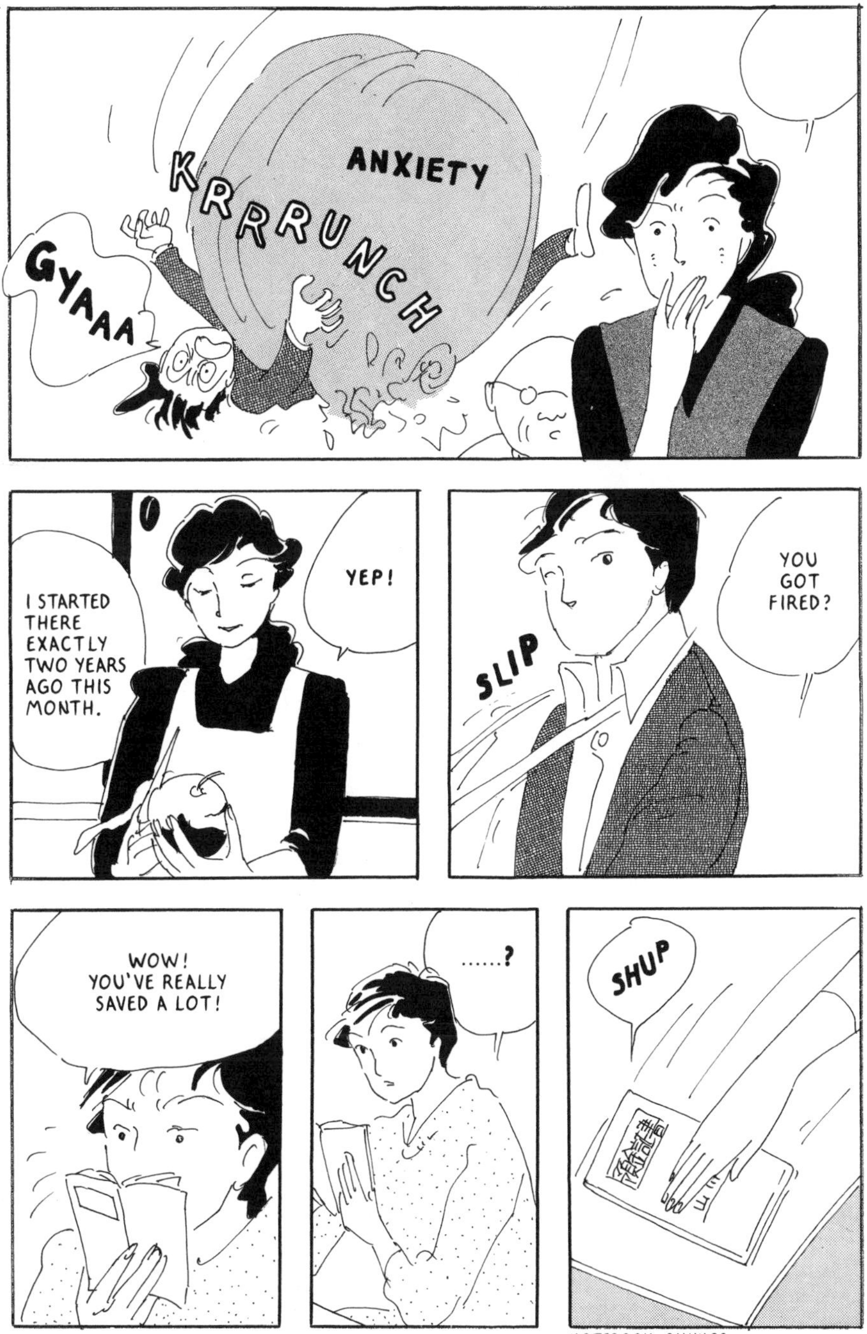
ANXIETY
KRRRUNCH
GYAAA
YOU GOT FIRED?
SLIP
YEP!
I STARTED THERE EXACTLY TWO YEARS AGO THIS MONTH.
SHUP
......?
WOW! YOU'VE REALLY SAVED A LOT!

NOTEBOOK: SAVINGS

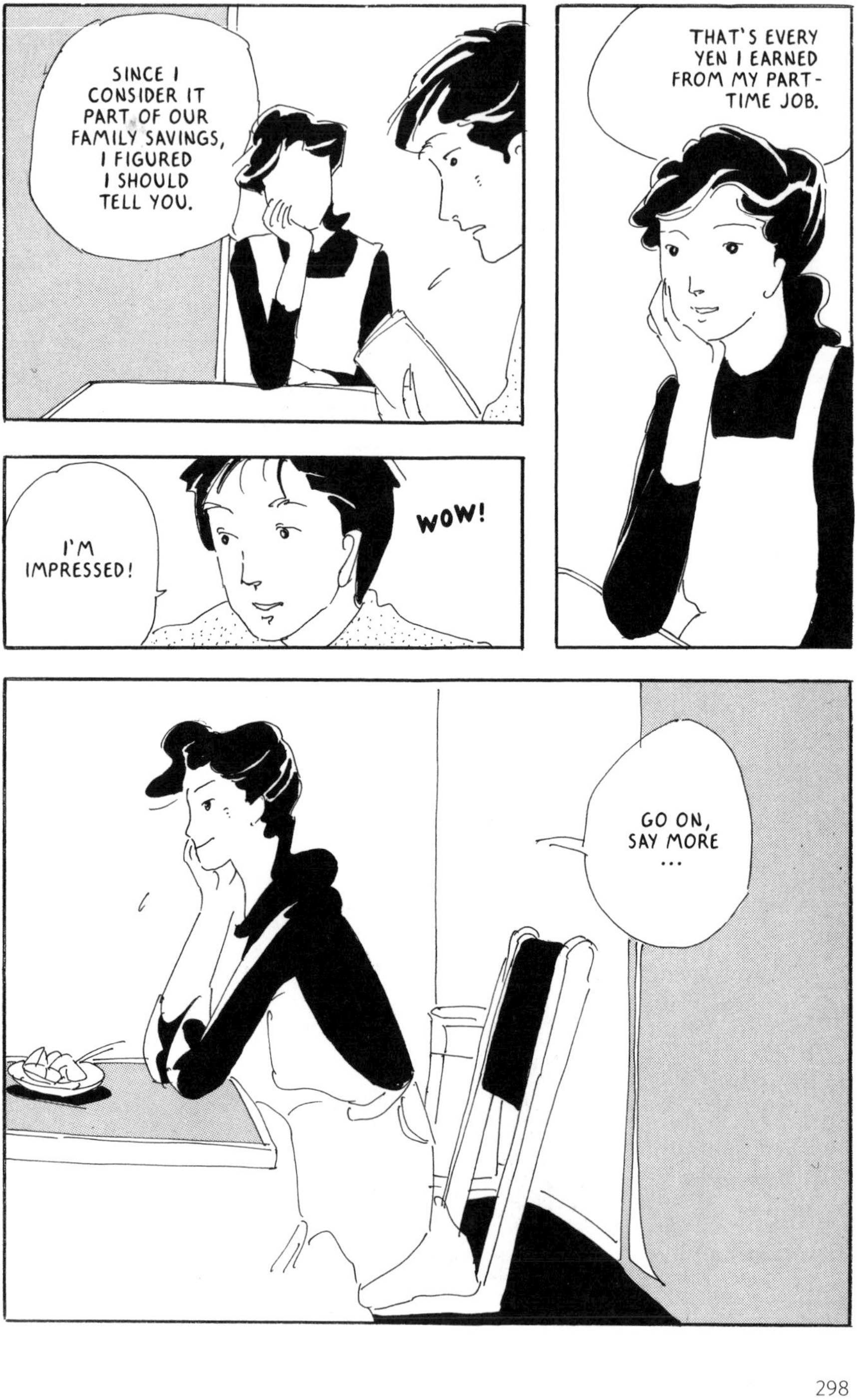
THAT'S EVERY YEN I EARNED FROM MY PART-TIME JOB.
SINCE I CONSIDER IT PART OF OUR FAMILY SAVINGS, I FIGURED I SHOULD TELL YOU.
WOW!
I'M IMPRESSED!
GO ON, SAY MORE ...

Haircut

BOO HOO

BOO HOO HOO

SNIFFLE SNIFFLE

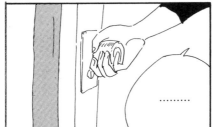

....

SNIFFLE SNIFFLE

BOO HOO HOO

I'M HOME!

WHAT HAPPENED?!

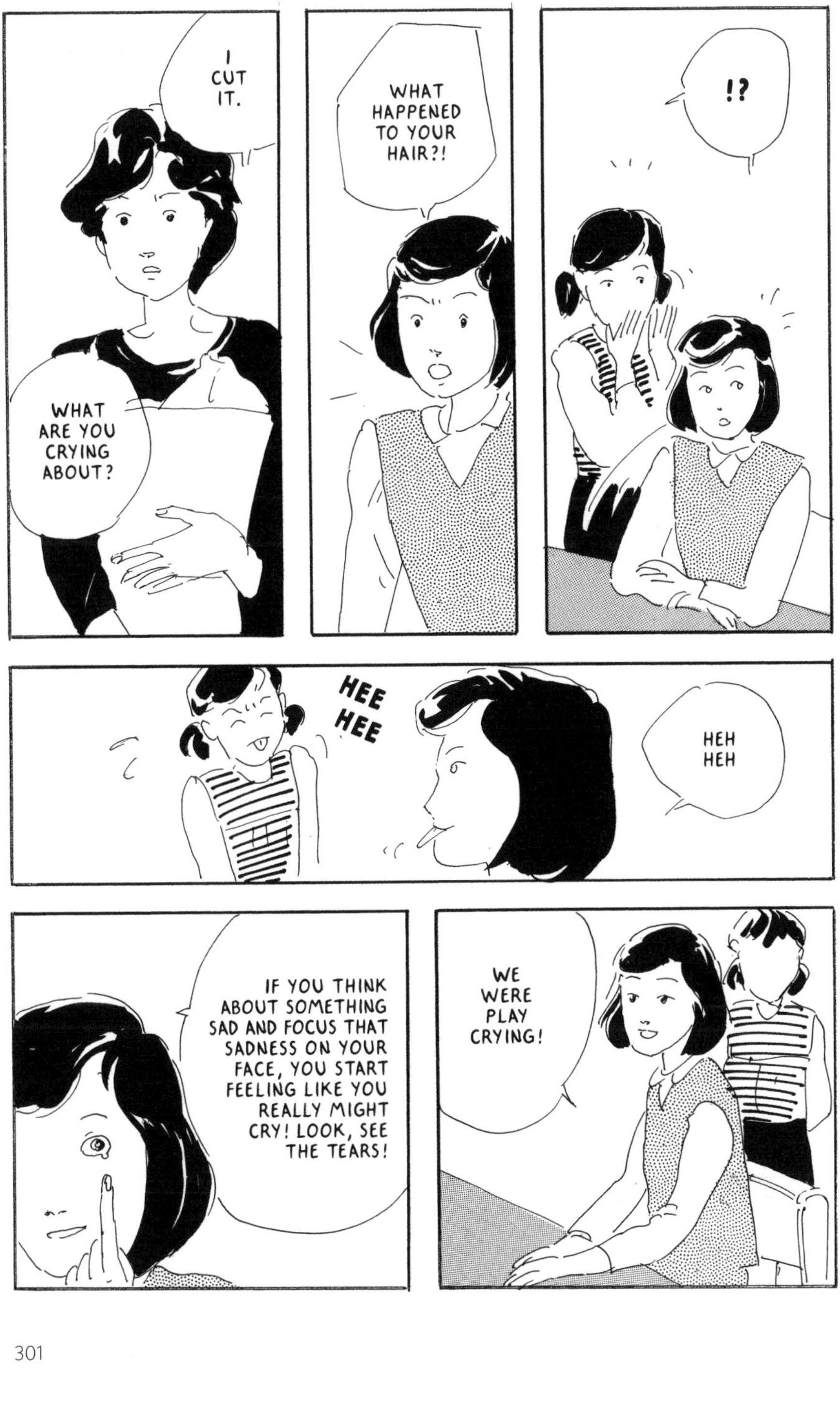
!?
WHAT HAPPENED TO YOUR HAIR?!
I CUT IT.
WHAT ARE YOU CRYING ABOUT?
HEH HEH
HEE HEE
WE WERE PLAY CRYING!
IF YOU THINK ABOUT SOMETHING SAD AND FOCUS THAT SADNESS ON YOUR FACE, YOU START FEELING LIKE YOU REALLY MIGHT CRY! LOOK, SEE THE TEARS!

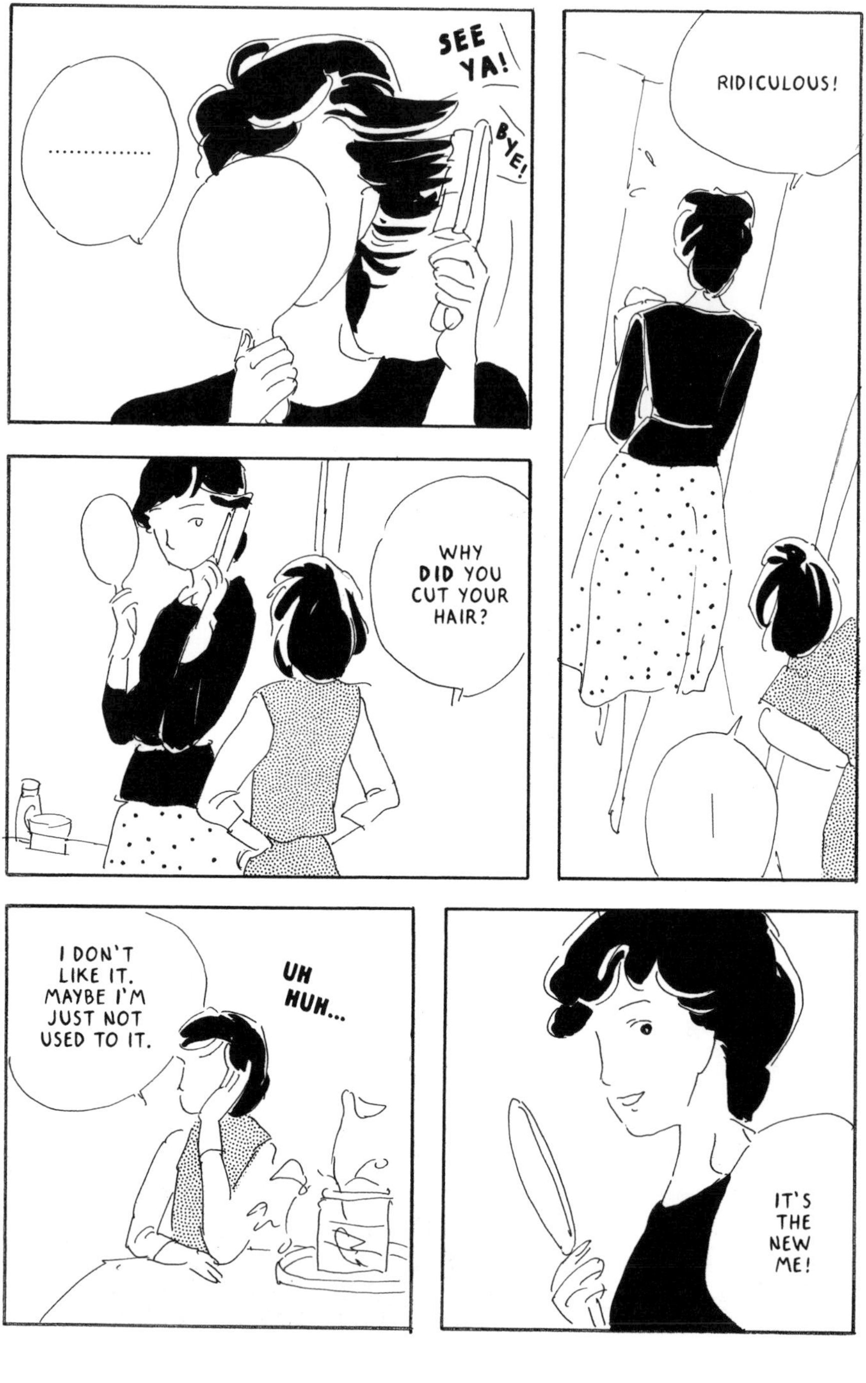
RIDICULOUS!
SEE YA!
BYE!
....
WHY **DID** YOU CUT YOUR HAIR?
IT'S THE NEW ME!
UH HUH...
I DON'T LIKE IT. MAYBE I'M JUST NOT USED TO IT.

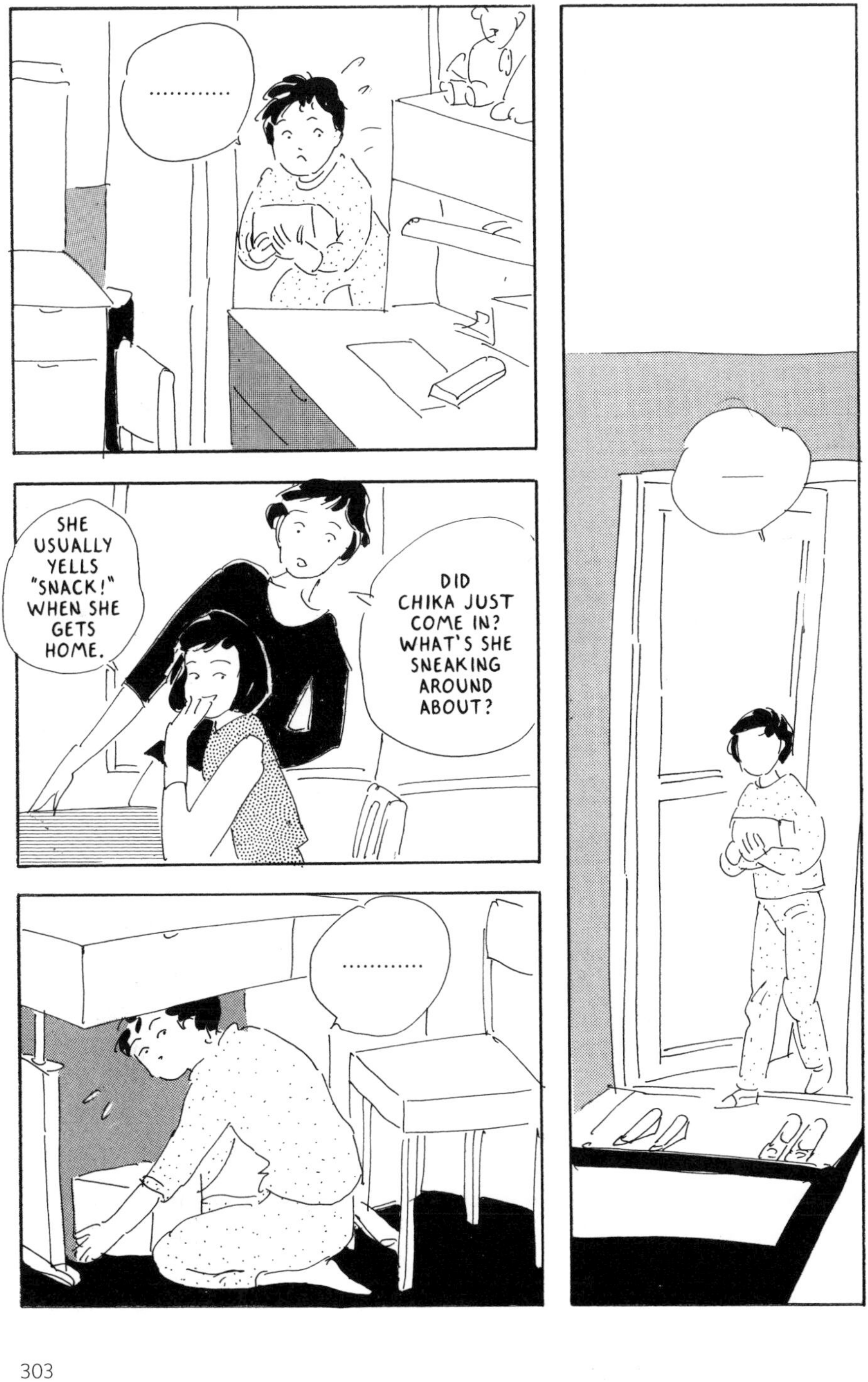
—
....
DID CHIKA JUST COME IN? WHAT'S SHE SNEAKING AROUND ABOUT?
SHE USUALLY YELLS "SNACK!" WHEN SHE GETS HOME.
....

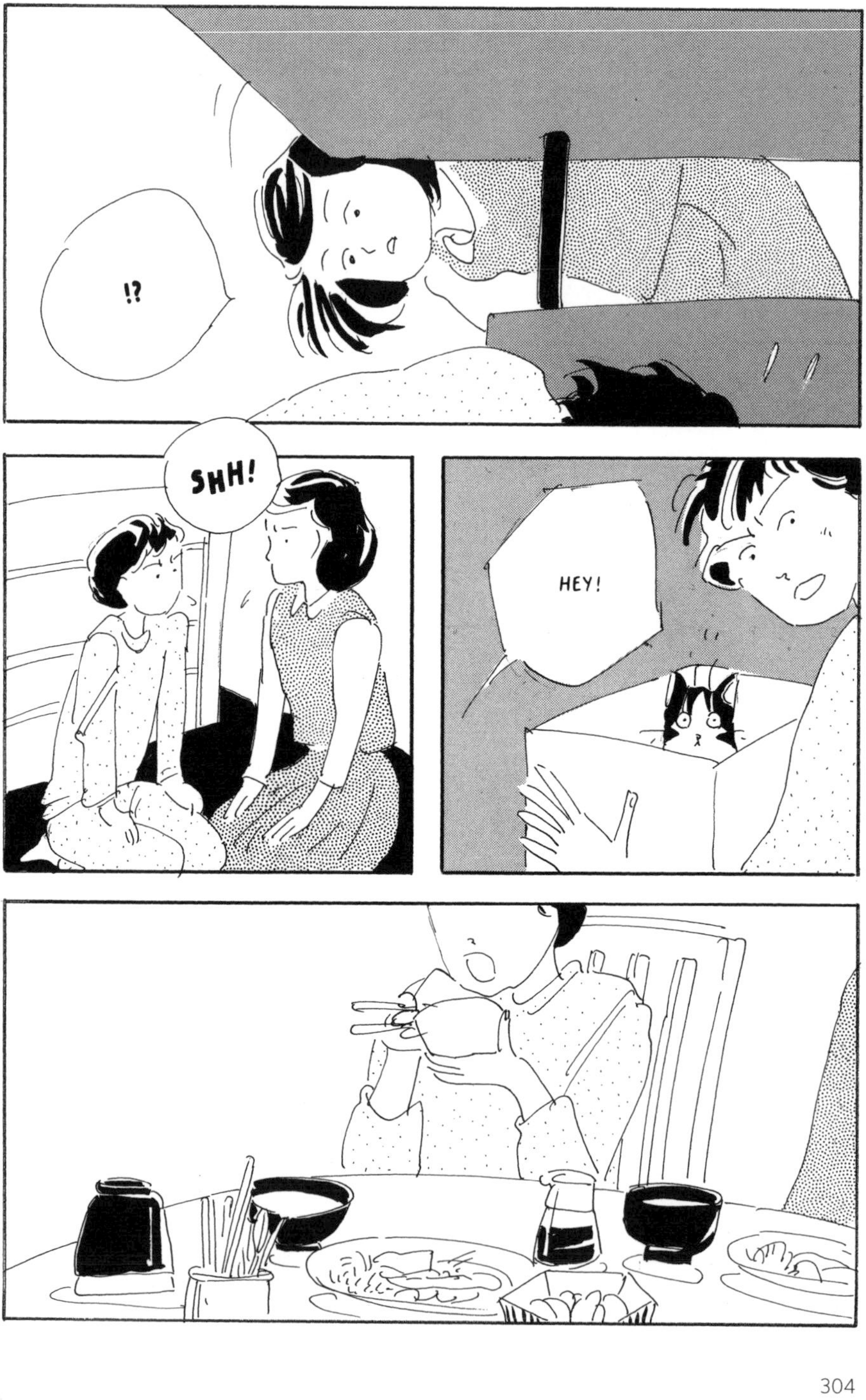
!?
HEY!
SHH!

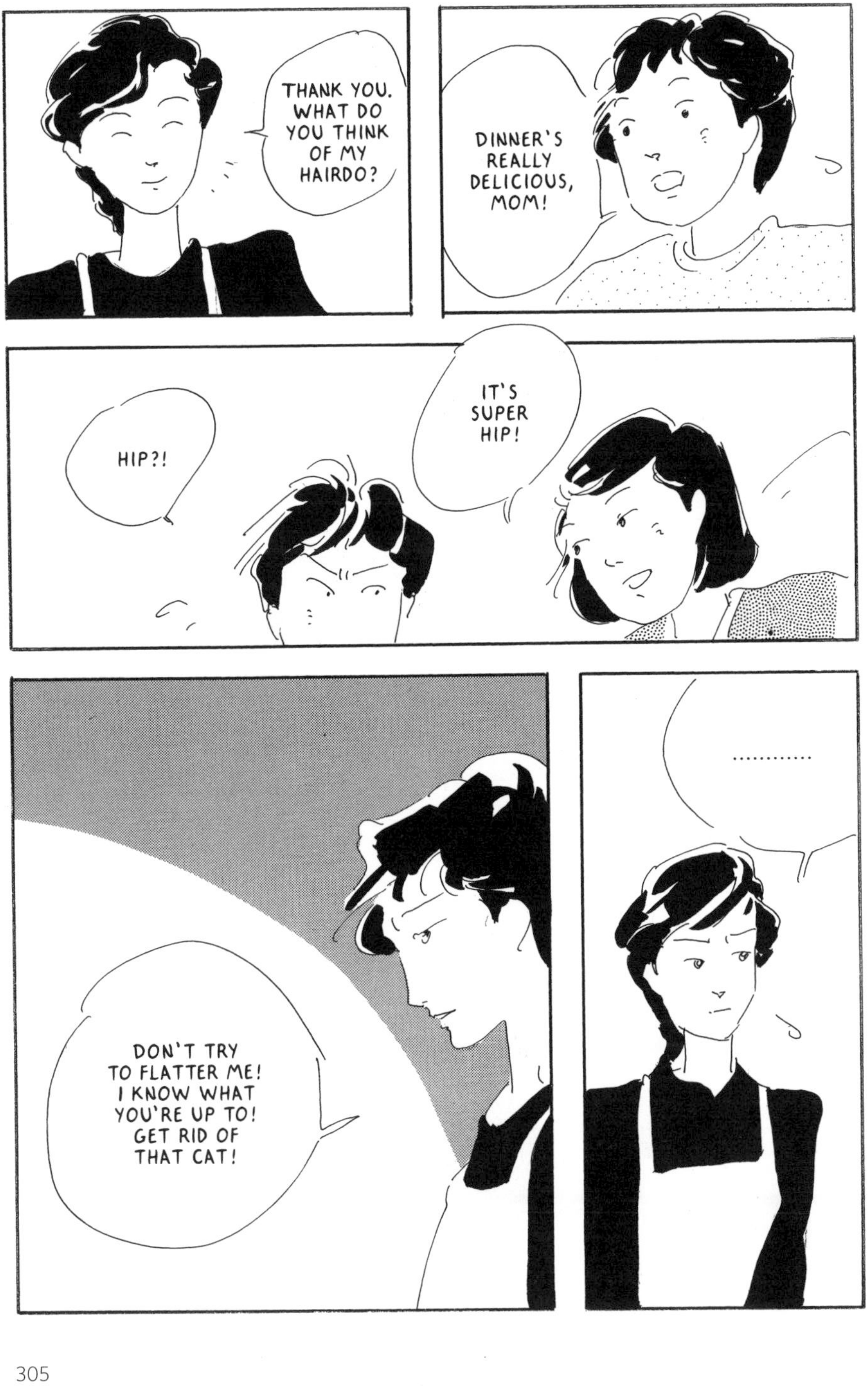
DINNER'S REALLY DELICIOUS, MOM!
THANK YOU. WHAT DO YOU THINK OF MY HAIRDO?
IT'S SUPER HIP!
HIP?!
....
DON'T TRY TO FLATTER ME! I KNOW WHAT YOU'RE UP TO! GET RID OF THAT CAT!

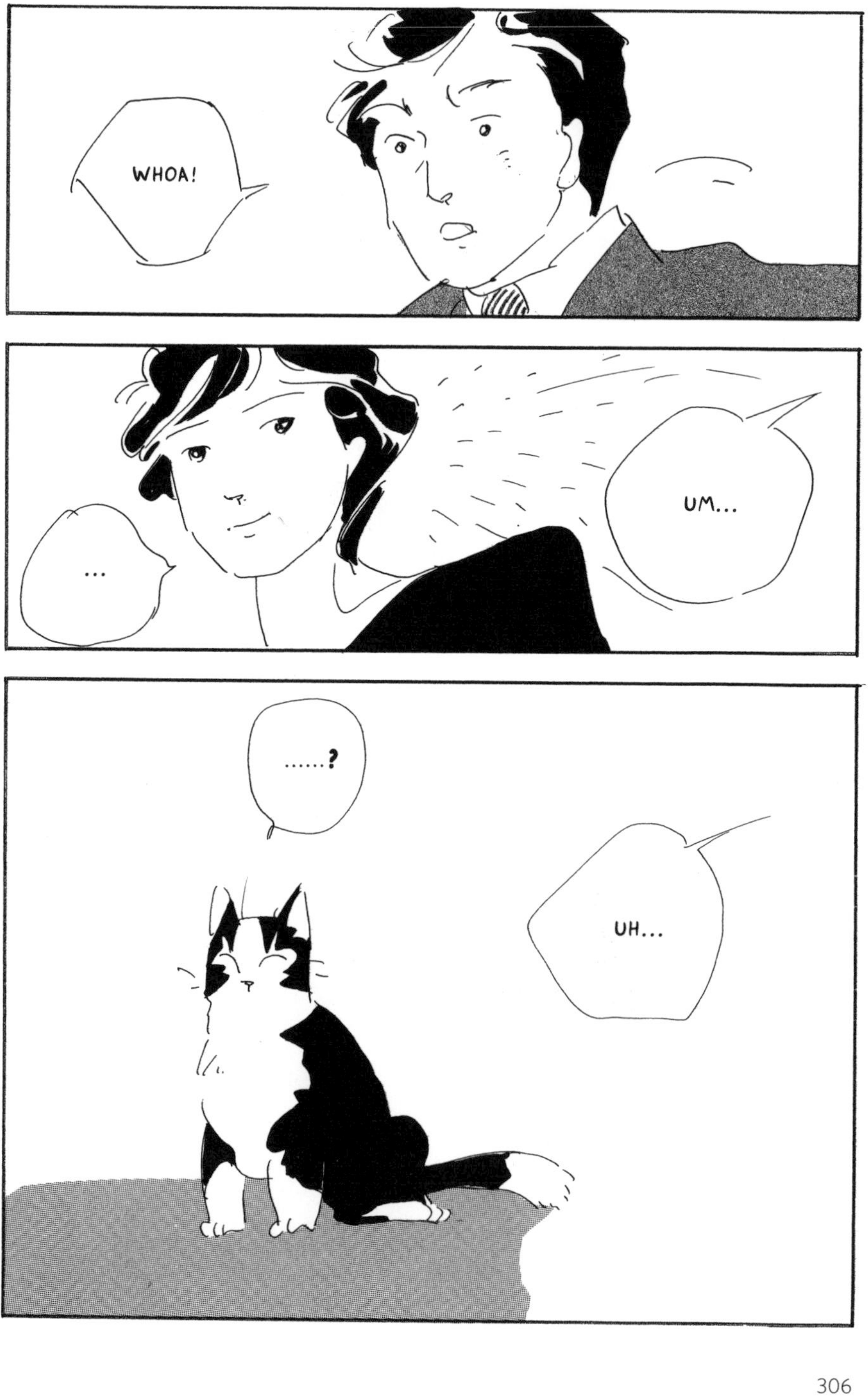
WHOA!
UM...
...
UH...
......?

Back On My Feet

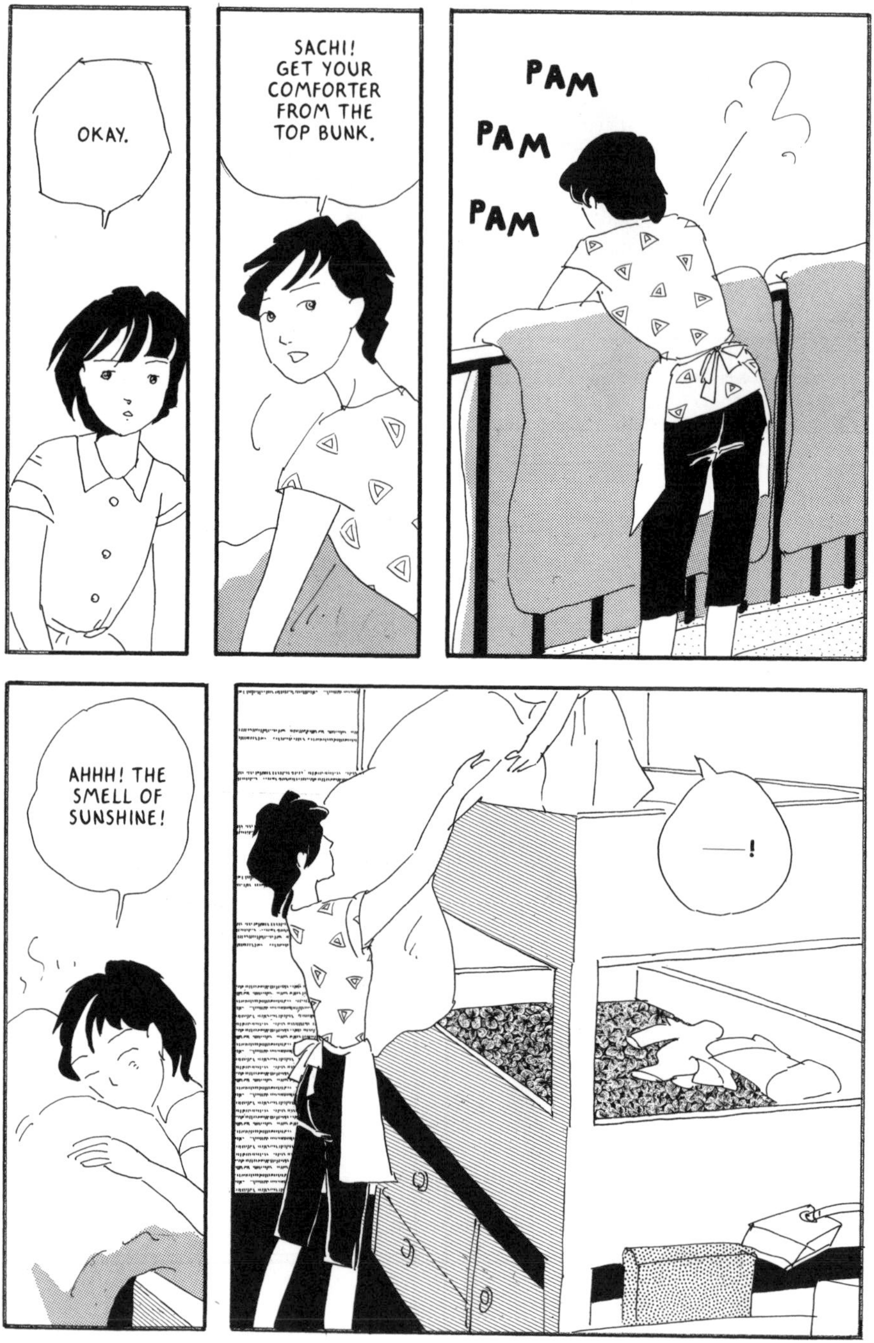
PAM
PAM
PAM
SACHI! GET YOUR COMFORTER FROM THE TOP BUNK.
OKAY.
——!
AHHH! THE SMELL OF SUNSHINE!

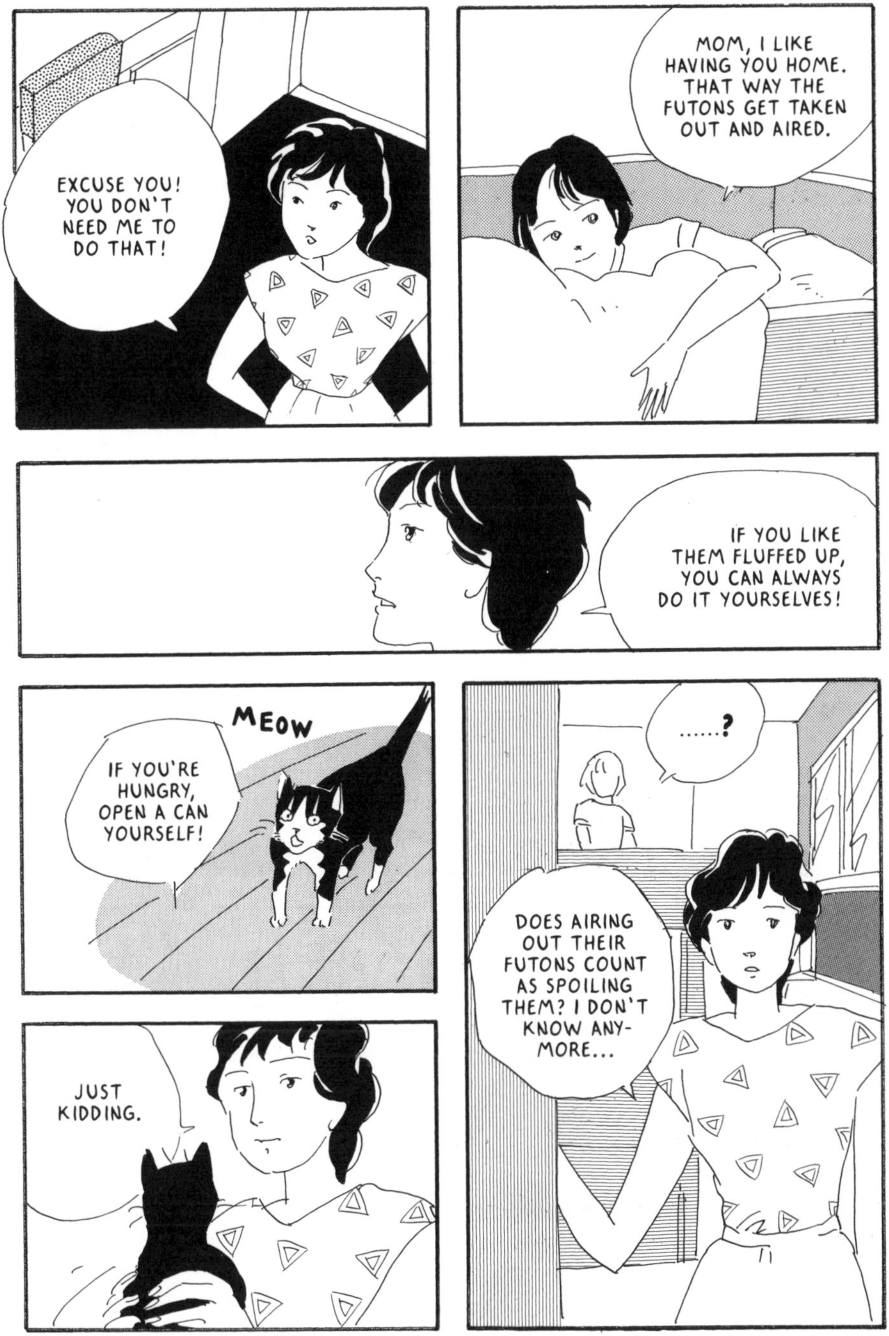
MOM, I LIKE HAVING YOU HOME. THAT WAY THE FUTONS GET TAKEN OUT AND AIRED.
EXCUSE YOU! YOU DON'T NEED ME TO DO THAT!
IF YOU LIKE THEM FLUFFED UP, YOU CAN ALWAYS DO IT YOURSELVES!
......?
DOES AIRING OUT THEIR FUTONS COUNT AS SPOILING THEM? I DON'T KNOW ANY-MORE...
MEOW
IF YOU'RE HUNGRY, OPEN A CAN YOURSELF!
JUST KIDDING.

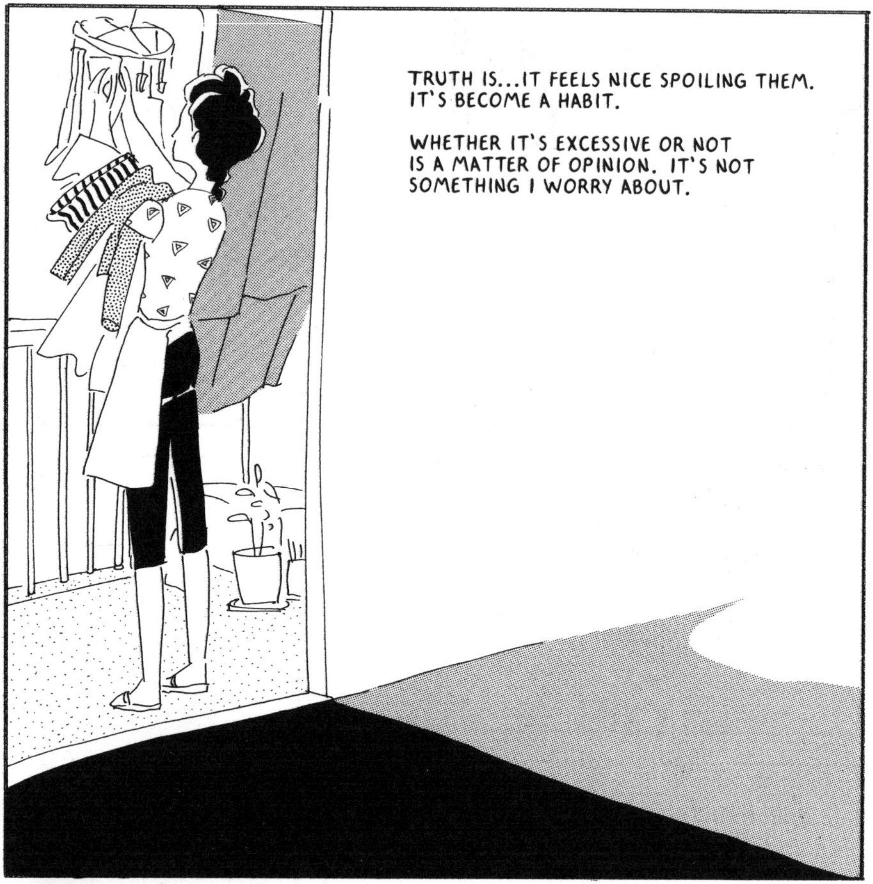
TRUTH IS...IT FEELS NICE SPOILING THEM. IT'S BECOME A HABIT.
WHETHER IT'S EXCESSIVE OR NOT IS A MATTER OF OPINION. IT'S NOT SOMETHING I WORRY ABOUT.

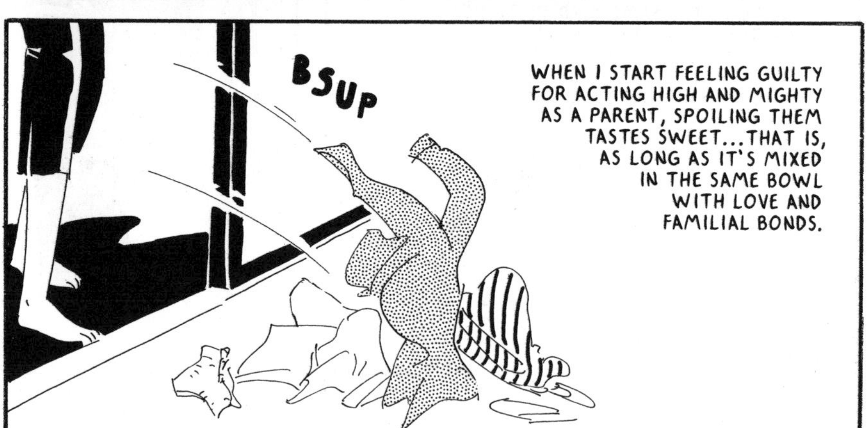
WHEN I START FEELING GUILTY FOR ACTING HIGH AND MIGHTY AS A PARENT, SPOILING THEM TASTES SWEET...THAT IS, AS LONG AS IT'S MIXED IN THE SAME BOWL WITH LOVE AND FAMILIAL BONDS.
BSUP

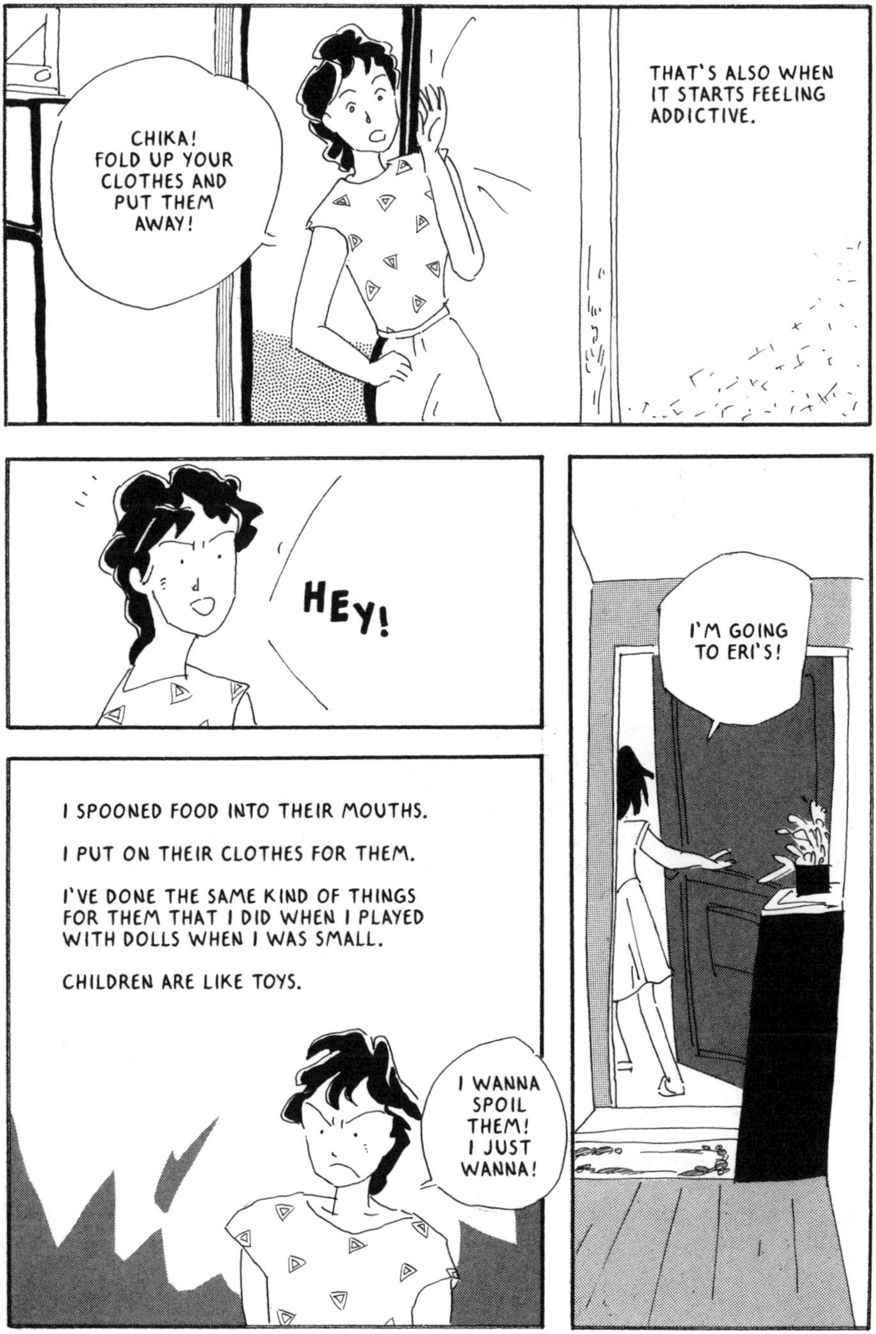
THAT'S ALSO WHEN IT STARTS FEELING ADDICTIVE.
CHIKA! FOLD UP YOUR CLOTHES AND PUT THEM AWAY!
I'M GOING TO ERI'S!
HEY!
I SPOONED FOOD INTO THEIR MOUTHS.
I PUT ON THEIR CLOTHES FOR THEM.
I'VE DONE THE SAME KIND OF THINGS FOR THEM THAT I DID WHEN I PLAYED WITH DOLLS WHEN I WAS SMALL.
CHILDREN ARE LIKE TOYS.
I WANNA SPOIL THEM! I JUST WANNA!

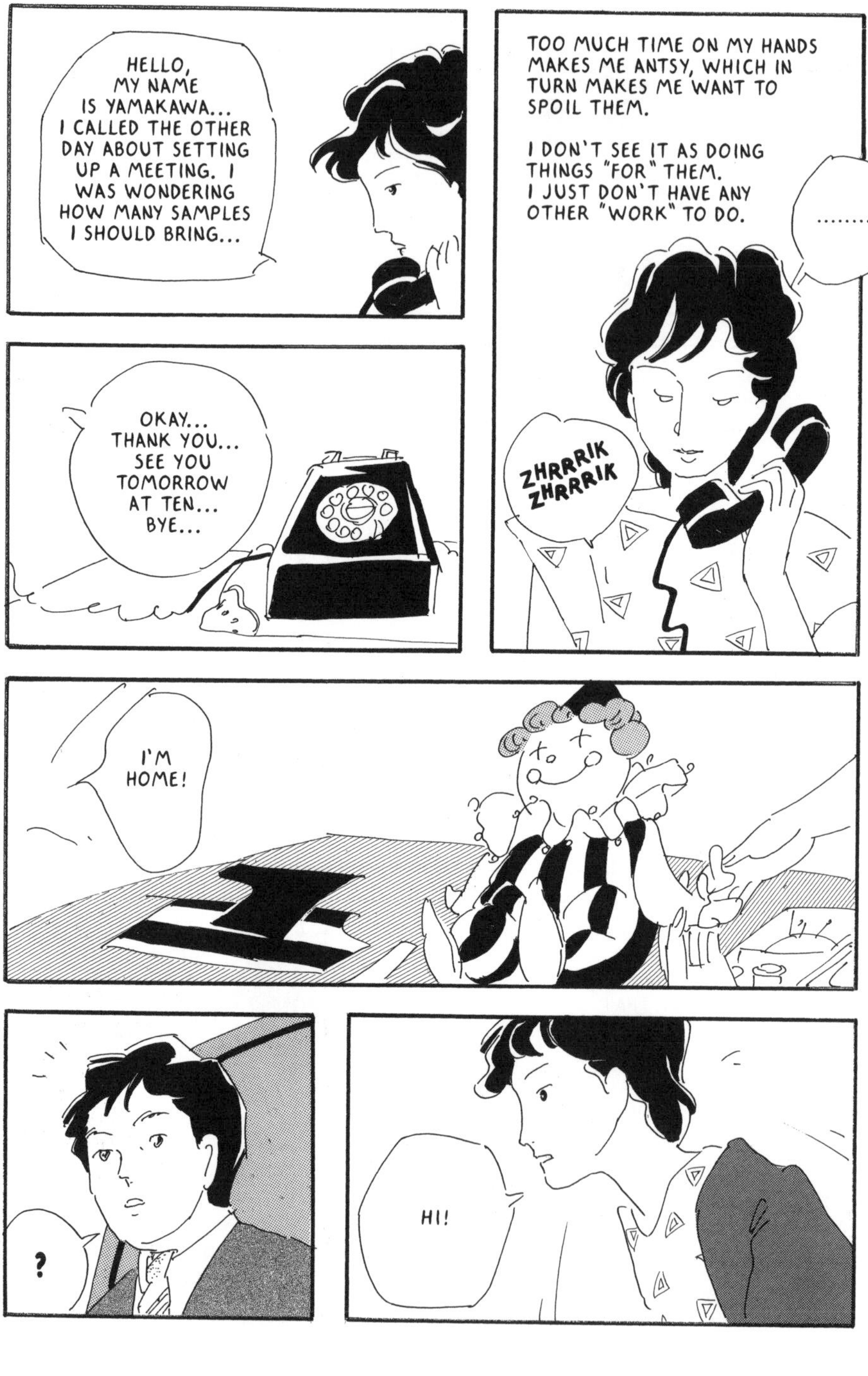
TOO MUCH TIME ON MY HANDS MAKES ME ANTSY, WHICH IN TURN MAKES ME WANT TO SPOIL THEM.
I DON'T SEE IT AS DOING THINGS "FOR" THEM. I JUST DON'T HAVE ANY OTHER "WORK" TO DO.
....
ZHRRRIK ZHRRRIK
HELLO, MY NAME IS YAMAKAWA... I CALLED THE OTHER DAY ABOUT SETTING UP A MEETING. I WAS WONDERING HOW MANY SAMPLES I SHOULD BRING...
OKAY... THANK YOU... SEE YOU TOMORROW AT TEN... BYE...
I'M HOME!
HI!
?

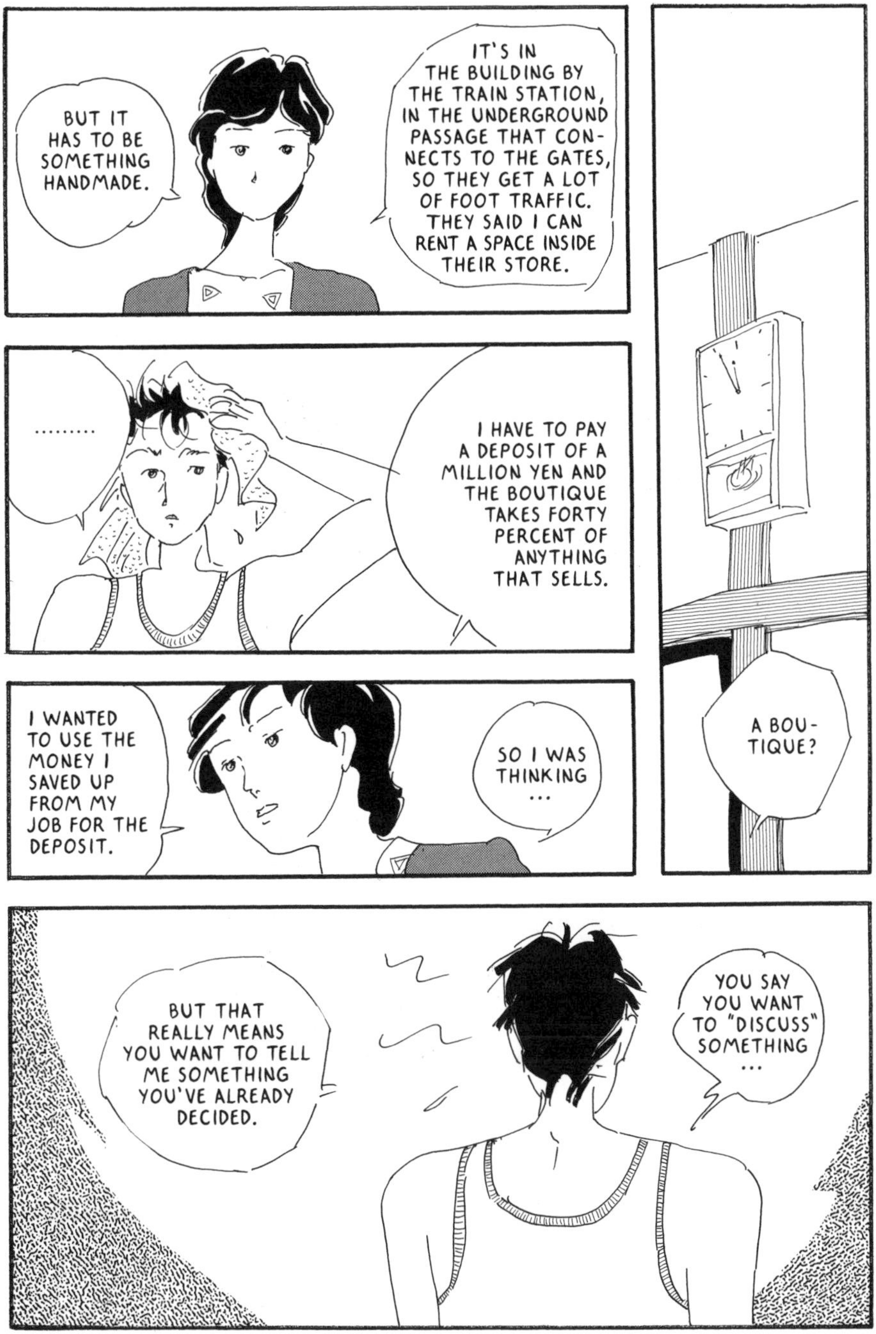
A BOUTIQUE?
IT'S IN THE BUILDING BY THE TRAIN STATION, IN THE UNDERGROUND PASSAGE THAT CONNECTS TO THE GATES, SO THEY GET A LOT OF FOOT TRAFFIC. THEY SAID I CAN RENT A SPACE INSIDE THEIR STORE.
BUT IT HAS TO BE SOMETHING HANDMADE.
I HAVE TO PAY A DEPOSIT OF A MILLION YEN AND THE BOUTIQUE TAKES FORTY PERCENT OF ANYTHING THAT SELLS.
....
SO I WAS THINKING ...
I WANTED TO USE THE MONEY I SAVED UP FROM MY JOB FOR THE DEPOSIT.
YOU SAY YOU WANT TO "DISCUSS" SOMETHING ...
BUT THAT REALLY MEANS YOU WANT TO TELL ME SOMETHING YOU'VE ALREADY DECIDED.

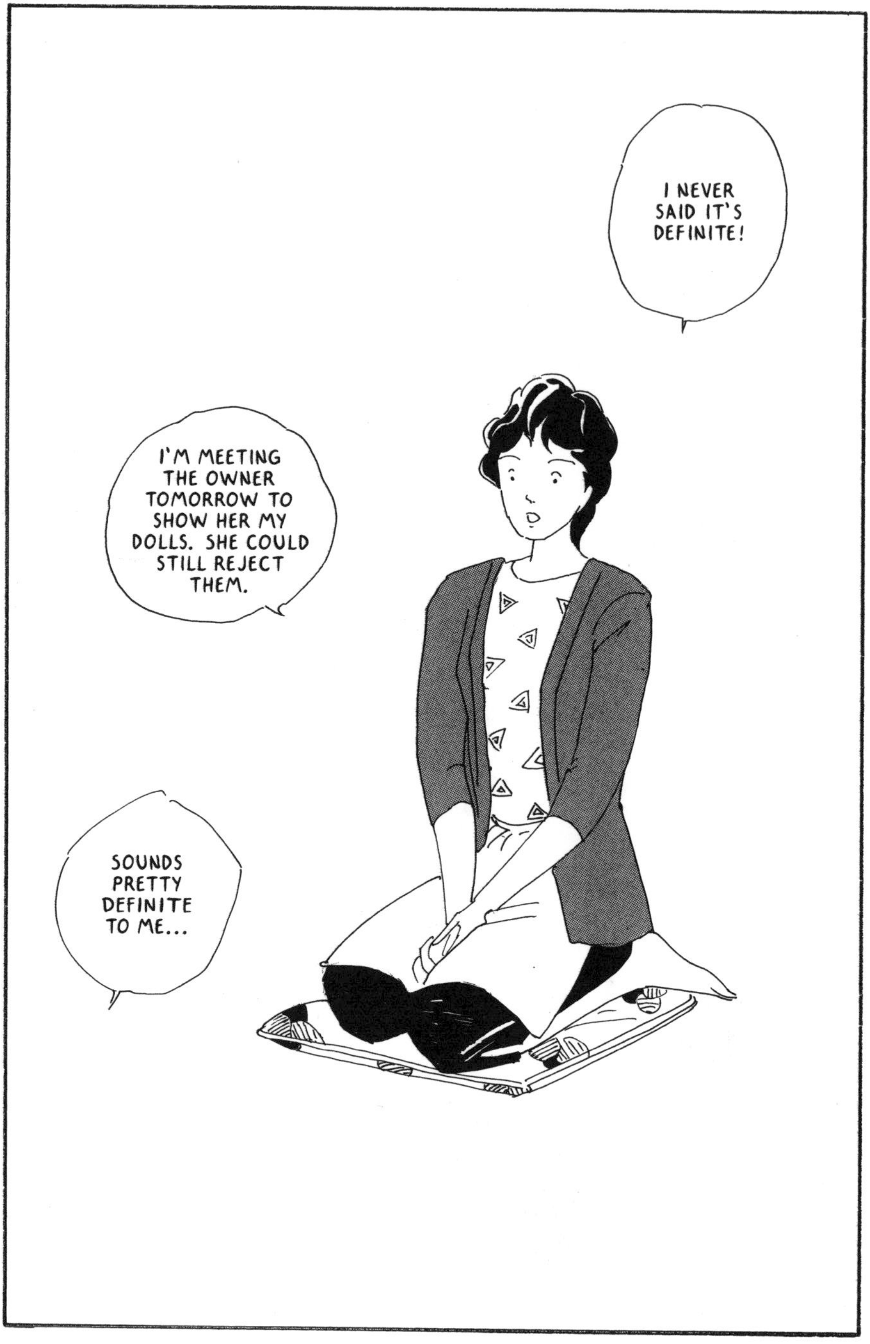
I NEVER SAID IT'S DEFINITE!
I'M MEETING THE OWNER TOMORROW TO SHOW HER MY DOLLS. SHE COULD STILL REJECT THEM.
SOUNDS PRETTY DEFINITE TO ME...

Yamakawa Chiharu

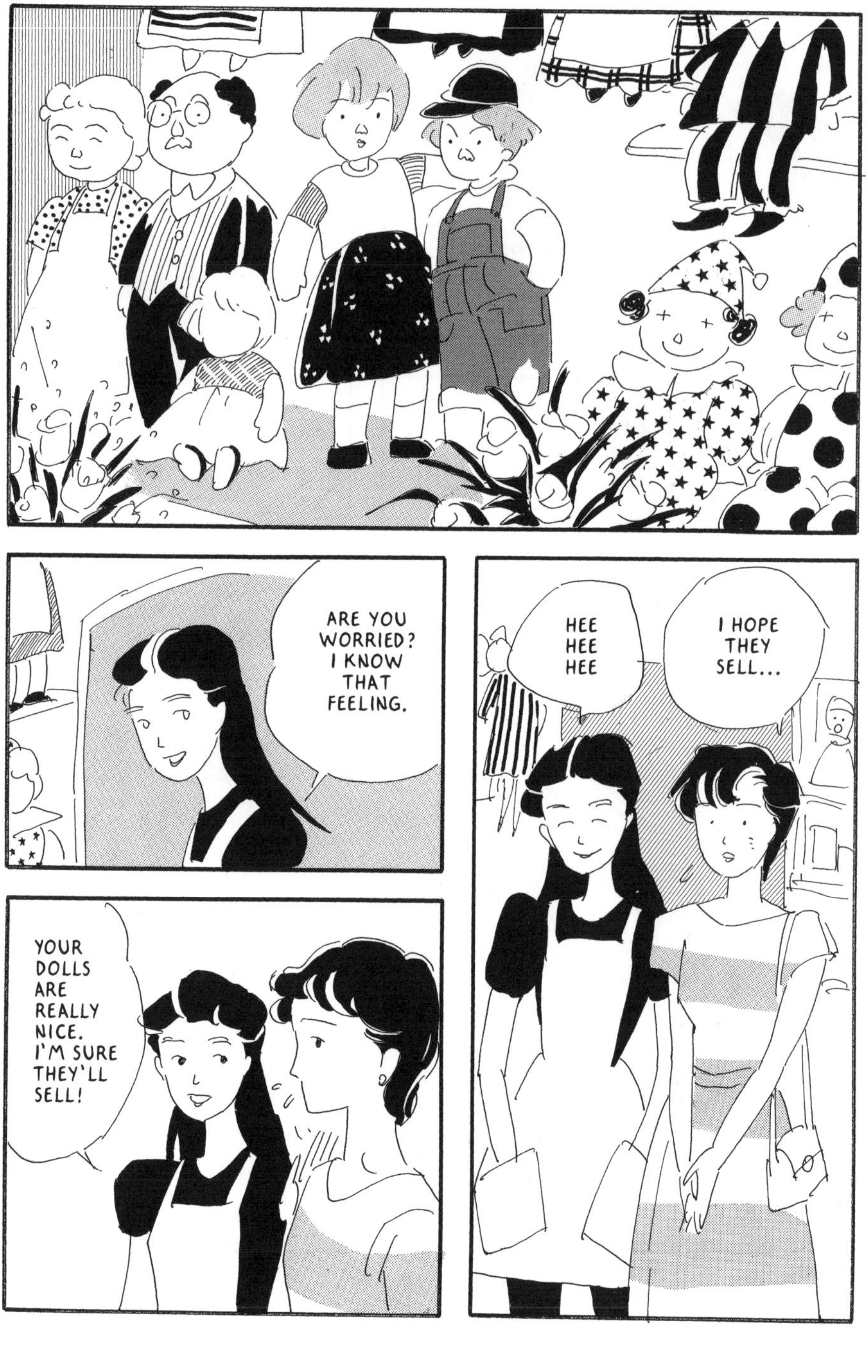
I HOPE THEY SELL...
HEE HEE HEE
ARE YOU WORRIED? I KNOW THAT FEELING.
YOUR DOLLS ARE REALLY NICE. I'M SURE THEY'LL SELL!

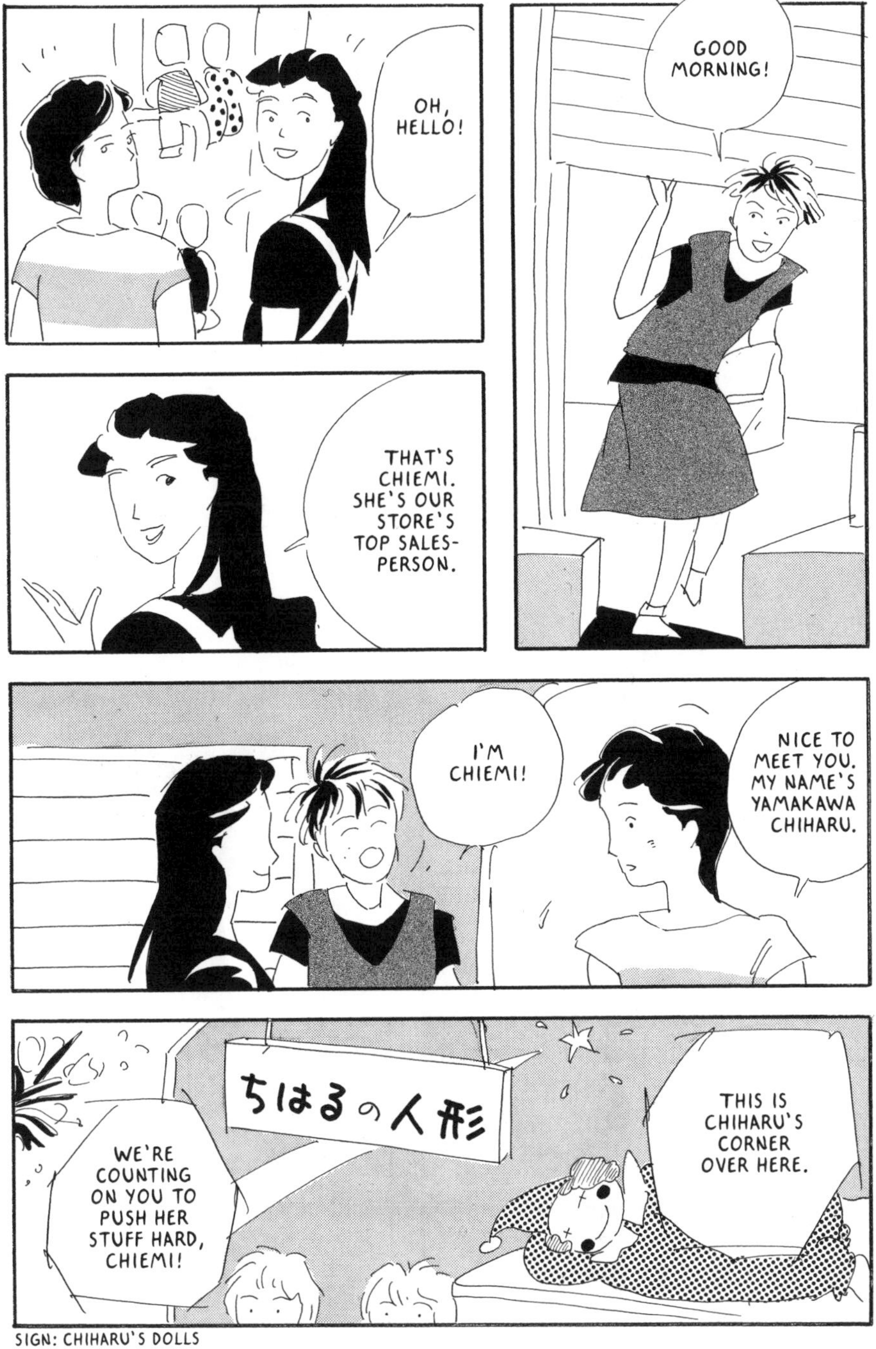
GOOD MORNING!
OH, HELLO!
THAT'S CHIEMI. SHE'S OUR STORE'S TOP SALES-PERSON.
NICE TO MEET YOU. MY NAME'S YAMAKAWA CHIHARU.
I'M CHIEMI!
THIS IS CHIHARU'S CORNER OVER HERE.
ちはるの人形
WE'RE COUNTING ON YOU TO PUSH HER STUFF HARD, CHIEMI!

SIGN: CHIHARU'S DOLLS

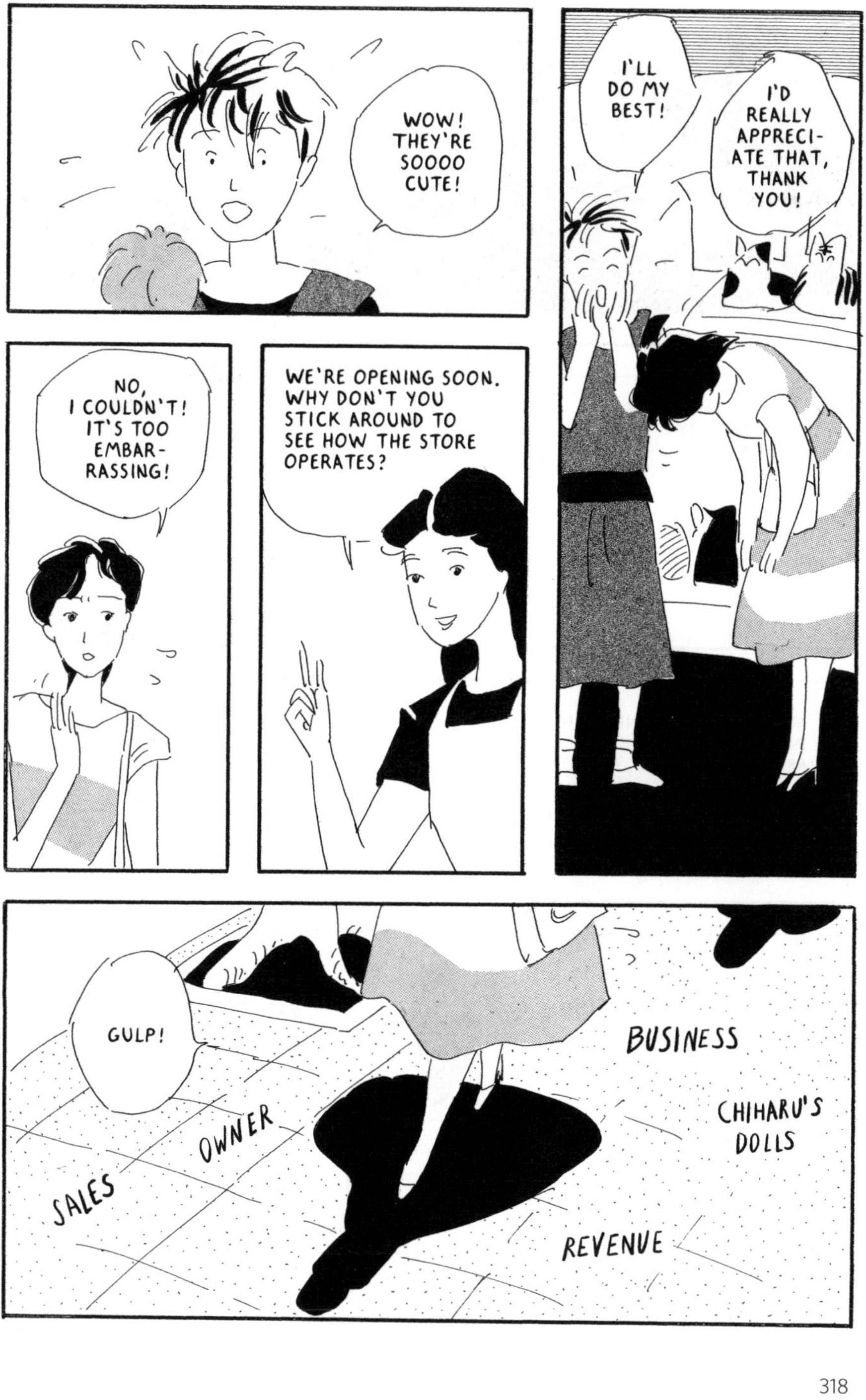
I'LL DO MY BEST!
I'D REALLY APPRECIATE THAT, THANK YOU!
WOW! THEY'RE SOOOO CUTE!
WE'RE OPENING SOON. WHY DON'T YOU STICK AROUND TO SEE HOW THE STORE OPERATES?
NO, I COULDN'T! IT'S TOO EMBARRASSING!
BUSINESS
CHIHARU'S DOLLS
GULP!
OWNER
REVENUE
SALES

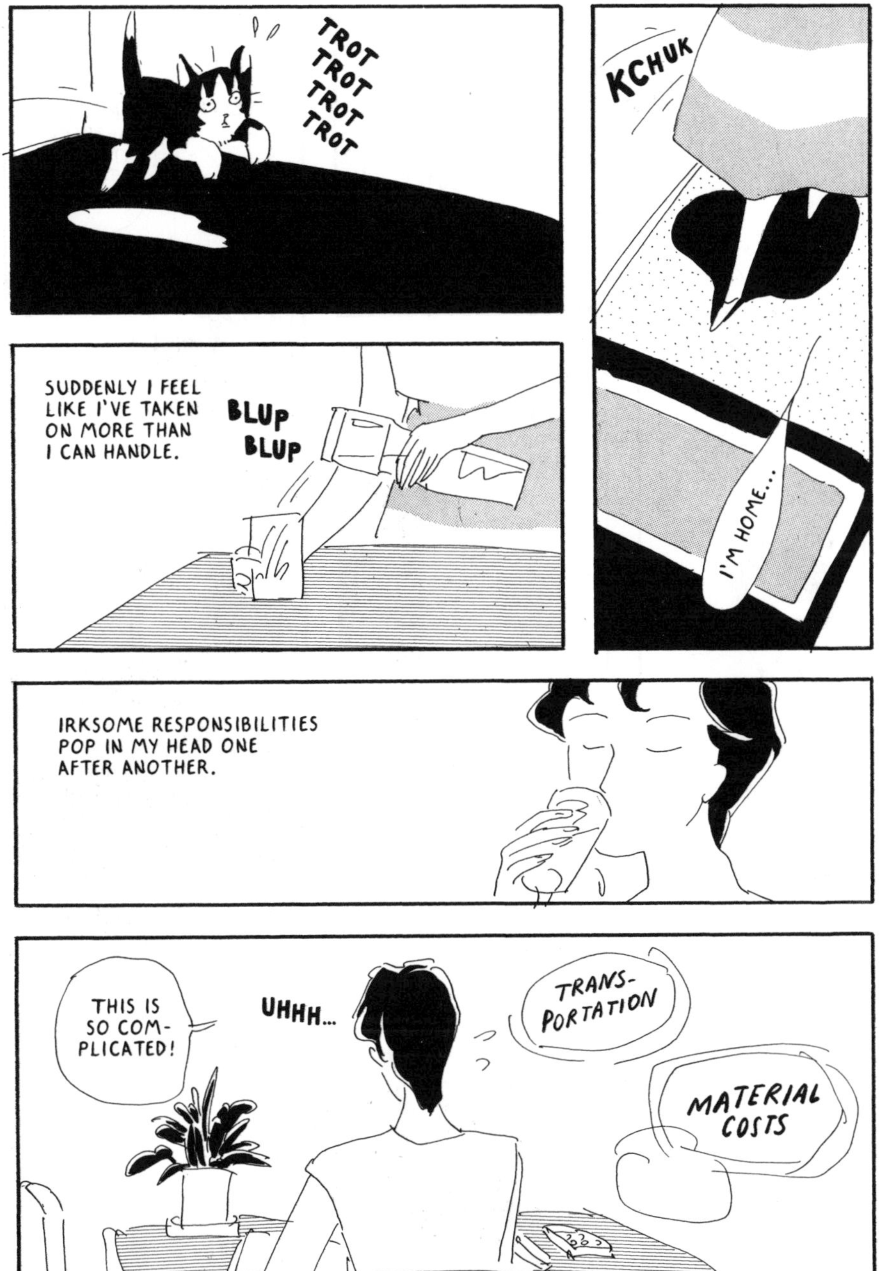
KCHUK
I'M HOME...
TROT TROT TROT TROT
SUDDENLY I FEEL LIKE I'VE TAKEN ON MORE THAN I CAN HANDLE.
BLUP BLUP
IRKSOME RESPONSIBILITIES POP IN MY HEAD ONE AFTER ANOTHER.
TRANS-PORTATION
MATERIAL COSTS
UHHH...
THIS IS SO COM-PLICATED!

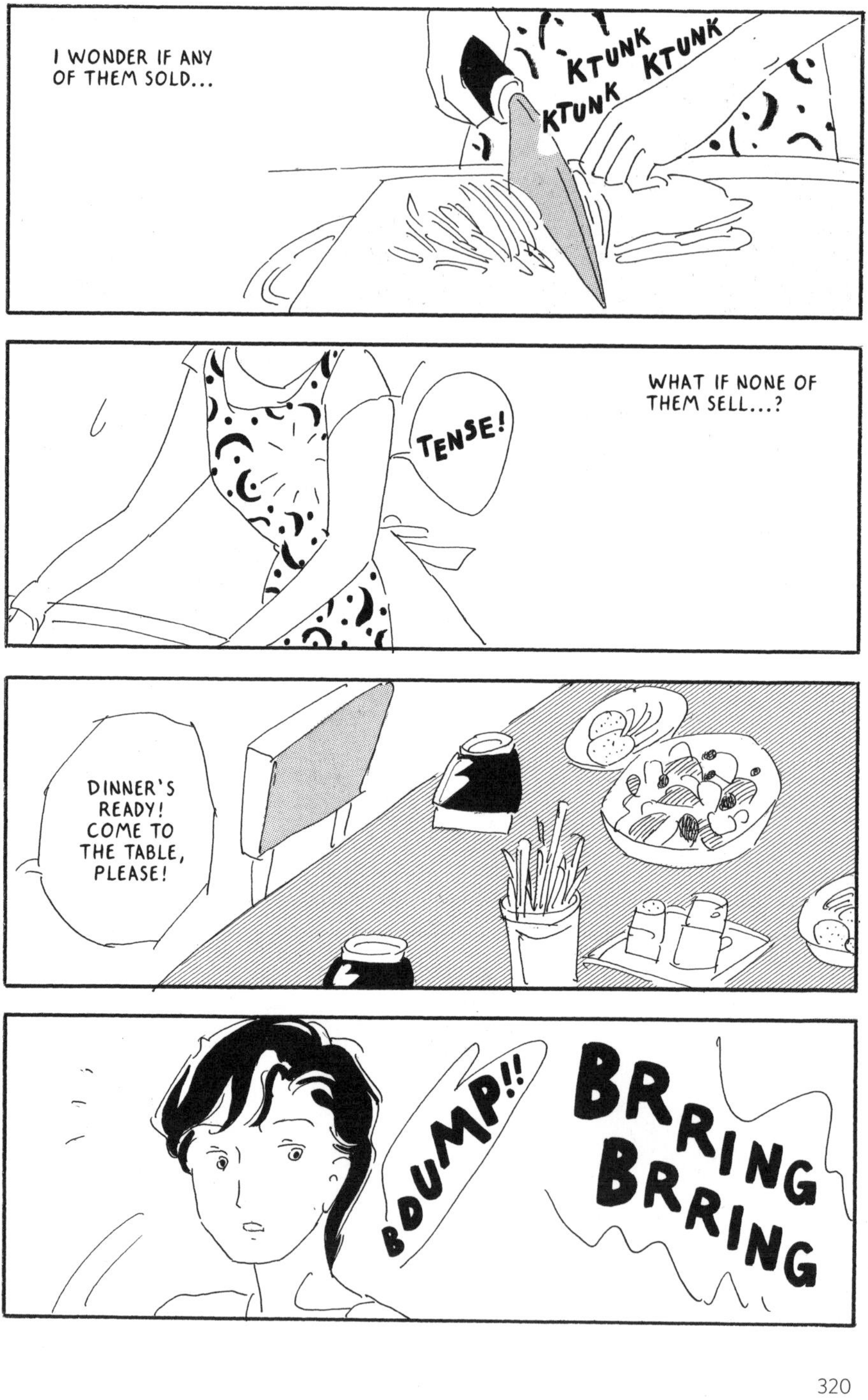
KTUNK KTUNK
KTUNK
I WONDER IF ANY OF THEM SOLD...
WHAT IF NONE OF THEM SELL...?
TENSE!
DINNER'S READY! COME TO THE TABLE, PLEASE!
BRRING BRRING
BDUMP!!

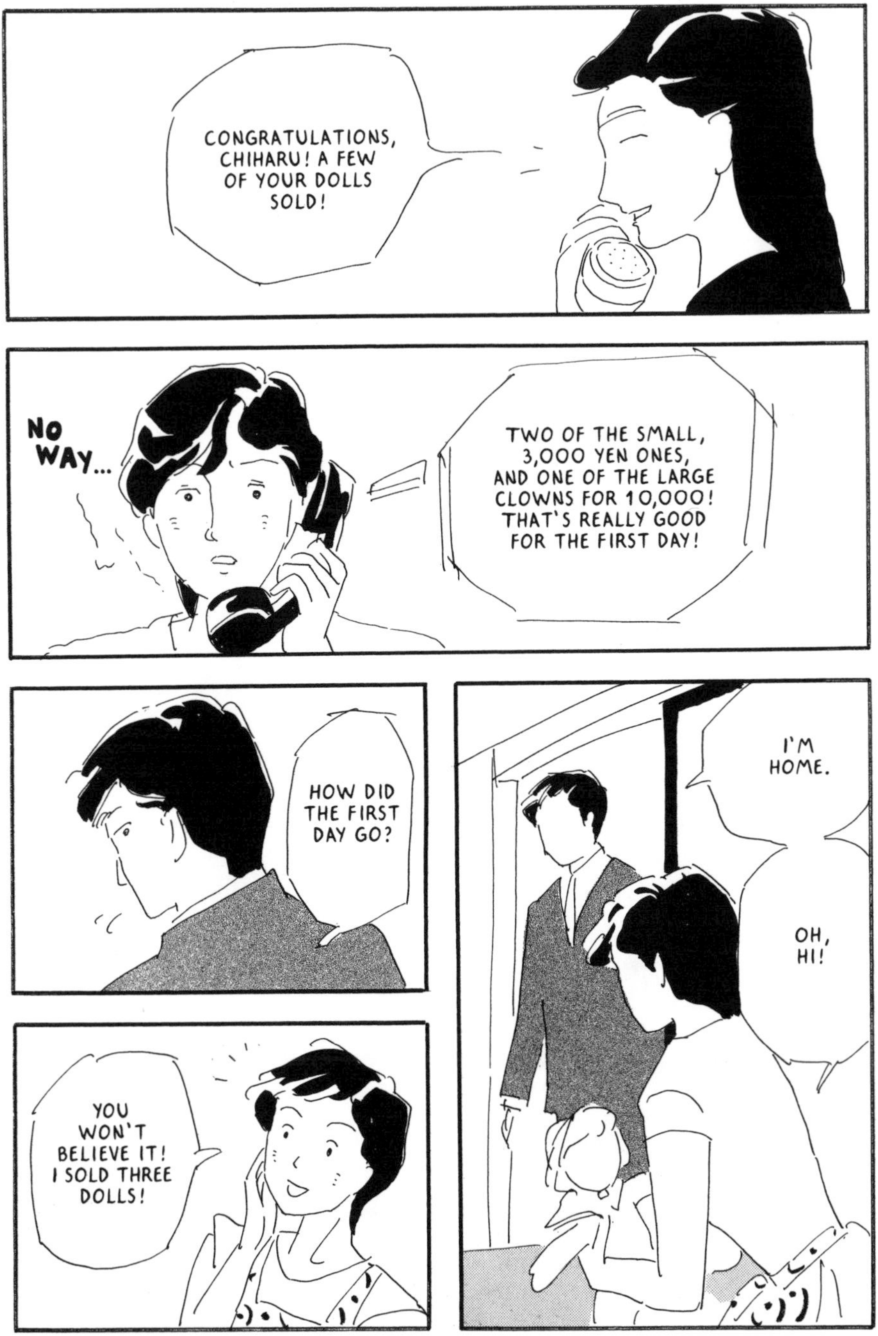
CONGRATULATIONS, CHIHARU! A FEW OF YOUR DOLLS SOLD!
TWO OF THE SMALL, 3,000 YEN ONES, AND ONE OF THE LARGE CLOWNS FOR 10,000! THAT'S REALLY GOOD FOR THE FIRST DAY!
NO WAY...
I'M HOME.
OH, HI!
HOW DID THE FIRST DAY GO?
YOU WON'T BELIEVE IT! I SOLD THREE DOLLS!

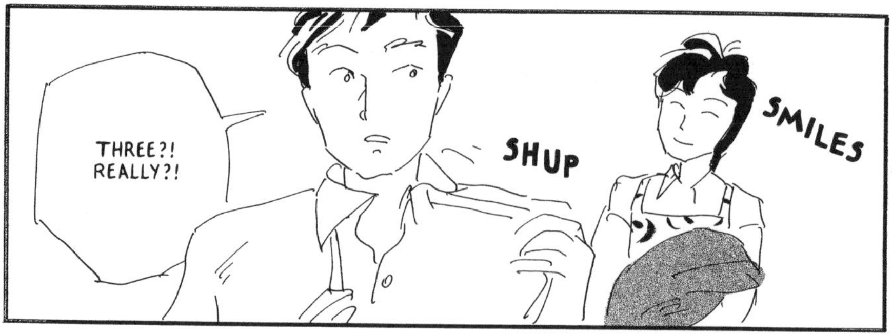
SMILES
SHUP
THREE?! REALLY?!

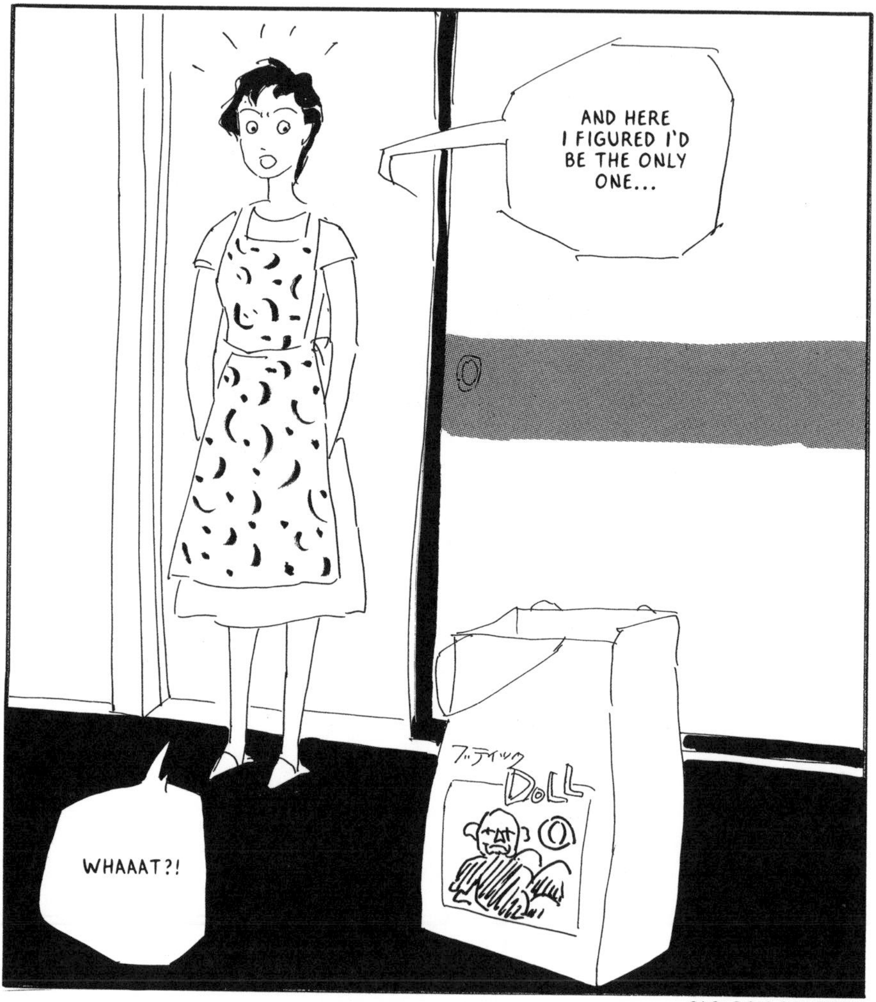
AND HERE I FIGURED I'D BE THE ONLY ONE...
ブティック
DOLL
WHAAAT?!

BAG: DOLL BOUTIQUE

Partner

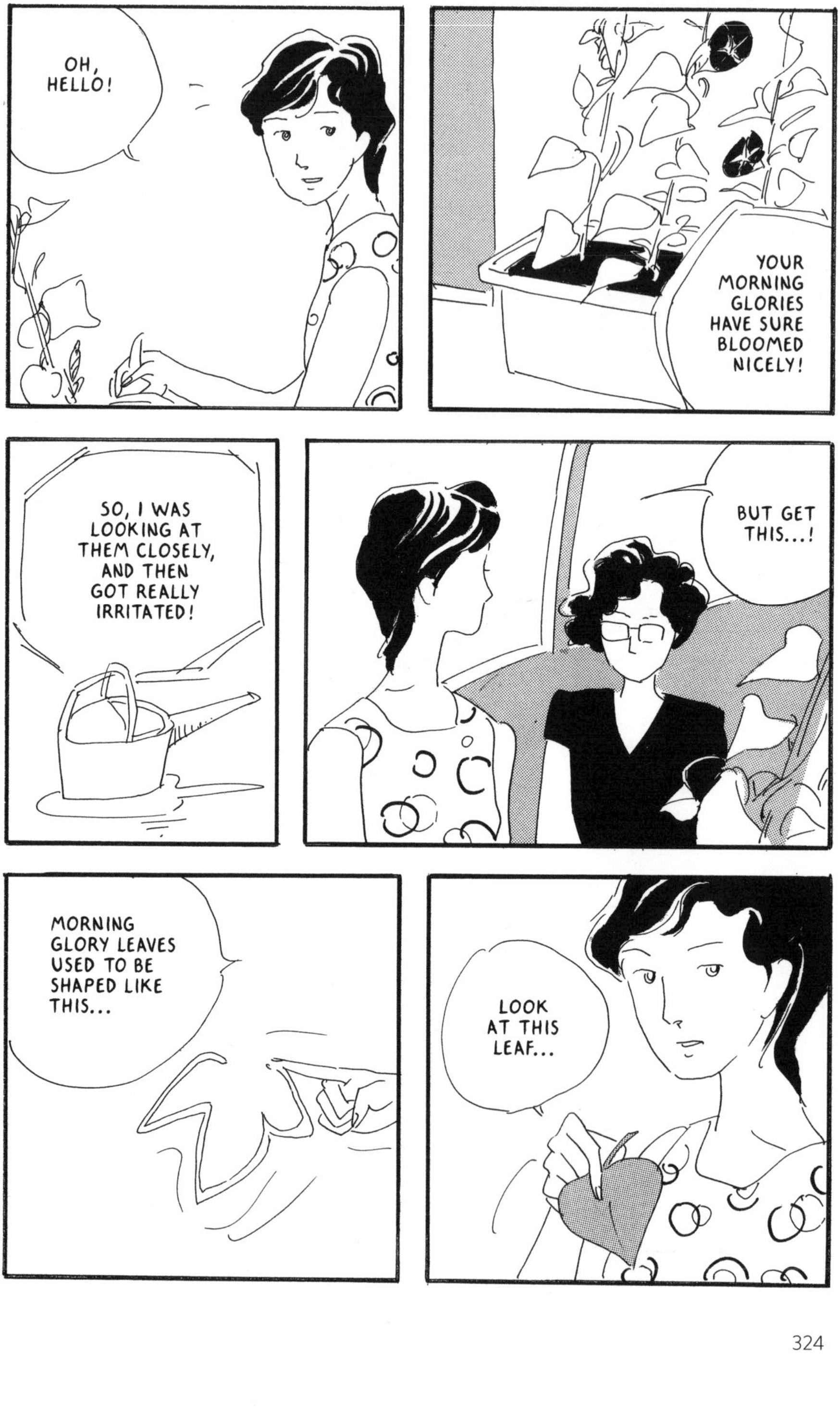
YOUR MORNING GLORIES HAVE SURE BLOOMED NICELY!
OH, HELLO!
BUT GET THIS...!
SO, I WAS LOOKING AT THEM CLOSELY, AND THEN GOT REALLY IRRITATED!
LOOK AT THIS LEAF...
MORNING GLORY LEAVES USED TO BE SHAPED LIKE THIS...

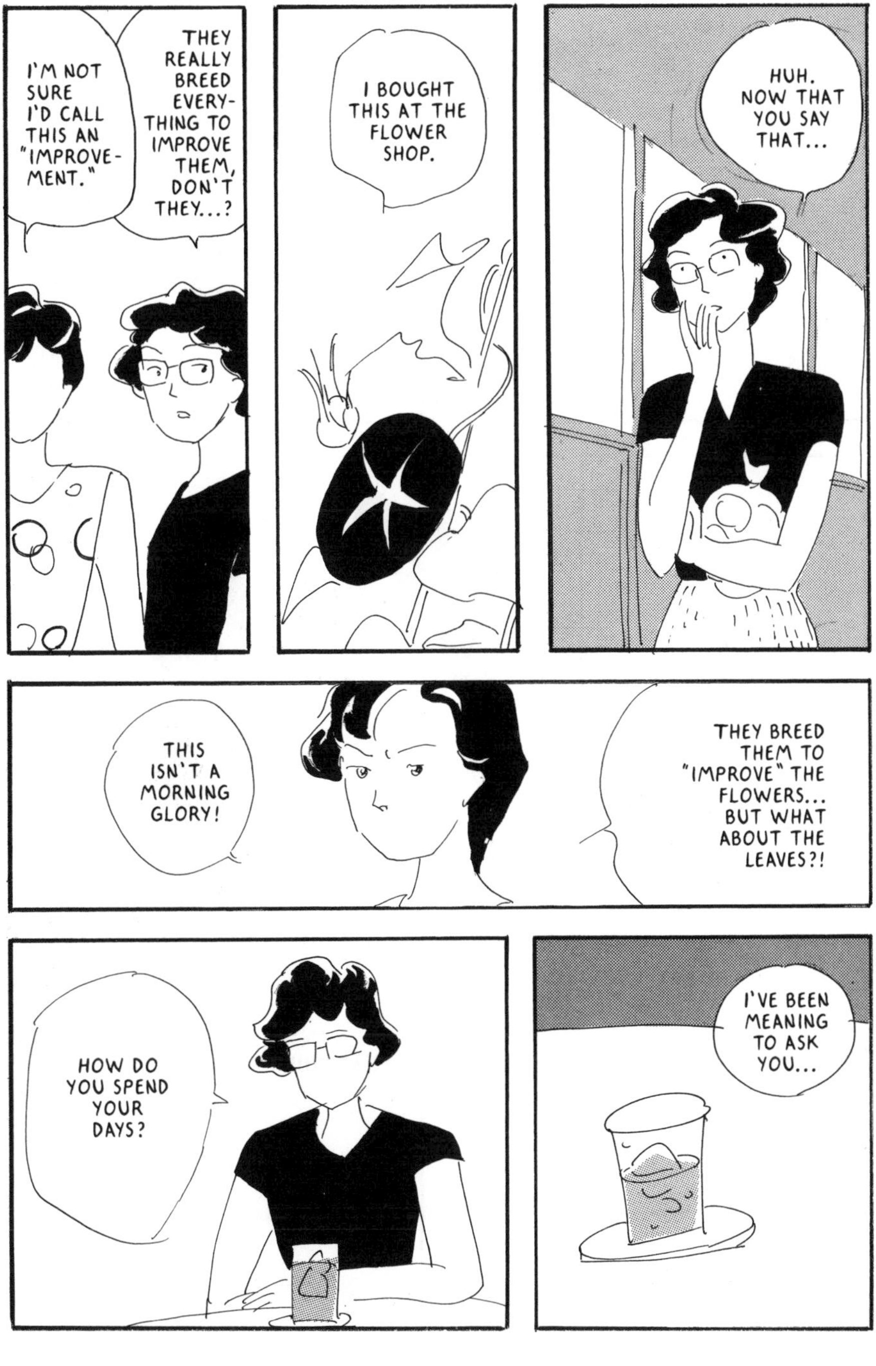
HUH. NOW THAT YOU SAY THAT...
I BOUGHT THIS AT THE FLOWER SHOP.
THEY REALLY BREED EVERYTHING TO IMPROVE THEM, DON'T THEY...?
I'M NOT SURE I'D CALL THIS AN "IMPROVEMENT."
THEY BREED THEM TO "IMPROVE" THE FLOWERS... BUT WHAT ABOUT THE LEAVES?!
THIS ISN'T A MORNING GLORY!
I'VE BEEN MEANING TO ASK YOU...
HOW DO YOU SPEND YOUR DAYS?

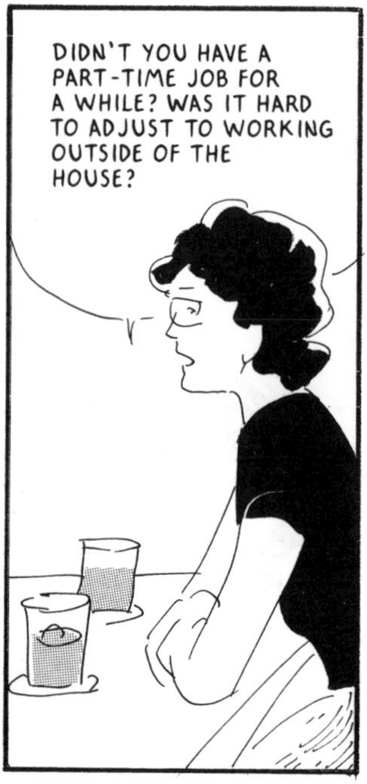
DIDN'T YOU HAVE A PART-TIME JOB FOR A WHILE? WAS IT HARD TO ADJUST TO WORKING OUTSIDE OF THE HOUSE?

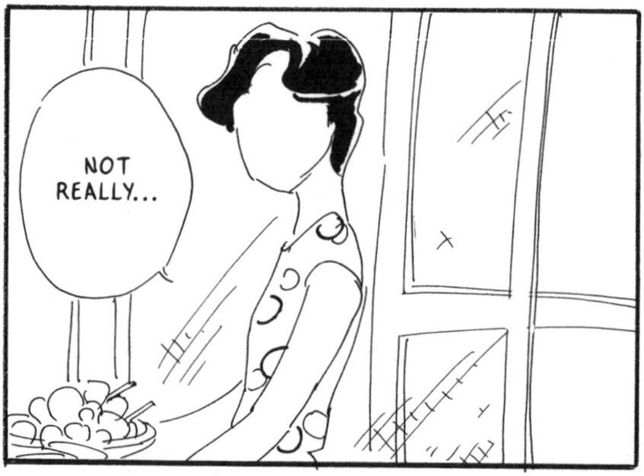
NOT REALLY...

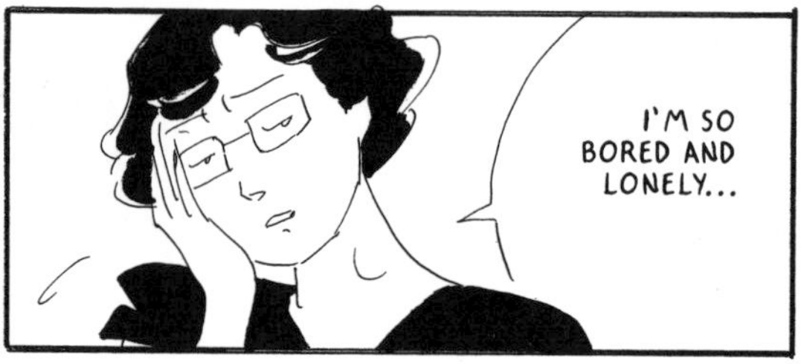
I'M SO BORED AND LONELY...

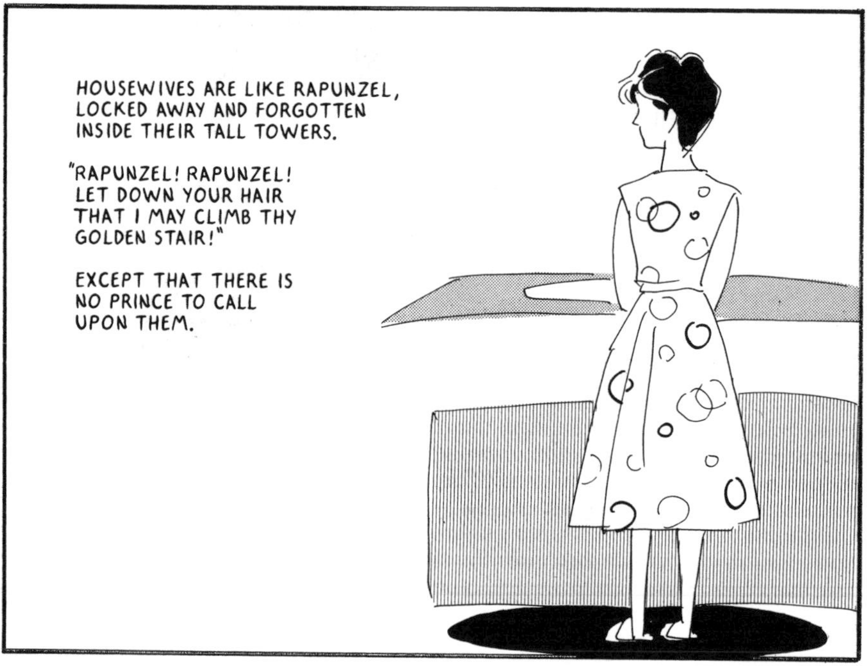
HOUSEWIVES ARE LIKE RAPUNZEL, LOCKED AWAY AND FORGOTTEN INSIDE THEIR TALL TOWERS.
"RAPUNZEL! RAPUNZEL! LET DOWN YOUR HAIR THAT I MAY CLIMB THY GOLDEN STAIR!"
EXCEPT THAT THERE IS NO PRINCE TO CALL UPON THEM.

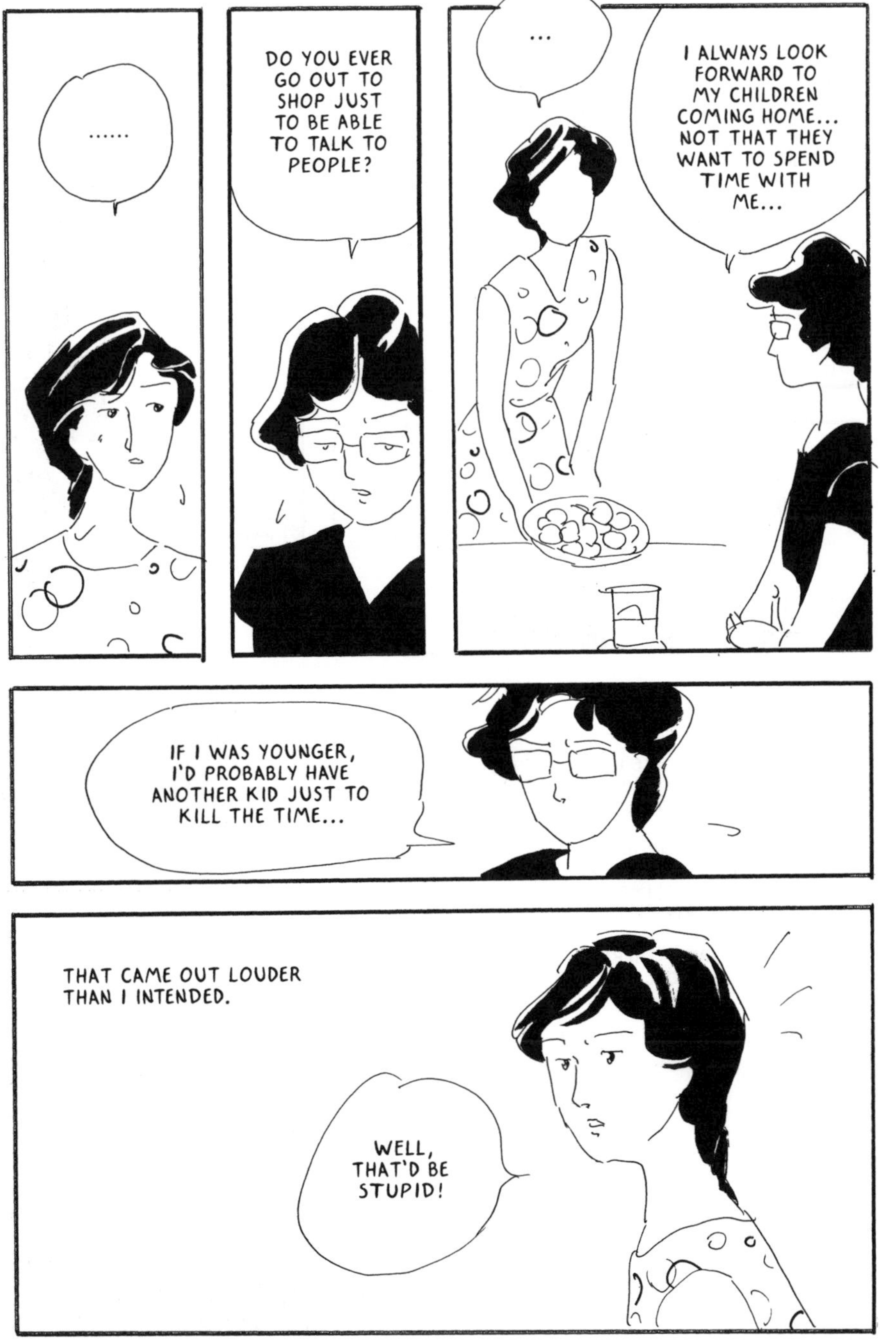
I ALWAYS LOOK FORWARD TO MY CHILDREN COMING HOME... NOT THAT THEY WANT TO SPEND TIME WITH ME...
...
DO YOU EVER GO OUT TO SHOP JUST TO BE ABLE TO TALK TO PEOPLE?
......
IF I WAS YOUNGER, I'D PROBABLY HAVE ANOTHER KID JUST TO KILL THE TIME...
THAT CAME OUT LOUDER THAN I INTENDED.
WELL, THAT'D BE STUPID!

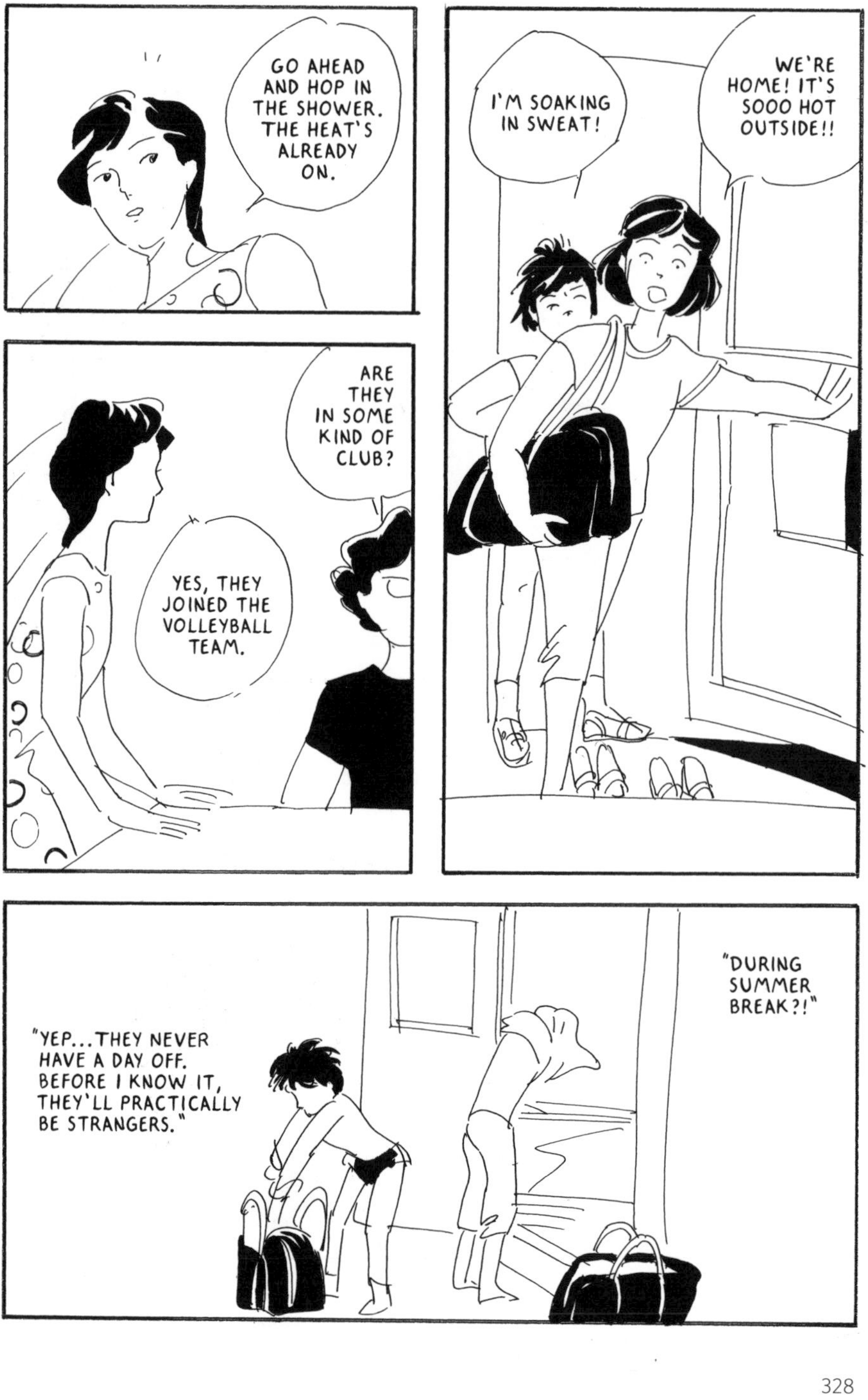
WE'RE HOME! IT'S SOOO HOT OUTSIDE!!
I'M SOAKING IN SWEAT!
GO AHEAD AND HOP IN THE SHOWER. THE HEAT'S ALREADY ON.
ARE THEY IN SOME KIND OF CLUB?
YES, THEY JOINED THE VOLLEYBALL TEAM.
"DURING SUMMER BREAK?!"
"YEP...THEY NEVER HAVE A DAY OFF. BEFORE I KNOW IT, THEY'LL PRACTICALLY BE STRANGERS."

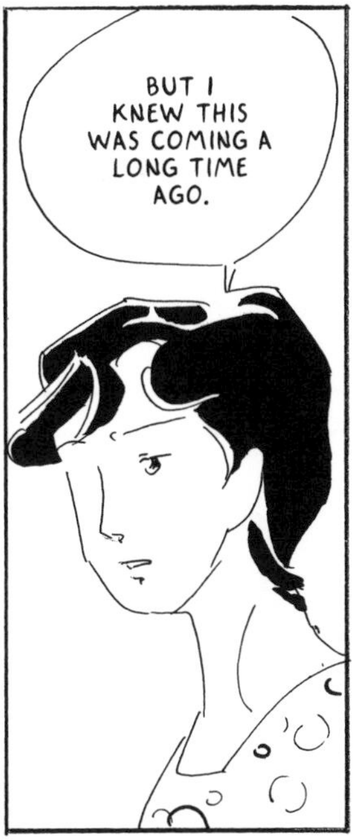
BUT I KNEW THIS WAS COMING A LONG TIME AGO.
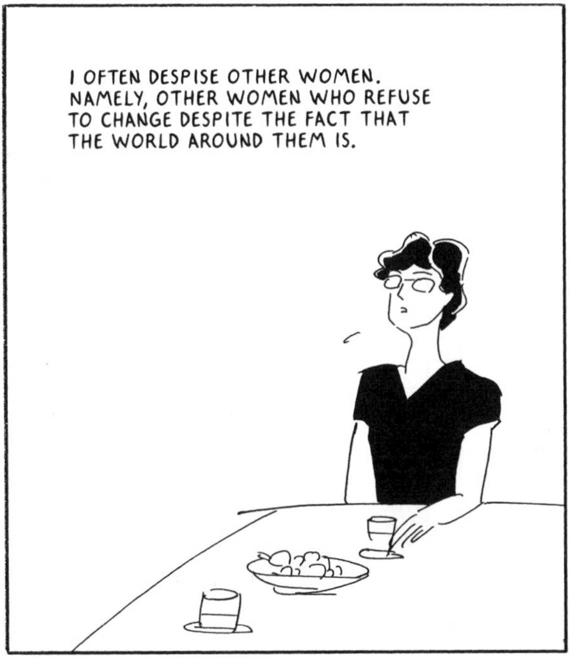
I OFTEN DESPISE OTHER WOMEN. NAMELY, OTHER WOMEN WHO REFUSE TO CHANGE DESPITE THE FACT THAT THE WORLD AROUND THEM IS.
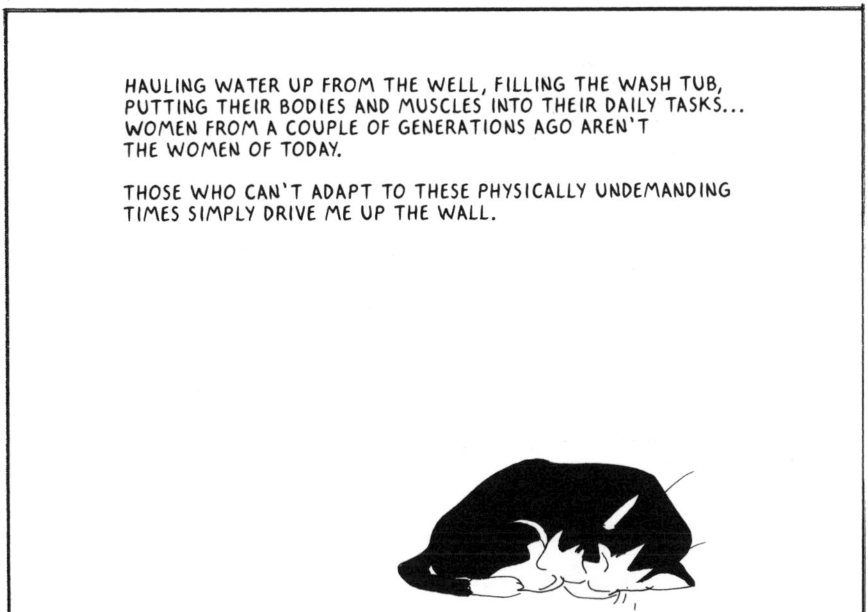
HAULING WATER UP FROM THE WELL, FILLING THE WASH TUB, PUTTING THEIR BODIES AND MUSCLES INTO THEIR DAILY TASKS... WOMEN FROM A COUPLE OF GENERATIONS AGO AREN'T THE WOMEN OF TODAY.
THOSE WHO CAN'T ADAPT TO THESE PHYSICALLY UNDEMANDING TIMES SIMPLY DRIVE ME UP THE WALL.

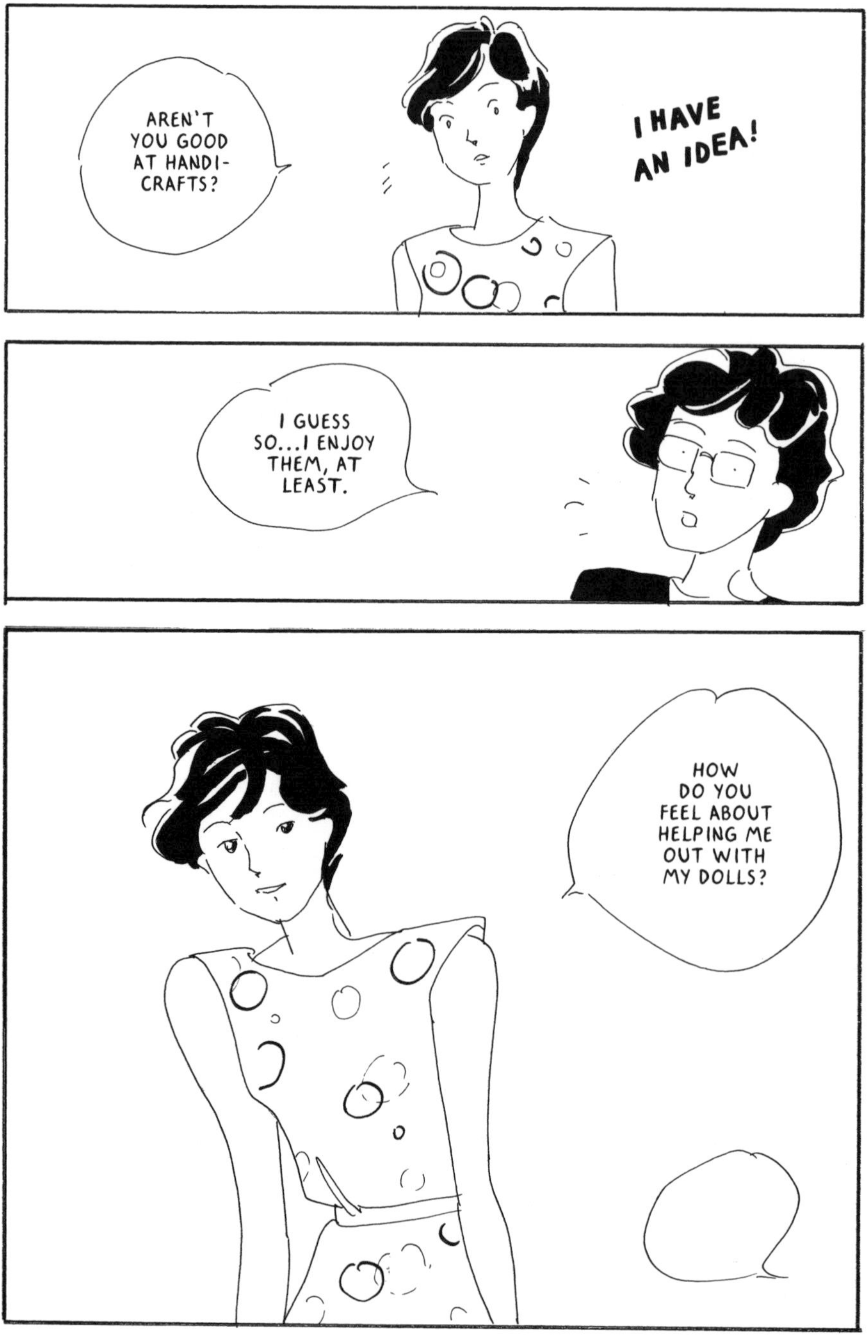
I HAVE AN IDEA!
AREN'T YOU GOOD AT HANDI-CRAFTS?
I GUESS SO...I ENJOY THEM, AT LEAST.
HOW DO YOU FEEL ABOUT HELPING ME OUT WITH MY DOLLS?

Rich Lady

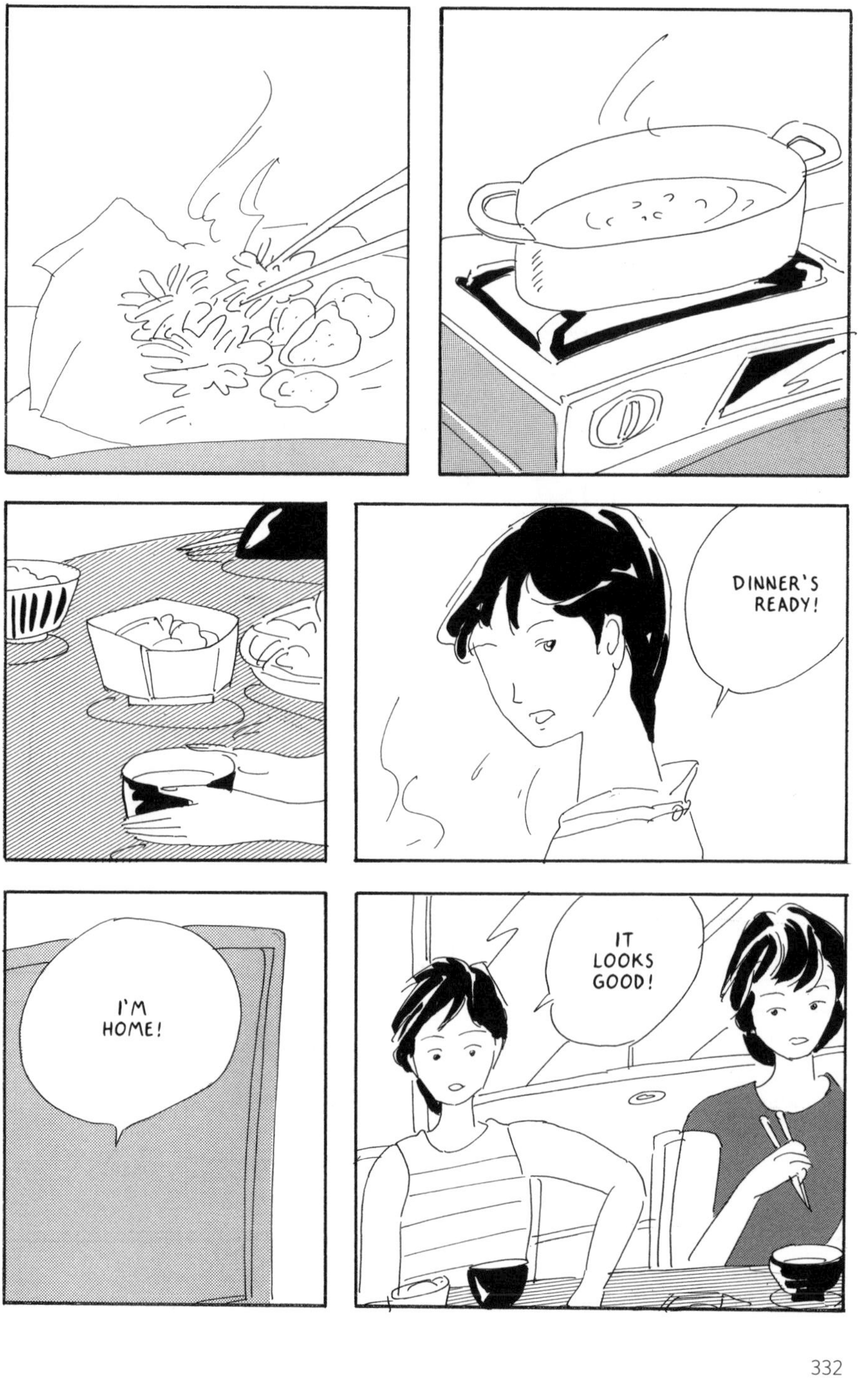
DINNER'S READY!
IT LOOKS GOOD!
I'M HOME!

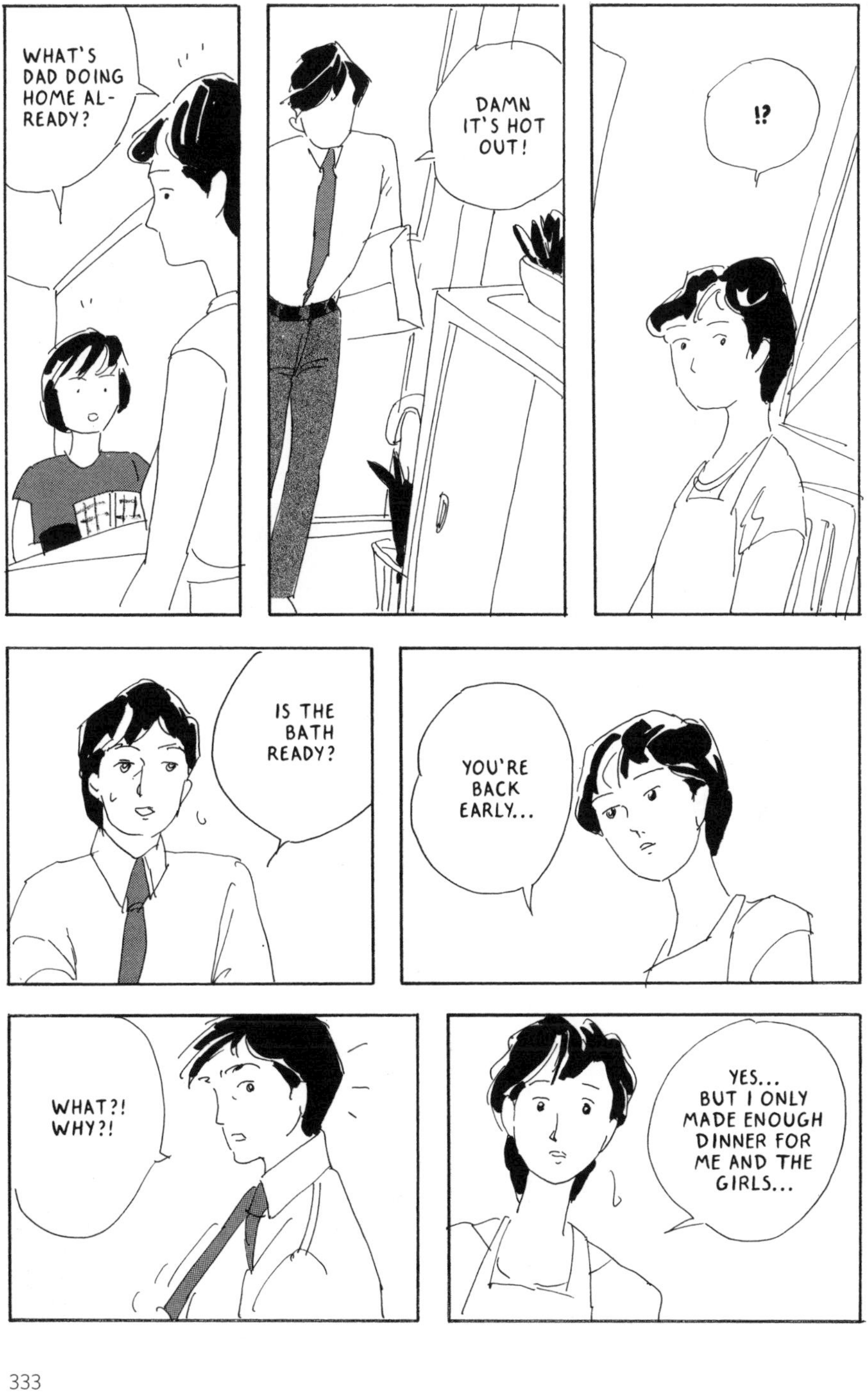
!?
DAMN IT'S HOT OUT!
WHAT'S DAD DOING HOME AL-READY?
YOU'RE BACK EARLY...
IS THE BATH READY?
YES... BUT I ONLY MADE ENOUGH DINNER FOR ME AND THE GIRLS...
WHAT?! WHY?!

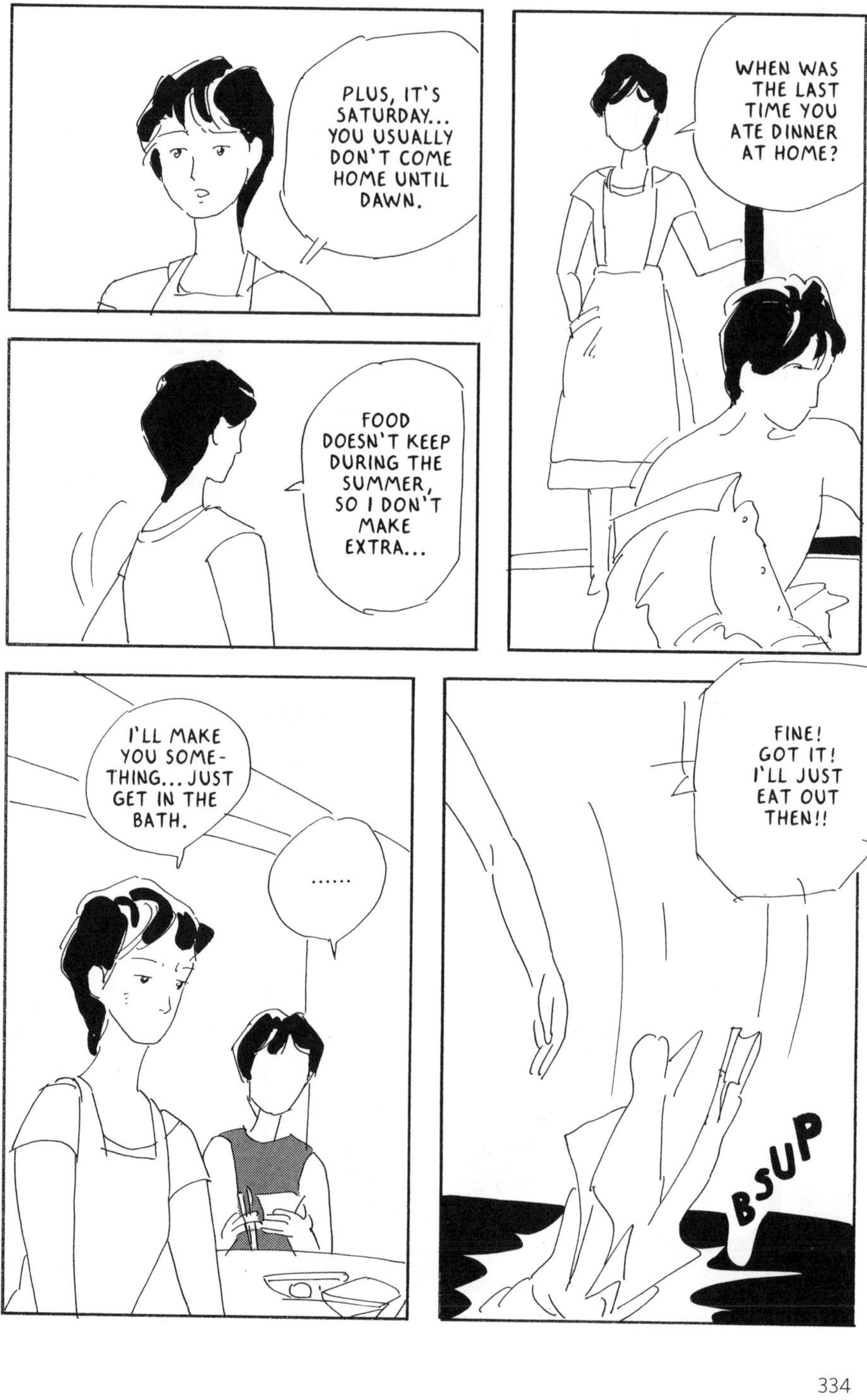
WHEN WAS THE LAST TIME YOU ATE DINNER AT HOME?
PLUS, IT'S SATURDAY... YOU USUALLY DON'T COME HOME UNTIL DAWN.
FOOD DOESN'T KEEP DURING THE SUMMER, SO I DON'T MAKE EXTRA...
FINE! GOT IT! I'LL JUST EAT OUT THEN!!
BSUP
I'LL MAKE YOU SOME-THING... JUST GET IN THE BATH.
......

WHAT HAPPENED? WHY ARE YOU HOME SO EARLY?
—
WHAT'S WRONG WITH ME COMING HOME EARLY?!
STOP TALKING BACK TO ME LIKE THE CHILDREN!
MUNCH MUNCH
I'M A MAN. THAT'S WHAT WE ARE... CHILDREN.
NO, YOU ARE NOT!
!?

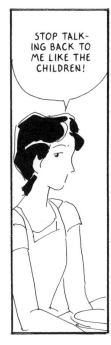

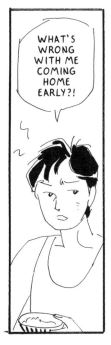

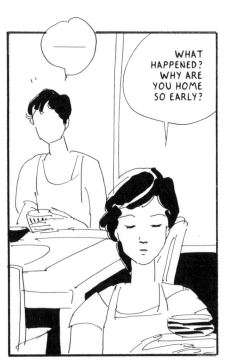

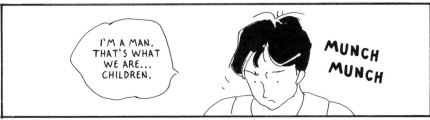

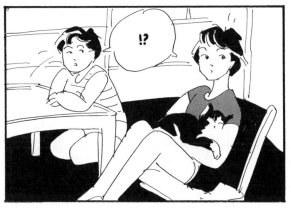

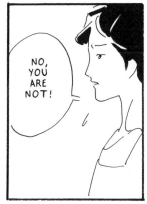

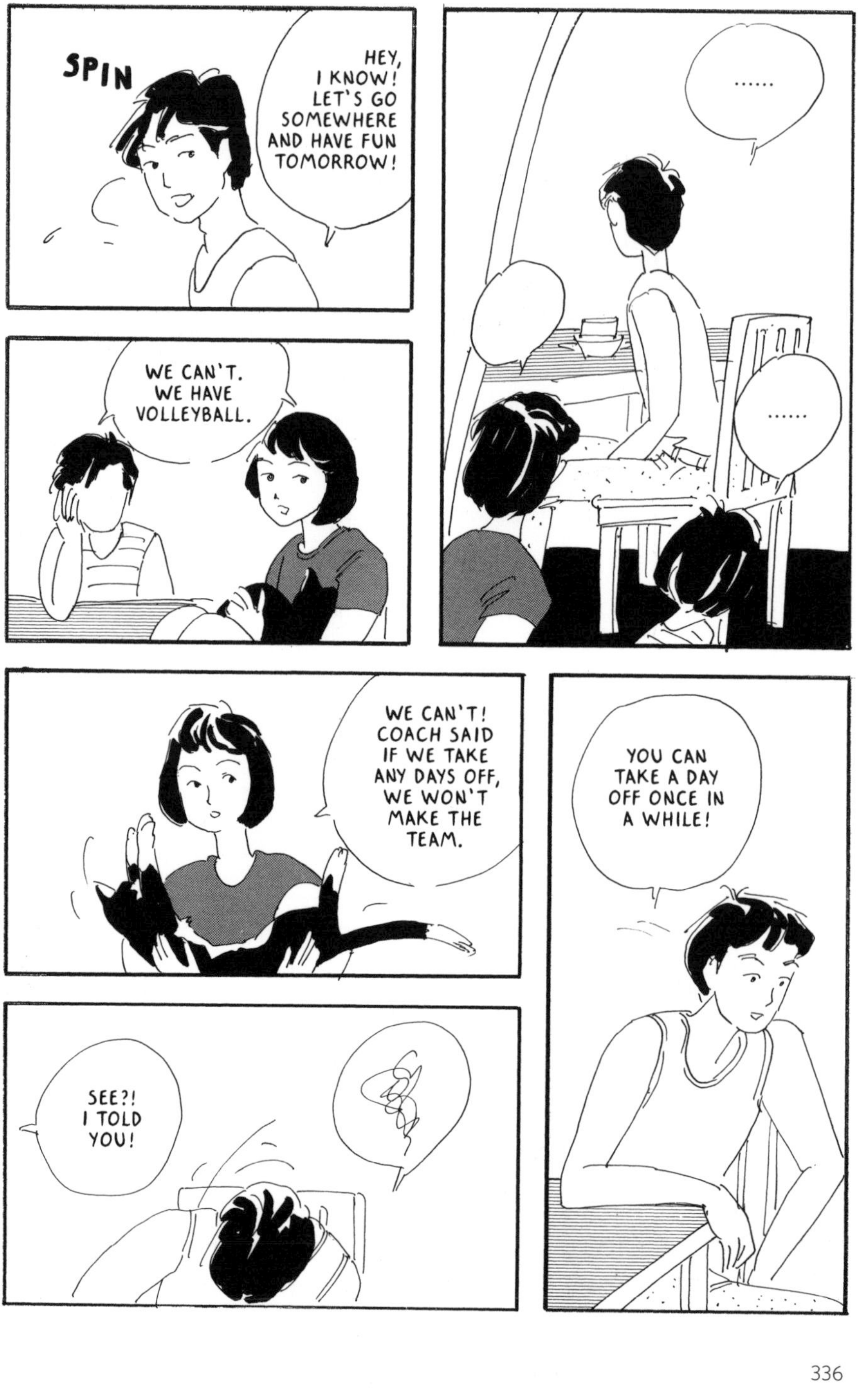
......
......
HEY, I KNOW! LET'S GO SOMEWHERE AND HAVE FUN TOMORROW!
SPIN
WE CAN'T. WE HAVE VOLLEYBALL.
YOU CAN TAKE A DAY OFF ONCE IN A WHILE!
WE CAN'T! COACH SAID IF WE TAKE ANY DAYS OFF, WE WON'T MAKE THE TEAM.
SEE?! I TOLD YOU!

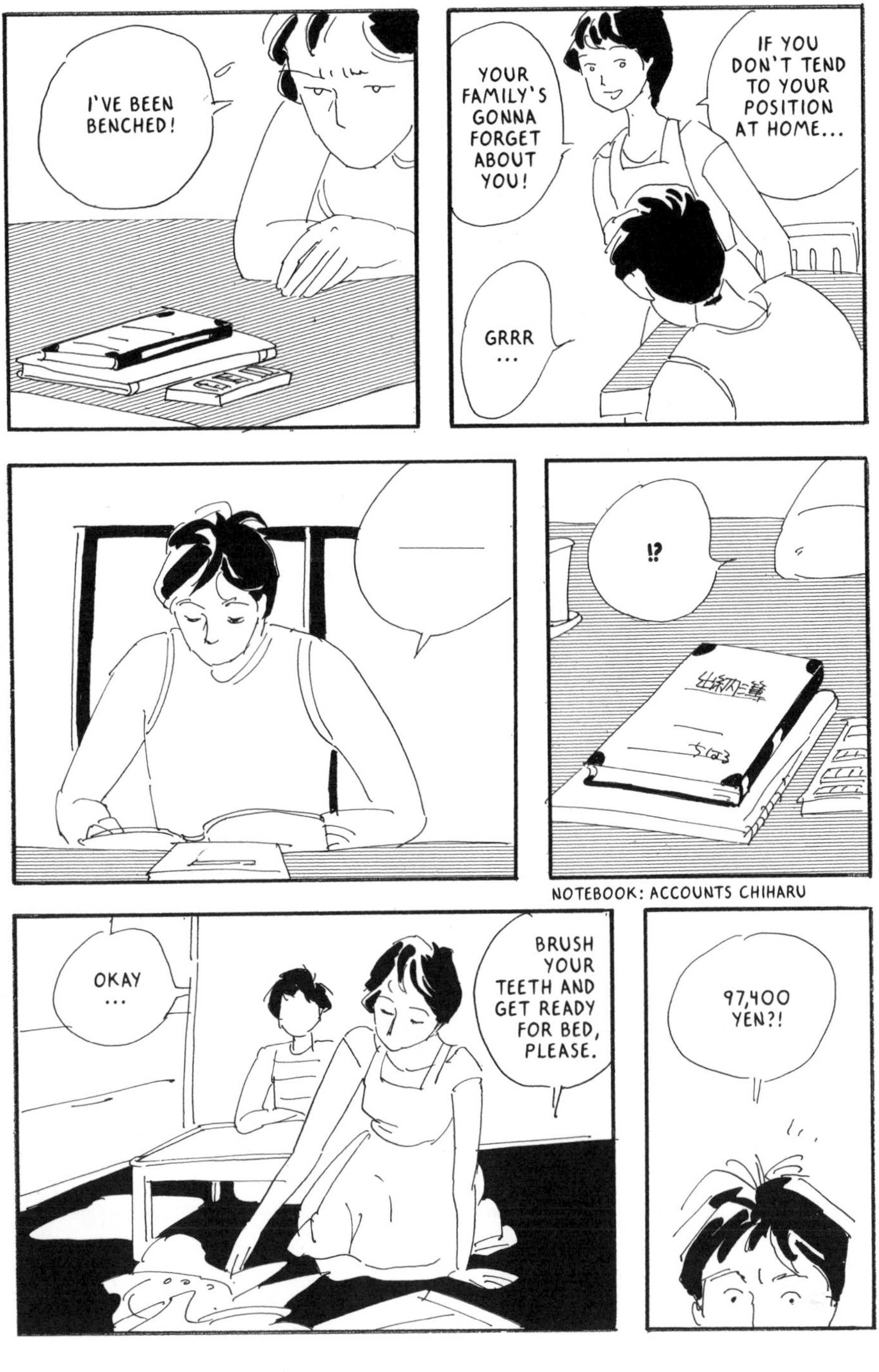
IF YOU DON'T TEND TO YOUR POSITION AT HOME...
YOUR FAMILY'S GONNA FORGET ABOUT YOU!
GRRR ...
I'VE BEEN BENCHED!
!?
NOTEBOOK: ACCOUNTS CHIHARU
97,400 YEN?!
BRUSH YOUR TEETH AND GET READY FOR BED, PLEASE.
OKAY ...

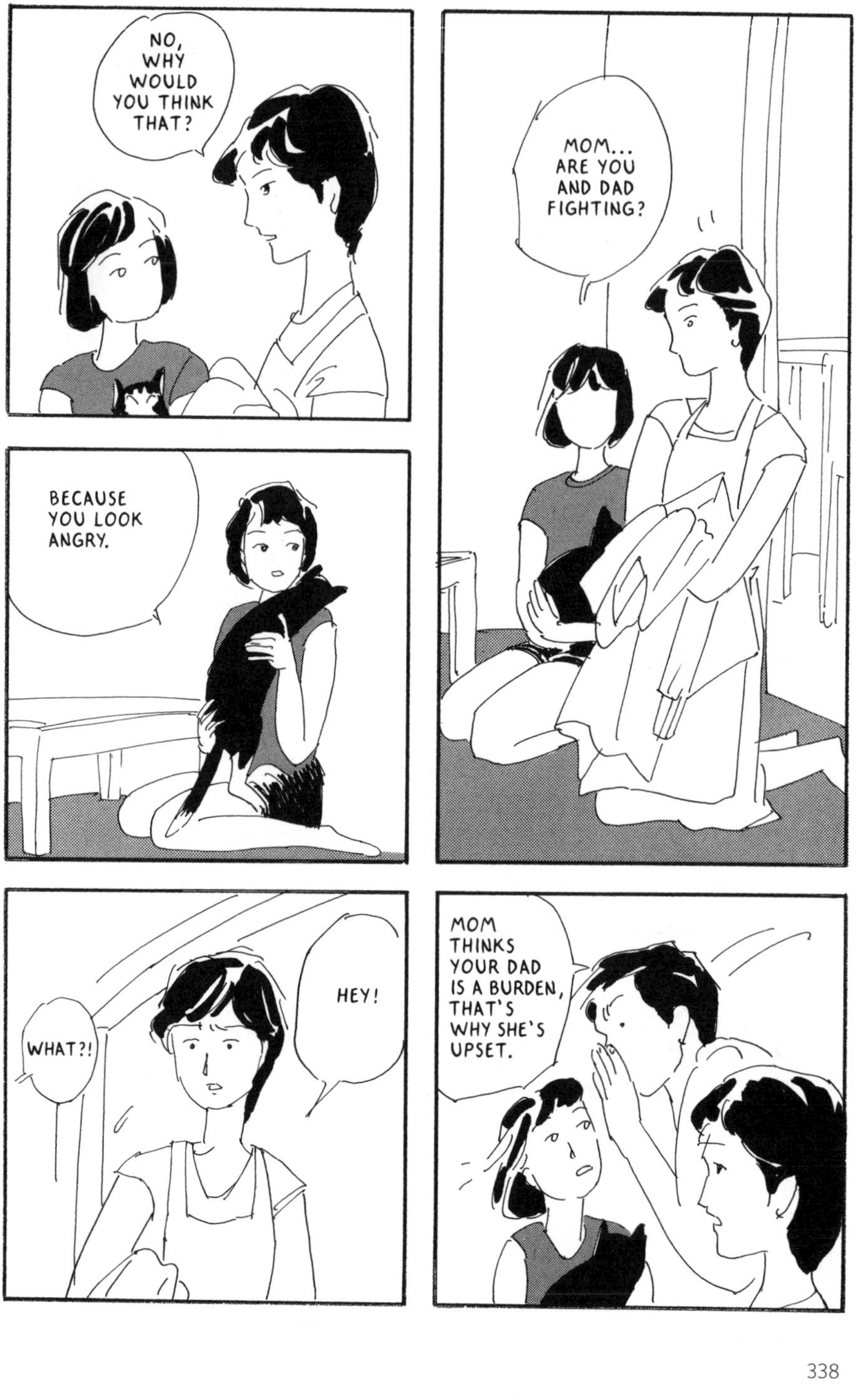
MOM... ARE YOU AND DAD FIGHTING?
NO, WHY WOULD YOU THINK THAT?
BECAUSE YOU LOOK ANGRY.
MOM THINKS YOUR DAD IS A BURDEN, THAT'S WHY SHE'S UPSET.
HEY!
WHAT?!

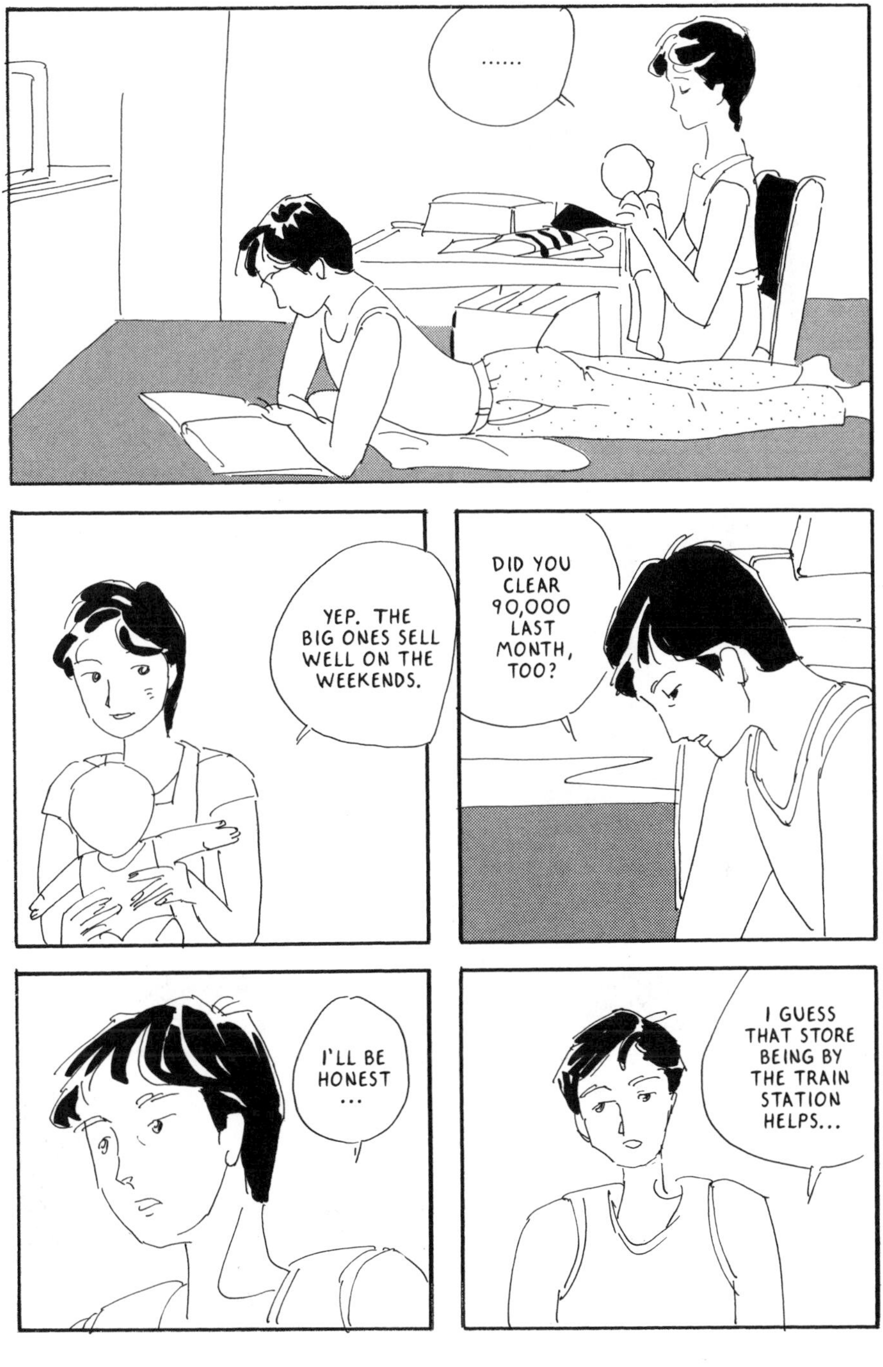
......
DID YOU CLEAR 90,000 LAST MONTH, TOO?
YEP. THE BIG ONES SELL WELL ON THE WEEKENDS.
I GUESS THAT STORE BEING BY THE TRAIN STATION HELPS...
I'LL BE HONEST ...

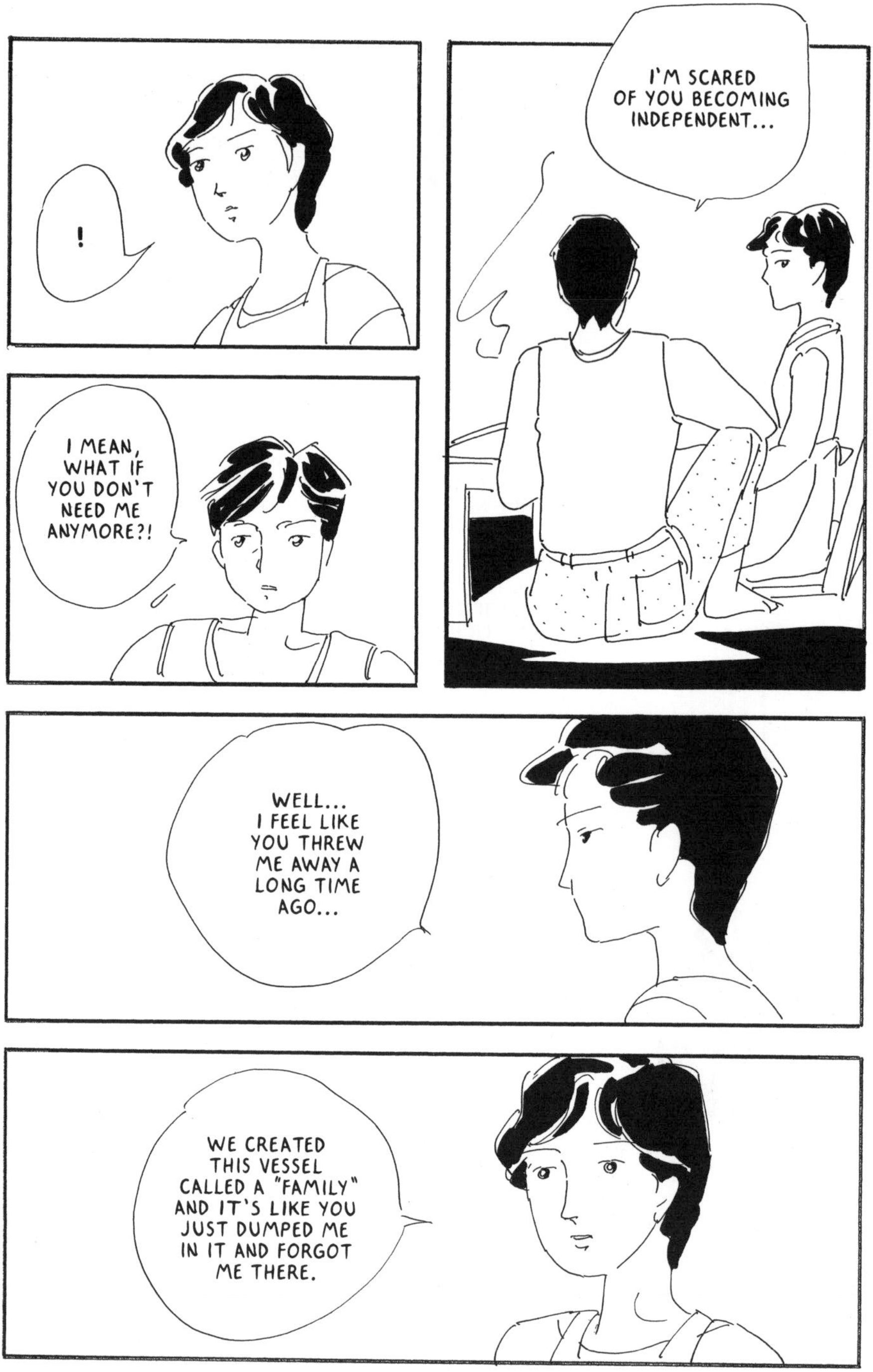
I'M SCARED OF YOU BECOMING INDEPENDENT...
!
I MEAN, WHAT IF YOU DON'T NEED ME ANYMORE?!
WELL... I FEEL LIKE YOU THREW ME AWAY A LONG TIME AGO...
WE CREATED THIS VESSEL CALLED A "FAMILY" AND IT'S LIKE YOU JUST DUMPED ME IN IT AND FORGOT ME THERE.

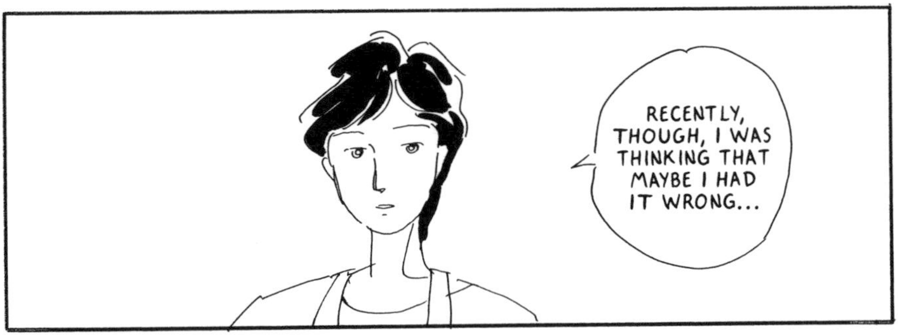
RECENTLY, THOUGH, I WAS THINKING THAT MAYBE I HAD IT WRONG...

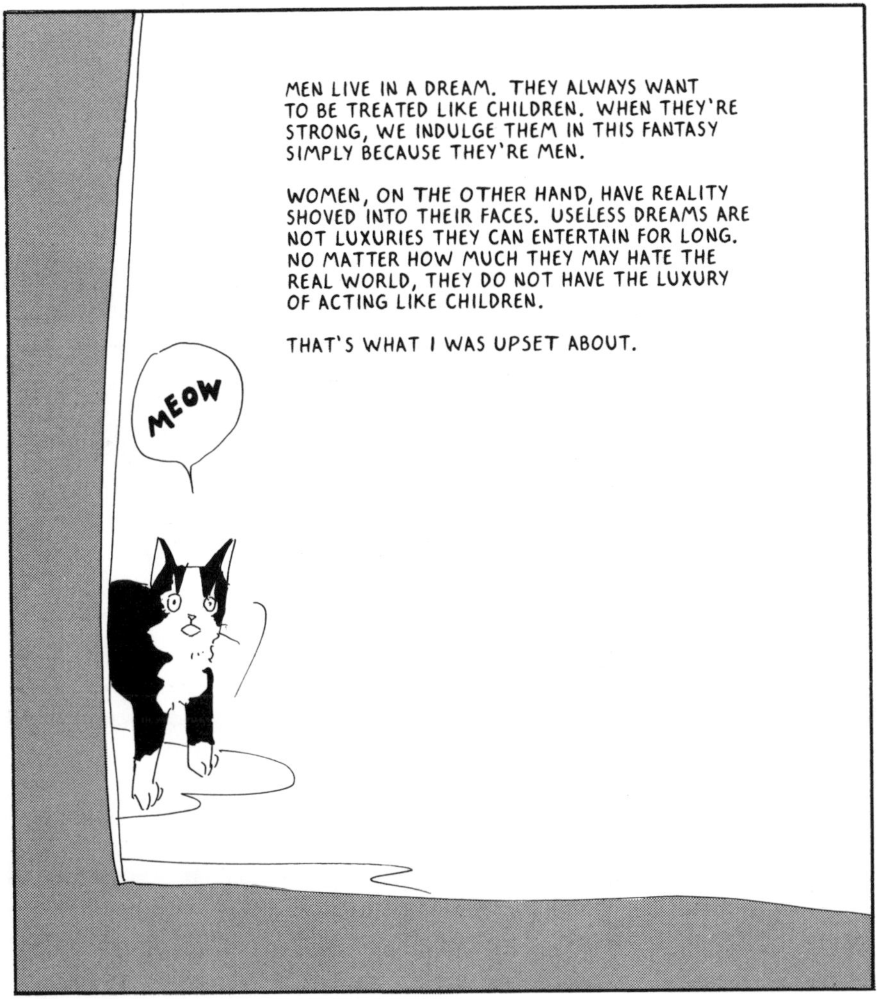
MEN LIVE IN A DREAM. THEY ALWAYS WANT TO BE TREATED LIKE CHILDREN. WHEN THEY'RE STRONG, WE INDULGE THEM IN THIS FANTASY SIMPLY BECAUSE THEY'RE MEN.
WOMEN, ON THE OTHER HAND, HAVE REALITY SHOVED INTO THEIR FACES. USELESS DREAMS ARE NOT LUXURIES THEY CAN ENTERTAIN FOR LONG. NO MATTER HOW MUCH THEY MAY HATE THE REAL WORLD, THEY DO NOT HAVE THE LUXURY OF ACTING LIKE CHILDREN.
THAT'S WHAT I WAS UPSET ABOUT.
MEOW

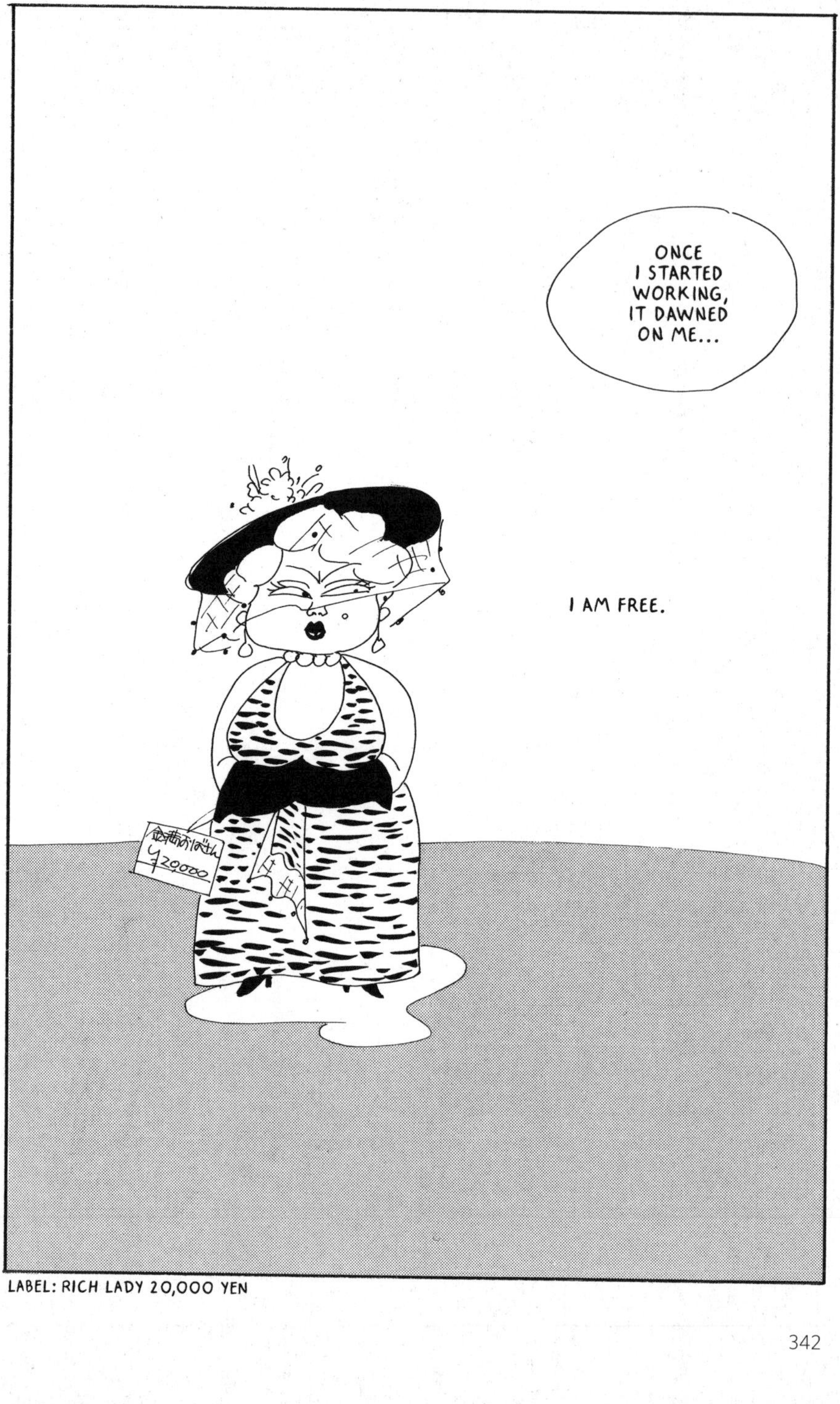
ONCE I STARTED WORKING, IT DAWNED ON ME...
I AM FREE.
金満おばさん
¥20,000

LABEL: RICH LADY 20,000 YEN

45 Yamada Murasaki, "'Myōri' o sagashite," *Garo mandara*, p. 275.

46 There is often confusion about Yamada's first two "comeback" works in *Garo*. "Sometimes in the Sunlight" was originally meant to be a series title, and is shared by both of the stories mentioned here, with the second subtitled "Sassy Cats." The first story has subsequently been reprinted independently under the title "My Back to Yours" ("Senaka awase"), while the first story in the *Sassy Cats* series, the redrawn cat piece, usually goes by "Sometimes in the Sunlight."

47 Email communication with Tetsuka Noriko, December 2021.

48 "Sumikko ga suki nan desu," p. 97.

49 Shiratori, p. 83.

50 Miyazaki Hayao and Yamane Sadao, in *Eiga Tenkū no Shiro Rapyuta Guide Book* (Tokyo: Tokuma shoten, 1986), p. 287.

51 While the literature on *shufu* is vast, even in English, pithy and suggestive synopses are provided in Ueno Chizuko, "Genesis of the Japanese Housewife," *Japan Quarterly* 34:2 (1987), pp. 130-42; and Ofra Goldstein-Gidoni, *Housewives of Japan: An Ethnography of Real Lives and Consumerized Domesticity* (New York: Palgrave Macmillan, 2012), pp. 37-52. For an ethnography of *shufu* conducted elsewhere in the suburbs of Tokyo and overlapping with the period in question, see Anne E. Imamura, *Urban Japanese Housewives: At Home and in the Community* (Honolulu: University of Hawai'i Press, 1987).

52 On the Equal Employment Opportunity Act (EEOA) and related labor trends, see Vera Mackie, *Feminism in Modern Japan: Citizenship, Embodiment, and Sexuality* (Cambridge University Press, 2003), pp. 179-90; and Nakamatsu Tomoko, "'Part-Timers' in the Public Sphere: Married Women, Part-Time Work, and Activism," in *Feminism and the State in Modern Japan*, ed. Vera Mackie (Papers of the Japanese Studies Centre, Melbourne, 1995), pp. 75-87. For the relationship between the EEOA and the rise of women's comics, see Ogi, "Female Subjectivity and *Shoujo* (Girls) *Manga* (Japanese Comics)."

53 Saitō, "Sei e no nigai kakusei to ai o egaku," p. 348.

54 *Tōkyō nosutarujia*, pp. 26-31.

55 "Sumikko ga suki nan desu," p. 97.

56 *Tōkyō nosutarujia*, pp. 65-73. Yamada's typical daily schedule in the mid '80s is detailed in the manga "Yamakawa sensei no 24 jikan," *Comic Again* (c. 1984–85), rpt. in *Yamada Murasaki sakuhinshū* vol. 3 (Tokyo: Chikuma shobō, 1992), pp. 155-70.

57 *Mantenboshi mita*, pp. 137-38.

58 *Tōkyō nosutarujia*, pp. 199-201.

59 This video can be found at https://www.nicovideo.jp/watch/sm5803776. Yamada appears from 1:42 to 2:00.

60 *Tōkyō nosutarujia*, p. 215. She also commented on her campaign in *Dōzo okatte ni* (Tokyo: Chūō kōron, 1999), pp. 205-7.

61 "Atogaki," *Otogi zōshi* (Tokyo: Chūō kōron sha, 1997), pp. 250-51.

62 An informative and personal account of the artist's later life is also provided by her daughter, Yamada Yū, in "Neko mo hito mo fuetari hettari," in Yamada Murasaki, *Neko no fushigi banashi* (Tokyo: Kōyōkan, 2021), pp. 166-74.

63 Shiratori, pp. 86-88.

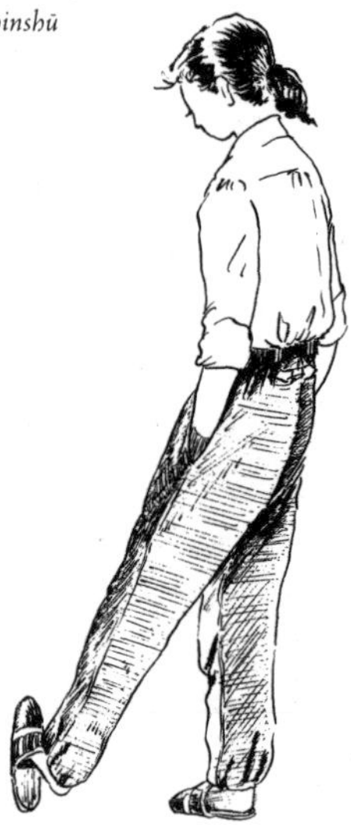

24   In her diary, Yamada complains that lack of critical feedback from the editors of COM was one of the reasons she finally decided to submit work to Garo, despite COM's pleads not to feed the competition. Out of loyalty, she waited more than a year to finally approach Garo, keeping it a secret from Akiyama Mitsuru, her editor at COM. This according to diary entries dated January 19 and May 15, 1970. Thank you to Yamada Yū for sharing portions of her mother's diary with me.

25   *Tōkyō nosutarujia*, p. 115.

26   "'70 nen ni tobidashita shinjin tachi," p. 167.

27   Yamada, "Aieru," *Comic Again* (November 1984), rpt. in *Sora ni ochiru* (Tokyo: Kawade shobō shinsho, 1985), pp. 108-13.

28   Diary, entry dated May 21, 1970.

29   Yamada Murasaki, "Shinnai hanmon: shōjo manga no genjō," *Manga komyunikeeshon* no. 1 (May 1971), p. 3.

30   On *Apple Core*, see Nakajima Takashi, "COM to *Appuru koa*: Gura kon kansai shibu tenmatsuki," *Biranzi* no. 27 (March 2011), pp. 112-36; and Nakajima, "40-nen me no gura kon shibu dayori: COM kara tobitachi," in *COM: 40-nen me no shūkangō*, pp. 152-53. The latter includes a period photo with Yamada. Among the zine's other notable contributors are Hino Hideshi, who drew a single-panel cartoon for volume one, and Takeuchi Osamu, one of Japan's leading manga scholars, who contributed manga and drew two of the covers. In 2015, Nakajima self-published a 92-page booklet titled *Sora tobu manga: Appuru koa* (Appuru koa of fukkan suru kai) that included an assortment of manga from *Apple Core*'s five issues and various reminisces from contributors. Thank you to Nakajima Takashi and Takeuchi Osamu for help sourcing information and images about this era.

31   On COM's central role in manga fanzine networks and the relationship between shōjo manga fandom and the formation of Comic Market, see Shimotsuki Takanaka, *Komikku maaketto sōseiki* (Tokyo: Asahi shinbun shuppan, 2008). Though the authors touch on COM's role only briefly, in English see Patrick W. Galbraith, *Otaku and the Struggle for Imagination in Japan* (Durham & London: Duke University Press, 2019), pp. 25-28; and Nagayama Kaoru, *Erotic Comics in Japan: An Introduction to Eromanga*, trans. Patrick W. Galbraith and Jessica Bauwens-Sugimoto (Amsterdam University Press, 2021), pp. 55-56.

32   Yamada Murasaki and Yoshihara Sachiko interview, "Neko yori mo hito o egakitai," *La Mer* (January 1990), rpt. in "*Ki no ue de neko ga miteiru* shohyōshū," p. 9, a pamphlet supplement to *Ki no ue de neko ga miteiru* (Tokyo: Shichōsha, 2010).

33   "Sumikko ga suki nan desu," p. 94.

34   "Sumikko ga suki nan desu," p. 94.

35   *Tōkyō nosutarujia*, p. 34.

36   Yamada Murasaki, *Mantenboshi mita* (Tokyo: Yamato shobō, 1985), p. 47.

37   Shiratori Chikao, '*Garo*' ni jinsei o sasageta otoko: zenshin henshūsha no kokuhaku (Tokyo: Kōyōkan, 2021), pp. 243-44.

38   Shiratori, pp. 244-45.

39   Shiratori, p. 247.

40   "Sumikko ga suki nan desu," pp. 95-96.

41   "Sumikko ga suki nan desu," pp. 92, 96.

42   *Mantenboshi mita*, p. 103.

43   "Aieru," p. 112.

44   Shiratori, pp. 245-46.

4   In 2001, a rebooted *Garo* ran a feature on women cartoonists, including an overview of landmarks in its support of them going back to Tsurita in the '60s: "*Garo* to josei sakka no kankei," *Garo* (August 2001), pp. 36-38.

5   Arikawa Yū, "Yamada Muraski: shufu no iru fūkei," *Eureka* (July 1981), p. 65.

6   Frederik L. Schodt, *Dreamland Japan: Writings on Modern Manga* (San Francisco: Stone Bridge Press, 1996), p. 155.

7   *Secret Comics Japan: Underground Comics Now* (VIZ Media, 2000), pp. 58, 98.

8   Yamada Murasaki and Yamanaka Jun interview, "'Katei' no iu no wa ima demo ichiban no nazo desu," *Garo* no. 337 (February/March 1993), p. 24. Unless otherwise noted, biographical details about Yamada's youth come from this interview, pp. 24-32, the chronology on page 44 of the same issue, or interviews and emails with the artist's daughter, Yamada Yū, between October and December 2021. Also essential, for both biographical and bibliographic information, was Shiratori Chikao's labyrinthine blog, http://shiratorichikao.blog.fc2.com.

9   Yamada Murasaki, *Tōkyō nosutarujia* (Tokyo: Fureeberu kan, 1991), pp. 138-40.

10   *Tōkyō nosutarujia*, pp. 181-83.

11   *Tōkyō nosutarujia*, p. 16. The only known period document related to the Weeping Love Strings is a pamphlet listing their scheduled performance at the Mitaka Popular Music Festival (January 30, 1966).

12   The first of two works by Hagio to appear in *COM* was "Poochi de shōjo ga koinu to" (January 1971), which she submitted to *COM* in the late '60s while still a high school student and prior to her debut in Kōndasha's *Nakayoshi* in 1969. *COM* decided to finally publish the story when they were faced with a page shortfall due to a chapter of Tezuka's *Phoenix* being under length.

13   According to Ishii Fumio in a roundtable conversation between former *COM* editors, "'*COM* no jidai' o kataru jidai," *Pafu* (May 1979), p. 52. On *COM*, see also Shimotsuki Takanaka, ed., *COM: 40-nen me no shūkangō* (Tokyo: Asahi shinbun shuppan, 2011).

14   See Ryan Holmberg and Mitsuhiro Asakawa, "The Life and Art of Kuniko Tsurita," in Kuniko Tsurita, *The Sky Is Blue with a Single Cloud* (Drawn & Quarterly, 2020), pp. v-xli.

15   On Okada's rejection by *Garo*, see *Okada Fumiko sakuhinshū: Odessey 1966–2005*, vol. 2 (Tokyo: Fukkan dotto komu, 2018), p. 270. The notes in this two-volume anthology offer many leads regarding Okada's influence on major shōjo manga artists. On Hagio being inspired by Okada's work, see Hagio Moto, "Okada saijin no koto," in Okada Fumiko, *Garasu dama* (Tokyo: Asahi sonorama, 1976), pp. 226-29. Yamada specified Okada's two-part "Red Vines" ("Akai tsurukusa," *COM*, November–December 1968), about a young French painter who loses his mind after his father dies, as not only the reason she submitted work to the magazine, but also why she started drawing comics seriously. See Saitō Shinji, "Sei e no nigai kakusei to ai o egaku," *Asashi gurafu* (April 23, 1982), revised rpt. in *Shinkirari* (Tokyo: Shōgakukan Creative, 2009), p. 346.

16   "'Katei' to iu no wa ima demo ichiban no nazo desu," p. 28.

17   "Senpyō," *COM* (May 1969), p. 240.

18   "Senpyō," *COM* (July 1969), p. 240.

19   Yamada, "Sumikko ga suki nan desu. Ushiro no hō kara damette mitete, sore ga futto katachi ni nattari," *Kōkoku hihyō* (March 1985), p. 90.

20   "'70 nen ni tobidashita shinjin tachi," *COM* (May/June 1970), p. 154.

21   Yamada Murasaki, "Shisha no tamashi ni mayou koto naki yō ni," *Pafu* (May 1979), pp. 42-43.

22   "Sumikko ga suki nan desu," p. 91.

23   Yamada Murasaki, "Shitsumon ga arimasu" [1970], rpt. in *Hōsenka* (Tokyo: Buronzu-sha, 1980), pp. 175, 178.

expanded opportunities and freedoms gained by Japanese women in the '80s constituted reluctant reforms at best. The "salaryman" family model—with its breadwinning husband, caretaker wife and mother, and ideally two children—has definitely taken a beating since the '80s, with increasingly more Japanese women delaying or refusing to get married or have children, and prioritizing their own freedom and careers over those of the men who are officially tasked with running the economy. What ones finds in *Talk To My Back* is not the dismissal or collapse of this traditional system, but rather an exploration of how to turn its fissures and broken ideals into a springboard for something positive for all members of the middle class nuclear family, and particularly the "female head of household." Despite dramatic differences in style, tone, and focus between them, Yamada and her younger peers in "ladies' comics" would probably agree that, in lieu of dramatic institutional changes that even today do not seem to be forthcoming, the main avenue to woman's liberation is money. Or, as the last chapter of *Talk To My Back* puts it, being "a rich old lady."

A note in closing. As mentioned at the beginning of this essay, quick summaries often name Yamada as one of the "three daughters of *Garo*." However, there are good reasons to retire this appellation. Not only is it inherently sexist in its suggestion that all women are attached to and dependent upon family, belonging to their fathers as children until they marry and belong instead to their husbands as wives. (Male artists are also often grouped into threes, but they are rarely called "sons.") In Yamada's particular case, the name is also highly misleading, considering she was a thirty-something mother at the time, her resistance to the codes of girlish femininity in shōjo manga, and the fact that her work for *Garo* rarely dealt with youth culture or the frustrations of being treated like a "daughter" into young adulthood. Her life as a woman, as much as her work as a cartoonist, stands as an inspiring if at times heartbreaking testimony of resilience against Japanese patriarchy, particularly as it reigned over the home, but also in other departments of life and business, including the manga industry.

ENDNOTES

1   Numbers based on a rough count from the index in *Garo mandara*, ed. Garo shi hensan iinkai (Tokyo: TBS buritanika, 1991). All translations in this essay are by Ryan Holmberg, unless otherwise noted. In addition to the individuals named below, thanks also to Tracy Hurren, Megan Tan, Shirley Wong, Lucia Gargiulo, Fujimoto Yukari, Kajiya Kenji, and James Welker for their help with this essay.

2   Fusami Ogi, "Female Subjectivity and *Shoujo* (Girls) *Manga* (Japanese Comics): *Shoujo* in Ladies' Comics and Young Ladies' Comics," *Journal of Popular Culture* (Spring 2003), p. 780. See also Kinko Ito, *A Sociology of Japanese Ladies' Comics: Images of the Life, Loves, and Sexual Fantasies of Adult Japanese Women* (The Edwin Mellen Press, 2010). In Japanese, see Fujimoto Yukari, *Watashi no ibasho wa doko ni aru no ka? shōjo manga ga utsusu kokoro no katachi* (Tokyo: Gakuyō shobō, 1998); and Sugimoto Shōgo, *Okazaki Kyōko ron: shōjo manga, toshi, media* (Tokyo: Shinyōsha, 2012), pp. 11-66.

3   For an overview of the ways in which the meaning of "shōjo" was shifting in this era in manga, see Jennifer S. Prough, *Straight From the Heart: Gender, Intimacy, and the Cultural Production of Shōjo Manga* (Honolulu: University of Hawai'i Press, 2011), especially pp. 1-56. For a canonical view of the history and aesthetics of shōjo culture until the '70s, see Deborah Shamoon, *Passionate Friendship: The Aesthetics of Girls' Culture in Japan* (Honolulu: University of Hawai'i Press, 2012).

The two first met in the summer of 1984, when Yamada guest-lectured for a course Seirindō president Nagai Katsuichi was teaching at the International Animation Institute in Hiroo, where Shiratori was a student. Shiratori joined Seirindō that winter, initially as a part-timer. Because they lived on the same train line (Mita), Shiratori (who resided in Sugamo) was tasked with fetching artwork from Yamada (in Nishidai). They became friendly as the last two standing during the *Garo* crew's frequent boozing all-nighters, often heading home together on the same train. Within a year of things turning romantic, circa 1985–86, Shiratori moved in with Yamada and her two daughters. They officially got married in 2002. In 2006, she joined the Faculty of Manga at Kyoto Seika University, moving to Kyoto with Shiratori in 2007.

This new appointment didn't last long, however. In April 2009, Yamada suffered a stroke, and passed away on May 5th, at the age of sixty. On his own deathbed in 2017 (leukemia), Shiratori began writing about his time as an editor of *Garo*, from the '80s through the magazine's tumultuous last days in the mid '90s, published posthumously as a book first in 2019, then in an expanded edition in 2021. It goes into heartbreaking detail about Yamada's failing health and recurrent hospitalization going back to 2002, when she had her right kidney removed after a benign tumor was discovered (renal angiomyolipoma), then her ongoing struggle with pancreatitis and diabetes. Based on highly personal blog posts and addressed to his late partner, the relevant passages are hard to read. At the same time, they attest to how Yamada finally found true love and happiness later in her life.[62]

. . .

From a certain perspective, Yamada's work appears distinctly conservative. As mentioned at the beginning of this essay, when one reads about the rise of "women's manga" in the '80s and '90s, usually highlighted are artists and works that foreground ribald expressions of female sexuality, an anarchic embrace of consumer capitalism, baroque displays of fashion, and sassy dismissals of men who seek to use them or hinder their freedoms, oftentimes expressed through parodies of shōjo aesthetics. By the early '90s, "ladies' comics" had become almost synonymous with pornography for women, oftentimes figured as "call girls" or unmarried OL ("office ladies," secretaries and clerical workers) navigating workplace frustrations, experiences of sexual harassment, and romantic and career hopes. In other words, the avant-garde of women's manga is traditionally represented by artists who were not only themselves young, but focused on the experiences and aspirations of young women in their late teens to twenties, unmarried, childless, with beaucoup expendable income and limited familial obligations. Sympathetic to this groundswell, not only did *Garo* actively include more women in its pages, Seirindō also proactively published books by rising women artists active in other magazines. Three of Uchida Shungiku's first four books (1985–86) and two of Sakurazawa Erica's first four (1987) were thus published by Seirindō. Though ultimately nothing came of it, Okazaki Kyōko was apparently a huge *Garo* fan and was overjoyed when Seirindō approached her to see if she had extra material for a book.[63]

Yet, as the avant-garde hardly represents the totality of important and socially engaged cultural production, so youth culture only speaks to and for a specific demographic. While the dating and shopping and partying goes on, there are still people who have to run companies and tend households, who are responsible for keeping the electricity on, putting food on the table, and making sure children get to school on time and do their homework. Even revolutions rarely sweep away the old, and the

Yamada had been exploring since the late '60s, now within a historical and fantastical frame. There is even one about cats and mice. Struggling with the new subject matter as well as with poor health, *Otogi Zōshi* took Yamada more than three years to finish, finally getting published in 1997. In the afterword, she writes, "As I was reading various texts in order to better interpret classical texts visually, I was moved again by just how beautiful old Japanese picture scrolls can be. The longer I looked, the deeper I felt that Japanese have been weaving together words and pictures on the same surface since ancient times. This also renewed my awe for the medium of manga."[61] To that end, her comicalization is drawn in a style that crosses the geometry and sparse abstraction of old emaki (picture scrolls) and Nara ehon (medieval illustrated books) with her own minimalist line and spatial compositions.

The personally most significant manga Yamada drew aside from *Sassy Cats* and *Talk To My Back*, however, was *Blue Sky* (*Buruu sukai*), serialized in the longstanding and reputable woman's magazine *Fujin Kōron* (*Wives' Review*) for two years between 1991 and 1992. The most directly autobiographical of her mature work, it tells the story of a single mother in her thirties who runs a bar, trying to find new love after a disastrous marriage with the father of her two children. The images of her overbearing and selfish ex seem a tame reflection of Yamada's own abusive ex, even when he's angrily declaring his right to show up at their old apartment and call on the kids whenever he wants. The woman's new boyfriend, on the other hand, a kind and earnest man twelve years the protagonist's junior, is clearly modeled on Yamada's own partner, Shiratori Chikao, who was not twelve but seventeen years younger.

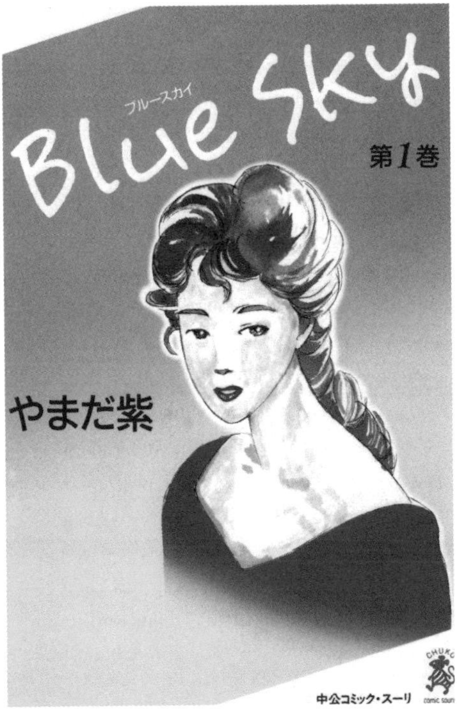
Blue Sky
ブルースカイ
第1巻
やまだ紫
中公コミック・スーリ
Yamada, *Blue Sky* vol. 1 (Chūō kōron, October 1992)

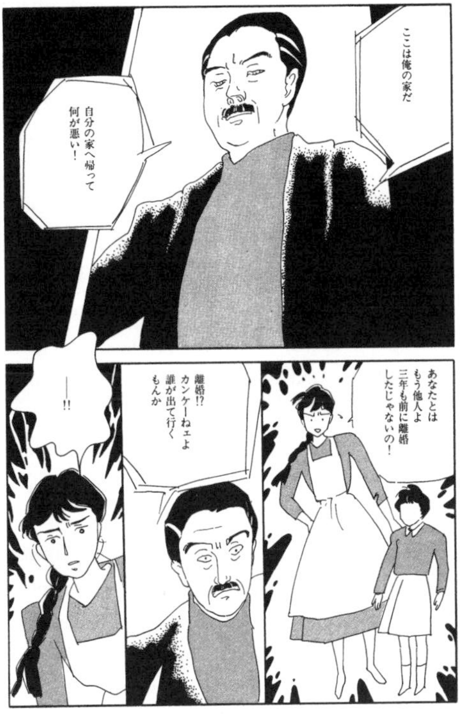
ここは俺の家だ
自分の家へ帰って何が悪い！
あなたとはもう他人よ三年も前に離婚したじゃないの！
離婚!? カンケーねェよ誰が出て行くもんか
――!!

なんと…
Yamada, *Otogi Zōshi* (Chūō Kōron, April 1997)

housewives with regards to care of the home, children, and elderly; the stark gender wage gap; the all-too-common occurrence of sexual assault; and the exploitative nature of sex work in Japan. In her allotted twenty seconds, Yamada says, "Our culture has long held that women standing up to men is unsightly. The negative consequences of that tradition have fallen almost entirely on the shoulders of women, who have been forced to accept a subservient position. People speak of the progress of civilization, but for women nothing has changed since the Meiji period."[59] Alas, all ten Earth Club candidates lost in the 1989 election. Yamada never ran for office again. "Though it started as something of a joke," she reminisced in 1991, "I began thinking there might be some kind of hope at the end of the tunnel, so I let myself get duped into going along with it. Indeed, I did glimpse something, but unfortunately that something was 'hopelessness' instead. In this country, if you aren't backed by money and political organizations, and don't have bile coursing through your veins, you'll never be able to muster the power to persuade others. What gets politicians riled up is not their country or its citizens, but their own self-advancement alone. When I realized that, and that I was nothing more than a powerless citizen, I felt utter despair."[60]

Nonetheless, she continued writing about related topics for a wide variety of venues, including a three-year stint as a columnist for *The Mainichi Shimbun* (1994–97), one of the country's biggest daily newspapers. Four books of her essays were published in her lifetime: *I Saw the Star-Studded Sky* (*Mantenboshi mita*, 1985), *Tokyo Nostalgia* (1991), *Life Chat with Wildcat* (*Yamaneko jinsei hōdan*, 1995), and *Do as You Wish* (*Okatte ni*, 1996), the last a collection of her *Mainichi* articles, which was reedited and reissued as a pocket paperback (*Dōzo okatte ni*) in 1999. Reading her essays today, one is struck by how many of the issues she complains about remain neglected in Japan, from public smoking and food waste, to prejudice against single mothers and the disabled, and the dogged refusal of the government to allow married couples to have separate surnames.

In the mid '90s, Yamada was commissioned by Chūō Kōron to draw a volume in their series *Manga: The Classics of Japan* (*Manga: Nihon no koten*). She chose a handful of stories from *Otogi Zōshi*, a collection of folktales from the medieval period, among them the well-known "Issun bōshi" about a miniature boy and "Shūten dōji" about a woman-eating demon. The stories she adapted touch on the blessings of childbirth, marriage between young star-crossed lovers, the power and seduction of female beauty, and princes in shimmering kimono freeing their brides-to-be from curses through love and bravery. Together they read as an exploration of the same themes of love, family, and childbirth that

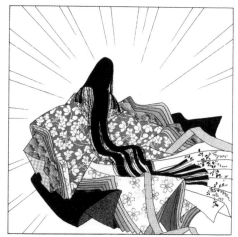

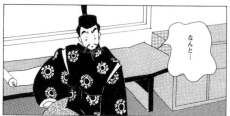

Yamada also returned to the crossing of poetry and comics with which she began her career. Most famous is *A Cat Watches from the Trees* (*Ki no ue de neko ga miteiru*, 1983–92), serialized in the poetry journal *La Mer*. Covering a wide range of topics, it lifts the daily life "comics poetry" of *Sassy Cats* out of panel breakdowns and spreads them out into a collection of two-page-spread, poetry-and-image pairs, known in Japanese as *shigashū*. After commencing this series, Yamada found her postbox bombarded with self-published and small press poetry collections, and invitations to talk at poetry symposia.[58] In 1985, for a special issue of *Contemporary Poetry Journal* (*Gendai shi techō*) about the interrelation between comics and poetry, she collaborated with poet Isaka Yōko on a piece titled "Resonance" ("Kyōkan"), using dispersed and overlapping panel frames to evoke a sense of poetic expansion. This led to a more sustained collaboration with Isaka titled *Les Enfants Rêveurs* (*Yume no maigo tachi*, 1988–90), originally serialized in *Garo*, comprising a group of linked short stories about womanhood and childrearing. In March 2010, the same *Contemporary Poetry Journal* dedicated an entire, posthumous issue to Yamada's work. She was also a frequent essayist in venues major and minor on the topics of love, marriage, childcare, homemaking, food politics, patriarchy, public etiquette, and pets, most of all cats.

In 1989, Yamada even ran for political office—perhaps the only mangaka ever to do so. She was one of ten women candidates running for the House of Councillors through the Earth Club (Chikyū kurabu), a political party created by songwriter, folk musician, and activist Yamamoto Kōtarō (male) that was dedicated to a wide range of environmental and feminist issues. Judging from a composite campaign video online, among the main issues shared by the party's candidates were: the oppressive nature of Japanese patriarchy; the heavy burden put upon

オカリナを吹くこども
こどもは昔その父と樽の湯舟につかり
母は写真をとった
母の手から一枚の写真がすべり落ちる
その一枚が
母の全身の力を呼びおこす
共鳴
井坂洋子
やまだ紫

息を吹き
少しずつ大きくしていく
肺が疲れているのがわかる

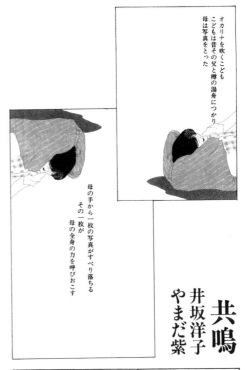

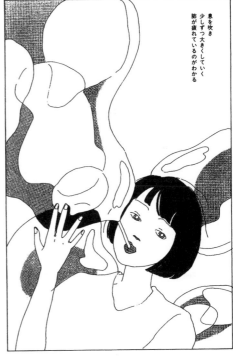

Yamada & Isaka Yōko, top: "Resonance," *Contemporary Poetry Journal* (October 1985); bottom: "Dog Time," from *Les Enfants Rêveurs*, *Garo* (August 1988)

6. RENAISSANCE WOMAN

The success of *Sassy Cats* and *Talk To My Back* led to Yamada receiving commissions from a number of venues, most of them more monied than *Garo*. As with *Talk To My Back*, most of the works sourced from her personal experiences as a wife, mother, and lover.

A Shimmering Pale Color (*Yurari usuiro*, 1983–84), serialized in Kōdansha's *Comic Morning*, deals more frontally and unforgivingly with men's infidelity. It was made into a movie in 1986, titled *Bed In* (Nikkatsu Studios) and directed by Konuma Kaoru, known for his softcore Roman Porno films in the '70s. For Nihon Bungeisha's *Comic Baku* (home to Tsuge Yoshiharu's *The Man Without Talent*, 1985–86), Yamada drew *His Majesty, Mr. Goldfish* (*Kingyō no tonosama*, 1984–85). Inspired by her own grandfather, the series is about a domineering and fussy patriarch enfeebled by age and a stroke, and a granddaughter who tolerates and loves him despite his overbearing ways, dated gender views, and non-relation by blood—an important motif in Yamada's interrogation of the dynamics and presumed naturalness of the Japanese family system. For the magazine *Shinsen* (*Fresh*), she drew *The Burden of Happiness* (*Shiawase tsubute*, 1984–85), about a young wife who is threatened with being abandoned by her husband on the eve of the birth of their first child, though he changes course in the nick of time. She also drew another group of cat stories for *Garo* in the mid '80s, *This Is How Cats Have Come and Gone* (*Kōshite neko ga fuetari hettari*, 1985–86), these more casual and cartoony.

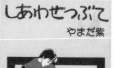

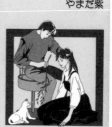

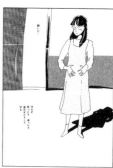

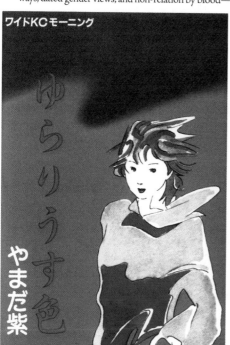

しあわせつぶて
やまだ紫
Yamada, *The Burden of Happiness* (Seirindō, September 1986)

ワイドKCモーニング
ゆらりうす色
やまだ紫
Yamada, *A Shimmering Pale Color* (Kōdansha, June 1984)

スー
スー
スー

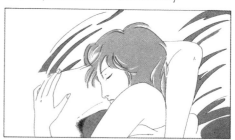

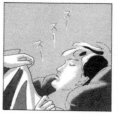

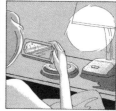

based on a knotted jumble of love and illusion and misunderstanding."[54] As evidenced in *Talk To My Back*, and due no doubt to her own negative experiences in marriage as well as her success in raising two children by herself, she had limited sympathy for women who failed to find an identity for themselves beyond the roles of wife and mother, who sank into boredom and depression once their children and husbands no longer needed their constant care or affection. In fact, outside of family relations, there is little camaraderie amongst women in Yamada's work whatsoever, from her earliest years to her last.

As the following quote from 1985 suggests, Yamada appears to have thought of her manga as a kind of corrective, and a potential source of inspiration for beleaguered mothers. At the same time, she worried if her work was making its way into the desired hands. "My fans? Actually, the vast majority of them are young men. The couple of times I've done signings at bookstores, everyone who came were guys in, like, high school and college. They'll ask me to make the books out to their moms, because they want to give it to them. Or to their girlfriends. It's interesting how many times that's happened. I imagine they're reading the books themselves, too, but that they were buying them as presents really made me happy. To be honest, I really wish housewives would read my work. But it's hard since my work doesn't get around all that much. Housewives don't really buy manga for themselves. They just read whatever weekly magazines their husbands leave around."[55]

When it came to her career, Yamada's feelings were split even more drastically. She acknowledged that, without being blessed with a profession that allowed her to work freelance from home, she would have never been able to maintain both halves of being a working mother. At the same time, she also insisted that cartooning productively required maintaining a strict separation between work and family, the bleeding of one into the other inside her manga notwithstanding. "It's spring break," she once wrote. "I am not fond of when my daughters have long breaks. Since I am used to having the house to myself during the day, I cannot relax when I sense someone nearby. I may spread out drawing paper on my desk and take my pen in hand, but my antennae are already distracted by the presence of my daughters." When her daughters were young, she commenced work after they went to bed at around ten at night, making them breakfast and bento lunches at dawn, then sleeping after they left for school. Once they got older, she worked from afternoon into the night—or through the night, as deadlines frequently demanded—though making sure to wake up by noon to tend to business calls.[56]

Yet, she did not like it when critics, based primarily on the content of her manga, collapsed her identity as an artist and a mother. In 1985, a year after *Talk To My Back* had ended, she concluded her first collection of essays with the following diatribe:

"Yamada Murasaki? Oh, you mean that person who draws housewife manga?"... People have been labeling me and my work in all sorts of ways. "Housewife manga," "mother manga" [mama manga], "watakushi manga" [quasi-autobiographical "I manga"]. They'll even add to the end of my author profile "a mommy-cartoonist, with daughters such-and-such an age." It makes me mad. I'm a working professional. It's equivalent to saying that, without adding the social roles of "housewife" and "mother," my personality has no flavor. Do other people get called "a daddy golfer," "a newlywed critic," "a step-daughter-bullying domestic life critic," or "an actress with a delinquent son"? Why are only women with children saddled with their family and children in their work? When I'm working, it's me and only me.[57]

Yamada identified as a manga artist, and Yamada identified as a *shufu*, and she thought *shufu* should read her manga—but "*shufu* cartoonist" be damned.

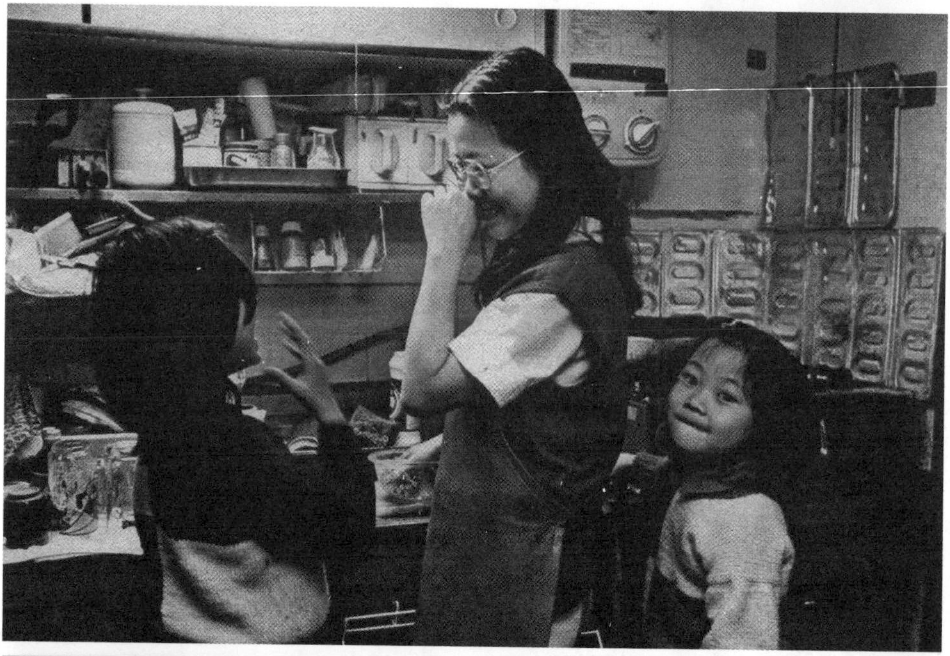

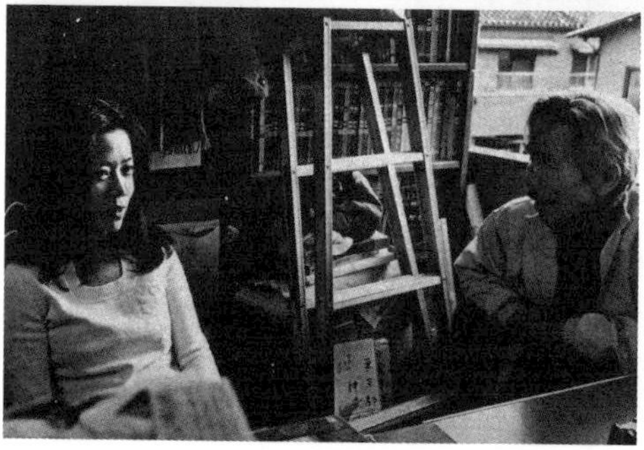

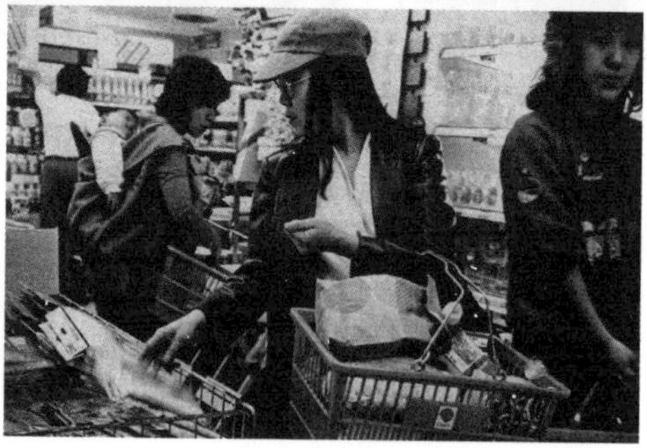

Asahi Graph, photos by Hashimoto Shōkō: Yamada in her kitchen with her daugthers, at Seirindō with Nagai Katsuichi, and shopping

at the offices of *Garo*, as well as shopping at the grocery store and laughing with her kids in the kitchen, this landmark article may be one of the earliest instances of a Japanese cartoonist being publicly identified and praised as both an artist and a stay-at-home mother. However, the important thing to note here is that Yamada is not a "professional housewife" whose identity and economic well-being depends on her husband—after all, she was separated and awaiting divorce at the time—but rather a single working mother without whom there would be no family at all.[53] For Yamada, the working mother was the true "female head of household."

In the early '90s, Yamada described the majority of *shufu* as "samurai without a sword" (*marugoshi*), meaning someone with an ostensibly respectable title but no true defenses with which to protect themselves, in this case due to economic dependence on their husbands and limited work experience outside the home. "*Shufu* is not an occupation," she declared, "it is a personal matter. It is a social service. It is volunteer work. It is uncompensated service

猫と主婦のいる風景

新進マンガ家 やまだ紫 の世界

二人の娘をもつ主婦やまだ紫氏（33）の猫と漫画が静かなブームを呼んでいる。猫のしなやかな姿態に主婦の繊細な生活感情を仮託するモノローグあるいは散文語のような世界が同性ばかりでなく多くの人々の心を捉えているのである。求龍の氏がスケッチする共に本誌に特に書き下ろしてもらった新作を掲載する。

文・斎藤頼明　写真・橋本陽子

東京電力

貼紙止めこと

NO.

"A Landscape of Cats and Housewives..." *Asahi Graph* (April 23, 1982), photo by Hashimoto Shōkō

ceilings. *Talk To My Back*, with its anxious chat about returning to work after children enter their teens might give the impression that few Japanese wives had jobs. However, by the mid '80s, almost half of married women were employed, though the majority of them only as part-timers. Part of the reason for that, of course, was that workplaces were inhospitable to women. In 1985, after years of grass-roots struggle, the Japanese government passed the Equal Employment Opportunity Act, ostensibly designed to redress egregious imbalances in employ-ment opportunities, hiring practices, labor contracts, and pay between men and women. But with no defined legal requirements and no penalties for non-compliance, the law was essentially toothless, with many companies responding to the legislation and the publicity around it by creating new categories of casual employment to institutionalize older forms of sexual discrimination. Essentially, the law was designed to protect working housewives as casual laborers—that is, as a pool of cheap and expendable workforce for Japanese companies to tap into as needed—not to create conditions in which women could pursue more rewarding and secure long-term careers.[52] The vulnerability of middle-aged, part-time working women is addressed explicitly in the latter chapters of *Talk To My Back*.

As was fairly typical of women of her generation, Yamada was of two minds about the term *shufu*. She proudly self-identified as *shufu*, yet squirmed when she was labeled as such by others in her professional life, and vocally spoke out against the sexist conditions under which most *shufu* labored. "I love the word *shufu*," she said in an interview with *Asahi Graph* in 1982, in an article titled "A Land-scape of Cats and Housewives: The World of Rising Cartoonist Yamada Murasaki." With numerous pho-tographs of Yamada at home drawing and chatting assert their independence, and with her husband, who is not the worst man, who is in fact kind and responsible by period standards, though he regularly works late, tends little to family affairs, cheats on his wife, and is unable to see her as much more than caretaker of his children and domestic servant. The true heart of *Talk To My Back*, however, is the protagonist's relationship to herself, her need to find new standards of self-worth after the roles of wife and mother wear thin and fears of having been dumped and forgotten inside "this vessel called a family" begin to gnaw at her soul, to borrow a phrase from the manga's last pages.

Despite Yamada's honest engagement with the realities of marriage and motherhood, she is surprisingly generous when it comes to those for whom she is expected to sacrifice, as she had been in her depictions of overbearing mothers in her early twenties. When the protagonist's husband has an affair, she finds reasons to excuse it. After all, she herself has "cheated" on the ideals of the breadwinner-model family by working a part-time job without her husband's "permission," and then by starting her own business creating sewn dolls, where she finally finds freedom. Yamada saves her harshest criticism instead for society at large, particularly its false promises of eternal satisfaction within a monogamous, gender-imbalanced, nuclear family. "Now that we've woken from the dream, what are we going to do?" the protagonist of *Talk To My Back* thinks to herself, rubbing her husband's head affectionately in the last panel of the chapter titled "Waking from the Dream."

In its day, *Talk To My Back* was often described as a "*shufu* manga," using a word that is often translated as "housewife," though is better rendered as "female head of household." Though it can be used for single mothers, as well as for married women who work part-time outside of the house, *shufu* primarily evokes "professional housewives" (*sengyō shufu*)

who commit the vast majority of their time and energy to housework, childcare, and supporting their husbands' near-total investment in their jobs and leisure outside the home and family. It is a term many women feel ambivalently about and many men use disparagingly, regardless of whether they recognize the fact that *shufu* names a social role without which postwar Japan's gender-segregated, company-centered society would not have been able to function. Since the '50s, it has been a centerpiece in feminist debates about the restricted place of women in Japanese society and the stranglehold the patriarchy exerts on the definition and inner shape of the Japanese family. It also has, to this day, many defenders among women, who see housewifery as a respectable life choice, an essential and demanding "job," a position of power and autonomy in the home, and a guarantee of freedom and leisure not granted to their overworked husbands. In the early '80s, when *Talk To My Back* was drawn, though the "salaryman" model was still hegemonic among middle-class families, "professional housewifery" was undergoing a new round of interrogation, under the pressures of radical feminist movements, increased political activism on the part of urban married women, rising stagflation, and a so-called "midlife crisis" of what baby boomer *shufu* should do to combat the malaise that followed their children growing older and more independent.[51]

One of the things they did, naturally, was engage in wage labor outside the home. When Yamada drew *Talk To My Back*, the demographics of Japanese labor were undergoing rapid changes. The country's salaried workforce at the time was sixty-five percent male, but among salaried employees were vast differences based on gender. Since young women were expected to abandon their jobs after marriage or childbirth to focus on their husbands and children, positions open to them were generally unskilled, lower paying, and insecure, with few benefits and very low glass

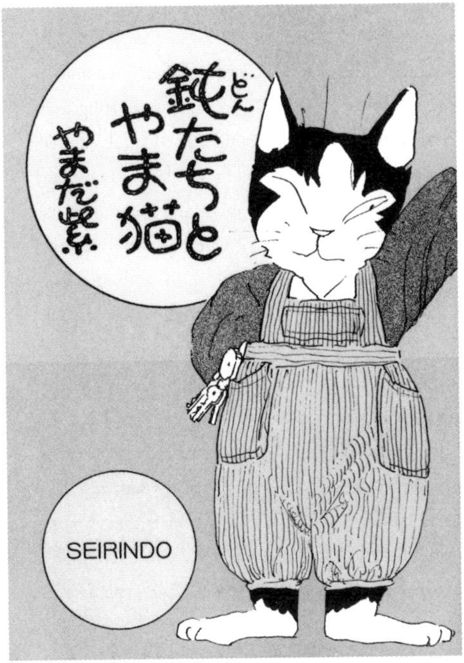
鈍たちとやま猫
やまだ紫
SEIRINDO

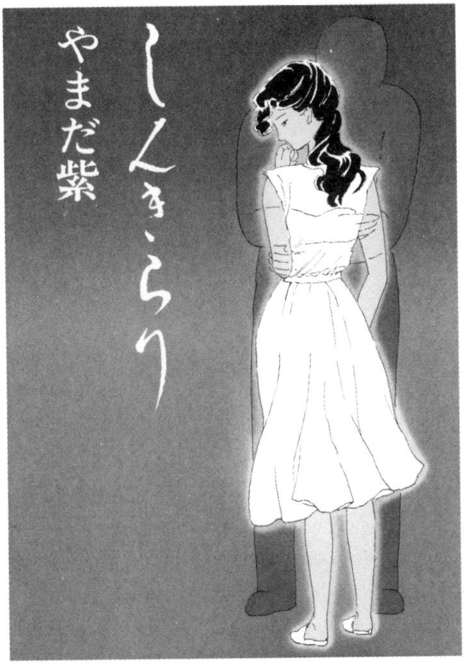
しんきらり
やまだ紫

Yamada, left: *Dumdums and Wildcat* (Seirindō, October 1981); right: *Talk To My Back* vol. 1 (Seirindō, August 1982)

by Hayashi Seiichi. Tetsuka Noriko, who oversaw production of the book and helped Yamada by affixing screentones and filling in black areas when deadlines approached, recalls the first volume selling especially well, at least over 10,000 copies.[47] In the mid '80s, Yamada claimed her books had sold somewhere in the vicinity of 20,000 copies, though she didn't specify which ones.[48] The Japanese title, *Shinkirari* (literally *A Flash of Light*), is a neologism pulled from a poem by Kawano Yūko, who herself often wrote about love and marriage. It has been included as an epigraph in all book editions, including the present one.

With *Talk To My Back*, Yamada's drawing had become suppler, more fluid, with wispier lines and looser fill, evocative of fashion illustration, but with a heightened degree of abstraction that characterized many so-called "new wave" manga of the time. "Since I didn't have much faith in my own drawing skills, I compensated with more lines, but that only made my work messy. So, I was always looking for techniques that would reduce the number of lines," said Yamada, paraphrased by Shiratori, in describing her mature style as an original solution to the simplification required of cartooning.[49] In an interview in 1986, Miyazaki Hayao cited *Talk To My Back* as an example of what's possible when Japanese cartooning's (including animation's) historical tendencies toward non-naturalistic abstraction and emotional expressionlessness are pushed to an extreme, forcing the reader/viewer to use their imagination.[50] Her late '60s and early '70s work had been fairly humorless; now, occasional self-deprecating gags lighten the mood. Leaving behind the homey wood structures of her *COM* years, *Talk To My Back* is set in a *danchi* apartment similar to the one in which Yamada herself lived in Nishidai. The chapters sashay across deftly constructed snapshots of the housewife protagonist's relationship with her two young daughters as they mature and begin to

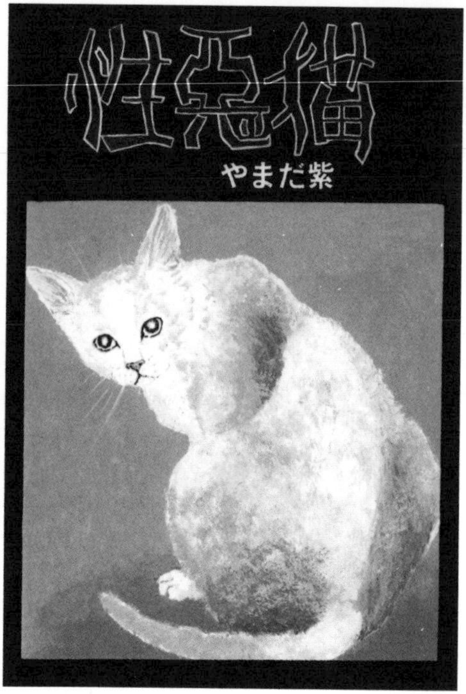
性悪猫
やまだ紫

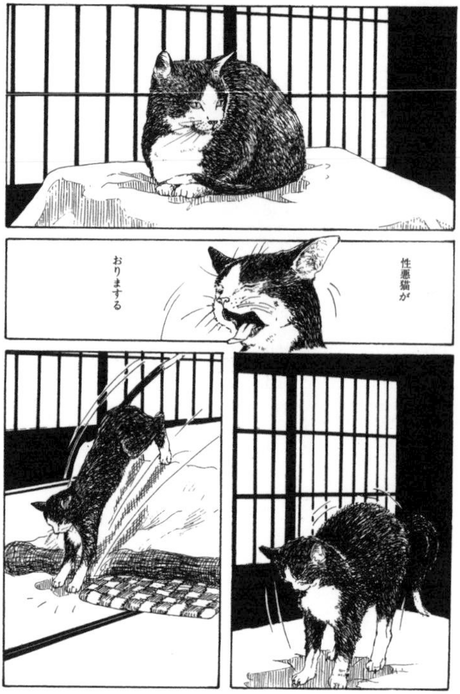
性悪猫が
おりまする

Yamada, left: "Sassy Cats" part 1, *Garo* (February/March 1979); right: *Sassy Cats* (Seirindō, August 1980)

small comforts and precious moments of daily life within the confined spaces of one's home, told through the eyes of house cats and the strays that pass through their yards.[46] Balancing between careful naturalistic drawings and pithy lyrical texts in a rural dialect, *Sassy Cats* (*Shōwaru neko*, 1979–80) marked the further development of the "comics poetry" for which Yamada had been praised during her *COM* years. Its success in book form (August 1980)—reportedly one of Seirindō's first true bestsellers—convinced Yamada that she might be able to support herself and her children on comics. A collection of her *COM* stories, *Touch-me-not* (*Hōsenka*), was published a few months later by Buronzu-sha, a publisher otherwise specializing in off-kilter and exquisitely drawn, ero-grotesque gekiga. A second collection of hers from Seirindō, *Dumdums and Wildcat* (*Dontachi to yamaneko*), comprising an assortment of *Garo* stories mostly created after *Sassy Cats*, was published in October 1981. While the volume is bookended by two comical pieces starring a loudmouthed feline—inspired by Miyazawa Kenji's "Wildcat and the Acorns" (1924)—the rest is comprised of realistically rendered stories about female identity on the borderlines of marriage and motherhood, foreshadowing what would come next in *Talk To My Back*.

Commenced soon after she and her husbanded separated, *Talk To My Back* was serialized in *Garo* in two phases between February/March 1981 and September 1982 (ending with the chapter "Waking from the Dream"), and December 1982 and October 1984. It has been collected numerous times as a book, initially as two volumes, and thrice as a single volume. The first half was published for the first time as a book in August 1982, with a cover resembling an *enka* album, designed by illustrator and *Garo* editor Minami Shinbō and with calligraphy consciously shōjo-esque manga she ever published, though she was often solicited by girls' magazines. "When you show your artwork to those kind of magazines," she explained in the mid '80s, "it has to be like [other shōjo manga]. With flowers for no reason. The costumes have to be pretty. The eyes can't be small. You should make your layouts bolder with diagonals, things like that. It's all very boring to me. But if they insist that's what girls want, it doesn't matter how hard you push, that door is not going to open for you." In contrast, "Drawing for men's magazines is pretty easy. Maybe it's because they publish work with varying tempos."[41] And elsewhere, speaking again about being approached by shōjo magazines, "When it's just women together, and there's this obsession with things being just for girls or women, the stuffiness of it all has always made me refuse the offer."[42] The only other manga she is known to have published in young women's magazines are two pieces for Shūeisha's *Seventeen* in 1984, one a redraw of her *COM* story "That's Mine"—commissions she agreed to, apparently, only because the editor begged her and allowed her to draw in her own, non-shōjo style.[43]

Beyond that one-off contribution to *Gals Life*, and a group of comical strips about *danchi* life titled "My Neighbor Hiromi" ("Tonari no Hiromi san") for the *Gurakon*-inspired magazine *Dakkusu* (December 1978), resurgent Yamada published exclusively in *Garo*. This is a surprising choice given her precarious financial situation, since Seirindō was so poor that it had been unable to pay contributors to its flagship magazine since the early '70s. On the other hand, they let her draw whatever she wanted. "Having swallowed her pride for so long drawing ads and fill-in illustrations for money, the natural creative energies she had repressed exploded across the pages of *Garo*," writes Shiratori. He also explains that she opted not to draw for bigger

publishers due to their obsession with sales figures and popularity, their condescending and paternalistic editorial meddling, and her own personal experiences of sexual harassment.[44] "Among the editors at big companies," wrote Yamada in 1991, glossing over the uglier parts of her experience, "are men who hardly deserve that job title. They show up to meetings with artists as the money-wielding representatives of their companies, ordering artists to draw in accordance with the company's wishes. When you don't draw as they say, they rub salt in your wounds while chuckling and claiming they're just being friendly. Many of them did not become editors because they like manga. They only see manga superficially as a fad. While artists are always trying to give birth to their next work, these editors demand that you keep rebirthing the same child as before. *Garo* always patiently waits until you're ready to give birth again." Given that she calls the editors "*karera*" (plural masculine pronoun) and describes artistic creation in maternal terms, the gender implications of her critique are clear enough, even if she doesn't outright condemn the system as part of the patriarchy.[45]

With both of her kids in elementary school, the perspective of Yamada's work had flipped: whereas in her *COM* years it was girls and young women negotiating mothers, now it was young mothers negotiating children, husbands, and the balance between social responsibilities as a housewife and self-respect as a woman. In the December 1978 issue of *Garo*, she published "Sometimes in the Sunlight" ("Tokidoki hidamari de"), about two friends in their twenties, a young woman and a man, with mismatched feelings for one another. This was followed by "Sassy Cats" (February/March, 1979), a redraw of her story for *Apple Core* in 1973, and the first in a series of short, poetic comics about domesticity, motherhood, and the

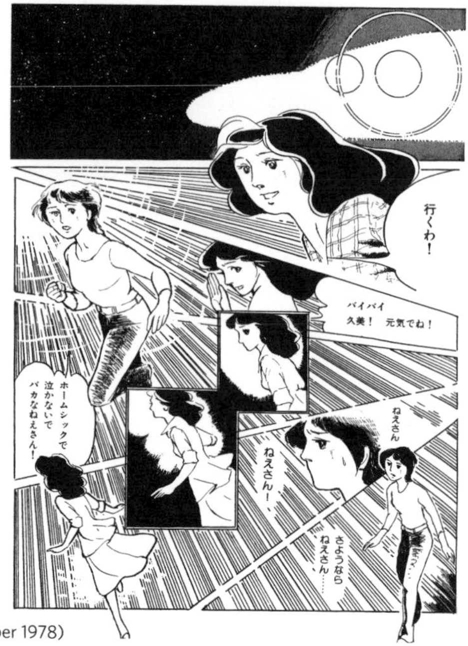
行くわ！
バイバイ
久美！ 元気でね！
ねえさん
ねえさん！
ホームシックで
泣かないで
バカなねえさん！
さようなら
ねえさん……

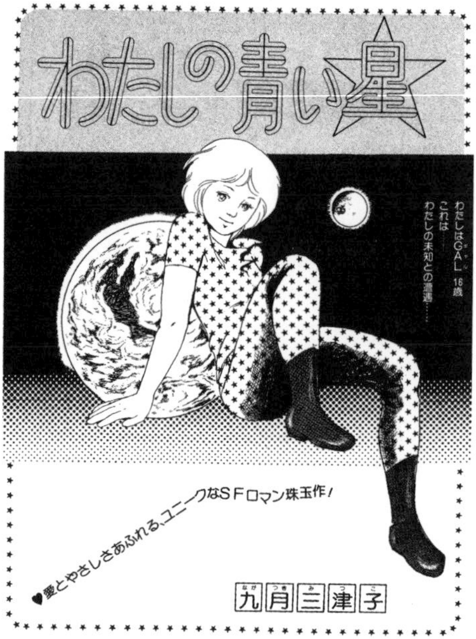
わたしの青い星
わたしはGAL 16歳
これは……
わたしの未知との遭遇……
♥愛とやさしさあふれる、ユニークなSFロマン珠玉作！
九月三津子

Nagatsuki Mitsuko [Yamada], "My Blue Star," *Gals Life* (September 1978)

is not known), she also worked on a couple of multi-page comics, though never published them.

Her first "comeback" work is often left off chronologies, since it was published under a pseudonym, Nagatsuki Mitsuko (literally "September Mitsuko," referring to her birth month and given first name), used so she wouldn't be caught by her husband. Titled "My Blue Star" ("Watashi no aoi hoshi"), it appeared in the inaugural issue of *Gals Life* (September 1978). Published by Shufu no tomo, an esteemed publisher of magazines and books for women founded way back in 1917, *Gals Life* reads like a late teen girl's version of the hip young men's magazines proliferating in those years, with its features about American life and fashion, news about movies and bands, romantic advice, and a sampling of shōjo manga tackling teen and young adult themes. "My Blue Star," thirty pages long and advertised as a "science-fiction romance," is about two sisters and a bearded male dreamer named Rai. As the sisters tease each other about their competing affections for Rai, it turns out that he is actually an alien who has come to Earth to study love, compassion, and other emotions lacking on his home planet. He is also the sisters' father, their mother having committed suicide when Rai first revealed his spaceship to her. At the end of the story, the elder sister decides to leave with Rai as his time on earth comes to an end, while the younger sister stays behind to tend to her beloved, verdant "blue star," Earth.

For all intents and purposes, "My Blue Star" is shōjo manga. The figures don't have the stereotypical big eyes, long thin legs, or flashy outfits. The relationship between the sisters echoes those in Yamada's *COM* work, which in turn were inspired by her own life. But the magical romantic father figure, the missing mother, and the science fiction escapism is typical of the genre. Given her vocal distaste for shōjo manga in the early '70s, one assumes economic necessity was what primarily drove her to draw "My Blue Star." At any rate, it was the last present, when she got home from the hospital, she found traces of him having been with his lover at their home.[37]

This "hell of marriage" just about sabotaged Yamada's artistic career. At the same time, it was her skills as an artist that provided her and her daughters a lifeline.

Amidst this torture, she began to think of escaping her so-called "home." She feared she might be killed. She knew she couldn't raise her children with such a father. But in order to pull that off, she needed to be economically independent. Her future had been bright as a rising cartoonist, but the little savings she had quickly disappeared covering daily expenses. When I asked her how that could be, she said, "My husband hardly ever gave me any money for living expenses…"

Scared because she never knew when her husband might get violent again, she secretly began drawing in resistance. As this was in the days before cellphones and email, she had to use public phones to get in touch with editors. Under the guise of going to the supermarket to shop, she smuggled artwork out of the house and slipped it to them during quick meetings at cafés. Despite such unimaginable circumstances, she said her desire to make art remained unabated.

I recall her saying that drawing illustrations for ads paid well, even if you don't get credited by name. She also drew what the industry calls "throwaway illustrations" [sute katto], drawings to fill blank space in magazines. Little by little, she thus started saving up money. Of course, the responsibilities of childcare and housework fell entirely on her shoulders. She had no public assistance of any kind, and had to figure out living expenses all by herself.

She used to say that only someone who has been married and has born children can understand just how extreme her hardships were. She had absolutely nobody or nothing to depend on. Her life was not just some cheap, lachrymose story or flimsy

melodramatic make-believe. It was "reality" itself in all its horrible ferocity.[38]

Yamada separated from her husband in 1981, with him moving out of their apartment in Nishidai. Their divorce was finalized in 1983. She asked for nothing but custody of her two children and the apartment, and that is all she ever got. "You know how you open your eyes in the morning?" she told Shiratori. "I thanked the morning sun simply knowing that I wouldn't be hit that day."[39] Or as she told an interviewer in 1985, "Not having my husband around has been a huge relief. I know I'm probably not supposed to say this publicly, but to be honest, I'd like to shout it loud enough so that everyone will hear. Things have gotten so much easier. Life has become truly enjoyable… After I got divorced, I reassessed my personality. Until then, I was the kind of woman who stays quiet and says nothing even when they're upset. I'd just frown and wash the dishes loudly. I couldn't muster a smile even when I was out shopping. I was probably insufferable. But once my husband left, I bloomed like a flower. My body danced. I couldn't stand still. I'd dance and blab about how I was feeling while waiting for the elevator, completely unaware of what I was doing. My kids even used to ask me to stop because I was embarrassing them." Ironically, she added, "Had my marriage gone well, I probably wouldn't be drawing manga now, so I guess I have my husband to thank for that. Thanks for putting me through hell!"[40]

5. THE SO-CALLED HOUSEWIFE CARTOONIST

By the time of their separation, Yamada had been actively, if secretly, drawing again for a few years. In addition to the spot illustrations Shiratori mentions (since these were done anonymously or under a pen name, and she never archived them, how many she drew and for what venues

1985 for *Kōkoku Hihyō* (*Advertising Critique*), in a special feature about women creators, Yamada suggested vaguely that her quick disenchantment with being married had less to do with "feeling like she was losing herself" and more with realizing that she had naively "expected too much of men," which was perhaps unfair to them as well.[34] In her many essays from the '80s and '90s, she often wrote about daily life as a mother and a woman in the world, sometimes about the sobering reality and politics of love, coupling, and marriage, and occasionally about exhausted and broken relationships. "Do you really think your children will grow up happy if they have to watch their mother hate their dad? Are you sure they won't end up mistrusting and hating both of their parents? By gritting your teeth and repeating to yourself, like some magical spell, that as long as you can put up with it everything will be fine, don't you realize that you're only forcing days of misery upon your children?" she wrote in the early '90s, speaking from experience.[35] It's also easy to read biographically into the following statement she made in the mid '80s: "Men who don't talk big and do nothing. Men who don't bluff. Men who don't hit women. Men who don't yell. Men who don't force their debts upon others. Men who don't ignore their parents. Men who don't leave things broken after their dalliances are exposed. Men who don't threaten to ditch their family and assets. Men who don't tell women that they'll dry up if they don't fuck more. Men who, instead of getting irritated and barking at women when they're hungry, quietly ask them to go to the kitchen to fix them tea-on-rice or ramen. Those are the kind of men I like."[36] These were high standards in the '80s.

In a book published in 2019, and thus years after the artist's death in 2009, Yamada's partner, *Garo* editor Shiratori Chikao, provided a painfully vivid glimpse of how horrible things were during her first marriage. The citation below is long, but it reveals much about why Yamada viewed marriage, men, and the patriarchy the way she did. After reading it, one can only marvel at how little bitterness colors her manga, especially considering the extent to which daily life experiences informed her art. Shiratori refers to Yamada as Mitsuko, her given first name.

It's not like she chose to stop drawing. Even if she had wanted to publish new work, the situation she was in made that impossible. She got married in October 1971, and on the very day she began living together with her husband, he suddenly got drunk and violent. "From now on, you shut up and do as I say, got it?!" Whenever she'd try to work in his presence, he'd accuse her of mocking him and hit and kick her. Though trying her best to put up with the situation, when she finally couldn't take it anymore, she went to his parents and asked them to do something about his outbursts. But all they did was snicker coldly and reply, "Are you sure you aren't to blame?"

When her husband sobered up, he'd see her bruises and prostrate himself before her, apologizing and vowing never to do it again. That same night, he'd start drinking again. One time, he slammed her head into a heavy dresser repeatedly and so hard that it cracked the wood. She began bleeding profusely and ran out of the house in panic. She burst into the police station that was in the traffic circle in front of the high-rise where she lived. But all the police did was chuckle and say, "Oh, it was your husband? Well, there's nothing we can do about that."

Today, the term "DV" [domestic violence] is widely accepted. Even when it is confined to the home, battery is battery and a crime is a crime. Thirty years ago, however, neither the police nor local municipal authorities would get involved, jointly citing the "sanctity of private space" [minji fukainyū]. It may be hard to believe, but when Mitsuko's second daughter was born, not only did her husband refuse to help or be fanzine and self-published manga fair were mainly male fans of shōjo manga, particularly those by the Shōwa 24 Group and especially Hagio, whose work some of them first encountered in COM. Its participants, on the other hand, were at first overwhelmingly female, before shifting for a time to male otaku fans of bishōjo in the late '70s and '80s. A pillar of the amateur otaku scene of the '80s and '90s and today dominated by women creators, Comiket annually draws tens of thousands of vendors across multiple events and hundreds of thousands of attendees, making it the largest such gathering in the world.[31]

Garo, meanwhile, was engaged in other directions, spelunking the dreamworlds pioneered by Tsuge Yoshiharu and nurturing the seeds of punky hetauma and the post-'60s subculture scene. Many leading Garo artists cameoed with work in COM, including Hayashi, Katsumata, Takita Yū, Abe Shin'ichi, Tsuge Tadao, and most frequently Kusunoki Shōhei. Abe and Kawasaki Yukio both had submissions featured in COM's amateur section before becoming Garo regulars. Yamada, however, is the only artist to have debuted and cut her teeth in COM, and be nurtured by its more extensive and inclusive amateur networks, before flourishing as a mature artist in Garo. If Yamada is to be regarded a forerunner of comics for women outside of the framework of shōjo manga, top supporting credits must go to the open-mindedness and foresight of COM rather than to the experimentalism of Garo, which, hamstrung by the sexism that characterized much of the Japanese counter-culture, took more than a decade to catch up with the inclusiveness that COM had already embraced in the late '60s.

4. THANKS FOR HELL

Yamada's contributions to Big Comic and Apple Core would be the last manga she published until 1978—a hiatus of five years. One could hardly hope for a more promising career step than a story in Shōgakukan's leading adult magazine. But then life—or more specifically, the patriarchy and social expectations of womanhood—intervened.

In October 1971, at the age of twenty-four, Yamada got married to one of the members of the folk group she had been in as a teenager. As expected of women in Japan, she put a lid on her career and refocused her life toward the home. She and her husband moved into a small apartment in Takashimadaira, in the northwest outskirts of Tokyo. It was on the thirteenth floor of the massive Nishidai Apartments, one of the many reinforced concrete danchi housing blocks that mushroomed around Japanese cities between the late '50s and '70s as mass-produced promises of the suburban, middle-class, nuclear family dream. Her first daughter, Momo, was born in August 1973; her second daughter, Yū, in November 1974. "I was really into the idea of marriage," Yamada recalled in 1989. "So, I stopped working right after getting married, put all my energy into the children and housework, and then started feeling like a carriage horse."[32] On another occasion, she explained in more detail, "I really had big dreams about marriage. I was raised in a household without a father, so I was super jealous of normal families. Cleaning the house, doing the laundry, washing the dishes, and so on while living in a proper house—I couldn't think of a better life. But once you get to doing it, then you realize how unnatural it all is."[33]

For a while, Yamada continued working for the design studio she joined after high school. But once her husband took to heavy drinking, violence, gambling, and philandering, even hopes for a conventionally compromised life as a Japanese wife began to unravel. Yamada herself wrote little about the details of her first marriage. In an interview in

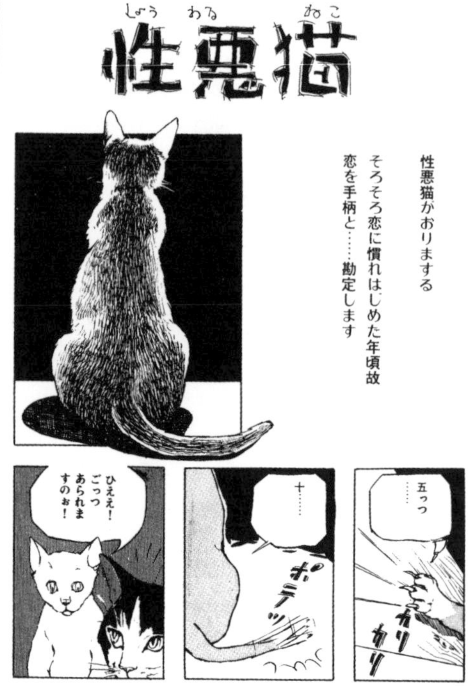
しょう わる ねこ
性悪猫
性悪猫がおりまする
そろそろ恋に慣れはじめた年頃故
恋を手柄と……勘定します
五っつ……
カリ
カリ
十……
ポテッ
ひええ！ごっつあられますのお！

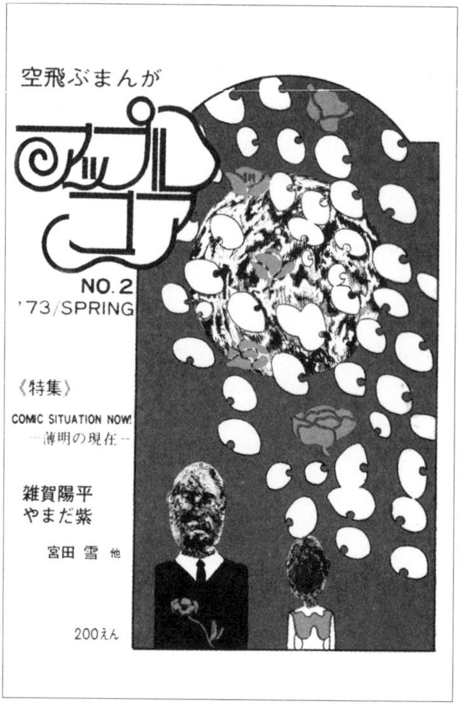
空飛ぶまんが
アップルコア
NO.2
'73/SPRING
《特集》
COMIC SITUATION NOW!
—薄明の現在—
雑賀陽平
やまだ紫
宮田 雪 他
200えん

Cover of *Apple Core* no. 2 (March 1973); Yamada, "Sassy Cats," in the same issue

COM was called *Grand Companion* (shortened to *Gurakon*). It initially occupied the back pages of the magazine before being printed as an independent, insert pamphlet. When *COM* folded at the end of 1971, *Grand Companion* lived on in the form of numerous short-lived zines and pamphlets, some sponsored by Mushi Pro, like *Manga Communication*, in which Yamada's "The Current State of Shōjo Manga" appeared in May 1971. *Apple Core*, founded the following year, was another such spin-off.

Many regions had their own local *Gurakon* club, initially sponsored by *COM*. That of the Kansai region—encompassing Osaka, Kobe, and Kyoto—was overseen by one Nakajima Takashi. In addition to creating zines, they hosted film screenings and other events. After one such event in Osaka in August 1971 featuring Tezuka's animated shorts, Yamada participated in a roundtable with no less than "the God of Manga" himself. Founded by Nakajima in late 1972, *Apple Core* was created to continue nurturing the local Kansai amateur scene beyond *Grand Companion*'s passing. Mushi Pro at first promised support, but financial troubles ultimately prevented them from doing so. Among the *COM* and *Grand Companion* regulars who contributed artwork were Kimura Minori, Akuta Maki, and Yamada. For the first issue, Yamada was supposed to participate in a collaborative work with Kimura and Akuta, but missed the deadline. In apology, she drew a longer work for issue two (March 1973) titled "Sassy Cats" ("Shōwaruneko"), which she redrew for *Garo* in 1978. For issue four (January 1974), Yamada contributed a group of illustrated poems like those she published in *COM* in 1970.[30]

Out of such coterie zines and amateur networks would come Comic Market (Comiket), initiated in 1975. Interestingly, the founders of this famous

In closing, she recommends that, instead of complaining about negative public and industry opinion, authors should put their feet down and declare, "We refuse to draw shōjo manga!!" However, since at the beginning of this essay Yamada expresses a desire to draw shōjo manga, as she did in the *COM* roundtable and does in her diary, one should read this screed less as a condemnation of comics for or about girls per se, than of the way that the conventions of shōjo manga limited what was possible for that demographic. One might thus consider Yamada's *COM* work as "girls' comics" outside the confines of shōjo manga, which was hampered not just by narrow societal views about young femininity—equating it too often with cuteness, innocence, and virginity—but also for having far fewer venues open to experimentation than did shōnen manga or gekiga.

And so, when Yamada decided to branch out beyond *COM*, she approached male-dominated forums. Just prior to her anti-shōjo manga broadside, she published her first story in *Garo* (February 1971). A year later, in 1972, after *COM*'s shuttering in December 1971, she submitted a story to *Big Comic*, Shōgakukan's leading manga magazine for adults, winning its coveted "newcomer prize." Advertised in English on its cover into the twenty-first century as "Comics for Men," *Big Comic* was created in 1968 as Shōgakukan's answer to dynamic magazines like

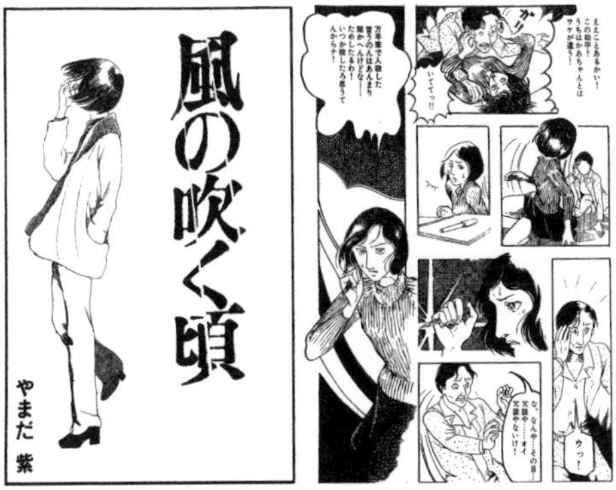

ええことあるかい！
この助平！
うちはかあちゃんとはワケが違う！
ガッ
いててっ!!
ウっ！
な、なんや…その目…
冗談や……オイ
冗談やないけ！
万年筆で人殺した
言うのんはあんまり
聞かへんけどな……
ためしたるわ！
いつか殺したろ思うてんからナ！
風の吹く頃
やまだ紫

Yamada, "When the Wind Blew," *Big Comic* (May 15, 1973)

Garo and Futabasha's *Manga Action*. Among the many iconic series it published were Saitō Takao's *Golgo 13* (1968–present) and Tezuka's *Swallowing the Earth* (*Chikyū o nomu*, 1968–69) and *Ayako* (1972–73). Though the magazine was marketed to men, in its attempt to appeal to a truly mass audience *Big Comic* also recruited women creating work about mature themes outside shōjo manga modes, thus enabling Ichinoseki Kyō's debut in 1975 and Saitō Nazuna's in 1986. Accompanied by tempered praise from Shirato Sanpei, Yokoyama Mitsuteru, and Fujiko Fujio, Yamada's winning submission, "When the Wind Blew" ("Kaze no fuku koro"), was finally published in a supplemental issue dated May 15, 1973. About a young woman who murders her estranged father after he won't stop harassing her and her hardworking mother and then ends up in prison, this nihilistic story, with its impressive combination of expressivity and fluidity in Yamada's increasingly naturalistic draftsmanship, is stylistically closest perhaps to the work of Miyaya Kazuhiko and Aoyanagi Yūsuke, *COM*'s leading young male talents.

The only other works Yamada appears to have published in the early '70s were two short works for *Apple Core*, a coterie zine created in the aftermath of *COM*'s demise. In addition to having hosted Tezuka's *Phoenix*, *COM* is best remembered for its proactive support of aspiring cartoonists and the clubs, zines, and self-published comics they created locally across Japan. In this, it was inspired by the amateur submissions pages in kashihon anthologies like *Machi* and that in *Garo*, but most of all *Manga Shōnen* (1948–55), where Tezuka first began drawing *Phoenix* in 1954, where Ishinomori debuted, and where many future stars of both postwar kids' manga and kashihon gekiga first tested their skills. Taking its name from a cross-regional network of amateur groups during the age of kashihon manga, the amateur section in

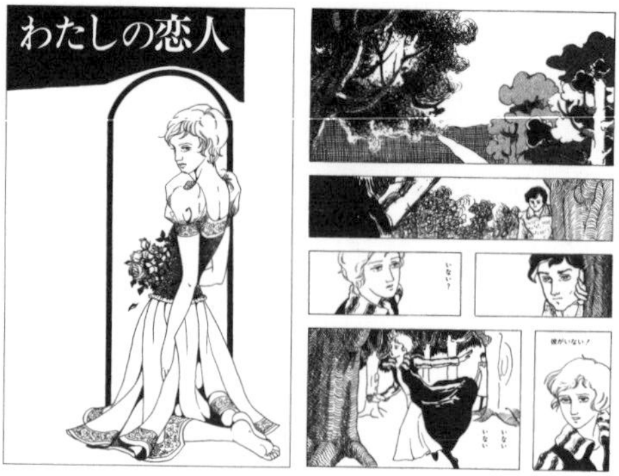
わたしの恋人

Yamada, "My Lover," *Funny* (May 1970)

two shōjo manga she is known to have published. About a young woman who falls in love with a tree, and her jealous human boyfriend whom she kills and buries at the tree's foot to nourish its roots, "My Lover" reflects Yamada's youthful consumption of world literature more than the typical tropes of shōjo romance. The open linework, flatness, and sparse, hand-drawn patterning speak as much to the influence of fashion and other forms of illustration as that of her contemporaries in manga. To my knowledge, the only other items Yamada published in *Funny* were art nouveau-esque portraits of young women framed by flowers for the magazine's romantic advice column. According to her diary, she drew another story for *Funny* before learning that the magazine had folded, due most immediately to its head editor's sudden death in a car accident, though ensured by poor sales. She also approached mainstream girls' magazines like Shūeisha's *Margaret* and *Seventeen*, but was told by their male editors that neither her style nor her stories were what girls wanted.[27]

"I don't think I'll publish anything I'm not confident about ever again," wrote Yamada in her diary about "My Lover."[28] Within a year, private embarrassment about struggling with drawing shōjo manga morphed into public disgust for the genre. In the first issue of *Manga Communication* (May 1971), a pamphlet published by Mushi Pro dedicated to the integration of theory and practice, Yamada came knives-out with an article titled "Cross-Examining Myself: The Current State of Shōjo Manga" ("Shinnai hanmon: shōjo manga no genjō"). After opening with expressions of sympathy for the fact that shōjo manga and women cartoonists are generally disparaged by the manga industry, Yamada writes that the real problem is the quality of the comics themselves. "Those weak stories, for example, or their random way of concluding. You'll have a three-hundred-page magazine, and everything will look the same without any kind of individuality. It'd be more honest to call shōjo manga 'love play manga.' All that head-over-heels and bent-out-of-shape falling in love stuff, over and over again, never tiring of the same romantic subject. One series ends and the next begins, but the only things that change are the characters' names and the circumstances of their romance and who they're in love with. Be it with someone poor or rich, a prince or a playboy, the romance never transcends Cinderella's world. Only the characters' eyes are drawn with any kind of dedication. The rest just feels slapped together."[29]

As a result, adds Yamada, not only is it impossible to identify with the characters, who utterly lack reality as human figures, but it's hard to regard what the authors are doing as much more than "playing a foreign love game" inside the bubble of their work desks. Though she admits she lacks knowledge about what it's like as an insider in the field, she blames the stultification of the genre on "a lack of competitive desire to make something that is truly one's own," reinforced by a culture of incestuous academicism in which newcomers only study and develop their style on the basis of other shōjo manga. "As women experience the pains of child birth, so cartoonists should experience the pains of creation. Yet, with shōjo manga, however much the characters suffer and cry and shout, I can't help but feel that they're just being abused by their authors as an outlet for their own frustrations."

alike have warm, unassuming, tactile grains. In "That's Mine" ("Are wa watashi no," October 1969), Yamada's third story for *COM*, a young girl and her estranged mother work through their personal differences via the avatars of a crude but affectionately handmade and sturdy doll versus a shiny but fragile store-bought one. In her only work for *Garo* in this early period, "Oh, the Ways of the World" ("Aa sekensama," February 1971), a young woman walks the streets of her neighborhood, bristling at the brusqueness of the people she passes, before finding peace in the simple laughter of a comedy show on television at her acquaintance's home.[24]

In the early '90s, Yamada described the neighborhood of Setagaya, where she grew up, in terms that resonate with the aesthetics of her early manga. "Everyone in the neighborhood knew everyone else from birth. Anyone who passed in front of your house, even if you didn't know their name, you at least recognized them. If you made eye contact, you exchanged pleasantries. Things were more congenial and time moved more slowly back then. Pretty much every household had elderly family members, who had lots of time on their hands and helped raise the children. The deep significance of this is something I have thought about since becoming an adult."[25] It was a world, she also claimed, whose intergenerational connections and relaxed cadence had since been practically wiped out by urban development and suburbanization. Yet, even when her work shifted setting in the '80s to the high-rises that replaced the neighborhood Tokyo of her postwar youth, Yamada remained sensitive to the soft poetry of place and people—of slants of sunlight through a window, the peaceful nothingness of personal downtime, the comforting rhythm of kitchen sounds—as well as the ways that older forms of family continued to shape romantic relations and gender norms.

3. SAY NO TO SHŌJO MANGA

Like her contemporary Tsurita Kuniko (whose work could otherwise not be more different), Yamada regarded shōjo manga with a high degree of ambivalence. In the span of a couple of years in the early '70s, that ambivalence soured into loathing. In the same period, and I don't think coincidentally, Yamada suffered two misfortunes: the shuttering of *COM* and getting married.

Though Yamada never mentions shōjo manga in recollections of comics she read in her youth, her *COM* work resonates with the genre in various ways. Her superimposed imagery, internal monologues, and poetic dispersal of words were features that had become increasingly popular in comics marketed to girls. Family tensions, especially among sisters and mothers, feature prominently in her work, as they did in shōjo manga. She deals centrally with the struggles of young girls trying to adapt to the complexities and compromises of the adult world, and the sobering impact that has on their childish fantasies and dependencies, as did many shōjo manga. Of course, such general stylistic and thematic similarities are distinguished in Yamada's work by an earthy realism alien to shōjo manga, and in most cases for Yamada such motifs are biographically rooted. Furthermore, her work is practically devoid of the stereotypical visual codes of "girlish" femininity, the romantic beaus, and the magical realist fantasies that governed shōjo manga. Nonetheless, when asked about how she might like to branch out as a cartoonist in the 1970 *COM* roundtable, Yamada replied, "I want to draw shōjo manga"—an expression of interest in the genre, but one that also implies that she regarded her own work as something distinct.[26]

Soon after, Mushi Pro gave her a chance to do just that. For the May 1970 issue of *Funny*, Mushi Pro's short-lived shōjo manga venture, Yamada drew "My Lover" ("Watashi no koibito"), one of only

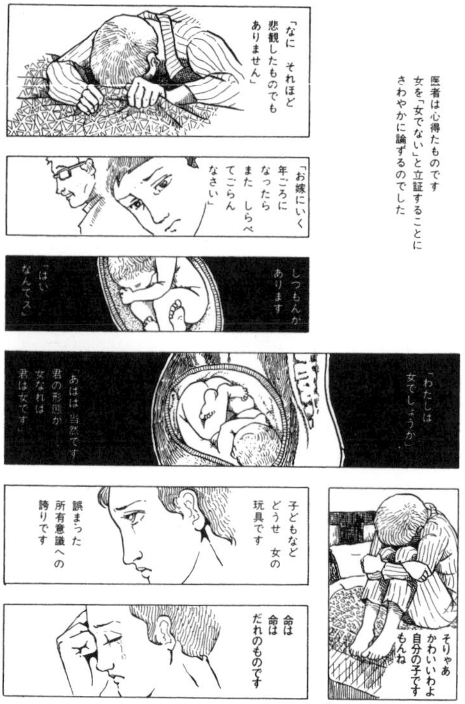
医者は心得たものです
女を「女でない」と立証することに
さわやかに論ずるのでした
「なに　それほど悲観したものでもありません」
「お嫁にいく年ごろになったらまた　しらべてごらんなさい」
しつもんかあります
「はいなんてス」
「わたしは女でしょうか」
「あはは 当然です君の形態か女なれは君は女です」
そりゃあかわいいわよ自分の子ですもんね
子どもなどどうせ　女の玩具です
誤まった所有意識への誇りです
命は命はだれのものです

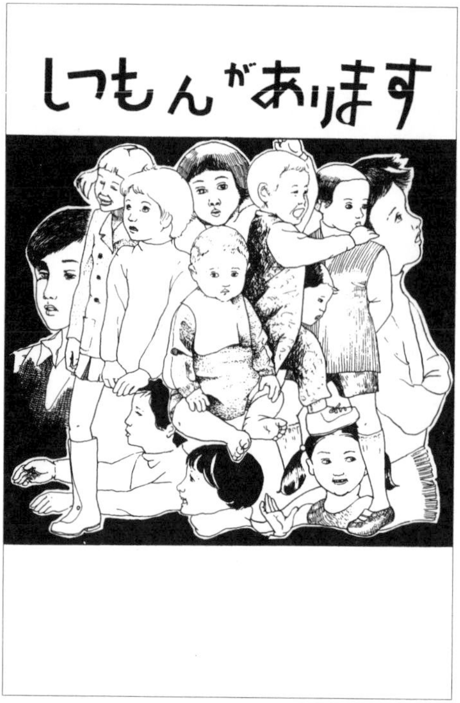
しつもんがあります

Yamada, "I Have a Question," *COM* (August 1970)

Yamada used wide gutters, as did Okada, which has the effect of separating panels out so that they serve dual function as narrative units and standalone illustrations. Women's domestic spaces dominate, particularly living rooms and kitchens. Images and stories are built around objects and activities associated with those spaces, most of all fabrics—simple articles of clothing, kimonos, futons, knitting, hand-sewn dolls—but also wooden dressers, kitchen knives and cutting boards, boiling kettles, chopped food. Though Yamada's draftsmanship could be stiff and unsteady at this early stage in her career, the linework is gentle and the hatching delicate, and the pacing of panels at once patient and fluid. Everything looks handmade, without the dramatic lines, stark tonal contrasts, and affixed screentones typical of manga at the time. Inanimate things and human relationships

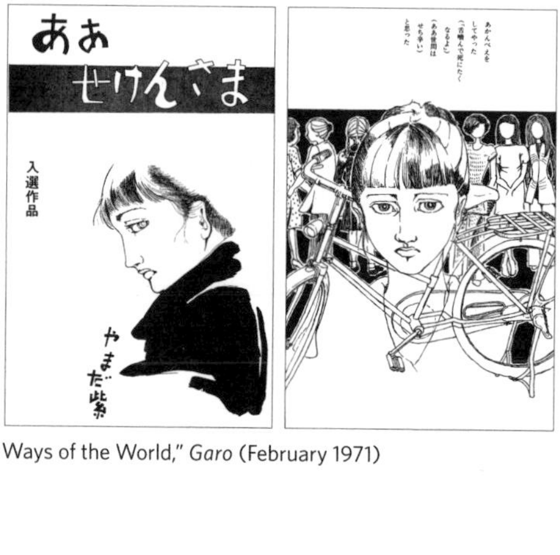
ああ
せけんさま
入選作品
やまだ紫

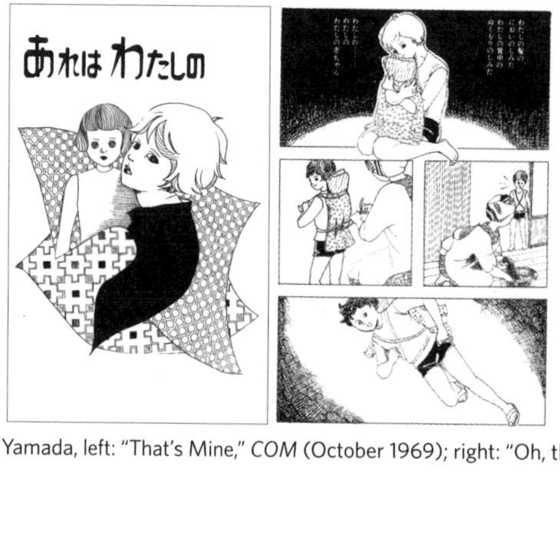
あれは わたしの

Yamada, left: "That's Mine," *COM* (October 1969); right: "Oh, the Ways of the World," *Garo* (February 1971)

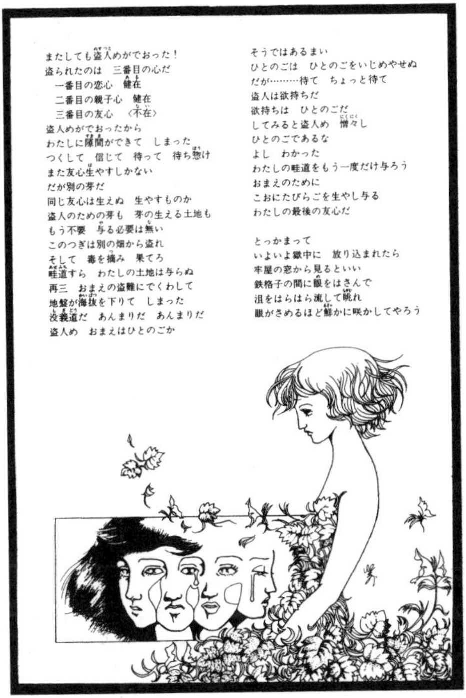
またしても盗人めがでおった！
盗られたのは　三番目の心だ
一番目の恋心　健在
二番目の親子心　健在
三番目の友心　〈不在〉
盗人めがでおったから
わたしに隙間ができて　しまった
つくして　信じて　待って　待ち惚け
また友心生やすしかない
だが別の芽だ
同じ友心は生えぬ　生やすものか
盗人のための芽も　芽の生える土地も
もう不要　与る必要は無い
このつぎは別の畑から盗れ
そして　毒を摘み　果てろ
畦道すら　わたしの土地は与らぬ
再三　おまえの盗難にでくわして
地盤が海抜を下りて　しまった
没義道だ　あんまりだ　あんまりだ
盗人め　おまえはひとのごか
そうではあるまい
ひとのごは　ひとのごをいじめやせぬ
だが………待て　ちょっと待て
盗人は欲持ちだ
欲持ちは　ひとのごだ
してみると盗人め　憎々し
ひとのごであるな
よし　わかった
わたしの畦道をもう一度だけ与ろう
おまえのために
こおにたびらごを生やし与る
わたしの最後の友心だ
とっかまって
いよいよ獄中に　放り込まれたら
牢屋の窓から見るといい
鉄格子の間に眼をはさんで
泪をはらはら流して眺れ
眼がさめるほど鮮かに咲かしてやろう

Yamada, "Poems to the Empyrean" no. 3, *COM* (May-June 1970)

nothing about the quality of your work. You had no choice but to become your own editor. I suppose that was probably the way it should have been."[21]

Despite a lack of guidance from *COM*'s editors, Yamada developed quickly as an artist, crafting a style that was so her own that it's hard to provide an art historical gloss. Informed by the artist's own compromised upbringing, her stories are miniature anthropological studies of young womanhood and family life in postwar Japan. They spotlight difficult but loving relationships between mothers, daughters, and grandmothers, between younger and older sisters, and between female friends after one or both marry or have children. They are constructed around common but important life events: a grandmother's death, a mother's remarriage, a graduating high school student's desire for independence, a young woman's yearning to have children. Though none of these were new topics in manga, they were still fairly rare. And in contrast to most contemporary shōjo manga, there is little fantasy in Yamada's work and little melodrama. Romance is of a sober and functional nature, and when men figure at all they usually do so as passive, soft-spoken background and ballast.

She also contributed a series of single-page, illustrated poems to *COM*, collectively titled "Poems to the Empyrean" ("Sora e no uta," March–December 1970). Some of them are so close in theme and detail to her manga that one suspects they were drafted before she switched focus to cartooning. In general, though, her word choices are flat and emotional sentiments pedestrian; as an artist of words, Yamada really didn't come into her own until the late '70s. She herself admitted in the '80s that complicated contemporary poetry eluded her, and that she really only understood the more straightforward poetry of the early twentieth century.[22]

Her manga, on the other hand, shimmer with a degree of realism found nowhere else in manga at the time, further enlivened by pithy verses minus the clichés of flowers and seasons often plied by male cartoonists, like Hayashi Seiichi (an influence) and Kamimura Kazuo, who presumed to speak for women's experiences. In "Onions and Carrots" ("Tamanegi to ninjin," April 1970), for example, two sisters deal with the absence of a father who died when they were still young and the desires of a mother who wishes to remarry. Elder sister welcomes the prospective step-father into the house, graciously, but with a glass of water reeking of onions. In "I Have a Question" ("Shitsumon ga arimasu," August 1970), a young woman learns that she cannot have children. "Am I still a woman?" she asks her doctor. "Is she still a woman?" she asks herself about a friend, who already has an infant, but recently aborted a second pregnancy.[23]

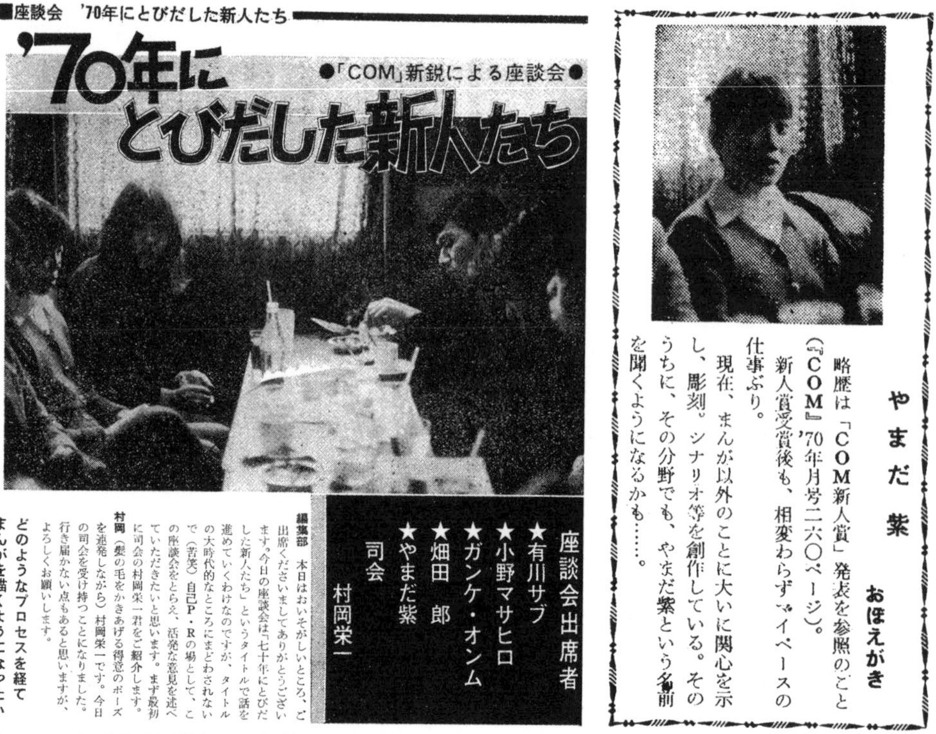
■座談会 '70年にとびだした新人たち

'70年にとびだした新人たち

●「COM」新鋭による座談会●

座談会出席者
★有川サブ
★小野マサヒロ
★ガンケ・オンム
★畑田 郎
★やまだ紫
司会 村岡栄一

編集部 本日はおいそがしいところ、ご出席くださいましてありがとうございます。今日の座談会は「七十年にとびだした新人たち」というタイトルで話を進めていくわけなのですが、タイトルの大時代的なところにまどわされないで（苦笑）自己P・Rの場として、この座談会をとらえ、活発な意見を述べていただきたいと思います。まず最初に司会の村岡栄一君をご紹介します。

村岡 （髪の毛をかきあげる得意のポーズを連発しながら）村岡栄一です。今日の司会を受け持つことになりました。行き届かない点もあると思いますが、よろしくお願いします。

どのようなプロセスを経てまんがを描くようになったか

やまだ 紫 **おぼえがき**

略歴は「COM新人賞」発表を参照のこと（『COM』'70年月号二六〇ページ）。新人賞受賞後も、相変わらずマイペースの仕事ぶり。

現在、まんが以外のことに大いに関心を示し、彫刻。シナリオ等を創作している。そのうちに、その分野でも、やまだ紫という名前を聞くようになるかも……。

"Newcomers bustin' out in 1970: a roundtable with *COM*'s cutting-edge," *COM* (May-June 1970), with Yamada at left; artist profile

wanted to write, so it could've gone either way. I just couldn't find anyone to publish my writing. When I first started thinking I wanted to make art, I couldn't make up my mind whether I wanted it to be through words or pictures. All I knew was that I wanted to commit to one or the other seriously." After apologizing to her manga-fanatical colleagues for saying that comics was simply the only field that she had success publishing in, she adds, "I wanted to illustrate my texts with my own pictures. That's probably how I would describe how I work."[20] These comments are interesting in that, while providing insight into the roots of Yamada's artistic practice, they also suggest that the proactive amateur submission contests within manga periodicals in the '60s not only provided a forum for aspiring cartoonists, but also made cartoonists out of aspiring artists and writers, including musicians and poets. The artist profile accompanying this roundtable claims that Yamada also dabbled in sculpture and screenwriting.

In 1979, in a special feature about *COM* in *Pafu* (one of the many magazines inspired by *COM* and the fan networks that grew out of it), Yamada commented as follows about the vibe around being a novice contributor to *COM*. "Because everyone's work was published as-is, I think it was easy for readers to relate to the magazine. Once I became a contributor, however, I remember being overcome with irrepressible fear. Some of the people at *COM* were really scary. The same people who were encouraging and kind to amateur submitters, or strict with words of wisdom, offered absolutely no direction once you started actually publishing in the magazine. When you finished drawing something, you'd take it to the publisher, but aside from deciding whether they were going to publish it or not, they said "delicate sensitivities that pulse through the poem" on which the manga is supposedly based. Furthermore, "Its ability to revive in the reader memories of one's early youth by capturing the feudal mood of the Japanese family through a distinctive pictorial style strikes the heart with sadness."[17]

Two months later, in the July 1969 issue, Yamada was awarded "Newcomer of the Month" for her story "Touch-me-not" ("Hōsenka," referring to the flower), about a young girl who, despite her grandmother's warnings, befriends another girl who is experiencing troubles at home: an alcoholic father whose rampages finally force the mother to leave town with her daughter. The flower of the title, like the fingernails of "My Left Hand…," serves as a metaphorical leitmotif appearing at the beginning and end of the story, in this case referring to the plant's seed pod which springs open beneath the nurturing sun, like children do when loved. Riffing on Yamada's story structure, COM describes

the manga as "a work born out of the knotting of poetry and pictures. What poetry cannot visualize is filled out with pictures, and what pictures cannot relay is expressed in poetry." Yamada is also praised for succeeding in capturing "how children are forced to rise and sink with the undulations of real life" better than any other submitter to COM.[18] Once again, her drawing is described as wanting. But as the artist herself once said about this period, "My drawing was horribly crude. I didn't know anything about how to draw comics. I used ballpens. I put India ink in fountain pens. It was a mess."[19]

In early 1970, Yamada took part in a roundtable between new artists in COM. The conversation opens with the participants being asked about why they first started drawing comics. After the others talk about how they loved drawing pictures from a young age and used to submit work to kashihon anthologies like Machi, Yamada says, "In my case, I wasn't particular about manga really. I also really

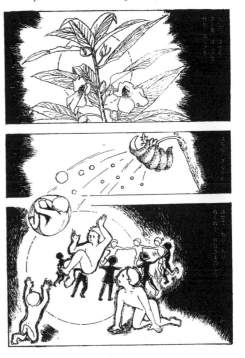

Yamada, "Touch-me-not," COM (July 1969)

as a shōjo manga artist. So did Nagashima Shinji, who drew for the magazine additional chapters of his *Cruel Stories of a Cartoonist* (*Mangaka zankoku monogatari*, 1961–64), a series about aspiring cartoonists that had appealed to both young men and women since its commencement in the early '60s. As a result, *COM*'s readership was reportedly twenty to thirty percent female.[13] Hoping to expand that audience and provide women artists a venue of their own, Mushi Pro created *Funny* (1969–70, '73), a shortlived monthly comics magazine for young women that is oftentimes named as a precursor to "ladies' comics" of the '80s, though it was essentially a shōjo manga magazine targeted at a high teen readership.

Meanwhile, *Garo* remained dense with darkly drawn stories about male angst, with no lack of sexist asides and rape scenes. The only regular woman cartoonist in *Garo* in the '60s and early '70s was Tsurita, who thrived despite experiencing subtle and overt forms of sexual discrimination and harassment at the hands of the magazine's editors and artists.[14] Okada Fumiko's work was rejected by *Garo* before being picked up by *COM*, which promptly made her its first amateur star. Her ethereal storybook imagery, abstract paneling, many European literary and artistic references, metaphor-laden interior monologue, and imaginative mix of comics and poetry inspired other aspiring women to submit work to *COM*, including Hagio and Yamada.[15] Even young women without personal experience of Seirindō's inner workings suspected that the environment there was less than hospitable. Yamada, for example, was a fan of *Garo*, particularly of the work of Hayashi Seiichi, Katsumata Susumu, and Tsuge Yoshiharu. But when asked later in life why she didn't submit her work initially to *Garo*, she responded tellingly, "The magazine was filled with men, most of whom were older than me." She also felt intimidated by their skills as artists. *COM*, on the other hand, was

●「青春・実験まんがコース」佳作第1位●
ひだり手の…
やまだ 紫

Yamada, "My Left Hand...," *COM* (May 1969)

"filled with all sorts of amateurs. At a glance, it just seemed easier to slide into that scene."[16]

Yamada was one of the first women amateurs to become a regular in *COM*. After a few rejected submissions, she debuted in the May 1969 issue, where her "My Left Hand..." ("Hidari te no...") received first place in the "Youth/Experimental" division of the magazine's amateur section. As would become typical of Yamada's early work, "My Left Hand..." depicts the adult world from the perspective of a child, in this case a young girl of about eight struggling to understand her elder sister's romantic troubles and decision to get married—something Yamada herself had recently experienced, when her sister got married and moved out of the apartment they were sharing with their mother. The title refers to the little girl's difficulty with cutting her fingernails with her left hand without her sister's help, a metaphor for her own burgeoning independence. The layered imagery, the frequency of faces in flat side and three-quarter profile, and the abstraction of the girl's thoughts as poetic phrases seem influenced by Okada's work. As with other featured submissions in *COM*, "My Left Hand..." was given points in various categories by the magazine's editors and resident critics, with Yamada scoring higher in those pertaining to story theme and construction, and lower on qualities of her drawing. In their comments, they describe the manga as the "distillation" of the pen name Murasaki Neko, literally "Violet Cat," in honor, first of all, of her lifelong love of cats, which inspired some of her most popular manga. According to her daughter, Yamada Yū, "Murasaki" was inspired by Edo Murasaki, a shade of bluish purple traditionally produced by textile dyers in Edo (Tokyo), an industry her mother knew well from having worked in it as a child. She also liked the poetic connotations of the kanji for "murasaki," which pairs "kono" (this/that which is closest to me) as its top element with "ito" (thread/a thing that binds and gives color) as its bottom half. Purples had been associated with nobility, luxuriance, and the Buddhist Pure Land for over a thousand years in Japan. And of course, as a female nom de plume, Murasaki immediately evokes Heian noblewoman Murasaki Shikibu, author of *The Tale of Genji* (early eleventh century), the first novel in Japan, if not the world.

In 1967, Yamada began working for a design studio, though which one and doing what exactly is unknown. Her manga suggest at least some professional experience with fashion illustration. She would continue working for them into the '70s. She also took art lessons at a design school, though dropped out before graduating. And, as a supplement to her poetry practice, she started drawing comics, using a new pen name, Yamada Murasaki—Yamada Violet.

2. COMICS POETRY AND *COM*

Though her name is today associated primarily with *Garo*, Yamada began her cartooning career in the pages of Tezuka Osamu's rival magazine, *COM*, debuting there in 1969 and publishing eight stories and a handful of illustrated poems before the magazine's demise in 1971.

Like *Garo*, *COM* was founded and overseen by a male artist, and staffed largely with male editors. The vast majority of critics who wrote for the magazine

were also men. But unlike *Garo's* founder Shirato Sanpei—who, aside from a few manga in the late '50s and early '60s for a cross-gender audience, drew almost exclusively for boys and young men—Tezuka was one of the progenitors of postwar shōjo manga and had been challenging gender norms through that genre since his era-defining *Princess Knight* (*Ribon no kishi*, 1953–56). When Tezuka and his publishing company, Mushi Pro, created *COM* in late 1966, they did so with a conscious effort to make it gender inclusive. From the beginning, there were many works by women artists, essays about shōjo manga, and interviews with young women creators. The magazine's second most regular contributor (after Tezuka) was a woman, Yashiro Masako, who had been active in the kashihon market since the early '60s. Kimura Minori, who otherwise drew for shōjo magazines, wrote some of her most famous and socially astute stories for *COM*. Among the many women who debuted through the magazine's amateur submissions section were, in addition to Yamada, Okada Fumiko, Takemiya Keiko, Motoyama Reiko, and Yamagishi Ryōko. Hagio Moto might also have debuted there, had editors not sat on her submission until 1971.[12]

Even the pillar manga by male veterans in *COM* had cross-gender appeal. Both Tezuka's *Phoenix* (1967–71) and Ishinomori Shōtarō's experimental *Jun* (1967–71) stem from a genre—science fiction—that was highly popular among young women. The ethereal layouts and melancholic pacing of *Jun* clearly resonate with the aesthetics of shōjo manga, while its self-positionings as a "poem comic" (*poemu komikku*) resonated with the high-brow literary references and breathless poetic mood that were increasingly informing the genre. Ishinomori himself had debuted as a shōjo manga author and is oftentimes credited with pioneering its open, complex layouts. Matsumoto Leiji, another *COM* regular, also began

Mizuki Shigeru. She remembers being shocked by Shirato Sanpei's *The Legend of Kagemaru* (*Ninja bugeichō*, 1959–62), and a little titillated by a notorious scene in which a lead female character is raped and dismembered by rampaging ninja. She also read lots of Tezuka and loved Disney movies.

Toward the end of elementary school, she started reading literature in earnest. Every month, her grandmother bought her a new volume in a series of literary classics for kids, comprising both Japanese and foreign titles. She loved Miyazawa Kenji, Natsume Sōseki, and Akutagawa Ryūnosuke. But the novel that made the deepest impression on her as a kid was Frances Hodgson Burnett's *Little Lord Fauntleroy* (1885–86). When her grandmother saw her crying while reading it, she too cried, as she often did despite her daily displays of strength and acts of courage. The experience, Yamada said, taught her the value of emotional vulnerability despite a culture that usually rebuked children prone to tears for being weak and immature.[10] In later years, she also became a fan of Mishima Yukio.

With child labor laws practically non-existent at the time, Yamada also worked. "In sixth grade, there was this thing I really wanted. But since I couldn't beg my mother for anything, I decided to get a job and buy it myself." Eleven years old and on her own initiative, she found a part-time job at a dyer's shop over winter break—another subject that appears occasionally in her manga. "You'll laugh if I tell you what I wanted, but it was this foreign-made toy kitchen set, made out of aluminum. These were the years when *The Donna Reed Show*, *Father Knows Best*, and *Lassie* were on TV, showing kitchens with ovens and moms baking and pulling chocolate cakes out of them. I saw a foreign kitchen set just like that in the window of a toy store in Sangenjaya. I wanted it so badly. It was this amazingly well-made miniature. It had a pot and a frypan. The oven door opened and everything."

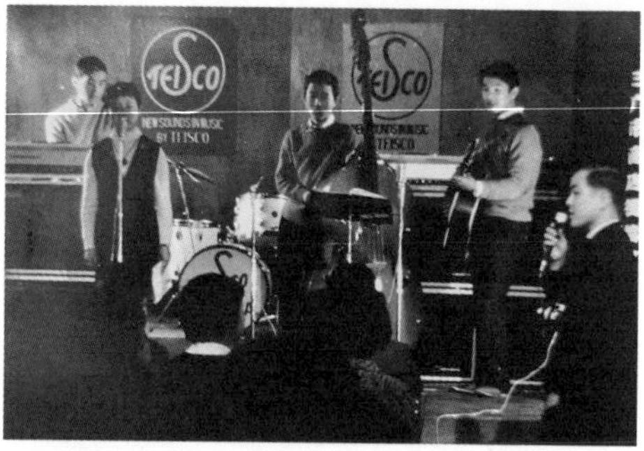
TEISCO
TEISCO
Yamada with the Weeping Love Strings, c. 1965-66

In 1963, Yamada entered Fujimigaoka High School, a private all-girls' school located in Sasazuka, Shibuya. She had recently begun living with her mother and elder sister, in an apartment block in Sangenjaya, staying there until she got married in 1971. Looking back at those years, Yamada described herself as a "potato girl" (*imo ane*), an old term for a frumpy and unstylish young woman. Still, she was hip enough to form a folk band with four guys, she as the vocalist. Named Weeping Love Strings, they performed some original songs, but primarily covers of foreign icons like Joan Baez and Peter, Paul, and Mary. "My generation," she recalled later, "was baptized by pop music in our adolescence. This was a little before the Beatles' shock. Paul Anka, Neil Sedaka, Connie Franics, Itō Yukari, and Hirota Mieko weren't bad, but real-deal American pop was a culture shock."[11] She could be referring to surf bands like the Ventures (who were huge in Japan), perhaps the Beach Boys, or the folk musicians her own band covered.

More decisively, Yamada also wrote poetry. In 1966, soon after graduating high school, she joined a poetry circle run by a friend called Shichinin (Seven People), after the number of people initially in the group. Serendipitously, one of the original seven quit soon after she joined, rectifying the misnomer. Yamada remained involved with Shichinin until 1970, publishing numerous mimeographed zines with them. It was as a poet that she started using the freedoms allowed by alt-manga could also be accessed by wives and mothers in their thirties to address issues important to their personal lives as they navigated family, husbands, and encroaching middle age. She was also possibly the first cartoonist in Japan to be framed in the press as a mother and "housewife," and possibly the first to publicly embrace those roles, even if with caveats.

"We should have recognized her importance earlier," wrote Arikawa in 1981, addressing Japanese readers. But in the English-speaking world—where analyses of gender and sexuality have dominated writing on Japanese art and pop culture for well over two decades now, and translations of manga from the '80s have never been in short supply, including ones by women—we, too, should have recognized Yamada's groundbreaking importance earlier.

1. YOUNG MURASAKI

"My earliest years were crazy bleak," Yamada said in an interview for *Garo* in 1993, on the occasion of a special issue dedicated to her. "We were poor, and I only had one parent," she explained. "I was a timid kid. The adults around me were all super scary. I was always afraid of being scolded for screwing something up, so I was careful about everything I did. I was the kind of kid who is always trying to read adults' moods."[8]

Yamada Murasaki was born Yamada Mitsuko on September 5, 1948, in Setagaya, Tokyo, in the neighborhood of Taishidō. Few Japanese had it easy after World War II, particularly those who lived in cities, which had been ravished by American firebombs. The chaos and severity of that era turned Yamada's family upside down, like it did many others. When she was born, her father had tuberculosis. So did her elder sister, two years her senior. Out of fear that infant Mitsuko would catch what was then a crippling and often fatal disease, she moved in with her grandparents, who also lived in Taishidō, in a tiny three-tatami-room (less than fifty square feet). "I never asked, so I don't know when exactly I started living with them. According to my grandmother, I was still nursing. But since there was no one to nurse me, apparently they gave me goat's milk," she recalled. "I was raised by goats!"

In July 1950, before she reached two, Yamada's father succumbed to his illness. The only thing she remembered about him is his funeral. His death forced her mother to work full-time, meaning even less time for her to see her daughter. Even when her mother did visit, she was too overwhelmed and exhausted to pay her daughter much attention or indulge her needs. Yamada's grandmother was functionally her mother. And as her sister lived with her mother, Yamada essentially grew up as a single child. The emotional difficulty of this complicated family situation figures centrally in her earliest manga for *COM*, and appears in her '80s and '90s work as isolated motifs. She was also close to her grandfather (technically her step-grandfather), whom she once described as a strict but fair disciplinarian, a stereotypically taciturn and upright adult of the Meiji generation.[9]

For enjoyment, Yamada drew and did little else. When adults praised her skills, they often described her as "just like your father," which always brought a smile to her face. Her father had been a professional artist, designing things like textiles and theatrical stage sets. He was so near-sighted that he was nearly blind, which kept him from being conscripted into the military during the war. He was assigned instead to draw large pictures of planes to be installed as decoys at Japanese airfields. In elementary school, Yamada started regularly winning prizes for her art. Around the age of ten, in the late '50s, she became a fan of "rental book" kashihon manga, particularly the work of Saitō Takao, Kojima Gōseki, and the artist most closely associated with the magazine through the '80s, publishing in almost every issue between 1979 and 1986, and in more issues than not for the rest of the decade. She also had close personal relationships with many of its artists and staff, particularly Nemoto Takashi and Ebisu Yoshikazu, with whom she often played all-night sessions of mahjong. In the mid '80s, she became romantically involved with, and later married, *Garo* editor Shiratori Chikao (1965–2017), editor of the aforementioned *Secret Comics Japan*, and facilitator of *Comics Underground Japan*. Thus, Yamada, the woman artist who was most intimately part of the *Garo* family, was ironically also the one who created the least stereotypically "*Garo*-esque" work.

She holds a similarly ambivalent position within the history of women's manga at large. Though Yamada is one of the first cartoonists in Japan to deal with the difficulties of womanhood in a realistic, critical, and sustained way, and outside the thematic and pictorial conventions of shōjo manga and its preference for fantasy, she is rarely named among the leaders of "women's manga." In a rare acknowledgement of her pioneering role, critic Arikawa Yū wrote in 1981, "Rather than shōjo manga or diehard fan manga, she was already drawing women's manga from the time of her debut. Whether it be her grandmother, her mother, or her older sister, she depicted the lives of the women connected to her own with an artistry that was careful and honest. We should have recognized her importance earlier."[5] In *Dreamland Japan: Writings on Modern Manga* (1996), Frederik L. Schodt offers snapshots of three women artists who had been associated with *Garo*: Sugiura, Uchida, and Yamada, whose work, Schodt writes, "often transcends manga and takes on the quality of poetry and feminist literature."[6] In *Secret Comics Japan*, Shiratori describes Yamada as the "first lady of manga" and a pioneer who "realistically and poetically depicted the casual, everyday life of women."[7] But since then, you hardly ever find her name mentioned in the teeming literature about gender and women's issues in Japanese manga and popular culture, even in Japan, where every serious scholar and fan knows her work.

This oversight is due to a number of factors. Since she rarely drew in a recognizable shōjo style and almost never published in shōjo magazines, Yamada's oeuvre falls into a blind spot in surveys of comics for a female audience in Japan, as does Tsurita's. Just by looking at her work, you probably wouldn't guess that Yamada was born less than a year before Hagio Moto and most others of the Shōwa 24 (1949) Group—which makes her work unrecognizable to and unlocatable within the standard historical narratives of shōjo and women's manga. It has not helped that she worked on the margins of the comics industry in *Garo*, a magazine not typically associated with the '80s upsurge in women's comics, and before that, *COM*. But such is oftentimes the fate of the pioneer, and Yamada was a decade ahead of her time not once but twice: in the early '70s, when she drew about family relations in a realistic and quasi-autobiographical way when few other women cartoonists did so; and again in the '80s, when she drew about marriage and motherhood at a time when "women's comics" usually signified ribald expressions of young female sexuality à la Sakurazawa, Uchida, and Okazaki, all of whom were still in their twenties. Aged thirty with two children and an abusive husband when she returned to comics in 1978, Yamada was not just a veteran as an artist when the "women's comics" boom hit, but also in life, having had to struggle on the domestic frontlines with the worst of Japanese patriarchy after getting married in 1971. As a single mother when she drew *Talk To My Back*, her most famous work, Yamada was arguably the first cartoonist to demonstrate that the expressive were upwards of nineteen different such magazines, and by 1991 four dozen, many of which provided pornography for women.[2] In the late '70s and early '80s, women creators recognized as pioneers in dealing frontally with young female sexuality outside of a shōjo (girls') manga mold were cutting their teeth in erotic and pulp magazines for men, among them Kondō Yōko, Sakurazawa Erica, Okazaki Kyōko, and Uchida Shungiku. Oftentimes, you will find this work referred to collectively as "ladies' comics" (redeiizu komikku), though in Japan that term primarily signifies erotic comics for heterosexual women—as made explicit in another period name, "women H cartoonists" (onna no ko H mangaka), in which "H" stands for "hentai," meaning raunchy, lewd, and perverted. There is also "joryū manga," literally "female-style comics," recycling an outdated term for women authors in literature, though it's rarely used now. Many people defer to the conveniently nebulous "women's comics" (josei manga) to describe manga by women for women about real-life women's issues, usually outside of the generic conventions of shōjo manga. However, as even so-called "girls' comics" (shōjo manga) have dealt frequently with adult themes and have been read by adults of all genders since the mid '70s, the nomenclature remains fluid and confusing.[3]

Though rarely mentioned in the literature on women's manga, Garo, despite its sexist past, was so reshaped by this revolution that it became one of its galvanizing forces. Leading figures like Kondō (who debuted in Garo in 1979), Sakurazawa, and Uchida published some of their most iconic work in Garo in the '80s and '90s. More than three dozen different women artists featured in the magazine during that same period, while Seirindō published dozens of books by women, not all of whom were regular contributors to Garo. In fact, by the mid '90s, so many women had published within Garo and other

"alt-manga" venues like Comic Baku and Comic Again, and in such a wide variety of styles and subject matter, that the male and lowbrow focus of the English-language anthologies mentioned above can be judged to reflect more the bias of their male editors than actual trends on the ground in Japan. No doubt, the deskilled hetauma of Ebisu Yoshikazu, Terry Johnson (Yumura Teruhiko), and Nemoto Takashi, and the exquisitely drawn surrealism and "erotic grotesque" of Hanawa Kazuichi and Maruo Suehiro, are defining developments of '80s Japanese subculture. Yet none of those quintessentially "alternative" aesthetics speaks to the role Garo played in another important aspect of that transitional decade: women's empowerment and their increased visibility as artistic creators beyond the sphere of shōjo manga.[4]

Yamada Murasaki (1948–2009) occupies a unique position within this watershed, one that is multi-faceted and indisputable, but oftentimes overlooked because of the anomalous nature of her work and career. Of the many women who published in Garo in the '80s, only Tsurita (1947–85) was older, and only by a year—which is surprising to learn considering how strongly Tsurita is associated with the '60s and Yamada with the '80s. The other women active in Garo's pages in the '80s were born in the late '50s and '60s, including the two artists Yamada is most often grouped with, Kondō Yōko (b. 1957) and Sugiura Hinako (1958–2005). Having debuted in COM in 1969 and been awarded a major prize by Shōgakukan's Big Comic in 1972 before stepping away from the industry for many years for personal reasons, Yamada was already an established and respected artist before reemerging in Garo in the late '70s. As a measure of her stature and experience, both Kondō and Sugiura briefly worked as her assistant in the early '80s; Haga Yuka, who also drew for Garo, moonlighted with her later in the decade. Of the "three daughters of Garo," Yamada remained

THE LIFE AND ART OF YAMADA MURASAKI

Ryan Holmberg

What is your image of alternative manga? It probably doesn't include many suburban housewives with school-age children, or many disconnected white-collar dads. It probably isn't composed of limpid, minimalist artwork with elegantly flowing lines, like you find here, in Yamada Murasaki's *Talk To My Back* (*Shinkirari*, 1981–84). And, I imagine, it includes probably relatively few women creators.

Not that women who published in alt-manga venues haven't been translated into English. Within the handful of anthologies of comics sourced from the pages of *Garo*, the original and most famous alt-manga periodical, there are a number of contributions by women working in a variety of modes. Nekojiru's cute surrealism and Nananan Kiriko's snapshots of high school girl life were included in *Sake Jock: Comics from Today's Japanese Underground* (Fantagraphics, 1995). Nekojiru, Migiwa Pan, Yamada Hanako, and Carol Shimoda appeared in *Comics Underground Japan* (Blast Books, 1996), collectively suggesting that something like a mock "girlie" and riot grrrl spirit informed Japanese comics. Nananan, the romantic-surrealist Tsuno Yūko, and goth kawaii Mizuno Junko were translated in *Secret Comics Japan: Underground Comics Now* (Viz Media, 2000), offering a range of work wide enough to reveal that alt-manga by women defies neat categorization. This was reaffirmed by *Ax: Alternative Manga* (Top Shelf, 2009), sourced from *Garo*'s successor, by featuring Kondoh Akino on its cover, and comics by Kondoh, Akiyama Ayuko, Nishioka Brosis, Gotō Yuka, Fujieda Namie, Tomozawa Mimiyo, and Seiko Erisawa. But with barely a quarter of the contributors across these anthologies being women, the dominant impression is that alt-manga has been dominated by men, and that the expressive freedoms enabled by venues like *Garo* have largely served male fantasies of an angsty, scatological, psycho-sexual sort.

This bias is not wholly misrepresentative of actual trends in Japan. Until the late '70s, *Garo* published the work of less than a dozen women cartoonists, and only two with any regularity: Tsurita Kuniko, author of the acclaimed anthology *The Sky Is Blue with a Single Cloud* (D+Q, 2020), and the largely forgotten Naka Keiko. This compared to over a hundred different male artists in the same period, many with extended serials and multiple short stories.[1] In contrast, Tezuka Osamu's rival periodical, *COM* (1967–71, '73), hosted dozens of women contributors, many of whom became major figures in women's comics, among them Okada Fumiko, Takemiya Keiko, Hagio Moto, Kimura Minori, and—author of the present volume—Yamada Murasaki. It was not until 1979–80 and the rise of the so-called "three daughters of *Garo*" (*Garo sannin musume*)—Yamada Murasaki (again), Kondō Yōko, and Sugiura Hinako—that this gender imbalance began to right in a substantive way. 1971 was also the year that Seirindō, the publisher of *Garo*, hired its first full-time woman editor, Tetsuka Noriko (b. 1955), who currently keeps the flame of classic alt-manga burning as president of the publishing house Seirinkōgeisha, with its flagship periodical *Ax*.

Meanwhile, elsewhere in the manga industry, comics specifically for adult women were burgeoning. In 1980, Kōdansha inaugurated what is regarded as the first successful manga magazine dedicated to young adult women, the monthly *Be Love*, an outgrowth of the magazine *Young Lady*. By 1985, there

Facing page: *Asahi Graph* (April 23, 1982), photo by Hashimoto Shōkō: Yamada at home working

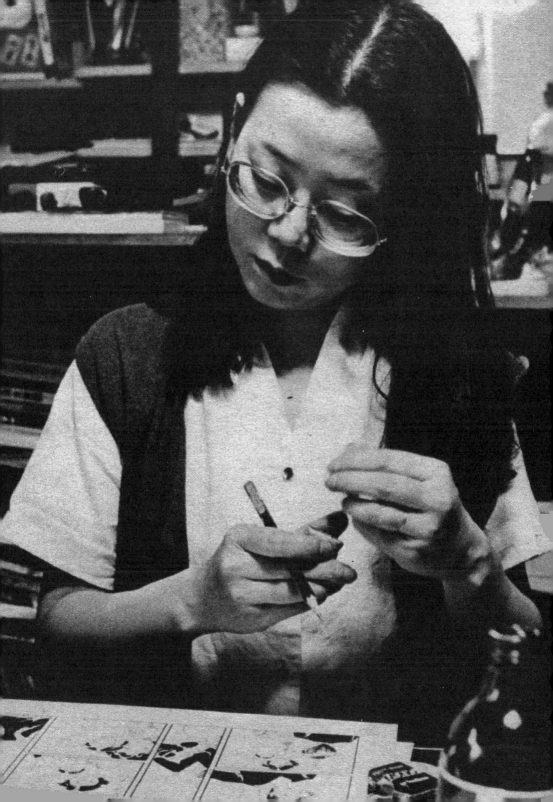

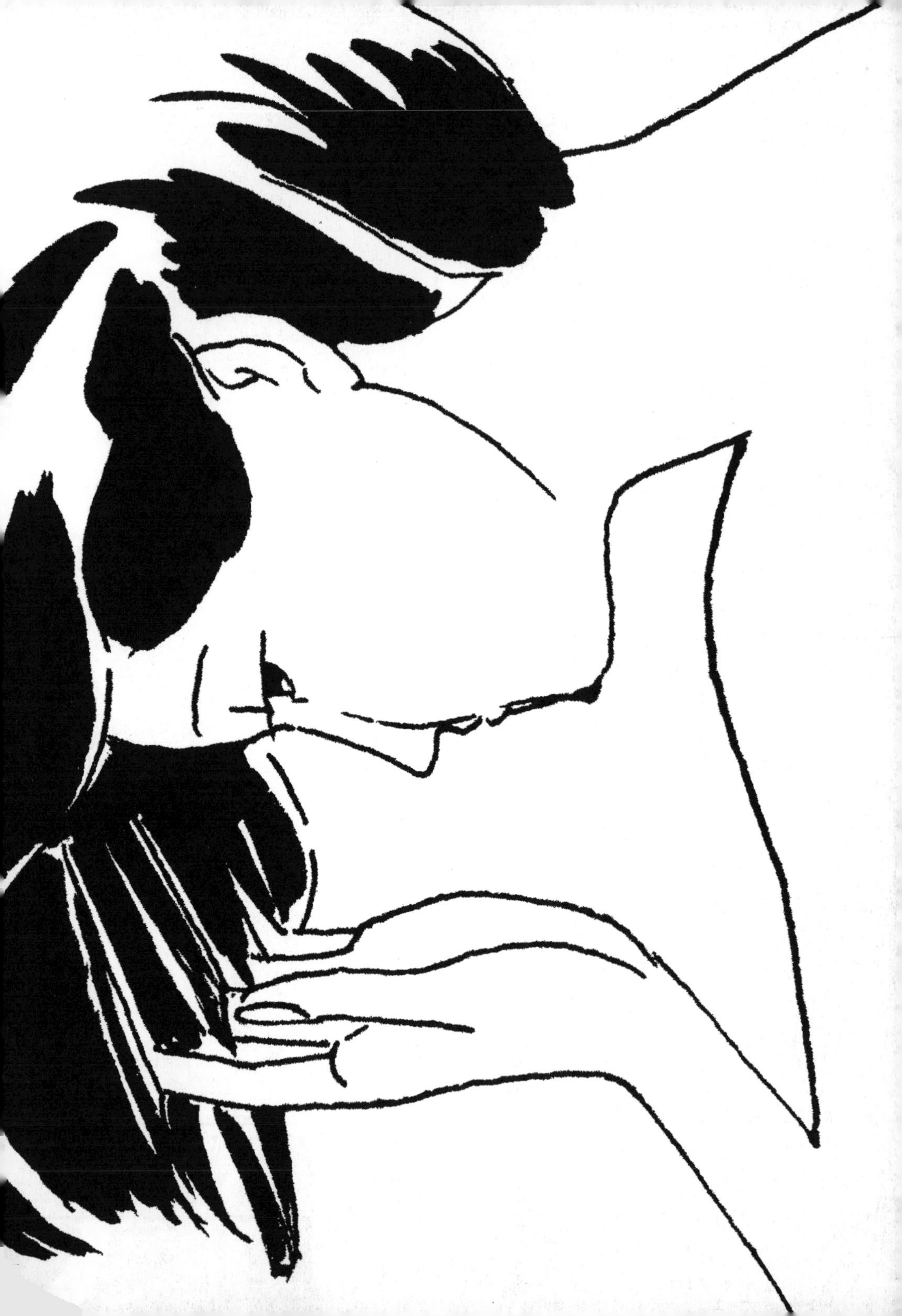

drawnandquarterly.com

Cataloguing data available from
Library and Archives Canada

FSC
www.fsc.org
MIX
Paper | Supporting
responsible forestry
FSC® C005748

Printed in Turkey
First edition: July 2022
ISBN 978-1-77046-563-3
10 9 8 7 6 5 4 3 2 1

Published in the USA by Drawn & Quarterly, a
client publisher of Farrar, Straus and Giroux. Published
in Canada by Drawn & Quarterly, a client publisher of
Raincoast Books. Published in the United Kingdom by
Drawn & Quarterly, a client publisher of Publishers Group UK.

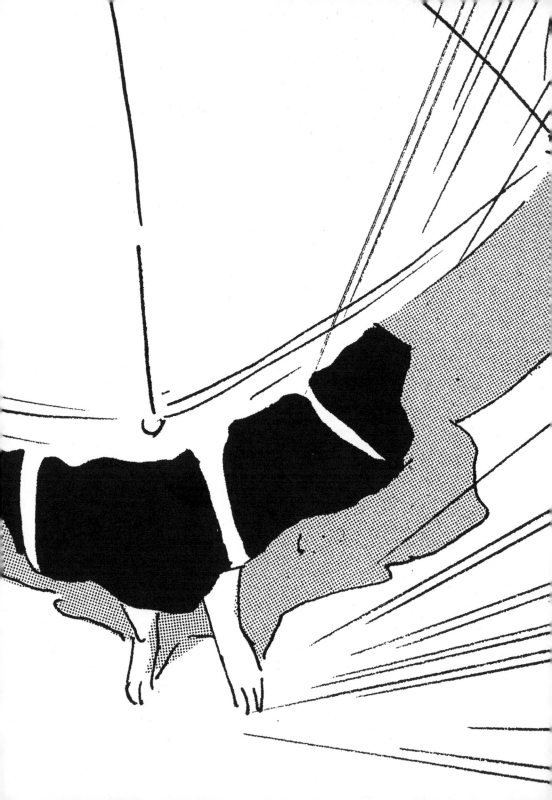

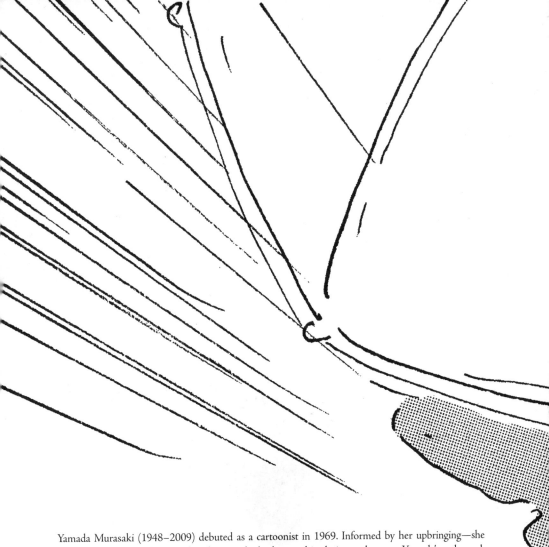

Yamada Murasaki (1948–2009) debuted as a cartoonist in 1969. Informed by her upbringing—she was raised mainly by her grandmother—and a background in design and poetry, Yamada's early work was unique in form and content, offering realistic portraits of young women negotiating complicated family situations and the passage to adulthood. In the late '70s, after having a family of her own, her work shifted to young mothers negotiating children, husbands, and the balance between social responsibilities as a housewife and self-respect as a woman. Yamada published manga in practically every issue of *Garo* from 1978 to 1986, and is considered the first cartoonist to use the artistic freedoms of alternative manga to explore motherhood and domesticity with an unromantic eye.

Ryan Holmberg is an award-winning translator and historian of Japanese comics. He has worked on over two dozen books with such publishers as Drawn & Quarterly, New York Review Comics, and Breakdown Press. He is the author of *The Translator Without Talent* (Bubbles, 2020) and *Garo Manga: The First Decade, 1964–1973* (Center for Book Arts, 2010). A full bibliography of his work can be found at www.mangaberg.com.

This book is presented in the traditional Japanese manner
and is meant to be read from right to left. The cover
at the opposite end is considered the front.

To begin reading the manga, please flip the book over
and start at the other end. For the historical essay,
turn this page and read from left to right.